Essentials of Criminal Justice

FIFTH EDITION

Larry J. Siegel
University of Massachusetts–Lowell

Joseph J. Senna
Northeastern University

THOMSON

WADSWORTH

Australia • Brazil • Canada • Mexico • Singapore • Spain • United Kingdom • United

THOMSON

™

WADSWORTH

Senior Acquisitions Editor, Criminal Justice: Carolyn
  Henderson Meier
Development Editor: Shelley Murphy
Assistant Editor: Jana Davis
Editorial Assistant: Rebecca Johnson
Technology Project Manager: Susan DeVanna
Marketing Manager: Terra Schultz
Marketing Assistant: Jaren Boland
Marketing Communications Manager: Linda Yip
Project Manager, Editorial Production: Jennie Redwitz
Creative Director: Rob Hugel
Art Director: Vernon Boes
Print Buyer: Barbara Britton

Permissions Editor: Kiely Sisk
Production Service: Linda Jupiter, Jupiter Productions
Text Designer: Lisa Delgado
Photo Researcher: Linda Rill
Copy Editor: Lunaea Weatherstone
Proofreader: Mary Kanable
Illustrator: John and Judy Waller, Scientific Illustrators
Indexer: Paula C. Durbin-Westby
Cover Designer: Yvo
Cover Illustration: Sally Wern Comport
Cover Printer: Phoenix Color Corp
Compositor: Pre-Press Company, Inc.
Text Printer: Courier Corporation/Kendallville

Library of Congress Control Number: 2005931399

ISBN 0-495-00602-5

Thomson Higher Education
10 Davis Drive
Belmont, CA 94002-3098
USA

For more information about our products, contact us at:
Thomson Learning Academic Resource Center
1-800-423-0563

For permission to use material from this text or product, submit a request online at
http://www.thomsonrights.com.
Any additional questions about permissions can be submitted by e-mail to
thomsonrights@thomson.com.

Dedication

To my children, Eric, Andrew, Julie, and Rachel;
my grandchildren, Kayla and Jack;
and to my wife, Therese J. Libby.
LARRY J. SIEGEL

To my children, Joseph, Peter, Stephen, and Christian,
and to my wife, Janet.
JOSEPH J. SENNA

About the Authors

LARRY J. SIEGEL was born in the Bronx in 1947. While attending City College of New York in the 1960s, he was swept up in the social and political currents of the time. He became intrigued with the influence contemporary culture had on individual behavior: Did people shape society or did society shape people? He applied his interest in social forces and human behavior to the study of crime and justice. After graduating CCNY, he attended the newly opened program in criminal justice at the State University of New York at Albany, earning both his M.A. and Ph.D. degrees there. After completing his graduate work, Dr. Siegel began his teaching career at Northeastern University, where he was a faculty member for nine years. He has also held teaching positions at the University of Nebraska–Omaha and Saint Anselm College in New Hampshire. He is currently a professor at the University of Massachusetts–Lowell.

Dr. Siegel has written extensively in the area of crime and justice, including books on juvenile law, delinquency, criminology, and criminal procedure. He is a court certified expert on police conduct and has testified in numerous legal cases. The father of four and grandfather of two, Larry Siegel and his wife, Terry, now reside in Bedford, New Hampshire, with their two cockapoos, Watson and Cody.

JOSEPH J. SENNA was born in Brooklyn, New York. He graduated from Brooklyn College, Fordham University Graduate School of Social Service, and Suffolk University Law School. Mr. Senna spent over sixteen years teaching law and justice courses at Northeastern University. In addition, he served as an assistant district attorney, director of Harvard Law School Prosecutorial Program, and consultant to numerous criminal justice organizations. His academic specialties include areas of criminal law, Constitutional due process, criminal justice, and juvenile law.

Mr. Senna lives with his wife and sons outside of Boston.

Brief Contents

Contents

(Career Profiles

Chapter 1 • Ross Wolf
Division Chief of the Orange County
Sheriff's Office Reserve Unit, Orange
County, Florida

Chapter 2 • John A. Graham
United States Customs Service, Corpus
Christi, Texas

Chapter 3 • David Sher
Defense Attorney, Arlington, Virginia

Chapter 4 • Terry McAdam
Forensic Scientist, Washington State
Patrol Crime Lab, Tacoma, Washington

Chapter 5 • Tom Kukowski
Police Captain of the Criminal Investiga-
tions Bureau of the Milwaukee Police
Department, West Allis, Wisconsin

Chapter 6 • Lee Libby
Detective Sergeant (retired), Seattle Police
Department, Seattle, Washington;
Professor of Criminal Justice, Washington
Shoreline Community College

Chapter 7 • Jeff Czarnec
Detective (retired), Manchester, New
Hampshire; now teaching at Hesser
College, Manchester, New Hampshire

Chapter 8 • Tim Bakken
Attorney/Prosecutor; Professor in the
Department of Law at the United States
Military Academy at West Point, New
York

Chapter 9 • Ralph C. Martin II
Attorney; Partner at Bingham
McCutchen LLP and Managing Principal
of Bingham Consulting Group, Boston,
Massachusetts

Chapter 10 • Wade Schindler
Court Forensics Expert, Adjunct
Professor of Criminal Justice and Crimi-
nology at Tulane University, Tulane
University, New Orleans, Louisiana

Chapter 11 • Tim Kenny
Judge, Criminal Division of the 3rd
Circuit Court, Wayne County (Detroit),
Michigan

Chapter 12 • Debra Heath-Thornton
Crime Victim Advocate; Associate
Professor of Criminal Justice and
Sociology at Messiah College, Grantham,
Pennsylvania

Chapter 13 • Debra Rasouliyan
Program Director, Women for Women
(in-custody substance abuse treatment),
Atlanta Detention Center, Atlanta,
Georgia

Chapter 14 • Rachel Anita Jung
Training Officer III, Executive
Development Manager, Staff Develop-
ment Bureau, Arizona Department of
Corrections, Phoenix, Arizona

Chapter 15 • Kathryn Sellers
Developed a Drug Outpatient Program
for juveniles found guilty of drug/alcohol
related crimes; Court Referral Officer,
Virginia

(Preface

On April 21, 2004, a grand jury indicted Michael Jackson—the "King of Pop"—on ten felony counts, setting off one of the most highly publicized cases of the decade. Among the charges:

- 1 count of attempting a lewd act upon a minor (3 to 5 years)
- 4 counts of lewd acts involving a minor under the age of 14 (each count carries a mandatory sentence of 3 to 8 years)
- 4 counts of administering an intoxicating agent (each count carries the potential for a 16-month to 3-year sentence)
- 1 conspiracy count involving 28 separate acts, including child abduction, false imprisonment, and extortion (2 to 4 years plus a $10,000 fine)

The prosecution, led by Santa Barbara District Attorney Tom Sneddon, claimed that Jackson sexually molested a teenage boy between February and March of 2003 at his famed Neverland Ranch. During the trial, the prosecution attempted to paint Jackson as a pedophile who routinely provided kids with liquor and wine (which Jackson allegedly called "Jesus Juice"), showed them pornographic films, shared his bed with them, and, most damaging, engaged in frequent bouts of sexual molestation. Jackson's legal defense retaliated by painting the accuser and his family as greedy opportunists who concocted a story to extort money from a millionaire celebrity. They claimed that the alleged victim was controlled by his mother, who was intent on taking advantage of Jackson's generosity and love of children. Rather than a molester, Jackson was an innocent, childlike adult who, if anything, was simply too lavish in his affection for needy kids.

In one bizarre twist, the boy's mother claimed that Jackson had held the family hostage in the wake of the television broadcast of "Living with Michael Jackson" (BBC News, February 4, 2003), during which Jackson admitted to British interviewer Martin Bashir that he had slept in the same bed with young boys. At one point in the documentary Jackson is seen with his 13-year-old accuser, who rests his head on Jackson's shoulder and talks enthusiastically about the singer. The accuser's mother claimed that Jackson's fear of the impact the documentary would have on the public drove him and his staff to intimidate and restrain the family—at which point the media became an actual player in the case rather than just an outside reporter of what was happening.

And the trial itself quickly turned into a media circus. Reporters arrived from around the world. Actors recreated court testimony on nightly entertainment programs, celebrities were served with subpoenas, a gag order was placed on comedian Jay Leno, and so on. The turning point in the case may have come on May 11, 2005, when former child actor Macaulay Culkin denied that Jackson molested him when he spent time at the Neverland Ranch. Culkin's testimony reassured jurors that Jackson was not an evil predator; it was particularly important to counterbalance testimony that Jackson had paid millions to other boys in prior molestation cases. On June 13, 2005, the jury found Jackson not guilty of the charges, ending one of the most bizarre cases in the annals of American jurisprudence.

INTRODUCTION TO CRIMINAL JUSTICE

The Jackson case raises many questions about the American criminal justice system. Does the system treat celebrities more leniently than the average citizen? Conversely, are prosecutors overzealous in their pursuit of high-profile defendants such as Michael Jackson, Kobe Bryant, or Martha Stewart? Should the media be allowed to broadcast intimate details about a defendant's life? Should a defendant's prior behavior be considered by jurors?

While the Jackson case was certainly unique, it reminds us of the great impact crime, law, and justice have had on the American consciousness. Few defendants can afford high-priced defense teams or call famous witnesses such as Macaulay Culkin or Jay Leno to testify on their behalf as could Jackson. Nonetheless, each year the criminal justice system routinely processes millions of cases involving theft, violence, drug trafficking, and other crimes. How does this vast enterprise costing billions of dollars and involving millions of people operate? What are its most recent trends and policies? How effective are its efforts to control crime? What efforts are being made to improve its efficiency?

Essentials of Criminal Justice was written in an attempt to help answer these questions and many others in a concise, forthright, interesting, and objective manner. The book lays a groundwork for the study of criminal justice by analyzing and describing the agencies of justice and the procedures they use to identify and treat criminal offenders. It covers what most experts agree are the critical issues in criminal justice and analyzes their impact on the justice system. Our primary goals in writing the text have always been these:

1. To provide students with a thorough, up-to-date knowledge of the criminal justice system.
2. To be as readable and interesting as possible.
3. To be objective and unbiased.
4. To describe the most current methods of social control and analyze their strengths and weaknesses.
5. And finally, to strike the right balance between brevity and comprehensiveness.

Every attempt has been made to make the presentation of material interesting, balanced, and objective. No single political or theoretical position dominates the text; instead, the many diverse views that shape criminal justice and characterize its interdisciplinary nature are presented. The text includes topical information on recent cases and events to enliven and illustrate the presentation. We hope that in *Essentials of Criminal Justice* we have provided a text that is informative and accurate, interesting, comprehensive yet succinct, well-organized, up to date, and objective, as well as provocative and thought-provoking.

ORGANIZATION

Essentials of Criminal Justice is divided into five parts. Part One gives the student a basic introduction to crime, law, and justice. The first chapter covers the agencies of justice and the formal justice process, as well as introducing students to the informal justice system, which involves discretion, deal-making, and plea bargains. Chapter 1 also discusses the major perspectives on justice and shows how they shape justice policy. Chapter 2 discusses the nature and extent of crime and victimization: How is crime measured? Where and when does it occur? Who commits crime? Who are its victims? What social factors influence the crime rate? Chapter 3 provides a discussion of the criminal law and its relationship to criminal justice. It covers the legal definition of crime, the defenses to crime, and issues in Constitutional procedural law. Chapter 4 is new to the Fifth Edition (see below for more details) and focuses on two increasingly important areas of concern to the field: cybercrime and terrorism.

Part Two provides an overview of law enforcement. These chapters cover the history and development of police departments, the functions of police in modern society, issues in policing, and the police and the rule of law. In addition to such foundational topic coverage, these chapters also emphasize community policing, technology and policing, recent developments/changes in police procedure, and other timely topics.

Part Three is devoted to the adjudication process, from pretrial indictment to the sentencing of criminal offenders. In this section, individual chapters focus on the organization of the court system, pretrial procedures, the criminal trial, and sentencing (including bail, sentencing, and capital punishment).

Part Four focuses on the correctional system, including probation and the intermediate sanctions of house arrest, intensive supervision, and electronic monitoring. While the traditional correctional system of jails, prisons, community-based corrections, and parole are discussed at length, there is a new focus on restorative justice programs in the Fifth Edition (see below for more details). Such issues as the prison and jail overcrowding crisis, correctional treatment, super-maximum-security prisons, and inmate re-entry are discussed.

Finally, Part Five explores the juvenile justice system and includes coverage of the development of juvenile justice, the legal rights of juveniles, and the changing view of the juvenile offender.

THE FIFTH EDITION

Because criminal justice is a dynamic, ever-changing field of scientific inquiry, this text has been thoroughly updated and revised to reflect the field's evolving concepts and processes as well as the most critical legal cases, research, and policy initiatives. Among the most important enhancements we have made to the text are the inclusion of a brand-new chapter on terrorism and cybercrime and a more concise or "leaner" treatment of material throughout the text to keep pace with the evolving learning styles of today's students.

Another key change to the Fifth Edition is the incorporation of chapter-opening career profiles that describe in detail the backgrounds and activities of working professionals in the criminal justice system. These vignettes have been created to offer students insight into various criminal justice careers: how people choose them, what educational background they require, what such professionals do on the job every day, and what they see as their greatest challenges. A complete list of career profiles can be found on page xi, and we owe each of these people a special note of thanks for allowing us to interview them.

Chapter-by-Chapter Changes

- **Chapter 1, Crime and Criminal Justice.** This chapter has been streamlined and reorganized to provide a more manageable introduction to criminal justice. In particular, the discussion of perspectives of justice has been rewritten to provide a more concise overview, and the discussion of the wedding cake model of justice is more succinct than in previous editions. This chapter also features a new section on ethics in criminal justice, which looks at the ethical dilemmas facing police, prosecutors, and correctional agents. Finally, a new **Policies, Programs, and Issues in Criminal Justice** box ("Should Drugs be Legalized?") has been created to examine this important issue and present evidence from both sides of the debate.

- **Chapter 2, The Nature of Crime and Victimization.** The data included in this chapter has been carefully updated, particularly in the sections on international crime trends and the factors that influence crime rates. The chapter also reviews recent research on using hidden cameras to observe crime, crime trends and patterns, and the validity of self-report data, and includes a new **Race, Culture, and Gender in Criminal Justice** box titled "International Crime Trends."

- **Chapter 3, Criminal Law: Substance and Procedure.** This chapter has been carefully updated and rewritten to explain criminal law in simpler, clearer language. The sections on history and the sources of criminal law in particular have been made more clear and concise. And we have included a new discussion of ex post facto laws, as well as an analysis of *Lawrence v. Texas,* in which the Supreme Court declared that laws banning sodomy were unconstitutional.

- **Chapter 4, Criminal Justice in the New Millennium: Terrorism, Homeland Security, and Cybercrime.** Because agencies of the criminal justice system are now being called upon to confront new forms of criminality, a new chapter has been added that covers terrorism, homeland security, and cybercrime. The chapter discusses the factors that may cause someone to become a terrorist and the background of the contemporary terrorist. It reviews the findings of the 9/11 Commission and the agencies/positions that were created to lead the fight against terrorism, including the Department of Homeland Security and the Director of National Intelligence. Local- and state-level antiterrorism strategies are discussed. We also cover the USA Patriot Act and its impact on society. The chapter then turns to cybercrime and discusses its definition, the various forms it takes, and what is being done to thwart cybercriminals.

- **Chapter 5, Police in Society: History and Organization.** This chapter now covers the post-9/11 reorganization of the FBI and the Bureau of Alcohol, Tobacco, Firearms, and Explosives; salaries of law enforcement officers; and the use of new technologies such as virtual information and Web-based facial recognition systems.

- **Chapter 6, The Police: Role and Function.** In this chapter, we review current community- and problem-oriented policing programs. There is an updated analysis of CompStat, the program that has helped the NYPD bring the city's crime rate down, as well as new information on structural changes in detective bureaus and detection methods. The chapter also covers new research on female police officers and precinct-level efforts to ensure that officers are respectful of citizens.

- **Chapter 7, Issues in Policing: Professional, Social, and Legal.** This thoroughly revised chapter covers research into how police departments are reluctant to change and the effects of education on police performance. The chapter includes updated discussion of racial profiling and new data from the most recent survey of police contacts with civilians. Helpful new exhibits on "Models of Police Review Boards" and the "Office of Citizen Complaints" (OCC) in San Francisco have also been added to the chapter to clarify key points.

- **Chapter 8, Courts, Prosecution, and the Defense.** This chapter features new research that finds that African-American women are actually less likely to support prosecution of domestic violence than Caucasian women despite the fact that additional research indicates that court protection orders can reduce the incidence of repeat violence. New programs discussed include Santa Barbara's Elder Abuse Unit and Mason County, Washington's effort to have fees paid to fund crime victim programs. There is a new **Policy, Programs, and Issues in Criminal Justice** box titled "Ethical Issues in Defense: Should Defense Attorneys Tell the Truth?" and the court technology material includes a new section on information sharing.

- **Chapter 9, Pretrial Procedures.** Coverage of the role prosecutors play in plea bargaining has been updated, as has coverage of recent efforts to reduce plea negotiations in serious felonies. The chapter contains a recent study indicating that bail may be racially or ethnically biased and that African-American and Hispanic defendants receive less favorable treatment than whites charged with similar offenses. Finally, research on the types of offenders who succeed in pretrial programs has been added.

- **Chapter 10, The Criminal Trial.** A new section on the right to be competent at trial details research on the conditions necessary for a person to be considered mentally incompetent. The section on the level of proof needed for conviction has been updated, and there is additional material on the presentation of evidence at a criminal trial. New research focusing on racism and jury selection is included and there is analysis of a recent federal case in which the courts refused to extend the right of the press to attend deportation hearings.

- **Chapter 11, Punishment and Sentencing.** This chapter reviews a number of important cases, including *Blakely v. Washington,* in which the Supreme Court concluded that Washington state's sentencing guidelines were a violation of a defendant's Sixth Amendment rights; *United States v. Booker,* which held that the federal guidelines were unconstitutional; and *Roper v. Simmons* (2005), in which the Supreme Court set 18 years as the age at which a defendant can be sentenced to death. The **Race, Culture, and Gender in Criminal Justice** box "Race and Sentencing" has also been updated to include recent research that finds that on average African Americans receive 20 percent longer sentences than whites.

- **Chapter 12, Community Sentences: Probation, Intermediate Sanctions, and Restorative Justice.** This chapter looks at the explosive growth of probation, the use of probation abroad, and new restorative justice techniques in alternative sanctions. It covers recent research that shows—surprisingly—that males convicted of sexual offenses seem to do quite well on probation. Also covered is Maryland's HotSpot probation initiative. And we even devote some time to Jennifer Wilbanks, the notorious "runaway bride," and her sentence to intermediate sanctions. Finally, a **Race, Culture, and Gender in Criminal Justice** box looks at "Restorative Cautioning in England."

- **Chapter 13, Corrections: History, Institutions, and Populations.** This chapter includes updated discussion of trends in correctional populations and shows how sentencing changes influence corrections. Also included is new material on ultra-maximum-security prisons and another look at the increasingly important issue of elderly inmates.

- **Chapter 14, Prison Life: Living in and Leaving Prison.** This chapter features new material on prisoner re-entry and parole as well as a new **Policy, Programs, and Issues in Criminal Justice** box on "Therapeutic Communities" and a **Race, Culture, and Gender in Criminal Justice** box on "Monitoring High-Risk Offenders in New Zealand." There is new material on sexual assault in prisons, and the Prison Rape Reduction Act of 2003 is covered in some detail.

- **Chapter 15, Juvenile Justice.** The final chapter of the book has been thoroughly revised and updated. The new book *Juvenile Justice in the Making,* by historian David Tanenhaus, is discussed and a new exhibit sets out Hawaii's Family Court project. Also covered in this chapter are the Fast Track Project, a national juvenile treatment effort, and the Children at Risk (CAR) program, a highly regarded rehabilitation effort.

LEARNING TOOLS

We have created a comprehensive, proven learning system designed to help students get the most out of their first course in criminal justice. In addition to the many changes already mentioned, we have included a wealth of new photographs to appeal to visual learners and make material more relevant and meaningful. Carefully updated tables and figures highlight key chapter concepts. New "Learning Objectives" sections appear at the start of every chapter to help students chart their course, while new "Concept Summaries" appear throughout the chapters to enable students to check their understanding of key concepts as they work. Marginal definitions of key terms, concise, bulleted end-of-chapter summaries, and a comprehensive end-of-book glossary all help students master the material, and Internet research links appearing in the text's margins let students explore topics further via the Web.

We have also included a number of thematic boxes to highlight and amplify text coverage and introduce students to some of the field's most crucial programs, policies, and issues.

Policy, Programs, and Issues in Criminal Justice These boxes help students think critically about current justice issues, policies, and practices. Some of the new boxes focusing on cutting-edge issues/policies include:

- Should Drugs Be Legalized? (Ch. 1)
- Ex Post Facto Laws (Ch. 3)
- Operation Atlas (Ch. 4)
- The Problem of Elderly Inmates (Ch. 13)
- Therapeutic Communities (Ch. 14)
- The Fast Track Project (Ch. 15)

Race, Culture, and Gender in Criminal Justice These boxes are aimed at helping students achieve a better understanding of diversity concerns in the justice system and spotlight such issues as:

- Criminal Groups/Terrorist Groups: One and the Same? (Ch. 4)
- Racial Profiling (Ch. 7)
- Restorative Cautioning in England (Ch. 12)
- Monitoring High-Risk Offenders in New Zealand (Ch. 14)

Criminal Justice and Technology These boxes review how some of the more recent scientific advances can aid the justice system. New technologies covered include:

- Crime Mapping (Ch. 5)
- Less-than-Lethal Weapons (Ch. 7)

SUPPLEMENTS

The most extensive package of supplemental aids available for a criminal justice text accompanies this edition. Many separate items have been developed to enhance the course and to assist instructors and students. Available to qualified adopters. Please consult your local sales representative for details.

For the Instructor

Instructor's Edition Designed just for instructors, the *Instructor's Edition* includes a visual walkthrough that illustrates the key pedagogical features of the text, as well as the media and supplements that accompany it. Use this handy tool to quickly learn about the many options this text provides to keep your class engaging and informative.

Instructor's Resource Manual with Test Bank An improved and completely updated *Instructor's Resource Manual with Test Bank* has been developed by Lynn Newhart of Rockford College. The manual includes learning objectives, detailed chapter outlines, key terms, class discussion exercises, lecture suggestions, term paper topics, and a test bank. Each chapter's test bank contains approximately 80 questions in multiple-choice, true-false, fill-in-the-blank, and essay formats, with a full answer key. The test bank is coded according to difficulty level and Bloom's taxonomy, and it also includes the page numbers in the main text where the answers can be found. The Resource Integration Guide within the manual will help you maximize your use of the rich supplements package that comes with the text by integrating media, Internet, video, and other resources. A transition guide will make it easier for you to update your syllabi if you are changing from another text to *Essentials of Criminal Justice*, Fifth Edition, and will also help you correlate the material in the text with other textbooks you may have used. The *Instructor's Resource Manual* is backed up by ExamView, a computerized test bank available for IBM-PC compatibles and Macintosh computers.

ExamView® Computerized Testing Create, deliver, and customize tests and study guides (both print and online) in minutes with this easy-to-use assessment and tutorial system. ExamView offers both a Quick Test Wizard and an Online Test Wizard that guide you step by step through the process of creating tests. You can build tests of up to 250 questions using up to 12 question types. Using ExamView's complete word processing capabilities, you can enter an unlimited number of new questions or edit existing questions.

WebTutor™ ToolBox on Blackboard and WebCT A powerful combination: easy-to-use course management tools and content from this text's rich companion website all in one place. You can use ToolBox as is from the moment you log on—or, if you prefer, customize the program with web links, images, and other resources.

Classroom Presentation Tools for the Instructor

Multimedia Manager for Criminal Justice: A Microsoft® PowerPoint® Link Tool This valuable resource is a one-stop shop containing all of the art from the book as well as interactive learning tools that will enhance your classroom lectures. In addition, you can choose from the ready-made dynamic slides offered or customize your own with the art files provided from the text.

JoinIn™ on TurningPoint® Enhance your students' interaction with you, your lecture, and each other. This exciting new response system supplement allows you to transform your classroom and assess student progress with instant in-class quizzes and polls. The TurningPoint software lets you pose book-specific questions and display students' answers seamlessly within the Microsoft PowerPoint slides of your own lecture, in conjunction with the "clicker" hardware of your choice.

The Wadsworth Criminal Justice Video Library So many exciting, new videos—so many great ways to enrich your lectures and spark discussion of the material in this text. View our full video offerings and download clip lists with running times at www.cj.wadsworth.com/videos. Your Thomson Wadsworth representative will be happy to provide details on our video policy by adoption size. The library includes these selections and many others:

- *ABC Videos:* Feature short, high-interest clips from current news events as well as historic raw footage going back 40 years. Perfect for discussion starters or to enrich your lectures and spark interest in the material in the text, these brief videos provide students with a new lens through which to view the past and present, one that will greatly enhance their knowledge and understanding of significant events and open up to them new dimensions in learning. Clips are drawn from such programs as *World News Tonight, Good Morning America, This Week, PrimeTime Live, 20/20,* and *Nightline,* as well as numerous ABC News specials and material from the Associated Press Television News and British Movietone News collections. Your Thomson Wadsworth representative will be happy to provide a complete listing of videos and policies.

- *60 Minutes DVD:* Featuring 12-minute clips from CBS's *60 Minutes* news program, this DVD will give you a way to explore a topic in more depth with your students without taking up a full class session. Topics include the Green River Killer, the reliability of DNA testing, and California's Three Strikes Law. Produced by Wadsworth, CBS, and Films for the Humanities.

- *The Wadsworth Custom Videos for Criminal Justice:* Produced by Wadsworth and Films for the Humanities, these videos include short five- to ten-minute segments that encourage classroom discussion. Topics include white-collar crime, domestic violence, forensics, suicide and the police officer, the court process, the history of corrections, prison society, and juvenile justice.

- *CNN® Today:* Integrate the up-to-the-minute programming power of CNN and its affiliate networks right into your course. This video features short, high-interest clips perfect for launching your lectures.

- *Oral History Project:* Developed in association with the American Society of Criminology, the Academy of Criminal Justice Society, and the National Institute of Justice, these videos will help you introduce your students to the scholars who have developed the criminal justice discipline. Compiled over the last several years, each video features a set of guest lecturers—scholars whose thinking has helped to build the foundation of present ideas in the discipline. Vol. 1: Moments in Time; Vol. 2: Great Moments in Criminological Theory; Vol. 3: Research Methods.

- *COURT TV Videos:* One-hour videos presenting seminal and high-profile cases, such as the interrogation of Michael Crowe and serial killer Ted Bundy, as well as crucial and current issues such as cybercrime, double jeopardy, and the management of the prison on Riker's Island.

- *A&E American Justice:* Forty videos to choose from, on topics such as deadly force, women on death row, juvenile justice, strange defenses, and Alcatraz.

- *Films for the Humanities:* Nearly 200 videos to choose from on a variety of topics such as elder abuse, supermax prisons, suicide and the police officer, the making of an FBI agent, domestic violence, and more.

For the Student

Criminal JusticeNow™ This unique, interactive online resource is the most exciting assessment-centered student learning tool ever offered for this course. *Criminal JusticeNow* determines students' unique study needs by having them take a chapter pre-test and then offering them personalized learning plans that focus their study time on the concepts they need to master. Study plan resources include video clips with questions, interactive diagrams, animations, learning modules, PowerPoint lectures, career profiles, topic reviews, an e-book, and more. Once the student has completed his personalized study plan, a post-test evaluates his improved comprehension of chapter content. At any time the student can view her pre- or post-test scores, and all scores and gradable assignments flow directly into the instructor's grade book.

Study Guide An extensive student guide has been developed and updated for this edition by Lynn Newhart of Rockford College. Because students learn in different ways, the guide includes a variety of pedagogical aids to help them, as well as integrated art and figures from the main text. Each chapter is outlined and summarized, major terms and figures are defined, and self-tests are provided.

Companion Website
http://cj.wadsworth.com/siegel_ess5e
http://info.wadsworth.com/0534615333
The book-specific website provides many chapter-specific resources: chapter outlines, chapter summary and review, the author's own videotaped chapter introductions, the book glossary, flash cards, tutorial quizzing, a final exam, ABC video clips with questions, and content-rich audio files for use with students' iPods. The site also features Internet exercises, InfoTrac College Edition® exercises, a discussion forum, and multi-step learning modules (Concept Builders) that present key concepts with case examples followed by essay questions in which students apply their knowledge and critical-thinking skills.

The Wadsworth Criminal Justice Resource Center
www.cj.wadsworth.com
Now includes a direct link to "Terrorism: An Interdisciplinary Perspective," an intriguing site that provides thorough coverage of terrorism in general and the issues surrounding the events of September 11. The site also features information on conventions and grants as well as an interactive criminal justice timeline, hundreds of links to popular criminal justice sites, and much more.

Careers in Criminal Justice 3.0 Interactive CD-ROM Filled with self-assessment and profiling activities, this unique CD is designed to help students investigate and focus on the criminal justice career choices that are right for them. The CD includes many outstanding features:

- The Career Rolodex features video testimonials from a variety of practicing professionals in the field and information on hundreds of specific jobs, including descriptions, employment requirements, and more.

- The Interest Assessment gives students a direct link to the Holland Personalized Self-Assessment Test, which is designed to help them decide which careers suit their personalities and interests.

- The Career Planner features helpful tips and worksheets on résumé writing, interviewing techniques, and successful job search strategies.

- Links for Reference offer direct links to federal, state, and local agencies where students can get contact information and learn more about current job opportunities.

Wadsworth's Guide to Careers in Criminal Justice, Third Edition This handy guide will give students information on a wide variety of career paths, including requirements, salaries, training, contact information for key agencies, and employment outlooks.

Handbook of Selected Supreme Court Cases, Third Edition This supplementary text provides briefs of key cases that have defined the administration of justice in this country, along with citations and commentary.

Current Perspectives: Readings from InfoTrac College Edition These readers, which are designed to give students a deeper taste of special topics in criminal justice, include free access to InfoTrac College Edition. The timely articles are selected from within InfoTrac College Edition by experts in each topic. They are available free when bundled with the text.

- Terrorism and Homeland Security
- Juvenile Justice
- Public Policy

Terrorism: An Interdisciplinary Perspective Available for bundling with each copy of *Essentials of Criminal Justice*, Fifth Edition, this 80-page booklet (with companion website) discusses terrorism in general and the issues surrounding the events of September 11, 2001. This information-packed booklet examines the origins of terrorism in the Middle East, focusing on Osama bin Laden in particular, as well as issues involving bioterrorism, the specific role played by religion in Middle Eastern terrorism, globalization as it relates to terrorism, and the reactions to and repercussions of terrorist attacks.

Crime Scenes 2.0: An Interactive Criminal Justice CD-ROM Recipient of several *New Media Magazine* Invision Awards, this interactive CD-ROM allows your students to take on the roles of investigating officer, lawyer, parole officer, and judge in excitingly realistic scenarios. Available free when bundled with every copy of the text. An online instructor's manual for the CD-ROM is also available.

Mind of a Killer CD-ROM (bundle version) Voted one of the top 100 CD-ROMs by an annual *PC Magazine* survey, *Mind of a Killer* gives students a chilling glimpse into the realm of serial killers with over 80 minutes of video *and* 3D simulations, and extensive mapping system, a library, and much more.

Internet Guide for Criminal Justice, Second Edition Internet beginners will appreciate this helpful booklet. With explanations and the vocabulary necessary for navigating the Web, it features customized information on criminal justice–related websites and presents Internet project ideas.

Internet Activities for Criminal Justice, Second Edition This completely revised 96-page booklet shows how to best utilize the Internet for research through searches and activities.

Criminal Justice Internet Explorer, Third Edition This colorful brochure lists the most popular Internet addresses for criminal justice–related websites. It includes URLs for corrections, victimization, crime prevention, high-tech crime, policing, courts, investigations, juvenile justice, research, and fun sites.

ACKNOWLEDGMENTS

Many people helped make this book possible. Those who reviewed this fifth edition and made suggestions that I attempted to follow to the best of my ability, as well as all those who reviewed previous editions, are as follows:

Kelly Asmussen, Peru State University

E. Elaine Bartgis, Fairmont State College

Richard Becker, North Harris County College

Joe W. Becraft, Portland Community College

Julia Foster Beeman, University of North Carolina, Charlotte

Daniel James Bell, Southwest Texas State University

Bruce Bikle, Portland State University

Michael B. Blankenship, Memphis State University

Ronald R. Brooks, Clinton Community College

Kathleen A. Cameron, Arizona State University

Stephen M. Cox, Central Connecticut State University

Paul Cromwell, Wichita State University

Chris W. Eskridge, University of Nebraska–Omaha

Tom Fields, Cape Fear Community College

Jacqueline Fitzgerald, Temple University

Janet Foster Goodwill, Yakima Valley Community College

Verna Henson, Texas State University

Kathrine Johnson, Kentucky State University

William Kelly, Auburn University

Daniel A. Klotz, Los Angeles Valley College

Pearl Jacobs, Sacred Heart University

Patricia Joffer, South Dakota State University

Mark Jones, East Carolina University

Barry McKee, Bristol Community College

Terry Miller, Valencia Community College

Donald A. Nypower, Montgomery County Community College

Gregory Russell, Arkansas State University

Gary Thompson, Monroe Community College

Cecilia Tubbs, Jefferson State Community College

Ellen F. Van Valkenburgh, Jamestown Community College

Margaret Vandiver, University of Memphis

Special thanks must also go to Kathleen Maguire and Ann Pastore, editors of the *Sourcebook of Criminal Justice;* the staff at the Institute for Social Research at the University of Michigan; and the National Criminal Justice Reference Service.

The form and content of this new edition were directed by our terrific new editor Carolyn Henderson Meier. It has been a pleasure working with Carolyn and our other colleagues at Thomson Wadsworth: the delightful developmental editor (as well as singer and drummer) Shelley Murphy; the fantastic Jennie Redwitz, our favorite production manager; the fabulous Linda Jupiter, production editor and personal confidante; the marvelous Linda Rill, photo editor and friend; the captivating Terra Schultz, our marketing manager; and Susan DeVanna, technology project manager.

Larry Siegel
Bedford, NH

PART 1

The Nature of Crime, Law, and Criminal Justice

A nationwide search began when eight-months-pregnant Laci Peterson, a 27-year-old substitute teacher in Modesto, California, disappeared on Christmas Eve 2002. Her grieving husband, Scott, told her family and police that she had simply vanished from their home while he was on a fishing trip. She was going to take a walk in a nearby park, he said, and never came back. When her body and that of her unborn child were found four months later, Scott was charged with two counts of murder.

Though Laci's parents and relatives at first believed that Scott Peterson could not have harmed his wife, their trust was broken when detectives told them that Scott was having an affair with a massage therapist named Amber Frey and had also taken out a $250,000 life insurance policy on Laci.

Scott pleaded not guilty to two counts of murder. During the trial, the defense first tried to blame the murder on transients who were in the park at the time Laci disappeared and then floated a theory of mistaken identity (i.e., Laci looked like a prosecutor who lived in the neighborhood and it may have been a revenge killing). The prosecution presented evidence of Scott's infidelity and suspicious activity: he was seen carrying a large wrapped object out of his house the night Laci disappeared; his "fishing trip" was in the vicinity of where her body was recovered. As the jury deliberated, it seemed they were hopelessly deadlocked. Two jurors were replaced, the foreman (who asked to be replaced) and a juror who was supposedly conducting independent research on the case. On November 12, 2004, the reconstituted jury brought back a guilty verdict; Scott was sentenced to death soon after.

How can such crimes as the killing of Laci Peterson be explained? Are they a product of an abnormal mind, or the result of social and economic factors? Are crimes like this common? Is the murder rate on the increase or in decline? What factors must a jury consider in order to find Scott guilty of murder in the first degree? And what should be done with a criminal such as Scott Peterson? Should he be sentenced to death? Or would you spare his life? What would be the moral and ethical thing to do?

The first section of *Essentials of Criminal Justice* deals with these issues in some detail. Chapter 1 reviews the criminal justice process, chapter 2 analyzes the nature and extent of crime, chapter 3 looks at criminal law and its processes, while chapter 4 reviews some of the emerging issues confronting the justice system. ∎

1 CRIME AND CRIMINAL JUSTICE

2 THE NATURE OF CRIME AND VICTIMIZATION

3 CRIMINAL LAW: SUBSTANCE AND PROCEDURE

CHAPTER 1

Crime and Criminal Justice

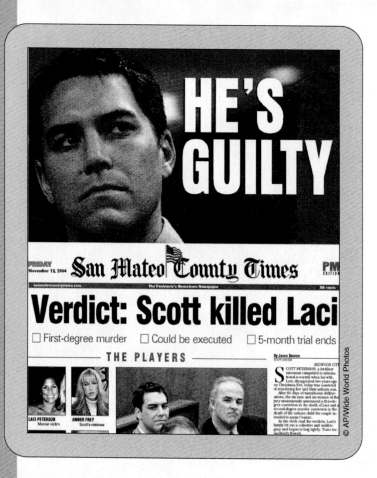

HE'S GUILTY

FRIDAY
November 12, 2004

San Mateo County Times

PM EDITION

The Peninsula's Hometown Newspaper

50 cents

Verdict: Scott killed Laci

☐ First-degree murder   ☐ Could be executed   ☐ 5-month trial ends

THE PLAYERS

By Jason Dearen
STAFF WRITER

REDWOOD CITY

SCOTT PETERSON, a fertilizer salesman catapulted to international notoriety when his wife, Laci, disappeared two years ago on Christmas Eve, today was convicted of murdering her and their unborn son.

After 66 days of tumultuous deliberations, the six men and six women of the jury unanimously announced a first-degree conviction in the death of Laci and a second-degree murder conviction in the death of the unborn child the couple intended to name Conner.

As the clerk read the verdicts, Laci's family let out a collective and audible gasp and began to sob lightly. Tears trickled down.

LACI PETERSON
Murder victim

AMBER FREY
Scott's mistress

© AP/Wide World Photos

ROSS WOLF'S law enforcement career began when he went on a ride-along with a college friend who was a sheriff's deputy with Florida's Orange County Sheriff's Office (OCSO). In the course of one shift, he found his calling. He went through an auxiliary academy and started working as a volunteer deputy. Four years later, he completed the course at the state of Florida Basic Law Enforcement Academy and started working full-time for the OCSO. After transferring to the Criminal Investigations unit he spent several years as a detective.

Though many contemporary law enforcement officers have college degrees, Ross's educational experience is beyond the norm: he holds a B.A., a master's degree in Public Administration, and a doctoral degree in Higher Education Administration and Leadership, all from the University of Central Florida in Orlando. He also has attended numerous in-service training sessions, gaining certificates from the Florida Depart-

Chapter Outline

Chapter Objectives

1. Be able to define the concept of criminal justice
2. Distinguish between the study of criminal justice and criminology
3. Be aware of the long history of crime in America
4. Discuss the development of the criminal justice system
5. Be familiar with the agencies of the criminal justice system
6. Trace the formal criminal justice process
7. Know what is meant by the term "informal criminal justice system"
8. Discuss the "wedding cake" model of justice
9. Be familiar with the various perspectives on justice
10. Understand the issues concerning ethics in criminal justice

ment of Law Enforcement in Instructor Techniques, Criminal Law, Investigative Interviews, and Field Training Officer.

Though Ross Wolf's educational credentials qualify him to teach at the university level, he did not want to give up his law enforcement career. Currently, he is the Division Chief for the Orange County Sheriff's Office Reserves. He leads a unit of more than 70 men and women who each have various specialties in law enforcement. They work in assignments such as SWAT, marine patrol, background investigations, criminal investigations, aviation, public information, and other law enforcement specialties. Though he holds an administrative position, Ross Wolf spends part of a typical day in the field, going on patrol, assisting in special details (like fundraisers for charitable organizations and parades), proactive arrest details (like drug stings), and teaching at the local police academy. The entire OCSO Reserve Unit has been recognized as one of the most progressive volunteer police organizations in the country.

Ross Wolf's career, which gives him the opportunity to help society and serve the public, illustrates the wonderful career prospects presented by the criminal justice system. The system needs talented and educated people because the public relies on the agencies of the criminal justice system to provide solutions to the crime problem and to shape the direction of crime policy.

Criminal justice may be viewed or defined *as the system of law enforcement, adjudication, and correction that is directly involved in the apprehension, prosecution, and control of those charged with criminal offenses.* This loosely organized collection of agencies is responsible for, among other matters, protecting the public, maintaining order, enforcing the law, identifying transgressors, bringing the guilty to justice, and treating criminal behavior. The public depends on this vast system, employing more than two million people and costing taxpayers more than $165 billion a year, to protect them from evil-doers and to bring justice to their lives.

This text serves as an introduction to the study of criminal justice. Those who study criminal justice typically engage in describing, analyzing, and explaining the behavior of those agencies, authorized by law and statute, to dispense justice—police departments, courts, and correctional agencies—and through their scholarly efforts, help them to identify effective and efficient methods of crime control.

This chapter introduces some basic issues, beginning with a discussion of the history of crime in America and the development of criminal justice. The major organizations and **criminal justice processes** of the criminal justice system are then introduced so that you can develop an overview of how the system functions. Because there is no single view of the underlying goals that help shape criminal justice, the varying perspectives on what criminal justice really is or should be are set out in some detail.

Criminal Justice ⚖ Now™
Learn more about Crime by viewing the "Klan Member" "In the News" video clip.

■ IS CRIME A RECENT DEVELOPMENT?

Crime and violence have existed in the United States for more than two hundred years. In fact, the crime rate may actually have been much higher in the nineteenth and early twentieth centuries than it is today.[1] Guerilla activity was frequent before, during, and after the revolutionary war. Bands supporting the British—the Tories—and the American revolutionaries engaged in savage attacks on each other, using hit-and-run tactics, burning, and looting.

The struggle over slavery during the mid-nineteenth century generated decades of conflict, crimes, and violence, including a civil war. After the war, night riders and the Ku Klux Klan were active in the South, using vigilante methods to maintain the status quo and terrorize former slaves. The violence spilled over into bloody local feuds in the hill country of southern Appalachia. Factional hatreds, magnified by the lack of formal law enforcement and grinding poverty, gave rise to violent attacks and family feuding.

After the Civil War, former Union and Confederate soldiers headed west with the dream of finding gold or starting a cattle ranch; some resorted to murder, theft, and robbery, such as the notorious John Wesley Hardin (who is alleged to have killed 30 men, studied law in prison, and became a practicing attorney before his death!), Billy the Kid, and Johnny Ringo. Opposing them were famous lawmen such as Wyatt Earp and Bat Masterson (who became a sports columnist in New York after hanging up his guns!).

criminal justice process The decision making points from the initial investigation or arrest by police to the eventual release of the offender and his or her reentry into society; the various sequential criminal justice stages through which the offender passes.

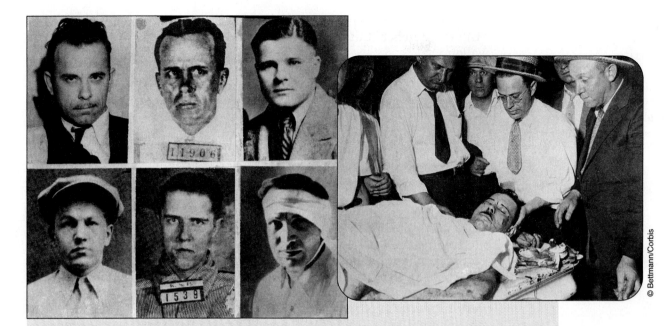

At the turn of the last century, rural outlaws became mythic figures. At left are photos of the FBI's six most wanted men in 1934. Charles "Pretty Boy" Floyd (left photo, top right) was a folk hero among the sharecroppers of eastern Oklahoma. Floyd robbed as many as thirty banks, filing a notch in his pocket watch for each of the ten men he killed. Floyd was shot dead by police on October 19, 1934. John Dillinger (left photo, top left and right photo) became the nation's premier bank robber until he was killed in front of a Chicago movie house on July 22, 1934. After his death, his body was put on view at the morgue. Hordes of people came to view America's most notorious criminal.

Although the Civil War generated western gunslingers, it also produced widespread business crime. The great robber barons bribed government officials and intrigued to corner markets and obtain concessions for railroads, favorable land deals, and mining and mineral rights on government land. The administration of President Ulysses Grant was tainted by numerous corruption scandals.

Crime at the Turn of the Twentieth Century

From 1900 to 1935, the nation experienced a sustained increase in criminal activity. This period was dominated by Depression-era outlaws, including the infamous "Ma" Barker (and her sons Lloyd, Herman, Fred, and Arthur), Bonnie Parker and Clyde Barrow, and Charles "Pretty Boy" Floyd. Notorious bank robber John Dillinger cut a swath through the Midwest until he was slain on Sunday, July 22, 1934 in a shootout with federal agents in front of a Chicago movie house.

While these relatively small and mobile outlaw gangs were operating in the Midwest, organized gangs flourished in the nation's largest cities. The first criminal gangs formed before the Civil War in urban slums, such as the Five Points and Bowery neighborhoods in New York City. Though they sported colorful names, such as the Plug Uglies, the Hudson Dusters, and the Dead Rabbits, they engaged in mayhem, murder, and extortion. These gangs were the forerunners of the organized crime families that developed in New York and then spread to Philadelphia, Chicago, New Orleans, and other major urban areas. They were the subject matter of the 2002 film

Gangs of New York with Daniel Day-Lewis playing the gang leader William "Bill the Butcher" Cutting and Leonardo DiCaprio as his rival, Amsterdam Vallon.

Criminal Justice ⚖ Now™

Learn more about Criminal Justice by viewing the "Jackson Trial" "In the News" video clip.

■ DEVELOPING THE CRIMINAL JUSTICE SYSTEM

The emergence of criminal gangs and groups in the nineteenth century coincided with the development of formal agencies of criminal justice. In 1829 the first police agency, the London Metropolitan Police, was developed to keep the peace and identify criminal suspects. In the United States, police agencies began to appear during the mid-nineteenth century. The penitentiary, or prison, was created to provide nonphysical correctional treatment for convicted offenders; these were considered "liberal" innovations that replaced corporal or capital punishment.

Although significant and far-reaching, these changes were rather isolated developments. As criminal justice developed over the next century, these fledgling agencies of justice rarely worked together in a systematic fashion. It was not until 1919—when the Chicago Crime Commission, a professional association funded by private contributions, was created—that the work of the criminal justice system began to be recognized.[2] This organization acted as a citizens' advocate group and kept track of the activities of local justice agencies. The commission still carries out its work today.

In 1931 President Herbert Hoover appointed the National Commission of Law Observance and Enforcement, which is commonly known today as the Wickersham Commission. This national study group made a detailed analysis of the U.S. justice system and helped usher in the era of treatment and rehabilitation. The final report found that thousands of rules and regulations governed the system and made it difficult for justice personnel to keep track of the system's legal and administrative complexity.[3]

The Modern Era of Justice

The modern era of criminal justice can be traced to a series of research projects, first begun in the 1950s, under the sponsorship of the American Bar Foundation.[4] Originally designed to provide in-depth analysis of the organization, administration, and operation of criminal justice agencies, the ABF project discovered that the justice system contained many procedures that heretofore had been kept hidden from the public view. The research focus then shifted to an examination of these previously obscure processes and their interrelationship—investigation, arrest, prosecution, and plea negotiations. It became apparent that justice professionals used a great deal of personal choice in decision making, and showing how this discretion was used became a prime focus of the research effort. For the first time, the term *criminal justice system* began to be used, a view that justice agencies could be connected in an intricate yet often unobserved network of decision making processes.

Federal Involvement in Criminal Justice

In 1967, the President's Commission on Law Enforcement and Administration of Justice (the Crime Commission), which had been appointed by President Lyndon Johnson, published its final report, entitled *The Challenge of Crime in a Free Society*.[5] This group of practitioners, educators, and attorneys was given the responsibility of creating a comprehensive view of the

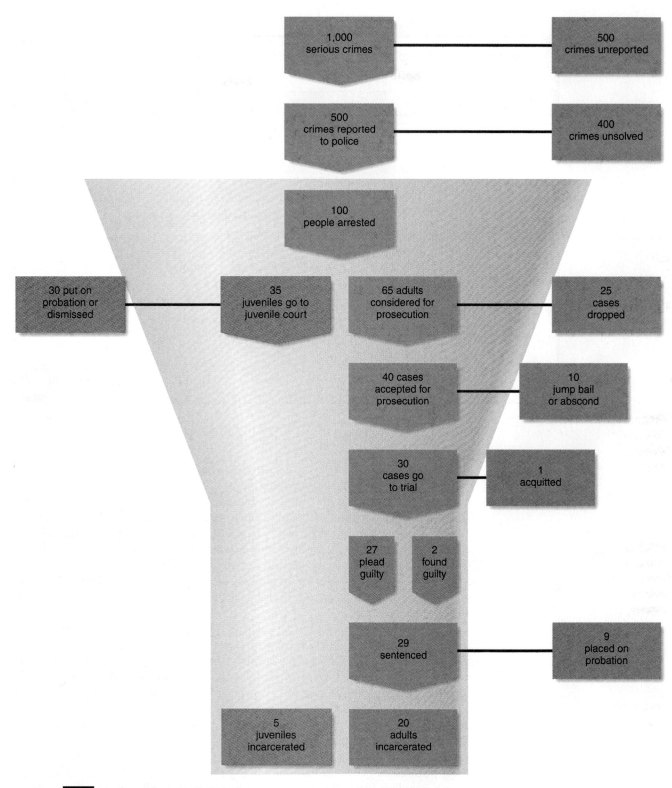

Figure 1.3 The criminal justice funnel

Sources: Gerard Rainville and Brian Reaves, *Felony Defendants in Large Urban Counties, 2000* (Washington, D.C.: Bureau of Justice Statistics, 2003); Matthew Durose and Patrick Langan, *Felony Sentences in State Courts, 2002* (Washington, D.C.: Bureau of Justice Statistics, 2004).

Concept Summary 1.1

The interrelationship of the criminal justice system and the criminal justice process

The System: Agencies of Crime Control	The Process
1. Police	1. Contact
	2. Investigation
	3. Arrest
	4. Custody
2. Prosecution and defense	5. Complaint/charging
	6. Grand jury/preliminary hearing
	7. Arraignment
	8. Bail/detention
	9. Plea negotiations
3. Court	10. Adjudication
	11. Disposition
	12. Appeal/postconviction remedies
4. Corrections	13. Correction
	14. Release
	15. Postrelease

rights and procedures, many are settled in an informal pattern of cooperation between the major actors in the justice process. For example, police may be willing to make a deal with a suspect in order to gain his cooperation, and the prosecutor may bargain with the defense attorney to gain a plea of guilty as charged in return for a promise of leniency. Law enforcement agents and court officers are allowed tremendous discretion in their decision to make an arrest, bring formal charges, handle a case informally, substitute charges, and so on. Crowded courts operate in a spirit of getting the matter settled quickly and cleanly, rather than engage in long, drawn-out criminal proceedings with an uncertain outcome.

Whereas the traditional model regards the justice process as an adversarial proceeding in which the prosecution and defense are combatants, most criminal cases are actually cooperative ventures in which all parties get together to work out a deal; this is often referred to as the **courtroom work group**.[13] Made up of the prosecutor, defense attorney, judge, and other court personnel, the courtroom work group helps streamline the process of justice through the extensive use of deal making and plea negotiation. Rather than looking to provide a spirited defense or prosecution, cooperation rather than conflict between prosecutor and defense attorney appears to be the norm. It is only in a few widely publicized criminal cases involving rape or murder that the adversarial process is called into play. Consequently, upward of 80 percent of all felony cases and over 90 percent of misdemeanors are settled without trial.

The "Wedding Cake" Model of Justice

Samuel Walker, a justice historian and scholar, has come up with a rather unique way of describing this informal justice process: he compares it to a four-layer cake, as depicted in Figure 1.4.[14]

courtroom work group The phrase used to denote that all parties in the adversary process work together in a cooperative effort to settle cases with the least amount of effort and conflict.

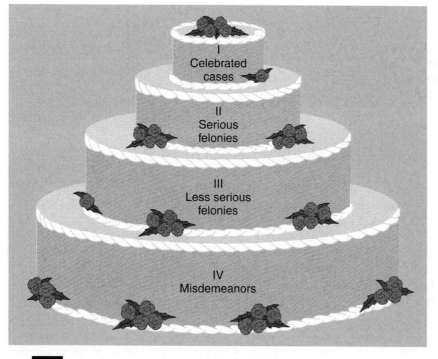

Figure 1.4 **The criminal justice "wedding cake"**
Source: Based on Samuel Walker, *Sense and Nonsense About Crime* (Belmont, Calif.: Wadsworth, 2001).

Level I The first layer of Walker's model is made up of the celebrated cases involving the wealthy and famous, such as O. J. Simpson and Michael Jackson, or the not-so-powerful who victimize a famous person—for example, John Hinckley, Jr., who shot President Ronald Reagan. Other cases fall into the first layer because they are widely reported in the media and become the subject of a TV investigation, such as Scott Peterson, convicted of killing his wife, Laci.

Cases in the first layer of the criminal justice wedding cake usually receive the full array of criminal justice procedures, including competent defense attorneys, expert witnesses, jury trials, and elaborate appeals. Because of the media focus on Level I cases and the Hollywood treatment of them, the public is given the impression that most criminals are sober, intelligent people and most victims are members of the upper classes, a patently false impression

Level II The second layer contains serious felonies—rapes, robberies, and burglaries. Police, prosecutors, and judges all agree that these are serious cases, worthy of the full attention of the justice system. The seriousness of the offense places them in the Level II category:

- They are committed by experienced, repeat offenders.
- The amount of money stolen in a burglary or larceny is significant.
- Violent acts are committed by a stranger who uses a weapon.
- Robberies involve large amounts of money taken by a weapon-wielding criminal.

Offenders in such Level II cases receive a full jury trial and, if convicted, can look forward to a prison sentence.

Level III Though they can also be felonies, crimes that fall in the third layer of the wedding cake are either less serious offenses, committed by young or first-time offenders, or involve people who knew each other or were otherwise related. Level III crimes may be dealt with by an outright dismissal, a plea bargain, reduction in charges, or most typically, a probationary sentence.

Level IV The fourth layer of the cake is made up of the millions of misdemeanors—disorderly conduct, shoplifting, public drunkenness, and minor assault—that are handled by the lower criminal courts in assembly-line fashion. Few defendants insist on exercising their constitutional rights, because the delay would cost them valuable time and money, and punishment is typically a fine or probation.[15]

The wedding cake model of informal justice is an intriguing alternative to the traditional criminal justice flowchart. Criminal justice officials handle individual cases quite differently, yet there is a high degree of consistency with which particular types or classes of cases are dealt in every legal jurisdiction. For example, police and prosecutors in Los Angeles and Boston will each handle the murder of a prominent citizen in similar fashion. They will also deal with the death of an unemployed street person killed in a brawl in a similar manner. The model is useful because it helps us realize that public opinion about criminal justice is often formed on the basis of what happened in an atypical case.

Criminal Justice ⚖ Now™

Learn more by exploring the "Drug Control Strategies" Vocabulary Check activity.

▎PERSPECTIVES ON JUSTICE

Though it has been more than thirty-five years since the field of criminal justice began to be the subject of both serious academic study and attempts at unified policy formation, significant debate continues over the actual meaning of *criminal justice* and how the problem of crime control should be approached. After decades of effort in research and policy analysis, it is clear that criminal justice is far from a unified field. Practitioners, academics, and commentators alike have expressed irreconcilable differences concerning its goals, purpose, and direction. Considering the complexity of criminal justice, it is not surprising that no single view, perspective, or philosophy dominates the field. What are the dominant views of the criminal justice system today? What is the role of the justice system, and how should it approach its tasks? The different perspectives on criminal justice are discussed next.

Crime Control Perspective

People who hold the **crime control perspective** believe that the proper role of the justice system is to prevent crime through the judicious use of criminal sanctions. Because the public is outraged by violent crimes, it demands an efficient justice system that hands out tough sanctions to those who choose to violate the law.[16] If the justice system were allowed to operate in an effective manner, unhampered by legal controls, potential criminals would be deterred from committing law violations. Those who did commit a crime would be apprehended, tried, and punished so that they would never dare risk committing a crime again. Crime rates trend upward, the argument goes, when criminals do not sufficiently fear apprehension and punishment. If the efficiency of the system could be increased and the criminal law could be toughened, crime rates would eventually decline. Effective law enforcement, strict mandatory punishment, incarceration of dangerous criminals, and the judicious use of capital punishment are the keys to reducing crime rates. Though crime control may be expensive, reducing the pains of criminal activity is well worth the price. If punishment was swift, certain, and severe, few would be tempted to break the law.

crime control perspective A model of criminal justice that emphasizes the control of dangerous offenders and the protection of society. Its advocates call for harsh punishments as a deterrent to crime, such as the death penalty.

Crime control advocates do not want legal technicalities to help the guilty go free and tie the hands of justice. They lobby for the abolition of legal restrictions that control a police officer's ability to search for evidence and interrogate suspects. They want law enforcement officers to be able to profile people at an airport in order to identify terrorists, even if it means singling out people because of their gender, race, or ethnic origin. They are angry at judges who let obviously guilty people go free because a law enforcement officer made an unintentional procedural error.

In sum, the key positions of the crime control perspective are:

- The purpose of the justice system is to deter crime through the application of punishment.
- The more efficient the system, the greater its effectiveness.
- The justice system is not equipped to treat people, but rather, to investigate crimes, apprehend suspects, and punish the guilty.

Rehabilitation Perspective

If the crime control perspective views the justice system in terms of protecting the public and controlling criminal elements, then advocates of the **rehabilitation perspective** view crime as an expression of frustration and anger created by social inequality and the justice system as a means of caring for and treating people who have been the victims of this inequity. According to this view, crime can be controlled by giving people the means to improve their lifestyle and helping them overcome any personal and or psychological problems caused by their life circumstances.

rehabilitation perspective A model of criminal justice that views its primary purpose as helping to care for people who cannot manage themselves. Crime is an expression of frustration and anger created by social inequality that can be controlled by giving people the means to improve their lifestyle through conventional endeavors.

According to the rehabilitation perspective, at-risk kids can be successfully treated before they become career criminals. Here, students at the Missouri Division of Youth Services' Rosa Parks Center "circle up" to resolve a problem. Part of these juvenile offenders' rehabilitation involves learning anger management and peaceful ways to resolve disputes. With its low recidivism rates, this program is gaining attention from other states that currently treat juvenile offenders harshly.

The rehabilitation concept assumes that people are at the mercy of social, economic, and interpersonal conditions and interactions. Criminals themselves are the victims of racism, poverty, strain, blocked opportunities, alienation, family disruption, and other social problems. They live in socially disorganized neighborhoods that are incapable of providing proper education, health care, or civil services. Society must help them in order to compensate for their social problems.

Rehabilitation advocates believe that government programs can help reduce crime on both a societal (macro-) and individual (micro-) level. On the macro- or societal level, rehabilitation efforts are aimed at preventing crimes before they occur. If legitimate opportunities increase, crime rates decline.[17] This goal may be achieved at the neighborhood level by increasing economic opportunities through job training, family counseling, educational services, and crisis intervention. On a micro- or individual level, rehabilitation efforts are aimed at known offenders who have already violated the law. The best method to reduce crime and recidivism (repeat offending) rates is to help offenders produce through intensive one-on-one counseling prosocial changes in attitudes and improved cognitive thinking patterns.[18] Although the public may want to "get tough" on crime, many are willing to make exceptions, for example, by advocating leniency for younger offenders.[19]

The key provisions of the rehabilitation model are:

- In the long run, it is better to treat than punish.
- Criminals are society's victims.
- Helping others is part of the American culture.

Due Process Perspective

According to the **due process perspective,** the justice system should be dedicated to providing fair and equitable treatment to those accused of crime.[20] This means providing impartial hearings, competent legal counsel, equitable treatment, and reasonable sanctions to ensure that no one suffers from racial, religious, or ethnic discrimination.

Those who advocate the due process orientation are quick to point out that the justice system remains an adversarial process that pits the forces of an all-powerful state against those of a solitary individual accused of a crime. If concern for justice and fairness did not exist, the defendant who lacked resources could easily be overwhelmed; miscarriages of justice are common. Numerous criminal convictions have been overturned because newly developed DNA evidence later shows that the accused could not have committed the crimes; many of the falsely convicted spend years in prison before their release.[21] Evidence also shows that many innocent people have been executed for crimes they did not commit.[22] Because such mistakes can happen, even the most apparently guilty offender deserves all the protection the justice system can offer.

The key positions advocated by due process supporters include:

- Every person deserves their full array of constitutional rights and privileges.
- Preserving the democratic ideals of American society takes precedence over the need to punish the guilty.
- Because of potential errors, decisions made within the justice system must be carefully scrutinized.
- Steps must be taken to treat all defendants fairly regardless of their socioeconomic status.

due process perspective Due process is the basic constitutional principle based on the concept of the privacy of the individual and the complementary concept of limitation on governmental power; a safeguard against arbitrary and unfair state procedures in judicial or administrative proceedings. Embodied in the due process concept are the basic rights of a defendant in criminal proceedings and the requisites for a fair trial. See Glossary for further details.

Multimillionaire murder defendant Robert Durst is shown copies of record by assistant prosecutor Joel Bennet, right, as defense attorney Mike Ramsey looks on during the prosecution's cross-examination on October 28, 2003, in Galveston, Texas. The son of a New York City real estate tycoon, Durst was accused of murder for killing a neighbor at a low-rent Galveston apartment house where they both lived, then dismembering the victim and throwing the body parts into Galveston Bay. Durst was found not guilty despite what appeared to be overwhelming evidence. The case illustrates the due process principle that a fair trial is critical for a defendant to prove his or her innocence to a jury of their peers.

© 2005 AP/Wide World Photos

- Illegally seized evidence should be suppressed even if it means that a guilty person will go free.
- Despite the cost, the government should supply free legal counsel at every stage of the justice system to prevent abuse.

Nonintervention Perspective

Supporters of the **nonintervention perspective** believe that justice agencies should limit their involvement with criminal defendants. They believe that regardless of whether intervention is designed to punish or treat people, the ultimate effect of any involvement is harmful and will have long-term negative effects. Once involved with the justice system, criminal defendants develop a permanent record that follows them for the rest of their lives. They may be watched and kept under surveillance. Bearing an official label disrupts their personal and family life and harms their own self-image; they may view themselves as bad, evil, outcasts, troublemakers, or crazy. Official labels then may promote rather than reduce the continuity in antisocial activities.[23] When people are given less stigmatized forms of punishment, such as probation, they are less likely to become repeat offenders.[24]

Fearing the harmful effects of stigma and labels, noninterventionists have tried to place limitations on the government's ability to control people's lives. They have called for the **decriminalization** (reduction of penalties) and **legalization** (lawful and non-criminal) of nonserious **victimless crimes,** such as the possession of small amounts of marijuana (see the following Policy, Programs, and Issues in Criminal Justice box).

Noninterventionists have sponsored the removal of nonviolent offenders from the nation's correctional system, a policy referred to as **deinstitutionalization.** They support the placement of first offenders who commit minor

nonintervention perspective A justice philosophy that emphasizes the least intrusive treatment possible. Among its central policies are decarceration, diversion, and decriminalization. In other words, less is better.

decriminalization Reducing the penalty for a criminal act but not actually legalizing it.

legalization The removal of all criminal penalties from a previously outlawed act.

victimless crime An act that is in violation of society's moral code and therefore has been outlawed—for example, drug abuse, gambling, and prostitution. These acts are linked together because, although they have no external victim, they are considered harmful to the social fabric.

deinstitutionalization The movement to remove as many offenders as possible from secure confinement and treat them in the community.

Policy, Programs, and Issues in Criminal Justice

Should Drugs Be Legalized?

A keystone of the noninterventionist perspective is decriminalization of recreational drug usage. According to this view, like it or not, drug use is here to stay. Using mood-altering substances is customary in almost all human societies; no matter how hard we try, people will find ways of obtaining psychoactive drugs. Banning drugs serves to create generation after generation of people who are considered criminals, who might otherwise have been productive citizens. It also creates networks of illegal drug manufacturers and distributors, many of whom use violence as part of their standard operating procedures. Though some may charge that drug use is immoral, is it any worse than the unrestricted use of alcohol and cigarettes, both of which are addicting and unhealthy? Far more people die each year because they abuse these legal substances than the numbers who are killed in drug wars or from using illegal substances (an estimated 85,000 people die each year from alcohol-related causes and another 435,000 from tobacco compared to about 17,000 related to illegal drugs, including suicide, homicide, motor-vehicle injury, HIV infection, pneumonia, violence, hepatitis, and overdoses).

Reformer Ethan Nadelmann of the Drug Policy Alliance is an outspoken critic of the ongoing "war" against drugs. Nadelmann argues persuasively that everyone has a stake in ending the war on drugs, whether they be a parent concerned about protecting children from drug-related harm, a social justice advocate worried about racially disproportionate incarceration rates, an environmentalist seeking to protect the Amazon rainforest, or a fiscally conservative taxpayer seeking to save money. U.S. federal, state, and local governments have spent hundreds of billions of dollars trying to make America drug-free. Yet heroin, cocaine, methamphetamine, and other illicit drugs are cheaper, purer, and easier to get than ever before. Moreover, Nadelmann suggests that many of the problems the drug war claims to resolve are in fact caused by the drug war itself. For example, public health problems such as HIV and hepatitis C are all

increased by laws that restrict access to clean needles. The drug war is not the promoter of family values that some would have us believe, he argues. Children of inmates are at risk for educational failure, joblessness, addiction, and delinquency. In a recent publication (2003), Nadelmann castigates the federal government's strict law enforcement approach to drug control. By and large, he says, the more punitive the approach, the greater the harms that result. The United States represents 5 percent of the world's population and 25 percent of the world's prison population. Nearly half a million people are behind bars on drug charges—more than all of western Europe (with a bigger population) incarcerates for all offenses. The stand against the use of marijuana for medical purposes shows the futility of the get-tough approach. Almost 80 percent of Americans believe marijuana should be legally available as a medicine, when recommended by a doctor. Every state ballot initiative on the issue has won. Now even state legislatures are approving medical marijuana. The U.S. Institute of Medicine says marijuana has medicinal value. Yet the federal government continues to forbid marijuana use.

Liberals are not the only critics of current drug control policy. Judge James P. Gray, a political conservative, is also an outspoken critic of America's antidrug policies. In his book *Why Our Drug Laws Have Failed and What We Can Do About It* (2001), Gray decries the program of massive imprisonment and demonization of drug users that has flowed from making drugs illegal. Illegality is futile because it amounts to an attempt to repeal the law of supply and demand, which is an impossible task. Criminalizing drugs raises the price of the goods, which encourages growers and dealers to risk their lives to sell drugs for huge profits. Gray also argues that antidrug efforts have eroded civil liberties and due process, giving police too much power to seize assets and confiscate property or money from criminals in order to obstruct further criminal activity. Few of those whose assets have been seized are later charged with crime. Some form of legalization would help reduce these problems. However, rather than condone drug use, Gray calls for a program of drug maintenance (allowing addicts a monitored drug intake) and controlled distribution (in which government-regulated drugs are sold in a controlled fashion). Gray goes so far as to suggest that generically packaged drugs such as marijuana could be sold by pharmacists, with a steep tax that would fund rehabilitation programs and drug education.

Against Legalization

At a recent hearing (2003) on legalization of marijuana for medical purposes in Maryland, John P. Walters, director of the Office of National Drug Control Policy (ONDCP), stated:

> We owe people with debilitating medical conditions the best that science has to offer—not the results of interest group lobbying and political compromise. Research has not demonstrated that smoked marijuana is safe and effective medicine. Legalizing smoked marijuana under the guise of medicine is scientifically irresponsible and contradictory to our high standards for approval of medications. The legislation being considered in Maryland for so-called medical marijuana would also mean more availability of a dangerous drug in our neighborhoods. The citizens of Maryland deserve better.

Walters and other legalization opponents are of the opinion that legalization may harm the well-being of the community by creating health and social damage. Individuals do not have the right to harm society even if it means curbing their freedom and personal choices—that is, the right to use drugs. If injured by their drug use, individuals would have to be cared for by the community at a very substantial cost to citizens who do not use drugs. Legalization would result in an increase in the nation's rate of drug usage, creating an even larger group of nonproductive, drug-dependent people, who must be cared for by the rest of society. If drugs were legalized and freely available, users might significantly increase their daily intake. In countries like Iran and Thailand, where drugs are cheap and readily available, narcotic-use rates are high.

The problems of alcoholism should serve as a warning of what can happen when controlled substances are made readily available. If legalized, the number of drug-dependent babies could begin to match or exceed the number who are delivered with fetal alcohol syndrome. Drunk-driving fatalities, which today number about twenty-five thousand per year, could be matched by deaths caused by driving under the influence of pot or crack. And though distribution would be regulated, adolescents would likely have the same opportunity to obtain potent drugs as they now have with beer and other forms of alcohol.

Critical Thinking

In the final analysis, and after considering all the issues in this ongoing debate, should drugs be legalized? What is the logic of banning marijuana while dangerous substances such as scotch and bourbon are readily available in stores?

InfoTrac College Edition Research

To find out what former drug czar and value guru Will Bennett thought of the Pottawatomie County decision, go to InfoTrac College Edition and read: "Statement of Empower America Co-Director William J. Bennett on the Supreme Court's Decision in *Pottawatomie County v. Earls*," *US Newswire*, June 27, 2002, p1008178n9466.

Sources: Ali Mokdad, James Marks, Donna Stroup, and Julie Gerberding, "Actual Causes of Death in the United States, 2000," *Journal of the American Medical Association 10* (2004): 1242–1243; Press Release, "White House Drug Czar, Chair of Congressional Black Caucus Rep. Elijah Cummings and Maryland Community Leaders Discuss Harms of 'Medical Marijuana' and Warn of Dangers of Marijuana Legalization," March 24, 2003, www.whitehousedrugpolicy.gov/news/press03/032403.html, accessed on August 3, 2005; Ethan Nadelmann, "The U.S. Is Addicted to War on Drugs." *Globe and Mail*. May 20, 2003; James P. Gray, *Why Our Drug Laws Have Failed and What We Can Do About It: A Judicial Indictment of the War on Drugs* (Philadelphia: Temple University Press, 2001); Erich Goode, *Between Politics and Reason: The Drug Legalization Debate* (New York: St. Martin's Press, 1997); David Courtwright, "Should We Legalize Drugs? History Answers No," *American Heritage* (February/March 1993): 43–56; Ethan Nadelmann, "America's Drug Problem," *Bulletin of the American Academy of Arts and Sciences 65* (1991): 24–40; Ethan Nadelmann, "Should We Legalize Drugs? History Answers Yes," *American Heritage* (February/March 1993): 41–56.

crimes in informal, community-based treatment programs, a process referred to as **pretrial diversion.**

Noninterventionists fear that efforts to help or treat offenders may actually stigmatize them beyond the scope of their actual offense; this is referred to as **widening the net of justice.** Their efforts have resulted in rulings stating that these laws can be damaging to the reputation and the future of offenders who have not been given an opportunity to defend themselves from the charge that they are chronic criminal sex offenders.[25] As a group, noninterventionist initiatives have been implemented to help people avoid the stigma associated with contact with the criminal justice system.

The key elements of the nonintervention perspective include:

- The justice process stigmatizes offenders.
- Stigma locks people into a criminal way of life.
- Less is better. Decriminalize, divert, and deinstitutionalize whenever possible.

Justice Perspective

According to those holding the **justice perspective,** the greatest challenge facing the American criminal justice system is its ability to dispense fair and equal justice to those who come before the law. It is unfair for police to issue a summons to one person for a traffic violation while letting a second offender off with a warning or to have two people commit the same crime but receive different sentences or punishments. Unequal and inconsistent treatment produces disrespect for the system, suspiciousness, and frustration; it also increases the likelihood of recidivism. Therefore, law violators should be evaluated on the basis of their current behavior, not on what they have done in the past (they have already paid for that behavior) nor on what they may do in the future (since future behavior cannot be accurately predicted). The treatment of criminal offenders must be based solely on present behavior: punishment must be equitably administered and based on "just deserts."

The justice perspective has had considerable influence in molding the nation's sentencing policy. There has been an ongoing effort to reduce discretion and guarantee that every offender convicted of a particular crime receives equal punishment. There have been a number of initiatives designed to achieve this result, including mandatory sentences requiring that all people convicted of a crime receive the same prison sentence. *Truth-in-sentencing laws* now require offenders to serve a substantial portion of their prison sentence behind bars, limiting their eligibility for early release on parole.[26]

The key elements of the justice perspective are:

- People should receive equal treatment for equal crimes.
- Decision making in the justice system must be standardized and structured by rules and regulations.
- Whenever possible, individual discretion must be reduced and controlled.
- Inconsistent treatment produces disrespect for the system.

Restorative Justice Perspective

According to the concept of restorative justice, the criminal justice system should promote a peaceful and just society; the justice system should aim for peacemaking, not punishment.[27]

The **restorative justice perspective** draws its inspiration from religious and philosophical teachings ranging from Quakerism to Zen. Advocates of

pretrial diversion A program that provides nonpunitive, community-based alternatives to more intrusive forms of punishment such as jail or prison.

widening the net of justice The charge that programs designed to divert offenders from the justice system actually enmesh them further in the process by substituting more intrusive treatment programs for less intrusive punishment-oriented outcomes.

justice perspective A view of justice that holds that all people should be treated equally before the law. Equality may be best achieved through the control of individual discretion in the justice process.

restorative justice perspective A view of criminal justice that advocates peaceful solutions and mediation rather than coercive punishments.

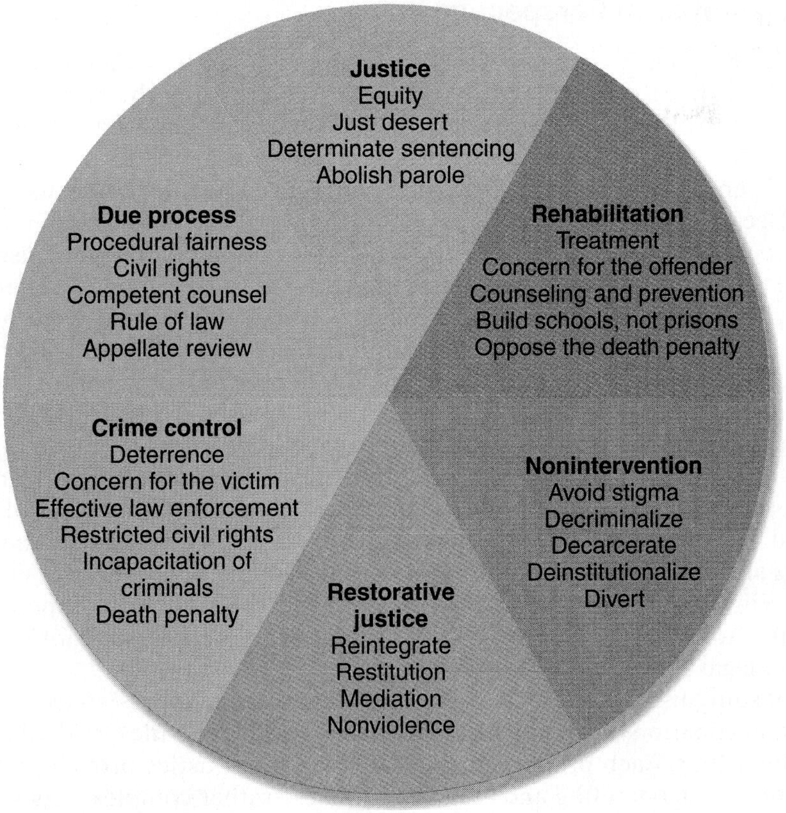

Justice
Equity
Just desert
Determinate sentencing
Abolish parole

Due process
Procedural fairness
Civil rights
Competent counsel
Rule of law
Appellate review

Rehabilitation
Treatment
Concern for the offender
Counseling and prevention
Build schools, not prisons
Oppose the death penalty

Crime control
Deterrence
Concern for the victim
Effective law enforcement
Restricted civil rights
Incapacitation of
criminals
Death penalty

Nonintervention
Avoid stigma
Decriminalize
Decarcerate
Deinstitutionalize
Divert

Restorative justice
Reintegrate
Restitution
Mediation
Nonviolence

Figure 1.5 **Perspectives on justice: Key concerns and concepts**

restorative justice view the efforts of the state to punish and control as encouraging crime rather than discouraging crime. The violent, punishing acts of the state are not dissimilar from the violent acts of individuals.[28] Therefore, mutual aid rather than coercive punishment is the key to a harmonious society. Without the capacity to restore damaged social relations, society's response to crime has been almost exclusively punitive.

According to restorative justice, resolution of the conflict between criminal and victim should take place in the community in which it originated and not in some far-off prison. The victim should be given a chance to voice his story, and the offender can directly communicate his need for social reintegration and treatment. The goal is to enable the offender to appreciate the damage he has caused, to make amends, and to be reintegrated back into society.

Restorative justice programs are now being geared to these principles. Police officers, as elements of community policing programs, are beginning to use mediation techniques to settle disputes rather than resort to formal arrest.[29] Mediation and conflict resolution programs are common features in many communities. Financial and community service restitution programs as an alternative to imprisonment have been in operation for more than two decades.

The most important elements of the restorative justice model are:

- Offenders should be reintegrated back into society.
- Coercive punishments are self-defeating.
- The justice system must become more humane.

The various perspectives are summarized in Figure 1.5.

Perspectives in Perspective

Advocates of each view have attempted to promote their vision of what justice is all about and how it should be enforced. During the past decade, the crime control and justice models have dominated. Laws have been toughened and the rights of the accused curtailed, the prison population has grown, and the death penalty has been employed against convicted murderers. Because the crime rate has been dropping, these policies seem to be effective; they may be questioned if crime rates once again begin to rise. At the same time, efforts to rehabilitate offenders, to provide them with elements of due process, and to give them the least intrusive treatment have not been abandoned. Police, courts, and correctional agencies supply a wide range of treatment and rehabilitation programs to offenders in all stages of the criminal justice system. Whenever possible, those accused of crime are treated informally in nonrestrictive, community-based programs, and the effects of stigma are guarded against. Although the legal rights of offenders are being closely scrutinized by the courts, the basic constitutional rights of the accused remain inviolate. Guardians of the process have made sure that defendants are allowed the maximum protection possible under the law. For example, criminal defendants have been awarded the right to competent legal counsel at trial; merely having a lawyer to defend them is not considered sufficient legal protection.

In sum, understanding the justice system today requires analyzing a variety of occupational roles, institutional processes, legal rules, and administrative doctrines. Each predominant view of criminal justice provides a vantage point for understanding and interpreting these rather complex issues. No single view is the right or correct one. Each individual must choose the perspective that best fits his or her own ideas and judgment—or they can all be discarded and the individual's own view substituted.

Criminal Justice ⚖ Now™

*Learn more about **Careers in Criminal Justice** by exploring the "On the Job" feature **DEA Special Agent Recruiter.***

❚ ETHICS IN CRIMINAL JUSTICE

The general public and criminal justice professionals are also concerned with the application of ethics in the criminal justice system.[30] Both would like every police officer on the street, every district attorney in court, and every correctional administrator in prison to be able to discern what is right, proper, and moral, to be committed to ethical standards, and to apply equal and fair justice. These demands are difficult because justice system personnel are often forced to work in an environment where moral ambiguity is the norm. For example, should a police officer be forced to arrest, a prosecutor charge, and a correctional official punish a woman who for many years was the victim of domestic abuse and who in desperation retaliates against her abusive spouse? Who is the victim here and who is the aggressor? And what about the parent who attacks the man who has sexually abused her young child; should she be prosecuted as a felon? But what happens if the parent mistakenly attacks and injures the wrong person? Can a clear line be drawn between righteous retribution and vigilante justice? As students of justice, we are concerned with identifying the behavioral standards that should govern each of the elements of justice. If these can be identified, is it possible to find ways to spread these standards to police, court, and correctional agencies around the nation?

Ethics in criminal justice is an especially important topic today considering the power granted to those who control the justice system. We rely on the justice system to exert power over people's lives, to be society's instrument of social control, and thereby grant the system and its agents the authority to deny people their personal liberty on a routine basis. A police officer's ability to arrest and use force, a judge's power to sentence, and a correctional administrator's ability to punish an inmate give them considerable personal power that must be governed by ethical considerations. Without ethical decision making, it is possible that individual civil rights will suffer and personal liberties, guaranteed by the U.S. Constitution, trampled upon. The need for an ethical criminal justice system is further enhanced by cyber-age advances in record keeping and data recording. Agents of the criminal justice system now have immediate access to our most personal information, ranging from arrest record to medical history. Issues of privacy and confidentiality—which can have enormous economic, social, and political consequences—are now more critical than ever. Ethical issues transcend all elements of the justice system. Yet each branch has specific issues that shape their ethical standards, which are discussed in the following sections.

© 2005 AP/Wide World Photos

The television wall tells the Microsoft story as CNBC's Tom Costello gives a report from the NASDAQ MarketSite in New York's Times Square on June 28, 2001. A federal appeals court in the District of Columbia unanimously reversed the breakup of Microsoft, ruling that although the software giant violated antitrust laws, the trial judge engaged in "serious judicial misconduct" by making derogatory comments about the company. Should a defendant go free because a judge erred? While the Microsoft case was a civil matter, what about a murder trial? Should a conviction be overturned because the judge made derogatory comments about the killer?

Ethics and Law Enforcement

Ethical behavior is particularly important in law enforcement because, quite simply, police officers have the authority to deprive people of their liberty. And, in carrying out their daily activities, they also have the right to use physical and even deadly force.

Depriving people of liberty and using force are not the only police behaviors that require ethical consideration. Police officers maintain considerable discretion when they choose whom to investigate, how far the investigation should go, and how much effort is required—for example, undercover work, listening devices, or surveillance. In carrying out their duties, police officers must be responsive to the public's demand for protection while at the same time remaining sensitive to the rights and liberties of those they must deter and/or control. In this capacity, they serve as the interface between the power of the state and the citizens it governs. This duality creates many ethical dilemmas. Consider the following:

- Should law enforcement agents target groups whom they suspect are heavily involved in crime and violence or does this lead to racial/ethnic profiling? Is it unethical for a security agent to pay closer attention to a young Arab male getting on an airline flight than she gives to a well-groomed American soldier from upstate New York? After all, there have been no terrorist activities among army personnel, and the 9/11 terrorists were of Arab descent. But don't forget that clean-cut Tim McVeigh, who grew up in rural Pendleton, New York, and spent more than three years in the Army, went on to become the Oklahoma City bomber. How can police officers balance their need to protect public security with the ethical requirement that they protect citizens' legal rights?

- Should police officers tell the truth even if it means that a guilty person goes free? For example, a police officer stops a car for a traffic violation and searches it illegally. He finds a weapon used in a particularly heinous shooting in which three children were killed. Would it be ethical for the officer to lie on the witness stand and say the gun was laying on the car seat in plain sight (thereby rendering its seizure legal and proper)? Or should he tell the truth and risk having the charges dismissed, leaving the offender free to kill again?

- Should police officers be loyal to their peers even when they know they have violated the law? A new officer soon becomes aware that his partner is taking gratuities from local gangsters in return for looking the other way and allowing their prostitution and bookmaking operations to flourish. Should the rookie file a complaint and turn in his partner? Will she be labeled a "rat" and lose the respect of her fellow officers? After all, gambling and prostitution are not violent crimes and do not really hurt anyone? Or do they?

How can law enforcement officers be aided in making ethical decisions? Various national organizations have produced model codes of conduct that can serve as behavioral guides. One well-known document created by the International Association of Chiefs of Police says in part:

> As a law enforcement officer my fundamental duty is to serve mankind; to safeguard lives and property; to protect the innocent against deception, the weak against oppression or intimidation, and the peaceful against violence or disorder; and to respect the constitutional rights of all men to liberty, equality, and justice . . . [31]

Ethics and the Court Process

Ethical concerns do not stop with an arrest. As an officer of the court and the "people's attorney," the prosecutor must seek justice for all parties in a criminal matter and should not merely be hunting a conviction. To be fair, prosecutors must share evidence with the defense, not use scare tactics or intimidation, and represent the public interest. It would be inexcusable and illegal for prosecutors to suppress critical evidence, a practice which might mean that the guilty walk free and the innocent are convicted.

Prosecutorial ethics become tested when the dual role of a prosecutor causes them to experience role conflict. On the one hand, a prosecutor represents the people and has an obligation to present evidence, uphold the law, and obtain convictions as vigorously as possible. In the adversary system, it is the prosecutor who takes the side of the victim and upon whom they count for justice.

But as a fair and impartial officer of the court, the prosecutor must oversee the investigation of crime and make sure that all aspects of the investigation meet constitutional standards. If during the investigation it appears that the police have violated the constitutional rights of suspects—for example, by extracting an illegal confession or conducting an illegal search—the prosecutor has an ethical obligation to take whatever action is necessary and appropriate to remedy legal or technical errors, even if it means rejecting a case in which the defendant's rights have been violated. Moreover, the canon of legal ethics in most states forbids the prosecutor from pursuing charges when there is no probable cause and mandates that all evidence that might mitigate guilt or reduce the punishment be turned over to the defense.

Defense Attorney As an officer of the court, along with the judge, prosecutors, and other trial participants, the defense attorney seeks to uncover the basic facts and elements of the criminal act. In this dual capacity of being both a defensive advocate and an officer of the court, the attorney is often confronted with conflicting obligations to his client and profession. Suppose, for example, a client confides that she is planning to commit a crime. What are the defense attorney's ethical responsibilities in this case? Obviously, the attorney would have to counsel the client to obey the law; if the attorney assisted the client in engaging in illegal behavior, the attorney would be subject to charges of unprofessional conduct and even criminal liability.

© 2005 AP/Wide World Photos

Ana White testifies at Suffolk Superior Court during the trial of Harold Parker, Luis Vasquez, his brother Ismael Vasquez, and Scott Davenport in Boston. White testified as part of a deal with prosecutors in which she pleaded guilty to lesser charges in exchange for her testimony against the four men charged in the killing of Io Nachtwey in November 2001. Is it ethical to grant leniency to a killer who is willing to testify against her co-conspirators? Why should someone be spared punishment because they are willing to "rat out" their accomplices?

Ethics and Corrections

Ethical issues do not stop once a defendant has been convicted. The ethical issues in punishment are too vast to discuss here, but include the following:

- Is it fair and ethical to execute a criminal? Can capital punishment ever be considered as a moral choice?

- Should people be given different punishments for the same criminal law violation? Is it fair and just when some convicted murderers and rapists receive probation for their crimes while others are sentenced to prison for the same offense?

- Is it fair to grant leniency to criminals who agree to testify against their co-conspirators and therefore allow them to benefit from their perfidy while others not given the opportunity to "squeal" are forced to bear the full brunt of the law?

- Should some criminal inmates be granted early release because they can persuade the parole board they have been rehabilitated while others, not as glib, convincing, or well spoken, are forced to serve their entire sentence behind bars?

Ethics are also challenged by the discretion afforded to correctional workers and administrators. Discretion is involved when a correctional officer decides to report an inmate for disorderly conduct, which might jeopardize his or her parole. And while the Supreme Court has issued many rulings relating to prisoners' rights, they are not at the scene of the prison to make sure that their mandates are carried out in an orderly fashion.

Correctional officers have significant coercive power over offenders. They are under a legal and professional obligation not to use unnecessary force or take advantage of inmate powerlessness. Examples of abuse would be an officer who beats an inmate, or a staff member who coerces sex from an inmate. These are abuses of power and the possibility for them exists because of the powerlessness of the offender relative to the correctional professional. A recent national survey uncovered evidence showing that this breach of ethics is significant: During 2004, an estimated 8,210 allegations of sexual violence were reported by correctional inmates. About 42 percent of the reported allegations of sexual violence involved staff-on-inmate sexual misconduct and 11 percent involved staff sexual harassment of inmates. In other words, staff members were involved in more cases of sexual violence and harassment in correctional facilities than were inmates![32]

Ethical considerations transcend all elements of the justice system. Making ethical decisions is an increasingly important task in a society that is becoming more diverse, pluralistic, and complex every day.

SUMMARY

- Criminal justice refers to the agencies that dispense justice and the process in which justice is carried out.
- America has experienced crime throughout most of its history.
- In the Old West justice was administered by legendary lawmen like Wyatt Earp.
- There was little in the way of a formal criminal justice system until the nineteenth century when the first police agencies were created.
- The term *criminal justice system* became prominent around 1967, when the President's Commission on Law Enforcement and the Administration of Justice began a nationwide study of the nation's crime problem.
- Criminal justice is a field that uses knowledge from various disciplines in an attempt to understand what causes people to commit crimes and how to deal with the crime problem.
- Criminal justice consists of the study of crime and of the agencies concerned with its prevention and control.
- On an ideal level, the criminal justice system functions as a cooperative effort among the primary agencies—police, courts, and corrections.
- The process consists of the actual steps the offender takes from the initial investigation through trial, sentencing, and appeal.
- In many instances, the criminal justice system works informally to expedite the disposal of cases.
- Criminal acts that are very serious or notorious may receive the full complement of criminal justice processes, from arrest to trial. However, less serious cases are often settled when a bargain is reached between the prosecution and the defense.

- The role of criminal justice can be interpreted in many ways. People who study the field or work in its agencies bring their own ideas and feelings to bear when they try to decide on the right course of action to take or recommend. Therefore there are a number of different perspectives on criminal justice today.
- The crime control perspective is oriented toward deterring criminal behavior and incapacitating serious criminal offenders.
- The rehabilitation model views the justice system as a treatment agency focused on helping offenders. Counseling programs are stressed over punishment and deterrence strategies.
- The due process perspective sees the justice system as a legal process. Their concern is that every defendant receives the full share of legal rights granted under law.
- The nonintervention model is concerned about stigma and helping defendants avoid a widening net of justice; these advocates call for the least intrusive methods possible.
- The justice model is concerned with making the system equitable. The arrest, sentencing, and correctional process should be structured so that every person is treated equally.
- The restorative justice model focuses on finding peaceful and humanitarian solutions to crime.
- The justice system must deal with many ethical issues. It is sometimes difficult to determine what is fair and just and balance it with the need to protect the public.

KEY TERMS

criminal justice process 4
Law Enforcement Assistance
    Administration (LEAA) 7
social control 7
in-presence requirement 10
nolle prosequi 10
grand jury 10

true bill of indictment 10
courtroom work group 14
crime control perspective 16
rehabilitation perspective 17
due process perspective 18
nonintervention perspective 19
decriminalization 19

legalization 19
victimless crime 19
deinstitutionalization 19
pretrial diversion 22
widening the net of justice 22
justice perspective 22
restorative justice perspective 22

REVIEW QUESTIONS

1. Can there be a single standard of ethics that is applied to all criminal justice agencies? Or is the world too complex to legislate morality and ethics?

2. Describe the differences between the formal and informal justice systems. Is it fair to treat some offenders informally?

3. What are the layers of the criminal justice "wedding cake"? Give an example of a crime for each layer.

4. What are the basic elements of each model or perspective on justice? Which best represents your own point of view?

5. How would each perspective on criminal justice consider the use of the death penalty as a sanction for first-degree murder?

CHAPTER 2

The Nature of Crime and Victimization

KIDNAPPED

LAST SEEN AT CARLOS & CHARLIES
MONDAY, MAY 29, 2005 1:30AM
NATALEE HOLLOWAY
CAUCASIAN AMERICAN FEMALE
BLUE EYES / LONG BLOND HAIR
5'4" 110 LBS.   18 YEARS OLD

ANY INFORMATION
PLEASE CALL 587-6222
OR CALL POLICE STATION 100

© 2005 AP/Wide World Photos

JOHN A. GRAHAM'S career in criminal justice began when as a young man he received a job as a deputy sheriff before he was old enough to buy a firearm. After serving as a city police officer and a U.S. Border Patrol agent, he started a career with the United States Customs Service. His work did not stop him from getting an advanced education. He went to Texas A&M University at Corpus Christi, where he earned an undergraduate degree in Political Science and Secondary Special Education, a Master of Science Degree in Education and a Master of Public Administration, both with an emphasis in Criminal Justice Administration.

Graham finds customs work challenging. He has conducted investigations into drug smuggling, marine enforcement, air surveillance, underwater search and recovery, money laundering, child pornography,

Chapter Outline

Chapter Objectives

1. Be able to discuss how crime is defined
2. Be familiar with how crime is measured
3. Discuss the differences between survey data and record data
4. Recognize the trends in the crime rate
5. Comment on the factors that influence crime rates
6. Be familiar with international crime trends
7. Know the various crime patterns
8. Understand the concept of the criminal career
9. Be able to discuss the characteristics of crime victims
10. Distinguish between the various views of crime causation

murder, and kidnapping, testified in court, worked on task force operations, and written hundreds of reports.

Customs agents work long hours, and twenty-four-hour days are not abnormal. A moving surveillance might require driving from Texas to Chicago, straight through with no sleep or rest for two or more days. Reports, office notices, meetings, public information presentations, and training are all part of the job. Training is constant and consistent with lots of travel involved. A customs agent has to be able to adapt to the situation immediately, with no break in concentration or purpose. Therefore it is imperative to develop new skills to meet the never-ending challenges. The job of a special agent, regardless of the agency, is a tough but rewarding field of employment.

gents of the criminal justice system, such as customs agents, must develop accurate information about crime—where it occurs, who commits it, and why—in order to design valid strategies for its control. It would be foolish to create a gang control strategy based on job creation if being unemployed was not related to joining a gang. It would be ineffective to create a sex-offender registry if research shows that registering sex offenders causes them to commit even more crimes. Justice experts must develop accurate measures of criminal behavior because otherwise they cannot be sure whether a particular policy, process, or procedure has the effect its creators envisioned. For example, a state may enact a new law requiring that anyone who uses a firearm to commit a crime serve a mandatory prison term. The new statute is aimed directly at reducing the incidence of such violent crimes as murder, armed robbery, and assault. The effectiveness of this statutory change cannot be demonstrated without hard evidence that the use of firearms actually declines after the law is instituted and that the use of knives or other weapons does not increase. Without being able to measure crime accurately, it would be impossible either to understand its cause or to plan its elimination.

This chapter will review some of the basic questions about crime addressed by criminal justice professionals: How is crime defined? How is crime measured? How much crime is there, and what are its trends and patterns? Why do people commit crime? How many people become victims of crime, and under what circumstances does victimization take place?

Criminal Justice ⚖ Now™

*Learn more about **Defining Crime** by going through the Learning Module.*

▌HOW IS CRIME DEFINED?

The justice system centers around crime and its control. While for most of us the concept of "crime" seems rather simple—a violation of criminal law—the question remains: Why are some acts considered a violation of the law and others, seemingly more serious, legal and noncriminal? There are actually three views of how and why some behaviors become illegal and considered crimes while others remain noncriminal.

Criminal Justice ⚖ Now™

*Learn more about **Models of Criminal Justice** by exploring the Review and Reinforce activity.*

Consensus View

According to what is known as the **consensus view of crime,** behaviors that become crimes are those that (1) are essentially harmful to a majority of citizens living in society and therefore (2) have been controlled or prohibited by the existing criminal law. Using this definition, criminal law is a set of rules, codified by state authorities, that express the norms, goals, and values of *the vast majority of society*. The definition implies that criminal law and the crimes it defines represent the *consensus* of public opinion and that there is general agreement about which behaviors society needs to control and which should be beyond state regulation.

The consensus view rests on the assumption that criminal law has a social control function—restraining those whose behavior would otherwise endanger the social framework by taking advantage of others' weakness for their own personal gain. Criminal law works to control behaviors that are inherently destructive and dangerous in order to maintain the existing social fabric and ensure the peaceful functioning of society. The consensus view is so named because it infers that the great majority of citizens agree that certain behaviors must be outlawed or controlled and that criminal law is designed to protect citizens from social harm.

consensus view of crime *The belief that the majority of citizens in a society share common ideals and work toward a common good and that crimes are acts that are outlawed because they conflict with the rules of the majority and are harmful to society.*

Conflict View

According to the **conflict view of crime,** the ongoing class struggle between the rich and poor, the haves and have-nots, controls the content of criminal law and thereby the definition of crime. According to this view, criminal law is created and enforced by the ruling class as a mechanism for controlling dissatisfied, have-not members of society. The law is the instrument that enables the wealthy to maintain their position of power and control the behavior of those who oppose their ideas and values or who might rebel against the unequal distribution of wealth.[1] Laws defining property crimes, such as larceny and burglary, are created in order to protect the wealth of the affluent. Drug laws are developed to ensure that workers will be productive, clearheaded, and sober. Laws defining violent crimes are created to keep the angry and frustrated lower classes under control. People who violate these laws are subject to severe punishments. In contrast, business and white-collar crimes receive relatively lenient punishments considering the extent of the harm and damage they cause.

Interactionist View

Falling between the consensus and conflict visions, the **interactionist view of crime** suggests that criminal law is structured to reflect the preferences and opinions of people who hold social power in a particular legal jurisdiction. These people use their influence to impose their definition of right and wrong on the rest of the population. Crimes are outlawed behaviors simply because the law defines them as such, and not because they are inherently evil or immoral acts. So, for example, it is illegal to purchase marijuana and hashish, while liquor and cigarettes are sold openly even though far more people die of alcoholism and smoking than from drug abuse each year.[2]

The interactionist view of crime is focused on the role of people who dedicate themselves to shaping the legal process.[3] These **moral entrepreneurs** wage campaigns (*moral crusades*) to control behaviors they view as immoral and wrong (such as abortion) or, conversely, to legalize behaviors they consider harmless social eccentricities (such as smoking marijuana). The basics of these views are set out in Concept Summary 2.1.

Though these views of crime differ, they generally agree (1) that criminal law defines crime; (2) that the definition of crime is constantly changing and evolving; (3) that social forces mold the definition of crimes; and (4) that

Criminal Justice ⚖ Now ™

Learn more about Types of Crime by exploring the "Domestic Violence Part I" Role Play activity.

Criminal Justice ⚖ Now ™

Learn more by exploring the Mala Prohibita and Morality Review and Reinforce activities.

conflict view of crime (or critical view of crime) *The belief that the law is controlled by the rich and powerful who shape its content to ensure their continued economic domination of society. The criminal justice system is an instrument of social and economic repression.*

interactionist view of crime *Criminal law reflects the values of people who use their social and political power to shape the legal system.*

moral entrepreneurs *People who wage moral crusades to control criminal law so that it reflects their own personal values.*

Concept Summary 2.1

Definition of crime

Consensus View	Conflict View	Interactionist View
• The law defines crime. • Agreement exists on outlawed behavior. • Laws apply to all citizens equally.	• The law is a tool of the ruling class. • Crime is a politically defined concept. • "Real crimes" are not outlawed. • The law is used to control the underclass.	• Moral entrepreneurs define crime. • Crimes are illegal because society defines them that way. • Criminal labels are life-transforming events.

Using pepper spray, Pittsburgh police arrest antiwar demonstrators as they protest United States involvement in the war in Iraq, during an unpermitted march on March 30, 2003. The FBI's Uniform Crime Report program tallies arrests and reports them on a yearly basis.

© 2005 AP/Wide World Photos

criminal law has a social control function. Therefore, as used here, the term **crime** is defined as follows:

> Crime is a violation of social rules of conduct, interpreted and expressed by a written criminal code, created by people holding social and political power. Its content may be influenced by prevailing public sentiments, historically developed moral beliefs, and the need to protect public safety. Individuals who violate these rules may be subject to sanctions administered by state authority, which include social stigma and loss of status, freedom, and on occasion, their lives.

Criminal Justice ⚖ Now™

Learn more by viewing the "Tyco" and "WorldCom" "In the News" video clips.

HOW IS CRIME MEASURED?

In addition to understanding how an act becomes a crime, it is important for criminal justice scholars to measure the nature, extent, and trends in the crime rate. They use a variety of techniques to study crime and its consequences. The following sections review in some detail some of the most important of these methods.

Record Data

A significant proportion of criminal justice data comes from the compilation and evaluation of government and social agency records, including schools, courts, police departments, social service centers, and corrections departments.

Records can be used for a number of purposes. Correctional records can be analyzed in an effort to determine what types of inmates adjust to prison and which inmates are more likely to fail after they reenter society. Educational records are important indicators of intelligence, academic achievement, school behavior, and other information that can be related to criminal behavior patterns. However, records of local police departments, compiled and analyzed by the Federal Bureau of Investigation (FBI) are the most important source of crime statistics; this data is discussed in detail below.[4]

crime A violation of societal rules of behavior as interpreted and expressed by a criminal legal code created by people holding social and political power. Individuals who violate these rules are subject to sanctions by state authority, social stigma, and loss of status.

Official Crime Data: The Uniform Crime Report (UCR)

The FBI's **Uniform Crime Report (UCR)** is the best known and most widely cited source of criminal statistics.[5] Data from the UCR is published in an annual volume called *Crime in the United States* and serves as the nation's **official crime statistics.**

How is the UCR compiled? The FBI receives records from over seventeen thousand police departments serving a majority of the U.S. population. Its main unit of analysis involves **index (Part I) crimes:** criminal homicide, forcible rape, robbery, aggravated assault, burglary, larceny/theft, motor vehicle theft, and arson. Exhibit 2.1 defines these crimes. Local police departments compute all reported incidents involving these crimes and send the information to the FBI. The Bureau tallies the local police reports, and then compiles the number of known offenses by city, county, standard metropolitan statistical area, and geographical divisions of the United States. Besides these statistics, the UCR also provides a number of other important pieces of crime data. Most importantly, it calculates the number and characteristics (age, race, and gender) of individuals who have been arrested for these and all other crimes—**nonindex (Part II) crimes**—such as prostitution and drug trafficking.

The UCR uses three methods to express crime data. First, the number of crimes reported to the police and arrests made are expressed as raw figures (for example, in 2003 16,503 murders occurred). Second, crime rates per one hundred thousand people are computed. That is, when the UCR indicates that the murder rate was about 5.76 in 2003, it means that almost six people in every one hundred thousand were murdered between January 1 and December 31, 2004. This is the equation used:

$$\frac{\text{Number of reported crimes}}{\text{Total U.S. population}} \times 100,000 = \text{Rate per } 100,000$$

Third, the FBI computes changes in the number and rate of crime over time. For example, murder rate decreased about 3.6 percent between 2003 and 2004.

How Accurate Is the UCR? The UCR's accuracy has long been suspect. Many serious crimes are not reported to police and therefore are not counted by the UCR. The reasons for not reporting vary:

- Victims consider the crime trivial or unimportant and therefore choose not to call police.
- Some victims fail to report because they do not trust the police and/or have little confidence in their ability to solve crime.
- People without property insurance believe it is useless to report theft.
- Some victims fear reprisals from an offender's friends or family.
- Some victims have "dirty hands" and are involved in illegal activities themselves. They do not want to get involved with police.

Because of these and other factors, less than half of all criminal incidents are reported to the police.

The way police departments record and report criminal activity also affects the validity of UCR statistics. Some departments may define crimes loosely—reporting a trespass as a burglary or an assault on a woman as an attempted rape—whereas others pay strict attention to FBI guidelines. Some make systematic errors in UCR reporting, for example, counting an arrest only after a formal booking procedure, although the UCR requires arrests to be counted if the suspect is released without a formal charge. These reporting practices may help explain interjurisdictional differences in crime.[6]

 To access Crime in the United States, go to "Web Links" on your Siegel Essentials of Criminal Justice 5e website: http://cj.wadsworth.com/siegel_ess5e.

Uniform Crime Report (UCR) The FBI's yearly publication of where, when, and how much serious crime occurred in the prior year.

official crime statistics Compiled by the FBI in its Uniform Crime Reports, these are a tally of serious crimes reported to police agencies each year.

index (Part I) crimes The eight crimes that, because of their seriousness and frequency, the FBI reports the incidence of in the annual Uniform Crime Report. Index crimes include murder, rape, assault, robbery, burglary, arson, larceny, and motor vehicle theft.

nonindex (Part II) crimes All other crimes plus the eight index crimes. The FBI records all arrests made for Part II crimes including race, gender, and age information.

Exhibit	2.1	FBI index crimes

Criminal Homicide

Murder and nonnegligent manslaughter. The willful (nonnegligent) killing of one human being by another. Deaths caused by negligence, attempts to kill, assaults to kill, suicides, accidental deaths, and justifiable homicides are excluded. Justifiable homicides are limited to the killing of a felon by a law enforcement officer in the line of duty and the killing of a felon by a private citizen.

Manslaughter by negligence. The killing of another person through gross negligence. Traffic fatalities are excluded. While manslaughter by negligence is a Part I crime, it is not included in the crime index.

Forcible Rape

The carnal knowledge of a female forcibly and against her will. Included are rapes by force and attempts or assaults to rape. Statutory offenses (no force used—victim under age of consent) are excluded.

Robbery

The taking or attempting to take anything of value from the care, custody, or control of a person or persons by force or threat of force or violence and/or by putting the victim in fear.

Aggravated Assault

An unlawful attack by one person on another for the purpose of inflicting severe or aggravated bodily injury. This type of assault is usually accompanied by the use of a weapon or by means likely to produce death or great bodily harm. Simple assaults are excluded.

Burglary

Breaking or entering. The unlawful entry of a structure to commit a felony or a theft. Attempted forcible entry is included.

Larceny/Theft *(except motor vehicle theft)*

The unlawful taking, carrying, leading, or riding away of property from the possession or constructive possession of another. Examples are thefts of bicycles or automobile accessories, shoplifting, pocket picking, or the stealing of any property or article that is not taken by force and violence or by fraud. Attempted larcenies are included. Embezzlement, "con" games, forgery, worthless checks, etc., are excluded.

Motor Vehicle Theft

The theft or attempted theft of a motor vehicle. A motor vehicle is self-propelled and runs on the surface and not on rails. Specifically excluded from this category are motorboats, construction equipment, airplanes, and farming equipment.

Arson

Any willful or malicious burning or attempt to burn, with or without intent to defraud, a dwelling, house, public building, motor vehicle or aircraft, personal property of another, and so on.

Source: Federal Bureau of Investigation, *Crime in the United States*, 2004 (Washington, D.C.: U.S. Government Printing Office, 2005).

 To access the **UCR**, go to "Web Links" on your Siegel Essentials of Criminal Justice 5e website: http://cj.wadsworth.com/siegel_ess5e.

Some critics take issue with the way the FBI records data and counts crimes. For example, according to the *Hierarchy Rule*, in a multiple offense incident, only the most serious crime is counted. So if an armed bank robber commits a robbery, assaults a patron as he flees, steals a car to get away, and damages property during a police chase, only the robbery is reported because it is the most serious offense.

Although these issues are troubling, the UCR continues to be one of the most widely used sources of criminal statistics.

Survey Data

Surveys are designed to have people respond to questions about their values, attitudes and behavior. For example, a sample of ten thousand high school seniors can be selected at random and asked about the frequency of their use of alcohol and drugs and their attitudes toward drug usage. If the survey sample is carefully drawn and the subjects randomly selected, it is possible to make accurate estimates of drug use among the total population of millions of high school seniors in the United States.

Because survey instruments typically include questions measuring the subject's behaviors, attitudes, beliefs, and abilities, they can provide information on the background and personal characteristics of offenders that otherwise would remain unknown. Surveys also provide a valuable source of information on particular crime problems—such as drug use—that are rarely reported to police and may therefore go undetected.

Surveys can be used to measure the nature and extent of criminal victimization. Some are conducted with relatively small groups in an effort to find out if personal status influences victimization risk. For example, a recent (2004) survey of gang members found that when youth join gangs they become more likely to both commit crimes and experience violent victimization. The survey found that many youths join gangs for security, but in reality gang membership offers little in the way of protective value and much in the way of danger.[7]

Victim Surveys: The National Crime Victimization Survey (NCVS)

One of the most important sources of crime data is the federally funded **National Crime Victimization Survey (NCVS).** This yearly survey uses a large, carefully drawn sample of citizens who are queried about their experiences with criminal activity during the past year. By assessing victimizations, the NCVS enables crime experts to estimate the total number of criminal incidents that occur each year, including those that are never reported to police.[8]

How is the NCVS conducted? Samples of housing units are selected using a complex, multistage sampling technique. Each year, data is obtained twice annually from a large nationally representative sample of about 75,000 persons in 42,000 households.[9] Those contacted are asked to report on the frequency, characteristics, and consequences of criminal victimization for such crimes as rape, sexual assault, robbery, assault, theft, household burglary, and motor vehicle theft.

Because of the care with which the samples are drawn and the high completion rate, NCVS data is considered a relatively unbiased, valid estimate of all victimizations for the target crimes included in the survey. Yet, like the UCR, the NCVS may also suffer from some methodological problems. As a result, its findings must be interpreted with caution. Some of the potential problems are listed in Exhibit 2.2.

www To access data from the NCVS on the Web, go to "Web Links" on your Siegel Essentials of Criminal Justice 5e website: http://cj.wadsworth.com/siegel_ess5e.

National Crime Victimization Survey (NCVS) The ongoing victimization study conducted jointly by the Justice Department and the U.S. Census Bureau that surveys victims about their experiences with law violation.

| Exhibit | 2.2 | Validity issues in the NCVS |

- Victims may overreport due to their misinterpretation of events; for example, a lost wallet may be reported as stolen or an open door may be viewed as a burglary attempt.
- Victims may underreport because they are embarrassed about reporting crime to interviewers, afraid of getting in trouble, or simply forget an incident.
- There may be an inability to record the personal criminal activity of those interviewed, such as drug use or gambling; murder is not included for obvious reasons.
- Sampling errors may produce a group of respondents that does not represent the nation as a whole.
- An inadequate question format may invalidate responses; some groups, such as adolescents, may be particularly susceptible to error because of question format.

Self-Report Surveys

You may have read newspaper reports that teenage drug use has been on the rise (or is falling). How can the daily substance abuse of American teenagers possibly be calculated? Drug use is something that teens rarely talk freely about with strangers, especially those who work in the criminal justice system! The answer to this dilemma can be found in the use of self-report surveys that ask teens about their substance abuse. A self-report survey, such as the annual Monitoring the Future (MTF) study conducted by the Institute of Social Research at the University of Michigan, can provide information on the percentage of students who use drugs, trends in drug use, and the type of adolescent who becomes a drug user.[10]

 To access the **Monitoring the Future** website, go to "Web Links" on your Siegel Essentials of Criminal Justice 5e website: http://cj.wadsworth.com/siegel_ess5e.

Self-report surveys are most often anonymously administered to large groups of subjects. It is assumed that subjects will be willing to accurately describe their illegal activities because the survey instruments are typically unsigned, the respondent cannot be identified, and their answers are confidential. Self-reports are viewed as a mechanism to get at the "dark figures of crime," those criminal acts missed by official statistics. Exhibit 2.3 illustrates some typical self-report items.

Most self-report studies such as MTF involve school-administered surveys measuring juvenile delinquency and youth crime.[11] Because school attendance is universal, a school-based self-report survey represents a cross section of the community. However, self-reports are not restricted to youth crime. They are also used to examine the offense histories of prison inmates, drug users, and other segments of the population. They can be used to estimate the number of criminal offenders who have previously been unknown to the police. These respondents represent many criminals who have never figured in official crime statistics, some of whom may even be serious or **chronic offenders.**[12] In sum, self-reports provide an appreciable amount of information about offenders that cannot be found in official statistics.

Are Self-Reports Valid? Critics of self-report studies frequently suggest that it is unreasonable to expect people to candidly admit illegal acts. They have nothing to gain, and the ones taking the greatest risk are the ones with official records who may be engaging in the most criminality. Some people may exaggerate their criminal acts, forget some of them, or be confused about what is being asked. Some surveys contain an overabundance of trivial offenses, such as shoplifting small amounts of items or using false identification, often lumped together with serious crimes, to form a total crime index. Consequently, comparisons between groups can be highly misleading.

chronic offender A delinquent offender who is arrested five or more times before he or she is eighteen and who stands a good chance of becoming an adult criminal; these offenders are responsible for more than half of all serious crimes.

Exhibit **2.3** **Self-report survey questions**

Please indicate how often in the past 12 months you did each act. (Check the best answer.)

	Never did act	1 time	2–5 times	6–9 times	10+ times
Stole something worth less than $50					
Stole something worth more than $50					
Used cocaine					
Been in a fistfight					
Carried a weapon such as a gun or knife					
Fought someone using a weapon					

Response rate is also critical. Even if 90 percent of a school population voluntarily participates in a self-report survey, researchers can never be sure whether the few who refuse to participate or are absent that day account for a significant portion of the school's population of persistent, high-rate offenders.[13] It is also unlikely that the most serious chronic offenders in the teenage population are the most willing to cooperate with university-based criminologists administering self-report tests.[14] For example, persistent substance abusers tend to underreport the frequency of their drug use.[15]

While these charges are troubling, criminologists have used a variety of techniques to verify self-report data.[16] For example, the "known group" method compares youths who are known to be offenders with those who are not to see whether the former report more delinquency. There is evidence that kids known to be active delinquents self-report more crime than those who are not involved in criminality.[17] Research shows that when kids are asked if they have ever been arrested or sent to court their responses accurately reflect their true life experiences.[18]

Criminal Justice ⚖ Now ™
Learn more by exploring the "Discretion" Review and Reinforce activity.

Alternative Data Sources

In addition to these primary data sources, there are a number of alternative methods used by criminal justice researchers:

Observation The systematic observation, recording, and deciphering of behavior types within a sample or population is another common method of criminal justice data collection. Some observation studies are conducted in the field, where the researcher observes subjects in their natural environments; other observations take place in a contrived, artificial setting or a laboratory. For example, children will watch a violent TV program in a university psychology lab, and researchers will record their behavior to determine whether it undergoes a discernible change. In one recent study, researchers Dean Dabney, Richard Hollinger, and Laura Dugan used a hidden camera to observe shoplifters in a large department store. They found that the most important predictor of shoplifting was in-store behavior (and personal characteristics such as age, gender, or race): shoplifters left the store without purchasing anything, and spent time checking out surveillance and tampering with products.[19]

Interviews Some criminal justice researchers conduct in-depth interviews with a small sample of offenders. This kind of study provides insights into the causes of crime that surveys and records cannot capture. In one study criminologists Emily Gaarder and Joanne Belknap interviewed delinquent girls sent to adult prisons and found that many had troubled lives that set them on a criminal career path.[20] One girl told them how her father had attacked her, yet her mother shortly let him return home:

> I told her I'd leave if he came back, but she let him anyway. I was thinking, you know, she should be worrying about me. I left and went to my cousin's house. Nobody even called me. Mom didn't talk to me for two weeks, and Dad said to me, "Don't call." It was like they didn't care. I started smoking weed a lot then, drinking, skipping school, and shoplifting. . . . I had no (delinquency) record before this happened.

In-depth interviews help crime experts develop a more complete understanding of the social and personal forces that have shaped the lives of young offenders.

Life Histories Another technique of criminal justice data collection is the **life history.** This method uses personal accounts of individuals who have had experience in crime, deviance, and other related areas. Diaries or autobi-

life history *A research method that uses the experiences of an individual as the unit of analysis, such as using the life experience of an individual gang member to understand the natural history of gang membership.*

ographies can be used; sometimes an account is given to an interested second party to record "as told to."[21] Life histories provide insights into the human condition that other, less personal research methods cannot hope to duplicate.

Compatibility of Crime Data Sources

Are the various sources of crime data compatible? Each has strengths and weaknesses. The FBI survey is carefully tallied and contains data on the number of murders and people arrested, information that the other data sources lack. However, this survey omits the many crimes that victims choose not to report to police, and it is subject to the reporting caprices of individual police departments.

The NCVS contains unreported crime and important information on the personal characteristics of victims, but the data consists of estimates made from relatively limited samples of the total U.S. population, so that even narrow fluctuations in the rates of some crimes can have a major impact on findings. It also relies on personal recollections that may be inaccurate. Furthermore, the NCVS does not include data on important crime patterns, including murder and drug abuse.

Self-report surveys can provide information on the personal characteristics of offenders—such as their attitudes, values, beliefs, and psychological profiles—that is unavailable from any other source. Yet, at their core, self-reports rely on the honesty of criminal offenders and drug abusers, a population not generally known for accuracy and integrity.

Despite these differences, the data sources seem more compatible than was first believed. Although their tallies of crimes are certainly not in sync, the crime patterns and trends they record are often similar.[22] For example, all three sources generally agree about the personal characteristics of serious criminals (such as age and gender) and where and when crime occurs (such as urban areas, nighttime, and summer months).

Criminal Justice ⚖ Now™

Learn more about Crime Trends by exploring the "Burglary Part I" Role Play activity.

▌CRIME TRENDS

What do the various sources of crime data tell us about the nature, extent, and trends in crime? Criminal behavior is not new to this century.[23] Studies have indicated that a gradual increase in the crime rate, especially in violent crime, occurred from 1830 to 1860. Following the Civil War, this rate increased significantly for about fifteen years. Then, from 1880 up to the time of World War I—with the possible exception of the years immediately preceding and following the war—the number of reported crimes decreased. After a period of readjustment, the crime rate steadily declined until the Depression (about 1930), when another crime wave was recorded. Crime rates increased gradually following the 1930s until the 1960s, when the growth rate became much greater. The homicide rate, which had actually declined from the 1930s to the 1960s, also began a sharp increase that continued through the 1970s.

As Figure 2.1 shows, the crime rate peaked in the mid-1990s when police recorded about 14.6 million crimes. Since then both the number of crimes and the rate of crime declined for the remainder of the decade. Even the teen murder rate, which had remained stubbornly high, underwent a significant decline.[24]

The overall decline in crime is reflected in both the property and violent crime rates. The violent crime rate trended downward for most of the 1990s;

Rate per 100,000 population

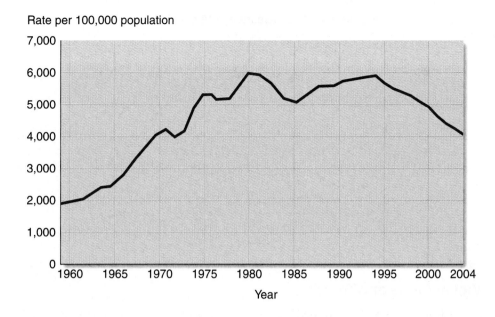

Figure 2.1
Crime rate trends
After years of steady increase, crime rates declined from 1993 through 2004.
Source: FBI, Uniform Crime Report, 2003; updated September 2005.

between 1994 and 2004, the violent crime rate declined by one third (33 percent). Particularly encouraging has been the continuing decline in the number and rate of murders. Figure 2.2 illustrates homicide rate trends since 1900. Note how the rate peaked around 1930, then fell, began to rise dramatically around 1960, and peaked once again in 1991, when the number of murders topped twenty-four thousand for the first time in U.S. history.

The property crime rate also declined about one quarter (25 percent) between 1994 and 2004. Property crimes reported in the UCR include larceny, motor vehicle theft, and arson. FBI data indicates that property crime rates declined during the past decade, though the drop was not as dramatic as that experienced in violent crimes.

Criminal Justice ⚖ Now ™
*Learn more about **Crime Trends** by exploring the **Crime Rate Trends** and **Homicide Rate Trends** Animated Artwork.*

Rate per 100,000 population

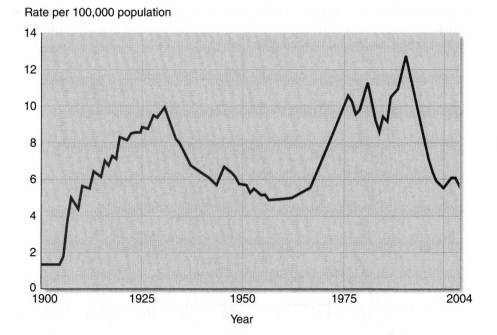

Figure 2.2
Homicide rate trends, 1900–2004
Source: FBI, Uniform Crime Report, updated September 2005.

Figure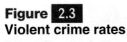
Violent crime rates

Source: Shannan Catalano,
Criminal Victimization 2004
(Washington, D.C.: Bureau of
Justice Statistics, 2005).

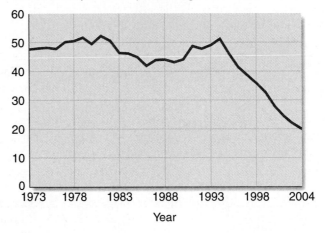

Violent crime per 1,000 persons age 12 or older

Victim Rates and Trends

According to the NCVS, Americans age twelve and older experienced approximately 24 million violent and property victimizations in 2004.

- Of the 24 million victimizations:
    - 77 percent (18.6 million) were property crimes
    - 22 percent (5.1 million) were crimes of violence
    - 1 percent were personal thefts.
- For every 1,000 persons age 12 or older, there occurred:
    - 1 rape or sexual assault
    - 1 assault with injury
    - 2 robberies
- About 22 percent of all violent crime incidents were committed by an armed offender; 6 percent by an offender with a firearm.
- Males, African Americans, and youths are more likely to be victimized than members of other groups/statuses.[25]

The NCVS reports significant declines in the violent (see Figure 2.3) and property crime (see Figure 2.4) rates during the past decade, trends that reflect the declines found in the UCR.

Figure 2.4
Property crime rates

Source: Shannan Catalano,
Criminal Victimization 2004
(Washington, D.C.: Bureau of
Justice Statistics, 2005).

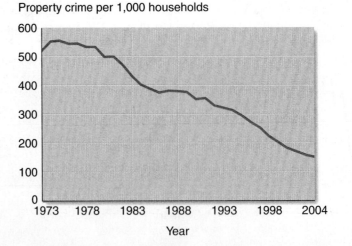

Property crime per 1,000 households

The factors that help explain the upward and downward movements in crime rates are discussed in the following Policy, Programs, and Issues in Criminal Justice feature.

Arrest Trends Currently, about 13.5 million people are arrested each year, 2 million for index crimes and the rest for non-index crimes including 1.7 million drug arrests. Over the past decade the number of arrests has trended downward, echoing the decline in the crime rate. One exception is arrests for drug violations (see Figure 2.5), which appears to be in an upward spiral since 1990.

Slightly more than 20 percent of all reported index crimes are cleared by arrest each year. Violent crimes are more likely to be solved than property crimes because police devote more resources to the more serious acts. For these types of crimes, witnesses (including the victim) are frequently available to identify offenders, and in many instances the victim and offender were previously acquainted. Murder cases are typically cleared by arrest more frequently than any other crime. Because it is the most visible and important crime, detectives work aggressively to solve murder cases regardless of where they occur or the characteristics of homicide victims.[26]

Self-Report Trends

Self-reports indicate that the number of people who break the law is far greater than the number projected by official statistics. Almost everyone surveyed is found to have violated some law; the most common offenses are truancy, substance abuse, petty theft, shoplifting, fighting, and vandalism.[27]

Yet the incidence of self-reported criminality has been relatively stable. While a self-reported crime wave has not occurred, neither has there been a sharp decline in reported behavior. Table 2.1 on page 46 shows the percentage of youths who self-report delinquency in the most recent Monitoring the Future (MTF) survey. Note that about 9 percent of all high school seniors stole something worth more than $50 during the past year and 13 percent report hurting someone so badly that the victim required medical care.

The Monitoring the Future study is also used to measure teen drug use. Data suggests that drug use has declined during the past two decades (with a few exceptions such as inhalants and oxycontin).[28] But the MTF findings show that drug use has certainly not disappeared: today, about 15 percent of 8th graders, 31 percent of 10th graders, and 39 percent of 12th graders used drugs in the past year; about half of all 12th graders have used drugs at least once in their lifetime.

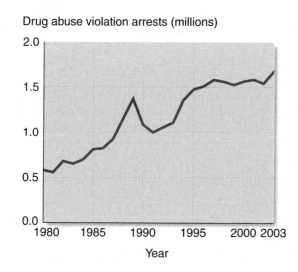

Drug abuse violation arrests (millions)

Year

**Figure 2.5
Drug abuse violation arrests, 1980–2003**

Source: FBI, Uniform Crime Report, 2004.

Policy, Programs, and Issues in Criminal Justice

Factors That Have an Impact on Crime Rates

What are the most important influences on fluctuations in the crime rate? Criminologists have identified a variety of social, economic, personal, and demographic factors that influence crime rate trends. Some of the most important factors are discussed here.

Age
Because the teenage population has extremely high crime rates, a change in the general population age distribution may have a significant influence on crime trends: when the number of young males increases, so too do crime rates. With the "graying" of society in the 1980s and a decline in the birthrate, it is not surprising that the overall crime rate declined between 1991 and 2000. The number of juveniles should be increasing over the next decade, and some criminologists fear that this will signal a return to escalating crime rates. However, the number of senior citizens is also expanding and their presence in the population may have a moderating effect on crime rates (seniors do not commit much crime), offsetting the effect of teens.

Economy
There is debate over the effects the economy has on crime rates. Some criminologists believe that a poor economy actually helps lower crime rates because unemployed parents are at home to supervise children and guard their possessions. Because there is less money to spend, a poor economy reduces the number of valuables worth stealing. Also, it seems unlikely that law-abiding, middle-aged workers will suddenly turn to a life of crime if they are laid off during an economic downturn. Recent research by Gary Kleck and Ted Chiricos confirms that the unemployment/crime rate relationship is modest.

Although a poor economy may lower crime rates in the short run, long-term periods of sustained economic weakness and unemployment in a particular area can eventually increase crime rates when measured at the local or neighborhood level. It is

also possible that a long-term sustained economic recession may produce increases in the crime rate.

Social Problems
As the level of social problems increases—such as the number of single-parent families, dropout rates, level of racial conflict, and teen pregnancies—so too do crime rates. For example, crime rates are correlated with the number of unwed mothers in the population. It is possible that children of unwed mothers need more social services than children in two-parent families. As the number of kids born to single mothers increases, the child welfare system will be taxed and services depleted. As the teenage birthrate began to drop in the late 1980s and 1990s, so too did crime rates.

Racial conflict may also increase crime rates. Areas undergoing racial change, especially those experiencing a migration of minorities into predominantly white neighborhoods, seem prone to significant increases in their crime rate. Whites in these areas may be using violence to protect what they view as their home turf. Racially motivated crimes actually diminish as neighborhoods become more integrated and power struggles diminish.

Abortion
In a controversial work, John J. Donohue III and Steven D. Levitt found empirical evidence that the recent drop in the crime rate can be attributed to the availability of legalized abortion. Donohue and Levitt suggested that the crime rate drop began approximately eighteen years after *Roe v. Wade* legalized abortions. They found that states that legalized abortion before the rest of the nation were the first to experience decreasing crime and that states with high abortion rates have seen a greater fall in crime since 1985.

Guns
The availability of firearms may influence the crime rate, especially the proliferation of weapons in the hands of teens. There is evidence that more guns than

ever before are finding their way into the hands of young people. Surveys of high school students indicate that between 6 and 10 percent carry guns at least some of the time. Guns also cause escalation in the seriousness of crime. As the number of gun-toting students increases, so too does the seriousness of violent crime as, for example, a schoolyard fight turns into murder.

Gangs

Another factor that affects crime rates is the explosive growth in teenage gangs. Surveys indicate that there are more than 850,000 gang members in the United States. Boys who are members of gangs are far more likely to possess guns than non–gang members; criminal activity increases when kids join gangs.

Drug Use

Some experts tie increases in the violent crime rate between 1980 and 1990 to the crack cocaine epidemic, which swept the nation's largest cities, and drug-trafficking gangs, which fought over drug turf. These well-armed gangs did not hesitate to use violence to control territory, intimidate rivals, and increase market share. As the crack epidemic has subsided, so too has the violence in cities such as New York and in other metropolitan areas where the crack epidemic was rampant.

Justice Policy

Some law enforcement experts have suggested that a reduction in crime rates may be attributed to aggressive police practices that target "quality of life" crimes such as panhandling, graffiti, petty drug dealing, and loitering. By showing that even the smallest infractions will be dealt with seriously, aggressive police departments may be able to discourage potential criminals from committing more serious crimes.

It is also possible that tough laws targeting drug dealing and repeat offenders with lengthy prison terms can affect crime rates. The fear of punishment may inhibit some would-be criminals. Lengthy sentences also help boost the nation's prison population. Placing a significant number of potentially high-rate

offenders behind bars may help stabilize crime rates. Some ex-criminals have told researchers that they stopped committing crimes because they perceived higher levels of street enforcement and incarceration rates.

Crime Opportunities

Crime rates may drop when market conditions change and an alternative criminal opportunity develops. For example, the decline in the burglary rate over the past two decades may be explained in part by the abundance and subsequent decline in price of commonly stolen merchandise such as VCRs, TVs, and cameras. In contrast, in 2005 subway crime increased in New York when thieves began targeting people carrying iPods.

Critical Thinking

1. Do you agree that the factors listed here contribute to fluctuations in the crime rate? If not, why?
2. What other factors may increase or reduce crime rates?

InfoTrac College Edition Research

Can fear of gangs and their contribution to the crime rate lead to an overzealous response by police? To find out, read Diane Schaefer, "Police Gang Intelligence Infiltrates a Small City," *Social Science Journal 39* (2002): 95–108.

Sources: Gary Kleck and Ted Chiricos, "Unemployment and Property Crime: A Target-Specific Assessment of Opportunity and Motivation as Mediating Factors," *Criminology 40* (2002): 649–680; Michael Brick, "An iPod Crime Wave? How Terrible. On Second Thought," *New York Times*, May 2, 2005; Steven Messner, Lawrence Raffalovich, and Richard McMillan, "Economic Deprivation and Changes in Homicide Arrest Rates for White and Black Youths, 1967–1998: A National Time Series-Analysis," *Criminology 39* (2001): 591–614; John Laub, "Review of the Crime Drop in America," *American Journal of Sociology 106* (2001): 1820–1822; John J. Donohue III and Steven D. Levitt, "Legalized Abortion and Crime" (June 24, 1999, unpublished paper, University of Chicago); Darrell Steffensmeier and Miles Harer, "Making Sense of Recent U.S. Crime Trends, 1980 to 1996/1998: Age Composition Effects and Other Explanations," *Journal of Research in Crime and Delinquency 36* (1999): 235–274; Desmond Ellis and Lori Wright, "Estrangement, Interventions, and Male Violence Toward Female Partners," *Violence and Victims 12* (1997): 51–68; Bruce Johnson, Andrew Golub, and Jeffrey Fagan, "Careers in Crack, Drug Use, Drug Distribution, and Nondrug Criminality," *Crime and Delinquency 41* (1995): 275–295.

Table 2.1	Self-reported delinquent activity, high school seniors, during past 12 months		
Type of Crime	**Total %**	**Committed Only Once (%)**	**Committed More Than Once (%)**
Set fire on purpose	4	2	2
Damaged school property	13	6	7
Damaged work property	7	3	4
Auto theft	5	2	3
Auto part theft	6	3	3
Breaking and entering	23	10	13
Theft of less than $50	27	13	14
Theft of more than $50	9	4	5
Shoplifting	28	12	15
Gang fight	19	10	9
Hurt someone badly enough so that they needed medical care	13	6	7
Used force to steal	4	2	2
Hit teacher or supervisor	3	1	2
Got into serious fight	14	7	7

Source: *Monitoring the Future, 2003* (Ann Arbor: Institute for Social Research, 2004).

What the Future Holds

Speculating about the future of crime trends is always risky because current conditions can change rapidly. Some criminologists predict that a significant increase in teen violence may soon occur. There are approximately fifty million school-age children in the United States, many under age ten; this is more than we have had for decades. Though many come from stable homes, others lack stable families and adequate supervision. These are some of the children who will soon enter their prime crime-committing years.[29]

Other experts dispute the fact that we are in for a big upswing in the crime rate. Even if teens commit more crime in the future, their contribution may be offset by the growing senior citizen and elderly population, a group with a relatively low crime rate.[30]

It is also possible that economic, technological, and social factors could help moderate the crime rate.[31] Technological developments such as the rapid expansion of e-commerce on the Internet have created new classes of crime. Another trend may the globalization of crime. While the crime rate has declined during the past decade in the United States, it seems to be increasing abroad, as the following Race, Culture, and Gender in Criminal Justice feature shows.

Criminal Justice ⚖ Now™

Learn more by viewing the "Brazil Guns" "In the News" video clip.

▌CRIME PATTERNS

By studying crime data, experts can determine if there are stable patterns in the crime rate, which may help us to better understand where crime occurs, who commits crime, and why they violate the law. What are these enduring and stable patterns?

Ecological Patterns

There are distinct ecological patterns in the crime rate:

- Rural and suburban areas have much lower crime rates than large metropolitan centers, suggesting that urban problems—overcrowding, poverty,

Race, Culture, and Gender in Criminal Justice

International Crime Trends

How do crime rates in the United States compare to those abroad? Despite what some people think, while crime rates are trending downwards in the United States, they are rapidly increasing abroad:

- The United States in 1980 clearly led the Western world in overall crime, but beginning a decade later, there was a marked decline in U.S. crime rates. Overall crime rates for the U.S. dropped below those of England and Wales, Denmark, and Finland.

- No matter what part of the world, over a five-year period, two out of three of the inhabitants of big cities are victimized by crime at least once. Risks of being victimized are highest in Latin America and (sub-Saharan) Africa.

- While homicide rates are still high in the United States, other nations, especially those experiencing social or economic upheaval, have higher rates. Today, Colombia has about 63 homicides per 100,000 people and South Africa has 51, compared to fewer than 6 in the United States. During the past decade there were more homicides in Brazil than in the United States, Canada, Italy, Japan, Australia, Portugal, Britain, Austria, and Germany combined. Why are crime rates so high in nations like Brazil? Law enforcement officials link the upsurge in violence to drug trafficking, gang feuds, vigilantism, and disputes over trivial matters, in which young, unmarried, uneducated males are involved.

- Until 1990, U.S. rape rates were higher than those of any Western nation, but by 2000, Canada took the lead. The lowest reported rape rates were in Asia and the Middle East. Violence against women is, like most serious crime, related to economic hardship.

- As of 2000, countries with more reported robberies than the United States included England and Wales, Portugal, and Spain. Countries with fewer reported robberies include Germany, Italy, and France, as well as Middle Eastern and Asian nations.

- As of 2000, the United States had lower burglary rates than Australia, Denmark, Finland, England and Wales, and Canada. It had higher reported burglary rates than Spain, Korea, and Saudi Arabia.

- Australia, England and Wales, Denmark, Norway, Canada, France, and Italy now have higher rates of vehicle theft than the United States.

- Contrary to the common assumption that Europeans are virtually unarmed, the 15 countries of the European Union have an estimated 84 million firearms, 67 million of which (80 percent) are in civilian hands. With a total population of 375 million people, this amounts to 17.4 guns for every 100 people.

Why are crime rates increasing around the world while leveling off in the United States? In some developing nations, crime rates may be spiraling upward because they are undergoing a rapid change in their social and economic makeup. In Eastern Europe, for example, the fall of Communism has brought about a transformation of the family, religion, education, and economy. These changes increase social pressures and can result in crime rate increases. Other societies, such as China, are undergoing rapid industrialization as traditional patterns of behavior are disrupted by urbanization, and the shift from agricultural to industrial and service economies. In some areas, such as Asia and the Middle East, political turmoil has resulted in a surge in their crime rates.

Critical Thinking
The United States is notorious for employing much tougher penal measures than Europe. Do you believe our tougher measures explain why crime is declining in the U.S. while increasing abroad?

InfoTrac College Edition Research
What is being done in Europe to combat the latest crime boom? To find out, use *international crime* as a key term on InfoTrac College Edition.

Sources: Gene Stephens, "Global trends in crime: Crime varies greatly around the world, statistics show, but new tactics have proved effective in the United States. To keep crime in check in the twenty-first century, we'll all need to get smarter, not just tougher." *The Futurist* 37 (2003): 40–47; Graeme Newman, *Global Report on Crime and Justice* (New York: Oxford University Press, 1999); Gary Lafree and Kriss Drass, "Counting Crime Booms Among Nations: Evidence for Homicide Victimization Rates, 1956–1998," *Criminology* 40 (2002): 769–801; the Small Arms Survey, 2003, www.smallarmssurvey.org, accessed on August 4, 2005; Pedro Scuro, *World Factbook of Criminal Justice Systems: Brazil* (Washington, D.C.: Bureau of Justice Statistics, 2003).

social inequality, narcotics use, and racial conflict—are related to crime rates.

- Crime rates are highest in the summer months, most likely because (1) people spend so much time outdoors and are less likely to secure their homes and (2) schools are closed and young people have greater opportunity for criminal activity.

- Crime rates are also related to the region of the country. The West and South usually have significantly higher rates than the Midwest and New England.

Gender Patterns

UCR arrest data consistently shows that males have a much higher crime rate than females. The UCR arrest statistics indicate that the overall male-female arrest ratio is about 3.5 male offenders to 1 female offender; for serious violent crimes, the ratio is closer to 5 males to 1 female. However, in recent years female crime rates are increasing at a faster pace than males and producing gender convergence.

How can gender differences in the crime rates be explained? A number of views have been put forward:

- Males are stronger and better able to commit violent crime.
- Hormonal differences make males more aggressive.
- Girls are socialized to be less aggressive than boys and consequently develop moral values that strongly discourage antisocial behavior.[32]
- Girls have better verbal skills and use them to diffuse conflict.
- Males are granted greater personal freedom and therefore have more opportunities to commit crime. Girls are subject to greater parental control.

These views, however, are now being challenged by the rapid rise in the female crime rate.[33] As gender role differences at home, school, and the workplace have narrowed, so too have crime rates. As a result, there has been a rise in female participation in traditionally male-oriented forms of criminality such as violent crime and juvenile gang membership.[34]

Racial Patterns

Official crime data indicates that minority group members are involved in a disproportionate share of criminal activity. According to UCR reports, African Americans make up about 12 percent of the general population, yet they account for about 37 percent of Part I violent crime arrests and 29 percent of property crime arrests. They also are responsible for a disproportionate number of Part II arrests (except for alcohol-related arrests, which detain primarily white offenders). How can racial differences in the crime rate be explained? There are a number of competing views on this issue:

- Police are more likely to arrest racial minorities because of discriminatory patterns such as racial profiling.
- Differential opportunity, powerlessness, and other social problems in the United States have resulted in a higher African-American crime rate. The high rate of crime committed by African Americans is an expression of their anger and frustration at an unfair social order.[35]
- African-American families are forced to reside in some of the nation's poorest communities that cannot provide economic opportunities. The resulting sense of hopelessness increases the incentive to commit crime.

Crimes are more common in urban areas in the West and South. Here, a police helicopter hovers over a Target store in Culver City, California, after gunmen invaded the closed discount store and ordered employees to the floor in a botched robbery attempt. Other police and sheriff's forces can be seen on the ground outside the store. Two people were arrested, no shots were fired, and no one was injured.

According to most experts, when and if inter-racial economic, social, and educational differences converge, so too will crime rates.

Class Patterns

Official data indicates that crime rates are highest in deprived, inner-city areas and that the level of poverty and social disorganization in an area can predict its crime rate. Why are lower-class neighborhoods more crime prone than affluent communities?

- Communities that lack economic and social opportunities also produce high levels of stress and strain, and residents may then turn to criminal behavior to relieve their frustration.[36]
- Family life is disrupted, and law-violating youth groups and gangs thrive in a climate where adult supervision has been undermined.[37]
- Socially disorganized neighborhoods lack the ability to exert social control over their residents. Lack of informal social control significantly increases the likelihood that residents will engage in criminality.
- Crime rates are high in deteriorated areas where the disadvantaged and the affluent live in close proximity. In these neighborhoods, social differences are magnified, and less affluent residents perceive a feeling of relative deprivation that results in a higher crime rate.[38]

Criminal Justice ⚖ Now™

Learn more about by exploring the "Drug Bust Part I" Role Play activity.

- People living in lower-class neighborhoods experience poverty, dilapidated housing, poor schools, broken families, drugs, and street gangs. Deteriorating neighborhoods attract law violators, i.e., the "broken windows" have been linked to high crime rates.

Regardless of the reason, the crime data tells us that rates of violent and property crime are higher in impoverished areas.

Age Patterns

Official statistics tell us that young people are arrested at a disproportionate rate to their numbers in the population; victim surveys generate similar findings for crimes in which assailant age can be determined. As a general rule, the peak age for property crime is believed to be sixteen and for violence, eighteen (see Figure 2.6). In contrast, the elderly are particularly resistant to the temptations of crime; elderly males age sixty-five and over are predominantly arrested for alcohol-related matters (public drunkenness and drunk driving) and elderly females for larceny (shoplifting). The elderly crime rate has remained stable for the past twenty years.

When violence rates surged in the 1980s, the increase was due almost entirely to young people; the adult violence rate remained rather stable. How can the age-crime relationship be explained?

- Young people are part of a youth culture that favors risk taking, short-run hedonism, and other behaviors that may involve them in law violation. The high-risk lifestyle of most youths ends as they mature and become involved in forming a family and a career.[39]

- Adolescents are psychologically immature and are therefore unlikely to appreciate the wrongfulness of their antisocial acts or their destructive consequences.

- Youths have limited financial resources and may resort to theft and drug dealing for income.

- Young people have the energy, strength, and physical skill needed to commit crime, all of which erode with age.[40]

- Adolescents are aware that the juvenile justice system is not as punitive as the adult court system and are therefore more likely to risk committing criminal acts.

Figure 2.6
The relationship between age and serious crime arrests
Source: FBI, Uniform Crime Reports, 2004.

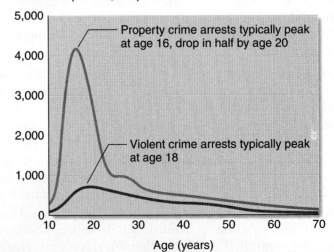

Arrest rate per 100,000 persons

Property crime arrests typically peak at age 16, drop in half by age 20

Violent crime arrests typically peak at age 18

Age (years)

Career Patterns: The Chronic Offender

One of the most important patterns discovered in the crime rate is that some people who begin committing crime at a very early age maintain a high rate of criminal violations throughout their lifetime. These *chronic offenders* are immune to both the ravages of age and the punishments of the justice system. More important, this small group may be responsible for a significant portion of all serious criminal behavior.

Chronic offenders can be distinguished from conventional criminals. The latter category contains law violators who may commit and be apprehended for a single instance of criminal behavior, usually of relatively minor seriousness— shoplifting, simple assault, petty larceny, and so on. The chronic offender is one who has serious and persistent brushes with the law, who is building a career in crime, and whose behavior may be excessively violent and destructive.

The concept of the chronic offender is most closely associated with the research efforts of Marvin Wolfgang and his associates at the University of Pennsylvania. In 1972, Wolfgang, Robert Figlio, and Thorsten Sellin published a landmark study entitled *Delinquency in a Birth Cohort.*[41] Wolfgang, Figlio, and Sellin used official records to follow the criminal careers of a cohort of 9,945 boys born in Philadelphia in 1945 until they reached age eighteen in 1963. They found:

- About two-thirds of the cohort (6,470) never had contact with police authorities.

- About one third (3,475) had at least one contact with the police during their minority.

- Of the repeat offenders, a relatively small subgroup (627 boys) were arrested five times or more. These were the chronic offenders who made up 6 percent of the total (600 out of 10,000).

- The chronic offenders were responsible for 5,305 arrests, or 51.9 percent of the total. They committed 71 percent of the homicides, 73 percent of the rapes, 82 percent of the robberies, and 69 percent of the aggravated assaults.

- Arrest and punishment did little to chronic offenders. In fact, punishment was inversely related to chronicity—the stricter the sanctions they received, the more likely they were to engage in repeated criminal behavior.

Since the Philadelphia survey was carried out, a number of other independent studies, including one of a larger Philadelphia cohort of children born in 1958, have also confirmed the existence of a repeat offender.[42] Here are some of the key findings about chronic offenders:

- Chronic offender research indicates that young persistent offenders grow up to become adult repeat offenders. This phenomenon is referred to as *persistence* or continuity of crime.

- Chronic delinquents who commit the most serious violent acts as young-sters have the greatest chance of later becoming adult offenders.[43]

- Youthful offenders who persist are more likely to abuse alcohol, get into trouble while in military service, become economically dependent, have lower aspirations, get divorced or separated, and have a weak employment record.

The chronic offender concept has had a great impact on the criminal justice system. If a small group of offenders commits almost all of the serious crime, then it stands to reason that their incarceration might have an appreciable influence on the crime rate. This thought pattern has been

Criminal Justice ⚖ Now™
Learn more about by exploring the "Drug Bust Part I" Role Play activity.

The victim data tells us that men are much more likely than women to be victims of violent crime, but females are more likely to be victims of sexual assault. The Reverend Don Kimball, left, and his attorney, Chris Andrian, sit in front of molestation victim Ellen Brem while listening to the testimony of others allegedly molested by Kimball, in Sonoma County Superior Court in Santa Rosa, California. Convicted of molesting Brem twenty years earlier when she was thirteen, Kimball, an inactive minister, was sentenced to seven years in prison.

responsible for the recent spate of "get-tough" laws designed to put habitual offenders behind bars for long periods of time. As a consequence of these get-tough sentences, the prison population has trended upward as crime rates have fallen.

Victim Patterns

The various sources of crime and victim data can also provide a snapshot of the social and demographic characteristics of its victims. What are these characteristics?

Gender Gender affects victimization risk. Men are much more likely than women to be victims of robbery and aggravated assault; they are also more likely to experience theft, but the differences are less pronounced. Although females are far more likely to be the victim of sexual assault, thousands of men are sexually assaulted each year.

When men are the victims of violent crime, the perpetrator is usually described as a stranger. Women are much more likely to be attacked by a relative than men are; about two-thirds of all attacks against women are committed by a husband or boyfriend, family member, or acquaintance. In two-thirds of sexual assaults as well, the victim knows the attacker.

Age Young people face a much greater victimization risk than older persons do. Victim risk diminishes rapidly after age twenty-five. The elderly, who are thought of as being the helpless targets of predatory criminals, are actually much safer than their grandchildren. People over age sixty-five, who make up 14 percent of the population, account for 1 percent of violent victimizations; teens aged twelve to nineteen, who also make up 14 percent of the population, typically account for more than 30 percent of crime victims.

What factors explain the age-victimization association?

- Adolescents often stay out late at night, go to public places, and hang out in places where crime is most likely to occur.

- Teens face a high victimization risk because they spend a great deal of time in the presence of their adolescent peers, the group most likely to commit crime.

Income The poorest Americans might be expected to be the most likely victims of crime, since they live in areas that are crime-prone: inner-city, urban neighborhoods. The NCVS does in fact show that the least affluent (annual incomes of less than $7,500) are by far the most likely to be victims of violent crimes, and this association occurs across all gender, racial, and age groups.

Marital Status Unmarried or never married people are victimized more often than married people or widows and widowers. These relationships are probably influenced by age, gender, and lifestyle:

- Unmarried people tend to be younger, and young people have the highest victim risk.

- Widows, who are more likely to be older women, suffer much lower victimization rates because they interact with older people, are more likely to stay home at night, and avoid public places.

Race African Americans experience violent crime victimizations at a higher rate than other groups. NCVS data shows that African Americans have strikingly higher rates of violent personal crime victimizations than do whites. Although the race-specific risk of theft victimization is more similar, African Americans are still more likely to be victimized than whites.

Crimes committed against African Americans tend to be more serious than those committed against whites. African Americans experience higher rates of aggravated assault, whereas whites are more often the victims of simple assault. African Americans are about three times as likely to become robbery victims as whites. Young African-American males are also at great risk for homicide victimization. They face a murder risk four or five times greater than that of young African-American females, five to eight times higher than that of young white males, and sixteen to twenty-two times higher than that of young white females.[44]

Why do these discrepancies exist? One clear reason is that young black males tend to live in the largest U.S. cities, in areas beset by alcohol and drug abuse, poverty, racial discrimination, and violence. Forced to live in the most dangerous areas, their lifestyle places them in the highest at-risk population group.

Ecological Factors There are distinct ecological patterns in the victim rate:

- Most victimizations occur in large urban areas; rural and suburban victim rates are far lower.
- Most incidents occur during the evening hours (6 P.M. to 6 A.M.). More serious crimes take place after 6 P.M.; less serious, before 6 P.M.
- The most likely site for a victimization—especially a violent crime such as rape, robbery, and aggravated assault—is an open, public area such as a street, park, or field.
- One of the most dangerous public places is a public school building. About 10 percent of all U.S. youth aged twelve to nineteen (approximately two million) are crime victims while on school grounds each year.
- An overwhelming number of criminal incidents involve a solo victim.
- Most victims report that their assailant was not armed (except for the crime of robbery, where about half the offenders carry weapons). The use of guns and knives is about equal, and there does not seem to be a pattern of a particular weapon being used for a particular crime.

Victim-Offender Relationships The NCVS can tell us something about the characteristics of people who commit crime. This information is available only on criminals who actually came in contact with the victim through such crimes as rape, assault, or robbery.

- About 50 percent of all violent crimes are committed by strangers. The other half of violent crimes are committed by people who were known to the victim, including family members, spouses, parents, children, and siblings.
- Women seem much more likely than men to be victimized by acquaintances; a majority of female assault victims know their assailants.
- A majority of victims report that the crime was committed by a single offender over the age of twenty.

- About 25 percent of victims indicate that their assailant was a young person twelve to twenty years of age. This may reflect the criminal activities of youth gangs and groups in the United States.

- Whites are the offenders in a majority of single-offender rapes and assaults; there is no racial pattern in single-offender robberies. However, multiple-offender robberies are more likely to be committed by African Americans.

Repeat Victimization   Does prior victimization enhance or reduce the chances of future victimization? Stable patterns of behavior may encourage victimization, and a few people who maintain these patterns may become "chronic victims," constantly the target of predatory crimes.

Most research does in fact show that individuals who have had prior victimization experiences have a significantly higher chance of repeat victimization than do people who have been nonvictims.[45] Research also shows that households that have experienced victimization are the ones most likely to experience it again.[46] Repeat victimizations are most likely to occur in areas with high crime rates; one study found that during a four-year period, 40 percent of all trauma patients in an urban medical center in Ohio were repeat victims.[47]

Some combination of personal and social factors may possibly encourage victimization risk. Most revictimizations happen soon after a previous crime, suggesting that repeat victims share some personal characteristics that make them a magnet for predators.[48] Not fighting back, not reporting crime to police, and re-purchasing stolen goods may encourage repeat victimization.

Criminal Justice ⚖ Now™
Learn more about Theories of Criminal Behavior by going through the Learning Module.

CAUSES OF CRIME AND VICTIMIZATION

Although the various sources of criminal statistics can tell us about the nature of crime patterns and trends, knowing why an individual commits crime in the first place is also important. Such knowledge is critical if programs are to be devised to deter or prevent crime. If, for example, people commit crime because they are poor and desperate, the key to crime prevention might be a job program and government economic aid. If, however, the root cause of crime is a poor family life marked by conflict and abuse, then providing jobs will not help lower the crime rate; family counseling and parenting skills courses would prove to be more effective.

There is still a great deal of uncertainty about the "real" cause of crime. Some of the more popular explanations are discussed in the following sections.

Choice Theory: Because They Want To

One prominent view of criminality is based on the writings of Cesare Beccaria (1738–1794), who believed people want to achieve pleasure and avoid pain. Therefore, he concluded, crimes must provide some pleasure to the criminal. To deter crime, pain must be administered in an appropriate amount to counterbalance the pleasure obtained from crime. His views are today known as the **classical theory of crime.**[49]

In its contemporary form, referred to as rational choice theory (or simply **choice theory**), crime is viewed as a reasoned choice:

1. All people of their own free will can choose between conventional or criminal behaviors.

2. Most people have the potential to violate the law because crime promises great rewards and requires less effort for greater gain.

classical theory of crime The view that people choose to commit crime after weighing potential costs and benefits.

choice theory The school of thought holding that people will engage in delinquent and criminal behavior after weighing the consequences and benefits of their actions. Delinquent behavior is a rational choice made by a motivated offender who perceives the chances of gain outweigh any perceived punishment or loss.

3. However, people will refrain from antisocial acts if they believe:

   a. That the severity of the punishment they will receive for their actions will outweigh any potential gain.

   b. That there is a substantial likelihood or certainty that they will be caught and punished.

   c. That punishment will be swift and timely.

4. The punishments threatened by the existing criminal law are the primary deterrent to crime.

People commit crime if they believe it will provide immediate benefits without the threat of long-term risks. For example, before concluding a drug sale, experienced traffickers will mentally balance the chances of making a large profit with the consequences of being apprehended and punished for drug dealing. They know that most drug deals are not detected and that the potential for enormous, untaxed profits is great. They evaluate their lifestyle and determine how much cash they need to maintain their standard of living, which is usually extravagant. They may have borrowed to finance the drug deal, and their creditors are not usually reasonable if loans cannot be repaid promptly. They also realize that they could be the target of a "sting" operation by undercover agents and, if caught, will get a long mandatory sentence in a forbidding federal penitentiary. If they conclude that the potential for profits is great enough, their need for cash urgent, and the chances of apprehension minimal, they will carry out the deal. If, however, they believe that the transaction will bring them only a small profit and a large risk of apprehension and punishment, they may forgo the deal as too risky.

The decision to commit a specific crime is thus a matter of personal decision making based on a weighing of available information.[50] Experienced criminals may not fear punishment because they know from experience that the risk of apprehension for committing crime is actually quite low. Experienced criminals may also hang out with criminal friends who convince them that the rewards of crime are greater than the risks.[51] Crime, then, is a matter of personal choice.

In sum, according to this view, crimes are events that occur when offenders decide to risk crime after considering:

- Personal factors such as the need for money, excitement, experience, or revenge
- Situational factors (how well a target is protected, the risk of apprehension, the chance for hurting bystanders)
- Legal factors (the efficiency of police, the threat of legal punishment, the effect of a prior criminal record on future punishment)

Sociobiological Theory: It's in Their Blood

During the nineteenth century, the first social scientists began to apply the scientific method to the study of society. Auguste Comte (1798–1857), a founder of social science, described how as society progressed people embraced a rational, scientific view of the world. Comte called this final stage the **positive stage,** and those who followed his writings became known as positivists. Those who embraced positivism relied on the strict use of empirical methods—factual, firsthand observation, and measurement of conditions and events—to test hypotheses.

The first positivists to study crime focused on biological factors that caused people to become violent and antisocial. Though this approach was

positive stage During the positive stage of human social development, people embrace rational scientific explanations for observed phenomenon.

abandoned in the twentieth century, in recent years there has been renewed interest in finding a biological basis of crime.

In its contemporary form referred to as **biosocial theory,** those who believe that crime has a biological basis maintain that elements of the environment (family life, community factors) interact with biological factors (neurological makeup) to control and influence behavior. For example, children who suffer deficits caused by birth complications will be predisposed to committing violent acts as they mature if they also are forced to grow up in a dysfunctional and negative home environment.[52]

Sociobiological theories can be divided into three broad areas of focus: biochemical factors, neurological problems, and genetic abnormalities.

Biochemical Factors Crime and violence are possibly functions of biochemical abnormality. Such biochemical factors as vitamin and mineral deficiencies, hormone imbalance, improper diet, environmental contaminants, and allergies have been linked to antisocial behavior.[53]

Biochemical studies suggest that some criminal offenders have abnormal levels of organic or inorganic substances in their bodies that influence their behavior and in some way make them prone to antisocial behavior. Potential inorganic triggers include lead, which can be ingested from the surrounding environment.[54] Organic factors linked to crime and aggression include abnormal hormonal activity. Some criminologists argue that gender differences in the crime rate can be linked to the male hormone testosterone and its assumed effect on behavior.[55]

Neurological Problems Another area of interest to biocriminologists is the relationship of brain activity to behavior. Biocriminologists have used the electroencephalogram to record the electrical impulses given off by the brain. Preliminary studies indicate that 50 to 60 percent of those with behavior disorders display abnormal recordings.[56]

People with an abnormal cerebral structure, referred to as *minimal brain dysfunction,* may experience periods of explosive rage that can lead to violent episodes.[57] Brain dysfunction is sometimes manifested as attention deficit/hyperactive disorder (ADHD), which has been linked to antisocial behavior. About 3 percent of all U.S. children, primarily boys, are believed to suffer from this disorder, and it is the most common reason children are referred to mental health clinics. The condition usually results in poor school performance, bullying, stubbornness, and a lack of response to discipline.[58]

Genetic Abnormalities Violent behavior is possibly inherited and a function of a person's genetic makeup. One approach to test this theory has been to evaluate the behavior of adopted children. If an adopted child's behavior patterns run parallel to those of his or her biological parents, it would be strong evidence to support a genetic basis for crime. Studies conducted in Europe have indicated that the criminality of the biological father is in fact a strong predictor of a child's antisocial behavior.[59] The probability that a youth will engage in crime is significantly enhanced when both biological and adoptive parents exhibit criminal tendencies.

Another method of studying the genetic nature of crime is to compare the behavior of twins. Using twin pairs, it has been found that genetic effects are a significant predictor of problem behaviors in children as young as three years old.[60] Whereas the behavior of some twin pairs seems to be influenced by their environment —that is, the twins are raised in similar circumstances and therefore equally influenced by their environment—others display behavior disturbances that can only be explained by their genetic similarity.[61]

biosocial theory The school of thought holding that human behavior is a function of the interaction of biochemical, neurological, and genetic factors with environmental stimulus.

Psychological Theory: It's in Their Heads

Sometimes when we hear of a particularly gruesome crime, we say of the criminal, "That guy must be crazy." It comes as no surprise, then, that some experts believe that criminality is caused by psychological factors.

There are actually a number of views on this subject.

Psychoanalytic Theory According to the **psychoanalytic view,** some people encounter problems during their early development that cause an imbalance in their personality.

The most deeply disturbed are referred to as psychotics who cannot restrain their impulsive behavior. One type of psychosis is schizophrenia, a condition marked by incoherent thought processes, a lack of insight, hallucinations, feelings of persecution, and so on. Schizophrenics may suffer delusions and feel persecuted, worthless, and alienated.[62] Other offenders may suffer from a garden variety of mood and behavior disorders that render them histrionic, depressed, antisocial, or narcissistic.[63] They may suffer from conduct disorders, which include long histories of antisocial behavior or mood disorders characterized by disturbance in expressed emotions. Among the latter is *bipolar disorder,* in which moods alternate between periods of wild elation and deep depression.[64] Some offenders are driven by an unconscious desire to be punished for prior sins, either real or imaginary. As a result, they may violate the law or even harm their parents to gain attention. According to the psychoanalytic view, crime is a manifestation of feelings of oppression and people's inability to develop the proper psychological defenses and rationales to keep these feelings under control. Criminality may allow these troubled people to survive by producing positive psychic results: it helps them to feel free and independent, and gives them the possibility of excitement and the chance to use their skills and imagination. It also provides them with the promise of positive gain, as well as allowing them to blame others for their predicament (for example, the police). Finally, it gives them a chance to rationalize their sense of failure ("If I hadn't gotten into trouble, I could have been a success").[65]

Social Learning Another psychological view is that criminal behavior is learned through interactions with others. One assumption is that people act aggressively because as children they experienced violence firsthand, either observing it at home or being its target from parents. Children model their behavior after the violent acts of adults. Observed and experienced violence may have an interactive effect: kids who live in high-crime neighborhoods and

© 2005 AP/Wide World Photos

Can psychological abnormality cause someone to kill and, if so, should she be spared the full extent of the law? Defendant Christine Wilhelm sits back as public defenders Jerome Frost, left, and John Turi confer in Troy, New York, during her trial on second-degree murder charges in the drowning of her four-year-old son, Luke. She was also accused of the attempted murder of her son Peter, then five, who escaped. Psychiatrists testified on behalf of Wilhelm, claiming she suffered from paranoid schizophrenia. Despite her history of mental illness, a jury convicted her of second-degree murder. Should someone like Wilhelm be sent to prison for her crimes?

psychoanalytic view This position holds that criminals are driven by unconscious thought patterns, developed in early childhood, that control behaviors over the life course.

witness violence in the community and at home, who are the direct victims of domestic and community-based violence, are the ones most likely to commit crime.[66]

One area of particular interest to **social learning** theorists is whether the media can influence violence. Studies have shown that youths exposed to aggressive, antisocial behavior on television and in movies are likely to copy that violent behavior. Laboratory studies generally conclude that violence on television can lead to aggressive behavior by children and teenagers who watch such programs.[67] Whether the evidence obtained in controlled laboratory studies can be applied to the real world is still being debated.[68] Considering that the average child watches more than twenty hours of TV a week, any link between TV violence and criminal behavior is important.

Criminal Personality Psychologists have explored the link between personality and crime. Evidence shows that aggressive youth have unstable personality structures often marked by hyperactivity, impulsiveness, and instability.

One area of particular interest to criminology is the identification of the **psychopathic** (sometimes referred to as the **antisocial** or **sociopathic**) **personality.** Psychopaths are believed to be dangerous, aggressive, antisocial individuals who act in a callous manner. They neither learn from their mistakes nor are deterred by punishment.[69] Although they may appear charming and have at least average intelligence, psychopaths lack emotional depth, are incapable of caring for others, and maintain an abnormally low level of anxiety. They are likely to be persistent alcohol and drug abusers.[70]

The concept of the psychopathic personality is important for criminology, because it has been estimated that somewhere between 10 and 30 percent of all prison inmates can be classified as psychopaths or sociopaths or as having similar character disorders.[71] Psychopathy has also been linked to the phenomenon of serial murder.[72]

What causes a psychopathic personality to develop?

- Having a psychopathic parent, parental rejection and lack of love during childhood, and inconsistent discipline are all contributing factors.[73]

- Physical abnormality, especially the activity of the autonomic nervous system, may be a factor. Psychopaths may have lower arousal levels than normal.[74]

- Another view is that the psychopathic personality is imprinted at birth and is relatively unaffected by socialization or experience.[75]

Social Structure Theory: Because They're Poor

At the same time that biological positivists were dominating criminology, others were developing the field of sociology to scientifically study the major social changes that were taking place in nineteenth century society. Émile Durkheim (1858–1917), one of the founders of sociology, considered crime as normal and necessary because it produced social change. Without crime, society was doomed to conformity and inertia.[76]

The social positivist tradition is still alive today. Because crime patterns have a decidedly social orientation, sociological explanations of crime have predominated in criminology.

According to one branch of social positivism, **social structure theory,** the United States is a stratified society. The contrast between the lifestyles of the wealthiest members of the upper class and the poorest segment of the lower class is striking. The gap between the richest and the poorest Americans seems to be growing wider; the number of families living in poverty

social learning *The view that behavior patterns are modeled and learned in interactions with others.*

psychopathic (antisocial, sociopathic) personality *Psychopaths are chronically antisocial individuals who are always in trouble, and who do not learn from either experience or punishment. They are loners who engage in frequent callous and hedonistic behaviors, are emotionally immature, and lack responsibility, judgment, and empathy.*

social structure theory *The view that a person's position in the social structure controls behavior. Those in the lowest socioeconomic tier are more likely to succumb to crime-promoting elements in their environment, whereas those in the highest tier enjoy social and economic advantages that insulate them from crime-producing forces.*

doubled in the past decade. About twenty million high school dropouts face dead-end jobs, unemployment, and social failure. Because of their meager economic resources, lower-class citizens are often forced to live in poor areas marked by substandard housing, inadequate health care, renters rather than homeowners, poor educational opportunities, underemployment, and despair. These indicators of neighborhood disorder are highly predictive of crime rates.[77]

The problems of lower-class culture are particularly acute for racial and ethnic minorities who have an income level significantly below that of whites and an unemployment rate almost twice as high. In addition, they face the burden of racism and racial stereotyping. Research shows that whites are averse to living in or visiting black neighborhoods because they consider them crime-ridden even if these neighborhoods actually have relatively low crime rates.[78] Fear and suspicion may keep the races apart.

The crushing burden of urban poverty results in the development of a **culture of poverty.**[79] This culture is marked by apathy, cynicism, helplessness, and distrust. The culture is passed from one generation to another so that its members become part of a permanent underclass, "the truly disadvantaged."[80] The crushing effects of poverty may have an especially hard impact on minority group members who have comparably fewer resources to address ongoing social problems than whites.[81] Considering the social disability suffered by the impoverished, it is not surprising that they turn to crime as a means of support and survival. Forced to endure substandard housing and schools in deteriorated inner-city, socially disorganized neighborhoods, and cut off from conventional society, the urban poor are faced with a constant assault on their self-image and sense of worth. Criminal acts and drug dealing provide a means of survival in an otherwise bleak existence. Those living in impoverished neighborhoods are exposed to the opportunity to buy drugs and engage in antisocial acts.[82]

There are three independent yet overlapping branches within the social structure perspective: social disorganization, strain theory, and cultural deviance theory (outlined in Figure 2.7).

culture of poverty The crushing lifestyle of slum areas produces a culture of poverty, passed from one generation to the next, marked by apathy, cynicism, feelings of helplessness, and mistrust of social institutions, such as schools, government agencies, and the police.

Social disorganization theory focuses on conditions in the environment:
- Deteriorated neighborhoods
- Inadequate social control
- Law-violating gangs and groups
- Conflicting social values

Strain theory focuses on conflict between goals and means:
- Unequal distribution of wealth and power
- Frustration
- Alternative methods of achievement

Cultural deviance theory combines these two:
- Development of subcultures as a result of disorganization and stress
- Subcultural values in opposition to conventional values

CRIME

Figure 2.7   **The three branches of social structure theory**

Social Disorganization Theory According to this view, a socially disorganized area is one in which institutions of social control, such as the family, commercial establishments, and schools, have broken down and can no longer carry out their expected or stated functions.[83] Indicators of social disorganization include high unemployment, school dropout rates, deteriorated housing, low income levels, and large numbers of single-parent households. Delinquent gangs and youth groups soon form in disorganized areas and replace ineffective social institutions. Gangs can provide respect, protection, and financial security.[84] As gangs actively recruit new members and grow larger, residents experience conflict, despair, and hopelessness.[85] Those who can move out do, further destabilizing the neighborhood. Those remaining feel powerless and incapable of engaging in **collective efficacy** or acting cooperatively to solve neighborhood problems.[86] In neighborhoods that maintain collective efficacy, neighbors may become more active in informal crime control activities.[87] They may engage in surveillance practices, for example, by keeping an "eye out" for intruders when their neighbors go out of town.[88] In contrast, in less cohesive communities, (1) social control efforts are blunted, (2) crime rates increase, (3) neighborhood cohesiveness is weakened, in a never-ending cycle.[89]

Strain Theory Strain theory holds that crime is a function of the conflict between the *goals* people have and the *means* they can use to obtain them legally.[90] Social and economic goals are common to people in all economic strata, but ability to obtain these goals is class-dependent. Most people in the United States desire wealth, material possessions, power, prestige, and other life comforts. Members of the lower class are unable to achieve these symbols of success through conventional means. Consequently, they feel anger, frustration, and resentment. Lower-class citizens can either accept their condition and live out their days as socially responsible, if unrewarded, citizens, or they can choose an alternative means of achieving success, such as theft, violence, or drug trafficking. While there are other sources of strain, such as negative life experiences or losing a loved one, the strain produced by limited opportunities may help explain why lower-class areas have such high crime rates.[91]

Cultural Deviance Theory Combining elements of both strain and social disorganization, cultural deviance theory holds that because of strain and social isolation, a unique lower-class culture has developed in disorganized poverty-ridden neighborhoods. The independent **subcultures** maintain a unique set of values and beliefs that are in conflict with conventional social norms. Criminal behavior is an expression of conformity to lower-class subcultural values, which stress toughness, independence, and standing up to authority. These subcultural values are handed down from one generation to the next in a process called **cultural transmission.** Neighborhood youths who hold these values and use them as part of their own personal code of behavior are much more likely to join gangs and violate the law than those who reject the deviant subculture.

Social Process Theory: Socialized to Crime

A second branch of social positivism maintains that people commit crime as a result of the experiences they have while they are being socialized by the various organizations, institutions, and processes of society. People are most strongly influenced toward criminal behavior by poor family relationships, destructive peer-group relations, educational failure, and labeling by agents of the justice system. Although lower-class citizens have the added burdens of

collective efficacy *The ability of neighborhood residents to act cooperatively to maintain social control within communities.*

subculture *A substrata of society that maintains a unique set of values and beliefs.*

cultural transmission *The passing of cultural values from one generation to the next.*

Washington, D.C. sniper John Lee Malvo, left, was seventeen at the time of his arrest for murder. Social process theorists might argue that he learned his criminal ways from his stepfather, John Allen Muhammad, right, before participating in their murderous rampage, which left ten dead.

poverty and strain, even middle-class or upper-class citizens may turn to crime if their socialization is poor or destructive.

Social process theory points to research efforts linking family problems to crime as evidence that socialization, not social structure, is the key to understanding the onset of criminality. Family problems linked to criminality include inconsistent discipline, poor supervision, and the lack of a warm, loving, supportive parent-child relationship.[92] Parents who are supportive and effectively control their children in a noncoercive fashion—**parental efficacy**—are more likely to raise children who refrain from delinquency.[93] In contrast, the likelihood of delinquency increases if parents are unable to provide the type of family structure that gives children the ability to assert their individuality and regulate their own behavior.[94]

Educational experience has also been found to have a significant impact on criminality. Youths who fail at school and eventually drop out are the ones most likely to engage in criminal behavior; academic performance is a significant predictor of crime and delinquency.[95] One reason is that many schools are troubled and cannot provide an adequate academic experience. Data from a recent (2004) survey of high school students found that almost half report having seen other students carry knives at school, roughly one in ten report having seen other students carry guns at school, and more than one in five report being fearful of weapon-associated victimization at school.[96]

In a similar fashion, socialization within the peer group is also a significant influence on behavior. Children who maintain ties with a deviant

social process theory *The view that an individual's interactions with key social institutions—family, school, peer group—shape behavior.*

parental efficacy *The ability of parents to provide support and discipline in a noncoercive manner.*

peer group are the ones most likely to persist in criminal behavior into their adulthood.[97]

The social process approach has several independent branches. The first branch, *social learning theory*, suggests that people learn the techniques and attitudes of crime from close and intimate relationships with criminal peers; crime is a learned behavior. The second, *social control theory*, maintains that everyone has the potential to become a criminal but that most people are controlled by their bond to society. Crime occurs when the forces that bind people to society are weakened or broken. The third branch, *social reaction (labeling) theory*, says people become criminals when significant members of society label them as such and they accept those labels as a personal identity.

Put another way, social learning theory assumes people are born "good" and learn to be "bad"; social control theory assumes people are born "bad" and must be controlled in order to be "good"; social reaction theory assumes that whether "good" or "bad," people are controlled by the reactions of others.

Conflict Theory: It's a "Dog-Eat-Dog" World

In Europe, the writings of another social thinker, Karl Marx (1818–1883) described how economic, social, and political forces controlled human behavior and shaped society.[98] His thoughts were soon being applied to the study of crime and conflict.

Contemporary **conflict theory** views the economic and political forces operating in society as the fundamental causes of criminality. The criminal law and criminal justice systems are viewed as vehicles for controlling the poor members of society. The criminal justice system is believed to help the powerful and rich impose their particular morality and standards of good behavior on the entire society, while it protects their property and physical safety from the have-nots, even though the cost may be the legal rights of the lower class. Those in power control the content and direction of the law and legal system.

Crimes are defined in a way that meets the needs of the ruling classes. The theft of property worth $5 by a poor person can be punished much more severely than the misappropriation of millions by a large corporation. Those in the middle class are drawn into this pattern of control because they are led to believe that they too have a stake in maintaining the status quo and should support the views of the upper-class owners of production.[99]

An important aspect of conflict theory, radical feminist theory, tries to explain how capitalism places particular stress on women and to explicate the role of male dominance in female criminality.[100] Radical feminists view female crime as originating with the onset of male supremacy (patriarchy), the subsequent subordination of women, male aggression, and efforts of men to control women sexually.[101] They focus on the social forces that shape women's lives and experiences to explain female criminality. For example, they attempt to show how the sexual victimization of females is a function of male socialization because so many young males learn to be aggressive and exploitative of women. Exploited at home, female victims try to cope by running away and by engaging in premarital sex and substance abuse. The double standard means that female adolescents still have a much narrower range of acceptable behavior than male adolescents. Any sign of misbehavior is viewed as a substantial challenge to authority that requires immediate control. Feminist scholars view the female criminal as a victim of gender inequality.

conflict theory *The view that human behavior is shaped by interpersonal conflict and that those who maintain social power will use it to further their own needs.*

Developmental Theory: Life Is a Bumpy Road

Criminal Justice ⊛ Now™
Learn more by going through Types of Crime and System or Process Review and Reinforce activities.

While at Harvard University in the 1930s, Sheldon and Eleanor Glueck popularized research on the life cycle of delinquent careers. In a series of longitudinal research studies, they followed the careers of known delinquents to determine the factors that predicted persistent offending.[102] The Gluecks made extensive use of interviews and records in their elaborate comparisons of delinquents and nondelinquents.[103] Their work serves as the cornerstone for contemporary **developmental theory.**

According to developmental theory, even as toddlers, people begin relationships and behaviors that will determine their adult life course.[104] These transitions are expected to take place in order—beginning with completing school, entering the workforce, getting married, and having children. Some individuals, however, are incapable of maturing in a reasonable and timely fashion because of family, environmental, or personal problems. In some cases, transitions can occur too early—for example, when adolescents engage in precocious sex. In other cases, transitions may occur too late, such as when a student fails to graduate on time because of bad grades. Sometimes disruption of one trajectory can harm another. For example, teenage childbirth will most likely disrupt educational and career development. Because developmental theories focus on the associations between life events and deviant behaviors, they are sometimes referred to as life-course theories.

Disruptions in life's major transitions can be destructive and ultimately can promote criminality. Those who are already at risk because of socioeconomic problems or family dysfunction are the most susceptible to these awkward transitions. The cumulative impact of these disruptions sustains criminality from childhood into adulthood.

Because a transition from one stage of life to another can be a bumpy ride, the propensity to commit crimes is neither stable nor constant; it is a developmental process. A positive life experience may help some criminals desist from crime for a while, whereas a negative one may cause them to resume their activities. Criminal careers are said to be developmental because people are influenced by the behavior of those around them and in turn influence others' behavior. A youth's antisocial behavior may turn his more conventional friends against him; their rejection solidifies and escalates his antisocial behavior.

Developmental theory also recognizes that, as people mature, the factors that influence their behavior change.[105] At first, family relations may be most influential; in later adolescence, school and peer relations predominate. In adulthood, vocational achievement and marital relations may be the most critical influences.[106] For example, some antisocial children who are in trouble throughout their adolescence may manage to find stable work and maintain intact marriages as adults; these life events help them desist from crime. In contrast, the less fortunate adolescents who develop arrest records and get involved with the wrong crowd may find themselves limited to menial jobs and at risk for criminal careers.[107]

A Final Word

There are probably so many views of crime causation because there are so many types of crimes. It is possible that all explanations are partially correct: some people commit crime because they are poorly socialized; some succumb to the obstacles placed in their path by lower-class life; others have psychological or biological problems; some are victims of class conflict. The various forms of crime theory are summarized in Exhibit 2.4.

developmental theory The view that social interactions developed over the life course shape behavior. Some interactions, such as involvement with deviant peers, encourage law violations, whereas others, such as marriage and military service, may help people desist from crime.

Exhibit 2.4 **Concepts and theories of criminology: A review**

Theory	Major Premise
Choice Theory	People commit crime when they perceive that the benefits of law violation outweigh the threat and pain of punishment.
Biosocial Theory	
Biochemical	Crime, especially violence, is a function of diet, vitamin intake, hormonal imbalance, or food allergies.
Neurological	Criminals and delinquents often suffer brain impairment. Attention deficit disorder and minimum brain dysfunction are related to antisocial behavior.
Genetic	Delinquent traits and predispositions are inherited. The criminality of parents can predict the delinquency of children.
Psychological Theory	
Psychoanalytic	The development of personality early in childhood influences behavior for the rest of a person's life. Criminals have weak egos and damaged personalities.
Social learning	People commit crime when they model their behavior after others whom they see being rewarded for the same acts. Behavior is enforced by rewards and extinguished by punishment.
Social Structure Theory	
Social disorganization	The conflicts and problems of urban social life and communities control the crime rate. Crime is a product of transitional neighborhoods that manifest social disorganization and value conflict.
Strain	People who adopt the goals of society but lack the means to attain them seek alternatives, such as crime.
Social Process Theory	
Learning theory	People learn to commit crime from exposure to antisocial behaviors. Criminal behavior depends on the person's experiences with rewards for conventional behaviors and punishments for deviant ones. Being rewarded for deviance leads to crime.
Social control theory	A person's bond to society prevents him or her from violating social rules. If the bond weakens, the person is free to commit crime.
Self-control theory	Crime and criminality are separate concepts. People choose to commit crime when they lack self-control. People lacking self-control will seize criminal opportunities.
Conflict Theory	
Conflict theory	People commit crime when the law, controlled by the rich and powerful, defines their behavior as illegal. The immoral actions of the powerful go unpunished.
Radical feminist theory	The capital system creates patriarchy, which oppresses women. Male dominance explains gender bias, violence against women, and repression.
Developmental Theory	
Developmental theory	Early in life people begin relationships that determine their behavior through their life course. Life transitions control the probability of offending.

SUMMARY

- There are three views on how behaviors become crimes: the consensus, the conflict, and the interactionist.
- We get our information on crime from a number of sources, including surveys, records, interviews, and observations.
- One of the most important sources is the Uniform Crime Report compiled by the FBI. This national survey compiles criminal acts reported to local police. The acts are called index crimes (murder, rape, burglary, robbery, assault, larceny-theft, and motor vehicle theft).
- Questioning the validity of the UCR, critics point out that many people fail to report crime to police because of fear, apathy, or lack of respect for law enforcement. Many crime victims also do not report criminal incidents to the police because they believe that nothing can be done or that they should not get involved.
- The federal government also sponsors the National Crime Victimization Survey (NCVS), which asks people about their experiences with crime.
- A third form of information is self-report surveys, which ask offenders themselves to tell about their criminal behaviors.
- The various sources of criminal statistics tell us much about the nature and patterns of crime. Crime rates have been in a downward trend for about a decade.
- Changes in the crime rate have been attributed to the influence of drugs, the economy, age structure, social decay, and other factors. The crime patterns found in all three data sources may be more similar than some critics believe.
- Crime occurs more often in large cities during the summer and at night. Some geographic areas (the South and the West) have higher crime rates than others (the Midwest and New England).
- Arrest data indicates that males, minorities, the poor, and the young have relatively high rates of criminality.
- About 20 percent of all reported crimes are solved by police. However, a positive relationship exists between crime seriousness and the probability of a successful clearance; that is, murders and rapes are much more often solved than car thefts or larcenies.
- Victims of crime tend to be poor, young, male, and members of a minority group.
- Diverse schools of criminological theory approach the understanding of the cause of crime and its consequences. Some focus on the individual, whereas others view social factors as the most important element in producing crime.
- Developmental theories integrate social, individual, and societal level variables.

KEY TERMS

consensus view of crime 32
conflict view of crime 33
interactionist view of crime 33
moral entrepreneurs 33
crime 34
Uniform Crime Report (UCR) 35
official crime statistics 35
index (Part I) crimes 35
nonindex (Part II) crimes 35
National Crime Victimization
  Survey (NCVS) 37

chronic offender 38
life history 39
classical theory of crime 54
choice theory 54
positive stage 55
biosocial theory 56
psychoanalytic view 57
social learning 58
psychopathic (antisocial,
  sociopathic) personality 58

social structure theory 58
culture of poverty 59
collective efficacy 60
subculture 60
cultural transmission 60
social process theory 61
parental efficacy 61
conflict theory 62
developmental theory 63

REVIEW QUESTIONS

1. Why are crime rates higher in the summer than during other seasons?
2. What factors account for crime rate trends?
3. What factors are present in poverty-stricken urban areas that produce high crime rates?
4. It seems logical that biological and psychological factors might explain why some people commit crime. How would a biologist or a psychologist explain the fact that crime rates are higher in the West than in the Midwest? Or that there is more crime in the summer than in the winter?
5. Considering the patterns victimization takes, what steps should you take to avoid becoming a crime victim?

CHAPTER 3

Criminal Law: Substance and Procedure

Department of Justice

DAVID SHER graduated from American University's Washington College of Law and knew from the start that he wanted to be a trial lawyer. Beginning as a state prosecutor, he quickly learned that there are plenty of slippery slopes and sudden drops in every courtroom. Now a criminal defense attorney in the Washington, D.C., area, he applies his considerable skill, experience, and knowledge to defending his clients in cases ranging from gang fights to white-collar crimes.

On a typical day, David Sher will interview witnesses, investigate defense theories, draft pleadings, and serve as an advocate for his clients. Because most of his clients ultimately accept responsibility for their role in the alleged wrongdoing, it is up to attorney Sher to arrange for the best possible plea bargain to settle their case. To be an effective

Chapter Outline

Chapter Objectives

1. Know the similarities and differences between criminal law and civil law
2. Understand the concept of substantive criminal law and its history
3. Discuss the sources of the criminal law
4. Know what is meant by the term "ex post facto law"
5. Be familiar with the elements of a crime
6. Be able to discuss excuses and justification defenses for crime
7. Recognize that the criminal law is constantly evolving
8. Describe the role of the Bill of Rights in shaping criminal procedure
9. Know which amendments to the Constitution are the most important to the justice system
10. List the elements of due process of law.

criminal defense attorney, Sher says, you must be creative and tenacious in plea negotiations. Ironically, sometimes the biggest challenge he faces is not presented by the prosecution but by a client who is reluctant to take the deal. He has to persuade them that the plea is in their best interest and help them understand their rather precarious legal position: if they go to trial, they may spend a good portion of their lives behind bars. Though they may want to take their fight to court, sometimes a plea is their only chance of one day resuming a normal life. So Sher spends his time reassuring his clients, helping them deal with the difficulty of their situation, and at the same time using his legal savvy to maneuver the criminal justice system to serve his clients' best interests.

While legal practitioners like David Sher must be thoroughly familiar with the intricacies of the criminal law, a working knowledge of the law is critical for the criminal justice practitioner because, in our modern society, the rule of law governs almost all phases of human enterprise, including crimes, family life, property transfer, and the regulation of interpersonal conflict.

The law today can generally be divided into three broad categories:

- ***Substantive criminal law.*** The branch of the law that defines crimes and their punishment. It involves such issues as the mental and physical elements of crime, crime categories, and criminal defenses.

- *Procedural criminal law.* Those laws which set out the basic rules of practice in the criminal justice system. Some elements of the law of **criminal procedure** are the rules of evidence, the law of arrest, the law of search and seizure, questions of appeal, jury selection, and the right to counsel.

- *Civil law.* The set of rules governing relations between private parties, including both individuals and organizations (such as business enterprises and/or corporations). **Civil law** is used to resolve, control, and shape such personal interactions as contracts, wills and trusts, property ownership, and commerce. The element of civil law most relevant to criminal justice is **torts** or the law of personal injuries (Exhibit 3.1 sets out the various types of torts).

In some instances, a person who has been the victim of a criminal act may also sue the perpetrator for damages in a civil tort; some crime victims may forgo criminal action and choose to file a tort claim alone. It is also possible to seek civil damages from a perpetrator even if they are found not guilty of crime (for example, the families of Nicole Brown and Ron Goldman sucessfully sued O. J. Simpson for damages though he was found not guilty of murder) because the evidentiary standard in a tort action is less than is needed for a criminal conviction (perponderance of the evidence compared to beyond a reasonable doubt).

The government has the option to pursue a legal matter through the criminal process or file a tort action. White collar crimes, including mail, wire, tax-related and computer fraud, and money-laundering violations, often involve both criminal and civil penalties, giving the government the choice of pursuing one type of action or both.

Concept Summary 3.1 summarizes the main similarities and differences between criminal law and tort law.

substantive criminal law A body of specific rules that declare what conduct is criminal and prescribe the punishment to be imposed for such conduct.

criminal procedure The rules and laws that define the operation of the criminal proceedings. Procedural law describes the methods that must be followed in obtaining warrants, investigating offenses, effecting lawful arrests, conducting trials, introducing evidence, sentencing convicted offenders, and reviewing cases by appellate courts.

civil law All law that is not criminal, including torts (personal wrongs), contract, property, maritime, and commercial law.

tort A personal injury or wrong for which an action for damages may be brought.

Criminal Justice ⊕ Now™
Learn more by exploring the Civil Law Review and Reinforce activity.

THE HISTORICAL DEVELOPMENT OF THE CRIMINAL LAW

The roots of the criminal codes used in the United States can be traced back to such early legal charters as the Babylonian Code of Hammurabi (2000 B.C.), the Mosaic Code of the Israelites (1200 B.C.), and the Roman Twelve Tables

Exhibit 3.1 **Three categories of torts**

Intentional torts Injury that the person knew or should have known would occur through their actions—for example, a person attacks and injures another (assault and battery) after a dispute.

Negligent torts Injuries caused because a person's actions were unreasonably unsafe or careless—such as a traffic accident caused by a reckless driver.

Strict liability torts A particular action causes damage prohibited by statute—for example, a victim is injured due to a manufacturer making a defective product.

In some instances a person who has been the victim of a criminal act may also sue the perpetrator for damages in civil court. Sikh hate-crime victim Rajinder Singh Khalsa holds a photograph of himself taken after he was allegedly beaten on July 12, 2005, in New York by five men yelling ethnic and religious epithets in the mistaken belief that he was a Muslim. Besides the criminal charges against the alleged attackers, Khalsa plans to file a civil suit to be compensated for his monetary expenses and to send a message that the Sikh community is prepared to engage bias crimes with legal action.

© 2005 AP/Wide World Photos

Concept Summary   3.1

A comparison of criminal and tort law

Similarities

- Both share the goal of controlling unwanted behavior.
- Both impose legal sanctions
- Some common areas of legal action—for example, personal assault, control of white-collar offenses such as environmental pollution
- The payment of damages to the victim in a tort case serves some of the same purposes as the payment of a fine in a criminal case.

Differences

- Crime is a public offense. Tort is a civil or private wrong.
- The sanction associated with tort law is monetary damages. Only a violation of criminal law can result in incarceration or even death.
- In criminal law, the right of enforcement belongs to the state. The individual brings the action in civil law.
- In criminal law, monetary damages (fines) go to the state. In civil law, the individual receives damages as compensation for harm done.
- Level of proof is different. Criminal law, beyond reasonable doubt; tort law, preponderance of the evidence.

(451 B.C.). Some of the elements of these codes still influence contemporary legal regulations. For example, Hammurabi's concept of **lex talionis** (i.e., an eye for an eye) still guides proportionality in punishment; the Ten Commandments' prohibition against theft, violence, and perjury still holds sway.

During the sixth century, under the leadership of Byzantine emperor Justinian, the first great codification of law in the Western world was prepared. Justinian's *Corpus Juris Civilis,* or body of civil law, summarizes the system of Roman law that had developed over a thousand years. Rules and regulations to ensure the safety of the state and the individual were organized into a code and served as the basis for future civil and criminal legal classifications. Centuries later, French emperor Napoleon I created the French civil code, using Justinian's code as a model.[1]

The early formal legal codes were lost during the Dark Ages after the fall of Rome (500–1000 A.D.). Emerging Germanic societies developed legal systems featuring monetary compensation, called *wergild* (*wer* means "worth" and refers to what the person, and therefore the crime, was worth), for criminal violations. Guilt was determined by two methods: *compurgation,* which involved having the accused person swear an oath of innocence while being backed up by a group of twelve to twenty-five oath-helpers, who would attest to his or her character and claims of innocence, and *ordeal,* which was based on the principle that divine forces would not allow an innocent person to be harmed.

Determining guilt by ordeal involved such measures as having the accused place his or her hand in boiling water or hold a hot iron. If the wound healed, the person was found innocent; conversely, if the wound did not heal, the accused was deemed guilty. Another ordeal, trial by combat, allowed the accused to challenge his accuser to a duel, with the outcome determining the legitimacy of the accusation. Punishments included public flogging, branding, beheading, and burning.

Common Law and the Principle of Stare Decisis

Soon after Duke William of Normandy conquered England in 1066, a feat that transformed him into William the Conqueror, he sent his royal judges/administrators to travel throughout the land, holding court in each county of his new domain. When court was in session, the royal administrator, or judge, would summon a number of citizens who would, on their oath, tell of the crimes and serious breaches of the peace that had occurred since the judge's last visit. The royal judge then would decide what to do in each case, using local custom and rules of conduct as his guide in a system known as **stare decisis** (Latin for "to stand by decided cases").

The present English system of law came into existence during the reign of Henry II (1154–1189), when royal judges began to publish their decisions in local cases. This allowed judicial precedents to be established, and a national law to be established. Other judges began to use these written decisions as a basis for their decision making, and eventually a fixed body of legal rules and principles was produced. If the new rules were successfully applied in a number of different cases, they would become precedents, which would then be commonly applied in all similar cases. This unified system evolved into a **common law** of the country that incorporated local custom and practice into a national code. Crimes that were **mala in se,** inherently evil and depraved (such as murder, burglary, and arson) and which were the cornerstone of the common law, were joined by new **mala prohibitum** crimes such as embezzlement, which reflected existing social and economic conditions. The common law evolved continually. For example, in the *Carriers* **case** (1473), an English court ruled that a merchant who had been hired to transport merchandise was guilty of larceny (theft) if he kept the goods for his own purposes.[2] Before the *Carriers* case, it was not considered a crime under the common law when people kept

lex talionis (Latin for "law as retaliation") From Hammurabi's ancient legal code, the belief that the purpose of the law is to provide retaliation for an offended party and that the punishment should fit the crime.

stare decisis To stand by decided cases. The legal principle by which the decision or holding in an earlier case becomes the standard by which subsequent similar cases are judged.

common law Early English law, developed by judges, that incorporated Anglo-Saxon tribal custom, feudal rules and practices, and the everyday rules of behavior of local villages. Common law became the standardized law of the land in England and eventually formed the basis of the criminal law in the United States.

mala in se A term that refers to acts that society considers inherently evil, such as murder or rape, and that violate the basic principles of Judeo-Christian morality.

mala prohibitum Crimes created by legislative bodies that reflect prevailing moral beliefs and practices.

Carriers case A fifteenth-century case that defined the law of theft and reformulated the concept of taking the possession of another.

According to the principle of stare decisis, legal precedents followed common custom and practice. Before the trial by jury, legal disputes could be settled by a duel in which the survivor was considered the innocent party. It was believed that God intervened on behalf of the victor. The "wager of battel" was introduced in England by the Normans and was used in both civil and criminal disputes.

"Wager of Battel" from *Le Coutume de Normandie*, an illuminated manuscript (1450–1470).

something that was voluntarily placed in their possession, even if the rightful owner had only given them temporary custody of the merchandise. Breaking with legal tradition, the court acknowledged that the commercial system could not be maintained unless the laws of theft were expanded. The definition of larceny was altered in order to meet the needs of a growing free enterprise economic system. The definition of theft was changed to not only include the taking goods by force or stealth, but also by embezzlement and fraud.

Before the American Revolution, the colonies, then under British rule, were subject to the common law. After the colonies acquired their independence, state legislatures standardized common law crimes such as murder, burglary, arson, and rape by putting them into statutory form in criminal codes. As in England, whenever common law proved inadequate to deal with changing social and moral issues, the states and Congress supplemented it with legislative statutes, creating new elements in the various state and federal legal codes.

Similarly, statutes prohibiting such offenses as identity theft and the pirating of videotapes have been passed to control human behavior unknown at the time the common law was formulated.

SOURCES OF THE CRIMINAL LAW

The contemporary American legal system is codified by state and federal legislatures. Each jurisdiction precisely defines crime in its legal code and sets out the appropriate punishments. However, like its English common law roots, American criminal law is not static and is constantly evolving. For example, a state statute based on common law may define first degree murder as the "unlawful killing, with malice and premeditation, of one human being by another." Over time, state court decisions might help explain the meaning of the term *malice* or clarify whether *human being* only refers to someone "born and alive" or whether it can refer to an unborn fetus. For example, more than half the states have expanded their legal codes to include *feticide law*, which makes killing of an unborn fetus murder (see Exhibit 3.2 for an example).

The content of the law may also be influenced by judicial decision making. For example, a criminal offense may be no longer enforceable when an appellate judge rules that the statute is vague, deals with an act no longer of interest to the public, or is an unfair exercise of state control over an individual. Conversely, a judicial ruling may expand the scope of an existing criminal law, thereby allowing control over behaviors which heretofore were beyond its reach. For example, in 1990, 2 Live Crew, a prominent rap group, found its sales restricted in Florida as police began arresting children under 18 for purchasing the band's sexually explicit CD, *As Nasty as They Wanna Be*. The hit single, "Me So Horny," was banned from local radio stations. Prosecutors tried but failed to get a conviction after group members Luther Campbell, Christopher Wong-Won, and Mark Ross (the group also included DJ Mr. Mixx) were arrested at a concert. If members of the Crew had in fact been found guilty for using bad language, and the conviction was upheld by the state's highest appellate court, obscenity laws would have been expanded to cover people singing (or rapping in this case) objectionable music lyrics.

Constitutional Limits

Regardless of its source, all criminal law in the United States must conform to the rules and dictates of the U.S. Constitution.[3] Any criminal law that

Exhibit 3.2	Louisiana: Feticide in the first degree

First-degree feticide is:

1. The killing of an unborn child when the offender has a specific intent to kill or to inflict great bodily harm.
2. The killing of an unborn child when the offender is engaged in the perpetration or attempted perpetration of aggravated rape, forcible rape, aggravated arson, aggravated burglary, aggravated kidnapping, second degree kidnapping, assault by drive-by shooting, aggravated escape, armed robbery, first degree robbery, or simple robbery, even though he has no intent to kill or inflict great bodily harm.
3. Whoever commits the crime of first degree feticide shall be imprisoned at hard labor for not more than fifteen years.

Source: Louisiana First Degree Feticide Law LA R.S. 14:32.6.

conflicts with the various provisions and articles of the Constitution will eventually be challenged in the appellate courts and stricken from the legal code by judicial order (or modified to adhere to constitutional principles). In general, the Constitution has been interpreted to forbid any criminal law that violates a person's right to be treated fairly and equally; this principle is referred to as substantive due process. This means that before a new law can be created, the state must show that there is a compelling need to protect public safety or morals.[4]

Criminal laws have been interpreted as violating constitutional principles if they are too vague or overbroad to give clear meaning of their intent. A law forbidding adults to engage in "immoral behavior" could not be enforced because it does not use clear and precise language or give adequate notice as to which conduct is forbidden.[5] The Constitution also prohibits laws that make a person's status a crime. For example, becoming a heroin addict is not a crime, though laws can forbid the sale, possession, and manufacture of heroin. Finally, the Constitution limits laws that are overly cruel and/or capricious. While the use of the death penalty may be constitutionally approved, capital punishment would be constitutionally forbidden if it were used for lesser crimes such as rape or employed in a random, haphazard fashion.[6]

The Constitution also forbids *bills of attainder:* legislative acts that inflict punishment without a judicial trial. This device, used by the English kings to punish rebels and seize their property, was particularly troublesome to American colonials when it was used to seize the property of people considered disloyal to the crown; hence, attainder is forbidden in the Constitution. Nor does the Constitution permit the government to pass ex post facto laws, defined as:

- A law that makes an action, done before the passing of the law, and which was innocent when done, criminal; and punishes such action.

- A law that makes a crime more serious after the fact than it was when first committed.

- A law inflicts a greater punishment than was available when the crime was committed.

- A law which makes it easier to convict the offender than was present at the time she committed the crime.[7]

The following Policy, Programs, and Issues in Criminal Justice box discusses the concept of ex post facto laws in greater depth.

Crimes and Classifications

Each state and the federal government has developed its own body of criminal law that defines and grades offenses, sets levels of punishment, and classifies crimes into categories. Crimes are generally grouped into:

- Felonies, the most serious crimes punishable by imprisonment, such as criminal homicide, robbery, and rape, as well as such crimes against property as burglary and larceny.

- Misdemeanors, less serious crimes punishable by a jail term, that include petit (or petty) larceny, assault and battery, and the unlawful possession of marijuana.

- Violations (also called *infractions*), which are violations of city or town ordinances such as traffic violations or public intoxication, punishable by a fine. Some states consider violations civil matters, whereas others classify them as crimes.

Policy, Programs, and Issues in Criminal Justice

Ex Post Facto Laws

The Constitution forbids the passage of laws that retroactively punish people. That is, you cannot be punished for an act that was legal at the time of its occurrence. However, can you be treated or helped for a prior act? Can a state pass laws which apply retroactively if their intention is non-punitive? The Supreme Court made this point in three recent cases involving sex offenders.

Kansas v. Hendricks (1997)

Facts The Kansas Sexually Violent Predator Act allows for indefinite civil confinement for sexual predators after their criminal term has concluded. Hendricks, a habitual offender, was serving a prison term for sexual misconduct when the law was implemented. He appealed on the grounds that his ex post facto rights were violated because he now could be confined under a law that did not exist when he was first convicted.

Decision The Supreme Court upheld his confinement, concluding the act was non-punitive in nature and designed to treat rather than harm offenders. Therefore it did not violate the ex post facto provision, which forbids increasing punishment retroactively.

Smith v. Doe (2003)

Facts Under the Alaska Sex Offender Registration Act, an incarcerated sex offender or child kidnapper must register with the Department of Corrections within thirty days before their release. Even if convicted of a single, non-aggravated sex crime, the offender must register with authorities and provide information to authorities for fifteen years. The offender's information is forwarded to the Department of Public Safety, which maintains a central registry of sex offenders. Some of the data is kept confidential, while other information, such as the offender's name, aliases, address, photograph, and physical description, is published on the Internet. Both the act's registration and notification requirements were made retroactive to previously convicted offenders.

The petitioners were convicted of aggravated sex offenses and released from prison after completing rehabilitative programs for sex offenders. Although convicted before the act's passage, respondents were covered by its provisions and were required to register with authorities and make quarterly contacts. They brought suit to void the restrictions under the ex post facto clause, U.S. Constitution, art. 1, sec. 10, cl. 1.

Decision On review, the Supreme Court upheld the Alaska Sex Offender Registration Act's requirement that offenders who had been incarcerated prior to its passage be made to conform to its provisions because it is non-punitive. It ruled that the Alaska legislature's intent was to create a civil, non-punitive requirement for release that is designed to protect the public from sex offenders as the law's primary interest. The Court found that there was nothing in the statute's language that suggests that the Alaska legislature sought to create anything other than a civil scheme designed to protect the public from harm. The act does not impose physical restraint, and so does not resemble imprisonment, and there is no evidence that the act has led to substantial occu-

---

felony *A more serious offense that carries a penalty of incarceration in a state prison, usually for one year or more. Persons convicted of felony offenses lose such rights as the rights to vote, hold elective office, or maintain certain licenses.*

misdemeanor *A minor crime usually punished by less than one year's imprisonment in a local institution, such as a county jail.*

Distinguishing between a **felony** and a **misdemeanor** is sometimes difficult. Simply put, a felony is a serious offense, and a misdemeanor is a less serious one. *Black's Law Dictionary* defines the two terms as follows:

> A felony is a crime of a graver or more atrocious nature than those designated as misdemeanors. Generally it is an offense punishable by death or imprisonment in a penitentiary. A misdemeanor is lower than a felony and is generally punishable by fine or imprisonment otherwise than in a penitentiary.[8]

The felony–misdemeanor classification has a direct effect on the way an offender is treated within the justice system. Police may arrest a felon if there is either an arrest warrant issued by a court and/or probable cause they pational or housing disadvantages for former sex of-fenders that would not have otherwise occurred. Therefore requiring offenders convicted and or incarcerated prior to the law's passage to register and report is not illegal.

Stogner v. California (2003)

Facts In 1993, California enacted a new criminal statute of limitations permitting prosecution for sex-related child abuse within one year of a victim's report of the abuse to the police even if the statute of limitations had already run out. In 1998, Stogner was indicted for sex-related child abuse committed between 1955 and 1973. At the time those crimes were allegedly committed the limitations period was three years. Stogner argued his indictment was illegal on the ground that the ex post facto clause forbids revival of a previously time-barred prosecution.

Decision The Court ruled that a law enacted to allow criminal prosecutions after expiration of a previously applicable statute of limitations period violates the ex post facto clause. California's law extends the time in which prosecution is allowed and authorizes prosecutions that the passage of time had previously barred. Such laws are forbidden by the Constitution because they inflict punishments where the party was not, by law, liable to any punishment.

Significance of the Cases

All three cases show that the Court can use its discretion to interpret law in rather unusual ways. In *Smith v. Doe*, the Alaska law in question applied only to sex offenders and not other types of criminals. Isn't that a special form of "punishment"? It applied to every sex offender without allowing discretion and

imposed severe restrictions; yet the Court ruled that the burdens were non-punitive. As a group the cases show that the Court draws a clear distinction between a person being "treated" and a person who is being "punished" even though to an outsider the distinction between these two statuses may become muddled. In *Hendricks*, continued treatment was allowed even if it meant a longer period of confinement. In contrast, *Stogner* shows that when an ex post facto law is clearly punitive—that is, allows criminal prosecution—it will not be upheld by the Court.

Critical Thinking

In his dissent in *Smith v. Doe*, Justice Stevens wrote:

> In my opinion, a sanction that (1) is imposed on everyone who commits a criminal offense, (2) is not imposed on anyone else, and (3) severely impairs a person's liberty is punishment. It is therefore clear to me that the Constitution prohibits the addition of these sanctions to the punishment of persons who were tried and convicted before the legislation was enacted.

Do you agree with Stevens?

InfoTrac College Edition Research

To read more about the *Hendricks* case and the ex post facto clause, go to Wayne A. Logan, "The ex post facto clause and the jurisprudence of punishment," *American Criminal Law Review*, Summer 1998 v35 i4 p1261(1).

Sources: *Stogner v. California* No. 01-1757, Decided June 26, 2003; *Smith et al. v. Doe et al.* No. 01-729, Decided March 5, 2003; *Kansas v. Hendricks*, 117 S. Ct. 2072, 2078 (1997).

committed a crime. In contrast, misdemeanants may only be taken into custody with an arrest warrant and/or the police officer observed the infraction personally; this is known as the *in-presence requirement*. There are, however, some instances when police can make a misdemeanor arrest without observing its occurrence. For example, a number of jurisdictions have passed domestic violence prevention acts, which allow arrests based merely on the accusation of the injured party. These laws have been created in an effort to protect the target of the abuse from further attacks.[9]

If convicted, a person charged with a felony may be barred from certain fields of employment or some professions, such as law and medicine. A felony offender's status as an alien in the United States might also be affected, or the

Each state has developed its own body of criminal law and consequently determines its own penalties for the various crimes. However, even if a state legalizes an act, people who engage in it may still be law violators under federal law. Here, Robert Anton Wilson, right, who suffers from post-polio syndrome, receives marijuana from Jeremy Griffey, left, and Kathy Nicholson, second from left, both with the Wo/Men's Alliance for Medical Marijuana, at City Hall in Santa Cruz, California. Calling Santa Cruz a "sanctuary" from federal authorities, medical marijuana advocates, joined by city leaders, passed out pot to about a dozen sick and dying patients at City Hall. Should these people be punished for substance abuse violations?

offender might be denied the right to hold public office, vote, or serve on a jury.[10] These and other civil liabilities exist only when a person is convicted of a felony offense, not a misdemeanor.

Criminal Justice ⚛ Now™

Learn more by exploring the **Criminal Harm** *Review and Reinforce activity.*

▌THE LEGAL DEFINITION OF A CRIME

Almost all common law crime contains both mental and physical elements. Take, for example, the common law crime of burglary in the first degree. Alabama's is defined as shown in Exhibit 3.3.

Note that in order to commit the crime of armed burglary in Alabama (and elsewhere), an offender must do the following things:

- Willfully enter a dwelling
- Be armed or arm themselves after entering the house, or commit an actual assault on a person who is lawfully in the house
- Knowingly and intentionally commit the crime

actus reus An illegal act. The actus reus can be an affirmative act, such as taking money or shooting someone, or a failure to act, such as failing to take proper precautions while driving a car.

mens rea Guilty mind. The mental element of a crime or the intent to commit a criminal act.

For the prosecutor to prove a crime occurred, and that the defendant committed it, the prosecutor must show that the accused (1) engaged in the guilty act (**actus reus** or guilty act) and that (2) the act was intentional and purposeful (**mens rea** or guilty mind). Under common law, both the actus reus and the mens rea must be present for the act to be considered a crime.

| Exhibit | 3.3 | **Alabama definition of burglary in the first degree** |

Section 13A-7-5, Burglary in the First Degree

A person commits the crime of burglary in the first degree if he knowingly and unlawfully enters or remains unlawfully in a dwelling with intent to commit a crime therein, and if, in effecting entry or while in dwelling or in immediate flight there from, he or another participant in the crime: (1) is armed with explosives or a deadly weapon, or (2) causes physical injury to any person who is not a participant in the crime, or (3) uses or threatens the immediate use of a dangerous instrument. Burglary in the first degree is a Class A felony.

Sources: Alabama Criminal Code, Acts 1977, No. 607, p. 812, and sec. 2610; Acts 1979, No. 79-471, p. 862, and sec. 1; LegalTips.org, www.legaltips.org/Alabama/alabama_code/13A-7-5.aspx, accessed on August 11, 2005.

Thoughts of committing an act do not alone constitute a crime; there must also be an illegal act. Let us now look more closely at these issues.

Actus Reus

The actus reus is a *voluntary and deliberate* illegal act, such as taking someone's money, burning a building, or shooting someone; an accident or involuntary act would not be considered criminal. However, even an unintentional act can be considered a crime if it is the result of negligence and/or disregard for the rights of others. For example, a person cannot be held criminally liable for assault if while walking down the street he has a seizure and as a result his arm strikes another person in the face; his act was not voluntary and therefore not criminal. However, if this same person knew beforehand that he might have a seizure and unreasonably put himself in a position where he was likely to harm others—for instance, by driving a car—he could be criminally liable for his behavior because his actions were negligent and disregarded the rights of others.

In addition, there are occasions when the failure or omission to act can be considered a crime:

- *Failure to perform a legally required duty that is based on relationship or status.* These relationships include parent and child and husband and wife. If a husband finds his wife unconscious because she took an overdose of sleeping pills, he is obligated to save her life by seeking medical aid. If he fails to do so and she dies, he can be held responsible for her death. Parents are required to look after the welfare of their children; failure to provide adequate care can be a criminal offense.

- *Imposition by statute.* Some states have passed laws that require a person who observes an automobile accident to stop and help the other parties involved.

- *Contractual relationship.* These relationships include lifeguard and swimmer, doctor and patient, and babysitter or au pair and child. Because lifeguards have been hired to ensure the safety of swimmers, they have a legal duty to come to the aid of drowning persons. If a lifeguard knows a swimmer is in danger and does nothing about it and the swimmer drowns, the lifeguard can be held legally responsible for the swimmer's death.

The duty to act is a legal and not a moral duty. The obligation arises from the relationship between the parties or from explicit legal requirements. For example, a private citizen who sees a person drowning is under no legal obligation to save that person. Although we may find it morally reprehensible, the private citizen could walk away and let the swimmer drown without facing legal sanctions.

Criminal Justice ⚖ Now™
Learn more by exploring The Guilty Mind Review and Reinforce activity.

Mens Rea

For an act to constitute a crime, it must be done with deliberate purpose or criminal intent. A person who enters a store with a gun with the intention of stealing money indicates by his actions the intent to commit a robbery. Criminal intent is implied if the results of a person's action, though originally unintended, are certain to occur. For example, when Mohammed Atta and his terrorist band crashed aircraft into the World Trade Center on September 11, 2001, they did not intend to kill any particular person in the building. Yet the law would hold that Atta, or any other person, would be substantially certain that people in the building would be killed in the blast and that he therefore had the criminal intent to commit the crime of murder.

In some situations intent is derived from recklessness or negligence. A drunk driver may not have intended to kill her specific victim, yet her negligent and reckless behavior—driving while drunk—creates a condition that a reasonable person can assume may lead to injury.

The Relationship of Mens Rea and Actus Reus

To constitute a crime, the law requires a connection be made between the mens rea and actus reas thereby showing that the offender's conduct was the proximate cause of the criminal act. If, for example, a man chases a woman into the street intending to assault her, and the victim is struck by a car and killed, the accused cannot claim at trial that the death was an accident caused by the inopportune passing of the motor vehicle. The law holds that the victim would never have run into the street had she not been pursued by the defendant and therefore, (1) the defendant's reckless disregard for the victim's safety makes him responsible for her death and (2) his action was the proximate cause of her death. Exhibit 3.4 sets out common law crimes and their definitions.

Criminal Justice ⚖ Now™

*Learn more about **Strict Liability** by exploring the Review and Reinforce activity.*

Strict Liability

Certain statutory offenses exist in which mens rea is not essential. These offenses fall in a category known as public safety or **strict liability crimes.** A person can be held responsible for such a violation independent of the existence of intent to commit the offense. Strict liability criminal statutes generally include narcotics control laws, traffic laws, health and safety regulations, sanitation laws, and other regulatory statutes. For example, a driver could not defend herself against a speeding ticket by claiming that she was unaware of how fast she was going and did not intend to speed, nor could a bartender claim that a juvenile to whom he sold liquor looked quite a bit older. No state of mind is generally required where a strict liability statute is violated.[11] For example, consider the New York State law S 270.10: Creating a hazard, which is laid out in Exhibit 3.5.[12] Notice that the intent to commit this crime is not required for a conviction on charges of creating a hazardous condition.

Criminal Justice ⚖ Now™

*Learn more about **Criminal Defenses** by exploring the "Insanity Defense Standards" Vocabulary Check activity.*

strict liability crime Illegal act whose elements do not contain the need for intent or mens rea; usually, acts that endanger the public welfare, such as illegal dumping of toxic wastes.

CRIMINAL DEFENSES

In 1884, two British sailors, desperate after being shipwrecked for days, made the decision to kill and eat a suffering cabin boy who was on their lifeboat. Four days later, they were rescued by a passing ship and returned to England. English authorities, wanting to end the practice of shipwreck cannibalism, tried and convicted the two men for murder. Clemency was considered and a reluctant Queen Victoria commuted the death sentences to six months.[13] Were the seamen justified in killing a shipmate to save their lives? If they had not done so, it is likely they all would have died. Did they act out of necessity or

Exhibit   3.4   Common law crimes

	Crime	Definition	Example
Crimes against the person	First degree murder	Unlawful killing of another human being with malice afore-thought and with premeditation and deliberation.	A woman buys some poison and pours it into a cup of coffee her husband is drink-ing, intending to kill him. The motive—to get the insurance benefits of the victim.
	Voluntary manslaughter	Intentional killing committed under extenuating circum-stances that mitigate the killing, such as killing in the heat of passion after being provoked.	A husband coming home early from work finds his wife in bed with another man. The husband goes into a rage and shoots and kills both lovers with a gun he keeps by his bedside.
	Battery	Unlawful touching of another with intent to cause injury	A man seeing a stranger sitting in his favorite seat in the cafeteria goes up to that person and pushes him out of the seat.
	Assault	Intentional placing of another in fear of receiving an imme-diate battery.	A student aims an unloaded gun at her professor who believes the gun is loaded. The student says she is going to shoot.
	Rape	Unlawful sexual intercourse with a female without her consent.	After a party, a man offers to drive a young female acquaintance home. He takes her to a wooded area and, despite her protests, forces her to have sexual relations with him.
	Robbery	Wrongful taking and carrying away of personal property from a person by violence or intimidation.	A man armed with a loaded gun approaches another man on a deserted street and demands his wallet.
Inchoate (incomplete) offenses	Attempt	An intentional act for the pur-pose of committing a crime that is more than mere preparation or planning of the crime. The crime is not completed, however.	A person intending to kill another places a bomb in the second person's car, so that it will detonate when the ignition key is used. The bomb is discovered before the car is started. Attempted murder has been committed.
	Conspiracy	Voluntary agreement between two or more persons to achieve an unlawful object or to achieve a lawful object using means forbidden by law.	A drug company sells larger-than-normal quantities of drugs to a doctor, knowing that the doctor is distributing the drugs illegally. The drug company is guilty of conspiracy.
Crimes against property	Burglary	Breaking and entering of a dwelling house of another with the intent to commit a felony.	Intending to steal some jewelry and silver, a young man breaks a window and enters another's house.
	Arson	Intentional burning of a dwelling house of another.	A secretary, angry that her boss did not give her a raise, goes to her boss's house and sets fire to it.
	Larceny	Taking and carrying away the personal property of another with the intent to steal the property.	While a woman is shopping, she sees a diamond ring displayed at the jewelry counter. When no one is looking, the woman takes the ring and walks out of the store.

Exhibit	3.5	New York State law: Section 270.10: Creating a hazard

A person is guilty of creating a hazard when:

1. Having discarded in any place where it might attract children, a container which has a compartment of more than one and one-half cubic feet capacity and a door or lid which locks or fastens automatically when closed and which cannot easily be opened from the inside, he fails to remove the door, lid, locking or fastening device; or

2. Being the owner or otherwise having possession of property upon which an abandoned well or cesspool is located, he fails to cover the same with suitable protective construction.

Creating a hazard is a class B misdemeanor.

Sources: New York State Consolidated Laws, Article 270: Other Offenses Relating to Public Safety, Section 270.10: Creating a hazard (2002); http://wings.buffalo.edu/law/bclc/web/NewYork/ny3(b).htm, accessed on May 8, 2005.

malice? Can there ever be a good reason to take a life? Can we ever justify killing another? Before you answer, remember that we can kill in self-defense, to prevent lethal crimes, or in times of war (more on necessity defenses later).

When people defend themselves against criminal charges, they must refute one or more of the elements of the crime of which they have been accused. Defendants may deny the actus reus by arguing that they were falsely accused and the real culprit has yet to be identified. Defendants may also claim that while they did engage in the criminal act they are accused of, they lacked the mens rea, or mental intent, needed to be found guilty of the crime. If a person whose mental state is impaired commits a criminal act, it is possible for the person to excuse his criminal actions by claiming he lacked the capacity to form sufficient intent to be held criminally responsible. **Insanity,** intoxication, and ignorance are also among the types of excuse defenses.[14]

Another type of defense is justification. Here, the individual admits committing the criminal act, but maintains that the act was justified and that given the circumstances anyone would have acted in a similar manner; because they are justified they should not be held criminally liable. Among the justification defenses are necessity, duress, **self-defense,** and **entrapment.** We will now examine some of these defenses and justifications in greater detail.

Excuse Defenses

Excuses refer to situations in which the criminal defendants admit the physical act of crime but claim they are not responsible for it because they lacked free will. It is not their fault, they claim, because they had no control over their actions; therefore they should be "excused" from criminal responsibility.

Ignorance or Mistake People sometimes defend themselves by claiming that their actions were either a mistake or that they were unaware (ignorant) of the fact that their behavior was a crime. For example, they did not realize that they had stepped onto private property and were guilty of trespassing.

As a general rule, ignorance of the law is no excuse. According to the great legal scholar William Blackstone, "Ignorance of the law, which everyone is bound to know, excuses no man."[15] Consequently, a defendant cannot present a legitimate defense by saying he was unaware of a criminal law, had misinterpreted the law, or believed the law to be unconstitutional.

In some instances, mistake of fact, such as taking someone else's coat that is similar to your own, may be a valid defense. If the jury or judge as trier of fact determines that criminal intent was absent, such an honest mistake may remove the defendant's criminal responsibility. Mistake can also be used as a defense when the government failed to make enactment of a new law public

Criminal Justice ⚖ Now™

Learn more by exploring the ***Insanity Defense*** *by viewing the "In the News" video clip.*

insanity *A legal defense that maintains a defendant was incapable of forming criminal intent because he or she suffers from a defect of reason or mental illness.*

self-defense *A legal defense in which defendants claim that their behavior was legally justified by the necessity to protect their own life and property or that of another victim from potential harm.*

entrapment *A criminal defense that maintains the police originated the criminal idea or initiated the criminal action.*

or when the offender relies on an official statement of the law that is later deemed incorrect.

Insanity Insanity is a defense to criminal prosecution in which the defendant's state of mind negates his or her criminal responsibility. A successful insanity defense results in a verdict of "not guilty by reason of insanity."

Insanity is a legal category. As used in U.S. courts, it does not necessarily mean that everyone who suffers from a form of mental illness can be excused from legal responsibility. Many people who are depressed, suffer mood disorders, or have a psychopathic personality can be found legally sane. Instead, insanity means that the defendant's state of mind at the time the crime was committed made it impossible for that person to have the necessary mens rea to satisfy the legal definition of a crime. Thus, a person can be undergoing treatment for a psychological disorder but still be judged legally sane if it can be proven that at the time he committed the crime he had the capacity to understand the wrongfulness of his actions.

If a defendant uses the insanity plea, it is usually left to psychiatric testimony to prove that the person understood the wrongfulness of his actions and was therefore legally sane, or conversely, was mentally incapable of forming intent. The jury then must weigh the evidence in light of the test for sanity currently used in the jurisdiction.

Such tests vary throughout the United States; the commonly used tests are listed in Exhibit 3.6.

Intoxication As a general rule, intoxication, which may include drunkenness or being under the influence of drugs, is not considered a defense. However, a defendant who becomes involuntarily intoxicated under duress or by mistake may be excused for crimes committed. Involuntary intoxication may also lessen the degree of the crime; a judgment may be decreased from first- to second-degree murder because the defendant uses intoxication to prove the lack of the critical element of mens rea.

Age The law holds that a child is not criminally responsible for actions committed at an age that precludes a full realization of the gravity of certain types of behavior. Under common law, there is generally a conclusive presumption

Criminal Justice ⚖ Now™

Learn more by exploring the "Insanity" Review and Reinforce activity.

Exhibit 3.6	Various insanity defense standards		
Test	**Legal Standard of Mental Illness**	**Final Burden of Proof**	**Who Bears Burden of Proof**
M'Naghten	"Didn't know what he was doing or didn't know it was wrong"	Balance of probabilities	Defense
Irresistible impulse	"Could not control his conduct"	Beyond reasonable doubt	Prosecutor
Durham	"The criminal act was caused by his mental illness"	Beyond reasonable doubt	Prosecutor
Substantial capacity	"Lacks substantial capacity to appreciate the wrongfulness of his conduct or to control it"	Beyond reasonable doubt	Prosecutor
Present federal law	"Lacks capacity to appreciate the wrongfulness of his conduct"	Clear and convincing evidence	Defense

Source: Norval Morris, *Crime Study Guide: Insanity Defense* (Washington, D.C.: U.S. Department of Justice, 1986), p. 3.

of incapacity for a child under age seven, a reliable presumption for a child between the ages of seven and fourteen, and no presumption for a child over the age of fourteen. This generally means that a child under age seven who commits a crime will not be held criminally responsible for these actions and that a child between ages seven and fourteen may be held responsible. These common law rules have been changed by statute in most jurisdictions. Today, the maximum age of criminal responsibility for children ranges from age fourteen to seventeen or eighteen, while the minimum age may be set by statute at age seven or under age fourteen.[16]

Justification Defenses

Justifications refer to situations in which the defendants don't deny they committed a crime but claim that anyone in his or her situation would have acted in a similar fashion. Justification defenses deny mens rea: "I did a bad act, but I did it for all the right reasons."

Consent A person may not be convicted of a crime if the victim consented to the act in question. In other words, a rape does not occur if the victim consents to sexual relations; a larceny cannot occur if the owner voluntarily consents to the taking of property. Consent is an essential element of these crimes, and it is a valid defense where it can be proven or shown that it existed at the time the act was committed. In some crimes, such as statutory rape, however, consent is not an element of the crime and is considered irrelevant because the state presumes that young people are not capable of providing consent.

Self-Defense Defendants may justify their actions by saying they acted in self-defense. To establish the necessary elements to constitute self-defense, however, the defendant must have acted under a reasonable belief that he was in danger of death or great harm and had no means of escape from the assailant.

As a general legal rule, a person defending herself may use only such force as is reasonably necessary to prevent personal harm. A person who is assaulted by another with no weapon is ordinarily not justified in hitting the assailant with a baseball bat; a person verbally threatened is not justified in striking the other party. Persons can be found guilty of murder in the first degree if after being attacked during a brawl they shot and killed an unarmed person in self-defense. Despite the fact that it was the victim who initiated the fray and pummeled his opponent first; the imbalance in weaponry (gun versus fist) would mitigate a finding of self-defense.[17]

© 2005 AP/Wide World Photos

People can defend themselves by claiming self-defense. Here, Harvard graduate student Alexander Pring-Wilson points to the pocket in his jeans where he said he kept his knife, while on the stand at Middlesex Superior Court on October 5, 2004, in Cambridge, Massachusetts. Pring-Wilson said he was being brutally beaten by two men and feared for his life when he pulled a knife and fatally stabbed a Cambridge man. Testifying in his own murder trial, Pring-Wilson got on one knee in front of the jury, dramatically re-enacting the street fight that resulted in the death of 18-year-old Michael Colono and landed Pring-Wilson in jail on a first-degree murder charge. While the jury believed that Pring-Wilson was defending himself, they concluded that his use of a knife was excessive considering the circumstances.

To exercise the self-defense privilege, the danger to the defendant must be immediate; it is not justifiable to kill someone who threatened you with death a year ago. In addition, most jurisdictions require that the defendants prove that they sought alternative means of avoiding the danger, such as escape, retreat, or assistance from others, before they defended themselves with force.

In some instances women (or men) may kill their mates after years of abuse; this is known as *battered-wife syndrome* (or in cases involving child abuse, *battered-child syndrome*). While a history of battering can be used to mitigate the seriousness of the crime, a finding of not guilty most often requires the presence of imminent danger and the inability of the accused to escape from the assailant.

Entrapment Defendants can claim their criminal activity was justified because law enforcement agents use traps, decoys, and deception to induce criminal action; this is referred to as entrapment. It is generally legitimate for law enforcement officers to set traps for criminals by getting information about crimes from informers, undercover agents, and codefendants. Police officers are allowed to use ordinary opportunities for defendants to commit crime and to create these opportunities which involve a defendant in a crime. However, entrapment occurs when the police instigate the crime, implant criminal ideas, and coerce individuals into bringing about crime. In *Sherman v. United States* the United States Supreme Court found that the function of law enforcement is to prevent crime and to apprehend criminals, not to implant a criminal design originating with officials of the government in the mind of an innocent person.[18]

Duress In order to prove duress, defendants must show they have been forced into committing a crime in order to prevent death or serious harm to self or others. For example, a bank employee might be excused from taking bank funds if she can prove that her family was being threatened and that consequently she was acting under duress. But there is widespread general agreement that duress is no defense for an intentional killing.

Necessity Sometimes criminal defendants, like the two sailors who killed and ate the cabin boy, argue that they acted out of "necessity." To be successful, a defense of necessity must show that considering the circumstances and conditions at the time the crime occurred, the defendant (or any reasonable person) could not have behaved in any other fashion. For example, a husband steals a car to bring his pregnant wife to the hospital for an emergency delivery, or a hunter shoots an animal of an endangered species that was about to attack her child. The defense has been found inapplicable, however, in cases where defendants sought to shut down nuclear power plants or abortion clinics or to destroy missile components under the belief that the action was necessary to save lives or prevent a nuclear war.

Criminal Justice Now™

Learn more by exploring the "Duress" Review and Reinforce activity.

REFORMING THE CRIMINAL LAW

In recent years, many states and the federal government have been examining their substantive criminal law. In some instances what was formerly legal is now a crime and, in other instances, what was previously considered illegal has been legalized or decriminalized (in other words, the penalties have been reduced). An example of the former can be found in changes to the law of rape. In seven states, including California, it is now considered rape if (1) woman consents to sex, (2) the sex act begins, (3) she changes her mind during the act and tells her partner to stop, and (4) he refuses and continues. Before the legal change, such a circumstance was not considered rape.[19]

There are also many instances in which the law has been changed so what was considered illegal is now legal and non-criminal. For example, until recently sexual relations between consenting same-sex adults was punished as a serious felony under sodomy statutes. In an important 2003 case, *Lawrence v. Texas*, the Supreme Court declared that laws banning sodomy were unconstitutional if they restrict an adult's private sexual behavior and impose on their personal dignity. In its decision, the Court said

> Although the laws involved . . . here . . . to do not more than prohibit a particular sexual act, their penalties and purposes have more far-reaching consequences, touching upon the most private human conduct, sexual behavior, and in the most private of places, the home. They seek to control a personal relationship that, whether or not entitled to formal recognition in the law, is within the liberty of persons to choose without being punished as criminals. The liberty protected by the Constitution allows homosexual persons the right to choose to enter upon relationships in the confines of their homes and their own private lives and still retain their dignity as free persons.

As a result of the decision, laws banning same-sex relations between consenting adults in the U.S. are now unconstitutional and therefore non-enforceable.[20]

States may take action to decriminalize or legalize some crimes because the general public simply ignores the laws and law enforcement agents are reluctant to press charges even when they apprehend violators. Legal scholar Margaret Raymond calls these **penumbral crimes,** criminal acts defined by a high level of public non-compliance with the stated legal standard, an absence of stigma associated with violation of the stated standard, and a low level of law enforcement or public sanction.[21] Laws prohibiting the use of recreational drugs fall into this category: a majority of Americans have used marijuana (including some presidents!); those who use it are not banned, shunned, or stigmatized; and relatively few pot smokers are arrested or prosecuted. Because otherwise law-abiding people routinely violate these laws, they may be targets for penalty reduction and eventual legalization. For example, since the 55 mile per hour speed limit is so widely ignored, some states have increased limits to 65 and even 70 miles per hour.

Creating New Crimes

In some instances, new laws have been created to conform to emerging social issues. The ones discussed below illustrate the evolving nature of the criminal law:

Physician-Assisted Suicide Doctors helping people to end their life became the subject of a national debate when Dr. Jack Kevorkian began practicing what he calls **obitiatry,** helping people take their lives.[22] In an attempt to stop Kevorkian, Michigan passed a statutory ban on assisted suicide, reflecting what lawmakers believed to be prevailing public opinion; Kevorkian was convicted and imprisoned.[23]

Stalking More than 25 states have enacted **stalking** statutes, which prohibit and punish acts described typically as "the willful, malicious, and repeated following and harassing of another person."[24] Stalking laws were originally formulated to protect women terrorized by former husbands and boyfriends, although celebrities often are plagued by stalkers as well. In celebrity cases, these laws often apply to stalkers who are strangers or casual acquaintances of their victims.

penumbral crimes Criminal acts defined by a high level of public non-compliance with the stated legal standard, an absence of stigma associated with violation of the stated standard, and a low level of law enforcement or public sanction.

obitiatry Helping people take their own lives.

stalking The willful, malicious, and repeated following and harassing of another person.

Community Notification Laws These laws require the registration of people convicted of sex-related crimes, a response to concern about sexual predators moving into neighborhoods. One of the most well-known laws, New Jersey's "Megan's Law," was named after 7–year-old Megan Kanka of Hamilton Township, N.J., who was killed in 1994. Charged with the crime was a convicted sex offender who (unknown to the Kankas) lived across the street. On May 17, 1996, President Clinton signed Megan's Law, which contained two components:

- *Sex offender registration.* Requires the states to register individuals convicted of sex crimes against children.

- *Community notification.* Compels the states to make private and personal information on registered sex offenders available to the public.

While civil libertarians have expressed concern that notification laws may interfere with an offender's post-release privacy rights, recent research (2005) indicates that registered offenders find value in Megan's Law because it helps deter future abuse. When DNA collection is included in the law, it helps reduce false accusations and convictions.[25]

Anti-Cybercrime Laws Changing technology and the ever-increasing role of technology in our daily lives have also required modification in the criminal law. For example, a modification to Virginia's Computer Crimes Act (see Exhibit 3.7), which took effect in 2005, makes it a felony to engage in phishing—sending out bulk e-mail messages designed to trick consumers into revealing bank account passwords, Social Security numbers, and other personal information. Those convicted of selling the data or using it to commit another crime, such as identity theft, would face twice the prison time.

Environmental Crimes In response to the concerns of environmentalists, the federal government has passed numerous acts designed to protect the nation's well-being. Some of the most important are listed in Exhibit 3.8.

The Environmental Protection Agency, has successfully prosecuted significant violations of these and other new laws, including data fraud cases (such as private laboratories submitting false environmental data to state and federal environmental agencies); indiscriminate hazardous waste dumping that resulted in serious injuries and death; industry-wide ocean dumping by cruise ships; oil spills that caused significant damage to waterways, wetlands, and beaches; and illegal handling of hazardous substances such as pesticides and asbestos that exposed children, the poor, and other especially vulnerable groups to potentially serious illness.[26]

Exhibit **3.7**	**HB 2304 computer crimes; gathering personal information by deception (phishing); penalty**

Computer crimes; phishing; penalty. Makes it a Class 6 felony to fraudulently obtain, record, or access from a computer the following identifying information of another: (i) social security number; (ii) driver's license number; (iii) bank account numbers; (iv) credit or debit card numbers; (v) personal identification numbers (PIN); (vi) electronic identification codes; (vii) automated or electronic signatures; (viii) biometric data; (ix) fingerprints; (x) passwords; or (xi) any other numbers or information that can be used to access a person's financial resources, obtain identification, act as identification, or obtain goods or services. Any person who sells or distributes such information or uses it to commit another crime is guilty of a Class 5 felony.

Source: http://leg1.state.va.us/cgi-bin/legp504.exe?051+sum+HB2304, accessed on May 8, 2005.

| Exhibit | 3.8 | **Environmental protection laws** |

Federal Insecticide, Fungicide and Rodenticide Act (FIFRA), 7 USC sections 136–136y

Energy Supply and Environmental Coordination Act, 15 USC sections 791–798

Toxic Substances Control Act (TSCA), 15 USC sections 2601–2692

Federal Water Pollution Control Act (also known as the Clean Water Act), 33 USC sections 1251–1387

Safe Drinking Water Act, 42 USC sections 300f–300j-26

Noise Control Act, 42 USC sections 4901–4918, 42 USC section 4910 (criminal provision)

Solid Waste Disposal Act (including, in Subchapter III, *The Resource Conservation and Recovery Act* [RCRA]), 42 USC sections 6901–6992k

Clean Air Act, 42 USC sections 7401–7671

Federal Hazardous Material Transportation Statute, 49 USC sections 5101–5127

Source: Department of Justice, Environmental Crimes, www.usdoj.gov/usao/eousa/foia_reading_room/usam/title5/11menv.htm, accessed on August 11, 2005.

Changing Defenses

Criminal defenses are also undergoing rapid change. As society becomes more aware of existing social problems that may in part produce crime, it has become commonplace for defense counsels to defend their clients by raising a variety of new defenses based on preexisting conditions or syndromes with which their clients were afflicted. Examples might include "battered woman syndrome," "Vietnam syndrome," "child sexual abuse syndrome," "Holocaust survivor syndrome," and "adopted child syndrome." In using these defenses, attorneys are asking judges either to recognize a new excuse for crime or to fit these conditions into preexisting defenses. For example, a person who used lethal violence in self-defense may argue that the trauma of serving in the Vietnam War caused him to overreact to provocation. Or a victim of child abuse may use her experiences to mitigate her culpability in a crime, asking a jury, for example, to consider her background when making a death penalty decision. In some instances, exotic criminal defenses have been gender-specific. Attorneys have argued that their female clients' behavior was a result of their premenstrual syndrome (PMS) and that male clients were aggressive because of an imbalance in their testosterone levels. These defenses have achieved relatively little success in the United States.[27] Others contend that attorneys can turn the tables and use these defenses against the defendant. Some commentators have suggested that courts will ultimately view PMS as an aggravating condition in a crime prompting harsher penalties.

While criminal law reform may be guided by good intentions, it is sometimes difficult to put the changes into actual operation. Law reform may require new enforcement agencies to be created or severely tax existing ones. As a result the system becomes strained, and cases are backlogged.

Criminal Justice ⚖ Now™

Learn more by exploring the "Bill of Rights" Review and Reinforce activity.

CONSTITUTIONAL CRIMINAL PROCEDURE

Whereas substantive criminal law primarily defines crimes, the law of criminal procedure consists of the rules and procedures that govern the pretrial processing of criminal suspects and the conduct of criminal trials. The main source of the procedural law is the body of the Constitution and the first ten amendments added to the U.S. Constitution on December 15, 1791, collectively known as the **Bill of Rights.** The purpose of these amendments was to prevent the government from usurping the personal freedoms of citizens. The U.S. Supreme Court's interpretation of these amendments has served as the basis for the creation of legal rights of the accused. Of primary concern are the Fourth, Fifth, Sixth, and Eighth Amendments, which limit and control the manner in which the federal government operates the justice system. In addition, the due process clause of the Fourteenth Amendment has been interpreted to apply these limits on governmental action on the state and local level:

- The Fourth Amendment bars illegal "searches and seizures," a right especially important for the criminal justice system because it means that police officers cannot indiscriminately use their authority to investigate a possible crime or arrest a suspect. Stopping, questioning, or searching an individual without legal justification represents a serious violation of the Fourth Amendment right to personal privacy.

- The Fifth Amendment limits the admissibility of confessions that have been obtained unfairly. In the 1966 landmark case of *Miranda v. Arizona,* the Supreme Court held that a person accused of a crime has the right to refuse to answer questions when placed in police custody.[28] The Fifth Amendment also guarantees defendants the right to a grand jury, and protection from being tried twice for the same crime (double jeopardy). Its due process clause guarantees defendants the right to fundamental fairness and the expectation of fair trials, fair hearings, and similar procedural safeguards.

- The Sixth Amendment guarantees the defendant the right to a speedy and public trial by an impartial jury, the right to be informed of the nature of the charges, and the right to confront any prosecution witnesses. It also contains the right of a defendant to be represented by an attorney, a privilege which has been extended to numerous stages of the criminal justice process, including pretrial custody, identification and lineup procedures, preliminary hearing, submission of a guilty plea, trial, sentencing, and postconviction appeal.

- According to the Eighth Amendment, "Excessive bail shall not be required, nor excessive fines imposed, nor cruel and unusual punishments inflicted." Bail is a money bond put up by the accused to attain freedom between arrest and trial. Bail is meant to ensure a trial appearance, since the bail money is forfeited if the defendant misses the trial date. The Eighth Amendment does not guarantee a constitutional right to bail but rather prohibits the use of excessive bail, which is typically defined as an amount far greater than that imposed on similar defendants who are accused of committing similar crimes. The Eighth Amendment also forbids the use of cruel and unusual punishment. This prohibition protects both the accused and convicted offenders from actions regarded as unacceptable by a civilized society, including corporal punishment and torture.

- The Fourteenth Amendment is the vehicle used by the courts to apply the protection of the Bill of Rights to the states. It affirms that no state shall "deprive any person of life, liberty, or property, without due process of law." In essence, the same general constitutional restrictions previously applicable to the federal government can be imposed on the states.

Bill of Rights *The first ten amendments to the Constitution.*

▐ DUE PROCESS OF LAW

Criminal Justice⊕Now™

Learn more by exploring the "Comparison of Criminal and Tort Law" Animated Artwork.

The concept of due process, found in both the Fifth and Fourteenth Amendments, has been used to evaluate the constitutionality of legal statutes and to set standards and guidelines for fair procedures in the criminal justice system. In seeking to define the term, most legal experts believe that it refers to the essential elements of fairness under law.[29] This definition basically refers to the legal system's need for rules and regulations that protect individual rights.

Due process can actually be divided into two distinct categories, substantive and procedural. Substantive due process refers to the citizen's right to be protected from criminal laws which may be biased, discriminatory, and otherwise unfair. These laws may be vague or apply unfairly to one group over another.

In contrast, procedural due process seeks to ensure that no person will be deprived of life, liberty, or property without proper and legal criminal process. Basically, procedural due process is intended to guarantee that fundamental fairness exists in each individual case. Specific due process procedures include:

1. Prompt notice of charges
2. A formal hearing
3. The right to counsel or some other representation
4. The opportunity to respond to charges
5. The opportunity to confront and cross-examine witnesses and accusers
6. The privilege to be free from self-incrimination
7. The opportunity to present one's own witnesses
8. A decision made on the basis of substantial evidence and facts produced at the hearing
9. A written statement of the reasons for the decision
10. An appellate review procedure

Criminal Justice ⚖ Now™

Learn more by exploring the "Due Process" Review and Reinforce activity.

The Meaning of Due Process

Exactly what constitutes due process in a specific case depends on the facts of the case, the federal and state constitutional and statutory provisions, previous court decisions, and the ideas and principles that society considers important at a given time and in a given place.[30] Justice Felix Frankfurter emphasized this point in *Rochin v. California* (1952):

> Due process of law requires an evaluation based on a disinterested inquiry pursued in the spirit of science on a balanced order of facts, exactly and clearly stated, on the detached consideration of conflicting claims . . . on a judgment not ad hoc and episodic but duly mindful of reconciling the needs both of continuity and of change in a progressive society.[31]

The interpretations of due process of law are not fixed but rather reflect what society deems fair and just at a particular time and place. The degree of loss suffered by the individual (victim or offender) balanced against the state's interests also determines which and how many due process requirements are ordinarily applied. When the Supreme Court justices are conservative, as they are now, they are less likely to create new rights and privileges under the guise of due process. For example, the Court's decision in the case of *Sattazahn v. Pennsylvania* (2003) helped define the concept of double jeopardy. Sattazahn had been sentenced to death under a Pennsylvania law that requires that the sentencing jury must unanimously find that the case warranted capital punishment. If the jury cannot unanimously agree on the sentence, the court must then enter a life sentence. After he was convicted of murder, Sattazahn's jury became deadlocked on the sentence; the trial judge discharged them and

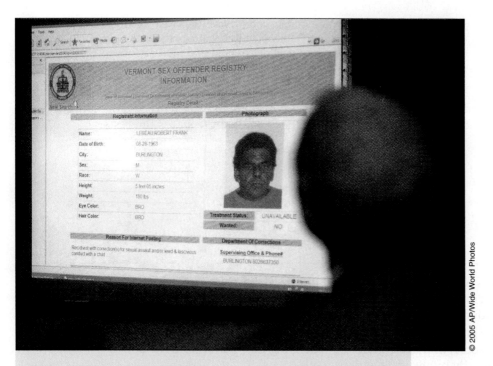

Vermont Attorney General Bill Sorrell looks at a web page during a news conference launching the state's new online sex offender registry in Williston, Vermont, on October 1, 2004. The registry includes information about 135 people who have been convicted of aggravated sexual assault, kidnapping and assault of a child, or repeated sexual offenses. The website will provide the public with a photograph of each offender, plus name and aliases and other information. Is it fair to put a person's photo on the Web and identify him as a danger to society after he has served his sentence? Should all people who break the law be treated in a similar fashion or is it fair to single some out for special treatment? Does this deny them their due process rights?

entered a life sentence. Later, Sattazahn appealed the conviction and received a new trial. At the second trial, the prosecutor again sought the death penalty and Sattazahn was again convicted, but this time the jury imposed a death sentence. Sattazahn appealed on the grounds that the imposition of the death sentence after he was originally awarded a life sentence was a violation of double jeopardy. However, the Supreme Court disagreed, finding that jeopardy was not compromised in this case. When a defendant is convicted of murder and sentenced to life imprisonment and succeeds in having the conviction set aside on appeal, jeopardy has not terminated, so that a life sentence imposed in connection with the initial conviction raises no double-jeopardy bar to a death sentence on retrial. The Court also concluded that double-jeopardy protections were not triggered in this case because the jury deadlocked at the first sentencing and made no findings with respect to the alleged aggravating circumstance; the result could not be called an "acquittal" within the context of double jeopardy. The Sattazahn Court could have ruled that the second capital sentence was a violation of the defendant's constitutional rights but chose not to, instead finding:

> Nothing in §1 of the Fourteenth Amendment indicates that any "life" or "liberty" interest that Pennsylvania law may have given petitioner in the first proceeding's life

Criminal Justice ⚖ Now™
Learn more by going through the ***"Decision Making in the Criminal Justice System"*** *Learning Module.*

Criminal Justice ⊛ Now™

*Learn more about **Careers in Criminal Justice** by exploring the "On the Job" feature **Deputy Public Defender.***

sentence was somehow immutable, and he was "deprived" of any such interest only by operation of the "process" he invoked to invalidate the underlying first-degree murder conviction. This Court declines to hold that the Due Process Clause provides greater double-jeopardy protection than does the Double Jeopardy Clause.[32]

This complicated case aptly illustrates how judicial interpretation controls the meaning of "double jeopardy" and how due process demands that the individual's rights must be balanced against the state's interests.

SUMMARY

- The criminal justice system is basically a legal system. Its foundation is the criminal law, which is concerned with people's conduct.

- The purpose of criminal law is to regulate behavior and maintain order in society. What constitutes a crime is defined primarily by the state and federal legislatures and reviewed by the courts. What is considered criminal conduct changes from one period to another. Social norms, values, and community beliefs play major roles in determining what conduct is antisocial.

- Crimes are generally classified as felonies or misdemeanors, depending on their seriousness.

- There are different elements, both mental and physical, in a crime.

- Crimes have a mental element known as mens rea or intent.

- The actus reas is the physical element of the crime. Thought alone is not enough and a crime must involve action.

- The law does not hold an individual blameworthy unless that person is capable of intending to commit the crime of which he is accused and that intent causes him to commit an illegal action.

- Persons can defend themselves against crime by denying they committed the act.

- They can also deny their intent to commit crime. They may claim that they were intoxicated, acted under duress or out of necessity, or in self-defense. It is possible to argue that the police entrapped them into committing crime. Such factors as insanity, a mental defect, or age mitigate a person's criminal responsibility.

- States periodically revise and update the substantive criminal law. The definitions of crime and criminal defense change to reflect existing social and cultural change.

- Procedural laws set out the rules for processing the offender from arrest through trial, sentencing, and release. An accused must be provided with the guarantees of due process under the Fifth and Fourteenth Amendments to the U.S. Constitution.

KEY TERMS

substantive criminal law 68
criminal procedure 68
civil law 68
tort 68
lex talionis 70
stare decisis 70
common law 70
mala in se 70

mala prohibitum 70
Carriers case 70
felony 74
misdemeanor 74
actus reus 76
mens rea 76
strict liability crime 78

insanity 80
self-defense 80
entrapment 80
penumbral crimes 84
obitiatry 84
stalking 84
Bill of Rights 87

REVIEW QUESTIONS

1. What are the specific aims and purposes of the criminal law? To what extent does the criminal law control behavior?

2. What kinds of activities should be labeled criminal in contemporary society? Why?

3. What is a criminal act? What is a criminal state of mind? When are individuals liable for their actions?

4. Discuss the various kinds of crime classifications. To what extent or degree are they distinguishable?

5. Numerous states are revising their penal codes. Which major categories of substantive crimes do you think should be revised?

6. Entrapment is a defense when the defendant was entrapped into committing the crime. To what extent should law enforcement personnel induce the commission of an offense?

7. What legal principles can be used to justify self-defense? As the law seeks to prevent, not promote, crime, are such principles sound?

8. What are the minimum standards of criminal procedure required in the criminal justice system?

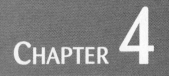

CHAPTER 4

Criminal Justice in the New Millennium: Terrorism, Homeland Security, and Cybercrime

© Mario Tama/Getty Images

TERRY MCADAM, a Graduate of the Royal Society of Chemistry (GRSC) at the University of Ulster (Northern Ireland) is the supervisor of the microanalysis section for the Washington State Patrol Crime Laboratory in Tacoma. In his role as a forensic scientist, he and his colleagues perform analysis on diverse types of evidence that are submitted to the crime lab. Cases may involve hairs, fibers, paint, glass, soils, explosives, shoeprints, or any other trace evidence material. Terry works closely with police agencies to prioritize which items of evidence will be analyzed and assigns cases to the scientists whose talents best match the type of evidence that has been submitted. He is also a senior responder on the Crime Scene Response Team (CSRT). They are available twenty-four hours a day to provide crime scene assistance to any police agency that is investigating a

Chapter Outline

Chapter Objectives

1. Be able to define terrorism and cybercrime
2. Know the factors that may cause someone to become a terrorist
3. Be familiar with the background of the contemporary terrorist
4. Know the findings of the 9/11 Commission
5. Understand the workings of the Department of Homeland Security
6. Be able to discuss local and state level antiterror initiatives
7. Know the USA Patriot Act and be able to discuss its impact on the American public
8. Discuss the various forms of cybercrime
9. Define the concept of cyberterrorism
10. Know what is being done to thwart cybercriminals

serious crime. The CSRT provides specialist services that include blood-stain pattern interpretation, bullet trajectory analysis, and crime scene assistance.

Terry's typical day on the job is never typical. In the morning he may testify in court on a homicide trial and then in the afternoon rush out with his CSRT colleagues to the scene of the brutal stabbing murder of a mother and daughter to gather evidence samples. While he finds the job rewarding, he cautions that because of TV shows such as *Crime Scene Investigation* (*CSI*) the public expects too much of forensic scientists and expects them to solve every case. While they are not magicians, they can provide the crucial link between the suspect and the crime scene for the detective or explain the science to the jury so that the prosecutor can win her case.

Criminal Justice⊕Now™

*Learn more about **Careers in Criminal Justice** by exploring the "On the Job" features **Criminal Investigator–High Tech Crimes** and **FBI Field Agent.***

To read about the **U.S. State Department**'s survey of terror activity around the globe, go to "Web Links" on your Siegel Essentials of Criminal Justice 5e website: http://cj.wadsworth.com/siegel_ess5e.

To learn more about **cybercrime,** go to "Web Links" on your Siegel Essentials of Criminal Justice 5e website: http://cj.wadsworth.com/siegel_ess5e.

terrorism *Premeditated, politically motivated violence perpetrated against noncombatant targets by subnational groups or clandestine agents.*

cybercrime *Illegal behavior that targets the security of computer systems and/or the data accessed and processed by computer networks.*

cyberterrorism *An attack against an enemy nation's technological infrastructure.*

Criminal Justice⊕Now™

Learn more by viewing the "To Order" "In the News" video clip.

CONTEMPORARY CHALLENGES OF THE CRIMINAL JUSTICE SYSTEM

The work of scientists such as Terry McAdam is critical if the criminal justice system is to meet its newest and greatest challenges. While efforts to control traditional crimes—murder, rape, robbery, drug trafficking—continue, emerging forms of criminal and illegal activity pose a significant threat to society. Because of their seriousness, potential for damage, and their effect on public morale, two of these contemporary challenges stand out in importance: **terrorism** and **cybercrime.** Neither appeared on the radar screen 20 years ago; today they dominate the news. Criminal justice agencies at the federal, state, and local levels have been forced to adapt to the threats they present.

One reason both cybercrime and terrorism present formidable challenges for the justice system is because both are evolving in complexity and seriousness. Terrorism involves the illegal use of force against innocent people to achieve a political objective. According to the U.S. State Department, the term *terrorism* means *premeditated, politically motivated violence perpetrated against noncombatant targets by sub-national groups or clandestine agents.*[1] The term *international terrorism* means terrorism involving citizens or the territory of more than one country. A terrorist group is any group practicing, or that has significant subgroups that practice, international terrorism.[2]

Confronting terrorism is also critical because of the lethal tactics now being used—bombings, killing hostages, chemical warfare, spreading toxic biological agents. Terror expert Thomas P. M. Barnett suggests that most people refrain from violent solutions to their problems because they enjoy the benefits of living in a society with a secure economic and social system. Even when they wage war, stable governments abide by a standard code of conduct that spells out appropriate and inappropriate behaviors. Because they or their group do not share in its benefits, terrorists not only are disinterested in maintaining the economic, social, and political structure, but they may be actively planning its destruction. They obey few rules of combat and will use any tactic, no matter how violent, to achieve their goals.[3] Agencies of the justice system have little experience with dealing with such ruthlessness.

Cybercrime, the second contemporary challenge facing the justice system, is defined here as *any illegal behavior that targets the security of computer systems and/or the data accessed and processed by computer networks.* Included within this category of crime are attacks against computers themselves—computer crimes such as implanting a computer virus, and illegal acts that target computer networks, including Internet crimes such as identity theft.

While at first glance cybercriminals present a far different challenge to law enforcement officials than terrorists, there is actually some common ground. Both groups rely on stealth and secrecy. Cyberspace may become an avenue for terrorist activity. Using the Internet as a theater of operations, cyberterrorists can mount attacks against an enemy nation's technological infrastructure, an action referred to as **cyberterrorism.**

This chapter looks at terror and cybercrime and reviews the efforts being made by the agencies of the criminal justice system to control their behavior and bring offenders to justice.

TERRORISM

While terrorism is sometimes viewed as a contemporary phenomenon, terrorism and terrorists have been around for quite some time. The term first appeared at the time of the French Revolution, when Edmund Burke, a noted British political philosopher, referred to the violence he observed in Paris as the "reign of terror."[4] Terror was also associated with the unrest in Russia, which led to the 1917 Bolshevik takeover. In May 1881, a terror group killed Czar Alexander II. After the revolution, Bolshevik leaders Vladimir Lenin and Leon Trotsky made terror an instrument of state policy. Terror has also been identified with the civil war in Ireland and the Irish Republican Army, considered to be the model for most contemporary terrorist organizations.[5]

Who Is the Terrorist?

Before terrorism can be effectively fought, controlled and eradicated, it is important for agents of the justice system to understand something about the kind of people who become terrorists, what motivates their behavior, and how their ideas are formed. Unfortunately, this is not an easy task. Terrorism researchers have generally concluded that there is no single personality trait or behavior pattern that distinguishes the majority of terrorists or sets them apart so they can be easily identified and apprehended. Some seem truly disturbed while many others have not suffered long-term mental illness or displayed sociopathic traits and/or tendencies; if that were so, bizarre or violent behavior in their early childhood would be a giveaway.[6] As such, there have been a number of competing visions of why terrorists engage in criminal activities such as bombings, shootings, and kidnappings to achieve a political end. Four stand out.

Psychological View While not all terrorists suffer from psychological deficits, enough do so that the typical terrorist can be described as an emotionally disturbed individual who acts out his or her psychoses within the confines of violent groups. According to this view, terrorist violence is not so much a political instrument as an end in itself; it is the result of compulsion or psychopathology. Terrorists do what they do because of a garden variety of emotional problems, including but not limited to self-destructive urges and disturbed emotions combined with problems with authority.[7]

The view that terrorists suffer psychological abnormality is quite controversial and some critics suggest that it is spurious. For example, it is possible that engaging in stressful terrorist activity results in the development of mental disorders and not vice versa.[8] Charles Ruby reviewed the literature on the psychology of terrorists and found little evidence that terrorists are psychologically dysfunctional or pathological. Ruby claims that terrorism is a form of politically motivated violence that is carried out by rational, lucid people who have valid motives; if they had more resources, terrorists would be military officers.[9]

Socialization View According to this view, if terrorists suffer psychological deficiencies it is because they have been poorly and improperly socialized.[10] Many have been raised to hate their opponents and learn at an early age that they have been victimized by some oppressor. Often, this socialization occurs in dysfunctional families in which the father was absent or even if present was a distant and cold figure.[11] Terrorists report that they were estranged from their fathers, whom they viewed as economically, socially, or politically weak and ineffective. Because of this family estrangement the budding terrorist may have been swayed to join a group or cult by a charismatic leader who serves as an alternative father figure. In this sense, terror groups, similar to what happens in urban street gangs, provide a substitute family-like environment, which can nurture a heretofore emotionally underprivileged youth.

Political/Religious/Social View Terrorists begin as members of minority political, social, and religious groups angered by their position of helplessness. Disenfranchised from the mainstream, harboring feelings of oppression, they believe that they have been victimized by a rival group, the government, or an outside force that they view as a threat, such as the United States.

Once the potential terrorists recognize that these conditions can be changed by an active reform effort that has not happened, they conclude that they must resort to violence to encourage change. The violence need not be aimed at a specific goal. Rather, terror tactics must help set in motion a series of events that enlist others in the cause and lead to long-term change. "Successful" terrorists believe that their "self-sacrifice" outweighs the guilt created by harming innocent people. They must be able to throw off the constraints of traditional religious beliefs, which hold that violence and killing are immoral. If their opponent is defined as godless, the use of suicide bombers to kill civilians is justified.[12] Terrorism, therefore, requires violence without guilt; the cause justifies the violence.

Alienation View Terrorist operatives are not poor or lacking in education. And yet lack of economic opportunity and recessionary economies are positively correlated with terrorism.[13] Terrorists may be motivated by feelings of alienation and failure to maintain the tools to compete in a post-technological society. For example, when Haruki Murakami interviewed members of the *Aum Shinrikyo*, a radical religious group that set off poison gas in a Tokyo subway in 1995, killing twelve and injuring five thousand, he found that the terrorists found modern society too complex to understand, with few clear-cut goals and values.[14] Surprisingly, the cult members he interviewed were relatively "ordinary" people; some were school dropouts with few prospects, but others were highly educated professionals. All seemed alienated from modern society, and some felt that a suicide mission would cleanse them from the corruption of the modern world.

The Contemporary Terrorist

Are these traditional views of terrorists still valid? Does the contemporary terrorist still fit the traditional mold? The criminal justice system is now confronting a new breed of terrorists, whose motivations are varied and whose sponsors are diverse.[15] Rather than achieving a political goal, such as a separate state or nation, many groups are motivated by religious and cultural values. They view their cause as a global war against their enemies' values and traditions. Consequently, contemporary terrorism may produce higher casualties: violence is a divine duty, justified by scripture, and the terrorist is absolved from guilt because their targets are blasphemers.[16]

Rather than a unified central command, these new terrorists are organized in far-flung nets or cells. Not located in any particular nation or area, they have no identifiable address.[17] They are capable of attacking anyone at any time with great destructive force. They may employ an arsenal of weapons of mass destruction—chemical, biological, nuclear—without fear of contaminating their own homeland, because in reality they may not actually have one.

Contemporary terrorists use technology—computers and the Internet—to attack their targets' economic infrastructure and actually profit from the resulting economic chaos by buying and/or selling securities in advance of their own attack![18] They may want to

Terrorist bombings strike fear into people all across the globe. Here, emergency services personnel assist evacuated passengers at Edgware Road following an explosion that ripped through London's underground tube network on July 7, 2005, killing more than 50 people. Blasts on the underground network and a city bus were seen as an effort to force Britain out of Iraq.

© Gareth Cattermole/Getty Images

bankrupt their opponents by forcing them to spend billions on terror defense.[19]

A Case Study: Osama bin Laden The prototype of this new generation is Osama bin Laden, a multimillionaire who has never personally suffered at the hands of the United States. His motivation may combine elements of socialization, religious and political oppression, personal alienation, and psychological deficits.[20]

Osama bin Laden was the favored son of a wealthy Saudi family. The fortune he has used to finance his terrorist activities derives from an inheritance of over $300 million. Rather than poverty and helplessness, his violent aggression may be motivated by some deep-rooted psychological deficits. Bin Laden is the only son of his late father's least favorite wife, who was a Syrian and not a Saudi. Though bin Laden may have been close to his mother, he may have felt driven to achieve stature in the eyes of his father and the rest of the family. He may have been willing to do anything to gain power and eclipse his father, who died when bin Laden was ten years old.

In other words, the impulse for his murderous actions may stem from bin Laden's unconscious efforts to gain his father's approval. He modeled his behavior after his father in many ways, including working with the Saudi royal family on construction projects. Bin Laden once told an interviewer of his desire to please his father: "My father was very keen that one of his sons should fight against the enemies of Islam. So I am the one son who is acting according to the wishes of his father." Perhaps this need for acceptance explains bin Laden's religious zeal, which is in excess of anyone else in his large extended family.

After his father's death, bin Laden was mentored by a Jordanian named Abdullah Azzam, whose motto was "Jihad and the rifle alone: no negotiations, no conferences, and no dialogues." When Azzam was killed in 1989 by a car bomb in Pakistan, bin Laden vowed to carry on Azzam's "holy war" against the West. He threw himself into the Afghan conflict against the Soviet Union, and when the Russians withdrew, was convinced that the West was vulnerable. "The myth of the superpower was destroyed not only in my mind but also in the minds of all Muslims," bin Laden has told interviewers.

Bin Laden's personal issues became cloaked in religious fervor that drew adherents to his **al Qaeda** organization, which grew sixfold from 1980 to 1992. His religiously inspired terrorist attacks are more likely to result in high casualties because they are motivated not by efforts to obtain political freedom or a national homeland but by cultural and religious beliefs. Because they are on a

al Qaeda *A terrorist network strongly opposed to the United States that distributes money and tactical support and training to a wide variety of radical Islamic terrorist groups.*

© AFP/Getty Images

Saudi-born alleged terror mastermind Osama bin Laden is seen in this video footage at an undisclosed location in Afghanistan. Bin Laden masterminded the September 11 attacks on the U.S and coordinates the al Qaeda terror network.

holy mission, his followers can justify in their minds the deaths of large numbers of people; after all, the violence is a divine duty justified by scripture.

Osama bin Laden and the al Qaeda group are the paradigm of the new terrorist organization. Bin Laden's masterminding of the September 11, 2001, attacks was not designed to restore his homeland or bring about a new political state but rather to have his personal value structure adopted by Muslim nations. His attack may have been designed to create the military invasion of Afghanistan, which he hoped to exploit for his particular brand of revolution. Some experts believe that bin Laden hoped that his acts would ignite the *umma*, or universal Islamic community. The media would show the Americans killing innocent civilians in Afghanistan and the umma would find it shocking that Americans nonchalantly caused Muslims to suffer and die. The ensuing outrage would open a chasm between the Moslem population of the Middle East and the ruling governments in states such as Saudi Arabia that have been allied with the West. On October 7, 2001, bin Laden made a broadcast in which he said that the Americans and the British "have divided the entire world into two regions—one of faith, where there is no hypocrisy, and another of infidelity, from which we hope God will protect us."

It is possible that bin Laden's true aim for the September 11 attacks was to cause an Islamic revolution within the Muslim world itself, in Saudi Arabia especially, and not to win a war with the United States. Bin Laden views the leaders of the Arab and Islamic worlds as hypocrites and idol worshipers, propped up by American military might. His attack was designed to force those governments to choose: you are either with the idol-worshiping enemies of God or you are with the true believers. The attack on the United States was merely an instrument designed to help his brand of extremist Islam survive and flourish among the believers who could bring down these corrupt governments. Americans, in short, were drawn into somebody else's civil war.

These new-generation terrorists, represented by bin Laden, are especially frightening because they feel no need to live to enjoy the fruits of victory. Because they do not hope to regain a homeland or a political victory, they are willing to engage in suicide missions to achieve their goals. The devoted members of al Qaeda are willing to martyr themselves because they believe they are locked in a life-or-death struggle with the forces of nonbelievers.

In some instances, these rootless people will band together with criminals to carry out their plots. Because their goals are vague, it is sometimes difficult to separate their political motives from their criminal ones. This is the topic of the following Race, Culture, and Gender in Criminal Justice feature.

Now that this new breed of terrorist has made his mark upon the world, how has the criminal justice system responded to the threat? What has been done to create homeland security?

Criminal Justice ⚖ Now™

Learn more about by exploring the "Agencies Responsible for Intelligence Gathering" Vocabulary Check activity.

HOMELAND SECURITY: THE CRIMINAL JUSTICE RESPONSE TO TERRORISM

After the 9/11 attacks, agencies of the criminal justice system began to focus their attention on combating the threat of terror. Even local police agencies created antiterror programs designed to protect their communities from the threat of attack. How should the nation best prepare itself to thwart potential attacks? The **National Commission on Terrorist Attacks Upon the United States** (also known as the 9/11 Commission), an independent, bipartisan commission was created in late 2002, and given the mission of preparing an in-depth report of the events leading up to the 9/11 attacks. Part of their goal was to create a comprehensive plan to ensure that no further attacks of that magnitude take place. Among their numerous recommendations are those included in Exhibit 4.1.

National Commission on Terrorist Attacks Upon the United States An independent, bipartisan commission created in 2002, which prepared an in-depth report of the events leading up to the 9/11 attacks.

Exhibit	4.1	Key recommendations of the 9/11 Commission

- Develop a comprehensive coalition strategy against Islamist terrorism, using a flexible contact group of leading coalition governments and fashioning a common coalition approach on issues like the treatment of captured terrorists.
- Devote a maximum effort to the parallel task of countering the proliferation of weapons of mass destruction.
- Address problems of screening people with biometric identifiers across agencies and governments, including our border and transportation systems, by designing a comprehensive screening system that addresses common problems and sets common standards. As standards spread, this necessary and ambitious effort could dramatically strengthen the world's ability to intercept individuals who could pose catastrophic threats
- Develop a National Counterterrorism Center (NCTC) that would borrow the joint, unified command concept adopted in the 1980s by the American military in a civilian agency, combining the joint intelligence function alongside the operations work.
- The NCTC would build on the existing Terrorist Threat Integration Center and would replace it and other terrorism "fusion centers" within the government. The NCTC would become the authoritative knowledge bank, bringing information to bear on common plans. It should task collection requirements both inside and outside the United States.
- National Intelligence Director should be established with two main jobs: (1) to oversee national intelligence centers that combine experts from all the collection disciplines against common targets—like counterterrorism or nuclear proliferation; and (2) to oversee the agencies that contribute to the national intelligence program, a task that includes setting common standards for personnel and information technology. This National Intelligence Director (NID) should be located in the Executive Office of the President and report directly to the president, yet be confirmed by the Senate.

Source: The National Commission on Terrorist Attacks Upon the United States, *The 9/11 Commission Report*, www.9-11commission.gov, accessed on August 13, 2005.

To monitor the more than 500 million people who cross into America, the commission recommended that a single agency should be created to screen border crossings. They also recommended creation of an investigative agency to monitor all aliens in the United States and to gather intelligence on the way terrorists travel across borders. The commission suggested that people who wanted passports be tagged with biometric measures to make them easily identifiable.

In response to the commission report, a **Director of National Intelligence (DNI)** charged with coordinating data from the nation's primary intelligence gathering agencies was created (see Concept Summary 4.1 on page 102). The DNI serves as the principal intelligence adviser to the president and the statutory intelligence adviser to the National Security Council. On February 17, 2005, President George W. Bush named U.S. Ambassador to Iraq John Negroponte to be the first person to hold the post; he was confirmed on April 21, 2005. Also reporting to the DNI is the staff of the newly created National Counterterrorism Center (NCTC), which is staffed by terrorism experts from the CIA, FBI, and the Pentagon; the Privacy and Civil Liberties Board; and the National Counterproliferation Center. The NCTC serves as the primary organization in the United States government for analyzing and integrating all intelligence possessed or acquired by the government pertaining to terrorism and counterterrorism, excepting purely domestic counterterrorism information.

While the Commission report outlines what has already been done, what has not been done, and what needs to be done, agencies of the justice system have begun to respond to the challenge.

The Law Enforcement Response to Terrorism

In the aftermath of the September 11, 2001, attacks, even before the 9/11 Commission made its report, it became obvious that the nation was not prepared to deal adequately with the threat of terrorism. One reason is the very

Director of National Intelligence (DNI) Government official charged with coordinating data from the nation's primary intelligence-gathering agencies.

Race, Culture, and Gender in Criminal Justice

Criminal Groups/Terrorist Groups: One and the Same?

Sometimes terrorist groups become involved in common-law crimes such as drug dealing and kidnapping, even selling nuclear materials. According to terrorism expert Chris Dishman, these illegal activities may on occasion become so profitable that they replace the group's original focus. For example, Burmese terror groups, which were formed with a political focus, now actively cultivate, refine, and traffic opium and heroin out of the Golden Triangle (the border between Burma, Thailand, and Laos), and some have even moved into the methamphetamine market. They engage in what some consider *narcoterrorism* while others may view it as criminal drug trafficking for profit.

In some cases there has been such close cooperation between organized criminal groups and terrorists that the line between being a terrorist organization with political support and an organized criminal group engaging in illicit activities for profit becomes blurred. Terrorism expert Rollie Lal has found numerous ties between criminals and terrorists. He claims that the Dubai-based Indian criminal Aftab Ansari used ransom money he earned from kidnappings to help fund the September 11, 2001, terrorist attacks. The Pakistan-based Indian crime boss Dawood Ibrahim has pursued dual careers as both a criminal and terrorist leader.

Lal argues that the connections between criminals and terrorists exist on a variety of levels, including logistical support in weapons purchases, shared routes, training, and some ideological overlap. At the tactical level, terrorist groups rely on organized crime networks to provide them with the necessary weaponry and munitions to undertake attacks and insurgencies. The routes that have been carefully constructed by criminal networks to engage in such illicit activities as drug smuggling can also be used for transporting goods on behalf of terrorist groups. Conversely, criminal gangs can turn to terrorist groups to provide needed training in the use of guns and explosives, and also to provide safe passage through terrorist-controlled territory for a price. Criminal syndicates in the Middle East and South Asia are also closely connected to terrorist groups via the illegal drug trade. Money earned from drug trafficking supports both criminal and terrorist activity.

The association between criminal and terrorist groups is most potent when it concerns the threat of nuclear arms. In December 2001 six men were arrested by Russian security forces as they were making a deal for weapons-grade uranium. Some of the men were members of the Balashikha criminal gang, who were in possession of two pounds of top-grade radioactive material, which can be used to build

nature of American society. Because we live in a free and open nation, it is extremely difficult to seal the borders and prevent the entry of terrorist groups. In his book *Nuclear Terrorism* (2004), Graham Allison, an expert on nuclear weapons and national security, describes the almost superhuman effort it would take to seal the nation's borders from nuclear attack. Every day, 30,000 trucks, 6,500 rail cars, and 140 ships deliver more than 50,000 cargo containers into the United States. And while fewer than 5 percent ever get screened, those that do are given non-physical inspections using external detectors, which may not detect nuclear weapons or fissile material. The potential for terrorists to obtain bombs is significant: there are approximately 130 nuclear research reactors in 40 countries. Two dozen of these have enough highly enriched uranium for one or more nuclear bombs. If terrorists can get their hands on fissile material from these reactors, they could build a crude but working nuclear bomb within a year. But they may not have to build their own bomb. They may be able to purchase an intact device on the black market. Russia alone has thousands of nuclear warheads and material for many thousands of additional weapons; all of these remain vulnerable to theft. Terrorists may also be able to buy the knowledge to construct bombs. In one weapons. They were asking $30,000 for the deadly merchandise. Since 1990 there have been a half-dozen cases involving theft and transportation of nuclear material and other cases involving people who offered to sell agents material not yet in their possession. These are the known cases; it is impossible to know if client states have already purchased enriched uranium or plutonium. The Russians are not alone. When Pakistani scientist Abdul Qadeer Khan transferred nuclear material from Pakistan to North Korea, Libya, and Iran, he relied on the assistance of criminal networks. Khan used false papers and front companies in several countries to transfer the nuclear technology to other nations, and used government cargo planes to assist in deliveries to North Korea. Khan's middleman was a Dubai-based Sri Lankan businessman, Buhary Ayed Abu Tahir. He arranged for a Malaysian company to manufacture nuclear components for shipping to Libya, and for Libyan technicians to be trained in the use of machines that were part of the nuclear program. Tahir also assisted Khan in the transfer of centrifuge units from Pakistan to Iran.

How can the criminal gang/terrorist group association be stopped? Lal argues that terrorist groups will be able to continue operations as long as they can acquire the needed weaponry, financing, and personnel. Closing this access is difficult, but crucial. In addition to military cooperation to interdict terrorists, much more attention needs to be paid to pro-moting the rule of law, combating corruption, and improving judicial proceedings in areas where terrorists have taken refuge. Police capabilities in urban areas need to be much improved if they are to locate and disrupt criminal networks. International cooperation on extradition laws must also be strengthened, so that criminals cannot easily elude arrest by fleeing the country.

Critical Thinking

1. Are the conditions that produce terrorism the same that produce criminal gangs? Are criminals and terrorists cut from the same cloth?

2. Can the existing agencies of justice be an effective deterrent to terrorist groups or are more specialized agencies required to combat terrorism?

InfoTrac College Edition Research
To learn more about the dangers of *nuclear terrorism*, use it as a key term on InfoTrac College Edition.

Sources: Rollie Lal, "Terrorists and Organized Crime Join Forces," *International Herald Tribune*, May 24, 2005; Chris Dishman, "The Leaderless Nexus: When Crime and Terror Converge," *Studies in Conflict and Terrorism 28* (2005): 237–253; Jeffrey Kluger, "The Nuke Pipeline: The Trade in Nuclear Contraband Is Approaching Critical Mass. Can We Turn Off the Spigot?" *Time*, December 17, 2001, 40; Chris Dishman, "Terrorism, Crime, and Transformation," *Studies in Conflict and Terrorism 24* (2001): 43–56.

well-known incident, Pakistan's leading nuclear scientist, A. Q. Khan, sold comprehensive "nuclear starter kits" that included advanced centrifuge components, blueprints for nuclear warheads, uranium samples in quantities sufficient to make a small bomb, and even provided personal consulting services to assist nuclear development.[21]

Sensing this problem, law enforcement agencies around the country began to realign their resources to combat future terrorist attacks. In response to 9/11, law enforcement agencies undertook a number of steps: increasing the number of personnel engaged in emergency response planning; updating response plans for chemical, biological, or radiological attacks; and reallocating internal resources or increasing departmental spending to focus on terrorism preparedness.[22] Actions continue to be taken on the federal, state, and local levels.

Federal Law Enforcement

One of the most significant changes has been a realignment of the Federal Bureau of Investigation (FBI), the federal government's main law enforcement

Concept Summary 4.1

The nation's intelligence gathering agencies

Federal Bureau of Investigation (FBI)	Conducts counterintelligence *within* the United States.
Defense Intelligence Agency (DIA)	Performs foreign intelligence and counterintelligence for the Secretary of Defense and Joint Chiefs of Staff.
National Reconnaissance Office (NRO)	Manages the nation's satellite reconnaissance programs.
Air Force (Marine, Army, and Navy) Intelligence	Conducts, collects, and processes intelligence data for the Air Force. The Army, Navy, and Marine Corp. maintain similar organizations.
Department of State's Bureau of Intelligence and Research	Produces political and economic intelligence for the State Department.
Department of Energy (DOE)	Collects political, economic, and technical information concerning foreign energy matters.
Department of the Treasury	Collects information on foreign, financial, and monetary matters.
Department of Homeland Security	Gathers intelligence to prevent terrorist attacks within the United States.
Central Intelligence Agency (CIA)	Responsibilities include collecting foreign intelligence, conducting counterintelligence, and developing intelligence gathering techniques.
National Geospatial-Intelligence Agency (formerly the National Imagery and Mapping Agency)	A combat support agency of the Department of Defense, supporting the Secretary of Defense, the Director of Central Intelligence, and national-level policymakers in the areas of other imagery, imagery intelligence, and geospatial information.
Coast Guard Intelligence	Deals with information related to U.S. maritime borders and Homeland Security.
Department of Energy	Performs analyses of foreign nuclear weapons, nuclear nonproliferation, and energy security-related intelligence issues in support of U.S. national security policies, programs, and objectives.

Source: United States Intelligence Community, www.intelligence.gov/1-members.shtml

agency (see chapter 5 for more on the FBI). The FBI has already announced a reformulation of its priorities, making protecting the United States from terrorist attack its number one commitment. It is now charged with coordinating intelligence collection with the Border Patrol, Secret Service, and the CIA. The FBI must also work with and share intelligence with the National Counterterrorism Center (NCTC)

To carry out its newly formulated mission, the FBI is expanding its force of agents. In addition to recruiting candidates with the traditional background in law enforcement, law, and accounting, the Bureau is concentrating on hiring agents with scientific and technological skills as well as foreign-language proficiency in priority areas such as Arabic, Farsi, Pashtun, Urdu, all dialects of Chinese, Japanese, Korean, Russian, Spanish, and Vietnamese, and with other priority backgrounds such as foreign counterintelligence, counterterrorism, and military intelligence. Besides helping in counterterrorism activities, these agents will staff the new Cyber Division, which was cre-

Exhibit 4.2	**Key near-term actions to combat terrorism**

1. Restructure the Counterterrorism Division at FBI headquarters (redefine relationship between HQ and field; shift from reactive to proactive orientation).
2. Establish "flying squads" to coordinate national and international investigations.
3. Establish a national Joint Terrorism Task Force.
4. Substantially enhance analytical capabilities with personnel and technology (expand use of data mining, financial record analysis, and communications analysis to combat terrorism; establish Office of Intelligence).
5. Build a national terrorism response capability that is more mobile, agile, and flexible.
6. Permanently shift additional resources to counterterrorism.
7. Augment overseas capabilities and partnerships.
8. Target recruitment to acquire agents, analysts, translators, and others with specialized skills and backgrounds.
9. Enhance counterterrorism training for FBI and law enforcement partners.

Source: Adapted from Federal Bureau of Investigation, *The FBI Strategic Plane 2004–2009,* www.fbi.gov/publications/strategicplan/stategicplantext.htm#ct, accessed on August 31, 2005.

ated in 2001 to coordinate, oversee, and facilitate FBI investigations in which the Internet, online services, and computer systems and networks are the principal instruments or targets of terrorists. Exhibit 4.2 describes some of the other actions the FBI has undertaken to combat terrorist activities.

Department of Homeland Security (DHS)

Soon after the 2001 attack, President George W. Bush proposed the creation of a new cabinet-level agency called the **Department of Homeland Security (DHS)** and assigned it the following mission:

- Preventing terrorist attacks within the United States
- Reducing America's vulnerability to terrorism
- Minimizing the damage and recovering from attacks that do occur

On November 19, 2002, Congress passed legislation authorizing the creation of the DHS and assigned it the mission of providing intelligence analysis and infrastructure protection, strengthening the borders, improving the use of science and technology to counter weapons of mass destruction, and creating a comprehensive response and recovery division.

Organization and Mission of the DHS

Rather than work from ground up, the DHS combined a number of existing agencies into a super-agency that carried out the following missions:

Border and Transportation Security The Department of Homeland Security is responsible for securing our nation's borders and transportation systems, which include 350 ports of entry. The department manages who and what enters the country, and works to prevent the entry of terrorists and the instruments of terrorism while simultaneously ensuring the speedy flow of legitimate traffic. The DHS also is in charge of securing territorial waters, including ports and waterways.

Emergency Preparedness and Response The Department of Homeland Security ensures the preparedness of emergency response professionals, provides the federal government's response, and aids America's recovery from terrorist attacks and natural disasters. The department is responsible for reducing the loss of life and property and protecting institutions from all types

 The Department of Homeland Security provides the unifying core for the vast national network of organizations and institutions involved in efforts to secure our nation from terror. To visit this site, go to "Web Links" on your Siegel Essentials of Criminal Justice 5e website: http://cj.wadsworth.com/siegel_ess5e.

Department of Homeland Security (DHS) *Federal agency responsible for preventing terrorist attacks within the United States, reducing America's vulnerability to terrorism, and minimizing the damage and recovering from attacks that do occur*

A U.S. Customs and Border Patrol official from the Anti-Terrorism Contraband Enforcement Team inspects bags of Canadian lentils imported by sea at a U.S. Customs warehouse on June 2, 2004, in Wilmington, California. After passing the bags' container through a large X-ray machine, inspectors determined it might be carrying suspicious or possibly terrorist material. The container was moved to the Wilmington warehouse where the cargo was manually inspected and reloaded. Before 9/11, most inspections of container cargo were conducted for narcotics smuggling. With Department of Homeland Security now controlling more of the overall anti-terrorist campaign, inspections for weapons of mass destruction in ports have been stepped up. The Port of Los Angeles–Long Beach receives more than three million containers annually. Inspectors are on the lookout for dirty bombs, weapons smuggling, or terrorist contraband. Surveillance of the waterways inside the port area has been stepped up. The L.A.–L.B. port facility is the West Coast's energy hub for natural gas imports as well as oil and gasoline refining.

of hazards through an emergency management program of preparedness, mitigation, response, and recovery.

Chemical, Biological, Radiological, and Nuclear Countermeasures The Department of Homeland Security leads the federal government's efforts in preparing for and responding to the full range of terrorist threats involving weapons of mass destruction. To do this, the department sets national policy and establishes guidelines for state and local governments. It directs exercises and drills for federal, state, and local chemical, biological, radiological, and nuclear (CBRN) response teams and plans. The department is assigned to prevent the importation of nuclear weapons and material.

Information Analysis and Infrastructure Protection The department analyzes information from multiple available sources, including, the CIA and FBI, in order to assess the dangers facing the nation. It also analyzes law enforcement and intelligence information.[23]

The DHS has numerous and varied duties. It is responsible for port security and transportation systems and manages airport security with its Transportation Security Administration (TSA). It has its own intelligence section, and it covers every special event in the United States including political conventions.

At the time of this writing the DHS is undergoing a significant reorganization. Among the proposed changes include:

- Increase overall preparedness, particularly for catastrophic events
- Create better transportation security systems to move people and cargo more securely and efficiently
- Strengthen border security and interior enforcement and reform immigration processes
- Enhance information sharing with our partners
- Improve DHS financial management, human resource development, procurement and information technology
- Realign the DHS organization to maximize mission performance[24]

It is expected that the proposed changes will improve the efficiency of the DHS and make it a more effective antiterror organization.

State Law Enforcement Efforts to Combat Terrorism

In the wake of the 9/11 attacks, a number of states have beefed up their intelligence-gathering capabilities and aimed them directly at homeland security. California has introduced the California Anti-Terrorism Information

Criminal Justice ⊕ Now™

Learn more by viewing the "Security" "In the News" video clip.

Center (CATIC), a statewide intelligence system designed to combat terrorism. It divides the state into five operational zones, and links federal, state, and local information services in one system. Trained intelligence analysts operate within civil rights guidelines and utilize information in a secure communications system; information is analyzed daily.[25] CATIC combines both machine-intelligence with information coming from a variety of police agencies. The information is correlated and organized by analysts looking for trends. Rather than simply operating as an information gathering unit, CATIC is a synthesizing process. It combines open-source public information with data on criminal trends and possible terrorist activities. Processed intelligence is designed to produce threat assessments for each area and to project trends outside the jurisdiction. The CATIC system attempts to process multiple sources of information to predict threats. By centralizing the collection and analytical sections of a statewide system, California's Department of Justice may have developed a method for moving offensively against terrorism.

California is not alone in implementing antiterror legislation. Alabama is the first state in the nation to create its own legislatively enacted cabinet-level Department of Homeland Security. Its mission is to protect lives and safeguard property, and if required, to respond to any acts of terrorism occurring in Alabama. To accomplish this mission, the Alabama Department of Homeland Security works closely with both public and private sector stakeholders in a wide range of disciplines: law enforcement, emergency management, emergency medical, fire services, public works, agriculture, public health, public safety communications, environmental management, military, transportation, and more.

Since its inception, the Alabama Department of Homeland Security has administered more than $70 million in federally appropriated homeland security grants.

Local Law Enforcement

Federal law enforcement agencies are not alone in responding to the threat of terrorism. And, of course, nowhere is the threat of terrorism being taken more seriously than in New York City, one of the main targets of the 9/11 attacks, which has established a new Counterterrorism Bureau.[26]

 To visit the **NYPD** website, go to "Web Links" on your Siegel Essentials of Criminal Justice 5e website: http://cj.wadsworth.com/siegel_ess5e.

Teams within the bureau have been trained to examine potential targets in the city and are now attempting to insulate them from possible attack. Viewed as prime targets are the city's bridges, the Empire State Building, Rockefeller Center, and the United Nations. Bureau detectives are assigned overseas to work with the police in several foreign cities, including cities in Canada and Israel. Detectives have been assigned as liaisons with the FBI and with Interpol, in Lyon, France. The city is now recruiting detectives with language skills from Pashtun and Urdu to Arabic, Fujianese, and other dialects. The existing New York City Police Intelligence Division has been revamped, and agents are examining foreign newspapers and monitoring Internet sites. The department is also setting up several backup command centers in different parts of the city in case a terror attack puts headquarters out of operation. Several backup senior command teams have been created so that if people at the highest levels of the department are killed, individuals will already have been tapped to step into their jobs.

The Counterterrorism Bureau has assigned more than one hundred city police detectives to work with FBI agents as part of a Joint Terrorist Task Force. In addition, the Intelligence Division's seven hundred investigators now devote 35 to 40 percent of their resources to counterterrorism, up from about 2 percent before January 2002. The department is also drawing on the expertise of other institutions around the city. For example, medical specialists have been enlisted to monitor daily developments in the city's hospitals to detect any suspicious outbreaks of illness that might reflect a biological attack. And the police are now conducting joint drills with the New York Fire Department to avoid the problems in communication and coordination that marked the emergency response on September 11.

A comprehensive antiterror program now being conducted in New York is called Operation Atlas, discussed in the following Policy, Programs, and Issues in Criminal Justice box.

Criminal Justice ⊛ Now™

Learn more by viewing the "Drug Museum" "In the News" video clip.

THE LAW AND TERRORISM

Soon after the September 11 terrorist attacks, the U.S. government enacted several laws focused on preventing further acts of violence against the United States and creating greater flexibility in the fight to control terror activity. Most importantly, Congress passed the **USA Patriot Act (USAPA)** on October 26, 2001. The bill is over 342 pages long, creates new laws, and makes changes to over fifteen different existing statutes. Its aim is to give sweeping new powers to domestic law enforcement and international intelligence agencies in an effort to fight terrorism, to expand the definition of terrorist activities, and to alter sanctions for violent terrorism. While it is impossible to discuss every provision of this sweeping legislation here, a few of its more important elements will be examined.

The USA Patriot Act

USAPA expands all four traditional tools of surveillance—wiretaps, search warrants, pen/trap orders (installing devices that record phone calls), and subpoenas. The Foreign Intelligence Surveillance Act (FISA) that allows domestic operations by intelligence agencies is also expanded. USAPA gives greater power to the FBI to check and monitor phone, Internet, and computer records without first needing to demonstrate that they were being used by a suspect or target of a court order.

The government may now serve a single wiretap, or pen/trap order, on any person regardless of whether that person or entity is named in a court order. Prior to this act, telephone companies could be ordered to install pen/trap devices on their networks that would monitor calls coming to a surveillance target and to whom the surveillance target made calls; the USAPA extends this monitoring to the Internet. Law enforcement agencies may now also obtain the e-mail addresses and websites visited by a target, and e-mails of the people with whom they communicate. It is possible to require that an Internet service provider install a device that records e-mail and other electronic communications on its servers, looking for communications initiated or received by the target of an investigation. Under USAPA, the government does not need to show a court that the information or communication is relevant to a criminal investigation, nor does it have to report where it served the order or what information it received.

The act also allows enforcement agencies to monitor cable operators and obtain access to their records and systems. Before the act, a cable company had to give prior notice to the customer, even if that person was a target of an investigation. Information can now be obtained on people with whom the cable subscriber communicates, the content of the person's communications, and the person's subscription records; prior notice is still required if law enforcement agencies want to learn what television programming a subscriber purchases.

The act also expands the definition of "terrorism" and enables the government to monitor more closely those people suspected of "harboring" and giving "material support" to terrorists (sections 803, 805). It increases the authority of the U.S. attorney general to detain and deport noncitizens with little or no

Policy, Programs, and Issues in Criminal Justice

Operation Atlas

Since the beginning of the war with Iraq in March of 2003, the city of New York has implemented a new, comprehensive program to protect the city and its citizens from future acts of terrorism. Under Operation Atlas, the New York Police Department has stepped up efforts to protect major city landmarks and transportation hubs. The program is broken up into four sections: increased personnel deployment, transit system security, counterterrorism, and increased coverage. It is hoped that a combination of these four core elements increases security throughout New York.

Personnel Deployment
The NYPD has not only increased the number of patrol officers but has also deployed specialized teams and agencies throughout the city. The department has increased deployments of harbor patrol units, aviation patrol, and emergency services units. Harbor patrols now pay special attention to commuter ferries around the city. The city has also deployed COBRA (Chemical, Ordnance, Biological or Radiological Actions) units. These units are specially trained in responding to attacks of weapons of mass destruction. Bomb-sniffing dogs are deployed at ferry entrances. Several units have been created:

- Archangel teams, which are comprised of emergency services, bomb experts, and investigators
- Hammer teams, made up of police officers and firefighters who are specially trained in hazardous material incidents
- Patrol units; NYPD has deployed heavily armed patrols in undercover vehicles throughout the city.

Transit System
The transit system has also received increased protection from the city. Highway units are on extended tours of duty and conducting checkpoints at all bridges. The city is towing any vehicles parked in front of high profile targets. Train Order Maintenance Sweeps (TOMS) are being deployed, whose mission is to deter low-level fare evaders in an attempt to prevent larger attacks. Undercover patrols are used to ride the subway system looking for problems, and radiation detectors are monitoring the system. In terms of increased foot traffic, the department has increased the number of officers in high traffic locations like Times Square and the major train stations.

Counterterrorism
The city's Counterterrorism Bureau has already been discussed. However, under Operation Atlas, counterterrorism inspectors work twelve hour shifts that provide for twenty-four-hour coverage of the city. High risk targets, like the financial district, are under constant surveillance. The Counterterrorism Bureau now provides city businesses with terrorism updates. The department also has in place policies in the event of another attack, including citywide searches for radioactive devices.

Increased Coverage
The city has created a framework for increased coverage in case of a terror attack:

- Each patrol commander has plans in place to act as a separate police department in the event that the central headquarters is disabled.
- Thousands of school safety officers have been empowered to act in case of emergency to evacuate citizens and help with department resources.
- The NYPD conducts daily assessments of high profile targets. These include houses of worship, hotels, museums, and city landmarks, and any foreign missions or heads of state that may need to be protected on a day-to-day basis. Also, the city has increased surveillance of fuel depots and sites that could store radioactive materials. The city is in communication with garage owners to stay alert for vehicles that may be linked to terrorist attacks.

Each of these strategies and increases in coverage and intelligence gathering have been designed to make New York City a more difficult target for terrorists and help in recovery if another attack takes place.

Critical Thinking
1. Do counterterror initiatives such as Operation Atlas compromise citizens' due process rights and interfere with their privacy? Even if they do, is it a price worth paying?
2. If members of a particular population group, such as Muslims and people of Arab descent, are suspected of terror activity, should people who fit that profile be subject to searches and surveillance? Is this racial profiling?

InfoTrac College Edition Research
In order to find out more about what police agencies are doing to battle terrorists, use *counterterrorism* in a key word search on InfoTrac College Edition.

Source: Operation Atlas (2003), www.nyc.gov/html/nypd/html/atlas.html, accessed on May 26, 2005.

judicial review. The attorney general may certify that he has "reasonable grounds to believe" that a noncitizen endangers national security and is therefore eligible for deportation. The attorney general and secretary of state are also given the authority to designate domestic groups as terrorist organizations, and deport any noncitizen who is a member.

Civil Rights and the USA Patriot Act Although law enforcement agencies may applaud these new laws, civil libertarians are troubled because they view the act as eroding civil rights. Some complain that there are provisions that permit the government to share information from grand jury proceedings and from criminal wiretaps with intelligence agencies. First Amendment protections may be violated because the Patriot Act authority is not only limited to true terrorism investigations but covers a much broader range of activity involving reasonable political dissent. Some have called for its repeal.

At the time of this writing the Patriot Act is up for congressional renewal and proponents are optimistic that it will be maintained. Another version referred to as Patriot Act II has also been contemplated. The new act is more sweeping and includes such measures as removing court-ordered prohibitions against police agencies spying on domestic groups and granting federal law enforcement agencies powers to conduct searches and surveillance based on intelligence gathered in foreign countries, without first obtaining a court order. Patriot II provides for the automatic denial of bail for persons accused of terrorism-related crimes. The burden of proof would be on alleged terrorists to demonstrate why they should be released on bail, rather than the government being required to demonstrate why they should be held. While Patriot II has been met with opposition, and its passage seems remote, some provisions are now being included in other congressional bills.

Communications Assistance for Law Enforcement Act (CALEA)

The Patriot Act is not the only legislation helping law enforcement in the conflict with terrorists. Some new laws are designed to aid agencies keeping surveillance on suspected terrorist groups. When Congress passed the **Communications Assistance for Law Enforcement Act (CALEA)** in 1994, it aided law enforcement's ability to monitor suspects. The act required that communication equipment manufacturers and carriers design equipment, facilities, and services that are compatible with electronic surveillance needs.[27] Under the law, telecommunications carriers must ensure that equipment has the capability to facilitate the isolation and interception of communications content and call-identifying information and make it easy to deliver these data to law enforcement agencies.[28] CALEA allows that upon issue of a court order or other lawful authorization, communication carriers must be able to: (1) expeditiously isolate all wire and electronic communications of a target transmitted by the carrier within its service area; (2) expeditiously isolate call-identifying information of a target; (3) provide intercepted communications and call-identifying information to law enforcement; and (4) carry out intercepts unobtrusively, so targets are not made aware of the electronic surveillance, and in a manner that does not compromise the privacy and security of other communications. Under CALEA the government reimburses telecommunications carriers for the costs of developing software to intercept communications.

Communications Assistance for Law Enforcement Act (CALEA) A law requiring communication equipment manufacturers to design equipment, facilities, and services that are compatible with electronic surveillance needs.

Criminal Justice Now™

Learn more about Cybercrime by exploring the Vocabulary Check activity.

CYBERCRIME

The changes wrought by the Internet to our society—including business, education, government, and personal communication—are evident all around us, and still very much in flux. The cyber revolution has permeated virtually every facet of our lives. Unfortunately, that revolution has entered the criminal arena as well. For just as millions of people around the globe have incorporated the Internet and advanced information technology into their daily endeavors, so have criminals, terrorists, and adversarial foreign nations. Whether we like it or not, cyber crime presents the most fundamental challenge for law enforcement in the 21st century. By its very nature, the cyber environment is borderless, affords easy anonymity and methods of concealment to bad actors, and provides new tools to engage in criminal activity. A criminal sitting on the other side of the planet is now capable of stealthily infiltrating a computer network in this country to steal money, abscond with proprietary information, or shut down e-commerce sites. To deal with this problem, law enforcement must retool its work force, its equipment, and its own information infrastructure.[29]

So claims Michael Vatis, Director of the National Infrastructure Protection Agency. This new form of criminality presents a compelling challenge for the justice system because (1) it is rapidly evolving with new schemes being created daily, (2) it is difficult to detect through traditional channels, and (3) its control demands that agents of the justice system develop technical skills which match those of the perpetrators.

Why has cybercrime become so important? Information technology (IT) has become an intricate part of daily life in most of industrialized societies. It is the key to the economic system and will become more important as major industries shift their manufacturing plants to other areas of the world where production is much cheaper. IT is responsible for the **globalization** phenomenon or the process of creating transnational markets, politics, and legal systems—in other words, creating a global economy. The Internet coupled with ever more powerful computers is now the chosen medium to provide a wide range of global services, ranging from entertainment and communication to research and education.

The cyber age has also generated an enormous amount of revenue. Spending on IT and telecommunications will grow by more than 6 percent each year, soon reaching about $2 trillion.[30] Today there are more than 1 billion people are using e-mail and 240 million are mobile Internet users. Magnifying the importance of the Internet is the fact that many critical infrastructure functions are now being conducted online, ranging from banking to control of shipping on the Mississippi River.[31]

Criminal entrepreneurs view this vast pool as a target for cybercrimes and their incidence is growing rapidly. One recent survey found that 78 percent of employers had detected employee abuse of Internet access privileges (for example, downloading pirated software or inappropriate use of e-mail systems) and 38 percent suffered unauthorized access or misuse on their web.[32] With the continuing growth of e-commerce, payment-card fraud on the Internet has increased from $1.6 billion in 2000 to almost $16 billion today.[33]

What are some of the major forms of cybercrime?[34] Typically, cybercrimes are divided into two broad categories: computer crime in which the target is the computer hardware and the offender wishes to compromise its integrity, and Internet crime in which the target is both the computer network and the information it transports. However, there is a third type of cybercrime on the horizon, cyberterrorism, in which terrorist attacks are carried out against computer hardware, the Internet, or both. All three forms of cybercrime are discussed below.

www Cybercrime is being felt around the world. To find out what the **British government is doing to control cybercrime's** spread, go to "Web Links" on your Siegel Essentials of Criminal Justice 5e website: http://cj.wadsworth.com/siegel_ess5e.

Computer Crime

The widespread use of computers to record business transactions has encouraged some people to use them for illegal purposes. Computer crimes generally fall into one of five categories:

- Theft of services, in which the criminal uses the computer for unauthorized purposes or an unauthorized user penetrates the computer system.

globalization The process of creating transnational markets, politics, and legal systems in order to develop a global economy.

Computer viruses are an important element of cybercrime. The "Mydoom" worm appeared on January 26, 2004, and became the fastest spreading worm ever, responsible for 30 percent of e-mail traffic. The virus, believed to have its origins in Russia, appears as an e-mail attachment, which then replicates to other e-mail addresses if opened.

Included within this category is the theft of processing time and services not entitled to an employee.

- Use of data in a computer system for personal gain.
- Unauthorized use of computers employed for various types of financial processing to obtain assets.
- Theft of property by computer for personal use or conversion to profit. For example, using a computer to illegally copy and sell software.
- Making the computer itself the subject of a crime—for example, when a virus is placed in it to destroy data.

Computer crimes have become so common that standardized terms have been created to describe individual methods of criminality:

Virus A virus is a program that disrupts or destroys existing programs and networks, causing them to perform the task for which the virus was designed.[35] The virus is then spread from one computer to another when a user sends out an infected program on a disk or memory device or it is downloaded via the Internet. Worms are similar to viruses, but use computer networks or the Internet to self-replicate and send themselves to other users, generally via e-mail, without the aid of the operator.

Trojan Horse A programmer installs a program that appears desirable, but which actually contains something harmful. For example, what appears to be a free game contains codes that erase every file in the computer's directory. The Trojan horse's contents could also be a virus or worm, which then spreads the damage.

Salami Slice An employee sets up a dummy account in the company's computerized records. A small amount—even a few pennies—is subtracted from customers' accounts and added to the account of the thief. Even if they detect the loss, customers don't complain because a few cents is an insignificant amount to them. The pennies picked up here and there eventually amount to thousands of dollars in losses.

Superzapping Most computer programs used in business have built-in antitheft safeguards. Superzappers use software that bypasses computer security programs to allow unauthorized access to data. However, employees can use a repair or maintenance program to supersede the antitheft program. Some tinkering with the program is required, but the superzapper is soon able to issue commands and install programs without going through normal file routines, bypassing not only security restrictions but also leaving no trail to the programmer. They may then order the system to issue checks to his or her private account.

Logic Bomb A set of instructions secretly inserted into a program that is designed to execute if a particular condition is satisfied, e.g., the "bomb" lies dormant until a particular date is reached or command entered. When exploded, the logic bomb may delete data or corrupt files or have other harmful effects. Logic bombs are a type of virus because they deliver their payload after a specific triggering event occurs.

The logic bomb secretly attached to a company's computer system. The new program monitors the company's work and waits for a sign of error to appear, some illogic that was designed for the computer to follow. Illogic causes the logic bomb to kick into action and exploit the weakness. The way the thief exploits the situation depends on his or her original intent—theft of money or defense secrets, sabotage, or the like.

The Extent of Computer Crime

An accurate accounting of computer crime will probably never be made because so many offenses go unreported. Sometimes company managers refuse to report the crime to police lest they display their incompetence and vulnerability to stockholders and competitors.[36] In other instances, computer crimes go unreported because they involve low-visibility acts such as copying computer software in violation of copyright laws.[37]

How much computer crime is there? One important source is the Computer Crime and Security Survey conducted by the Computer Security Institute (CSI) with the participation of the Federal Bureau of Investigation's Computer Intrusion Squad. Based on a survey of about 500 computer security practitioners in U.S. corporations, government agencies, financial institutions, medical institutions, and universities, the latest survey available (2004) indicates that the threat from computer crime and other information security breaches is quite significant.[38] Highlights of the *Computer Crime and Security Survey* include the following:

- Overall financial losses totaled $141,496,560. This is down significantly from 530 respondents reporting $201,797,340 in 2003 (from the 500 respondents).

- In a shift from previous years, the most expensive computer crime was denial of service. Theft of intellectual property, the prior leading category, was the second most expensive last year.

- The vast majority of organizations in the survey do not outsource computer security activities. Among those organizations that do outsource some computer security activities, the percentage of security activities outsourced is quite low.

In addition to these losses, the Business Software Alliance (BSA), a professional watchdog group, found in its most recent survey (2004) 35 percent of the software installed on personal computers worldwide was pirated in 2004, a one percentage point decrease from 36 percent in 2003. Yet, losses due to piracy increased from $29 billion to $33 billion.[39] In 2004, more than $59 billion was spent on commercial packaged PC software, up from $51 billion in 2003. But over $90 billion was actually installed, up from $80 billion the year before. Among the key findings:

- Piracy rates decreased in 37 countries; they increased in 34 countries. They remained consistent in 16 countries.

- In more than half the 87 countries studied, the piracy rate exceeded 60 percent. In 24 countries, the piracy rate exceeded 75 percent.

- The countries with the highest piracy rates were Vietnam (92 percent), Ukraine (91 percent), China (90 percent), Zimbabwe (90 percent), and Indonesia (87 percent).

- The countries with the lowest piracy rates were the United States (21 percent), New Zealand (23 percent), Austria (25 percent), Sweden (26 percent), and the United Kingdom (27 percent).

- The emerging markets in Asia Pacific, Latin America, Eastern Europe, and the Middle East and Africa account for over one-third of PC shipments today, but only a tenth of spending on PC software.

Internet Crime

The second form of cybercrime—Internet crime—has now become routine. While it is impossible to list and discuss every element of this newly emerging problem, a few of the most important areas are described below.

Distributing Illegal Sexual Material The Internet is an ideal venue for selling and distributing obscene material. One reason is that it is difficult to identify perpetrators and, even if they can be detected, even harder to prosecute. For example, in one well-known case, Landslide Productions Inc. of Fort Worth, Texas, operated as a highly profitable Internet-based pornography ring, taking in as much as $1.4 million in one month.[40] Landslide charged each customer approximately $29.95 per month for a gateway to child pornography websites.[41] However, the sites originated in Russia and Indonesia and therefore were off limits to control by U.S. authorities; they had a fee-sharing arrangement with Landslide's owners.

Denial of Service Attack Some Internet criminals threaten to or actually flood an Internet site with millions of bogus messages and/or orders so that site services will be tied up and unable to perform as promised. Unless the site operator pays extortion, the attackers threaten to keep up the interference until real consumers become frustrated and abandon the site.[42] The online gambling casino industry is particularly vulnerable to attack, especially when attacks coincide with a big sporting event such as the Super Bowl.[43]

Illegal Copyright Infringement For the past decade, groups of individuals have been working together to illegally obtain software and then "crack" or "rip" its copyright protections before posting it on the Internet; this is referred to as **warez.** Another form of illegal copyright infringement involves file-sharing programs that allow Internet users to download music and other copyrighted material without paying the artists and record producers their rightful royalties. Theft through the illegal reproduction and distribution of movies, software, games, and music is estimated to cost U.S. industries $19 billion worldwide each year. While some students routinely share files and download music, criminal copyright infringement represents a serious economic threat. In the 2005 case *MGM v. Grokster*, the Supreme Court ruled that companies that distribute devices with the object of promoting their use to infringe on copyrights are liable for the resulting acts of infringement by third parties such as people who use their software. The Court found that such software encourages people to illegally distribute copyrighted material on the

warez The practice of organized groups who trade in illegally obtained programs and other Internet content in violation of copyright licenses.

Internet. While not a criminal case, the Court's ruling opens the door for major lawsuits against those who distribute file sharing software.[44]

Internet Securities Fraud Some criminals use the Internet to intentionally manipulate the securities marketplace for profit. There are actually three major types of Internet securities fraud today:

- *Market manipulation.* An individual either posts erroneous and deceptive information online to artificially inflate the price of a stock (so they can sell previously purchased shares) or they post negative rumors, driving down the price of a stock so they can buy it at lower levels.[45]

- *Fraudulent offerings of securities.* Some cybercriminals create websites specifically designed to fraudulently sell securities. To make the offerings look more attractive than they are, assets may be inflated, expected returns overstated, and/or risks understated.

- *Illegal touting.* This crime occurs when individuals make securities recommendations and fail to disclose that they are being paid to disseminate their favorable opinions. Section 17(b) of the Securities Act of 1933 requires that paid touters disclose the nature, source, and amount of their compensation. If those who tout stocks fail to disclose their relationship with the company, information misleads investors into believing that the speaker is objective and credible rather than bought and paid for.

Identity Theft **Identity theft** occurs when a person uses the Internet to steal someone's identity and/or impersonate them to open a new credit card account or conduct some other financial transaction. Identity information can be gathered easily from confederates because people routinely share their name, address, phone numbers, personal information, credit card account numbers, and Social Security number (SSN) when making routine purchases over the Internet or in stores. An identity thief can fill out change of address cards at the post office and have someone else's mail sent to their own PO box. When people's credit card bills arrive, they (1) call the issuer and pretend to be the victim, (2) ask for a change in address on the account, and (3) purchase items over the Internet and have the merchandise sent to a new address. Some identity thieves engage in **phishing** by sending fraudulent e-mails or website pop-ups, to get victims to divulge sensitive financial information such as credit card numbers or social security numbers.

Ponzi/Pyramid Schemes This is an investment scheme in which investors are promised abnormally high profits on their investments. No investment is actually made. Early investors are paid returns with the investment money received from the later investors. The system usually collapses, and the later investors do not receive dividends and lose their initial investment.

Nondelivery of Goods/Services This involves the nondelivery of goods or services that were purchased or contracted remotely through the Internet. Online auction sites are a fertile ground for fraud. Goods may never be sent or, if they are, they may be damaged, counterfeit, or stolen.[46]

Cyberterrorism

The justice system must now also be on guard against attacks that integrate terrorist goals with cyber capabilities: cyberterrorism. While the term may be difficult to define, cyberterrorism can be seen as an effort by covert forces to disrupt the intersection where the virtual electronic reality of computers intersects with the physical world.[47] FBI expert Mark Pollitt defines

identity theft Using the Internet to steal someone's identity and/or impersonate them to open a new credit card account or conduct some other financial transaction.

phishing Slang for the processes used to acquire personal information used for identity theft and other fraudulent activities.

cyberterrorism as "the premeditated, politically motivated attack against information, computer systems, computer programs, and data which result in violence against noncombatant targets by subnational groups or clandestine agents."[48]

Terrorist organizations are now beginning to understand the power that cybercrime can inflict on their enemies even though, ironically, they come from a region where computer databases and the Internet are not widely used. Terrorist organizations are now adapting IT into their arsenal of terror, and agencies of the justice system have to be ready for a sustained attack on the nation's electronic infrastructure.

Why Terrorism in Cyberspace? Cyberspace is a handy battlefield for the terrorist because an attack can strike directly at a target that bombs won't effect: the economy of their target. Research by Sanjeev Gupta and his associates shows that terror attacks are associated with lower economic growth and higher inflation and reduced tax revenues. Cyberterrorism may result in a battered economy in which the government is forced to spend more on the military and cut back on social programs and education. These outcomes can weaken the terrorist's target and undermine their resolve to continue to resist.[49]

There is no loss of life and no need to infiltrate "enemy" territory. Terrorists can commit crimes from anyplace in the world and the costs are minimal. Nor do terror organizations lack for skilled labor to mount cyber attacks. There are a growing number of highly skilled experts who are available at reasonable costs in developing countries.

Cyber Attacks Has the United States already been the target of cyber attacks? While it may be difficult to separate the damage caused by hackers from deliberate attacks by terrorists, the Center for Strategic and International Studies has uncovered attacks on the National Security Agency, the Pentagon, and a nuclear weapons laboratory; operations were disrupted in all of these sites.[50] The financial service sector is a prime target and has been victimized by information warfare. Between January 1 and June 30, 2002, financial service firms received an average of 1,018 attacks per company, and 46 percent of these firms had at least one server attack during the period.[51]

What form may cyber attacks take in the future? Here are some possible scenarios:

- Viruses called "logic bombs" are implanted in an enemy's computer. They can go undetected for years until they are instructed through the Internet to overwhelm a computer system.
- Programs are used to allow terrorists to enter "secure" systems and disrupt or destroy the network.
- Using conventional weapons, terrorists overload a network's electrical system thereby threatening computer security.[52]
- Computers allow terrorist groups to remain connected and communicate covertly with agents around the world. Networks are a cost-effective tool for planning and striking.[53]
- The computer system of a corporation whose welfare is vital to national security—such as Boeing or Raytheon—is breached and disrupted.
- Internet-based systems used to manage basic infrastructure needs such as an oil pipeline's flow or water levels in dams are attacked and disrupted, posing a danger of loss of life and interruption of services.
- Cyberterrorists may directly attack the financial system. In ever-increasing numbers people are spending and investing their money electronically, using online banking, credit card payment, and online brokerage services. The

banking/financial system transacts billions of dollars each day through a complex network of institutions and systems. Efficient and secure electronic functioning is required if people are willing to conduct credit and debit card purchases, money transfers, and stock trading. A cyber attack can disrupt these transactions and interfere with the nation's economic well-being.[54]

- Terrorists can use the Internet to recruit new members and disseminate information. For example, Islamic militant organizations use the Internet to broadcast anti-Western slogans and information. An organization's charter and political philosophy can be displayed on its website, which can also be used to solicit funds.

Some experts question the existence of cyberterrorism, going so far as to claim that not a single case of cyberterrorism has yet been recorded, that hackers are regularly mistaken for terrorists, and cyberdefenses are more robust than is commonly supposed. Even so, some of these same skeptics recognize that the potential threat is still there, likely to increase, and steps must be taken to address the dangers ahead.[55]

Controlling Cybercrime

The proliferation of cybercrimes has created the need for new laws and enforcement processes. Since technology evolves so rapidly, enforcement presents challenges that are particularly vexing. There have been numerous organizations set up to provide training and support for law enforcement agents. In addition, new federal and state laws have been aimed at particular areas of high-tech crimes.[56] What are some of the new legislative initiatives designed to limit or control cybercrime?

Software Piracy The government has actively pursued members of the warez community, and some have been charged and convicted under the Computer Fraud and Abuse Act (CFAA), which criminalizes accessing computer systems without authorization to obtain information.[57] The Digital Millennium Copyright Act (DMCA) makes it a crime to circumvent antipiracy measures built into most commercial software and also outlaws the manufacture, sale, or distribution of code-cracking devices used to illegally copy software.[58]

Illegal Copyright Infringement The United States Criminal Code provides penalties for a first-time illegal copyright offender of five years incarceration and a fine of $250,000.[59] Other provisions provide for the forfeiture and destruction of infringing copies and all equipment used to make the copies.[60]

Identity Theft To meet the increasing threat, Congress passed the Identity Theft and Assumption Deterrence Act of 1998 (Identity Theft Act) to make it a federal crime when anyone:

> knowingly transfers or uses, without lawful authority, a means of identification of another person with the intent to commit, or to aid or abet, any unlawful activity that constitutes a violation of Federal law, or that constitutes a felony under any applicable State or local law.[61]

Violations of the act are investigated by federal investigative agencies such as the U.S. Secret Service, the FBI, and the U.S. Postal Inspection Service. In 2004, the Identity Theft Penalty Enhancement Act was signed into law. The act increases existing penalties for the crime of identity theft, establishes aggravated identity theft as a criminal offense, and establishes mandatory penalties for aggravated identity theft. According to the new law anyone who knowingly "transfers, possesses, or uses, without lawful authority" someone else's identification will be sentenced to an extra prison term of two years with no possibility of parole. Individuals committing identity fraud while engaged in crimes associated with terrorism—such as aircraft destruction, arson, airport violence, or kidnapping top government officials—will receive a mandatory sentence enhancement of five years.

Internet Pornography As noted previously, it is difficult to detect and control Internet pornography. Opponents of any controls warn that free speech may be violated. Congress has struggled to create legislation that will restrict usage without violating First Amendment rights. For example, the Child Online Protection Act (H.R. 3783), bans Web postings of material deemed "harmful to minors."[62] On May 13, 2002, the Supreme Court partly upheld the law when it ruled that the law's use of what it calls "community standards" to define what is harmful to children does not by itself make the law unconstitutional.[63] However, there may be future challenges to COPA on the grounds that it controls free speech.

Computer Crimes Congress has treated computer-related crimes as distinct federal offenses since the passage of the Counterfeit Access Device and Computer Fraud and Abuse Law in 1984.[64] The 1984 act protected classified United States defense and foreign relations information, financial institution and consumer reporting agency files, and access to computers operated for the government. The act was supplemented in 1996 by the National Information Infrastructure Protection Act (NIIPA), which significantly broadens the scope of the law. The key provisions of this act are set out in Exhibit 4.3.

Criminal Justice ⚖ Now™

Learn more by going through the "Rule of Law" Learning Module.

Enforcing Cyber Laws

How has the justice system responded to cybercrime? Most of the efforts are being made at the federal level. The government is now operating a number of

Internet pornography is now a multibillion dollar international crime. The men photographed here, Arhmet Ali, Antoni Skinner, David Hines, Andrew Barlow, Frederick Stephens, and Ian Baldock, together with Gavin Seagers (not shown), were sentenced at Kingston Crown Court, in southwest London, for distributing thousands of obscene images in the world's biggest Internet pedophile ring. Despite efforts to prosecute distributors, Internet distribution makes enforcement efforts quite difficult.

© Reuters/Corbis

Exhibit 4.3 Key provisions of the National Information Infrastructure Protection Act (NIIPA)

- NIIPA makes it a crime to access computer files without authorization or in excess of authorization, and subsequently to transmit classified government information.
- The act criminalizes gaining information without access or in excess of authorized access, from financial institutions the United States government, or private sector computers used in interstate commerce.
- Proscribes intentionally accessing a United States department or agency nonpublic computer without authorization. If the government or a government agency does not use the computer exclusively, the illegal access must affect the government's use.
- Prohibits accessing a protected computer, without or beyond authorization, with the intent to defraud and obtain something of value. There is an exception if the defendant only obtained computer time with a value less than $5,000 per year.
- Extends the protection against computer hacking by including interstate, government, and financial institution computers as "protected computers." Prohibits unauthorized access that causes damage regardless of whether or not the damage was "recklessly caused."
- Criminalizes knowingly causing the transmission of a program, code, or command, and as a result, intentionally causing damage to a protected computer (without regard as to authorization to access the computer). Company employees and other authorized users can be culpable for intentional damage to a protected computer. Makes unauthorized users, such as hackers, who cause the transmission of viruses responsible even if the transmission was not intentional because it was only reckless or negligent.
- Prohibits one with intent to defraud from trafficking in passwords, which either would permit unauthorized access to a government computer or affect interstate or foreign commerce.
- Makes it illegal to transmit in interstate or foreign commerce any threat to cause damage to a protected computer with intent to extort something of value. For example, hackers threatening to crash a system if not given system privileges or encrypting a company's data and demanding money for the key would be held criminally liable.

Source: Pub. L. No. 104-294, Title II, [sections] 201, 110 Stat. 3488, 3491-94 (1996).

organizations that are coordinating efforts to control cyber fraud. One approach is to create working groups that coordinate the activities of numerous agencies involved in investigating cybercrime. For example, the Interagency Telemarketing and Internet Fraud Working Group brings together representatives of numerous United States Attorneys' offices, the FBI, the Secret Service, the Postal Inspection Service, the Federal Trade Commission, the Securities and Exchange Commission, and other law enforcement and regulatory agencies to share information about trends and patterns in Internet fraud schemes.

Other Specialized Enforcement Agencies Specialized enforcement agencies are being created to fight cybercrime. The Internet Fraud Complaint Center, based in Fairmont, West Virginia, is run by the FBI and the National White Collar Crime Center.

It brings together about 1,000 state and local law enforcement officials and regulators. It then analyzes the fraud-related complaints for patterns, develops additional information on particular cases, and sends investigative packages to law enforcement authorities in the jurisdiction that appears likely to have the greatest investigative interest in the matter. In the first year of its operation, the center received 36,000 complaints, the majority involving auction fraud.

Law enforcement has made remarkable strides in dealing with identity theft as a crime problem over the last two years. Nonetheless, the problem is serious and may expand despite control efforts.

Private Security Efforts to Control and Combat Cybercrime Some private security companies now offer services to counter Internet criminals. For example, the Equifax Corporation has launched a credit-monitoring service

www The **Internet Fraud Complaint Center (IFCC)** was established as a partnership between the **Federal Bureau of Investigation (FBI)** and the **National White Collar Crime Center (NW3C)** to serve as a means to receive Internet-related criminal complaints, research, develop, and refer the criminal complaints to law enforcement agencies for any investigation they deem to be appropriate. To visit these websites, go to "Web Links" on your Siegel Essentials of Criminal Justice 5e website: http://cj.wadsworth.com/siegel_ess5e.

that alerts clients by e-mail whenever an inquiry is made of their credit file or a new account is opened under their name. Other firms already sell credit-monitoring services and several of them offer daily alerts.

Criminal Justice ⚖ Now™

*Learn more about **Careers in Criminal Justice** by exploring the "On the Job" features **Deportation Officer** and **Senior Deputy U.S. Marshal (Coordinator, Fugitive Apprehension Strike Task Force)**.*

What the Future Holds

The justice system's response to cybercrime and terrorism is constantly evolving. All too often it is moved by events, being reactive rather than proactive. For example, prior to 9/11, most local law enforcement agencies had little experience with terrorist-related incidents and most did little to prepare for attacks. After 9/11, the country went on high alert. State and local agencies began to develop antiterror strategies and responses. In response to 9/11, criminal justice agencies increased the number of personnel engaged in emergency response planning and antiterror activities. They have updated plans for chemical, biological, or radiological attacks and, to a lesser extent, mutual aid agreements. They have reallocated internal resources and increased departmental spending to focus on terrorism preparedness.[65]

In the future, rather than react to events, the justice system may go on the offensive. Using their technological prowess, efforts will be made to identify terrorists and cybercriminals and bring them to justice before they can carry out their attacks rather than wait for the attack and plan a reaction. To reach this goal, greater cooperation between agencies ranging from the FBI, to the Department of Homeland Security, and the National Counterterrorism Center with the Director of National Intelligence will be critical.

SUMMARY

- Two contemporary challenges stand out in importance for the justice system: terrorism and cybercrime.
- Terrorism generally involves the illegal use of force against innocent people to achieve a political objective.
- Confronting terrorism is also critical because of the extremely violent tactics they employ, including bombings, killing hostages, chemical warfare, and spreading toxic biological agents.
- Cybercrime involves use of the nation's rapidly growing computer and Internet systems to commit theft and fraud.
- Cyberterrorists may mount attacks against an enemy nation's technological infrastructure.
- The term "terrorism" first appeared at the time of the French Revolution, when Edmund Burke, a noted British political philosopher, referred to the violence he observed in Paris as the "reign of terror."
- Terrorism researchers have generally concluded that there is no single personality trait or behavior pattern that distinguishes the majority of terrorists.
- Some terrorists have psychological deficits, some have been raised in homes and socialized in families where the father was absent or even if present was a distant and cold figure. Some terrorists begin as members of minority political, social, and religious groups angered by their positions of helplessness. Some terrorists may be motivated by feelings of alienation and failure to maintain the tools to compete in a post-technological society.
- The criminal justice system is now confronting a new breed of terrorists, whose motivations are diverse and varied. The paradigm of this new breed is Osama bin Laden. They consider themselves true believers surrounded by blasphemers and have concluded that the future of religion itself, and therefore the world, depends on them and their battle against idol worship.
- Some terrorist groups have morphed into criminal gangs; some criminal gangs are involved in terror.
- After the 9/11 attacks, agencies of the criminal justice system began to focus their attention on combating the threat of terror. There is now a Director of National Intelligence (DNI) charged with coordinating data from the nation's primary intelligence gathering agencies.
- The Federal Bureau of Investigation (FBI) has announced a reformulation of its priorities, making

protecting the United States from terrorist attack its number one commitment.

- The Department of Homeland Security (DHS) was created to prevent terrorist attacks within the United States and to minimize the damage if an attack occurs.
- A number of states have beefed up their intelligence-gathering capabilities and aimed them directly at homeland security. California has introduced the California Anti-Terrorism Information Center (CATIC), a statewide intelligence system designed to combat terrorism. Alabama is the first state in the nation to create its own legislatively enacted cabinet-level Department of Homeland Security.
- New York has implemented a new, comprehensive program called Operation Atlas, to protect the city and its citizens from future acts of terrorism.
- The USA Patriot Act (USAPA) gives new powers to domestic law enforcement and international intelligence agencies in an effort to fight terrorism, to

expand the definition of terrorist activities, and to alter sanctions for violent terrorism.

- The Communications Assistance for Law Enforcement Act (CALEA) helps law enforcement's ability to monitor suspects.
- Criminal entrepreneurs have used the Internet to commit a variety of crime, including distributing illegal sexual material, denial of service attacks, illegal copyright infringement, Internet securities fraud, identity theft, ponzi/pyramid schemes, and nondelivery of goods/services.
- Computer crimes can involve theft of services, use of data in a computer system for personal gain, unauthorized use of computers, theft of property by computer, or destroying hardware.
- Cyberterrorism is an effort by covert forces to disrupt the place where the virtual electronic reality of computers intersects with the physical world.
- Cyberspace is a handy battlefield for the terrorist because an attack can strike directly at a target that bombs won't affect: the economy of his or her target.

KEY TERMS

terrorism 94
cybercrime 94
cyberterrorism 94
al Qaeda 97
National Commission on Terrorist Attacks Upon the United
  States 98

Director of National Intelligence
  (DNI) 99
Department of Homeland
  Security (DHS) 103
USA Patriot Act (USAPA) 106
Communications Assistance for
  Law Enforcement Act
  (CALEA) 108

globalization 109
warez 112
identity theft 113
phishing 113

REVIEW QUESTIONS

1. Would you be willing to give up some of your civil rights in order to aid the war on terror?
2. Should people who illegally download movies or music be prosecuted for theft?
3. Should terror suspects arrested in a foreign land be given all the rights and privileges as an American citizen accused of crime?

4. Should the Internet be more closely monitored and controlled to prevent the threat of cyberterrorism?
5. What groups in America might be the breeding ground of terrorist activity in the United States?

PART 2

The Police and Law Enforcement

A few years ago, the Richmond, Virginia, homicide rate was the second highest in the nation; gun toting had become a way of life. Then the local police, in cooperation with the U.S. Bureau of Alcohol, Tobacco, and Firearms, created Project Exile. This innovative program was designed to combat gun crime in a simple and direct fashion. Any time Richmond police found a gun on a drug dealer, user, convicted felon, or suspect in a violent crime, the case would be tried under federal statutes that carry mandatory sentences of at least five years without parole—and longer for repeated or aggravated offenses. To publicize the program, its slogan—*An Illegal Gun Gets You Five Years in Prison*—was splashed across billboards in high-crime neighborhoods and on city buses. A TV campaign spread the word over the airwaves. Since the program began, hundreds of gun offenders have been sent to prison and hundreds of guns have been removed from the street. Much to the program creators' delight, murders and armed robberies in Richmond dropped sharply after the program was instituted. Because of its success, Project Exile–type programs are being adopted in Atlanta, Georgia; Birmingham, Alabama; Fort Worth, Texas; New Orleans; Norfolk, Virginia; Philadelphia; Rochester, New York; and San Francisco. In Texas, the program's motto is "Gun crime means hard time," while in Rochester billboards on the side of city buses read: "You + illegal gun = federal prison."

Programs such as Project Exile typify the effort of modern police agencies to take an aggressive stance against crime. Rather than simply react after a crime occurs, local police are now cooperating with other governmental agencies and working in partnership with the general public to reduce area crime rates. Cracking down on gun crimes, patrolling crime-ridden schools, and acting as community change agents are but a few of the roles of the modern police. In the following three chapters the history, roles, and police profession will be discussed in some detail. We will be looking at legal, social, and professional issues in depth. ■

5   POLICE IN SOCIETY: HISTORY AND ORGANIZATION

6   THE POLICE: ROLE AND FUNCTION

7   ISSUES IN POLICING: PROFESSIONAL, SOCIAL, AND LEGAL

CHAPTER 5

Police in Society: History and Organization

© Steve Liss/Time Life Pictures/Getty Images

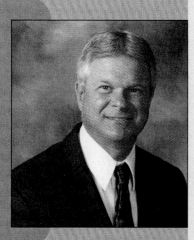

TOM KUKOWSKI earned his Bachelor of Science degree in Criminal Justice at the University of Wisconsin, Milwaukee, and holds a Master of Arts in Public Service Administration from Marquette University in Milwaukee. He is captain of the Criminal Investigations Bureau in the Milwaukee Police Department and oversees all investigations and investigators in the Investigations and Juvenile Crimes Bureaus. He is also in charge of the Drug Investigations Unit, the Forensic and Technical Services Unit, and the Gang Investigations Unit.

Why did Captain Kukowski choose a law enforcement career? Growing up just outside of the city of Milwaukee, he witnessed the social turmoil of the 1960s firsthand. He saw the National Guard being called in to patrol Milwaukee, and mandatory curfews being put in place and strictly enforced. As a young man he wanted to do something to end this conflict. He believed that rather than engaging in conflict that

Chapter Outline

Chapter Objectives

1. Describe policing in the eighteenth century
2. Discuss the development of law enforcement in colonial America
3. Analyze the problems of early police agencies
4. Discuss how reformers attempted to create professional police agencies
5. Discuss the problems of policing in the 1960s and '70s
6. Describe the major changes in law enforcement between 1970 and today
7. Be familiar with the major federal law enforcement agencies
8. Know the differences between state and county law enforcement
9. Describe how technology is changing police work
10. Discuss some of the future technological developments that may influence policing

increases differences and inflames emotions, there was common middle ground that could bring people together. Having a calm, reasoned approach, he thought, was the best way to resolve conflict. He brought this philosophy with him on the job, where he has used his resolution skills to resolve conflicts on an individual and community level.

As the commander of the Criminal Investigations Bureau, he is on call twenty-four hours a day, seven days a week, including all holidays. He responds to all serious violent crime calls, which include homicides, stabbings, shootings, and violent sexual assaults. He leads the investigations, making sure that evidence-gathering is thorough and in compliance with strict departmental and legal standards. His goal now is to find and implement an appropriate crime prevention strategy in a socially dynamic environment.

Criminal Justice ⊛ Now™
Learn more about Careers in Criminal Justice by exploring the "On the Job" features IRS Agent, Postal Inspector, and Fish and Wildlife Special Agent.

Law enforcement officers such as Tom Kukowski find that their responsibilities are immense; they may suddenly be faced with an angry mob, an armed felon, or a suicidal teenager and be forced to make split-second decisions on what action to take. At the same time, they must be sensitive to the needs of citizens who are often of diverse racial and ethnic backgrounds. When police are present and visible it creates a sense of security in a neighborhood and improves residents' opinions of the police.[1]

Unfortunately, many police officers feel unappreciated by the public they serve, a perception that may be due to the underlying conflicts inherent in the police role. Some officers take the job believing they will be proactive crime fighters who initiate actions against law violators; they may find their role is generally reactive, responding only when a citizen calls for service. The desire for direct action is often blunted because police are expected to perform many civic duties that in earlier times were the responsibility of every citizen: keeping the peace, performing emergency medical care, dealing with family problems, and helping during civil emergencies.

Most of us agree that a neighborhood brawl must be stopped, that shelter must be found for the homeless, and that the inebriated must be taken safely home, but few of us want to jump into the fray personally; we would rather "call the cops." The police officer has become a "social handyman" called in to fix up problems that the average citizen wishes would simply go away. Police officers are viewed as the "fire it takes to fight fire."[2] The public needs the police to perform those duties that the average citizen finds distasteful or dangerous, such as breaking up a domestic quarrel or dispersing rowdy youths. At the same time, the public resents the power the police have to use force, arrest people, and deny people their vices. Put another way, the average citizen wants the police to crack down on undesirable members of society while excluding his/her own behavior from legal scrutiny.

Because of these natural role conflicts, the relationship between the police and the public has been the subject of a great deal of concern. Citizens may be less likely to go to police for help, to report crimes, to step forward as witnesses, or to cooperate with and aid police if there is a schism between police and the public they serve. Victim surveys indicate that some citizens have so little faith in the police that they will not report even serious crimes, such as rape or burglary. In some communities, citizen self-help groups have sprung up to supplement police protection.[3] In return, police officers often feel ambivalent and uncertain about the public they are sworn to protect.

Because of this ambivalence and role conflict, more communities are adapting new models of policing that reflect the changing role of the police. Law enforcement administrators now recognize that police officers are better equipped to be civic problem solvers than effective crime fighters. Rather than ignore, deny, or fight this reality, police departments are being reorganized to maximize their strengths and minimize their weaknesses. What has emerged is the *community policing movement,* a new concept of policing designed to bridge the gulf between police agencies and the communities they serve.

The changing police role is of critical importance to the criminal justice system. The police are the gatekeepers of the criminal justice process. They initiate contact with law violators and decide whether to arrest them formally and start their journey through the criminal justice system, to settle the issue in an informal way (such as by issuing a warning), or to take no action at all. The strategic position of law enforcement officers, their visibility and contact with the public, and their use of weapons and arrest power kept them in the forefront of public thought for most of the twentieth century.

The public, especially the minority community, may applaud police efforts that have brought the crime rate down, but they are also concerned by

Empirical evidence shows that, in at least some jurisdictions, young African-American males are treated more harshly by the criminal and juvenile justice system than are members of any other group. Recent research shows that after being stopped for traffic violations, minorities are more likely to be searched and arrested than whites. Elements of institutional racism have become so endemic that terms such as "DWB" (Driving While Black) are now part of the vernacular, used to signify the fact that young African-American motorists are routinely stopped by police.

© 2002 AP/Wide World Photos

media reports of police officers who abuse their power by either using unnecessary force and brutality or routinely violating the civil rights of suspects. Even when community members believe police officers are competent and dependable, many question their priorities and often consider them disrespectful.[4]

Another concern is that police are racially and ethnically biased and use racial profiling to routinely stop young African-American males and search their cars. Some cynics suggest that police have created a new form of crime: *DWB*, "driving while black."[5] It is disturbing that recent (2005) research by Stephen Rice and Alex Piquero still finds that African Americans living in New York City were three times more likely than Caucasians to perceive that (1) police are racially biased, that (2) discrimination is widespread and unjustified, and that (3) they had personally experienced police bias.[6] Despite such reports, the majority of American citizens give their local police force high marks. Their appreciation is most pronounced when they view their neighborhoods as safe and people believe that police efficiency is a key to their protection.[7]

In this and the following two chapters, we will evaluate the history, role, organizational issues, and procedures of police agents and agencies and discuss the legal rules that control police behavior.

■ THE HISTORY OF POLICE

The origin of U.S. police agencies, like the origins of criminal law, can be traced to early English society.[8] Before the Norman Conquest, no regular English police force existed. Every person living in the villages scattered throughout the countryside was responsible for aiding neighbors and protecting the settlement from thieves and marauders. This was known as the *pledge system*. People were grouped in collectives of ten families, called

Criminal Justice ⚖ Now ™

Learn more about **The History of Police** *by exploring the "Early Forms of Law Enforcement" Vocabulary Check activity.*

tithings, and were entrusted with policing their own minor problems. When trouble occurred, the citizen was expected to make a **hue and cry.** Ten tithings were grouped into a **hundred,** whose affairs were supervised by a **constable** appointed by the local nobleman. The constable, who might be considered the first real police officer, dealt with more serious breaches of the law.[9]

Shires, which resembled the counties of today, were controlled by the **shire reeve,** who was appointed by the Crown or local landowner to supervise the territory and ensure that order would be kept. The shire reeve, a forerunner of today's **sheriff,** soon began to pursue and apprehend law violators as part of his duties.

In the thirteenth century, the **watch system** was created to help protect property in England's larger cities and towns. Watchmen patrolled at night and helped protect against robberies, fires, and disturbances. They reported to the area constable, who became the primary metropolitan law enforcement agent. In larger cities, such as London, the watchmen were organized within church parishes and were usually members of the parish they protected.

In 1326 the office of **justice of the peace** was created to assist the shire reeve in controlling the county. Eventually, these justices took on judicial functions in addition to their primary role as peacekeepers. The local constable became the operational assistant to the justice of the peace, supervising the night watchmen, investigating offenses, serving summonses, executing warrants, and securing prisoners. This system helped delineate the relationship between police and the judiciary, which has continued for more than 670 years.

Private Police and Thief Takers

As the eighteenth century began, rising crime rates encouraged a new form of private, monied police, who were able to profit both legally and criminally from the lack of formal police departments. These private police agents, referred to as *thief takers,* were universally corrupt, taking profits not only from catching and informing on criminals but also from receiving stolen property, theft, intimidation, perjury, and blackmail. They often relieved their prisoners of money and stolen goods and made more income by accepting hush money, giving perjured evidence, swearing false oaths, and operating extortion rackets. Petty debtors were especially easy targets for those who combined thief taking with the keeping of alehouses and taverns. While incarcerated, the health and safety of prisoners were entirely at the whim of the keepers, or thief takers, who were virtually free to charge what they wanted for board and other necessities. Court bailiffs who also acted as thief takers were the most passionately detested legal profiteers. They seized debtors and held them in small lockups where they forced their victims to pay exorbitant prices for food and lodging.

The thief takers' use of violence was notorious. They went armed and were prepared to maim or kill in order to gain their objectives. Before he was hanged in 1725, Jack Wild, the most notorious thief taker, "had two fractures in his skull and his bald head was covered with silver plates. He had seventeen wounds in various parts of his body from swords, daggers, and gunshots, [and] . . . his throat had been cut in the course of his duties."[10]

Henry Fielding, famed author of *Tom Jones,* along with Saunders Welch and Sir John Fielding, sought to clean up the thief-taking system. Appointed a city magistrate in 1748, Fielding operated his own group of monied police out of Bow Street in London, directing and deploying them throughout the city and its environs, deciding which cases to investigate and what streets to protect. His agents were carefully instructed on their legitimate powers and duties. Fielding's Bow Street Runners were a marked improvement over the earlier monied

tithing *In medieval England, a group of ten families who collectively dealt with minor disturbances and breaches of the peace.*

hue and cry *A call for assistance in medieval England. The policy of self-help used in villages demanded that everyone respond if a citizen raised a hue and cry to get their aid.*

hundred *In medieval England, a group of one hundred families that had the responsibility to maintain the order and try minor offenses.*

constable *In medieval England, an appointed official who administered and supervised the legal affairs of a small community.*

shire reeve *In medieval England, the senior law enforcement figure in a county; the forerunner of today's sheriff.*

sheriff *The chief law enforcement officer in a county.*

watch system *During the Middle Ages in England, men were organized in church parishes to guard at night against disturbances and breaches of the peace under the direction of the local constable.*

justice of the peace *Established in 1326 England, the office was created to help the shire reeve in controlling the county and later took on judicial functions.*

police because they actually had an administrative structure that improved record-keeping and investigative procedures.

Although an improvement, Fielding's forces were not adequate, and by the nineteenth century state police officers were needed. Ironically, almost 200 years later, private policing is now considered essential. Private police forces are a rapidly growing entity and in many instances local police work closely with private security firms and similar entities. In some gated communities and special tax assessment districts, property owners pay a special levy, in addition to their tax dollars, to hire additional private police, who may work in partnership with local law enforcement to investigate criminal activities.[11]

Creating Public Police

In 1829, Sir Robert Peel, England's home secretary, guided through Parliament an "Act for Improving the Police in and near the Metropolis." The Metropolitan Police Act established the first organized police force in London. Composed of over one thousand men, the London police force was structured along military lines; its members would be known from then on as *bobbies*, after their creator. They wore a distinctive uniform and were led by two magistrates, who were later given the title of commissioner. However, the ultimate responsibility for the police fell to the home secretary and consequently to the Parliament.

The early bobbies suffered from many of the same ills as their forebears. Many were corrupt, they were unsuccessful at stopping crime, and they were influenced by the wealthy. Owners of houses of ill repute who in the past had guaranteed their undisturbed operations by bribing watchmen now turned their attention to the bobbies. Metropolitan police administrators fought constantly to terminate cowardly, corrupt, and alcoholic officers, dismissing in the beginning about one-third of the bobbies each year.

Despite its recognized shortcomings, the London experiment proved a vast improvement over what had come before. It was considered so successful that the London Metropolitan Police soon began providing law enforcement assistance to outlying areas that requested it. Another act of Parliament allowed justices of the peace to establish local police forces, and by 1856 every borough and county in England was required to form its own police force.

Law Enforcement in Colonial America

Law enforcement in colonial America paralleled the British model. In the colonies, the county sheriff became the most important law enforcement agent. In addition to keeping the peace and fighting crime, sheriffs collected taxes, supervised elections, and handled a great deal of other legal business.

The colonial sheriff did not patrol or seek out crime. Instead, he reacted to citizens' complaints and investigated crimes that had occurred. His salary, related to his effectiveness, was paid on a fee system. Sheriffs received a fixed amount for every arrest made. Unfortunately, their tax-collecting chores were more lucrative than fighting crime, so law enforcement was not one of their primary concerns. In the cities, law enforcement was the province of the town marshal, who was aided, often unwillingly, by a variety of constables, night watchmen, police justices, and city council members. However, local governments had little power of administration, and enforcement of the criminal law was largely an individual or community responsibility. After the American Revolution larger cities relied on elected or appointed agents to serve warrants and recover stolen property, sometimes in cooperation with the thieves themselves. Night watchmen, referred to as "leatherheads" because of the leather helmets they wore, patrolled the streets calling the hour, equipped with a rattle to summon help and a nightstick to ward off lawbreakers. Watchmen were not widely respected: rowdy young men enjoyed tipping over the watch houses with the leatherhead inside, and a favorite saying in New York was "While the city sleeps the watchmen do too."[12]

In rural areas in the South, slave patrols charged with recapturing escaped slaves were an early, if loathsome, form of law enforcement.[13] In the western territories, individual initiative was encouraged by the practice of offering rewards for the capture of felons. If trouble arose, the town vigilance committee might form a posse to chase offenders. These **vigilantes** were called on to eradicate such social problems as theft of livestock through force or intimidation; the San Francisco Vigilance Committee actively pursued criminals in the mid-nineteenth century.

As cities grew, it became exceedingly difficult for local leaders to organize ad hoc citizen vigilante groups. Moreover, the early nineteenth century was an era of widespread urban unrest and mob violence. Local leaders began to realize that a more structured police function was needed to control demonstrators and keep the peace.

Early Police Agencies

The modern police department was born out of urban mob violence that wracked the nation's cities in the nineteenth century. Boston created the first formal U.S. police department in 1838. New York formed its police department in 1844; Philadelphia in 1854. The new police departments replaced the night-watch system and relegated constables and sheriffs to serving court orders and running jails.

At first, the urban police departments inherited the functions of the institutions they replaced. For example, Boston police were charged with maintaining public health until 1853, and in New York the police were responsible for street sweeping until 1881. Politics dominated the departments and determined the recruitment of new officers and promotion of supervisors. An individual with the right connections could be hired despite a lack of qualifications. Early police agencies were corrupt, brutal, and inefficient.[14] At first, police were expected to live in the area they patrolled, but as the nineteenth century grew to a close, officers left the most dangerous areas and commuted to work, thereby separating themselves from the people they were being asked to supervise and control.[15]

In the late nineteenth century, police work was highly desirable because it paid more than most other blue-collar jobs. By 1880 the average factory worker earned $450 a year, while a metropolitan police officer made $900 annually. For immigrant groups, having enough political clout to be appointed to the police department was an important step up the social ladder.[16] However, job security was uncertain because it depended on the local political machine staying in power.

Police work itself was primitive. There were few of even the simplest technological innovations common today, such as centralized record keeping. Most officers patrolled on foot, without backup or the ability to call for help. Officers were commonly taunted by local toughs and responded with force and brutality. The long-standing conflict between police and the public was born in the difficulty that untrained, unprofessional officers had in patrolling the streets of nineteenth-century U.S. cities and in breaking up and controlling labor disputes. Police were not crime fighters as we know them today. Their main role was maintaining order, and their power was almost unchecked. The average officer had little training, no education in the law,

vigilantes *A citizen group who tracked down wanted criminals in the Old West.*

Crowds line up on the sidewalk to view a group of New York mounted policemen parade on horseback on June 1, 1897.

and a minimum of supervision, yet the police became virtual judges of law and fact with the ability to exercise unlimited discretion.[17]

At mid-nineteenth century, the detective bureau was set up as part of the Boston police. Until then, thief taking had been the province of amateur bounty hunters, who hired themselves out to victims for a price. When professional police departments replaced bounty hunters, the close working relationships that developed between police detectives and their underworld informants produced many scandals, and consequently, high personnel turnover.

Police during the nineteenth century were regarded as incompetent and corrupt and were disliked by the people they served. The police role was only minimally directed at law enforcement. Its primary function was serving as the enforcement arm of the reigning political power, protecting private property, and keeping control of the ever-rising numbers of foreign immigrants.

Police agencies evolved slowly through the second half of the nineteenth century. Uniforms were introduced in 1853 in New York. The first technological breakthroughs in police operations came in the area of communications. The linking of precincts to central headquarters by telegraph began in the 1850s. In 1867 the first telegraph police boxes were installed; an officer could turn a key in a box, and his location and number would automatically register at headquarters. Additional technological advances were made in transportation. The Detroit Police Department outfitted some of its patrol officers with bicycles in 1897. By 1913 the motorcycle was being used by departments in the eastern part of the nation. The first police car was used in Akron, Ohio, in 1910, and the police wagon became popular in Cincinnati in 1912.[18] Nonpolice functions, such as care of the streets, had already begun to be abandoned after the Civil War.

The control of police departments by local politicians impeded effective law enforcement and fostered an atmosphere of graft and corruption. In the nineteenth century, big-city police were still not respected by the public, unsuccessful in their role as crime stoppers, and uninvolved in progressive activities.

Twentieth-Century Reform

In an effort to reduce police corruption, civic leaders in a number of jurisdictions created police administrative boards to reduce local officials' control over the police. These tribunals were responsible for appointing police administrators and controlling police affairs. In many instances, these measures failed because the private citizens appointed to the review boards lacked expertise in the intricacies of police work. Another reform movement was the takeover of some metropolitan police agencies by state legislators. Although police budgets were financed through local taxes, control of police was usurped by rural politicians in the state capitals. New York City temporarily lost authority over its police force in 1857. It was not until the first decades of the twentieth century that cities regained control of their police forces.

The Boston police strike of 1919 heightened interest in police reform. The strike came about basically because police officers were dissatisfied with their status in society. Other professions were unionizing and increasing their standards of living, but police salaries lagged behind. The Boston police officers' organization, the Boston Social Club, voted to become a union affiliated with the American Federation of Labor. The officers went out on strike on September 9, 1919. Rioting and looting broke out, resulting in Governor Calvin Coolidge's mobilization of the state militia to take over the city. Public support turned against the police, and the strike was broken. Eventually, all the striking officers were fired and replaced by new recruits. The Boston police strike ended police unionism for decades and solidified power in the hands of reactionary, autocratic police administrators. In the aftermath of the strike, various local, state, and federal crime commissions began to investigate the extent of crime and the ability of the justice system to deal with it effectively, and made recommendations to improve police effectiveness.[19] However, with the onset of the Depression, justice reform became a less important issue than economic revival, and for many years little changed in the nature of policing.

The Emergence of Professionalism

Around the turn of the twentieth century, a number of nationally recognized leaders called for measures to help improve and professionalize the police. In 1893 the International Association of Chiefs of Police (IACP), a professional society, was formed. The IACP called for creating a civil service police force and for removing political influence and control. The most famous police reformer of the time was August Vollmer. While serving as police chief of Berkeley, California, Vollmer instituted university training for young officers and helped develop the School of Criminology at the University of California at Berkeley. Vollmer's disciples included O. W. Wilson, who pioneered the use of advanced training for officers and was instrumental in applying modern management and administrative techniques to policing. During this period, police professionalism was equated with an incorruptible, tough, highly trained, rule-oriented department organized along militaristic lines. The most respected department was that of Los Angeles, which emphasized police as incorruptible crime fighters who would not question the authority of the central command.

Criminal Justice ⚖ Now™

Learn more by exploring the "Police and Professionalism" Review and Reinforce activity.

▎ CONTEMPORARY POLICING: 1960–2006

The modern era of policing can be traced from 1960 to the present time. What are the major events that occurred during this period?

Policing in the 1960s

Turmoil and crisis were the hallmarks of policing during the 1960s. Throughout this decade, the Supreme Court handed down a number of decisions designed to control police operations and procedures. Police officers were now required to obey strict legal guidelines when questioning suspects, conducting searches and wiretapping, and so on. As the civil rights of suspects were significantly expanded, police complained they were being "handcuffed by the courts."

Also during this time, civil unrest produced a growing tension between police and the public. African Americans, who were battling for increased rights and freedoms in the civil rights movement, found themselves confronting police lines. When riots broke out in New York, Detroit, Los Angeles, and other cities between 1964 and 1968, the spark that ignited conflict often involved the police. When students across the nation began marching in anti–Vietnam War demonstrations, local police departments were called on to keep order. Police forces were ill equipped and poorly trained to deal with these social problems; it is not surprising that the 1960s were marked by a number of bloody confrontations between the police and the public.

Confounding these problems was a rapidly growing crime rate. The number of violent and property crimes increased dramatically. Drug addiction and abuse grew to be national concerns, common among all social classes. Urban police departments could not control the crime rate, and police officers resented the demands placed on them by dissatisfied citizens.

Policing in the 1970s

The 1970s witnessed many structural changes in police agencies themselves. The end of the Vietnam War significantly reduced tensions between students and police. However, the relationship between police and minorities was still rocky. Local fears and distrust, combined with conservative federal policies, encouraged police departments to control what was perceived as an emerging minority group "threat."[20]

Increased federal government support for criminal justice greatly influenced police operations. During the decade, the Law Enforcement Assistance Administration (LEAA) devoted a significant portion of its funds to police agencies. Although a number of police departments used this money to purchase little-used hardware, such as antiriot gear, most of it went to supporting innovative research on police work and advanced training of police officers. Perhaps most significant, LEAA's Law Enforcement Education Program helped thousands of officers further their college education. Hundreds of criminal justice programs were developed on college campuses around the country, providing a pool of highly educated police recruits. LEAA funds were also used to import or transfer technology originally developed in other fields into law enforcement. Technological innovations involving computers transformed the way police kept records, investigated crimes, and communicated with one another. State training academies improved the way police learned to deal with such issues as job stress, community conflict, and interpersonal relations.

More women and minorities were recruited into police work. Affirmative action programs helped, albeit slowly, alter the ethnic, racial, and gender composition of U.S. policing.

Policing in the 1980s

As the 1980s began, the police role seemed to be changing significantly. A number of experts acknowledged that the police were not simply crime fighters and called for police to develop a greater awareness of community issues, which resulted in the emergence of the *community policing concept.*[21]

Police unions, which began to grow in the late 1960s, continued to have a great impact on departmental administration in the 1980s. Unions fought for and won increased salaries and benefits for their members. In many instances, unions eroded the power of the police chief to make unquestioned policy and personnel decisions. During the decade, chiefs of police commonly consulted with union leaders before making significant decisions concerning departmental operations.

Although police operations improved markedly during this time, police departments were also beset by problems that impeded their effectiveness. State and local budgets were cut back during the Reagan administration, while federal support for innovative police programs was severely curtailed with the demise of the LEAA.

Police-community relations continued to be a major problem. Riots and incidents of urban conflict occurred in some of the nation's largest cities.[22] They triggered continual concern about what the police role should be, especially in inner city neighborhoods.

Policing in the 1990s

The 1990s began on a sour note and ended with an air of optimism. The incident that helped change the face of American policing occurred on

Although police agencies are learning from the mistakes of the past, racial and ethnic conflict and charges of police brutality are still quite common. Here, police speak to protestors rallying against racial profiling and police brutality in front of the Ramparts police station in downtown Los Angeles. Some of the protestors, who urged police to arrest them, were later arrested peacefully.

© 2000 AP/World Wide Photos

March 3, 1991, when Rodney King and friend Bryant Allen were driving in Los Angeles, California. They refused to stop when signaled by a police car behind them but instead increased their speed; King, the driver, was apparently drunk or on drugs. When police finally stopped the car, they delivered fifty-six baton blows and six kicks to King in a period of two minutes, producing eleven skull fractures, brain damage, and kidney damage. They did not realize that their actions were being videotaped by an observer, who later gave the tape to the media. The officers involved were eventually tried and acquitted in a suburban court by an all-white jury, a decision which set off six days of rioting.[23]

The King case prompted an era of reform. Several police experts decreed that the nation's police forces should be evaluated not on their crime-fighting ability but on their courteousness, deportment, and helpfulness. Interest renewed in reviving an earlier style of police work featuring foot patrols and increased citizen contact. Police departments began to embrace new forms of policing that stressed cooperation with the community and problem solving. Ironically, urban police departments began to shift their focus to becoming community organizers at a time when technological improvements increased the ability to identify suspects. An ongoing effort was made to make departments more diverse, and African Americans began to be hired as chiefs of police, most notably in Los Angeles and Atlanta. The most notable achievements of police departments in the 1990s include:

- The intellectual caliber of the police rose dramatically.
- Police began to use advanced management techniques and applied empirical data to their decision making.
- Standards of police conduct climbed. Despite well-publicized incidents of brutality, police tended to treat the public more fairly, more equitably, and more civilly than they did in the 1960s.
- Police became more diverse in terms of race and gender.
- The work of the police became intellectually more demanding, requiring an array of new specialized knowledge about technology, forensic analysis, and crime.
- Civilian review of police discipline gradually became accepted by police.[24]

POLICING AND LAW ENFORCEMENT TODAY

Contemporary law enforcement agencies are still undergoing transformation. There has been an ongoing effort to make police "user friendly" by decentralizing police departments and making them responsive to community needs. Police and law enforcement agencies are also have to adapt to the changing nature of crime: they must be prepared to handle terrorism, Internet fraud schemes, and identity theft, as well as rape, robbery, and burglary.[25]

Policing and law enforcement today are divided into four broad categories: federal, state, county, and local policing agencies (and many subcategories within). There is no real hierarchy, and each branch has its own sphere of operations, though overlap may exist.

Federal Law Enforcement Agencies

The federal government has a number of law enforcement agencies designed to protect the rights and privileges of U.S. citizens; no single agency has unlimited jurisdiction, and each has been created to enforce specific laws and cope with particular situations. Federal agencies have no particular rank

Criminal Justice ⚖ Now™
Learn more by viewing the "Mexico Police" "In the News" video clip.

order or hierarchy of command or responsibility, and each reports to a specific department or bureau.

Federal Bureau of Investigation The FBI, a branch of the U.S. Department of Justice, originated from a force of special agents created by Attorney General Charles Bonaparte during the presidency of Theodore Roosevelt. These investigators were formalized in 1908 into a distinct branch of the government, the Bureau of Investigation, and the agency was later reorganized into the **Federal Bureau of Investigation (FBI),** under the direction of J. Edgar Hoover (1924–1972).

Today's FBI is not a police agency but an investigative agency with jurisdiction over all matters in which the United States is or may be an interested party. It limits its jurisdiction, however, to federal laws, including all federal statutes not specifically assigned to other agencies. Areas covered by these laws include espionage, sabotage, treason, civil rights violations, murder and assault of federal officers, mail fraud, robbery and burglary of federally insured banks, kidnapping, and interstate transportation of stolen vehicles and property. The FBI headquarters in Washington, D.C., oversees fifty-six field offices, approximately four hundred satellite offices known as resident agencies, four specialized field installations, and more than forty foreign liaison posts. The foreign liaison offices, each of which is headed by a legal attaché or legal liaison officer, work abroad with American and local authorities on criminal matters within FBI jurisdiction. In all, the FBI has approximately 30,000 employees, including more than 12,000 special agents and 17,000 support personnel who perform professional, administrative, technical, clerical, craft, trade, or maintenance operations.

The FBI mission has been evolving to keep pace with world events. With the end of the cold war and the reduction in East-West tensions, the FBI's counterintelligence mission was diminished. In some offices, agents were reassigned to anti-gang and drug control efforts.[26] As you may recall from Chapter 4, since 9/11 the FBI has dedicated itself to combating terrorism. Today, the FBI contains a number of independent divisions, which are described in Exhibit 5.1.[27]

These divisions are involved in carrying out the FBI mission, described as:

- Protecting the U.S. from terrorist attacks, from foreign intelligence operations, and from cyber-based attacks and high-technology crimes
- Combating public corruption at all levels
- Protecting civil rights
- Combating international and national organized crime, major white-collar crime, and significant violent crime
- Supporting law enforcement and intelligence partners
- Upgrading FBI technology

Drug Enforcement Administration Government interest in drug trafficking can be traced back to 1914, when the Harrison Act established federal jurisdiction over the supply and use of narcotics. A number of drug enforcement units, including the Bureau of Narcotics and Dangerous Drugs, were charged with enforcing drug laws. In 1973 these agencies were combined to form the **Drug Enforcement Administration (DEA),** another division of the U.S. Department of Justice.

DEA agents assist local and state authorities in investigating illegal drug use and carrying out independent surveillance and enforcement activities to control the importation of narcotics. For example, DEA agents work with foreign governments in cooperative efforts aimed at destroying opium and marijuana crops at their source—hard-to-find fields tucked away in the interiors

Federal Bureau of Investigation (FBI) The arm of the U.S. Justice Department that investigates violations of federal law, gathers crime statistics, runs a comprehensive crime laboratory, and helps train local law enforcement officers.

Drug Enforcement Administration (DEA) The federal agency that enforces federal drug control laws.

| Exhibit 5.1 | **Divisions of the FBI** |

- **National Security Division** coordinates investigative matters concerning foreign counterintelligence and counterterrorism. Activities include investigations into espionage, overseas homicide, protection of foreign officials and guests, domestic security, and nuclear extortion.
- **Criminal Investigative Division** coordinates investigations into illegal activities, including organized crime, violent crimes and property crimes of an interstate nature, crime on Indian reservations, crimes against U.S. citizens overseas, theft of government property, and investigations into white-collar crime.
- **FBI Laboratory,** established in 1932, is one of the largest and most comprehensive crime laboratories in the world. Laboratory activities include crime scene searches, special surveillance photography, latent-fingerprint examinations, forensic examinations of evidence (including DNA testing), court testimony, and other scientific and technical services.
- **Criminal Justice Information Services (CJIS) Division,** established in 1924, serves as the central repository for criminal justice information services in the FBI. The CJIS Division includes the Fingerprint Identification Program, National Crime Information Center Program, Uniform Crime Reporting Program, and the development of the Integrated Automated Fingerprint Identification System (IAFIS)—a new, computer-based system that can store, process, analyze, and retrieve millions of fingerprints in a relatively short period of time.
- **Information Resources Division (IRD)** provides centralized management and planning for information resources within the FBI. The IRD is responsible for the development of the National Crime Information Center (NCIC) 2000 project. The NCIC 2000 will enhance the existing NCIC system, which is used by federal, state, and local law enforcement agencies to locate wanted and missing persons, vehicles, boats, guns, and so on.
- **Training Division** manages the FBI Academy and trains FBI special agents and professional support staff as well as local, state, federal and international law enforcement personnel.
- **Administrative Services Division** manages FBI and non-FBI background investigations. This division is responsible for the management and security of all FBI facilities, in addition to managing and providing executive direction in all aspects of FBI personnel management matters, including but not limited to personnel assistance, personnel benefits, and personnel selection.

Source: FBI, *Organization*, www.fas.org/irp/agency/doj/fbi/org.htm, accessed on May 25, 2005.

of Latin America, Asia, Europe, and Africa. Undercover DEA agents infiltrate drug rings and simulate buying narcotics to arrest drug dealers.

Bureau of Alcohol, Tobacco, Firearms, and Explosives The ATF helps control sales of untaxed liquor and cigarettes, and through the Gun Control Act of 1968 and the Organized Crime Control Act of 1970, has jurisdiction over the illegal sales, importation, and criminal misuse of firearms and explosives. On January 24, 2003, the ATF's law enforcement functions were transferred to the Department of Justice (DOJ), and the ATF became the **Bureau of Alcohol, Tobacco, Firearms, and Explosives (ATF).** ATF's Strategic Plan is currently being revised to reflect the agency's new name and mission and function within the DOJ.

U.S. Marshals The **U.S. Marshals Service** is the nation's oldest federal law enforcement agency. Among their duties are included:

- *Judicial Security.* Protection of federal judicial officials, which includes judges, attorneys, and jurors. The U.S. Marshals Service also oversees each aspect of courthouse construction, from design through completion, to ensure the safety of federal judges, court personnel, and the public.
- *Fugitive Investigations.* Working with law enforcement authorities at federal, state, local, and international levels, the U.S. Marshals Service apprehends thousands of dangerous felons each year. The U.S. Marshals Service is the primary agency responsible for tracking and extraditing fugitives who are apprehended in foreign countries and wanted for prosecution in the United States.

www To reach the homepage of the Drug Enforcement Administration (DEA), go to "Web Links" on your Siegel Essentials of Criminal Justice 5e website: http://cj.wadsworth.com/siegel_ess5e.

Bureau of Alcohol, Tobacco, Firearms, and Explosives (ATF) Federal agency that has jurisdiction over the illegal sales, importation, and criminal misuse of firearms and explosives.

U.S. Marshals Service Federal agency whose jurisdiction includes protecting federal officials, transporting criminal defendants, and tracking down fugitives.

- *Witness Security.* The U.S. Marshals Service's Witness Security Program ensures the safety of witnesses who risk their lives testifying for the government in cases involving organized crime and other significant criminal activity. Since 1970, the U.S. Marshals Service has protected, relocated, and given new identities to over 7,500 witnesses.

- *Prisoner Services.* The U.S. Marshals Service houses over 47,000 federal unsentenced prisoners each day in federal, state, and local jails.

- *Justice Prisoner and Alien Transportation System (JPATS).* In 1995, the air fleets of the U.S. Marshals Service and the Immigration and Naturalization Service merged to create a more efficient and effective system for transporting prisoners and criminal aliens.

- *Asset Forfeiture Program.* The U.S. Marshals Service is responsible for managing and disposing of seized and forfeited properties acquired by criminals through illegal activities.

Internal Revenue Service (IRS) A division of the Treasury Department, the IRS, established in 1862, enforces violations of income, excise, stamp, and other tax laws. Its Intelligence Division actively pursues gamblers, narcotics dealers, and other violators who do not report their illegal financial gains as taxable income. For example, the career of Al Capone, the famous 1920s gangster, was brought to an end by the efforts of IRS agents.

To reach the Secret Service web page, go to "Web Links" on your Siegel Essentials of Criminal Justice 5e website: http://cj.wadsworth.com/siegel_ess5e.

Secret Service The **Secret Service135,** another Treasury agency, was originally charged with enforcing laws against counterfeiting. Today it is also accountable for the protection of the president and the vice president and their families, presidential candidates, and former presidents. The Secret Service maintains the White House Police Force, which is responsible for protecting the executive mansion, and the Treasury Guard, which protects the mint.

State Law Enforcement Agencies

Unlike municipal police departments, state police were legislatively created to deal with the growing incidence of crime in non-urban areas, a consequence of the increase in population mobility and the advent of personalized mass transportation in the form of the automobile. County sheriffs—elected officials with occasionally corrupt or questionable motives—had proven to be ineffective in dealing with the wide-ranging criminal activities that developed during the latter half of the nineteenth century. In addition, most local police agencies were unable to protect effectively against highly mobile lawbreakers who randomly struck at cities and towns throughout a state. In response to citizens' demands for effective and efficient law enforcement, state governors began to develop plans for police agencies that would be responsible to the state, instead of being tied to local politics and possible corruption.

The Texas Rangers, created in 1835, was one of the first state police agencies formed. Essentially a military outfit that patrolled the Mexican border, it was followed by the Massachusetts State Constables in 1865 and the Arizona Rangers in 1901. The states of Connecticut (1903) and Pennsylvania (1905) formed the first truly modern state police agencies.[28]

Today about twenty-three state police agencies have the same general police powers as municipal police and are territorially limited in their exercise of law enforcement regulations only by the state's boundaries. The remaining state police agencies are primarily responsible for highway patrol and traffic law enforcement.

Some state police, such as those in California, direct most of their attention to the enforcement of traffic laws. Most state police organizations are

Secret Service Federal law enforcement agency charged with enforcing laws against counterfeiting and protecting the lives of important political figures, including the president and the vice president and their families.

restricted by legislation from becoming involved in the enforcement of certain areas of the law. For example, in some jurisdictions, state police are prohibited from becoming involved in strikes or other labor disputes, unless violence erupts.

The nation's eighty-seven thousand state police employees (about fifty-six thousand officers and more than thirty thousand civilians) carry out a variety of functions besides law enforcement and highway safety, including maintaining a training academy and providing emergency medical services.[29] State police crime laboratories aid local departments in investigating crime scenes and analyzing evidence. State police also provide special services and technical expertise in such areas as bomb-site analysis and homicide investigation. Some state police departments, such as California's, are involved in highly sophisticated traffic and highway safety programs, including the use of helicopters for patrol and rescue, the testing of safety devices for cars, and the conducting of postmortem examinations to determine the causes of fatal accidents.

County Law Enforcement Agencies

The county sheriff's role has evolved from that of the early English shire reeve, whose primary duty was to assist the royal judges in trying prisoners and enforcing sentences. From the time of the westward expansion in the United States until municipal departments were developed, the sheriff was often the sole legal authority over vast territories.

Today, there are more than 3,000 county sheriffs' offices operating nationwide, employing more than 290,000 full-time employees, including about

State police have wide jurisdiction over criminal offenses. They may be called upon to apprehend escaped criminals. Here, Oklahoma Highway Patrol troopers Steve Harmon, left, and Eldon Mathews look over city maps of the Durant area as William Burton lies on the ground next to an Oklahoma Highway Patrol car, September 3, 2004, in Durant, Oklahoma. Police continued to search for an escaped prison inmate who led authorities on a chase that resulted in injury to an Oklahoma Highway Patrol trooper. Burton and inmate Audrey Allen Himes, 43, apparently walked away from the Howard McLeod Correctional Center in Atoka.

© 2005 AP/World Wide Photos

165,000 sworn personnel.[30] The duties of a sheriff's department vary according to the size and degree of development of the county. Nearly all sheriffs' offices provide basic law enforcement services such as routine patrol (97 percent), responding to citizen calls for service (95 percent), and investigating crimes (92 percent).

Other standard tasks of a typical sheriff's department are serving civil process (summons and court orders), providing court security, and operating the county jail. Less commonly, sheriffs' departments may serve as coroners, tax collectors, overseers of highways and bridges, custodians of the county treasury, and providers of fire, animal control, and emergency medical services; in years past, sheriffs' offices also conducted executions. Typically, a sheriff's department's law enforcement functions are restricted to unincorporated areas of a county, unless a city or town police department requests its help.

Some sheriffs' departments are exclusively law enforcement oriented; some carry out court-related duties only; some are involved solely in correctional and judicial matters and not in law enforcement. However, a majority are full-service programs that carry out judicial, correctional, and law enforcement activities. As a rule, agencies serving large population areas (over one million) are devoted to maintaining county correctional facilities, whereas those in smaller population areas are focused on law enforcement.

Criminal Justice Now™

Learn more by exploring the "Preserving the Peace" Review and Reinforce activity.

Metropolitan Law Enforcement Agencies

Local police form the majority of the nation's authorized law enforcement personnel. Metropolitan police departments range in size from the New York City Police Department with almost 40,000 full-time officers and 10,000 civilian employees, to rural police departments, which may have a single officer. At last count, the more than 13,000 local police departments nationwide had an estimated 565,000 full-time employees, including about 440,000 sworn personnel.[31] Metropolitan police departments are attracting applicants who value an exciting, well-paid job that also holds the opportunity to provide valuable community service. Salaries in municipal police agencies are becoming more competitive (see Table 5.1 below).

Most TV police shows feature the trials of big-city police officers, but the overwhelming number of departments actually have fewer than fifty officers and serve a population of under twenty-five thousand. Recent data indicated that seventy law enforcement agencies employed one thousand or more full-time sworn personnel, including forty-six local police departments with one thousand or more officers; these agencies accounted for about a third of all

Table 5.1 Minimum and maximum annual police officer salaries by rank

	Minimum Base	Maximum Base
Police chief	$68,337	$87,037
Deputy chief	59,790	75,266
Police captain	56,499	70,177
Police lieutenant	52,446	63,059
Police sergeant	46,805	55,661
Police corporal	39,899	49,299

Total earnings for local, state, and special police and detectives frequently exceed the base salary because of payments for overtime, paid vacation, and sick leave. Because police officers usually are covered by liberal pension plans, many retire at half-pay after 20 or 25 years of service.

Source: U.S. Department of Labor Bureau of Labor Statistics, www.bls.gov/oco/ocos160.htm, accessed on February 25, 2005.

| Exhibit 5.2 | Police activities |

- Criminal investigation
- Law enforcement
- Traffic enforcement
- Narcotics and vice control
- Accident investigation
- Radio communications
- Search and rescue
- Patrol and peacekeeping
- Order maintenance
- Emergency medical care
- Crime prevention
- Property and violent crime investigation
- Animal rescue
- Crowd control
- Fingerprint processing
- Death investigation
- Community development and organization

local police officers. In contrast, nearly eight hundred departments employed just one officer.

Regardless of their size, most individual metropolitan police departments perform a standard set of functions and tasks and provide similar services to the community (see Exhibit 5.2).

The police role is expanding, so procedures must be developed to help with special-needs populations, including AIDS-infected suspects, the homeless, and victims of domestic and child abuse.

These are only a few examples of the multiplicity of roles and duties assumed today by some of the larger urban police agencies around the nation. Smaller agencies can have trouble effectively carrying out these tasks; the hundreds of small police agencies in each state often provide duplicative services. Whether unifying smaller police agencies into "super-agencies" would improve services is often debated among police experts. Smaller municipal agencies can provide important specialized services that might have to be relinquished if they were combined and incorporated into larger departments. Another approach has been to maintain smaller departments but to link them via computerized information-sharing and resource management networks.[32]

TECHNOLOGY AND LAW ENFORCEMENT

Criminal Justice ⚖ Now™

Learn more by exploring the "Technological Capabilities of Police Departments" Animated Artwork.

Policing is relying more and more frequently on modern technology to increase effectiveness, and there is little doubt that the influence of technology on policing will continue to grow (see Figure 5.1).

Police officers now trained to prevent burglaries may someday have to learn to create high-tech forensic labs that can identify suspects involved in theft of genetically engineered cultures from biomedical labs.[33] Criminal investigation will be enhanced by the application of sophisticated electronic gadgetry: computers, cellular phones, and digital communication devices.

Police are becoming more sophisticated in their use of computer software to identify and convict criminals. For example, some have begun to use

Figure 5.1
Technological capabilities of police departments in large cities, 1990 and 2000
Source: Brian A. Reaves and Matthew J. Hickman, *Police Departments in Large Cities, 1990–2000* (Washington, D.C.: Bureau of Justice Statistics, 2002), p. 9.

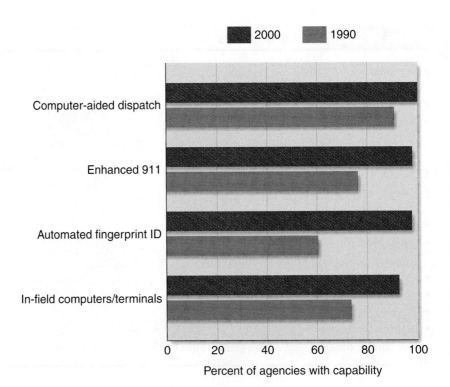

computer software to conduct analysis of behavior patterns, a process called *data mining,* in an effort to identify crime patterns and link them to suspects.[34] By discovering patterns in burglaries, especially those involving multiple offenders, computers can be programmed to recognize a particular way of working at crime and thereby identify suspects most likely to fit the working profile. Advanced computer software has helped in the investigations of Internet crime. For example, in one recent case that occurred in England, police used forensic software to show in court that a defendant had used a particular Internet search engine to find Web pages that contained information about child pornography and then followed links to sites that he used to obtain and view such pornography. The Internet evidence was used to obtain his conviction.[35]

It is now recognized that there are geographic "hot spots" where a majority of predatory crimes are concentrated. Computer mapping programs

Smart guns are designed so that they cannot be used by nonowners—they are useless if stolen. Here, Michael Recce, associate professor of information systems at New Jersey Institute of Technology and inventor of a smart gun, holds a prototype of the gun with grip recognition technology, during a news conference in Newark, New Jersey, January 6, 2004. The federal government is supporting efforts to create the first commercially marketable smart gun technology.

that can translate addresses into map coordinates allow departments to identify problem areas for particular crimes, such as drug dealing. Computer maps allow police to identify the location, time of day, and linkage among criminal events and to concentrate their forces accordingly. Crime mapping is discussed in the following Criminal Justice and Technology feature.

Information Technology

Crime mapping is not the only way technology can be used to improve the effectiveness of police resources. Budget realities demand that police leaders make the most effective use of their forces, and technology seems to be an important method of increasing productivity at a relatively low cost. The introduction of technology has already been explosive. In 1964, for example, only one city, St. Louis, had a police computer system; by 1968, ten states and fifty cities had state-level criminal justice information systems. Today, almost every city of more than fifty thousand people has some sort of computer-support services.[36]

One of the most important computer-aided tasks is the identification of criminal suspects. Computers now link neighboring agencies so they can share information on cases, suspects, and warrants. On a broader jurisdictional level, the FBI implemented the National Crime Information Center in 1967. This system provides rapid collection and retrieval of data about persons wanted for crimes anywhere in the fifty states.

Some police departments are using computerized imaging systems to replace mug books. Photos or sketches are stored in computer memory and easily retrieved for viewing. Several software companies have developed identification programs that help witnesses create a composite picture of the perpetrator. A vast library of photographed or drawn facial features can be stored in computer files and accessed on a terminal screen. Witnesses can scan through thousands of noses, eyes, and lips until they find those that match the suspect's. Eyeglasses, mustaches, and beards can be added; skin tones can be altered. When the composite is created, an attached camera prints a hard copy for distribution.

Criminal Identification

Computer systems now used in the booking process can also help in the suspect identification process. During booking, a visual image of the suspect is stored in a computer's memory, along with other relevant information. By calling up color photos on the computer monitor, police can then easily create a "photo lineup" of all suspects having a particular characteristic described by a witness. New computer software allows two-dimensional mug shots to be recreated on a three-dimensional basis. Effects on the three-dimensional image such as lighting and angles can also be changed to make a better recreation of an environment in which a crime has taken place.[37]

Automated Fingerprint Identification Systems

The use of computerized automated fingerprint identification systems (AFIS) is growing in the United States. Using mathematical models, AFIS can classify fingerprints and identify up to 250 characteristics (minutiae) of the print. These automated systems use high-speed silicon chips to plot each point of minutiae and count the number of ridge lines between that point and its four nearest neighbors, which substantially improves its speed and accuracy over earlier systems.

Criminal Justice and Technology

Crime Mapping

Crime maps offer police administrators graphic representations of where crimes are occurring in their jurisdiction. Computerized crime mapping gives the police the power to analyze and correlate a wide array of data to create immediate, detailed visuals of crime patterns. The most simple maps display crime locations or concentrations and can be used to help direct patrols to the places they are most needed. More complex maps can be used to chart trends in criminal activity, and some have even proven valuable in solving individual criminal cases. For example, a serial rapist may be caught by observing and understanding the patterns of his crime so that detectives may predict where he will strike next and stake out the area with police decoys.

Crime mapping makes use of new computer technology. Instead of archaic pin maps, computerized crime mappings let the police detect crime patterns and pathologies of related problems. It enables them to work with multiple layers of information and scenarios, and thus identify emerging hot spots of criminal activity far more successfully and target resources accordingly.

A number of the nation's largest departments are now using mapping techniques. The New York City Police Department's CompStat process relies on computerized crime mapping to identify crime hot spots. The Chicago Police Department has developed ICAM (Information Collection for Automated Mapping), designed to help police officers in analyzing and solving neighborhood crime problems. ICAM, operational in all of the department's twenty-five police districts, lets beat officers and other police personnel quickly and easily generate maps of timely, accurate crime data for their beats and larger units. The police use the information they develop to support the department's community policing philosophy.

Some mapping efforts cross jurisdictional boundaries. Examples of this approach include the Regional Crime Analysis System in the greater Baltimore-Washington area and the multijurisdictional efforts of the Greater Atlanta PACT Data Center. The Charlotte-Mecklenburg Police Department (North Carolina) uses data collected by other city and county agencies in its crime mapping efforts. By coordinating the tax assessor's, public works, planning, and sanitation departments, these police department analysts have made links between disorder and crime that have been instrumental in supporting the department's community policing philosophy.

Crime maps alone may not be a panacea that allows police agencies to significantly improve their effectiveness. Many officers are uncertain how to read maps and assess their data. To maximize the potential of this new technique, police agencies need to invest in training and infrastructure to allow the full capabilities of crime mapping to have an impact on their service efficiency.

Critical Thinking

1. Crime mapping represents one of the latest technological advances in the allocation of police resources to fight crime effectively. Is it possible that recent downturns in the crime rate reflect this emphasis on technology?

2. Does a growing police technology capability present a danger to personal privacy? How far should the police go in order to keep tabs on potentially dangerous people? For example, should DNA samples be taken at birth from all people and kept on file to match with genetic materials collected at crime scenes?

InfoTrac College Edition Research

To read more about developments in police technology, read Christina Couret, "Police and Technology: The Silent Partnership," *American City & County,* August 1999, vol. 114, issue 9, 31.

Sources: Derek Paulsen, "To map or not to map: Assessing the impact of crime maps on police officer perceptions of crime," *International Journal of Police Science & Management 6* (2004): 234–246; William W. Bratton and Peter Knobler, *Turnaround: How America's Top Cop Reversed the Crime Epidemic* (New York: Random House, 1998), 289; Jeremy Travis, "Computerized Crime Mapping," *NIJ News* (National Institute of Justice), January 1999.

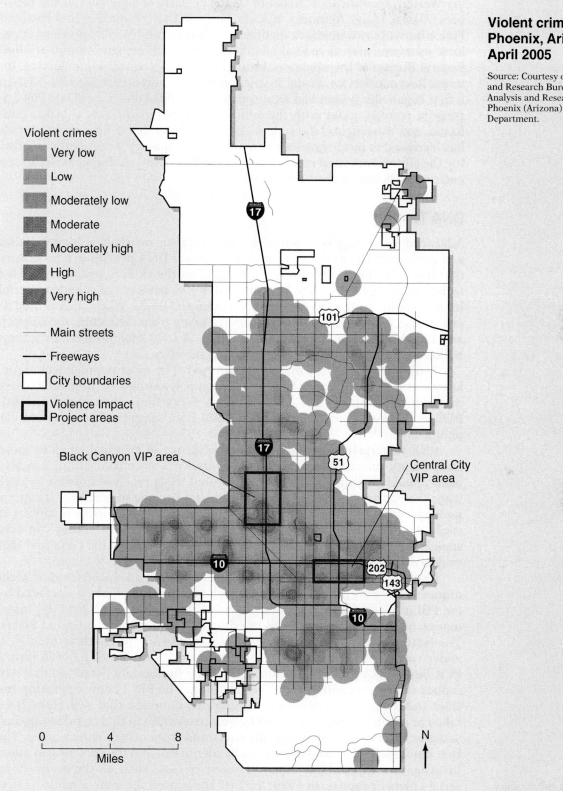

Violent crime map, Phoenix, Arizona, April 2005

Source: Courtesy of Planning and Research Bureau, Crime Analysis and Research Unit, Phoenix (Arizona) Police Department.

Violent crimes

Very low

Low

Moderately low

Moderate

Moderately high

High

Very high

Main streets

Freeways

City boundaries

Violence Impact Project areas

Black Canyon VIP area

Central City VIP area

0   4   8
Miles

N

Some police departments report that computerized fingerprint systems are allowing them to make over one hundred identifications a month from fingerprints taken at crime scenes. AFIS files have been regionalized. For example, the Western Identification Network (WIN) consists of eight central site members (Alaska, Idaho, Montana, Nevada, Oregon, Utah, Wyoming, and Portland Police Bureau), two interface members (California and Washington), multiple local members, and six federal members (Drug Enforcement Administration, Federal Bureau of Investigation, Immigration and Naturalization Service, Internal Revenue Service, Postal Inspection Service, and Secret Service).[38] When it first began, the system had a centralized automated database of 900,000 fingerprint records; today with the addition of new jurisdictions (Alaska, California, and Washington) the system's number of searchable fingerprint records has increased to more than fourteen million. Technology is constantly improving the effectiveness and reliability of the AFIS system, making it easier to use and more efficient in identifying suspects.[39]

DNA Testing

Advanced technology is also spurring new forensic methods of identification and analysis.[40] The most prominent technique is **DNA profiling,** a procedure that has gained national attention because of the O. J. Simpson trial. This technique allows suspects to be identified on the basis of the genetic material found in hair, blood, and other bodily tissues and fluids. When DNA is used as evidence in a rape trial, DNA segments are taken from the victim, the suspect, and blood and semen found on the victim. A DNA match indicates a four-billion-to-one likelihood that the suspect is the offender.

Two methods of DNA matching are used. The most popular technique, known as *RFLP* (restriction fragment length polymorphism), uses radioactive material to produce a DNA image on an X-ray film. The second method, *PCR* (polymerase chain reaction), amplifies DNA samples through molecular photocopying.[41]

DNA fingerprinting is now used as evidence in criminal trials in more than twenty states.[42] The use of DNA evidence to gain convictions has also been upheld on appeal.[43] Its use in criminal trials received a boost in 1997 when the FBI announced that the evidence has become so precise that experts no longer have to supply a statistical estimate of accuracy while testifying at trial ("The odds are a billion to one that this is the culprit"); they can now state in court that there exists "a reasonable degree of scientific certainty" that evidence came from a single suspect.[44]

Leading the way in the development of the most advanced forensic techniques is the Forensic Science Research and Training Center, operated by the FBI in Washington, D.C., and Quantico, Virginia. The lab provides information and services to hundreds of crime labs throughout the United States. The National Institute of Justice is also sponsoring research to identify a wider variety of DNA segments for testing and is involved in developing a PCR-based DNA-profiling examination using fluorescent detection that will reduce the time required for DNA profiling. The FBI is now operating the DNA Index System (NDIS), a computerized database that will allow DNA taken at a crime scene to be searched electronically to find matches against samples taken from convicted offenders and from other crime scenes. The first database will allow suspects to be identified, and the second will allow investigators to establish links between crimes, such as those involving serial killers or rapists. In 1999, the FBI announced the system made its first "cold hit" by linking evidence taken from crime scenes in Jacksonville, Florida, to ones in Washington, D.C., thereby tying nine crimes to a single offender.[45] When Timothy Spence was executed in Virginia on April 27,

DNA profiling The identification of criminal suspects by matching DNA samples taken from their person with specimens found at the crime scene.

1994, he was the first person convicted and executed almost entirely on the basis of DNA evidence.[46]

Communications

Computer technology is now commonplace in policing. Officers routinely and effectively use mobile-computer systems to make inquiries with local, state, and national criminal information databases.[47]

Many larger departments have equipped officers with portable computers, which significantly cuts down the time needed to write and duplicate reports.[48] Police can now use terminals to draw accident diagrams, communicate with city traffic engineers, and merge their incident reports into other databases. Pen computing, in which officers write directly on a computer screen, eliminates paperwork and increases the accuracy of reports.[49] To make this material more accessible to the officer on patrol, head-up display (HUD) units project information onto screens located on patrol car windshields; police officers can access computer readouts without taking their eyes off the road![50]

Future Tech

New investigation techniques are constantly being developed. Three examples include:

- *Genetic algorithms.* Using these mathematical models, a computerized composite image of a suspect's face will be constructed from relatively little information. Digitization of photographs will enable the reconstruction of blurred images. Videotapes of bank robbers or blurred photos of license plates—even bite marks—can be digitized using highly advanced mathematical models.

- *Augmented reality (AR) technology.* Now in the development stage, **augmented reality (AR) technology** will provide wearable components to supply computer-generated virtual information onto individuals' real-world view to improve and enhance their ability to accomplish tasks and missions. AR technology displays information in real time, in a way that enhances the individual abilities of people operating in the real world. (An example of AR technology is the virtual lines drawn by broadcasters on football fields to show the first down marker.) Uniformed patrol officers will have many potential uses for AR ranging from real-time language translation to the immediate display of real-time intelligence about crimes to facial and voice recognition data that will tell them if a suspect is wanted in another crime.[51]

- *ABIS (Automated Biometric Identification System)* is a Web-based facial recognition system that is now being designed to sift through millions of images to find duplicates prior to issuing an ID or clearing a passport. **ABIS** can be used by law enforcement agencies in facial searches or matching suspects who use false identities to their mug shots from past crimes.[52] ABIS may one day be mated to closed circuit TV (CCTV) surveillance systems. Today, second generation CCTV can be positioned to observe environments, such as harbors, airports, or freeways, and then link the recorded images to a computer system that can detect unusual behavior, unauthorized traffic, or surprising and unexpected changes and alert a human operator.[53] Closed circuit surveillance cameras armed with ABIS technology will be able to pick out and track wanted felons or terrorists using computer recorded facial recognition patterns. Big Brother will be watching you!

augmented reality (AR) technology Wearable components that supply computer-generated virtual information.

ABIS (Automated Biometric Identification System) Facial recognition system designed to sift through millions of images to find duplicates prior to issuing an ID or clearing a passport.

SUMMARY

- U.S. police agencies are modeled after their British counterparts.
- Early in British history, law enforcement was a personal matter. Later, constables were appointed to keep peace among groups of one hundred families.
- Early thief takers were private police who apprehended criminals for reward payments.
- The first organized police force was found by Sir Robert Peel in London.
- This rudimentary beginning was the seed of today's police departments.
- The first true U.S. police departments were formed in Boston, New York, and Philadelphia in the early nineteenth century.
- The earliest U.S. police departments were created because of the need to control mob violence, which was common during the nineteenth century. The police were viewed as being dominated by political bosses who controlled their hiring practices and policies.
- Reform movements begun in the 1920s culminated in the concept of professionalism in the 1950s and 1960s.
- Police professionalism was interpreted to mean tough, rule-oriented police work featuring advanced technology and hardware. However, the view that these measures would quickly reduce crime proved incorrect.

- The police experienced turmoil in the 1960s and 1970s, which led to reforms such as the hiring of women and minorities.
- Questions about the effectiveness of law enforcement has led to the development of community policing.
- There are several major law enforcement agencies. On the federal level, the FBI is the largest federal agency. Other agencies include the Drug Enforcement Administration, the U.S. Marshals, and the Secret Service.
- County-level law enforcement is provided by sheriff's departments who run jails and patrol rural areas.
- Most states maintain state police agencies who investigate crimes and patrol the roadways.
- Local police agencies engage in patrol, investigative, and traffic functions, as well as many support activities.
- Most police departments have begun to rely on advanced computer-based technology to identify suspects and collate evidence. Automated fingerprint systems and computerized identification systems have become widespread.

KEY TERMS

tithing 126
hue and cry 126
hundred 126
constable 126
shire reeve 126
sheriff 126
watch system 126
justice of the peace 126

vigilantes 128
Federal Bureau of Investigation (FBI) 134
Drug Enforcement Administration (DEA) 134
Bureau of Alcohol, Tobacco, Firearms, and Explosives (ATF) 135

U.S. Marshals Service 135
Secret Service 136
DNA profiling 144
augmented reality (AR) technology 145
ABIS (Automated Biometric Identification System) 145

REVIEW QUESTIONS

1. List the problems faced by today's police departments that were also present during the early days of policing.

2. Distinguish between the duties of the state police, sheriffs' departments, and local police departments.

3. Do you believe that the general public has greater respect for the police today than in the past? If so, why? If not, why not?

4. What are some of the technological advances that should help the police solve more crimes? What are the dangers of these advances?

5. Discuss the trends that will influence policing during the coming decade. What other social factors may affect police?

CHAPTER 6

The Police: Role and Function

LEE LIBBY began his police career in Seattle in July of 1970. It was a spontaneous career choice: he had not planned on becoming a police officer, but with a pregnant wife and little money, it seemed an ideal situation. He soon realized that he had made a wise career choice. Libby found policing to be physically and intellectually challenging and immensely rewarding in terms of personal accomplishment. He found himself surrounded by some of the finest men and women he had ever known, both personally and professionally.

Libby worked in a wide variety of assignments, including uniformed and plain clothes assignments and after being promoted worked in various uniformed and administrative capacities from patrol to crime prevention to sexual assault crimes. The job exposed him to experiences he never thought possible, such as meeting up with serial killer Ted Bundy. His assignments were varied and changed with promo-

Chapter Outline

Chapter Objectives

1. Understand the organization of police departments
2. Recognize the problems associated with the time-in-rank system
3. Discuss the concept of patrol and its effectiveness
4. Be familiar with aggressive and targeted policing
5. Know the similarities and differences between patrol and detective operations
6. Know what the term CompStat means
7. Be able to discuss the organization of police detectives
8. Understand the concept of community policing
9. Describe various community policing strategies
10. Discuss the concept of problem-oriented policing
11. Be familiar with the various police support functions

tions and re-assignments. As a sergeant in the Crime Prevention Division, he spent time directing the activities of both sworn and civilian personnel who devoted themselves to reducing the opportunity for crime to occur. Then as a detective sergeant in the Special Assault Unit, he was forced to deal with the consequences of some of the most horrible violent crimes that can be imagined. Libby believes that his greatest challenge as a police officer was to not let his identity be defined by his occupation—in other words, rather than believe "I *am* a police officer," he wanted to feel "I *work* as a police officer." Officers who were able to maintain their own identity were well balanced and had a better mental approach both to policing and to their lives away from policing. Libby retired from policing at the rank of detective sergeant and became a professor of criminal justice at Washington's Shoreline Community College.

As Lee Libby's career suggests, the police role, while rewarding, is extremely varied and complex. Officers are asked to serve as enforcers of the law in suburban communities, rural towns, and some of the toughest urban streets in America. While rural/suburban police tend to be generalists who focus on social problems ranging from public disorder to family dysfunction, urban police must confront heavily armed drug-dealing gangs on a regular basis.[1] In both instances, the public demands that the police "make them feel safe" and lose confidence in them if they fear crime in the streets.[2] Yet, these same officers who are called upon to allay the public's fears are criticized when their tactics become too aggressive.

This chapter describes the organization of police departments and their various operating branches: patrol, investigation, service, and administration. It discusses the realities and ambiguities of the police role and how the concept of the police mission has been changing radically. The chapter concludes with a brief overview of some of the most important administrative issues confronting today's U.S. law enforcement agencies.

Criminal Justice ⚖ Now™

Learn more about **The Police Organization** *by exploring the* **Bureaucracy Chain of Command** *and Review and Reinforce activities.*

THE POLICE ORGANIZATION

Most municipal police departments in the United States are independent agencies within the executive branch of government, operating without specific administrative control from any higher governmental authority.

On occasion, police agencies will cooperate and participate in mutually beneficial enterprises, such as sharing information on known criminals, or they may help federal agencies investigate interstate criminal cases. Aside from such cooperative efforts, police departments tend to be functionally independent organizations with unique sets of rules, policies, procedures, norms, budgets, and so on. The unique structure of police agencies greatly influences their function and effectiveness.

Most departments are still organized in a militaristic, hierarchical manner, as illustrated in Figure 6.1. Within this organizational model, each element of the department normally has its own chain of command. For example, in a large municipal department, the bureau of investigative services might have a deputy superintendent who serves as the director of the Detective Bureau, a captain who heads a particular division within the bureau (such as organized crime), a lieutenant who oversees individual cases and acts as liaison with other police agencies, and sergeants and inspectors who carry out the actual fieldwork. Smaller departments may have a captain as head of all detectives, while lieutenants supervise individual subsystems, such as robbery or homicide. At the head of the organization is the **police chief,** who sets policy and has general administrative control over all the department's various operating branches.

Most police departments employ a **time-in-rank system** for determining promotion eligibility. This means that before moving up the administrative ladder, an officer must spend a certain amount of time in the next lowest rank; a sergeant cannot become a captain without serving an appropriate amount of time as a lieutenant. Although this system is designed to promote fairness and limit favoritism, it also restricts administrative flexibility. Unlike in the private sector, where talented people can be pushed ahead in the best interests of the company, the time-in-rank system prohibits rapid advancement. A police agency would probably not be able to hire a computer systems expert with a Ph.D. and give her a command position in charge of its data-analysis section. The department would be forced to hire the expert as a civilian employee under the command of a ranking senior officer who may not be as technically proficient.

police chief *The top administrator of the police department, who sets policy and has general control over departmental policies and practices. The chief is typically a political rather than civil service appointee and serves at the pleasure of the mayor.*

time-in-rank system *For police officers to advance in rank they must spend an appropriate amount of time, usually years, in the preceding rank—that is, to become a captain, an officer must first spend time as a lieutenant.*

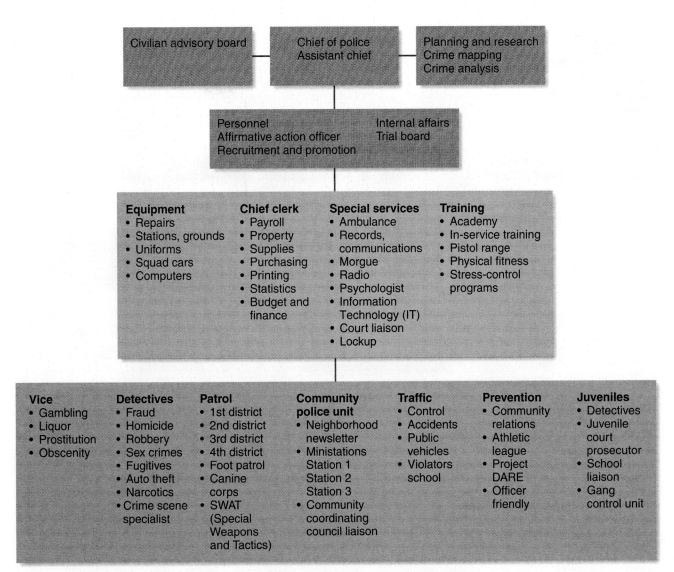

Figure 6.1 Organization of a traditional metropolitan police department

Under this rank system, a title can rarely be taken away or changed once it is earned. Inability to advance through the ranks convinces numerous educated and ambitious officers to seek private employment. The rank system also means that talented police officers cannot transfer to other departments or sell their services to the highest bidder. Time-in-rank ensures the stability—for better or worse—of police agencies.

THE POLICE ROLE

In countless books, movies, and TV shows, the public has been presented with a view of policing that romanticizes police officers as fearless crime fighters who think little of their own safety as they engage in daily shootouts. How close is this portrayal of a crime fighter to real life? Not very close, according to most research efforts. A police officer's crime-fighting efforts are only a small part of his or her overall activities. Studies of police work indicate that a significant portion of an officer's time is spent handling minor disturbances, service calls, and administrative duties. Police work, then, involves much more than catching criminals. Figure 6.2 shows the results of a national survey of police

Criminal Justice ⚖️ Now™

*Learn more about **The Police Role** by exploring the **Preventing Crime** Review and Reinforce activity.*

Figure 6.2
Police encounters with citizens

Source: Matthew Durose, Erica Schmitt, and Patrick Langan, *Contacts Between Police and the Public: Findings from the 2002 National Survey* (Washington, D.C.: Bureau of Justice Statistics, 2005).

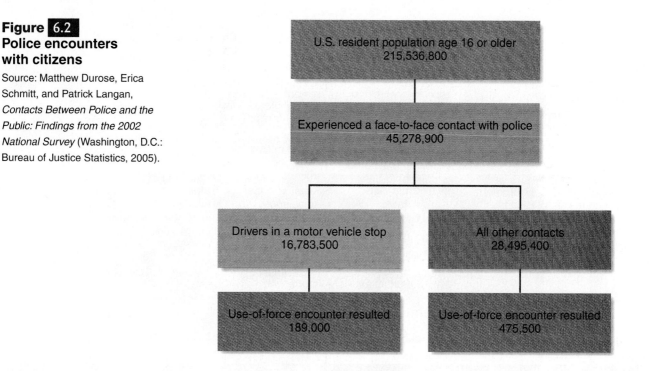

behavior.[3] This survey found that about 20 percent of all Americans (about forty-five million people) have contacts with the police each year. Most involve some form of motor vehicle or traffic-related issues. About five million annual contacts involve citizens asking for assistance—for example, responding to a neighbor's complaint about music being too loud during a party, or warning kids not to shoot fireworks. This survey indicates that the police role is both varied and complex. These results are not surprising when Uniform Crime Report (UCR) arrest data is considered. Each year, about seven hundred thousand local, county, and state police officers make about fourteen million arrests, or about twenty each. Of these, about two million are for serious index crimes (Part I), or about three per officer. Given an even distribution of arrests, it is evident that the average police officer makes fewer than two arrests per month and fewer than one felony arrest every four months.

These figures should be interpreted with caution because not all police officers are engaged in activities that allow them to make arrests, such as patrol or detective work. About one-third of all sworn officers in the nation's largest police departments are in such units as communications, antiterrorism, administration, and personnel. Even if the number of arrests per officer were adjusted by one-third, it would still amount to only nine or ten serious crime arrests per officer per year. So though police handle thousands of calls each year, relatively few result in an arrest for a serious crime such as a robbery and burglary; in suburban and rural areas, years may go by before a police officer arrests someone for a serious crime.

The evidence, then, shows that unlike their TV/film counterparts, the police role involves many activities that are not crime-related. While TV and movies show police officers busting criminals and engaging in high-speed chases, the true police role is much more complex. Police officers function in a variety of roles ranging from dispensers of emergency medical care to keepers of the peace on school grounds. Although officers in large urban departments may be called on to handle more felony cases than those in small towns, they too will probably find that most of their daily activities are not crime-related. What are some of the most important functions of police?

THE PATROL FUNCTION

Regardless of style of policing, uniformed patrol officers are the backbone of the police department, usually accounting for about two-thirds of a department's personnel.[4] Patrol officers are the most highly visible components of the entire criminal justice system. The major purposes of patrol are to

- Deter crime by maintaining a visible police presence
- Maintain public order (peacekeeping) within the patrol area
- Enable the police department to respond quickly to law violations or other emergencies
- Identify and apprehend law violators
- Aid individuals and care for those who cannot help themselves
- Facilitate the movement of traffic and people
- Create a feeling of security in the community[5]

Patrol officers' responsibilities are immense; they may suddenly be faced with an angry mob, an armed felon, or a suicidal teenager and be forced to make split-second decisions on what action to take. At the same time, they must be sensitive to the needs of citizens who are often of diverse racial and ethnic backgrounds. When police are present and visible it creates a sense of security in a neighborhood and improves residents' opinions of the police.[6]

Patrol Activities

Most experts agree that the great bulk of patrol efforts are devoted to what has been described as **order maintenance,** or **peacekeeping:** maintaining order and civility in their assigned jurisdiction.[7] Order-maintenance functions occupy the border between criminal and non-criminal behavior. The patrol officer's discretion often determines whether a noisy neighborhood dispute involves the crime of disturbing the peace or whether it can be controlled with street-corner diplomacy, and sending the combatants on their way. Similarly, teenagers milling around in the shopping center parking lot may be brought in and turned over to the juvenile authorities or handled in a less formal and often more efficient manner.

Criminal Justice Now™
Learn more by viewing the "Police Patrols" "In the News" video clip.

order maintenance (peacekeeping) The order-maintenance aspect of the police role involves peacekeeping, maintaining order and authority without the need for formal arrest, "handling the situation," and keeping things under control by using threats, persuasion, and understanding.

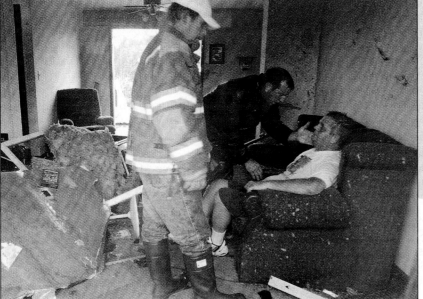

Police patrol means more than fighting crime. Here, Indiana State Police officer J. D. Maxwell checks Terry Martin of Ellettsville, fifty miles south of Indianapolis, after Martin survived a tornado that ripped the roof off his home. He said he got through the ordeal by lying in the fetal position next to his entertainment center after he failed to reach a closet in his bedroom in time. Twelve houses were destroyed and an apartment complex was damaged.

© 2002 AP/World Wide Photos

The primary role of police seems to be "handling the situation." Police encounter many troubling incidents that need some sort of "fixing up."[8] Enforcing the law might be one tool a patrol officer uses; threat, coercion, sympathy, and understanding might be others. Most important is keeping things under control so that there are no complaints that the officer is doing nothing at all or doing too much. The real police role, then, may be as a community problem solver.

Police officers actually practice a policy of selective enforcement, concentrating on some crimes but handling the majority in an informal manner. A police officer is supposed to know when to take action and when not to, whom to arrest and whom to deal with by issuing a warning or some other informal action. If a mistake is made, the officer can come under fire from peers and superiors, as well as the general public.

Does Patrol Deter Crime?

One of the primary goals of police patrol has been is to deter criminal behavior. The visible presence of patrol cars on the street and the rapid deployment of police officers to the scene of a crime are viewed as an effective method of crime control. Unfortunately, research efforts designed to measure the effectiveness of patrol have not supported its deterrence capability. The most widely heralded attempt at measuring patrol effectiveness was undertaken during the early 1970s in Kansas City, Missouri, where researchers divided fifteen separate police districts into three groups: one group retained normal patrol; the second (proactive) set of districts were supplied with two to three times the normal amount of patrol forces; and the third (reactive) group had its preventive patrol eliminated, with police officers responding only when summoned by citizens to the scene of a particular crime.[9] The Kansas City study found that these variations in patrol had little effect on the crime patterns in the fifteen districts. The presence or absence of patrol officers did not seem to affect residential or business burglaries, motor vehicle thefts, larceny involving auto accessories, robberies, vandalism, or other criminal behavior, nor did they influence citizens' attitudes toward the police, their satisfaction with police, or their fear of future criminal behavior. The findings of the Kansas City study were a stunning indicator that the presence of police patrol could do little to deter crime.

Proactive Patrol Although the mere presence of police may not be sufficient to deter crime, the manner in which they approach their task may make a difference. Police departments that use a proactive, aggressive law enforcement style may help reduce crime rates. Improving response time and increasing the number of patrol cars that respond per crime may be one way of increasing police efficiency.[10] Jurisdictions that encourage patrol officers to stop motor vehicles to issue citations and to aggressively arrest and detain suspicious persons also experience lower crime rates than jurisdictions that do not follow such proactive policies.[11] Departments that more actively enforce minor regulations, such as disorderly conduct and traffic laws, are also more likely to experience lower felony rates.[12]

Pinpointing why **proactive policing** works so effectively is difficult. It may have a **deterrent effect:** aggressive policing increases community perception that police arrest many criminals and that most violators get caught; criminals are scared to commit crimes in a town that has such an active police force! Proactive policing may also help control crime because it results in conviction of more criminals. Because aggressive police arrest more suspects, there are fewer left on the street to commit crime; fewer criminals produce lower crime rates.

Criminal Justice ⚖ Now™

*Learn more about **The Patrol Function** by exploring the **Preventive Patrol** Review and Reinforce activity.*

proactive policing A police department policy emphasizing stopping crimes before they occur rather than reacting to crimes that have already occurred.

deterrent effect Stopping or reducing crime by convincing would-be criminals that they stand a significant risk of being apprehended and punished for their crimes.

Aggressive police patrol efforts have been a critical success. The downturn in the New York City violent crime rate over the past decade has been attributed to aggressive police work aimed at lifestyle crimes: vandalism, panhandling, and graffiti.[13] Some commentators fear that aggressive policing will result in antagonism between proactive cops and the general public. However, recent research (2005) indicates that precinct-level efforts to ensure that officers are respectful of citizens helped lower the number of complaints and improved community relations.[14]

Targeting Crimes Evidence also shows that targeting specific crimes can be successful. One aggressive patrol program, known as the Kansas City Gun Experiment, was directed at restricting the carrying of guns in high-risk places at high-risk times. Working with academics from the University of Maryland, the Kansas City Police Department focused extra patrol attention on a "hot spot" high-crime area identified by computer analysis of all gun crimes. Over a twenty-nine-week period, the gun patrol officers made thousands of car and pedestrian checks and traffic stops and made over six hundred arrests. Using frisks and searches, they found twenty-nine guns; an additional forty-seven weapons were seized by other officers in the experimental area. There were 169 gun crimes in the target beat in the twenty-nine weeks prior to the gun patrol but only 86 while the experiment was under way, a decrease of 49 percent. Drive-by shootings dropped significantly, as did homicides, without any displacement to other areas of the city. It is possible that the weapons seized were taken from high-rate offenders who were among the most likely perpetrators of gun-related crimes; their "lost opportunity" to commit violent crimes may have resulted in an overall rate decrease. It is also possible that the gun sweeps caused some of the most violent criminals to be taken off the streets. And as word of the patrol got out, there may have been a general deterrent effect: people contemplating violent crime may have been convinced that apprehension risks were unacceptably high.[15] Can such aggressive programs targeting specific crimes work elsewhere? To find out, see the following Policy, Programs, and Issues in Criminal Justice for more on aggressive policing programs.

© Ed Kashi/Corbis

New technological breakthroughs are making it easier for law enforcement agencies to target crimes and crime-ridden areas. Chicago's Office of Emergency Management is the center for Chicago's criminal database, known as Citizen Law Enforcement Analysis and Reporting, or CLEAR. Superintendents and commanders keep close surveillance on the streets of Chicago from here. The cameras allow the crews to keep watch over criminal behavior and help them to decide when and where to send in the police on patrol.

Policy, Programs, and Issues in Criminal Justice

The Indianapolis Gun Control Program

During the mid-1990s, Indianapolis found itself in an unusual situation. Although the local economy was strong, the city also was experiencing record-setting levels of homicide at a time when homicide was declining in many comparable cities.

Local officials took several steps to address the problem. For example, they used data to identify where and when homicides were occurring. To produce the data, the Indianapolis Police Department (IPD) created the Indianapolis Management Accountability Program, or IMAP, an adaptation of the New York City Police Department's computer comparison statistics (CompStat) program.

IPD then applied directed patrol tactics in two areas of the city that had high concentrations of violent crime. *Directed patrol* involves assigning officers to a particular area to proactively investigate suspicious activities and to enforce existing gun, drug, traffic, and related laws. Officers assigned to directed patrol areas are freed from having to respond to calls for service. The most common approach in a directed patrol effort is to make traffic stops. The strategy generally includes increasing the number of police officers in a given location and the number of contacts with citizens.

IPD applied directed patrol tactics in two police districts in two different ways. Put in the simplest terms, the east district followed a *general deterrence strategy*, whereby it assigned many police officers who stopped many people, issued many citations, and made one felony arrest for every one hundred traffic stops. The north district, employing a *targeted deterrence strategy*, assigned fewer officers who stopped fewer people and issued fewer citations but made almost three times as many arrests for every one hundred stops. Officers in the north district were more likely to stop and arrest felons because they focused on specific suspicious behaviors and individuals.

Homicide went down in both districts, but the north district also reduced gun crime overall—and used fewer resources.

Directed patrol in the north target area reduced gun crime, homicide, aggravated assault with a gun, and armed robbery. In contrast, in the east target area

it had no effect on gun-related crime, except for a possible effect on homicide. Why? The north district's targeted deterrence approach probably sent a message of increased surveillance to those individuals most likely to commit violent gun-related crimes.

The results of the Indianapolis directed patrol program are consistent with a growing body of research that shows that when police identify a specific problem and focus their attention on it, they can reduce crime and violence. Directed police patrol led to sizable reductions in gun crime there. In addition, it did not shift crime to surrounding areas or harm police-community relations.

The finding that the community generally accepted the program supports the idea that crime control benefits need not generate police-citizen conflict. However, the lack of impact in Indianapolis's east target area, which used a more general deterrence model, and the potential strain that these types of police initiatives could have on police-community relations, suggest the need for continued research on both the benefits and the potential costs of such strategies.

Critical Thinking

1. Would you abandon traditional police patrol in favor of more directed, aggressive patrol tactics aimed at specific crimes? What are the advantages, if any, of the more traditional forms of patrol?

2. What other reforms might you make if you were the chief of police in a larger city?

 InfoTrac College Edition Research
To learn more about *new forms of police patrol*, use the phrase as a subject guide on InfoTrac College Edition.

Source: Edmund McGarrell, Steven Chermak, and Alexander Weiss, *Reducing Gun Violence: Evaluation of the Indianapolis Police Department's Directed Patrol* (Washington, D.C.: National Institute of Justice, 2002).

Making Arrests Can formal police action, such as an arrest, reduce crime? While the evidence is mixed, some research studies do show that contact with the police may cause some offenders to forgo repeat criminal behavior. Many first offenders will forgo criminal activity after undergoing arrest.[16] For example, an arrest for drunk driving reduces the likelihood of further driving while intoxicated.

Why do arrests deter crime? It is possible that news of increased and aggressive police arrest activity is rapidly diffused through the population and has an immediate impact on crime rates.[17] Arrests may also alter perceptions. An arrest for drunk driving may convince people that they will be re-arrested if they drink and drive.[18] Consequently, as the number of arrests per capita increases, crime rates go down.

Adding Patrol Officers One reason why patrol activity may be less effective than desired is the lack of adequate resources. Does adding more police help bring down the crime rate? At one time critics questioned whether adding police was effective because reviews of the existing research found that the actual number of law enforcement officers in a jurisdiction seemed to have little effect on area crimes.[19] However, during the past decade larger cities have expanded their police forces and crime rates plummeted (see Figure 6.3), a trend which indicates that adding police may in fact reduce crime rates.

The association between personnel size and crime rates has been supported by number of recent studies. Using a variety of methodologies, these studies have found that police presence may actually reduce crime levels and that adding police may bring crime levels down.[20] Evidence shows that cities with larger police departments that have more officers per capita than the norm also experience lower levels of violent crimes.[21]

Increasing police resources may improve the overall effectiveness of the justice system. When resources are lacking, many cases are dropped before they ever get to trial because it becomes difficult to gather sufficient evidence to ensure a conviction; prosecutors are likely to drop these cases.[22] Adding police resources improves the quality of police work with

Criminal Justice ⚖ Now™

*Learn more about **The Patrol Function** by exploring the "Incident-Driven Policing" and "Totality of the Circumstances" Review and Reinforce activities.*

Criminal Justice ⚖ Now™

Learn more about by exploring the "More Full-Time Police = Less Crime" Animated Artwork.

Figure 6.3
More full-time police means less crime

From 1990 to 2000, in cities with 250,000 or more residents, the number of UCR violent crimes decreased 34%, the number of UCR property crimes decreased 31%, and the number of full-time local police officers increased 17%. Source: Brian A. Reaves and Matthew J. Hickman, *Police Departments in Large Cities, 1990–2000* (Washington, D.C.: Bureau of Justice Statistics, 2002), p. 1.

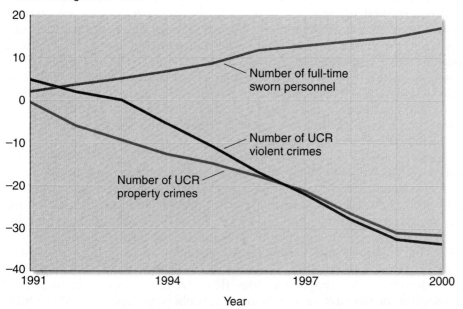

Percent change from 1990

Year

the spillover effect of increasing the effectiveness of the entire justice process.

Using Technology   Police departments have also relied on technology to help guide patrol efforts. The most well-known program, **CompStat,** was begun in New York City as a means of directing police efforts in a more productive fashion.[23] William Bratton, who had been appointed NYC police chief, wanted to revitalize the department and break through its antiquated bureaucratic structures. He installed CompStat, a computerized system that gave local precinct commanders up-to-date information about where and when crime was occurring in their jurisdictions. Part of the CompStat program, twice-weekly "crime-control strategy meetings," brought precinct commanders together with the department's top administrators, who asked them to report on crime problems in their precincts and tell what they are doing to turn things around. Those involved in the strategy sessions had both detailed data and electronic pin maps that showed how crime clustered geographically in the precinct and how patrol officers were being deployed. The CompStat program required local commanders to both demonstrate their intimate knowledge of crime trends and develop strategies to address them effectively. When ideas were presented by the assembled police administrators, the local commanders were required to demonstrate in follow-up sessions how they had incorporated the new strategies in their patrol plan. CompStat proved extremely successful and is generally credited with being a big part of why New York City's crime rate fell dramatically during the past decade.

Criminal Justice ⚖ Now™
*Learn more about by viewing the
"Columbia Arrest" "In the News"
video clip.*

THE INVESTIGATION FUNCTION

Since the first independent detective bureau was established by the London Metropolitan Police in 1841, criminal investigators have been romantic figures vividly portrayed in novels and in movies such as Clint Eastwood's *Dirty Harry* series and Mel Gibson's four *Lethal Weapon* films in which he plays the slightly mad Martin Riggs, who always seems to be shooting down helicopters with a handgun.[24] These fictional detectives shoot first and ask questions later and, when they do conduct an interrogation, think nothing of beating a confession out of the suspect. How accurate are these portrayals? Not very. The modern criminal investigator is most likely an experienced civil servant, trained in investigatory techniques, knowledgeable about legal rules of evidence and procedure, and at least somewhat cautious about the legal and administrative consequences of his or her actions.[25] The character of Gil Grissom—played by actor William Peterson—head of the *Crime Scene Investigation* team, may be a more realistic portrayal of the modern investigator than Dirty Harry. Although detectives are often handicapped by limited time, money, and resources, they are certainly aware of how their actions will one day be interpreted in a court of law.

Investigative services can be organized in a variety of ways. In New York, each borough or district has its own detective division that supervises investigators assigned to neighborhood police precincts (stations). Local squad detectives work closely with patrol officers to provide an immediate investigative response to crimes and incidents. New York City also maintains specialized borough squads—homicide, robbery, and special victims—to give aid to local squads and help identify suspects whose crimes may have occurred in multiple locations. There are also specialty squads that help in areas such as forensics. In smaller cities, detective divisions may be organized into sections or bureaus, such as homicide, robbery, or rape (see Exhibit 6.1).

CompStat A program originated by the New York City police that used carefully collected and analyzed crime data to shape policy and evaluate police effectiveness.

Criminal investigation is a key element of police work. Here, police officers scour a crime scene for evidence during the Washington, D.C., sniper investigation, October 19, 2002. Careful and coordinated detective work resulted in the identification of the snipers and the end to their deadly attacks.

© 2002 AP/World Wide Photos

How Do Detectives Detect?

Detectives investigate the causes of crime and attempt to identify the individuals or groups responsible for committing particular offenses. They may enter a case after patrol officers have made the initial contact, such as when a patrol car interrupts a crime in progress and the offenders flee before they can be apprehended. They can investigate a case entirely on their own, sometimes by following up on leads provided by informants. Sometimes detectives go undercover in order to investigate crime: a lone agent can infiltrate a criminal group or organization to gather information on future criminal activity. Undercover officers can also pose as victims to capture predatory criminals who have been conducting street robberies and muggings.[26]

In his recent study of investigation techniques, Martin Innes found that police detectives rely heavily on interviews and forensic evidence to create or manufacture a narrative of the crime, creating in a sense the "story" that sets out how, where, and why the incident took place.[27] To create their story, contemporary detectives typically use a three-pronged approach:[28]

- *Specific focus.* Interview witnesses, gather evidence, record events, and collect facts that are at the immediate crime scene.
- *General coverage.* (1) Canvass neighborhood and make observations (2); conduct interviews with friends, families, and associates; (3) contact coworkers or employers for information regarding victims and suspects; (4) construct victim/suspect timelines to outline their whereabouts prior to incident.
- *Informative.* Use modern technology to collect records of cell phones and pagers, computer hard drives (palm pilots, laptops, notebooks, desktops, and servers), diaries, notes, and documents. Informative includes data that persons of interest in the investigation use that, in turn, tell about their lives, interactions with others, and geographic connections. (See Concept Summary 6.1.)

Criminal Justice ⚖ Now™

Learn more about **The Investigative Function** *by exploring the* **"Burglary Part 2"** *Role Play activity.*

Exhibit 6.1   Detective bureau organization, Baton Rouge, Louisiana

Division I: Crimes Against Persons

Homicide, Armed Robbery, Juvenile/Sex Crimes, Major Assaults/Missing Persons, Computer Crimes

- The **Homicide** division is responsible for investigating all criminal calls where a death or life-threatening injury has occurred, any officer-involved shooting, or the attempted murder of a police officer.
- The **Armed Robbery** division is responsible for investigating all criminal calls involving all degrees of robbery.
- The **Juvenile/Sex Crimes** division is responsible for maintaining juvenile investigation records, cases of child abuse, and all types of sex crimes.
- The **Major Assaults** division is responsible for investigating a wide range of non-life-threatening felony personal crimes and missing person cases.
- The **Computer Crimes** division investigates crimes committed against persons or computer systems using the Internet, e-mail, or other electronic means.

Division II: Property Crimes

Burglary, Auto/Impound, Forgery, Felony Theft

- The **Burglary** division is responsible for coordinating all follow-up investigations of burglaries, as well as the recovery of stolen property from local pawn shops.
- The **Auto Theft/Impound** division is responsible for conducting follow-up investigations of auto thefts and unauthorized use of movables. The unit also coordinates all records and information relating to vehicles stored and impounded by the department and monitoring local towing services to insure compliance with applicable standards and ordinances.
- The **Forgery division** is responsible for investigating all crimes involving thefts by fraudulent use of access cards, and forgeries of negotiable documents.
- The **Felony Theft** unit is responsible for all felony theft investigations that do not fall under the Auto Theft, Burglary, or Forgery divisions. The office is also responsible for felony damage to property cases. Priority is placed on business embezzlement incidents.

Division III: Investigative Support

Evidence, Crime Scene, Polygraph, Crime Stoppers

- The **Evidence** division is responsible for the collection, storage, cataloguing, and disposition of all evidence and property seized by, or turned in to, the department.
- The **Crime Scene** division is responsible for assisting in investigations by taking photographs, sketching major crime scenes, collecting and tagging evidence, and performing various scientific tests on suspects and/or evidence as needed.
- The **Polygraph** division conducts all polygraph, or lie detector, tests given to recruits, employees, or criminal suspects.
- The **Crime Stoppers** office coordinates all facets of the Crime Stoppers program with local news media, businesses, and the public.

Division IV: Special Operations

Narcotics, School Drug Task Force, State and Federal Liaisons

- The **Narcotics** division is responsible for investigating crimes involving illegal drugs as well as related vice crimes. This division administers the HIDTA and LSP Task Forces.
- The **School Drug Task Force** investigates crimes involving narcotics, explosives and weapons in schools, school buses, and at school-sponsored events within the parish.
- **Liaison Detectives** assigned to outside state and federal agencies work jointly with these agencies to participate in multi-jurisdictional investigations

Source: Baton Rouge Louisiana Police Department, http://brgov.com/dept/brpd/criminal.htm, accessed on May 25, 2005.

Concept Summary 6.1

Investigative techniques

Immediate Specific Focus	Immediate General Coverage	Pending Informative
Specific witnesses	Neighborhood canvass	Cell phone records
Specific evidence	Friends, family, and associates	Computer hard drives
Specific events	Coworkers	Other records
Specific facts	Victim/suspect timelines	Private papers

Sting Operations

Another approach to investigation, commonly referred to as a **sting operation,** involves organized groups of detectives or patrol officers working in plain clothes who deceive criminals into openly committing illegal acts or conspiring to engage in criminal activity.

To sting criminals, some jurisdictions maintain **vice squads,** patrol officers working in plain clothes who focus on crimes of public morals such as prostitution or gambling. For example, female police officers may pose as prostitutes and arrest men who solicit their services.

While sting operations can be highly successful, they are also open to criticism.[29] Covert police activities have often been criticized as violating the personal rights of citizens while forcing officers into demeaning roles. Ironically, recent (2005) research by Mary Dodge and her associates found that rather than considering it demeaning, female officers find their sting work as make-believe prostitutes exciting; they consider it a stepping-stone for promotion.[30]

By its very nature, a sting involves deceit by police agents that often comes close to entrapment. Sting operations may encourage criminals to commit new crimes because they have a new source for fencing stolen goods. Innocent people may hurt their reputations by buying merchandise from a sting operation when they had no idea the items had been stolen. By putting the government into the fencing business, such operations blur the line between law enforcement and criminal activity.

Evaluating Investigations

Serious criticism has been leveled at the nation's detective forces for being bogged down in paperwork and relatively inefficient in clearing cases. One famous study of 153 detective bureaus by the Rand Corporation, a well-known think tank, found that a great deal of a detective's time was spent in unproductive work and that investigative expertise did little to solve cases; half of all detectives could be replaced without negatively influencing crime clearance rates.[31]

Although some question remains about the effectiveness of investigations, police detectives do make a valuable contribution to police work because their skilled interrogation and case-processing techniques are essential to eventual criminal conviction.[32] Nonetheless, a majority of cases that are solved are done so when the perpetrator is identified at the scene of the crime by patrol officers. Research shows that if a crime is reported while in progress, the police have about a 33 percent chance of making an arrest; the arrest probability declines to about 10 percent if the crime is reported one minute later, and to 5 percent if more than fifteen minutes have elapsed. As the time between the crime and the arrest grows, the chances of a conviction are also reduced, probably because the ability to recover evidence is lost. Put another way, once a crime has been

sting operation An undercover police operation in which police pose as criminals to trap law violators.

vice squad Police officers assigned to enforce morality-based laws, such as those on prostitution, gambling, and pornography.

completed and the investigation is put in the hands of detectives, the chances of identifying and arresting the perpetrator diminish rapidly.[33]

One reason for investigation ineffectiveness is that detectives often lack sufficient resources to carry out a lengthy ongoing probe of any but the most serious cases. Research shows the following:

- *Unsolved cases.* Almost 50 percent of burglary cases are screened out by supervisors before assignment to a detective for a follow-up investigation. Of those assigned, 75 percent are dropped after the first day of the follow-up investigation. Although robbery cases are more likely to be assigned to detectives, 75 percent of them are also dropped after one day of investigation.

- *Length of investigation.* The vast majority of cases are investigated for no more than four hours stretching over three days. An average of eleven days elapses between the initial report of a crime and the suspension of the investigation.

- *Sources of information.* Early in an investigation, the focus is on the victim; as the investigation is pursued, emphasis shifts to the suspect. The most critical information for determining case outcome is the name and description of the suspect and related crime information. Victims are most often the source of information; unfortunately, witnesses, informants, and members of the police department are consulted far less often. However, when these sources are tapped, they are likely to produce useful information

- *Effectiveness.* Preliminary investigations by patrol officers are critical. In situations where the suspect's identity is not known immediately after the crime is committed, detectives make an arrest in less than 10 percent of all cases.[34]

Criminal Justice ⚖ Now™

*Learn more about **The Investigative Function** by exploring the "Solving Cases" Review and Reinforce activity.*

Improving Investigations

A number of efforts have been made to revamp and improve investigation procedures. One practice has been to give patrol officers greater responsibility for conducting preliminary investigations at the scene of the crime. Another is to create specialized squads with special expertise in areas such as sex crimes or robbery. Technological advances in DNA and fingerprint identification have also aided investigation effectiveness. The *CSI* series has drawn attention to the developing field of forensics in police work, which uses a variety of sciences, mathematical principles, and problem-solving methods to identify perpetrators, including use of complex instruments and chemical, physical, and microscopic examining techniques. Today, forensic specialists can examine blood and other body fluids and tissues for the presence of alcohol, drugs, and poisons and compare body fluids and hair for typing factors, including DNA analysis. Analysis of a hair found at a crime scene can determine factors such as whether the hair belongs to a human or animal, the body area a hair came from, diseases the person or animal has, and, sometimes, race. Forensic scientists analyze trace physical evidence such as blood spatters, paint, soil, and glass to help reconstruct a crime scene and tell how the crime was committed. In addition to forensics, investigation is being improved by information technology, which allows investigators to compare evidence found at the crime scene with material collected from similar crimes by other police agencies.

Police agencies are now using a program called CopLink to facilitate this time-consuming task. CopLink integrates information from different jurisdictions into a single database that detectives can access when working on investigations.[35] The CopLink program allows investigators to search the entire database of past criminal records and computes a list of possible suspects even if only partial data is available, such as first or last name, partial license plate numbers, vehicle type, vehicle color, location of crime, and/or weapon used.

Detective work may also be improved if investigators are able to spend more time on each case, allowing them to carefully collect physical evidence at the scene of the crime, identify witnesses, check departmental records, and use informants. Research shows that in more serious cases, especially homicide investigations, where detectives are able to devote a lot of attention to a single crime, the likelihood increases that they will eventually be able to identify and arrest the culprit.[36]

COMMUNITY POLICING

For more than thirty years, police agencies have been trying to gain the cooperation and respect of the communities they serve. At first, efforts at improving the relationships between police departments and the public involved programs with the general title of **police-community relations (PCR).** Developed at the station house and departmental levels, these initial PCR programs were designed to make citizens more aware of police activities, alert them to methods of self-protection, and improve general attitudes toward policing.

A critical 1982 paper by George Kelling and James Q. Wilson advocated a new approach to improving police relations in the community, an approach that has come to be known as the **broken windows model.**[37] Kelling and Wilson made three points:

- *Neighborhood disorder creates fear.* Urban areas filled with street people, youth gangs, prostitutes, and the mentally disturbed are the ones most likely to maintain a high degree of crime.[38]

- *Neighborhoods give out crime-promoting signals.* A neighborhood filled with deteriorated housing, broken windows, and untended disorderly behavior gives out crime-promoting signals. Honest citizens live in fear in these areas, and predatory criminals are attracted to them.

- *Police need citizen cooperation.* If police are to reduce fear and successfully combat crime in these urban areas, they must have the cooperation, support, and assistance of the citizens.

According to the broken windows concept, a deteriorated neighborhood, whose residents are fearful, pessimistic, and despondent, is a magnet for crime. In contrast, neighborhoods where residents are civil to one another and where disorder is not tolerated send a different message: criminals are not wanted here, and criminal behavior will not be tolerated. To help achieve neighborhood stability, urban police departments must return to the earlier style of policing, in which officers on the beat had intimate contact with the people they served. Modern police departments generally rely on motorized patrol to cover wide areas, to maintain a visible police presence, and to ensure rapid response time. Although effective and economical, the patrol car removes officers from the mainstream of the community, alienating people who might otherwise be potential sources of information and help to the police.

The broken windows approach holds that police administrators would be well served by deploying their forces where they can encourage public confidence, strengthen feelings of safety, and elicit cooperation from citizens. Community preservation, public safety, and order maintenance—not crime fighting—should become the primary focus of patrol. Put another way, just as physicians and dentists practice preventive medicine and dentistry, police should help maintain an intact community structure rather than simply fight crime.

Criminal Justice ⚖ Now™
*Learn more by going through the **Police and the Community** Learning Module and the **Community Policing** Review and Reinforce activity.*

Criminal Justice ⚖ Now™
Learn more by exploring the "Broken Windows Theory" Review and Reinforce activity.

police-community relations (PCR) Programs developed by police departments to improve relations with the community and develop cooperation with citizens. The forerunner of the community policing model.

broken windows model The term used to describe the role of the police as maintainers of community order and safety.

Information about the Chicago Alternative Policing Strategy (CAPS) can be found at the Chicago Police Department's website. To reach this site go to "Web Links" on your Siegel Essentials of Criminal Justice 5e website: http://cj.wadsworth.com/siegel_ess5e.

foot patrol *Police patrols that take officers out of cars and put them on a walking beat in order to strengthen ties with the community.*

Implementing Community Policing

The community policing concept was originally implemented through a number of innovative demonstration projects.[39] Among the most publicized were experiments in **foot patrol,** which took officers out of cars and set them to walking beats in the neighborhood. Foot patrol efforts were aimed at forming a bond with community residents by acquainting them with the individual officers who patrolled their neighborhood, letting them know that police were caring and available. The first foot patrol experiments were conducted in cities in Michigan and New Jersey. An evaluation of foot patrol indicated that, although it did not bring down the crime rate, residents in areas where foot patrol was added perceived greater safety and were less afraid of crime.[40]

Since the advent of these programs, hundreds of communities have adopted innovative forms of decentralized, neighborhood-based community policing models. The federal government has encouraged the growth of community policing by providing billions of dollars to hire and train officers through its Office of Community Oriented Policing Services (COPS) program, which has given local departments more than $10 billion in aid since its inception.[41] According to the COPS program, community policing initiatives should follow the principles described in Exhibit 6.2.

Recent surveys indicate that there has been a significant increase in community policing activities and that certain core programs such as crime prevention have become embedded in the police role.[42] Community-oriented policing (COP) programs have been implemented in large cities, suburban areas, and rural communities.[43] The community policing concept is not only

Community policing has paid dividends for local police departments. Here, a group of Hispanic students listens to Community Policing Officer Corporal H. Borges, left, and Senior Police Attorney Arnetta Herring, right, June 2, 2003, at the Durham Police Department in Durham, North Carolina, during the Spanish-Speaking Citizens Police Academy. This program was so successful that a second academy was offered in 2004 and again it was met with the same level of community support and enthusiasm within the Durham Latino community. Typical academy sessions have police commanders discussing their core mission and explaining how police efforts support the community. Extensive interaction, discussion, and questions abound with translators assisting, as necessary, in the communication process.

Exhibit	6.2	Key elements of community policing

Organizational Elements

1. **Philosophy adopted organization-wide:** Police departments must integrate community policing concepts within the core of the organization and not treat it as a special program or add-on. Department-wide adoption of community policing is evidenced by the integration of the philosophy into mission statements, policies and procedures, performance evaluations and hiring and promotional practices, training programs, and other systems and activities that define organizational culture and activities.

2. **Decentralized decision-making and accountability:** In community policing, individual line officers are given the authority to solve problems and make operational decisions suitable to their roles, both individually and collectively. Leadership is required and rewarded at every level, with managers, supervisors, and officers held accountable for decisions and the effects of their efforts at solving problems and reducing crime and disorder within the community.

3. **Fixed geographic accountability and generalist responsibilities:** In community policing, the majority of staffing is geographically based. Appropriate personnel are assigned to fixed geographic areas for extended periods of time in order to foster communication and partnerships between individual officers and their community, and are accountable for reducing crime and disorder within their assigned area.

4. **Utilization of volunteer resources:** Community policing encourages the use of non-law-enforcement resources within a law enforcement agency. Examples of such resources might include police reserves, volunteers, Explorer Scouts, service organizations, and citizen or youth police academies.

5. **Enhancers:** There are a number of enhancers and facilitators that may assist departments in their transition to community policing. For example, updated technology and information systems can facilitate community policing by providing officers access to crime and incident data that supports problem analysis or increases uncommitted officer time by reducing time spent on administrative duties.

Tactical Elements

1. **Enforcement of laws:** Though community policing complements the use of proven and established enforcement strategies, emphasis is placed on identifying laws that need to be amended or enacted, then working with lawmakers and organizing citizen support efforts to change them.

2. **Proactive, crime prevention-oriented:** Under community policing, law enforcement focuses on crime prevention and proactively addressing the root causes of crime and disorder. The community actively engages in collaborating on prevention and problem-solving activities with a goal of reducing victimization and fear of crime.

3. **Problem-solving:** Police, community members, and other public and private entities work together to address the underlying problems that contribute to crime and disorder by identifying and analyzing problems, developing suitable responses, and assessing the effectiveness of these responses.

External Elements

1. **Public involvement and community partnerships:** Citizens serve as partners who share responsibility for identifying priorities, and developing and implementing responses. The public has "ownership" of the problem-solving process.

2. **Government, other agency partnerships:** Under community policing, other government agencies are called upon and recognized for their abilities to respond to and address crime and social disorder issues.

Source: The Office of Community Oriented Policing Services, www.cops.usdoj.gov/Default.asp?Item=36, accessed on August 19, 2005.

catching on in the United States; it has captured the interest of police departments around the world.[44] Community policing is being used in numerous countries, including Denmark, Finland, and Great Britain.

There is empirical evidence that some community policing efforts can reduce disorder and impact the crime rate.[45] The most successful programs give officers time to meet with local residents to talk about crime in the neighborhood and to use personal initiative to solve problems.

Although not all programs work (police-community newsletters and cleanup campaigns do not seem to do much good), the overall impression has been that patrol officers can actually reduce the level of fear in the community.

Some COP programs assign officers to neighborhoods, organize training programs for community leaders, and feature a bottom-up approach to deal with community problems: decision-making involves the officer on the scene, not a directive from central headquarters. Others have created programs for juveniles who might ordinarily have little to do other than get involved in gangs but are now directed at such activities as neighborhood cleanup efforts.[46]

Criminal Justice ⚖ Now™

Learn more by exploring the "Role and Function of the Police" Vocabulary Check activity.

CHANGING THE POLICE ROLE

Community policing also stresses sharing power with local groups and individuals. A key element of the community policing philosophy is that citizens must actively participate with police to fight crime.[47] This participation might involve providing information in area-wide crime investigations or helping police reach out to troubled youths. Among the other changes that have been linked to community policing initiatives include:

- *Neighborhood orientation.* To achieve the goals of COP, some police agencies have tried to decentralize, an approach sometimes referred to as **neighborhood-oriented policing (NOP).**[48] According to this view, problem solving is best done at the neighborhood level where issues originate, not at a far-off central headquarters. Because each neighborhood has its own particular needs, police decision-making must be flexible and adaptive. For example, neighborhoods undergoing change in racial composition may experience high levels of racially motivated violence and require special police initiatives to reduce tensions.[49] Some neighborhoods are highly organized and contain citizens who work together to solve problems (a condition known as **collective efficacy**) while others are fragmented and disorganized (anomic). The police must be able to distinguish between these situations and provide appropriate services. In the strong, organized area they might want to work with existing neighborhood groups, while in the anomic area they might want to use aggressive tactics to reduce crime and "take back the streets" before building relations with community leaders.[50]

- *Changing management styles.* Community policing also means the redesign of police departments' administration and management. Management's role must be reordered to focus on the problems of the community, not on the needs of the police department. The traditional vertical police organizational chart must be altered so that top-down management gives way to bottom-up decision-making. The patrol officer becomes the manager of his beat and a key decision-maker.

- *Changing recruitment and training.* Community policing requires that police departments alter their recruitment and training requirements. Future officers must develop community-organizing and problem-solving skills, along with traditional police skills. Their training must prepare them to succeed less on their ability to make arrests or issue citations and more on their ability to solve problems effectively.

Problem-Oriented Policing

Closely associated with yet independent from the community policing concept are **problem-oriented policing** strategies. Traditional police models focus on responding to calls for help in the fastest possible time, dealing with the situation, and then getting on the street again as soon as possible. In contrast, problem-oriented policing is proactive.

Problem-oriented policing strategies require police agencies to identify particular long-term community problems—street-level drug dealers,

neighborhood-oriented policing (NOP) *Community policing efforts aimed at individual neighborhoods.*

collective efficacy *Acting cooperatively to solve neighborhood problems. In neighborhoods that maintain collective efficacy, neighbors are active in informal social control activities.*

problem-oriented policing *A style of police operations that stresses proactive problem solving, rather than reactive crime fighting.*

prostitution rings, gang hangouts—and to develop strategies to eliminate them.[51] As with community policing, police departments must rely on local residents and private resources in order to be problem solvers. This means that police managers must learn how to develop community resources, design cost-efficient and effective solutions to problems, and become advocates as well as agents of reform.[52]

A significant portion of police departments are now using special units to confront specific social problems. Problem-oriented policing models are supported by the evidence that a great deal of urban crime is concentrated in a few "hot spots."[53] A significant portion of all police calls in metropolitan areas typically radiate from a relatively few locations: bars, malls, the bus depot, hotels, and certain apartment buildings.[54] By implication, concentrating police resources on these **hot spots of crime** could appreciably reduce crime.[55]

Problem-oriented strategies are being developed that focus on specific criminal problem areas and/or specific criminal acts. For example, a POP effort in Sarasota, Florida, aimed at reducing prostitution involved intensive, focused, and/or high-visibility patrols to discourage prostitutes and their customers, undercover work to arrest prostitutes and drug dealers, and collaboration with hotel and motel owners to identify and arrest pimps and drug dealers.[56]

Two POP efforts are described below.

Combating Auto Theft Because of problem-oriented approaches (combined with advanced technology), car thieves in many jurisdictions are no longer able to steal cars with as much ease as before. In order to reduce the high number of car thefts occurring each year, some police departments have invested in "bait cars," which are parked in high-theft areas and equipped with technology that alerts law enforcement personnel when someone has stolen the car. A signal goes off when either a door is opened or the engine starts. Then, equipped with Global Positioning Satellite (GPS) technology, police officers are able to watch the movement of the car. Some cars are also equipped with microscopic video and audio recorders, which allow officers to see and hear the suspect(s) within the car, and remote engine and door locks that can trap the thief inside. The technology has been used in conjunction with an advertising campaign to warn potential car thieves about the program. The system has been instituted in Vancouver, Canada, and Minneapolis, Minnesota, with impressive results. Motor vehicle theft dropped over 40 percent in Minneapolis over a three-year period in which bait cars were used and 30 percent in Vancouver within six months of being instituted. In addition to cutting down on auto theft, the system, which costs roughly $3,500 per car, decreases the chance of danger of high-speed pursuits, thereby increasing police officer safety.[57]

Reducing Violence There have been a number of efforts to reduce violence using problem-oriented community policing techniques. Police in Richmond, California, successfully applied problem-oriented policing techniques including citizen involvement to help reduce murder rates.[58] Problem-oriented techniques have also been directed at combating gang related violence. For example, the Tucson police department has created a Gang Tactical Detail, a unit aimed at proactively attacking neighborhood gang problems by targeting known offenders who have shown a propensity toward gang violence or criminal activity. Members of the tactical unit work directly with neighborhood community groups to identify specific gang problems within individual neighborhoods. Once the problem is identified, the unit helps devise a working solution combining community involvement, intergovernmental assistance, and law enforcement intervention. The officers of the Gang Tactical Detail attend meetings with community groups

hot spots of crime Places from which a significant portion of all police calls originate. These hot spots include taverns and housing projects.

to identify gang-related problems. They assist with gang awareness presentations for schools and/or civic groups.[59]

Another well-known program, Operation Ceasefire is a problem-oriented policing intervention aimed at reducing youth homicide and youth firearms violence in Boston. Evaluations of the program found Ceasefire produced significant reductions in youth homicide victimization and gun assault incidents in Boston that were not experienced in other communities in New England or elsewhere in the nation.[60]

Although programs such as these seem successful, the effectiveness of any street-level problem-solving effort must be interpreted with caution.[61] It is possible that the criminals will be displaced to other, "safer" areas of the city and will return shortly after the program is called a success and the additional police forces have been pulled from the area.[62] Nonetheless, evidence shows that merely saturating an area with police may not deter crime, but focusing efforts on a particular problem may have a crime-reducing effect.

The Challenges of Community Policing

The core concepts of police work are changing as administrators recognize the limitations and realities of police work in modern society. If they are to be successful, community policing strategies must be able to react effectively to some significant administrative problems.

Defining Community   Police administrators must be able to define the concept of community as an ecological area defined by common norms, shared values, and interpersonal bonds.[63] After all, the main focus of community policing is to activate the community norms that make neighborhoods more crime resistant. If, in contrast, community policing projects cross the boundaries of many different neighborhoods, any hope of learning and accessing community norms, strengths, and standards will be lost.[64] And even if natural community structures can be identified, it will be necessary for policing agencies to continually monitor the changing norms, values, and attitudes of the community they serve, a process that has the side effect of creating positive interactions between the community and the police.[65]

Defining Roles   Police administrators must also establish the exact role of community police agents. How should they integrate their activities with those of regular patrol forces? For example, should foot patrols have primary responsibility for policing in an area, or should they coordinate their activities with officers assigned to patrol cars? Should community police officers be solely problem identifiers and neighborhood organizers, or should they also be expected to be law enforcement agents who get to the crime scene rapidly and later do investigative work? Can community police teams and regular patrols work together, or must a department abandon traditional police roles and become purely community policing–oriented?

Changing Supervisor Attitudes   Some supervisors are wary of community policing because it supports a decentralized command structure. This would mean fewer supervisors, and consequently, less chance for promotion and a potential loss of authority.[66] It is not surprising, considering these misgivings, that more than a decade after the COP initiative began many police commanders still focus on the core values of order maintenance, crime fighting, and service at the expense of community policing.[67] They still use performance measures such as arrest and response time to evaluate subordinates, which makes it difficult for line-level officers to change their approach toward policing and embrace community policing goals.[68] Conversely, those supervisors who learn to actively embrace community policing concepts are the ones best able to encourage patrol officers to engage in self-initiated activities, including community policing and problem solving.[69]

Reorienting Police Values Research shows that police officers who have a traditional crime control orientation are less satisfied with community policing efforts than those who are public service–oriented.[70] In some instances officers holding traditional values may go as far as stigmatizing their own comrades assigned to community policing; their targets feel penalized by a lack of administrative support.[71]

Although this finding comes as no surprise, it is indicative of the difficulty police managers will face in convincing experienced officers, many of whom hold traditional law-and-order values, to embrace community policing models. Yet, it is unlikely that community policing activities can be successful unless police line officers are able to form a commitment to the values of community policing.[72]

Revise Training Because the community policing model calls for a revision of the police role from law enforcer to community organizer, police training must be revised to reflect this new mandate. If community policing is to be adopted on a wide scale, a whole new type of police officer must be recruited and trained in a whole new way. Retraining and reorienting police from their traditional roles into a more social service orientation may also be difficult. Most police officers do not have the social service skills required of effective community agents. Thus, community policing requires that police departments alter their training requirements. Future officers must develop community-organizing and problem-solving skills, along with traditional police skills.

Their training must prepare them to succeed less on their ability to make arrests or issue citations and more on their ability to solve problems, prevent crime effectively, and deal with neighborhood diversity and cultural values.[73]

Reorient Recruitment To make community policing successful, midlevel managers must be recruited and trained who are receptive to and can implement community-change strategies.[74] The selection of new recruits must be guided by a desire to find individuals with the skills and attitudes that support community policing. They must be open to the fact that community policing will help them gain knowledge of the community, give them opportunities to gain skill and experience, and help them engage in proactive problem solving.[75] Selecting people who find these values attractive and then providing training that accentuates the community vision of policing is essential to the success of the COP model.

Include the Entire Community Critics believe that community policing works best in stable, affluent areas. The challenge of community is to reach out to all people in all neighborhoods, including young people, and minorities who may previously have been left out of the process. As James Forman suggests, crime rate drops, especially declines in youth crime, may help make community policing more inclusive: people who were viewed as potential threats can now be seen as assets.[76]

Overcoming Obstacles

Although these are formidable obstacles to overcome, there is growing evidence that community and problem-oriented policing can work and fit well with traditional forms of policing.[77] Many police experts and administrators have embraced the community and problem-oriented policing concepts as revolutionary revisions of the basic police role. Community policing efforts have been credited with helping reduce crime rates in large cities such as New York and Boston. The most professional and highly motivated officers are the ones most likely to support community policing efforts.[78]

These results are encouraging, but there is no clear-cut evidence that community policing is highly successful at reducing crime or changing the traditional values and attitudes of police officers involved in the programs.[79] Some research does show that the arrest rate actually increases after COP programs have been implemented.[80] However, crime rate reductions in cities that have used COP may be the result of an overall downturn in the nation's crime rate rather than a result of community policing efforts.

Despite these professional obstacles, community policing has become a stable part of municipal police departments. The concept is also being exported around the world with varying degrees of success: while successful in some countries, other nations do not have the stability necessary to support community policing.[81] Where it is used, citizens seem to like community policing initiatives, and those who volunteer and get involved in community crime prevention programs report higher confidence in the police force and its ability to create a secure environment.[82]

Criminal Justice ⚖ Now™

Learn more about **Careers in Criminal Justice** *by exploring the "On the Job" features* **Police Officer** *and* **Bicycle Community Police Officer.**

■ SUPPORT FUNCTIONS

As the model of a typical police department indicates (see again Figure 6.1), not all members of a department engage in what the general public regards as "real police work"—patrol, detection, and traffic control. Even in departments that are embracing community- and problem-oriented policing, a great deal of police resources are actually devoted to support and administrative functions. There are too many tasks to mention in detail, but the most important include those discussed next.

Many police departments maintain their own personnel service, which carries out such functions as recruiting new police officers, creating exams to determine the most qualified applicants, and handling promotions and transfers. Innovative selection techniques are constantly being developed and tested. For example, the Behavioral-Personnel Assessment Device (B-PAD) requires police applicants to view videotaped scenarios and respond as if they were officers handling the situation; reviews indicate that this procedure may be a reliable and unbiased method of choosing new recruits.[83]

Larger police departments often maintain an **internal affairs** branch that is charged with policing the police. Internal affairs units process citizen complaints of police corruption, investigate what may be the unnecessary use of force by police officers, and even probe police participation in actual criminal activity, such as burglaries or narcotics violations. In addition, internal affairs divisions may assist police managers when disciplinary action is brought against individual officers. Internal affairs is a controversial function since investigators are feared and distrusted by fellow police officers. Nonetheless, rigorous self-scrutiny is the only way police departments can earn the respect of citizens. Because of these concerns it has become commonplace for police departments to institute citizen oversight over police practices and put in place civilian review boards that have the power to listen to complaints and conduct investigations. Civilian oversight is the subject of the following Policy, Programs, and Issues in Criminal Justice feature.

Most police departments are responsible for the administration and control of their own budgets. This task includes administering payroll, purchas-

internal affairs *The branch of the police department that investigates charges of corruption or misconduct made against police officers.*

While the media often glamorizes the law enforcement and crime fighting elements of policing, the police officer's role is varied and involves keeping the community safe and hazard-free. Here, a Kansas City, Missouri, police officer directs rush hour traffic at a darkened intersection. Freezing rain had left a heavy coat of ice on trees and power lines, resulting in a loss of power to large parts of the metropolitan area. Traffic control remains a significant part of the police role.

© 2002 AP/World Wide Photos

ing equipment and services, planning budgets for future expenditures, and auditing departmental financial records.

Police departments include separate units that are charged with maintaining and disseminating information on wanted offenders, stolen merchandise, traffic violators, and so on. Modern data management systems enable police to use their records in a highly sophisticated fashion. For example, officers in a patrol car who spot a suspicious-looking vehicle can instantly receive a computerized rundown on whether it has been stolen. Or, if stolen property is recovered during an arrest, police using this sort of system can determine who reported the loss of the merchandise and arrange for its return.

Another important function of police communication is the effective and efficient dispatching of patrol cars. Again, modern computer technologies have been used to make the most of available resources.[84]

Policy, Programs, and Issues in Criminal Justice

Civilian Review Boards

Two Rochester, New York, police officers arrest two young males allegedly for dealing drugs, and during the melee one youth is pushed through a plate glass window. The mother of one claims that these innocent young men were the victims of police brutality; they had merely been walking along the street when the officers approached.

At a hearing, the city's citizen review finds out that the arrestees had drugs in their possession, that the officers had remained polite and professional during the encounter, and that it was actually one of the boys who started the confrontation. The officers were exonerated by the review board.

Citizen oversight of police conduct can be a critical method of improving community relations, but it is also one that has caused conflict with police officers. Nonetheless, there has been a considerable increase in citizen oversight of police in the United States. Today there are slightly more than 100 citizen oversight agencies in the United States. The number continues to grow as new oversight agencies are established.

Typically, there are four models of oversight systems:

- Citizens investigate allegations of police misconduct and recommend a finding to the head of the agency.
- Officers investigate allegations and develop findings. Then, citizens review and recommend that the head of the agency approve or reject the findings.

- Complainants may appeal findings established by the police to citizens who review them and make recommendations to the head of the agency.
- An auditor investigates the process the police uses to accept and investigate complaints and reports to the agency and the community about the thoroughness and fairness of the process.

There are many variations on these basic models. The Minneapolis, Minnesota, civilian police review operates in two stages. First, paid, professional investigators and a director examine citizen complaints to determine if there is reasonable evidence that police misconduct occurred. Then, volunteer board members conduct closed-door hearings to decide whether they should support the allegations that came from the initial screening process in probable cause cases. And in Orange County, Florida, a nine-volunteer citizen review board holds hearings, open to the public and the media, on all cases involving the alleged use of excessive force and abuse of power after the sheriff's department has conducted an investigation.

Although police agencies in some communities have embraced citizen review, others find them troublesome. Departmental opposition is most likely when oversight procedures represent outside interference, oversight staff lack experience with and understanding of police work, and oversight processes are unfair. Most police administrators believe that their agencies should have the final say in matters of discipline,

In many departments, training is continuous throughout an officer's career. Training usually begins at a police academy, which may be run exclusively for larger departments or may be part of a regional training center servicing smaller and varied governmental units. More than 90 percent of all police departments require preservice training, including almost all departments in larger cities (population over one hundred thousand). The average officer receives more than five hundred hours of preservice training, including four hundred hours in the classroom and the rest in field training. Police in large cities receive over one thousand hours of instruction divided almost evenly between classroom and field instruction.[85] Among the topics usually covered are law and civil rights, firearms handling, emergency medical care, and restraint techniques.[86]

policies and procedures, and training, and some bridle at the hint of outside interference by nonprofessionals. In some communities local governments have established oversight bodies that act only in an advisory capacity and make nonbinding recommendations to law enforcement agencies.

Another familiar complaint is that civilians are unable to understand the complexities of police work. To compensate, candidates for the review board in Rochester, New York, attend a condensed version of a police academy run by the police department. The forty-eight-hour course involves three hours per evening for two weeks and two all-day Saturday sessions. The members use a shoot/don't shoot simulator, practice handcuffing, and learn about department policies and procedures, including the use-of-force continuum.

Many officers believe that review members hold them accountable for minor infractions, such as placing the wrong offense code on a citation or failing to record the end mileage on a vehicle transport. There is also the belief that the review process is often lengthy and that delays both harm the credibility of the oversight process and cause officers considerable stress as they wait for their cases to be decided. To overcome these problems, some police administrators have taken the initiative by helping to set up a citizen oversight system before being required to do so and then becoming involved in the planning process.

Despite serious reservations about citizen oversight, many law enforcement administrators have identified positive outcomes from having a review board in place. These include improving community relations, enhancing an agency's ability to police itself, and most important, improving an agency's policies and procedures. Citizen oversight bodies can recommend changes in the way the department conducts its internal investigation into alleged misconduct and also to improve department policies governing officer behavior.

Critical Thinking

1. Research conducted by Liqun Cao and Bu Huang shows that having a civilian review board is not a panacea that eliminates or significantly reduces citizen complaints. One reason is police resistance to civilian oversight. If you were the chief of police, would you want civilians to oversee how you ran your department or handled citizen complaints?

2. If you were the head of a civilian review board, how would you get the local police to accept your authority?

InfoTrac College Edition Research

Should there be civilian oversight over police? For one viewpoint, read Sidney L. Harring, "The Diallo Verdict: Another Tragic Accident in New York's War on Street Crime?" *Social Justice* 27 (2000): 9.

Sources: Samuel Walker, *Police Accountability: The Role of Citizen Oversight* (Belmont, Calif.: Wadsworth, 2001); Liqun Cao and Bu Huang, "Determinants of Citizen Complaints Against Police Abuse of Power," *Journal of Criminal Justice* 28 (2000): 203–213; Peter Finn, "Getting Along with Citizen Oversight," *FBI Law Enforcement Bulletin* 69 (2000): 22–27; Best Practices in Police Accountability website www.policeaccountability.org/issuefacts.htm, accessed on June 1, 2005.

After assuming their police duties, new recruits are assigned to field-training officers who break them in on the job. However, training does not stop here. On-the-job training is a continuous process in the modern police department and covers such areas as weapons skills, first aid, crowd control, and community relations. Some departments use roll call training, in which superior officers or outside experts address police officers at the beginning of the workday. Other departments allow police officers time off to attend annual training sessions to sharpen their skills and learn new policing techniques.

Police departments provide emergency aid to the ill, counsel youngsters, speak to school and community agencies on safety and drug abuse, and provide countless other services designed to improve citizen-police interactions.

Larger police departments maintain specialized units that help citizens protect themselves from criminal activity. They advise citizens on effective home security techniques or conduct Project ID campaigns—engraving valuables with an identifying number so that they can be returned if recovered after a burglary; police also work in schools teaching kids how to avoid drug use.[87] Police agencies maintain (or have access to) forensic laboratories that enable them to identify substances to be used as evidence and to classify fingerprints.

Planning and research functions include designing programs to increase police efficiency and strategies to test program effectiveness. Police planners monitor recent technological developments and institute programs to adapt them to police services.

SUMMARY

- Today's police departments operate in a military-like fashion; policy generally emanates from the top of the hierarchy.
- The most common law enforcement agencies are local police departments, which carry out patrol and investigative functions, as well as many support activities.
- Many questions have been raised about the effectiveness of police work. While some research efforts seem to indicate that police are not effective crime fighters, there is evidence that aggressive police work, the threat of formal action, and cooperation between departments can have a measurable impact on crime.
- Recent research indicates that adding police can help reduce crime rates.

- For some crimes, making arrests can help reduce criminal activity.
- There is little evidence that detectives solve many crimes.
- To improve effectiveness, police departments have developed new methods of policing that stress community involvement and problem solving.
- Community policing typically involves programs with law enforcement and community involvement.
- Police agencies face many challenges in transforming themselves into community-based problem solvers.
- Police departments contain many sub-areas, including training, communications, personnel, and other administrative systems.

KEY TERMS

police chief 150
time-in-rank system 150
order maintenance (peacekeeping) 153
proactive policing 154
deterrent effect 154
CompStat 158

sting operation 161
vice squad 161
police-community relations (PCR) 163
broken windows model 163
foot patrol 164

neighborhood-oriented policing (NOP) 166
collective efficacy 166
problem-oriented policing 166
hot spots of crime 167
internal affairs 170

REVIEW QUESTIONS

1. Should the primary police role be law enforcement or community service? Explain.

2. Should a police chief be permitted to promote an officer with special skills to a supervisory position, or should all officers be forced to spend "time in rank"? Why or why not?

3. Do the advantages of proactive policing outweigh the disadvantages? Explain.

4. Should all police recruits take the same physical tests, or are different requirements permissible for male and female applicants? Explain.

5. Can the police and the community ever form a partnership to fight crime? Why or why not? Does the community-policing model remind you of early forms of policing? Explain.

CHAPTER **7**

Issues in Policing: Professional, Social, and Legal

© 2005 AP/Wide World Photos

JEFF CZARNEC'S career with the Manchester, New Hampshire, police department involved a variety of different positions. During his more than two decades on the force, he served as an investigator assigned to the Juvenile Division, a public relations specialist, and a patrol and narcotics/vice investigator. His final assignment, as detective charged with managing and investigating all incidents and crimes against the elderly, was the assignment that proved to be the most challenging, taxing his abilities and requiring the greatest amount of time, energy, and commitment.

A typical day produced a wide variety of tasks. Along with the other day-shift detectives, Czarnec's tour of duty opened with a review of the previous day's reports and activities. Each and every report involving a victim aged fifty-five and older received his personal attention regard-

Chapter Outline

Chapter Objectives

1. Describe how the role of women in local police agencies has evolved over time
2. Discuss some of the problems of minority police officers
3. Be familiar with the concept of a police culture
4. Recognize the different types of police officer style
5. Be familiar with how police use discretion
6. Be able to discuss the issue of "racial profiling"
7. Know what is meant by "police stress"
8. Identify the problems of police use of violence and discuss different methods used to control the police use of force
9. Explain the concept of police corruption
10. Be familiar with search and seizure, interrogation, and the exclusionary rule

less of the incident or crime. These reported incidents ranged from the relatively minor to major cases such as financial exploitation involving losses in the millions of dollars, assaults resulting in injury or death, armed robberies, burglaries, and identity theft.

Czarnec attacked each case using a three-pronged approach:

- *Limit revictimization.* Using such techniques as mediation between offender and victim, or teaching victims how to protect themselves, Czarnec's first goal was to reduce the danger faced by the elderly client.

- *Provide support.* Czarnec established short- and long-term support for the elder victim via a trusted family member or friend, or barring that, by involving them with one of the various agencies entrusted with elder care such as Health and Human Services.

- *Aggressively pursue the case.* Czarnec sought to ensure resolution and closure for the elder victim in criminal court.

Helping the elderly provided the greatest satisfaction he derived during his law enforcement career. In addition to being involved with law enforcement issues, Jeff Czarnec currently teaches at Hesser College in Manchester, New Hampshire.

Police officers such as Jeff Czarnec must make critical decisions every day. They serve as the gatekeepers of the criminal justice process. They initiate contact with law violators and decide whether to formally arrest them and start their journey through the criminal justice system, settle the issue in an informal way (such as by issuing a warning), or simply take no action at all. The strategic position of law enforcement officers, their visibility and contact with the public, and their use of weapons and arrest power make police the most visible and controversial element of the criminal justice system.

During the politically charged 1960s, critics viewed police agencies as biased organizations that harassed minority citizens and stalked political dissidents. Since that tumultuous period, major efforts were undertaken in the nation's largest cities to curb police power. A great deal of progress has been made, though police agencies tend to be traditional organizations and resistant to change at the whim of public perceptions and attitudes.[1] Public concern over police behavior, fed by intense media scrutiny of police departments as well as individual police officers, has forced commanders to become more sensitive to their public image. Programs have been created to improve relations between police and community—to help police officers on the beat be more sensitive to the needs of the public and cope more effectively with the stress of their jobs. Police officers have also become better educated and are now attending programs in criminology and criminal justice in large numbers. After graduation they seem willing to stay on the job and contribute their academic experiences to improve police performance and enhance police-community relationships.[2]

Most citizens seem to approve of their local law enforcement agents; when surveyed, about two-thirds say they have a "great deal of confidence" in the police.[3] Although this is encouraging, approval is often skewed along racial lines. Surveys show that about 40 percent of African Americans give high marks compared to 70 percent of Caucasians. Minority citizens seem to be affected more adversely than whites when well-publicized incidents of police misconduct occur.[4] Compounding the problem is the fact that police behavior is now more visible than ever before because it is commonly captured on video; when police make the local news, these real accounts of the use of force can have an extremely negative impact on public perceptions of police behavior, especially in the minority community.[5] Race relations and racial profiling will be covered later in the chapter.

These developments are not lost on police officers, many of whom feel significant amounts of job-related stress, a condition which may lead them to develop negative attitudes and lose enthusiasm and commitment for the job.[6] There is evidence that police officers are all too often involved in marital disputes and even incidents of domestic violence, which may be linked to stress.[7] Stress and burnout become part of the job.[8] So is violence and danger: The latest data (2004) show that about 50 officers are feloniously killed in the line of duty and another 80 die in job-related accidents.[9] About half of the officers were killed while making arrests or conducting a traffic stop. There is good reason then for police officers to sometimes feel stress and anxiety.

This chapter focuses on these and other problems facing police officers in contemporary society. It looks at issues police face on the job, in court, and in society. We begin with a discussion of the makeup of the police and the police profession.

WHO ARE THE POLICE?

The composition of the nation's police forces is changing. Less than 50 years ago, police agencies were composed primarily of white males with a high school education who viewed policing as a secure position that brought them the respect of family and friends and took them a step up the social ladder. It was not uncommon to see police families in which one member of each new generation would enter the force. This picture has been changing and will continue to change. As criminal justice programs turn out thousands of graduates every year, an increasing number of police officers have at least some college education. In addition, affirmative action programs have slowly helped change the racial and gender composition of police departments to reflect community makeup. The following sections explore these changes in detail.

Demographic Makeup

With few exceptions the personnel in most early police departments were white and male, a condition that persisted through most of the twentieth century. However, the image of the police department as a bastion of white male dominance is either over or rapidly changing. For more than thirty years, U.S. police departments have made a concerted effort to attract women and minority police officers, and there have been some impressive gains.[10] From 1987 to 2000, minority representation among local police officers increased from 14.5 percent to 22.7 percent. In sheriffs' offices, minorities accounted for 17.1 percent of sworn personnel in 2000 compared to 13.4 percent in 1987. Women now make up more than 10 percent of police personnel (see Figure 7.1).

The reasons behind this effort are varied. Viewed in its most positive light, diversity initiatives by police departments are intended to field a more balanced force that truly represents the communities they serve. A heterogeneous police force can be instrumental in gaining the confidence of the community by helping dispel the view that police departments are generally bigoted or biased organizations.[11] Furthermore, women and minority police officers possess special qualities that can serve to improve police performance. Spanish-speaking officers can help with investigations in Hispanic neighbor-

Criminal Justice ⚖ Now ™
*Learn more about **Careers in Criminal Justice** by exploring the "On the Job" feature **Sr. Deputy Sheriff.***

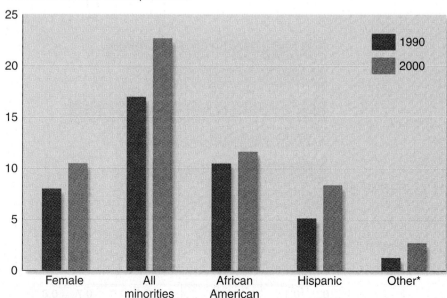

Percent of full-time sworn personnel

*Includes Asians, Pacific Islanders, American Indians, and Alaska Natives.

Figure 7.1
Female and minority local police officers, 1990 and 2000
Source: Matthew J. Hickman and Brian A. Reaves, *Local Police Departments 2000* (Washington, D.C.: Bureau of Justice Statistics, Law Enforcement Management and Administrative Statistics, 2003), p. 111.

hoods, while Asian officers are essential for undercover or surveillance work with Asian gangs and drug importers.

Criminal Justice☺Now™

Learn more by exploring the "Ratio of Minority Officers to the Minority Populations" Animated Artwork.

Minority Police Officers

The earliest known date of when an African American was hired as a police officer was 1861 in Washington, D.C.; Chicago hired its first African-American officer in 1872.[12] By 1890 an estimated two thousand minority police officers were employed in the United States. At first, African-American officers suffered a great deal of discrimination. Their work assignments were restricted, as were their chances for promotion. Minority officers were often assigned solely to the patrol of African-American neighborhoods, and in some cities they were required to call a white officer to make an arrest. White officers held highly prejudicial attitudes, and as late as the 1950s some refused to ride with African Americans in patrol cars.[13]

The experience of African-American police officers has not been an easy one. In his classic 1969 book, *Black in Blue*, Nicholas Alex pointed out that African-American officers of the time suffered from what he called **double marginality.**[14] On the one hand, African-American officers had to deal with the expectation that they would give members of their own race a break. On the other hand, they often experienced overt racism from their police colleagues. Alex found that African-American officers adapted to these pressures in a range of ways, from denying that African-American suspects should be treated differently from whites to treating African-American offenders more harshly than white offenders in order to prove their lack of bias. Alex offered several reasons why some African-American officers are tougher on African-American offenders: they desire acceptance from their white colleagues; they are particularly sensitive to any disrespect given them by African-American teenagers; and they view themselves as protectors of the African-American community. Ironically, minority citizens may actually be more likely to accuse a minority officer of misconduct than white officers, a circumstance that underscores the difficult position of the minority officer in contemporary society.[15]

However, these issues have become more muted as the number of minority officers has increased. Between 1990 and 2000 in larger cities (with populations over 250,000) Hispanic representation among officers increased from 9 percent to 14 percent, and African-American representation rose from 18 percent to 20 percent.[16] As Figure 7.2 shows, the ratio of minority police officers to minority population has been increasing over the past decade.

double marginality The social burden African-American police officers carry by being both minority group members and law enforcement officers.

Figure 7.2
Ratio of minority officers to the minority population, 1990–2000
Source: Brian A. Reaves and Matthew J. Hickman, *Police Departments in Large Cities, 1990–2000* (Washington, D.C.: Bureau of Justice Statistics, 2002).

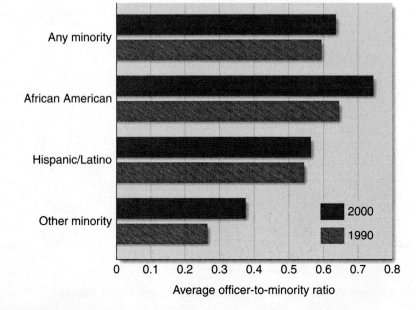

Average officer-to-minority ratio

Minority police officers now seem as self-assured as white officers.[17] They may, if anything, be more willing to use their authority to take official action than white officers: the higher the percentage of black officers on the force, the higher the arrest rate for crimes such as assault.[18] Minority officers appear to be experiencing some of the same problems and issues encountered by white officers.[19] For example, minority officers report feeling similar or somewhat higher rates of job-related stress and strain than white officers.[20] They deal with stress in a somewhat different fashion. Minority officers are more likely to deal with stress by seeking aid from fellow minority officers, whereas white officers are more likely to try to express their feelings to others, form social bonds, and try to get others to like them better.[21]

African-American and white police officers share similar attitudes toward community policing, although minority officers report being even more favorable to it than white officers.[22] African-American officers today may be far less detached and alienated from the local community than white or Hispanic officers.[23]

Women in Policing

In 1910, Alice Stebbins Wells became the first woman to hold the title of police officer (in Los Angeles) and to have arrest powers.[24] For more than half a century, female officers endured separate criteria for selection, were given menial tasks, and were denied the opportunity for advancement.[25] Some relief was gained with the passage of the 1964 Civil Rights Act and its subsequent amendments. Courts have consistently supported the addition of women to police forces by striking down entrance requirements that eliminated almost all female candidates but could not be proven to predict job performance, such as height and upper-body strength.[26] Women do not do as well as men on strength tests and are much more likely to fail the entrance physical than male recruits; critics contend that many of these tests do not reflect the actual tasks of police on the job.[27] Nonetheless, the role of women in police work is still restricted by social and administrative barriers that have been difficult to remove. Today, about 16 percent of all sworn officers in larger cities (with populations over 250,000) are women; in all, about 10 percent of sworn officers are female.[28]

Studies of policewomen indicate that they are still struggling for acceptance, believe that they do not receive equal credit for their job performance, and report that it is common for them to be sexually harassed by their co-workers.[29] One reason for this may be that many male police officers tend to view policing as an overtly masculine profession that is not appropriate for women. Surveys of male officers show that many do not think that women can handle the physical requirements of the job as well as men can.[30] Female police officers may also be targeted for more disciplinary action by administrators and, if cited, are more likely to receive harsher punishments than male officers—that is, a greater percentage receive punishments more severe than a reprimand.[31] Considering the sometimes hostile reception they get from male colleagues and supervisors, it may not come as a surprise that female officers report significantly higher levels of job-related stress than male officers.[32]

© Topical Press Agency/Getty Images

Alice Stebbins Wells of the Los Angeles Police Department, one of the first policewomen in the world, January 1, 1912.

Gender bias is certainly not supported by existing research on job performance that indicates that female officers are highly successful police officers.[33] Research shows that women were more likely than their male colleagues to receive support from the community and less likely to be charged with improper conduct. Because female officers seem to have the ability to avoid violent encounters with citizens and to deescalate potentially violent arrest situations, they are typically the target of fewer citizen complaints.[34]

Minority Women African-American women, who account for less than 5 percent of police officers, occupy a unique status. In a study of African-American policewomen serving in five large municipal departments, Susan Martin found that they do in fact perceive significantly more discrimination than both other female officers and African-American male officers.[35] However, white policewomen were significantly more likely to perceive sexual discrimination than African-American policewomen were.

Martin found that African-American policewomen often incur the hostility of both white women and African-American men, who feel threatened that they will take their place. On patrol, African-American policewomen are treated differently than are white policewomen by male officers. Neither group of women are viewed as equals: white policewomen are more likely to be seen as protected and coddled, whereas African-American policewomen are more likely to be viewed as passive, lazy, and unequal. In the station house, male officers show little respect for African-American women, who face "widespread racial stereotypes as well as outright racial harassment."[36] African-American women also report having difficult relationships with African-American male officers; their relationships are strained by tensions and dilemmas "associated with sexuality and competition for desirable assignments and promotions."[37] Surprisingly, there was little unity among the female officers. Martin concludes: "Despite changes in the past two decades, the idealized image of the representative of the forces of 'law and order' and protector who maintains 'the thin blue line' between 'them' and 'us' remains white and male."[38]

Despite these problems, the future of women in policing grows brighter every year.[39] Female officers want to remain in policing because it pays a good salary, offers job security, and is a challenging and exciting occupation.[40] These factors should continue to bring women to policing for years to come.

Criminal Justice ⚖ Now™

Learn more by exploring the Education in Law Enforcement Review and Reinforce activity.

Educational Characteristics

Though most law enforcement agencies still do not require recruits to have a college degree, the number requiring advanced education in the hiring and promotion process is growing. Surveys show that about 15 percent of local police departments and 11 percent of sheriffs' offices have required some college education for new officers.[41] Larger police departments are more likely to require education; between 1990–2000 the percentage of departments requiring new officers to have at least some college rose from 19 percent to 37 percent, and the percent requiring a two-year or four-year degree grew from 6 percent to 14 percent.[42] Another promising trend was this: although not requiring college credits for promotion, 82 percent of the departments recognized that college education is an important element in promotion decisions. The U.S. is not alone in this regard; police departments around the world are now encouraging recruits and in-service officers to gain college credits.[43]

For what type of major are police departments looking? About half the surveyed departments expressed a preference for criminal justice majors, most often because of their enhanced knowledge of the entire criminal justice system and issues in policing.

What are the benefits of higher education for police officers? Better communication with the public, especially minority and ethnic groups, is believed to be one benefit. Educated officers write better and more clearly and are more likely to be promoted. Police administrators believe that education enables officers to perform more effectively, generate fewer citizen complaints, show more initiative in performing police tasks, and generally act more professionally.[44] In addition, educated officers are less likely to have disciplinary problems and are viewed as better decision makers.[45] Studies have shown that college-educated police officers generate fewer citizen complaints and have better behavioral and performance characteristics than their less-educated peers; higher education is associated with greater self-confidence and assurance.[46]

Though education has its benefits, there is little conclusive evidence that educated officers are more effective crime fighters.[47] The diversity of the police role, the need for split-second decision making, and the often boring and mundane tasks police are required to do are all considered reasons why formal education may not improve performance on the street.[48] However, as the police role evolves from reactive crime fighter to active community change agent, it is likely that the trend toward having a more educated police force will continue.[49]

Criminal Justice⚖Now™
Learn more by exploring the Field Training Review and Reinforce activity.

THE POLICE PROFESSION

All professions have unique characteristics that distinguish them from other occupations and institutions. Policing is no exception. Police experts have long sought to understand the unique nature of the police experience and to determine how the challenges of police work shape the field and its employees. In this section, some of the factors that make policing unique are discussed in detail.

Criminal Justice⚖Now™
Learn more by going through the Police Operations Learning Module.

© 2005 AP/Wide World Photos

Law enforcement is a profession no different than medicine, law, or accounting. Its constituent members must deal with the day-to-day issues that confront them in their work environment. Here, San Diego police officers stand in support of their union representative during a city council meeting May 16, 2005. SDPD officers are wondering how they will meet their financial commitments if they are forced to take a 6.5 percent pay cut to help the city out of its financial crisis.

The Police Culture

Police experts have found that the experience of becoming a police officer and the nature of the job itself cause most officers to band together in a police subculture, characterized by **cynicism,** clannishness, secrecy, and insulation from others in society—the so-called **blue curtain.** Police officers tend to socialize with one another and believe that their occupation cuts them off from relationships with civilians. Joining the police subculture means always having to stick up for fellow officers against outsiders, maintaining a tough, macho exterior personality, and distrusting the motives and behavior of outsiders.[50] The code of silence demands that officers never turn in their peers even if they engage in corrupt or illegal practices.[51]

Some police experts have written of the core beliefs as being the heart of the police culture today:

- *Police are the only real crime fighters.* The public wants the police officer to fight crime; other agencies, both public and private, only play at crime fighting.

- *No one else understands the real nature of police work.* Lawyers, academics, politicians, and the public in general have little concept of what it means to be a police officer.

- *Loyalty to colleagues counts above everything else.* Police officers have to stick together because everyone is out to get the police and make the job more difficult.

- *It is impossible to win the war against crime without bending the rules.* Courts have awarded criminal defendants too many civil rights.

- *Members of the public are basically unsupportive and unreasonably demanding.* People are quick to criticize police unless they need police help themselves.

- *Patrol work is the pits.* Detective work is glamorous and exciting.[52]

The forces that support a police culture generally are believed to develop out of on-the-job experiences. Most officers, both male and female, originally join police forces because they want to help people, fight crime, and have an interesting, exciting, prestigious career with a high degree of job security.[53] Recruits often find that the social reality of police work does not mesh with their original career goals. They are unprepared for the emotional turmoil and conflict that accompany police work today.

Some experts fear that the police culture will divide officers from the people they serve and create an "us against the world" mentality, an independent police culture in which law violations may result in stigmatization and leveling of sanctions against those who occupy the "other" status.[54] Criminals are referred to as "terrorists" and "predators," terms that convey the fact that they are evil individuals ready to prey upon the poor and vulnerable. This vision may encourage and promote violence and brutality.

While at first glance the existence of an independent police subculture seems damaging, it may also have some benefits. Membership in the police culture helps recruits adjust to the rigors of police work and provides the emotional support needed for survival.[55] The culture encourages decisiveness in the face of uncertainty and the ability to make split-second judgments that may later be subject to extreme criticism. Officers who view themselves as *crime fighters* are the ones most likely to value solidarity and depend on the support and camaraderie of their fellow officers.[56] The police subculture encourages its members to draw a sharp distinction between good and evil. Officers, more than mere enforcers of the law, are warriors in the age-old battle between right and wrong.[57] Police officers perceive their working environment to be laden with danger; perception of danger has a unifying effect on officers.[58] And because criminals—"predators"—represent a real danger, the

Criminal Justice ⚖ Now™
Learn more about Police Subculture by exploring the Review and Reinforce activity.

cynicism *The belief that most people's actions are motivated solely by personal needs and selfishness.*

blue curtain *The secretive, insulated police culture that isolates officers from the rest of society.*

police culture demands that its members be both competent and concerned with the safety of their peers and partners.[59]

In sum, the police culture has developed in response to the insulated, dangerous lifestyle of police officers. Policing is a dangerous occupation, and the unquestioned support and loyalty of their peers is not something officers could readily do without.[60] While it is feared that an independent police culture may isolate police officers from the community and make them suspicious and mistrustful of the public they serve, it may also unify the police and improve the camaraderie and solidarity among their fellow officers.

The Police Personality

To some commentators, the typical police personality can be described as dogmatic, authoritarian, and suspicious.[61] Cynicism has been found at all levels of policing, including chiefs of police, and throughout all stages of a police career.[62] These negative values and attitudes are believed to cause police officers to be secretive and isolated from the rest of society, producing the blue curtain.[63]

How does cynicism develop? The police officer's working personality is shaped by constant exposure to danger and the need to use force and authority to reduce and control threatening situations.[64] Police feel suspicious of the public they serve and defensive about the actions of their fellow officers. There are two opposing viewpoints on the cause of this phenomenon. One position holds that police departments attract recruits who are by nature cynical, authoritarian, secretive, and so on.[65] Other experts maintain that socialization and experience on the police force itself cause these character traits to develop in officers. According to this view, as their experiences in the separate police culture develops, officers eventually embrace a unique set of personality traits that distinguishes them from the average citizen.[66]

In his classic study of police personality, *Behind the Shield* (1967), Arthur Neiderhoffer examined the assumption that as a function of their daily duties most police officers develop a personality base dominated by cynicism and mistrust.[67] Among his most important findings were that police cynicism did increase with length of service and that military-like police academy training caused new recruits to quickly become cynical about themselves.[68] Neiderhoffer found that rather being born that way, a police officer's personality was a product of police culture and training.

Despite popular belief and some research support, efforts to find and identify a classic "police personality" have been mixed. Although some research concludes that police values are different from those of the general adult population, other efforts reach an opposite conclusion; some have found that police officers are actually more psychologically healthy than the general population, less depressed and anxious, and more social and assertive.[69] Police officers have been found to value such personality traits as warmth, flexibility, and emotion; these qualities are far removed from rigidity and cynicism.[70] Since research has found evidence supportive of both viewpoints, no one position dominates on the issue of how the police personality develops, or even if one actually exists.

Policing Style

Policing encompasses a multitude of diverse tasks, including peacekeeping, criminal investigation, traffic control, and providing emergency medical service. Part of the socialization as a police officer is developing a working attitude, or style, through which to approach policing. For example, some police officers may view the job as a well-paid civil service position that stresses careful compliance with written departmental rules and procedures. Other officers may see themselves as part of the "thin blue line" that protects

Criminal Justice ⚖ Now™

*Learn more about **Police Operations** by exploring the "Drug Bust Part 2" Role Play activity.*

the public from wrongdoers. They will use any means to get the culprit, even if it involves such cheating as planting evidence on an obviously guilty person who has so far escaped arrest. Should the police bend the rules to protect the public? This has been referred to as the "Dirty Harry problem," after the popular Clint Eastwood movie character who routinely (and successfully) violated all known standards of police work.[71]

Several studies have attempted to define and classify police styles into behavioral clusters. These classifications, called *typologies,* attempt to categorize law enforcement agents by groups, each with a unique approach to police work. The purpose of such classifications is to demonstrate that the police are not a cohesive, homogeneous group, as many believe, but rather are individuals with differing approaches to their work.[72] The way police approach their task and their attitude toward the police role, as well as toward their peers and superior officers, have been shown to affect police work.[73]

An examination of the literature suggests that four styles of police work seem to fit the current behavior patterns of most police agents: the crime fighter, the social agent, the law enforcer, and the watchman. These are described in Exhibit 7.1.

Exhibit   7.1   The four basic styles of policing

The Crime Fighter

To the crime fighter, the most important aspect of police work is investigating serious crimes and apprehending criminals. Crime fighters focus on the victim and view effective police work as the only force that can keep society's "dangerous classes" in check. They are the "thin blue line" protecting society from murderers and rapists. They consider property crimes to be less significant, and believe that such matters as misdemeanors, traffic control, and social service functions would be better handled by other agencies of government. The ability to investigate criminal behavior that poses a serious threat to life and safety, combined with the power to arrest criminals, separates a police department from other municipal agencies. Crime fighters see diluting these functions with minor social service and nonenforcement duties as harmful to police efforts to create a secure society.

The Social Agent

The social agent believes that police should be involved in a wide range of activities without regard for their connection to law enforcement. Rather than viewing themselves as "criminal catchers," the social agents consider themselves as community problem solvers. They are troubleshooters who patch the holes that appear where the social fabric wears thin. They are happy to work with special-needs populations, such as the homeless, school kids, and those in need of emergency services. The social agent fits well in a community policing unit.

The Law Enforcer

According to this officer's view, duty is clearly set out in law. The law enforcer stresses playing it "by the book." Since the police are specifically charged with apprehending all types of lawbreakers, they see themselves as generalized law enforcement agents. Although law enforcers may prefer working on serious crimes—because they are more intriguing and rewarding in terms of achievement, prestige, and status—they see the police role as one of enforcing all statutes and ordinances. They perceive themselves neither as community social workers nor vengeance-seeking vigilantes; quite simply, they are professional law enforcement officers who perform the functions of detecting violations, identifying culprits, and taking the lawbreakers before a court. The law enforcer is devoted to the profession of police work and is the officer most likely to aspire to command rank.

The Watchman

The watchman style is characterized by an emphasis on maintaining public order as the police goal, rather than law enforcement or general service. Watchmen choose to ignore many infractions and requests for service unless they believe that the social or political order is jeopardized. Juveniles are "expected" to misbehave and are best ignored or treated informally. Motorists will often be left alone if their driving does not endanger or annoy others. Vice and gambling are problems only when the currently accepted standards of public order are violated. Like the watchman of old, this officer only takes action when and if a problem arises. The watchman is the most passive officer, more concerned with retirement benefits than crime rates.

Sources: William Muir, *Police: Streetcorner Politicians* (Chicago: University of Chicago Press, 1977); James Q. Wilson, *Varieties of Police Behavior* (Cambridge, Mass.: Harvard University Press, 1968).

Do Police Styles Actually Exist? Although officers who embrace a particular style of policing may emphasize one area of law enforcement over another, their daily activities will likely require them to engage in police duties they consider to be trivial or unimportant. Although some pure types exist, an officer probably cannot specialize in one area of policing while ignoring the others.[74]

It is possible that today's police officer is more of a generalist than ever before and that future police recruits will be required to engage in a great variety of police tasks.

POLICE DISCRETION

Style and role orientation may influence how police officers carry out their duties and the way they may use their **discretion.**[75] Police have the ability to deprive people of their liberty, arrest them and take them away in handcuffs, and even use deadly force to subdue them. A critical aspect of this professional responsibility is the personal discretion each officer has in carrying out his daily activities. Discretion can involve the selective enforcement of the law—as when a vice squad plainclothes officer decides not to take action against a tavern that is serving drinks after hours. Patrol officers use discretion when they decide to arrest one suspect for disorderly conduct but escort another home.

The majority of police officers use a high degree of personal discretion in carrying out daily tasks, sometimes referred to as *low-visibility decision making* in criminal justice.[76] This terminology suggests that, unlike members of almost every other criminal justice agency, police are neither regulated in their daily procedures by administrative scrutiny nor subject to judicial review (except when their behavior clearly violates an offender's constitutional rights). The public recognizes the right of police to use their discretion even if it means using force to control an unruly suspect while treating a more respectful one with deference and respect.[77]

The following sections describe the factors that influence police discretion and review suggestions for its control.

Legal Factors

Police discretion is inversely related to the severity of the offense. There is far less personal discretion available when police confront a suspect in a case involving murder or rape than there is with a simple assault or trespass. The likelihood of a police officer taking legal action then may depend on how the individual views the severity of the offense.

The perception of offense seriousness may be influenced by the relationship between the parties involved. An altercation between two friends or relatives may be handled differently than an assault on a stranger. Domestic violence cases are known to involve significant discretion. Police are reluctant to respond to these kinds of cases, intentionally delaying intervention in the hope that by the time they get there the problem will be settled.[78] Victims, they believe, are weak and needy people who fail to get help or change their abusive situation.[79] If, however, domestic abuse involves extreme violence, especially if a weapon is brandished or used, police are much more likely to respond with a formal arrest.[80] Police, therefore, use their discretion to separate what they consider nuisance cases from those serious enough to demand police action.

Criminal Justice⚖Now™
Learn more by going through the
Discretion *Learning Module.*

 How do police use discretion and what can be done to control behaviors that violate community standards? The answer to these questions may be found in a publication of the National Institute of Justice entitled ***"Broken Windows" and Police Discretion,*** by criminologist George Kelling. To reach this site go to "Web Links" on your Siegel Essentials of Criminal Justice 5e website: http://cj.wadsworth.com/siegel_ess5e.

discretion *The use of personal decision making and choice in carrying out operations in the criminal justice system. For example, police discretion can involve the decision to make an arrest; prosecutorial discretion can involve the decision to accept a plea bargain.*

Environmental Factors

The degree of discretion an officer will exercise is at least partially defined by the officer's living and working environment.[81] Police officers may work or dwell in a community culture that either tolerates eccentricities and personal freedoms or expects extremely conservative, professional, no-nonsense behavior on the part of its civil servants. Communities that are proactive and contain progressive governmental institutions also may influence a police officer's discretion. Police officers in communities that provide training in domestic violence prevention and maintain local shelters for battered women are more likely to take action in cases involving spousal abuse.[82]

An officer who lives in the community he or she serves is probably strongly influenced by and shares a large part of the community's beliefs and values and is likely to be sensitive to and respect the wishes of neighbors, friends, and relatives. Conflict may arise, however, when the police officer commutes to an assigned area of jurisdiction, which is often the case in inner-city precincts. The officer who holds personal values in opposition to those of the community can exercise discretion in ways that conflict with the community's values and result in ineffective law enforcement.[83]

A police officer's perception of community alternatives to police intervention may also influence discretion. A police officer may exercise discretion to arrest an individual in a particular circumstance if it seems that nothing else can be done, even if the officer does not believe that an arrest is the best possible example of good police work. In an environment that has a proliferation of social agencies—detoxification units, drug control centers, and child-care services—a police officer will obviously have more alternatives to choose from in deciding whether to make an arrest. In fact, referring cases to these alternative agencies saves the officer both time and effort—records do not have to be made out and court appearances can be avoided. Thus, social agencies provide greater latitude in police decision making.

Departmental Factors

The policies, practices, and customs of the local police department are another influence on discretion. These conditions vary from department to department and strongly depend on the judgment of the chief and others in the organizational hierarchy. Departments can issue directives aimed at influencing police conduct. Patrol officers may be asked to issue more tickets and make more arrests or to refrain from arresting under certain circumstances. Occasionally, a directive will instruct officers to be particularly alert for certain types of violations or to make some sort of interagency referral when specific events occur. For example, the department may order patrol officers to crack down on street panhandlers or to take formal action in domestic violence cases.[84]

The ratio of supervisory personnel to subordinates may also influence discretion: departments with a high ratio of sergeants to patrol officers may experience fewer officer-initiated actions than those in which fewer eyes are observing the action in the streets. It is also possible that supervisory style may influence how police use discretion. Robin Shepard Engel found that patrol officers supervised by sergeants who are "take-charge" types, and like to participate in high levels of activity in the field themselves, spend significantly more time per shift engaging in self-initiated and community-policing or problem-solving activities than they do in administrative activities. In contrast, officers with supervisors who spend time mentoring and coaching subordinates are more likely to devote significantly more time engaging in administrative tasks.[85] The size of the department may also determine officer discretion. In larger departments, looser control by supervisors seems to encourage a level of discretion unknown in smaller, more tightly run police agencies.

Peer Influence Police discretion is also subject to peer influence.[86] Police officers suffer a degree of social isolation because the job involves strange working conditions and hours, including being on twenty-four-hour call, and their authority and responsibility to enforce the law may cause embarrassment during social encounters. At the same time, officers must handle irregular and emotionally demanding encounters involving the most personal and private aspects of people's lives. As a result, police officers turn to their peers for both on-the-job advice and off-the-job companionship, essentially forming a subculture to provide a source of status, prestige, and reward.

The peer group affects how police officers exercise discretion on two distinct levels. In an obvious, direct manner, other police officers dictate acceptable responses to street-level problems by providing or withholding approval in office discussions. Second, officers who take their job seriously and desire the respect and friendship of others will take their advice, abide by their norms, and seek out the most experienced and most influential patrol officers on the force and follow their behavior models.

Situational Factors

The situational factors attached to a particular crime are another extremely important influence on police actions and behavior. Regardless of departmental or peer influences, the officer's immediate interaction with a criminal act, offender, citizen, or victim will weigh heavily on the use of discretionary powers.[87] Some research efforts find that police officers rely on **demeanor** (the attitude and appearance of the offender) in making decisions.[88]

If an offender is surly, talks back, or otherwise challenges the officer's authority, formal action is more likely to be taken.[89] When Joseph Schafer and Stephen Mastrofski surveyed police officers on the factors that influenced their decision to issue traffic citations, they found that motorists who behaved in a civil manner, accepted responsibility for their offense, and admitted their guilt were less likely to receive a ticket than those who displayed a less courteous demeanor. Of course, even the most well-mannered motorist was not immune from citation if they committed what was considered to be a very serious offense, such as speeding near a school shortly after classes had been dismissed.[90]

Is a suspect's demeanor really that important? Would an experienced police officer release an offender simply because they are polite and arrest another one who is bad tempered? David Klinger, a police officer turned criminologist, maintains that demeanor may not be as much of a factor in shaping discretion as most others believe. Klinger believes that the average officer is pretty used to bad demeanor and uncivil behavior, so it takes more than that to influence their discretion.[91] A person who struggles or touches police during a confrontation is a likely candidate for arrest; merely having a "bad attitude" is not enough to generate police retaliation.

The way in which a crime or situation is encountered may also influence discretion. If a police officer stumbles on an altercation or break-in, the discretionary response may be different than if the officer is summoned by police radio. If an act has received official police recognition, such as the dispatch of a patrol car, police action must be taken or an explanation made as to why it was not. If a matter is brought to an officer's attention by a citizen observer, the officer can ignore the request and risk a complaint or take discretionary action. In contrast, when an officer chooses to become involved in a situation, without benefit of a summons or complaint, maximum discretion

demeanor *The way in which a person outwardly manifests his or her personality.*

can be used. Even in this circumstance, however, the presence of a crowd or of witnesses may influence the officer's decision making.

And, of course, the officer who acts alone is also affected by personal matters—physical condition, mental state, police style, and whether he or she has other duties to perform. Other factors that might influence police are the use of a weapon, seriousness of injury, and the presence of alcohol or drugs.

Extralegal Factors

One often-debated issue is whether police take race, class, and gender into account when making arrest decisions. The research is mixed: some efforts show that the offender's age, gender, and racial characteristics are key determinants that shape the arrest process.[92] Others find that situational and legal factors are more important, while still another group finds that victim characteristics control police action (that is, police are more willing to make an arrest when the victim is older, white, affluent, and so on).[93] The question then is whether police discretion is shaped by such extralegal factors as age, gender, income, and race. Because this issue is so important, it is the topic of the Race, Culture, and Gender in Criminal Justice feature.

■ PROBLEMS OF POLICING

Law enforcement is not an easy job. The role ambiguity, social isolation, and threat of danger present in "working the street" are the police officer's constant companions. What effects do these strains have on police? This section discusses three of the most significant problems: job stress, violence, and corruption.

Police and Stress

The complexity of their role, the need to exercise prudent discretion, the threat of using violence and having violence used against them, and isolation from the rest of society all take a toll on law enforcement officers. It is not surprising, then, that police officers experience tremendous stress, a factor that leads some to alcoholism, depression, and even suicide. There is evidence that police officers are all too often involved in marital disputes and even incidents of domestic violence that may be linked to stress.[94] These developments are not lost on police officers, many of whom feel significant amounts of job-related stress, a condition which may lead them to develop negative attitudes and lose enthusiasm and commitment for the job.[95] Stress and burnout become part of the job.[96] Stress may not be constant, but at some time during their career (usually the middle years) most officers will feel the effects of stress.[97]

Causes of Stress A number of factors have been associated with job stress.[98] The pressure of being on duty twenty-four hours a day leads to stress and emotional detachment from both work and public needs. Policing is a dangerous profession and officers are at risk for many forms of job-related accidental deaths. Stress has been related to internal conflict with administrative policies that deny officers support and a meaningful role in decision making. Some officers may become stressed when they are forced to adapt to the demands of community-oriented policing, but are skeptical about the utility or effectiveness of this change in policy.[99] In addition, police suffer stress in their personal lives when they "bring the job home" or when their work hours are shifted, causing family disruptions.[100] Other stressors include poor

Race, Culture, and Gender in Criminal Justice

Racial Profiling

In the late summer of 1997, New Yorkers were shocked as an astounding case of police brutality began to unfold in the daily newspapers. On August 9, Abner Louima, 33, a Haitian immigrant, had been arrested outside Club Rendez-vous, a Brooklyn nightclub after a fight had broken out. Louima later claimed that the arresting officers had become furious when he protested his arrest, twice stopping the patrol car to beat him with their fists. When they arrived at the station house, two officers, apparently angry because some of the club-goers had fought with the police, led Louima to the men's room, removed his trousers, and attacked him with the handle of a toilet plunger, first shoving it into his rectum and then into his mouth, breaking his teeth. The officers also shouted racial slurs at Louima, while Louima screamed, "Why are you doing this to me? Why? Why?" After the beating Louima was rushed to a hospital for emergency surgery to repair a puncture in his small intestine and injuries to his bladder. Witnesses said Louima had no bruises or injuries when officers first took him into custody, yet when he arrived at the hospital three hours later he was bleeding profusely.

In the aftermath of the case, NYPD investigators granted departmental immunity to nearly 100 officers in order to gain information. By cracking the "blue curtain" of silence a number of police officers were given long prison sentences on charges of sexual abuse and first-degree assault.

The Louima case and other incidents involving the police and the minority community have reignited the long debate over whether police use race as a factor when making decisions such as stopping and questioning a suspect or deciding to make an arrest. In other words, does "racial profiling" influence police discretion?

Does Race Make a Difference?

Some experts question whether profiling and racial discrimination is widespread as currently feared. One approach has been to measure the attitudes minority citizens hold toward police. When Ronald Weitzer surveyed residents in three Washington, D.C., neighborhoods he found that African Americans value racially integrated police services and welcome the presence of both white and black police officers, a finding which would seem improbable if most white officers were racially biased. The African-American community is generally supportive of the local police, especially when officers respond quickly to calls for service. It is unlikely that African Americans would appreciate rapid responses from racist police.

Another approach is to directly measure whether police treat minority and majority citizens differently—that is, use racial profiling in making decisions. There are research efforts that show little evidence that police use racial profiling:

- David Eitle, Lisa Stolzenberg, and Stewart J. D'Alessio found that whites are more likely to be arrested for assaults than African Americans and that as the percentage of black police officers in a department increases this racial gap actually widens.
- Matt DeLisi and Robert Regoli found that whites are nine times more likely to suffer DWI arrests than blacks, a finding which would be unlikely if racial profiling was routine.
- Jon Gould and Stephen Mastrofski studied illegal police searches and found that race had little influence on police conduct. Though police may routinely conduct illegal searches the suspect's race did not influence their tactics.
- Joseph Schafer, David Carter, and Andra Katz-Bannister found that while race played some role in traffic stops, age and gender actually had a greater influence over police decision making.

Profiling Remains a Problem

In contrast to these views, many experts remain concerned about the police use of profiling and discrimination. While some studies find that minority citizens value police as highly as whites, others reach an opposite conclusion. There is also evidence that racial profiling exists and that state and local police officers routinely stopped black motorists at a rate far greater than their representation in the driving pool:

- The most recent national survey of contacts between the police and the public found that racial profiling is still a serious problem. While the likelihood of being stopped by police did not differ significantly between white (8.7 percent), black (9.1 percent), and Hispanic (8.6 percent) drivers, what happened after the stop can be interpreted as racial profiling: during the traffic stop, police were more likely to carry out some type of search on a black (10.2 percent) or Hispanic (11.4 percent)

(continued)

Race, Culture, and Gender in Criminal Justice *(continued)*

than a white (3.5 percent). Blacks and Hispanics are much more likely to be searched, handcuffed, arrested, and subjected to force or the threat of it.

- Brian Withrow looked at police practices in Wichita, Kansas, and found that black citizens are stopped at disproportionately higher rates than non-black citizens; black and Hispanic citizens are more likely to be searched and arrested than non-black and non-Hispanic citizens.

- Researchers at Northeastern University in Boston used four statistical tests to analyze 1.6 million traffic citations issued between April 1, 2001, and June 30, 2003, in 366 jurisdictions across Massachusetts: ticketing resident minorities disproportionately more than whites; ticketing all minorities disproportionately more than whites; searching minorities more often than whites; and issuing warnings to whites more often than minorities. According to the study, 15 police departments failed all four tests, 42 failed three tests, 87 failed two tests, and 105 failed one.

- Richard Lundman's analysis of citizens' encounters with police indicates that minority citizens are more likely to be stopped than whites but that searches of minority-driven vehicles are no more likely to yield drugs or contraband than searches of vehicles driven by Caucasians.

Is the Tide Turning?

After thoroughly reviewing the literature on police bias, Samuel Walker, Cassia Spohn, and Miriam DeLone conclude that police discriminate against racial minorities and that significant problems per-sist between the police and racial and ethnic communities in the United States. While their conclusions are troubling, recent efforts to control police discrimination may be achieving results. According to legal experts Dan Kahan and Tracey Meares, racial discrimination may be on the decline because minorities now possess sufficient political status to protect them from abuses within the justice system. And in the event that political influence is insufficient to control profiling, members of the minority community have used the court system to seek legal redress. For example, in a 2003 settlement, Cincinnati was forced to establish a $4.5 million settlement fund to compensate 16 people for instances of racial profiling. One plaintiff was held at gunpoint after being stopped for a traffic infraction while another had been shot in the back while running away, unarmed. Community policing efforts may also be helping police officers become more sensitive to issues that concern the public such as profiling.

While these signs are encouraging, as Candice Batton and Colleen Kadleck point out, racial profiling takes many different forms, making it sometimes hard to detect. Some experts argue that despite some progress, racial discrimination is still widespread in the justice system. In his book *No Equal Justice: Race and Class in the American Criminal Justice System*, constitutional scholar David Cole argues that, despite efforts to create racial neutrality, race-based double standards operate in virtually every aspect of criminal justice. These disparities allow the privileged to enjoy constitutional protections from police power without extending these protections across the board to minorities and the poor.

training, substandard equipment, inadequate pay, lack of opportunity, job dissatisfaction, role conflict, exposure to brutality, and fears about competence, success, and safety.[101] Some officers may feel stress because they believe that the court system favors the rights of the criminal and handcuffs the police; others might be sensitive to a perceived lack of support from governmental officials and the general public.[102] Some officers believe that their superiors care little about their welfare.[103]

Police psychologists have divided these stressors into four distinct categories:[104]

- *External stressors* include verbal abuse from the public, justice system inefficiency, and liberal court decisions that favor the criminal. What are

Critical Thinking

1. What, if anything, can be done to reduce racial bias on the part of police? Would adding minority officers help? Would it be a form of racism to assign minority officers to minority neighborhoods?

2. Would research showing that police are more likely to make arrests in inter-racial incidents than intra-racial incidents constitute evidence of racism?

3. Police spot three men of Middle Eastern descent carrying a large, heavy box into a crowded building. Should they stop and question them and demand to look into the carton? Is this racial profiling?

 InfoTrac College Edition Research
Use *racial profiling* as a key term to review articles on the use of race as a determining factor in the police use of discretion.

Sources: Matthew Durose, Erica Schmitt, and Patrick Langan, *Contacts between Police and the Public: Findings from the 2002 National Survey* (Washington, D.C.: Bureau of Justice Statistics, 2005); Richard Lundman, "Driver Race, Ethnicity, and Gender and Citizen Reports of Vehicle Searches by Police and Vehicle Search Hits," *Journal of Criminal Law & Criminology* 94 (2004): 309–350; Stephen Rice and Alex Piquero, "Perceptions of Discrimination and Justice in New York City," *Policing: An International Journal of Police Strategies and Management* 28 (2005): 98–117; Joseph Schafer, David Carter, and Andra Katz-Bannister, "Studying Traffic Stop Encounters," *Journal of Criminal Justice* 32 (2004): 159–170; Candice Batton and Colleen Kadleck "Theoretical and Methodological Issues in Racial Profiling Research," *Police Quarterly* 7 (2004): 30–64; David Eitle, Lisa Stolzenberg, and Stewart J. D'Alessio, "Police Organizational Factors, the Racial Composition of the Police, and the Probability of Arrest," *Justice Quarterly* 22 (2005): 30–57; Brian Withrow, "Race-Based Policing: A Descriptive Analysis of the Wichita Stop Study," *Police Practice & Research 5* (2004): 223–240; Amy Farrell, Jack McDevitt, Lisa Bailey, Carsten Andresen, and Erica Pierce, *Massachusetts Racial and Gender Profiling Final Report* (Boston, Mass.: Northeastern University, 2004) www.racialprofilinganalysis.neu.edu/IRJsite_docs/finalreport.pdf, accessed on August 21, 2005; Tom Tyler and Cheryl Wakslak, "Profiling and Police Legitimacy: Procedural Justice, Attributions of Motive, and Acceptance of Police Authority," *Criminology* 42 (2004): 253–281; Jon Gould and Stephen Mastrofski "Suspect Searches: Assessing Police Behavior Under the U.S. Constitution," *Criminology & Public Policy* 3 (2004): 315–362; Andrew E. Taslit, "Racial Auditors and the Fourth Amendment: Data with the Power to Inspire Political Action," *Law and Contemporary Problems* 66 (2003): 221–299; In re Cincinnati Policing, No. C-1-99-3170 (S.D. Ohio, 2003); Patrick A. Langan, Lawrence A. Greenfeld, Steven K. Smith, Matthew R. Durose, and David J. Levin, *Contacts between Police and the Public Findings from the 1999 National Survey* (Washington, D.C.: Bureau of Justice Statistics, 2001); Richard Felson and Jeff Ackerman, "Arrest for Domestic and Other Assaults," *Criminology* 39 (2001): 655–676; Ronald Weitzer, "White, Black or Blue Cops? Race and Citizen Assessments of Police Officers," *Journal of Criminal Justice* 28 (2000): 313–324; Sidney L. Harring, "The Diallo Verdict: Another 'Tragic Accident' in New York's War on Street Crime?" *Social Justice* 27 (2000): 9–14; Robert Worden and Robin Shepard, "Demeanor, Crime and Police Behavior: A Reexamination of the Police Services Study Data," *Criminology* 34 (1996): 83–105; Stephen Mastrofski, Robert Worden, and Jeffrey Snipes, "Law Enforcement in a Time of Community Policing," *Criminology* 33 (1995): 539–563; Thomas Priest and Deborah Brown Carter, "Evaluations of Police Performance in an African American Sample," *Journal of Criminal Justice* 27 (1999): 457–465; Matt De Lisi and Bob Regoli, "Race, Conventional Crime, and Criminal Justice: The Declining Importance of Skin Color," *Journal of Criminal Justice* 27 (1999): 549–557; David Cole, *No Equal Justice: Race and Class in the American Criminal Justice System* (New York: New Press, 2000); Randall Kennedy, *Race, Crime and the Law* (New York: Vintage Books, 1998); Dan M. Kahan and Tracey L. Meares, "The Coming Crisis of Criminal Procedure," *Georgetown Law Journal* 86 (1998): 1153–1184. David Kocieniewski, "Man Says Officers Tortured Him After Arrest," *New York Times*, August 13, 1997, 1; Ronald Weitzer, "Racial Discrimination in the Criminal Justice System: Findings and Problems in the Literature," *Journal of Criminal Justice* 24 (1996): 309–322; Samuel Walker, Cassia Spohn, and Miriam DeLone, *The Color of Justice, Race, Ethnicity and Crime in America* (Belmont, Calif.: Wadsworth, 1996), 115; Sandra Lee Browning, Francis Cullen, Liqun Cao, Renee Kopache, and Thomas Stevenson, "Race and Getting Hassled by the Police: A Research Note," *Police Studies* 17 (1994): 1–10.

perceived to be antipolice judicial decisions may alienate police and reduce their perceptions of their own competence.

- *Organizational stressors* include low pay, excessive paperwork, arbitrary rules, and limited opportunity for advancement.
- *Duty stressors* include rotating shifts, work overload, boredom, fear, and danger.
- *Individual stressors* include discrimination, marital difficulties, and personality problems.

The effects of stress can be shocking. Police work has been related to both physical and psychological ailments.[105] Police have a high rate of premature death caused by such conditions as heart disease and diabetes. They also experience a disproportionate number of divorces and other marital problems. Research indicates that police officers in some departments, but not all, have higher suicide rates than the general public.[106] Police who feel stress may not be open to adopting new ideas and programs such as community policing.[107]

Combating Stress Research efforts have shown that the more support police officers get in the workplace, the lower their feelings of stress and anxiety.[108] Consequently, departments have attempted to fight job-related stress by training officers to cope with its effects. Today, stress training includes diet information, biofeedback, relaxation and meditation, and exercise. Many departments include stress management as part of an overall wellness program also designed to promote physical and mental health, fitness, and good nutrition.[109] Some programs have included family members: they may be better able to help the officer cope if they have more knowledge about the difficulties of police work. Total wellness programming enhances the physical and emotional well-being of officers by emphasizing preventive physical and psychological measures.[110] Research also shows that because police perceive many benefits of their job and enjoy the quality of life it provides, stress reduction programs can help officers focus on the positive aspects of police work.[111]

Because stress is a critically important aspect of police work, further research is needed to create valid methods of identifying police officers under considerable stress and to devise effective stress reduction programs.[112]

Criminal Justice ⚖ Now™

*Learn more by exploring the **Reasonable Force** Review and Reinforce activity.*

Police Brutality

Police officers are empowered to use force and violence in pursuit of their daily tasks. Some scholars argue that the use of violent measures is the core of the police role.[113] It is not surprising, then, that **police brutality** is a worldwide issue not restricted to the United States. In fact, U.S. police departments are now much less violent than some others around the world. In one incident, thirty people were murdered on March 31, 2005, in Baixada Fluminense, a poor area outside Rio de Janeiro, Brazil, by rogue members of the state police force. In Brazil, police "extermination groups" kill for hire and sometimes engage in theft and kidnapping.[114] Despite such brutality, the Brazilian public seems indifferent since many of the police targets are poor and/or criminal.

How much force is being used by the police in the U.S. today?[115] Despite some highly publicized incidents that get a lot of media attention, the research data show that the use of force is not a very common event. A national (2005) survey on police contacts with civilians sponsored by the federal government found that in a single year, of the 45 million people who had one or more police contacts, about 1.5 percent (664,500 persons) reported that an officer used or threatened to use force.[116] African Americans (3.5 percent) and Hispanics (2.5 percent) were more likely than whites (1.1 percent) to experience police threat or use of force during the contact; young people (16–29) were almost three times more likely to experience force than people over 29. When force was applied, it was most likely to be "pushing" or "grabbing." In 19 percent of the 664,500 force incidents a police officer pointed a gun at the resident and 14 percent resulted in injury to the citizen. And while 24 percent of the combatants cursed at, insulted, or verbally threatened the officer(s) during the incident, three-quarters claimed that the force was excessive and more than 80 percent believed the officer acted improperly. So while 45 million people were contacted by police only 90,000 or so were injured. Is that far too many or relatively few?

police brutality Usually involves such actions as the use of abusive language, unnecessary use of force or coercion, threats, prodding with nightsticks, stopping and searching people to harass them, and so on.

Race and Force The routine use of force may be diminishing, but there is still debate over whether police are more likely to get rough with minority suspects. The national survey on police contacts with civilians found that African Americans and Hispanics were more likely than whites to experience police threat or use of force as a consequence of police contact. Cities with large black populations also experience the highest amount of lethal violence by police.[117]

Considering this evidence, it is not surprising that surveys of minority group members show they are more likely to disapprove of the police view of force than majority group members.[118] Minority citizens are much more likely to claim that police "hassle them"—stop them or watch them closely when they have done nothing wrong.[119] While any evidence of racial disparity is troubling, these are national data that must be interpreted with caution. Race may be only one element of the factors that determine the outcome of police-citizen encounters. Joel Garner's study of police encounters with citizens using a wide variety of samples taken in different locales found that race actually played an insignificant role in the decision to use force.[120] The Garner research and similar efforts indicates that a suspect's behavior is a much more powerful determinant of police response than age or race. William Terrill studied 3,544 police-suspect encounters and found that situational factors often influence the extent to which force is applied. Use of force seems to escalate when a police officer gives a suspect a second chance (i.e., "Dump the beer out of your car and I will let you go") but the suspect hesitates or defies the order. People who resist police orders or actually grapple with officers are much more likely to be the target of force than those who are respectful, passive, and noncombative. Members of certain subpopulations such as intravenous drug users may be more likely to perceive or experience police coercion and violence than the general population.[121] Moreover, the general public seems to understand the situational use of force: even people who condemn police violence are more supportive of its use if the officer is in danger or a suspect is confrontational.[122] So the evidence suggests that whether black or white, suspect behavior may be a more important determinant of force than their race or ethnicity.[123]

Donovan Jackson sits at the witness stand in a Los Angeles courtroom as the videotape of his arrest and beating plays on a laptop computer. Incidents such as the Jackson case give the impression that race plays a significant role in shaping police discretion.

Who Are the Problem Cops? There is evidence that only a small proportion of officers are continually involved in use-of-force incidents.[124] Why do these cops continually get involved in violent confrontations? Aggressive cops may over-react to the stress of police work while at the same time feel socially isolated. They believe that the true source of their frustration cannot be responded to directly so they take their frustrations out on readily available targets: vulnerable people in their immediate environment.[125]

What kind of police officer gets involved in problem behavior? Are some officers "chronic offenders"? Research seems to show that a few officers were in fact chronic offenders who accounted for a significant portion of all citizen complaints. The officers receiving the bulk of complaints tend to be young and less experienced.[126] Efforts to deal with these "problem cops" are now being undertaken in police departments around the nation.

Curing Violence Because incidents of brutality undermine efforts to build a bridge between police and the public, police departments around the United States have instituted specialized training programs to reduce them. A number of larger departments are instituting early warning systems to change the behavior of individual officers who have been identified as having performance problems. In most systems, problem officers are identified by their behavior profiles: citizen complaints, firearm discharge and use-of-force reports, civil litigation, resisting arrest incidents, and high-speed pursuits and vehicular damage. The initial intervention generally consists of a review by the officer's immediate supervisor, who advises the officer of the sanctions they face if problems continue; some cases are referred to counseling, training, or police psychologists. Early warning program evaluations indicate that they are quite successful.[127]

Some departments have developed administrative policies that stress limiting the use of force and containing armed offenders until specially trained backup teams are sent to take charge of the situation. Administrative policies have been found to be an effective control on use of deadly force, and their influence can be enhanced if given the proper support by the chief of police.[128]

Some cities are taking an aggressive, proactive stance to curb violent cops. Since 1977 the New York Police Department has been operating a Force-Related Integrity Testing program in which undercover officers pose as angry citizens in elaborate sting operations intended to weed out officers with a propensity for violence. In a typical encounter, officers responding to a radio call on a domestic dispute confront an aggressive husband who spews hatred at everyone around, including the police. The "husband" is actually an undercover officer from the Internal Affairs Bureau, who is testing whether the officers, some of whom have a history of civilian complaints, will respond to verbal abuse with threats or violence. The NYPD conducts about six hundred sting operations each year to test the integrity of its officers; several dozen are devoted to evaluating the conduct of officers with a history of abuse complaints.[129]

Perhaps the greatest factors in controlling the use of police brutality are the threat of civil judgments against individual officers who use excessive force, police chiefs who ignore or condone violent behavior, and the cities and towns in which they are employed.

Police and Deadly Force

As it is commonly used, the term *deadly force* refers to the actions of a police officer who shoots and kills a suspect who is fleeing from arrest, assaults a victim, or attacks an officer.[130] The justification for the use of deadly force can be traced to English common law, where almost every criminal offense was a felony and bore the death penalty. The use of deadly force in the course of arresting a felon was considered expedient, saving the state the burden of trial (the *fleeing-felon rule*).[131]

Although the media depicts hero cops in a constant stream of deadly shootouts in which scores of bad guys are killed, the actual number of people killed by the police each year is most likely between 250 and 300.[132] And some of these shootings may even be precipitated by the target as a form of suicide.[133] This tragic event has become so common that the term **suicide by cop** has been coined to denote victim-precipitated killings by police.[134]

While the police use of deadly force may not be as common as previously believed, it still remains a central part of the police role. Although it is difficult to get an accurate figure, at least 6,600 civilians have been killed by the police since 1976 and the true number is probably much higher.[135]

Factors Related to Police Shootings Is police use of deadly force a random occurrence, or are there social, legal, and environmental factors associated with it? The following patterns have been related to police shootings:

- *Exposure to violence.* The community violence hypothesis maintains that areas with high violence levels will also have higher numbers of police killings of citizens. A strong association has been found between police use of force and "gun density" (the proportion of suicides and murders committed with a gun).[136] Most police shootings involve suspects who are armed and either attack the officer or are engaged in violent crimes.

- *National crime rates.* A number of studies have found that fatal police shootings were closely related to reported violent crime rates and criminal homicide rates; police officers kill civilians at a higher rate in years when the general level of violence in the nation is higher.[137] The perception of danger may contribute to the use of violent means for self-protection.[138]

- *Community threat levels.* According to the threat hypothesis, more police are killed in cities with a large underclass[139] David Jacobs and Jason Carmichael found that cities that have the greatest economic and political subordination of minority group members are also the location of the highest number of officers killed and wounded.[140] Police violence rates are highest in cities where members of the minority community experience a distinct economic disadvantage compared to the white majority. Interestingly, when an African-American mayor is elected in these communities, police violence abates. Political empowerment may reduce African-American feelings of powerlessness and consequently result in less anger against the state, of which the police are the most visible officials.

- *Administrative policies.* The philosophy, policies, and practices of individual police chiefs and departments significantly influence the police use of deadly force.[141] Departments that stress restrictive policies on the use of force and have more control over officer behavior generally have lower shooting rates than those that favor tough law enforcement and encourage officers to shoot when necessary. Poorly written or ambivalent policies encourage shootings because they allow the officer at the scene to decide when deadly force is warranted, often under conditions of high stress and tension. Two other administrative policies may influence shootings:
  - *Staffing levels.* A relationship exists between police violence and the number of police officers on the street. Departments with inadequate

suicide by cop A form of suicide in which a person acts in an aggressive manner with police officers in order to induce them to shoot to kill.

staffing risk having their officers handle too many calls for service, make too many arrests, and increase the risk of exposure to stressful situations.

- *Lack of proper training and preparation.* Police officers who have not been adequately trained to deal with emergency situations may respond with unnecessary violence; proper training can help reduce these incidents by teaching proper preparations.[142]

Race and Police Shootings No other issue is as important to the study of the police use of deadly force as racial discrimination. A number of critics have claimed that police are more likely to shoot and kill minority offenders than whites. In a famous statement, Paul Takagi charged that police have "one trigger finger for whites and another for African Americans."[143] Takagi's complaint was supported by a number of research studies that showed that a disproportionate number of police killings involved minority citizens—almost 80 percent in some of the cities surveyed.[144]

Do these findings alone indicate that police discriminate in the use of deadly force? Some pioneering research by James Fyfe helps provide an answer to this question. In his study of New York City shootings over a five-year period, Fyfe found that police officers were most likely to shoot suspects who were armed and with whom they became involved in violent confrontations. Once such factors as being armed with a weapon, being involved in a violent crime, and attacking an officer were considered, the racial differences in the police use of force ceased to be significant. In fact, Fyfe found that African-American officers were almost twice as likely as white officers to shoot citizens. Fyfe attributes this finding to the fact that (1) African-American officers work and live in high-crime, high-violence areas where shootings are more common, and (2) African-American officers hold proportionately more line positions and fewer administrative posts than white officers, which would place them more often on the street and less often behind a desk.[145]

Controlling Deadly Force Because the police use of deadly force is such a serious problem, ongoing efforts have been made to control it. One of the most difficult issues in controlling the problem was the continued use of the fleeing-felon rule in a number of states. However, in 1985 the Supreme Court outlawed the indiscriminate use of deadly force with its decision in *Tennessee v. Garner.* In this case, the Court ruled that the use of deadly force against apparently unarmed and nondangerous fleeing felons is an illegal seizure of their person under the Fourth Amendment. Deadly force may not be used unless it is necessary to prevent the escape and the officer has probable cause to believe that the suspect poses a significant threat of death or serious injury to the officer or others. The majority opinion stated that where the suspect poses no immediate threat to the officer and no threat to others, the harm resulting from failing to apprehend the suspect does not justify the use of deadly force to do so: "A police officer may not seize an unarmed, nondangerous suspect by shooting him dead."[146]

With *Garner,* the Supreme Court effectively put an end to any local police policy that allowed officers to shoot unarmed or otherwise nondangerous offenders if they resisted arrest or attempted to flee from police custody. However, the Court did not ban the use of deadly force or otherwise control police shooting policy. Consequently, in *Graham v. Connor,* the Court created a reasonableness standard for the use of force: force is excessive when, considering all the circumstances known to the officer at the time he acted, the force used was unreasonable.[147] For example, an officer is approached in a threatening manner by someone wielding a knife. The assailant fails to stop when

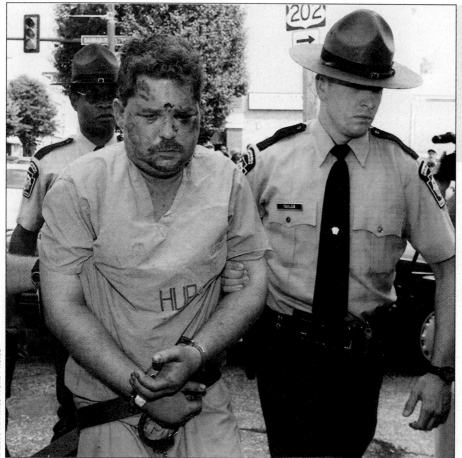

Murder suspect Dennis Czajkowski is escorted by Pennsylvania State Police Officers after being taken into custody for shooting two nurses he held captive at Norristown State Hospital. The police officer in charge of the investigation had given an order not to use deadly force.

warned and is killed by the officer, but it turns out later that the shooting victim was deaf and could not hear the officer's command. The officer would not be held liable if at the time of the incident he had no way of knowing the person's disability.

Individual state jurisdictions still control police shooting policy. Some states have adopted statutory policies that restrict the police use of violence. Others have upgraded training in the use of force. The Federal Law Enforcement Training Center has developed the FLETC use-of-force model, illustrated in Figure 7.3, to teach officers the proper method to escalate force in response to the threat they face. As the figure shows, resistance ranges from compliant and cooperative to assaultive with the threat of serious bodily harm or death. Officers are taught via lecture, demonstration, computer-based instruction, and training scenarios to assess the suspect's behavior and apply an appropriate and corresponding amount of force.[148]

Another way to control police shootings is through internal review and policymaking by police administrative review boards. New York's Firearm Discharge Review Board was established to investigate and adjudicate all police firearm discharges. Among the dispositions available to the board are the following:

Criminal Justice ⚖ Now™
*Learn more about **Use of Force** by going through the "**Proper Use of Force**" Learning Module.*

1. The discharge was in accordance with law and departmental policy.

2. The discharge was justifiable, but the officer should be given additional training in the use of firearms or in the law and departmental policy.

Figure 7.3
The Federal Law Enforcement Training Center's use-of-force model
Source: Franklin Graves and Gregory Connor, Federal Law Enforcement Training Center, Glynco, Georgia.

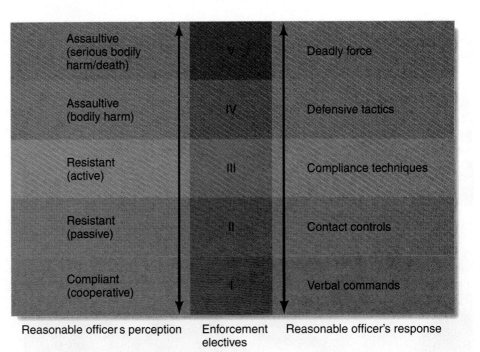

Reasonable officer's perception   Enforcement electives   Reasonable officer's response

3. The shooting was justifiable under law but violated departmental policy and warrants departmental disciplinary action.

4. The shooting was in apparent violation of law and should be referred to the appropriate prosecutor if criminal charges have not already been filed.

5. The officer involved should be transferred (or offered the opportunity to transfer) to a less sensitive assignment.

6. The officer involved should receive testing or alcoholism counseling.[149]

The review board approach is controversial because it can mean that the department recommends that one of its own officers be turned over for criminal prosecution.[150]

Nonlethal Weapons In the last few years, about a thousand local police forces have started using some sort of less-than-lethal weapon designed to subdue suspects. The most widely used nonlethal weapons are wood, rubber, or polyurethane bullets shot out of modified 37-mm pistols or 12-gauge shotguns. At short distances, officers use pepper spray and tasers, which deliver electric shocks with long wire tentacles, producing intense muscle spasms. Other technologies still in development include guns that shoot giant nets, guns that squirt sticky glue, and lights that can temporarily blind a suspect. New weapons are being developed that shoot bags filled with lead pellets; the weapons have a range of one hundred feet and pack the wallop of a pro boxer's punch.[151]

Recent research efforts indicate that nonlethal weapons may help reduce police use of force.[152] Greater effort must be made to regulate these nonlethal weapons and create effective policies for their use.[153] The Criminal Justice and Technology feature on page 202 reviews these weapons in some detail.

Police and Corruption

In July 1996, the elite antigang unit from the Los Angeles Police Department's Rampart Division raided gang-infested apartments at Shatto Place. Their target was the notorious 18th Street Gang, one of Los Angeles's most violent gangs. During the raid, police officers killed one gang member and wounded another. A departmental investigation found nothing wrong and exonerated the police involved. Then in 1999, Rafael A. Perez, an officer who took part in the raid, was caught stealing eight pounds of cocaine from police evidence lockers. After pleading guilty in September 1999, he bargained for a lighter sentence by telling departmental investigators about police brutality, perjury, planted evidence, drug corruption, and attempted murder within the Rampart Division and its antigang unit, known as CRASH (Community Resources Against Street Hoodlums). Perez told authorities that during the Shatto raid the victims may have been unarmed, so that the raiding officers resorted to a "throwdown"—slang for a weapon being planted to make a shooting legally justifiable. Perez's testimony resulted in at least twelve Rampart cops being fired or relieved from duty. But Perez was not done. He also said that he and his partner, Officer Nino Durden, shot an unarmed 18th Street Gang member named Javier Ovando, then planted a semiautomatic rifle on the unconscious suspect and claimed that Ovando had tried to shoot them during a stakeout. Their testimony had helped get Ovando, confined to a wheelchair for life because of the shooting, a twenty-three-year sentence for assault.[154] The Ramparts scandal has cost the city of Los Angeles more than $70 million from legal settlements; more than a dozen officers have been forced to leave the force; 100 criminal convictions have been overturned. Ovando has collected $15 million in damages from the city of Los Angeles. Perez was sentenced to two years in prison for violating Ovando's civil rights and three more for stealing cocaine from LAPD evidence lockers. Durden received a five-year prison sentence and was released in 2005.[155]

From their creation, U.S. police departments have wrestled with the problem of controlling illegal and unprofessional behavior by their officers. Corruption pervaded the American police when the early departments were first formed. In the nineteenth century, police officers systematically ignored violations of laws related to drinking, gambling, and prostitution in return for regular payoffs. Some actually entered into relationships with professional criminals, especially pickpockets. Illegal behavior was tolerated in return for goods or information. Police officers helped politicians gain office by allowing electoral fraud to flourish; some senior officers sold promotions to higher rank in the department.[156]

Since the early nineteenth century, scandals involving police abuse of power have occurred in many cities, and elaborate methods have been devised to control or eliminate the problem. Although most police officers are not corrupt, the few who are dishonest bring discredit to the entire profession.

Varieties of Corruption Police deviance can include a number of activities. In a general sense, it involves misuse of authority by police officers in a manner designed to produce personal gain for themselves or others.[157] However, debate continues over whether a desire for personal gain is an essential part of corruption. Some experts argue that police misconduct also involves such issues as the unnecessary use of force, unreasonable searches, or an immoral personal life and that these should be considered as serious as corruption devoted to economic gain.

Scholars have attempted to create typologies categorizing the forms that the abuse of police powers can take. When investigating corruption among police officers in New York City, the **Knapp Commission** classified abusers into two categories: **meat eaters** and **grass eaters.**[158] Meat eaters aggressively misuse police power for personal gain by demanding bribes, threatening legal action, or cooperating with criminals. Across the country, police officers have been accused, indicted, and convicted of shaking down club owners and other businesspeople.[159]

Knapp Commission A public body that led an investigation into police corruption in New York and uncovered a widespread network of payoffs and bribes.

meat eaters A term used to describe police officers who actively solicit bribes and vigorously engage in corrupt practices.

grass eaters A term to describe police officers who accept payoffs when everyday duties place them in a position to be solicited by the public.

Criminal Justice and Technology

Less-Than-Lethal Weapons

After the Supreme Court ruling in *Tennessee v. Garner*, law enforcement officers were prohibited from using deadly force to capture a fleeing, nonviolent, unarmed suspect. Because an alternative to deadly force was needed, police departments around the country turned to nonlethal weapons for use in many incidents. What are the most common nonlethal weapons being used today?

Pepper Spray

One of the most popular less-than-lethal weapons being used by law enforcement personnel is *oleoresin capsicum*, also known as pepper spray, which really is made from peppers. The product is so strong that when a target is sprayed, their eyes will automatically shut and they will experience shortness of breath. The use of pepper spray has become universal in a variety of scenarios, ranging from the subduing of an agitated individual to use against groups who are uncooperative and causing problems.

Some law enforcement agencies have adopted more high powered pepper spray models including the PepperBall System, a semi-automatic high pressure launcher that fires projectiles containing the strongest form of *oleoresin capsicum* and built to

burst on impact. The launcher is accurate up to thirty feet and can saturate an area up to one hundred feet, which allows police officers to safely stand back while incapacitating suspects. Now used by 1,200 agencies, including law enforcement, corrections, security, and other government agencies, the PepperBall projectiles impact with eight to ten foot-pounds of force to stop suspects without causing permanent injury. The PepperBall System is used for controlling violent suspects who may have barricaded themselves in a hard to reach area, as well as for riot control and hostage rescue.

Though billed as a nonlethal weapon, some critics fear that pepper spray is quite dangerous. After sixty-three people died after being exposed to pepper spray in three North Carolina counties, the federal government sponsored research to determine whether this nonlethal weapon was more lethal then previously believed. The research cleared use of the spray, finding that only two of the sixty-three deaths could be blamed on being pepper-sprayed; the other fatalities were attributed to drug use, illness, or a combination of the two. As a result, police are continuing to use incapacitating sprays and new ones are being developed despite some well-publicized incidents in which people have died after being hit by supposedly nonlethal pellets.

In contrast, grass eaters accept payoffs when their everyday duties place them in a position to be solicited by the public. Police officers have been investigated for taking bribes to look the other way while neighborhood bookmakers ply their trade.[160] The Knapp Commission concluded that the vast majority of police officers on the take are grass eaters, although the few meat eaters who are caught capture all the headlines. In 1993 another police scandal prompted formation of the **Mollen Commission,** which found that some New York cops were actively involved in violence and drug dealing.

Other police experts have attempted to create models to better understand police corruption. It may be possible to divide police corruption into four major categories:[161]

- *Internal corruption.* This corruption takes place among police officers themselves, involving both the bending of departmental rules and the outright performance of illegal acts. Chicago police officers conspired to sell relatively new police cars to other officers at cut-rate prices, forcing the department to purchase new cars unnecessarily. In Boston a major scandal hit the police department when a captain was indicted in an exam-tampering-and-selling scheme. Numerous officers bought promotion exams from the captain, while others had him lower the scores of rivals who were competing for the same job.[162]

Mollen Commission An investigatory body formed in New York City in 1993 to scrutinize police misconduct.

Beanbag Gun

Some law enforcement agencies are now using the beanbag gun, which delivers a projectile the size of a tea bag filled with lead birdshot. Once an assailant is hit by the projectile, he or she will experience a muscle spasm that will either drop them in their tracks or at least slow them down so they can easily be subdued by law enforcement agents.

While effective, beanbag guns have also caused injuries and deaths. At least twelve people have been killed in the United States and Canada after being struck by the beanbags. While the projectiles are supposed to unfold once they are released from the gun, when they malfunction, they can rip through the skin, resulting in devastating effects, especially when discharged too close to the target. Because of these concerns, beanbag guns are being used less frequently while new versions, lacking the sharp edges of previous projectiles, are being developed.

Tasers

Tasers fire electrified darts at fleeing individuals who, when hit, can experience up to 50,000 volts of electricity. The darts can travel approximately twenty feet and can pierce through two inches of clothing, attack the individual's central nervous system, and cause muscle contractions and temporary paralysis. Currently, 2,400 law enforcement agencies in the country are using Tasers.

Other weapons such as net launchers and sticky foams, two products that would also help capture fleeing offenders, are still being developed. So far safety issues regarding these products have deterred them from being used frequently.

Critical Thinking

1. Would the easy availability of nonlethal weapons encourage their use by police officers, increasing the risk of civilian injuries?
2. Would you prohibit most police officers from carrying firearms and rely more on nonlethal weapons? Should police in non-death-penalty states be allowed to shoot and kill criminal suspects even though they would not face death if they were caught, tried, and convicted?

InfoTrac College Edition Research

To read about the PepperBall System in more detail, go to "Law Enforcement Across the Nation Use PepperBall to Save Lives; Non-Lethal Weapon Helps Police and Civilians Avoid Death, Serious Injury," *PR Newswire*, June 9, 2003.

Sources: The National Institute of Justice, *The Effectiveness and Safety of Pepper Spray* (Washington, D.C.: U.S. Department of Justice, 2003); Patricia Biggs. "Officers take a shock, awe of Taser guns," *The Arizona Republic*, May 13, 2003, 1–2; Tamara Lush, "Deputies to test 50,000-volt weapon," *St. Petersburg Times*, March 17, 2003, 1–2; Jennifer LeClaire, "Police now carry guns, badges. . .beanbags," *The Christian Science Monitor*, December 18, 2001, 1–3; Jack Leonard, "Police Dropping 'nonlethal' beanbags as too dangerous," *The Nation*, June 3, 2002, 1–5; Terry Flynn, "Ft. Thomas police get non-lethal weapons," *The Cincinnati Enquirer*, June 15, 2001, 1–2.

- *Selective enforcement or nonenforcement.* This form occurs when police abuse or exploit their discretion. If an officer frees a drug dealer in return for valuable information, that is considered a legitimate use of discretion; if the officer does so for money, that is an abuse of police power.

- *Active criminality.* This is participation by police in serious criminal behavior. Police may use their positions of trust and power to commit the very crimes they are entrusted with controlling. In one recent case, retired officers Louis Eppolito, 56, and his former partner, Stephen Caracappa, 63, were arrested and charged with being on the payroll of organized crime while they were New York City police officers. Eppolito and Caracappa sold police files on key witnesses to the mob and are alleged to have participated directly and indirectly in eleven mob hits.[163]

- *Bribery and extortion.* This includes practices in which law enforcement roles are exploited specifically to raise money. Bribery is initiated by the citizen; extortion is initiated by the officer. Bribery or extortion can be a one-shot transaction, as when a traffic violator offers a police officer $100 to forget about issuing a summons. Or the relationship can be an ongoing one, in which the officer solicits (or is offered) regular payoffs to ignore criminal activities, such as gambling or narcotics dealing. This is known as "being on the pad."

Sometimes police officers accept routine bribes and engage in petty extortion without considering themselves corrupt; they consider these payments as some of the unwritten "benefits" of police work. *Mooching* involves receiving free gifts of coffee, cigarettes, meals, and so on in exchange for possible future acts of favoritism. *Chiseling* occurs when officers demand admission to entertainment events or price discounts; *shopping* involves taking small items, such as cigarettes, from a store whose door was accidentally left unlocked after business hours.[164]

Corrupt Departments It has also been suggested that entire police departments can be categorized on the basis of the level and type of corruption existing within them.[165] Three types of departments may exist:

- *"Rotten apples" and "rotten pockets."* This type of police department has a few corrupt officers ("rotten apples") who use their position for personal gain. When these corrupt officers band together, they form a "rotten pocket." Robert Daley described the activities of such a group in his book *Prince of the City*.[166] Agents of New York City's Special Investigations Unit kept money they confiscated during narcotics raids and used illegal drugs to pay off informers. *Prince of the City* tells the story of New York detective Frank Leuci, whose testimony against his partners before investigating committees made him an outcast in the police department. Rotten pockets help institutionalize corruption because their members expect newcomers to conform to their illegal practices and to a code of secrecy.

- *Pervasive unorganized corruption.* This type of department contains a majority of personnel who are corrupt but have little relationship to one another. Though many officers are involved in taking bribes and extortion, they are not cooperating with one another for personal gain.

- *Pervasive organized corruption.* This describes a department in which almost all members are involved in systematic and organized corruption. The Knapp Commission found this type of relationship in New York City's vice divisions, where payoffs and bribes were an organized and accepted way of police life.

The Causes and Control of Corruption No single explanation satisfactorily accounts for the various forms the abuse of power takes. One view puts the blame on the type of person who becomes a police officer. This position holds that policing tends to attract lower-class individuals who do not have the financial means to maintain a coveted middle-class lifestyle. As they develop the cynical, authoritarian police personality, accepting graft seems an all-too-easy method of achieving financial security.

A second view is that the wide discretion police enjoy, coupled with low visibility among the public and their own supervisors, makes them likely candidates for corruption. In addition, the code of secrecy maintained by the police subculture helps insulate corrupt officers from the law. Similarly, police managers, most of whom have risen through the ranks, are reluctant to investigate corruption or punish wrongdoers. Thus, corruption may also be viewed as a function of police institutions and practices.[167]

A third position holds that corruption is a function of society's ambivalence toward many forms of vice-related criminal behavior that police officers are sworn to control. Unenforceable laws governing moral standards promote corruption because they create large groups with an interest in undermining law enforcement. These include consumers who do not want to be deprived of their chosen form of recreation—people who gamble, wish to drink after the legal closing hour, or patronize a prostitute. Even though the consumers may not actively corrupt police officers, their existence creates a climate that tolerates active corruption by others.[168] Since vice cannot be controlled and the public apparently wants it to continue, the officer may have little resistance to inducements for monetary gain offered by law violators.

How can police misconduct be controlled? One approach is to strengthen the internal administrative review process in police departments. A strong and well-supported internal affairs division has been linked to lowered corruption rates.[169] However, asking police to police themselves is not a simple task. Officers are often reluctant to discipline their peers. For example, a 1999 review of disciplinary files found that hundreds of New York City police officers escaped punishment when their cases were summarily dismissed by the police department without ever interviewing victims or witnesses or making any other efforts to examine the strength of the evidence.[170]

Another approach, instituted by then New York Commissioner Patrick Murphy in the wake of the Knapp Commission, is the accountability system. This holds that supervisors at each level are directly accountable for the illegal behaviors of the officers under them. Consequently, a commander can be demoted or forced to resign if someone under his or her command is found guilty of corruption.[171] Close scrutiny by a department, however, can lower officer morale and create the suspicion that the officers' own supervisors distrust them.

Some departments have set up guidelines to help reduce corruption. In 1996 the city of Philadelphia agreed to implement a set of reforms to combat corruption in order to settle a lawsuit brought by civil rights organizations. The following were among the measures taken to reduce corruption:

- A policy mandating that all citizens' complaints be forwarded for investigation by the internal affairs division
- Development of computer files that contain all types of complaints and suits against individual officers that could be easily accessed during investigations
- A policy requiring that internal affairs give a high priority to any officer's claim that another officer was corrupt or used excessive force
- Mandatory reporting and recording of all incidents in which an officer used more than incidental force
- Training of officers to treat citizens without racial bias; assigning a deputy commissioner to monitor charges of race discrimination
- Reviewing all policies and practices to ensure they do not involve or have the potential for race bias[172]

Another approach is to create outside review boards or special prosecutors, such as the Mollen Commission in New York and the Christopher Commission in Los Angeles, to investigate reported incidents of corruption. However, outside investigators and special prosecutors are often limited by their lack of intimate knowledge of day-to-day operations. As a result, they depend on the testimony of a few officers who are willing to cooperate, either to save themselves from prosecution or because they have a compelling moral commitment. Outside evaluators also face the problem of the blue curtain, which is quickly closed when police officers feel their department is under scrutiny.

A more realistic solution to corruption, albeit a difficult one, might be to change the social context of policing. Police operations must be made more visible, and the public must be given freer access to controlling police operations. All too often, the public finds out about police problems only when a scandal hits the newspaper. Some of the vice-related crimes the police now deal with might be decriminalized or referred to other agencies. Although decriminalization of vice cannot in itself end the problem, it could lower the pressure placed on individual police officers and help eliminate their moral dilemmas.

Controlling Police Behavior

Politicians, legal experts, and police administrators have all sought to control police behavior so that its exercise may be both beneficial to citizens and nondiscriminatory.[173] One approach is to develop review boards that monitor police behavior and tactics and investigate civilian complaints. No two models are alike, but in the past thirty years about one hundred departments have adopted some form of civilian board. According to police authority Samuel Walker, there are a number of different models of civilian oversight (see Exhibit 7.2). In some jurisdictions, independent citizen agencies have full responsibility for receiving and investigating complaints. In others, citizens review the investigation of complaints conducted by the police department; some oversight agencies monitor or audit the complaint process. (See Exhibit 7.3 for a description of San Francisco's process.)

There are many variations on these basic models. The Minneapolis, Minnesota, civilian police review operates in two stages. First, paid, professional investigators and a director examine citizen complaints to determine if there is reasonable evidence that police misconduct occurred. Then, volunteer board members conduct closed-door hearings to decide whether they should support the allegations that came from the initial screening process in probable cause cases. In Orange County, Florida, a nine-volunteer citizen review board holds hearings, open to the public and the media, on all cases involving the alleged use of excessive force and abuse of power after the sheriff's department has conducted an investigation.

Although police agencies in some communities have embraced citizen review, others find them troublesome. Departmental opposition is most likely when oversight procedures represent outside interference, oversight staff lack experience with and understanding of police work, and oversight processes are unfair. Most police administrators believe that their agencies should have the final say in matters of discipline, policies and procedures, and training, and some bridle at the hint of outside interference by nonprofessionals. In some communities local governments have established oversight bodies that act only in an advisory capacity and make nonbinding recommendations to law enforcement agencies.

Another familiar complaint is that civilians are unable to understand the complexities of police work. To compensate, candidates for the review board in Rochester, New York, attend a condensed version of a police academy run by the police department. The forty-eight-hour course involves

Exhibit 7.2   **Models of police review boards**

Class I agencies are responsible for receiving and investigating citizen complaints.

Class II agencies review complaint investigations conducted by the police department.

Class III agencies hear appeals of complaint investigations and dispositions made by the police department.

Class IV agencies audit or monitor the police department's complaint process.

Class V is a new form of oversight. It involves non-sworn persons who are employed by the police department and who have some input or control over the complaint process.

Source: Samuel Walker, http://policeaccountability.org/modelsco.htm, accessed on February 26, 2005.

| Exhibit | 7.3 | Office of Citizen Complaints (OCC)—San Francisco |

- The OCC first became staffed and began its operations in 1983 and works directly with the Police Commission, a volunteer civilian body of five persons appointed by the mayor.
- The OCC receives, investigates, and makes findings on civilian complaints of on-duty misconduct (including acts and omissions) by sworn members of the San Francisco Police Department.
- Where the OCC sustains one or more allegations against one or more officers in a given case, the case can either go to the chief of police or to the Police Commission.
- The factors governing whether the Police Commission hears a case that has been sustained by the OCC include: severity of misconduct and of potential discipline; complexity of issues presented; degree of public interest in the matter.
- The chief of police either refers the case to the commission or hears it directly. The chief of police has disciplinary power to issue a ten-day suspension or less; the commission holds all greater disciplinary power, including the power to hear appeals from the chief's disciplinary decisions.
- Consistent with the Peace Officers' Bill of Rights, officers accused by OCC complaints receive notice of allegations against them, an opportunity to be heard by the OCC and to be represented during the investigative process, and notice of the outcome of the OCC's process.

Source: San Francisco, California, Office of Citizen Complaints, www.sfgov.org/site/occ_index.asp, accessed on August 21, 2005.

three hours per evening for two weeks and two all-day Saturday sessions. The members use a shoot/don't shoot simulator, practice handcuffing, and learn about department policies and procedures, including the use-of-force continuum.

Many officers believe that review members hold them accountable for minor infractions, such as placing the wrong offense code on a citation or failing to record the end mileage on a vehicle transport. There is also the belief that the review process is often lengthy and that delays both harm the credibility of the oversight process and cause officers considerable stress as they wait for their cases to be decided. To overcome these problems, some police administrators have taken the initiative by helping to set up a citizen oversight system before being required to do so and then becoming involved in the planning process.

Despite serious reservations about citizen oversight, many law enforcement administrators have identified positive outcomes from having a review board in place. These include improving community relations, enhancing an agency's ability to police itself, and most important, improving an agency's policies and procedures. Citizen oversight bodies can recommend changes in the way the department conducts its internal investigation into alleged misconduct and also to improve department policies governing officer behavior.[174]

POLICE AND THE RULE OF LAW

Court control over police conduct is sometimes vexing to police administrators. The police are charged with protecting the public and upholding the law. They want a free hand to enforce the law as they see fit, unencumbered by outside interference. The courts are charged with protecting the civil liberties of all citizens, even those accused of committing heinous crimes. The courts must balance the needs of efficient law enforcement with the constitutional rights of citizens.

In recent years, a more conservative U.S. Supreme Court has given police officers greater leeway to interrogate suspects, stop cars, detain drivers and

Criminal Justice ⚖ Now™
Learn more by viewing the "Code of Hammurabi" video clip.

their passengers, and search vehicles—often with the intent of finding illegal drugs or other contraband. However, although the balance may have tipped, the courts have by no means revoked the basic rights of American citizens to be protected from overzealous police work. Yet the question remains: Should personal rights have supremacy over public safety? Should guilty people be freed because the police made an error while carrying out their stated duties? Should a criminal be set free because the police officer failed to "read him his rights" or conducted a search that went beyond what is allowed by the law? The following section addresses these questions by reviewing the relationship between the police and the courts and discussing in some depth the legal cases that define the scope of police conduct—that is, what police can do and what they are prevented from doing.

The Police and the Courts

The police are charged with preventing crime and, failing to do so, investigating the case, gathering evidence, identifying the culprit, and making an arrest, all the while gathering sufficient evidence to convict the culprit at trial. To carry out these tasks, police officers need to be able to search for evidence, to seize items such as guns and drugs, and to question suspects, witnesses, and victims, because at trial, they need to provide prosecutors with sufficient evidence to prove guilt "beyond a reasonable doubt." This requirement means that soon after a crime is committed, they must make every effort to gather physical evidence, obtain confessions, and take witness statements that will stand up in court. Police officers also realize that evidence such as the testimony of a witness or a co-conspirator may evaporate before the trial begins. Then the case outcome may depend on some piece of physical evidence or a suspect's statement taken early during the investigation.

The need for police officers to gather evidence can conflict with the constitutional rights of citizens. Although police might prefer a free hand to search homes and cars for evidence, the Fourth Amendment restricts police activities by limiting searches and seizures only to those deemed "reasonable." When police wish to vigorously interrogate a suspect, they must honor the Fifth Amendment's prohibition against forcing people to incriminate themselves. The following sections address some of the key areas in which police operations have been restricted or curtailed by the courts.

Custodial Interrogation

After an arrest is made, police want to interrogate suspects, hoping they will confess to a crime, name co-conspirators, or make incriminating statements that can be used against them in court. But the Fifth Amendment guarantees people the right to be free from self-incrimination. The courts have used this phrase to prohibit law enforcement agents from using physical or psychological coercion while interrogating suspects under their control to get them to confess or give information. Confessions obtained from defendants through coercion, force, trickery, or promises of leniency are inadmissible because their trustworthiness is questionable.

The *Miranda* Rule In 1966, in the case of *Miranda v. Arizona*, the Supreme Court created objective standards for questioning by police after a defendant has been taken into custody.[175] Custody occurs when a person is not free to walk away, as when an individual is arrested. The Court maintained that before the police can question a person who has been arrested or is in custody, they must inform the individual of the Fifth Amendment right to be free from

© 2005 AP/Wide World Photos

Chicago Police Department Lt. Marty Ryczek shows off control panels to monitor video in the interview room at the police department's Area 1 headquarters. A new law that took effect on July 18, 2005, requires Illinois police to videotape homicide interrogations. The law was implemented because of fears that innocent men were being sent to death row after they issued false or coerced confessions.

self-incrimination. This is accomplished by the police issuing what is known as the ***Miranda* warning,** which informs the suspect that

- He has the right to remain silent.
- If he makes a statement, it can be used against him in court.
- He has the right to consult an attorney and to have the attorney present at the time of the interrogation.
- If he cannot afford an attorney, one will be appointed by the state.

If the defendant is not given the *Miranda* warning before the investigation, the evidence obtained from the interrogation cannot be admitted at trial. An accused person can waive his or her *Miranda* rights at any time. However, for the waiver to be effective, the state must first show that the defendant was aware of all the *Miranda* rights and must then prove that the waiver was made with the full knowledge of constitutional rights. People who cannot understand the *Miranda* warning because of their age, mental handicaps, or language problems cannot be legally questioned absent an attorney; if they can understand their rights, they may be questioned.[176]

Once the suspect asks for an attorney, all questioning must stop unless the attorney is present. And if the criminal suspect has invoked his or her *Miranda* rights, police officials cannot reinitiate interrogation in the absence of counsel even if the accused has consulted with an attorney in the meantime.[177]

The *Miranda* Rule Today The Supreme Court has used case law to define the boundaries of the *Miranda* warning since its inception. Although statements made by suspects who were not given the *Miranda* warning or received it improperly cannot be used against them in a court of law it is possible to use illegally gained statements and the evidence they produce in some well-defined instances:

1. Evidence obtained in violation of the *Miranda* warning can be used by the government to impeach defendants' testimony during trial, if they perjure themselves.[178]
2. At trial, the testimony of a witness is permissible even though his or her identity was revealed by the defendant in violation of the *Miranda* rule.[179]
3. It is permissible to use information provided by a suspect who has not been given the *Miranda* warning that leads to the seizure of incriminating evidence if the evidence would have been obtained anyway by other means or sources; this is now referred to as the **inevitable discovery rule.**[180]

Miranda *warning The result of two U.S. Supreme Court decisions (Escobedo v. Illinois and Miranda v. Arizona) that require police officers to inform individuals under arrest that they have a constitutional right to remain silent, that their statements can later be used against them in court, that they can have an attorney present to help them, and that the state will pay for an attorney if they cannot afford to hire one. Although aimed at protecting an individual during in-custody interrogation, the warning must also be given when the investigation shifts from the investigatory to the accusatory stage—that is, when suspicion begins to focus on an individual.*

inevitable discovery rule Evidence seized in violation of the Fifth Amendment's self-incrimination clause may be used in a court of law if a judge rules that it would have been found or discovered even if the incriminating statements had never been made.

4. Initial errors by police in getting statements do not make subsequent - statements inadmissible; a subsequent *Miranda* warning that is properly given can "cure the condition" that made the initial statements inadmissible.[181]

5. The admissions of mentally impaired defendants can be admitted in evidence as long as the police acted properly and there is a "preponderance of the evidence" that they understood the meaning of *Miranda*.[182]

6. The erroneous admission of a coerced confession at trial can be ruled a "harmless error" and therefore not automatically result in overturning a conviction.[183]

The Supreme Court has also ruled that in some instances the *Miranda* warning may not have to be given before a suspect is questioned and it has also narrowed the scope of *Miranda*, for example, by restricting the people with whom a suspect may ask to consult:

1. The *Miranda* warning applies only to the right to have an attorney present; the suspect cannot demand to speak to a priest, probation officer, or any other official.[184]

2. A suspect can be questioned in the field without a *Miranda* warning if the information the police seek is needed to protect public safety; in an emergency, suspects can be asked where they hid their weapons.[185] This is known as the **public safety doctrine.**

3. Suspects need not be aware of all the possible outcomes of waiving their rights for the *Miranda* warning to be considered properly given.[186]

4. An attorney's request to see the defendant does not affect the validity of the defendant's waiver of the right to counsel; police misinformation to an attorney does not affect waiver of *Miranda* rights.[187] A suspect's statements may be used if they are given voluntarily even though the suspect's family has hired an attorney and the statements were made before the attorney arrived. Only the suspect can request an attorney, not friends or family.

5. A suspect who makes an ambiguous reference to an attorney during questioning, such as "Maybe I should talk to an attorney," is not protected under *Miranda*; the police may continue their questioning.[188]

6. Initial errors by police in getting statements do not automatically make subsequent statements inadmissible; a subsequent *Miranda* warning that is properly given can "cure the condition" that disallowed use of the initial statements.[189] However, if police intentionally mislead suspects by questioning them before giving them a *Miranda* warning, their statements made after the warning is given are inadmissible in court. The "*Miranda* rule would be frustrated were the police permitted to undermine its meaning and effect."[190]

7. A voluntary statement given in the absence of the *Miranda* warning can be used to obtain evidence which can be used at trial. Failure to give the warning does not make seizure of evidence illegal per se.[191]

8. Failure to give a suspect a *Miranda* warning is not illegal unless the case actually becomes a criminal matter.[192] A "criminal case" at the very least requires the initiation of legal proceedings, and police questioning by itself does not constitute such a case.

Miranda is now a police institution. It is not surprising that today police administrators who in the past might have been wary of the restrictions forced by *Miranda* now actually favor its use.[193] One survey found that nearly 60 percent of police chiefs believe that the *Miranda* warning should be retained and the same number report that abolishing it would change the way the police function.[194]

 The Library of Congress contains more than 121 million items, some of them designated "treasures." One of the treasures is **Chief Justice Earl Warren's handwritten notes on the *Miranda* case.** To reach this site go to "Web Links" on your Siegel Essentials of Criminal Justice 5e website: http://cj.wadsworth.com/siegel_ess5e.

public safety doctrine *Statements elicited by police violation of the Fifth Amendment's self-incrimination clause may be used in a court of law if a judge rules that the questioning was justified in order to maintain public safety. So, for example, it would be permissible for police to ask a suspected terrorist where he planted a bomb and then use his statement in a criminal trial even though he had never been apprised of his Fifth Amendment (Miranda) rights.*

Search and Seizure

When conducting investigations, police officers want to collect evidence, seize it, and carry it away. They may wish to enter a suspect's home, look for evidence of a crime such as bloody clothes, drugs, the missing money, or a weapon, seize the evidence, and store it in the evidence room so it can later be used at trial.

But the manner in which police may seize evidence is governed by the search-and-seizure requirements of the Fourth Amendment of the U.S. Constitution, which was designed by the framers to protect a criminal suspect against unreasonable searches and seizures. Under normal circumstances, no search or seizure undertaken without a **search warrant** is lawful.

A search warrant is a court order authorizing and directing the police to search a designated place for evidence of a crime. To obtain a search warrant, the following procedural requirements must be met: (1) the police officer must request the warrant from the court; (2) the officer must submit an affidavit establishing the proper grounds for the warrant; and (3) the affidavit must state the place to be searched and the property to be seized. A warrant cannot be issued unless the presiding magistrate is presented with sufficient evidence to conclude that an offense has been or is being committed and the suspect is the one who committed the offense; this is referred to as the **probable cause** requirement. In other words, the presiding judge must conclude from the facts presented by the police that there is probable cause a crime has been committed and the person or place to be searched is materially involved in that crime; there must be solid evidence of criminal involvement.

Searches must also be reasonable under the circumstances of the crime. Police would not be able to get a warrant to search a suspect's desk drawer for a missing piano! Nor could a police officer obtain a warrant that allows them to tear down the walls of a person's house because it is suspected that they contain drugs. A search is considered unreasonable when it exceeds the scope of police authority or is highly invasive of personal privacy, even if it reveals incriminating evidence.

Warrantless Searches To make it easier for police to conduct investigations and to protect public safety, the Court has ruled that under certain circumstances a valid search may be conducted without a search warrant. The six major exceptions are search incident to a valid arrest, threshold inquiry (**stop and frisk**), automobile search, consent search, plain-sight search, and seizure of nonphysical evidence.

1. *Search incident to a valid arrest.* A warrantless search is valid if it is made incident to a lawful arrest. The reason for this exception is that the arresting officer must have the power to disarm the accused, protect himself or herself, preserve the evidence of the crime, and prevent the accused from escaping from custody. Because the search is lawful, the officer retains what he or she finds if it is connected with a crime. The officer is permitted to search only the defendant's person and the areas in the defendant's immediate physical surroundings that are under his or her control.[195]

2. *Stop and frisk.* A stop and frisk occurs where an officer does not have probable cause to arrest, but his or her suspicions are raised concerning the behavior of an individual. For example, the individual is found lurking behind a closed store. In such a case, the officer has a right to stop and question the individual, and if the officer has reason to believe that the person is carrying a concealed weapon, may frisk the subject—that is, pat down the person's outer clothing for the purpose of finding a concealed weapon. If an illegal weapon is found, then an arrest can be made and a

search warrant An order issued by a judge, directing officers to conduct a search of specified premises for specified objects or persons and bring them before the court.

probable cause The evidentiary criterion necessary to sustain an arrest or the issuance of an arrest or search warrant; less than absolute certainty or "beyond a reasonable doubt" but greater than mere suspicion or "hunch." Probable cause consists of a set of facts, information, circumstances, or conditions that would lead a reasonable person to believe that an offense was committed and that the accused committed that offense. An arrest made without probable cause may be susceptible to prosecution as an illegal arrest under "false imprisonment" statutes.

stop and frisk The situation when police officers who are suspicious of an individual run their hands lightly over the suspect's outer garments, to determine whether the person is carrying a concealed weapon. Also called a patdown or threshold inquiry, a stop and frisk is intended to stop short of any activity that could be considered a violation of Fourth Amendment rights.

search incident to the arrest performed.[196] Would it be legal to pat down a person merely because that person is standing in a high-crime neighborhood? Probably not. The Supreme Court suggests that an officer would need more suspicion—for example, if the person ran away when he spotted the police approaching.[197]

3. *Automobile search.* An automobile may be searched without a warrant if there is probable cause to believe that the car was involved in a crime.[198] Because automobiles are inherently mobile there is a significant chance that the evidence will be lost if the search is not conducted immediately; also, people should not expect as much privacy in their cars as in their homes.[199] Police officers who have legitimately stopped an automobile and who have probable cause to believe that contraband is concealed somewhere inside it may conduct a warrantless search of the vehicle that is as thorough as a magistrate could authorize by warrant. The Supreme Court has also ruled that police who have stopped a motorist for a routine traffic violation can conduct a search if they find probable cause that the vehicle has been involved in a crime—e.g., after stopping a car for an illegal U-turn, they spot drug paraphernalia in the front seat.[200]

   Because traffic stops can be dangerous, the Court has ruled that if a police officer perceives danger during a routine traffic stop he can order the driver and passengers from the car without suspicion and conduct a limited search of their persons to ensure police officer safety.[201] Police officers can search the car and passengers after a traffic stop as long as the search is reasonable and related to officer safety.[202]

4. *Consent search.* In a consent search, individuals waive their constitutional rights; therefore, neither a warrant nor probable cause need exist. A police officer stops a car because the driver has an outstanding traffic ticket that has never been paid. He asks if he can search the trunk and the driver gives consent. Any illegal contraband found in the trunk can be seized. However, for the search to be legal, the consent must be given voluntarily; threat or compulsion invalidates the search.[203] Although it has been held that voluntary consent is required, it has also been maintained that the police are under no obligation to inform individuals of their right to refuse the search. For example, police do not have to tell motorists they have stopped for a traffic violation that they are actually free to go before asking permission to search the car.[204]

5. *Plain-sight search.* Even when an object is in a house or other areas involving an expectation of privacy, the object can be freely inspected if it can be seen by the general public. If a police officer looks through a fence and sees marijuana growing in a suspect's fields, no search warrant is needed for the property to be seized. The articles are considered to be in plain view, and therefore a search warrant need not be obtained to seize.[205]

6. *Seizure of nonphysical evidence.* Police can seize nonphysical evidence, such as a conversation, if the suspects had no reason to expect privacy—for example, it would be legal for a police officer who overhears a conversation in which two people conspire to kill a third party to record the conversation and use the recording in a court of law.

Concept Summary 7.1 summarizes some notable Fourth and Fifth Amendment case doctrines and holdings.

The Exclusionary Rule

The most controversial issue revolving around the Court's control of police behavior is what is commonly known as the **exclusionary rule,** which provides that all evidence obtained by unreasonable searches and seizures is inadmis-

exclusionary rule *The principle that prohibits using evidence illegally obtained in a trial. Based on the Fourth Amendment "right of the people to be secure in their persons, houses, papers, and effects, against unreasonable searches and seizures," the rule is not a bar to prosecution because legally obtained evidence may be available that may be used in a trial.*

Concept Summary   7.1

Notable case doctrines and exceptions to the Fourth Amendment (search and seizure) and Fifth Amendment (self-incrimination) clauses

	Case Decision	Holding
Fourth Amendment Doctrine		
Expectation of privacy	*Katz v. United States* (1968)	Electronic eavesdropping is a search.
Plain view	*Arizona v. Hicks* (1967)	Fourth Amendment may not apply when the object is in plain view.
Open fields	*Oliver v. United States* (1984)	Police can search a field and curtilage if the marijuana can be seen from an airplane or a helicopter.
Stop and frisk	*Terry v. Ohio* (1967)	Police are authorized to stop and frisk suspicious persons.
Consent	*Schneckloth v. Bustamonte* (1973)	Consent to search must be voluntarily given.
Bus sweep	*Florida v. Bostick* (1991)	Police, after obtaining consent, may conduct a search of luggage without a search warrant or probable cause.
Warrant Requirements		
Probable cause	*Illinois v. Gates* (1983)	Probable cause to issue a warrant is based on a "totality of circumstances."
Home entry	*Kirk v. Louisiana* (2002)	Police need a warrant to enter a home absent probable cause and exigent circumstances.
Exceptions to the Warrant Requirement		
Federal requirement of exclusionary rule	*Weeks v. United States* (1914)	U.S. Supreme Court applied the exclusionary rule to federal prosecutions.
State application	*Mapp v. Ohio* (1961)	U.S. Supreme Court applied the exclusionary rule to state prosecutions.
Automobile search	*United States v. Ross* (1982)	Warrantless search of an auto is permissible when it is based on probable cause.
Search incident to arrest	*Chimel v. California* (1969)	Permissible scope for a search is the area "within the arrestee's immediate control."
Traffic stop	*Whren v. United States* (1996)	Traffic violation can be used as a pretext to stop suspicious vehicles.
Exceptions to the Exclusionary Rule		
Good faith	*United States v. Leon* (1984)	When police rely on "good faith" in a warrant, the evidence seized is admissible even if the warrant is subsequently deemed defective.
Good faith	*Arizona v. Evans* (1995)	Even though police arrested a man based on an erroneous warrant that resulted from a court employee's computer error, the evidence they found in a subsequent search is admissible.
Fifth Amendment Doctrine		
Self-incrimination	*Miranda v. Arizona* (1966)	Defendant must be given the *Miranda* warning before questioning begins.
Miranda warning	*Dickerson v. United States* (2000)	Congress cannot overrule the requirements that *Miranda* rights be read to criminal suspects.

sible in criminal trials. Similarly, it excludes the use of illegal confessions under Fifth Amendment prohibitions.

After police agencies were created in the mid-nineteenth century, evidence obtained by unreasonable searches and seizures was admitted by state and federal governments in criminal trials. The only criteria for admissibility were whether the evidence was incriminating and whether it would assist the judge or jury in reaching a verdict. Then, in 1914, the U.S. Supreme Court established the exclusionary rule in the case of *Weeks v. United States,* when it ruled that evidence obtained by unreasonable search and seizure must be excluded in a federal criminal trial.[206]

In 1961, the Supreme Court made the exclusionary rule applicable to state courts in the landmark decision of *Mapp v. Ohio.*[207]

Current Status and Controversy The U.S. Supreme Court, with its conservative bent of recent years, has been diminishing the scope of the exclusionary rule. It has created a **good faith exception** to the exclusionary rule: evidence is admissible in court if the police officers acted in good faith by first obtaining court approval for their search even if the warrant they received was deficient or faulty.[208] As long as the police tried to abide by legal rules, the evidence they seize is admissible in court even if the warrant contained some mistakes or errors. However, deliberately misleading a judge or using a warrant that the police know is deficient would be grounds to invoke the exclusionary rule.

Police administrators have long decried the exclusionary rule because it means that valuable evidence may not be usable at trial because the police made an error or failed to obtain a proper warrant. The most widely voiced criticism of the exclusionary rule, however, is that it allows guilty defendants to go free. Because courts frequently decide in many types of cases (particularly those involving victimless offenses, such as gambling and drug use) that certain evidence should be excluded, the rule is believed to result in excessive court delays and to affect plea-bargaining negotiations negatively. In fact, however, the rule appears to result in relatively few case dismissals. Research efforts show that prosecutions are lost because of suppression rulings less than 1 percent of the time.[209]

Suggested approaches to dealing with violations of the exclusionary rule include (1) criminal prosecution of police officers who violate constitutional rights, (2) internal police control, (3) civil lawsuits against state or municipal police officers, and (4) federal lawsuits against the government under the Federal Tort Claims Act (FTCA). Law professor Donald Dripps has derived a novel approach for modifying the exclusionary rule. His approach, which he labels the **contingent exclusionary rule,** would apply when a judge finds police testimony questionable but also concludes that the release of the guilty would be unpleasant and unwarranted. Rather than simply excluding the evidence, the judge could request that the prosecution or police pay a fee, similar in form to a fine, in order to use the evidence in court. Exclusion of the evidence would be contingent on the failure of the police department to pay the damages set by the court. The judge thereby could uphold the Constitution without freeing the guilty. The contingent exclusionary rule would force the prosecution to decide whether justice was worth the damages.[210]

In recent years the Court has given police greater latitude to search for and seize evidence and has eased restrictions on how police operate. However, even in this permissive environment research shows that police routinely violate suspects' rights when searching for evidence and that the majority of these incidents are never reviewed by the courts because the search was not followed up by arrest or citation.[211]

exclusionary rule The principle that prohibits using evidence illegally obtained in a trial. Based on the Fourth Amendment "right of the people to be secure in their persons, houses, papers, and effects, against unreasonable searches and seizures," the rule is not a bar to prosecution because legally obtained evidence may be available that may be used in a trial.

good faith exception The principle of law holding that evidence may be used in a criminal trial, even though the search warrant used to obtain it is technically faulty, if the police acted in good faith and to the best of their ability when they sought to obtain it from a judge.

contingent exclusionary rule A plan that would allow evidence seized in violation of the Fourth Amendment to be used in a court of law.

SUMMARY

- Social concerns also affect police operations.
- Today, many police officers seek higher education. The jury is still out on whether educated officers are actually more effective.
- Women and minorities are now being recruited into the police in increasing numbers. Research indicates that, with few exceptions, they perform as well or even better than other officers.
- The percentage of minorities on police forces reflects their representation in the general population, but the number of female officers still lags behind. Of greater importance is increasing the number of women and minorities in supervisory positions.
- Police departments today are faced with many critical problems in their development and relationship with the public.
- Police are believed to be insulated from the rest of society.
- Some experts hold that police officers have distinct personality characteristics marked by authoritarianism and cynicism.
- It is also alleged that police maintain a separate culture with distinct rules and loyalties.
- Four distinct police styles have been identified, and each influences the officer's decision making. The complexity and danger of the police role produce an enormous amount of stress that harms police effectiveness.
- There are many problems faced by contemporary police officers, including job stress.
- Force and violence are part of the police role though they are used in only about 1 percent of encounters with civilians.
- One critical concern is the police use of deadly force. Research indicates that anti-shooting poli-

cies can limit deaths resulting from police action. The Supreme Court has ruled that police cannot shoot unarmed fleeing felons.
- Another effort has been to identify and eliminate police corruption, which still mars the reputation of police forces.
- Over the past three decades, the U.S. Supreme Court has placed constitutional limitations on the police ability to conduct investigations.
- Under interpretations of the Fourth Amendment, police are required to use warrants to conduct searches except in some clearly defined situations.
- Police are required to have probable cause in order to obtain a warrant.
- The exceptions to the search warrant rule include searches of automobiles used in a crime, stop and frisk, searches incident to an arrest, consent searches, and searches of material in plain view.
- If police violate the legal rule controlling search and seizure, the evidence they collected cannot be used in court.
- Through the *Miranda* rule, the Supreme Court established a procedure required for all custodial interrogations that focuses on the need to warn criminal suspects of their right to remain silent and be advised by an attorney.
- Many issues concerning *Miranda* continue to be litigated. The Supreme Court has shaped *Miranda* protections, increasing them in some instances and reducing them in others.
- The exclusionary rule continues to be one of the most controversial issues in the criminal justice system. Even though the courts have curtailed its application in recent years, it still generally prohibits the admission of evidence obtained in violation of the defendant's constitutional rights.

KEY TERMS

double marginality 180
cynicism 184
blue curtain 184
discretion 186
demeanor 189
police brutality 194
suicide by cop 197

Knapp Commission 202
meat eaters 202
grass eaters 202
Mollen Commission 202
Miranda warning 209
inevitable discovery rule 210
public safety doctrine 210

search warrant 211
probable cause 211
stop and frisk 211
exclusionary rule 214
good faith exception 214
contingent exclusionary rule 214

REVIEW QUESTIONS

1. Should male and female officers have exactly the same duties in a police department? Explain your reasoning.

2. Do you think that an officer's working the street will eventually produce a cynical personality and distrust for civilians? Explain.

3. How can education help police officers?

4. Should a police officer who accepts a free meal from a restaurant owner be dismissed from the force? Why or why not?

5. A police officer orders an unarmed person running away from a burglary to stop; the suspect keeps running and is shot and killed by the officer. Has the officer committed murder? Explain.

6. Would you like to live in a society that abolished police discretion and used a full enforcement policy? Why or why not?

7. Should illegally seized evidence be excluded from trial, even though it is conclusive proof of a person's criminal acts? Might there be another way to deal with police violation of the Fourth Amendment—for example, making them pay a fine?

8. Have criminals been given too many rights by the courts? Should courts be more concerned with the rights of victims or the rights of offenders? Have the police been "handcuffed" and prevented from doing their job in the most efficient manner?

PART 3

Courts and Adjudication

The nation's court system is the location of some of the most critical decisions in the criminal justice system. Take, for instance, the decision by the Supreme Court in *Pottawatomie County et al. v. Earls* (2002). In its decision, the Court decided to uphold the student activities drug testing policy adopted by the Tecumseh, Oklahoma, School District. The policy requires all middle and high school students to consent to urinalysis testing for drugs if they wish to participate in any extracurricular activity. A federal appellate court had previously overruled the policy, holding that it violated the Fourth Amendment right to privacy.

The Supreme Court disagreed. It ruled that a search of schoolchildren may be reasonable when supported by "special needs" beyond the normal need for law enforcement; making sure that kids who participate in extracurricular activities are drug-free is one of those needs. The Court concluded that the students affected by this policy have a limited expectation of privacy and that the policy does not interfere with their personal lives. Under the policy, a faculty monitor waits outside the closed restroom stall for the student to produce a sample and must listen for the normal sounds of urination to guard against tampered specimens and ensure an accurate chain of custody. The Court did not see this as particularly intrusive or as an invasion of privacy. Furthermore, the only consequence of a failed drug test is to limit the student's privilege of participating in extracurricular activities. The Court ruled that this drug-testing policy is valid because preventing drug use by schoolchildren is an important governmental concern. Given the nationwide epidemic of drug use, and the evidence of drug use in Tecumseh schools that was presented, the Court concluded that the conditions necessary to allow such a testing policy were amply met by the school district.

Pottawatomie County et al. v. Earls is a case that illustrates the delicate balance between individual freedom and governmental concerns, which is reviewed by the court system every day. Kids who have never been in trouble and who are not suspected of taking drugs must hand over urine samples in order to get a part in the school play or go on a field trip. Is this a violation of their right to privacy? The Supreme Court said "No!" What do you think?

This section reviews the workings of the court system. Four chapters cover the structure of the courts: court personnel, early court processes, the criminal trial, and sentencing. ■

 CHAPTER 8

Courts, Prosecution, and the Defense

© 2003 AP/Wide World Photos

TIM BAKKEN received his B.S. degree with majors in English and psychology from the University of Wisconsin–Stevens Point, and then went on to earn his J.D. (*juris doctor*) degree in law and a Masters degree in counseling from the University of Wisconsin–Madison.

After law school, Tim Bakken became an assistant district attorney in New York City (Kings County/Brooklyn), where he specialized in homicide prosecutions. He enjoyed the adversarial system, arguing with defense lawyers in court and during trials, and was awed by his responsibilities. A mistake could have grave consequences, as the smallest error could result in someone evading justice and committing serious crimes or in an innocent person going to prison.

After serving as a prosecutor, Bakken worked for a law firm in New York and then decided to pursue a career teaching law. He enjoyed writing and creating, an essential component of a professor's career, as well as interactions with students and professors. But Bakken's job is a

Chapter Outline

Chapter Objectives

1. Be familiar with the state and federal court structure
2. Know the differences between limited and general courts
3. Describe how a case gets to the Supreme Court
4. Discuss the duties of a judge
5. Know what is meant by the term "Missouri Plan"
6. Identify the different types of judicial selection
7. Understand the role of the prosecutor
8. Recognize the role of prosecutorial discretion in the justice system
9. Be able to discuss the concept of right to counsel and role of the defense attorney
10. Explain how technology is changing the trial process

little different than most because he teaches law at the U.S. Military Academy at West Point. The mission of the institution is to prepare students for service as officers in the army and then for a "lifetime of service to the nation." The students he now teaches are somewhat atypical from other college students because the government covers all their expenses and even pays them a salary. After graduation, all West Point students must serve five years in the army, and all of them will serve one or more tours in Iraq or Afghanistan.

Tim Bakken's career illustrates the variety of options open to people who choose legal careers. Some may start as public defenders and then go on to the private sector, or—as in Bakken's case—move from prosecution to legal education. Regardless of their career paths, most attorneys cut their teeth within the court system.

The criminal court is the setting in which many of the most important decisions in the criminal justice system are made. Eyewitness identification, bail, trial, plea negotiations, and sentencing all involve court-made decisions. The criminal court is a complex social agency with many independent but interrelated subsystems: administrator, prosecutor, defense attorney, judge, and probation department. The entire process—from filing the initial complaint to final sentencing of the defendant—is governed by precise rules of law designed to ensure fairness. However, in today's crowded court system, such abstract goals are often impossible to achieve. The nation's court system is chronically under-budgeted and recent economic downturns have not helped matters.

These constraints have a significant impact on the way courts carry out justice. Quite often, the U.S. court system is the scene of accommodation and "working things out," rather than an arena for a vigorous criminal defense. Plea negotiations and other non-judicial alternatives, such as diversion, are far more common than the formal trial process. Consequently, U.S. criminal justice can be selective. Discretion accompanies defendants through every step of the process, determining what will happen to them and how their cases will be resolved. *Discretion* means that two people committing similar crimes will receive highly dissimilar treatment; most people convicted of homicide receive a prison sentence, but about 5 percent receive probation as a sole sentence; indeed, more murderers get probation than the death penalty.[1]

In this chapter, we examine the structure and function of the court system. The U.S. court system has evolved over the years into an intricately balanced legal process. To house this complex process, each state maintains its own state court organization and structure, and the federal court has an independent trial court system. These are described next.

Criminal Justice ⚖ Now™
Learn more about Jurisdiction by exploring the Review and Reinforce activity.

The **National Center for State Courts** is an independent, nonprofit organization dedicated to the improvement of justice. NCSC activities include developing policies to enhance state courts, advancing state courts' interests in the federal government, fostering state court adaptation to future changes, securing sufficient resources for state courts, strengthening state court leadership, facilitating state court collaboration, and providing a model for organizational administration. To reach this site, go to "Web Links" on your Siegel Essentials of Criminal Justice 5e website: http://cj. wadsworth.com/siegel_ess5e.

state courts of limited jurisdiction Generic terms referring to courts that have jurisdiction over misdemeanors and conduct preliminary investigations of felony charges.

STATE COURTS

Every state maintains its own court system. They are free to create as many courts as they wish, name courts what they like (in New York, felony courts are known as Supreme Courts!), and establish specialized courts that handle a single legal matter, such as drug courts and/or domestic courts. Consequently, no two court organizations are exactly alike. State courts handle a wide variety of cases and regulate numerous personal behaviors ranging from homicide to property maintenance.

Courts of Limited Jurisdiction

Depending on the jurisdiction in which they are located, **state courts of limited jurisdiction** are known by a variety of names—municipal courts, county courts, district courts, and metropolitan courts, to name but a few. Their name derives from the fact that the jurisdiction of these courts is limited to minor or less serious civil and criminal cases.

Courts of limited jurisdiction are restricted in the types of cases they may hear. Usually, they will handle misdemeanor criminal infractions, violations of municipal ordinances, traffic violations, and civil suits where the damages involve less than a certain amount of money (usually $1,000 or less). In criminal matters, they hear misdemeanors such as shoplifting, disorderly conduct, or simple assault. Their sanctioning power is also limited. In criminal matters, punishments may be limited to fines, community sentencing, or incarceration in the county jail for up to a year. In addition to their trial work, limited jurisdiction courts conduct arraignments, preliminary, and bail hearings in felony cases (before they are transferred to superior courts).

Some states separate limited courts into those that handle civil cases only and those that settle criminal cases. Included in the category of courts of limited jurisdiction are special courts, such as juvenile, family, and probate (divorce, estate issues, and custody) courts. State lawmakers may respond to a particular social problem, such as drug use, by creating specialized courts that focus on treatment and care for these special needs offenders. One of the most common is the family or juvenile court, which handles custody cases, delinquency, and other issues involving children (juvenile courts will be discussed further in Chapter 15). These newest types of specialty courts are discussed in the Policy, Programs, and Issues in Criminal Justice feature, "Specialized Courts: Drugs and Mental Health."

The nation's approximately 13,500 independent courts of limited jurisdiction are the ones most often accused of providing assembly-line justice. Because the matters they decide involve minor personal confrontations and conflicts—family disputes, divorces, landlord-tenant conflicts, barroom brawls—the rule of the day is "handling the situation" and resolving the dispute.

Courts of General Jurisdiction

Approximately two thousand **courts of general jurisdiction** exist in the United States, variously called felony, superior, supreme, county, or circuit courts. Courts of general jurisdiction handle the more serious felony cases (e.g., murder, rape, robbery) and civil cases where damages are over a specified amount, such as $10,000. Courts of general jurisdiction may also be responsible for reviewing cases on appeal from courts of limited jurisdiction. In some instances they will base their decision on a review of the transcript of the case, whereas in others they can actually grant a new trial; this latter procedure is known as the *trial de novo process*.

> **court of general jurisdiction**
> *A state or federal court that has jurisdiction over felony offenses and more serious civil cases (i.e., involving more than a dollar amount set by the legislature).*

Daryl Atkins sits in a York-Poquoson courtroom in York, Virginia, on July 25, 2005. Atkins, whose case led the U.S. Supreme Court to bar execution of the mentally retarded as unconstitutionally cruel, remained on death row nearly three years after the landmark ruling pending a new trial to decide whether his mental capacity renders him ineligible for the death penalty.

© 2005 AP/Wide World Photos

Policy, Programs, and Issues in Criminal Justice

Specialized Courts: Drugs and Mental Health

A growing phenomenon in the United States is the creation of specialty courts that focus on one type of criminal act, such as drug courts and gun courts. All cases within the jurisdiction that involve this particular type of crime are funneled to the specialty court, where presumably they will get prompt resolution.

Drug Courts

The **drug court** movement began in Florida to address the growing problem of prison overcrowding due in large part to an influx of drug-involved offenders. Drug courts were created to have primary jurisdiction over cases involving substance abuse and trafficking. The aim is to place nonviolent first offenders into intensive treatment programs rather than place them in jail or prison. Today there are more than three hundred drug courts across forty-three states, the District of Columbia, and Puerto Rico. Drug courts address the overlap between the public health threats of drug abuse and crime: crimes are often drug related; drug abusers are frequently involved with the criminal justice system. Drug courts provide an ideal setting to address these problems by linking the justice system with health services and drug treatment providers while easing the burden on the already overtaxed correctional system.

While some recent research finds that drug courts may not be as effective as originally believed, research by Denise Gottfredson and her associates conducted in the Baltimore City Drug Treatment Court (BCDTC) found that drug courts did seem to work for reducing crime in a population of offenders who were severely drug addicted. In one study conducted with Lyn Exum, Gottfredson used a carefully designed experimental model in which cases were randomly sent either to the drug court or a traditional court. The researchers found that drug court judges actually impose harsher sentences, but suspended these sentences conditional to compliance with the drug court regimen in drug testing and treatment and attending status hearings. Most importantly, within a twelve-month period, 48 percent of drug treatment court clients were arrested for new offenses, compared to 64 percent of the people handled in traditional courts. Among the more serious cases heard, 32 percent of drug court clients versus 57 percent of controls were rearrested. All things considered, defendants in cases handled in a traditional court suffered re-arrest at a rate nearly three times that of defendants in drug court.

This research finding is not unique. While methodological issues often make analysis difficult, reviews of drug court success have found that on balance they can help reduce recidivism rates.

Mental Health Courts

Based largely on the organization of drug courts, mental health courts focus their attention on mental health treatment to help people with emotional problems reduce their chances of re-offending. By focusing on the need for treatment, along with providing supervision and support from the community, mental health courts provide a venue for those dealing with mental health issues to avoid the trauma of jail or prison where they will have little if any access to treatment

Though mental health courts tend to vary in their approach, most share a few basic operating procedures:

• Most demand active participation by the defendant.

Courts of general jurisdiction are typically organized in judicial districts or circuits, based on a political division such as a county or a group of counties ("Superior Court for the Southern Tier"). They then receive cases from the various limited courts located within the county/jurisdiction. Some general courts separate criminal and civil cases so that some specialize in civil matters while others maintain a caseload that is exclusively criminal.

Appellate Courts

appellate court *A court that reconsiders a case that has already been tried in order to determine whether the measures used complied with accepted rules of criminal procedure and were in line with constitutional doctrines.*

If defendants believe that the procedures used were in violation of their constitutional rights, they may ask an **appellate court** to review the trial process. Appellate courts do not try cases; they review the procedures of the

- The participant must be diagnosed with a mental illness and a direct link must be established between the illness and the crime committed.

- Intervention must occur quickly; individuals must be screened and referred to the program either immediately after arrest or within three weeks.

- Once in the program, participants are closely monitored by case managers.

Although programs vary, most require that defendants plead guilty in exchange for entering the program. After "guilt" is established, participants are sent to live in a residential treatment facility where, with help from counselors, they develop a treatment plan, which is rigorous at first and then gradually less restrictive if improvement is shown. Most programs involve the use of medication to help overcome symptoms of the individual's illness.

While the mental health court concept seems beneficial, it has encountered a few operational difficulties. First, it is difficult to get community support for programs and institutions treating mentally ill offenders nor do residents want treatment centers to be located close to where they live—the "not in my neighborhood" syndrome. Second, most programs only accept the nonviolent mentally ill; those who are violence-prone are still lost in the correctional system without receiving the proper treatment.

It is also difficult to assess the benefits of having specialized mental health courts. With other specialized courts, measuring offender improvement is relatively easy. People sent to drug court programs must simply prove they can remain drug free. However, those involved with mental health court programs suffer from complex mental issues, and case managers must ensure that these individuals have gained control over their illness, which can be difficult to determine.

The mental health court movement has prompted development of juvenile mental health courts to treat troubled adolescents who have been accused of committing nonviolent crimes. Juvenile mental health court programs typically involve collaboration between the justice system, mental health professionals, and the parents of the young offenders to devise a treatment plan to treat the child, helping him or her avoid the standard juvenile justice system process.

Critical Thinking

1. Do you believe that specialized courts are needed for other crime types, such as sex offenses and/or domestic violence?

2. Should a judge preside over a specialized court or should it be administered by treatment personnel?

InfoTrac College Edition Research

To learn more about the *drug court* movement, use it as a subject guide on InfoTrac College Edition.

Sources: J. Scott Sanford and Bruce Arrigo, "Lifting the Cover on Drug Courts: Evaluation Findings and Policy Concerns," *International Journal of Offender Therapy and Comparative Criminology* 49 (2005): 239–259; John Goldkamp and Cheryl Irons-Guynn, *Emerging Judicial Strategies for the Mentally Ill in the Criminal Caseload: Mental Health Courts in Fort Lauderdale, Seattle, San Bernardino, and Anchorage* (Washington, D.C.: U.S. Department of Justice, Office of Justice Programs, 2000); Melissa Lackman and Susan Solomon, "CABF Endorses Juvenile Mental Health Courts," *Child & Adolescent Bipolar Foundation Bulletin* 4 (2003): 1; John Goldkamp, "The Impact of Drug Courts," *Criminology & Public Policy* 2 (2003): 197–206; Denise C. Gottfredson, Stacy Najaka, and Brook Kearley, "Effectiveness of Drug Treatment Courts: Evidence from a Randomized Trial," *Criminology & Public Policy* 2 (2003): 171–197; Denise C. Gottfredson and Lyn Exum, "The Baltimore City Drug Treatment Court: One-Year Results from a Randomized Study," *Journal of Research in Crime & Delinquency* 39 (2002): 337–357; Bureau of Justice Assistance, *Drug Night Courts: The Cook County Experience* (Washington, D.C.: National Institute of Justice, 1994); Terance Miethe, Hong Lu, and Eric Reese, "Reintegrative Shaming and Recidivism Risks in Drug Court: Explanations for Some Unexpected Findings," *Crime and Delinquency* 46 (2000): 522–541.

case to determine whether an error was made by judicial authorities. In some instances defendants can file an appeal if they believe that the law they were tried under was in violation of constitutional standards (i.e., the crime they were charged with, "being a public nuisance," was vague and ill defined) or if the procedures used in the case contravened principles of due process and equal protection or were in direct opposition to a constitutional guarantee (i.e., they were denied the right to have competent legal representation).

It is the role of the appellate court to decide whether the trial judge made a legal error that influenced the outcome of the case thereby denying the defendant a fair trial. Judicial error can include admitting into evidence illegally seized material, improperly charging a jury, allowing a prosecutor to ask witnesses improper questions, and so on. If upon review the appellate court decides that an error has been made, it can order a new trial or even allow the defendant to go free.

State criminal appeals are heard in one of the appellate courts in the fifty states and the District of Columbia. Each state has at least one **court of last resort,** usually called a state supreme court, which reviews issues of law and fact appealed from the trial courts; a few states have two high courts, one for civil appeals and the other for criminal cases. In addition, many states have established intermediate appellate courts (IAC) to review decisions by trial courts and administrative agencies before they reach the supreme court stage. Currently, thirty-nine states have at least one permanent IAC. Mississippi was the last state to create an IAC; it began operations in 1995.

Many people believe that criminal appeals clog the nation's court system because so many convicted criminals try to "beat the rap" on a technicality. Actually, criminal appeals represent a small percentage of the total number of cases processed by the nation's appellate courts. All types of appeals, including criminal ones, continue to inundate the courts, so most courts are having problems processing cases expeditiously.

State courts have witnessed an increase in the number of appellate cases each year. In the meantime, the number of judges and support staff has not kept pace. The resulting imbalance has led to the increased use of intermediate courts to screen cases.

Figure 8.1 illustrates the interrelationship of appellate and trial courts in a model state court structure. Each state's court organization, of course, may vary from this standard pattern. Though most states have a tiered court organization (lower, upper, and appellate courts), all vary in the way they have delegated responsibility to a particular court system and some have consolidated their courts into a single, unified system.

Criminal Justice ⚖ Now™
Learn more about *Federal Courts* by exploring the *Federal Judicial System* Animated Artwork.

FEDERAL COURTS

The legal basis for an independent federal court system is contained in Article 3, Section 1, of the U.S. Constitution, which provides that "the judicial power of the United States shall be vested in one Supreme Court, and in such inferior courts as Congress may from time to time ordain and establish." The important clauses in Article 3 indicate that the federal courts have jurisdiction over the laws of the United States and treaties and cases involving admiralty and maritime jurisdiction, as well as over controversies between two or more states and citizens of different states.[2] This complex language generally means that state courts have jurisdiction over most common law crimes, but that the federal system maintains jurisdiction over violations of federal criminal statute, civil suits between citizens of different states, or between a citizen and an agency of the federal government.

Within this authority, the federal government has established a three-tiered hierarchy of court jurisdiction that, in order of ascendancy, consists of the (1) U.S. district courts, (2) U.S. courts of appeals (circuit courts), and (3) the U.S. Supreme Court (see Figure 8.2).

U.S. District Courts

United States district courts, the trial courts of the federal system, were organized by Congress in the Judicial Act of 1789. Today ninety-four independent courts are in operation. Originally, each state was allowed one court; as the population grew, however, so did the need for courts so now some states have multiple jurisdictions.

U.S. district courts have jurisdiction over cases involving violations of federal laws, including civil rights abuses, interstate transportation of stolen

court of last resort A court that handles the final appeal on a matter. The U.S. Supreme Court is the official court of last resort for criminal matters.

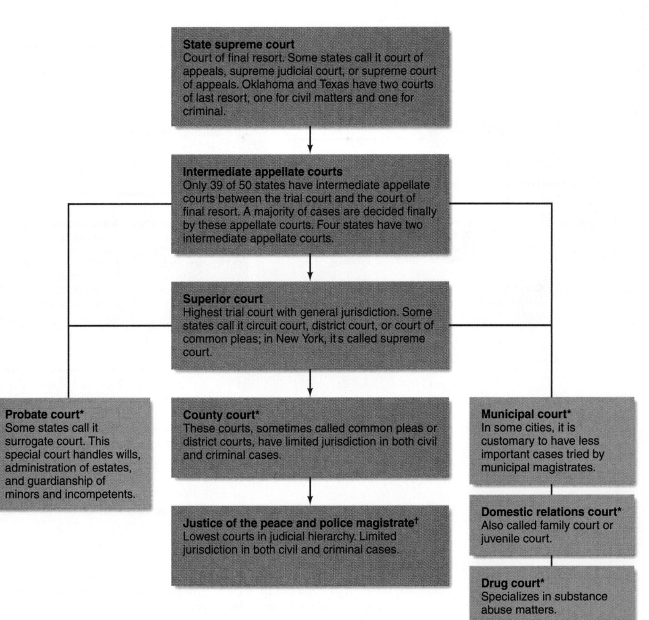

State supreme court
Court of final resort. Some states call it court of appeals, supreme judicial court, or supreme court of appeals. Oklahoma and Texas have two courts of last resort, one for civil matters and one for criminal.

Intermediate appellate courts
Only 39 of 50 states have intermediate appellate courts between the trial court and the court of final resort. A majority of cases are decided finally by these appellate courts. Four states have two intermediate appellate courts.

Superior court
Highest trial court with general jurisdiction. Some states call it circuit court, district court, or court of common pleas; in New York, it's called supreme court.

Probate court*
Some states call it surrogate court. This special court handles wills, administration of estates, and guardianship of minors and incompetents.

County court*
These courts, sometimes called common pleas or district courts, have limited jurisdiction in both civil and criminal cases.

Municipal court*
In some cities, it is customary to have less important cases tried by municipal magistrates.

Domestic relations court*
Also called family court or juvenile court.

Drug court*
Specializes in substance abuse matters.

Gun court
Handles felony gun cases.

Justice of the peace and police magistrate†
Lowest courts in judicial hierarchy. Limited jurisdiction in both civil and criminal cases.

Figure 8.1 A model of a state judicial system

*Courts of special jurisdiction, such as probate, family, or juvenile courts, and the so-called inferior courts, such as common pleas or municipal courts, may be separate courts or part of the trial court of general jurisdiction.

†Justices of the peace do not exist in all states. Where they do exist, their jurisdictions vary greatly from state to state.

Sources: American Bar Association, *Law and the Courts* (Chicago: ABA, 1974), 20; Bureau of Justice Statistics, *State Court Organization—1998* (Washington, D.C.: Department of Justice, 2000).

vehicles, and kidnappings. They may also hear cases on questions involving citizenship and the rights of aliens. The jurisdiction of the U.S. district court will occasionally overlap that of state courts. Citizens who reside in separate states and are involved in litigation of an amount in excess of $10,000 may choose to have their cases heard in either of the states or in the federal district court. Finally, federal district courts hear cases in which one state sues a resi-

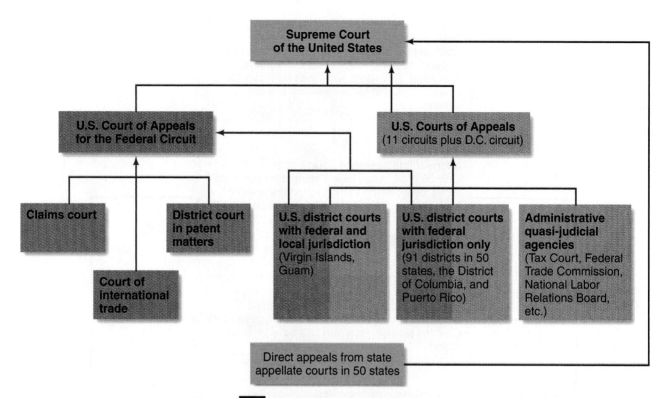

Figure 8.2 The federal judicial system

Sources: American Bar Association, *Law and the Courts* (Chicago: ABA, 1974), 21; updated information provided by the Federal Courts Improvement Act of 1982 and West Publishing Company, St. Paul, Minnesota.

dent (or firm) in another state, where one state sues another, or where the federal government is a party in a suit.

U.S. Courts of Appeals

There are thirteen judicial circuits, each with a court of appeals. The smallest court is the First Circuit with six judgeships, and the largest court is the Ninth Circuit, with 28 judgeships. Approximately forty thousand appeals are heard in these *U.S. circuit courts*. This name is derived from the historical practice of having judges ride the circuit and regularly hear cases in the judicial seats of their various jurisdictions. Today, appellate judges are not required to travel (although some may sit in more than one court), and each federal appellate court jurisdiction contains a number of associate justices who share the caseload. Circuit court offices are usually located in major cities, such as San Francisco and New York, and cases to be heard must be brought to these locations by attorneys.

The circuit court is empowered to review federal and state appellate court cases on substantive and procedural issues involving rights guaranteed by the Constitution. Circuit courts do not actually retry cases, nor do they determine whether the facts brought out during trial support conviction or dismissal. Instead, they analyze judicial interpretations of the law, such as the charge (or instructions) to the jury, and reflect on the constitutional issues involved in each case they hear.

Although federal court criminal cases make up only a small percentage of appellate cases, they are still of concern to the judiciary. Steps have been taken to make appealing more difficult. The U.S. Supreme Court has tried to limit the number of appeals being filed by prison inmates, which often represent a significant number of cases appealed in the federal criminal justice system.

The U.S. Supreme Court

The U.S. Supreme Court is the nation's highest appellate body and the court of last resort for all cases tried in the various federal and state courts.

The Supreme Court is composed of nine members appointed for lifetime terms by the president, with the approval of Congress. The Court has discretion over most of the cases it will consider and may choose to hear only those it deems important, appropriate, and worthy of its attention. The Court chooses some three hundred of the five thousand cases that are appealed each year, and only about one hundred of these receive full opinions.

When the Supreme Court decides to hear a case, it grants a **writ of certiorari,** requesting a transcript of the proceedings of the case for review. However, the Court must grant jurisdiction in a few instances, such as decisions from a three-judge federal district court on reapportionment or cases involving the Voting Rights Act.

When the Supreme Court rules on a case, usually by majority decision (at least five votes), its rule becomes a precedent or **landmark decision** that must be honored by all lower courts. If, for example, the Court grants a particular litigant the right to counsel at a police lineup, all similarly situated clients must be given the same right.

How a Case Gets to the Supreme Court The Supreme Court is unique in several ways.

- It is the only court established by constitutional mandate rather than federal legislation.
- It decides basic social and political issues of grave consequence and importance to the nation, such as the outcome of the 2000 presidential election.
- The Court shapes the future meaning of the U.S. Constitution by identifying a citizen's rights and liberties.

The device the Court uses to choose cases is the writ of certiorari. *Certiorari,* from the Latin term 'to be informed of," refers to an order a court issues so that it can review the decision and proceedings that occurred in a lower court. Under this procedure, an appellant requests a writ to be issued so that his/her case may be reviewed. If the writ is denied, the Supreme Court refuses to hear the appeal and the judgment in the lower court stands unchanged. If the writ is granted, the Supreme Court hears the appeal. For the appellant to be successful, at least four of the nine justices sitting on the Court must vote to grant the writ of certiorari even before the case can be considered for review. Generally, these votes are cast in a secret meeting attended only by the justices. More than 90 percent of the cases heard by the Court are brought by petition for a writ of certiorari.

After the Supreme Court decides to hear a case, it reviews written arguments referred to as legal briefs outlining the case and the points of law to be considered.

After the written material is reviewed, attorneys for each side in the case are allowed thirty minutes to present an oral argument before the court members. Then the justices normally meet in what is known as a *case conference* to discuss the case and vote to reach a decision. This procedure is outlined in Figure 8.3.

In reaching a decision, the Supreme Court reevaluates and reinterprets state statutes, the U.S. Constitution, and previous case decisions. Based on a review of the case, the Court either affirms or reverses the decision of the

 The Supreme Court maintains a website that has a wealth of information on its history, judges, procedures, cases filings, rules, opinions, and other Court-related material. To reach this site, go to "Web Links" on your Siegel Essentials of Criminal Justice 5e website: http://cj.wadsworth.com/siegel_ess5e.

writ of certiorari An order of superior court requesting that the record of an inferior court (or administrative body) be brought forward for review or inspection.

landmark decision A decision handed down by the U.S. Supreme Court that becomes the law of the land and serves as a precedent for similar legal issues.

Figure 8.3
Tracing the course of a case to the U.S. Supreme Court

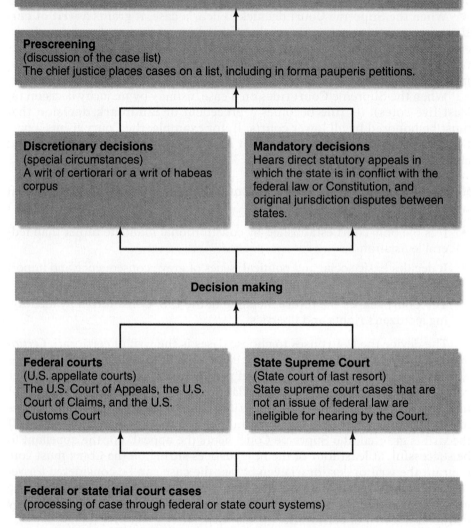

Full judicial decision by the U.S. Supreme Court
(majority and dissenting opinions)
The Court affirms or reverses lower court decisions. (Exception: The decision is not always a final judicial action. Lower courts may try the case again or, as in civil litigation, the case may be retried.) There is no appeal process beyond the U.S. Supreme Court.

Decision-making conferences by the justices
Four votes govern the acceptance or rejection of a case: (1) a decision and full opinion; (2) if the case is accepted, there may be a summary decision of a dismissal or affirmation of a lower-court decision (per curiam); (3) if the case is rejected, no explanation (reconsideration is possible); and (4) a rehearing after an unfavorable decision is possible.

Prescreening
(discussion of the case list)
The chief justice places cases on a list, including in forma pauperis petitions.

Discretionary decisions
(special circumstances)
A writ of certiorari or a writ of habeas corpus

Mandatory decisions
Hears direct statutory appeals in which the state is in conflict with the federal law or Constitution, and original jurisdiction disputes between states.

Decision making

Federal courts
(U.S. appellate courts)
The U.S. Court of Appeals, the U.S. Court of Claims, and the U.S. Customs Court

State Supreme Court
(State court of last resort)
State supreme court cases that are not an issue of federal law are ineligible for hearing by the Court.

Federal or state trial court cases
(processing of case through federal or state court systems)

lower court. When the justices reach a decision, and in the event that the Court's decision is split, the Chief Justice of the Court assigns a member of the majority group to write the opinion. Another justice normally writes a dissent, or minority, opinion; a single opinion may be written if the decision is unanimous. When the case is finished, it is submitted to the public and becomes the law of the land. The decision represents the legal precedents that add to the existing body of law on a given subject, change it, and guide its future development.

FEDERAL AND STATE COURT CASELOADS

This vast system has been overloaded by the millions of cases that are brought each year. State court systems now handle about 100 million new cases each year. That total includes:

- About 20 million civil and domestic cases
- Over 15 million criminal cases
- Two million juvenile cases
- More than 57 million traffic and ordinance violations (see Figure 8.4)

Though smaller, federal courts are equally burdened:

- More than 320,000 cases are filed each year in the district courts. Criminal cases have increased 55 percent since 1994. There are now more than 530 cases filed each year per judge, up from 339 in 1969.

Cases filed in state courts (millions)

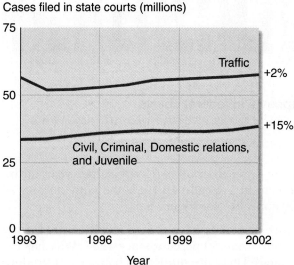

Total state court caseloads (millions)

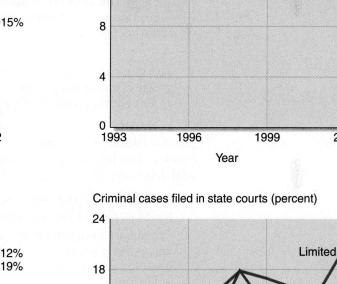

Cases filed in state courts by case type (millions)

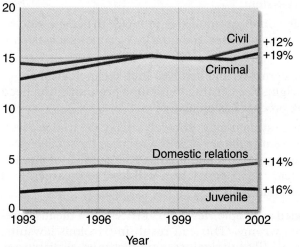

Criminal cases filed in state courts (percent)

Figure 8.4 **State court cases, 1993–2002**

Source: Brian Ostrom, Neal Kauder, and Robert LaFountain, *Examining the Work of State Courts, 2003* (Williamsburg, Va.: National Center for State Courts, 2004).

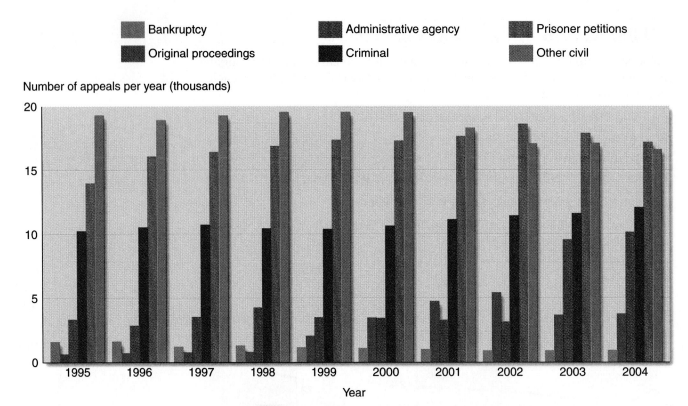

Figure 8.5 The growth of appeals in federal courts
Federal Court Management Statistics, *Court of Appeals, 2005* (Washington, D.C.: Administrative Office of the U.S. Courts).

- The circuit courts now hear more than 60,000 appeals per year, an increase of more than 25 percent in a decade. In 1969, the same number of circuit courts heard 10,000 appeals.[3] See Figure 8.5.

Both federal and state court caseloads have grown significantly for the past two decades, increasing more than 50 percent since 1984. Why has the court system become so congested? There are numerous factors that produce trial delay and court congestion:

- Rapidly increasing populations in some states, such as Nevada, has outpaced growth in the court system.

- Efforts are being made in some communities to lower the crime rate by aggressively prosecuting petty offenses and nuisance crimes such as panhandling or vagrancy.

- As the law becomes more complex, and involves such technological issues as intellectual property rights concerning computer programs, the need for a more involved court process has escalated.

- Reform efforts in the justice system may, ironically, delay the trial process. For example, the increase of mandatory prison sentences for some crimes may reduce the use of plea bargaining and increase the number of jury trials because defendants fear that a conviction will lead to incarceration and thus must be avoided at all costs.

Civil litigation has exploded as people view court process as a means of redressing all kinds of personal wrongs. This can result in frivolous lawsuits, such as when overweight people file suit against manufacturers, distributors, or sellers of food products charging them with responsibility for their obesity.[4] Increased civil litigation can add to the backlog because most courts handle both criminal and civil matters. If relief is to be found, it will probably be in the form of better administrative and management techniques that improve the use of existing resources. Another possible method of creating a more efficient court system is to unify existing state courts into a single administrative structure using modern management principles.

▌THE JUDICIARY

The judge is the senior officer in a court of criminal law. His/her duties are quite varied and far more extensive than might be expected:

- Their primary duty is to oversee the trial process. This means that, during trials, judges control the appropriateness of conduct, settle questions of evidence and procedure, and guide the questioning of witnesses.

- In a **jury trial** the judge must instruct jurors on which evidence is proper to examine and which should be ignored. The judge also formally charges the jury by instructing its members on what points of law and evidence they must consider to reach a decision of either guilty or not guilty.

- When a jury trial is waived, in a bench trial, the judge must decide whether the defendant is guilty as charged. If a defendant is found guilty, the judge must decide on the sentence (in some cases, this is legislatively

Criminal Justice ⚖ Now™

Learn more about **The Judiciary** *by exploring the* **Partisan Elections** *Review and Reinforce activity.*

jury trial The process of deciding a case by a group of persons selected and sworn in to serve as jurors at a criminal trial, often as a six- or twelve-person jury.

© 2005 AP/Wide World Photos

Ideally, the criminal trial process applies the law equally to all citizens, whether they are rich and powerful or poor and defenseless. Minnesota Attorney General Mike Hatch, center, looks up at the Chicago Circuit Courthouse as he escorts his two daughters, Elizabeth, left, and Annie, right, on June 7, 2005. Annie and Elizabeth were being tried for assaulting two Chicago police officers, resisting arrest, and damaging police property after celebrating Annie's 21st birthday in March 2004. After a bench trial, the young women were found not guilty as charged by Cook County Judge Colleen Sheehan.

Criminal Justice ⚖ Now™

Learn more about The Judiciary by exploring the "Burglary Part 3" Role Play activity.

determined), which includes choosing the type of sentence, its length, and in the case of probation, the conditions under which it may be revoked.

- The judge controls and influences court agencies: probation, the court clerk, the police, and the district attorney's office. Probation and the clerk may be under the judge's explicit control. In some courts, the operations, philosophy, and procedures of these agencies are within the magistrate's administrative domain. In others—where a state agency controls the probation department—the attitudes of the county or district court judge greatly influence the way a probation department is run and how its decisions are made.

While carrying out their duties, the judge must be wary of the legal controls placed on the trial process by the appellate court system. If an error is made, the judge's decision may be reversed causing at the minimum personal embarrassment. While some experts believe that fear of reversal may shape judicial decision-making, recent research by David Klein and Robert Hume indicates that judges may be more independent than previously believed. Judges relish using their judicial power as a policy-making tool to influence important social policies such as affirmative action or privacy.[5]

Criminal Justice ⚖ Now™

Learn more by exploring the Magistrate Review and Reinforce activity.

The Judge and the Justice System

Judicial attitudes and philosophy have a major impact on how the justice system operates. Judicial attitudes may extend way beyond the courtroom. Police policies may be directly influenced by the judge, whose sentencing discretion affects the arrest process. If a local judge usually chooses minimal sentences—such as a fine for a particular offense—the police may be reluctant to arrest offenders for that crime, knowing that doing so will basically be a waste of time. Similarly, if a judge is known to have a liberal attitude toward police discretion, the local department may be more inclined to engage in practices that border on entrapment or to pursue cases through easily obtained wiretaps. However, a magistrate oriented toward strict use of due process guarantees would stifle such activities by dismissing all cases involving apparent police abuses of personal freedoms.

The district attorney's office may also be sensitive to judicial attitudes. The district attorney might forgo indictments in cases that the presiding magistrate expressly considers trivial or quasi-criminal and in which the judge has been known to take only token action, such as the prosecution of pornographers.

Finally, the judge considers requests by prosecutors for leniency (or severity) in sentencing. The judge's reaction to these requests is important if the police and the district attorney are to honor the bargains they may have made with defendants to secure information, cooperation, or guilty pleas. For example, when police tell informers that they will try to convince the judge to go easy on them to secure required information, they will often discuss the terms of the promised leniency with representatives of the court. If a judge ignores police demands, the department's bargaining power is severely diminished, and communication within the criminal justice system is impaired.

Criminal Justice ⚖ Now™

Learn more about The Judiciary by exploring the Judicial Misconduct Review and Reinforce activity.

Judicial Qualifications

The qualifications for appointment to one of the existing thirty thousand judgeships vary from state to state and court to court. Most typically the potential judge must be a resident of the state, licensed to practice law, a member of the state bar association, and at least twenty-five years and less than seventy years of age. However, a significant degree of diversity exists in the basic qualification, depending on the level of court jurisdiction. Although almost every state requires judges to have a law degree if they are to serve on appellate courts or courts of general jurisdiction, it is not uncommon for municipal or town court judges to lack a legal background, even though they maintain the power to incarcerate criminal defendants for petty crimes such as vandalism.

Many methods are used to select judges, depending on the level of court jurisdiction. In some jurisdictions, judges are appointed officials, most typically by the state governor. In some states, in an effort to remove politics from judicial appointments, the governor's recommendations must be confirmed by the state senate, the governor's council, a special confirmation committee, an executive council elected by the state assembly, or an elected review board. Some states employ a judicial nominating commission that submits names to the governor for approval.

Another form of judicial selection is popular election. Judges may run as members of the Republican, Democratic, or other parties, or without party affiliation. Though this practice is used in a majority of states, there is no set procedure and each state sets its own terms of appointment. In some states judges are elected for fifteen-year terms while in others they're elected for four-year terms.[6]

The state of Missouri pioneered a nonpartisan method of selecting judges, referred to as the **Missouri Plan,** which is now used in some manner in more than thirty states. The plan consists of three parts:

1. A judicial nominating commission to select and nominate potential candidates for the bench. In Missouri, the judicial commission is composed of the chief justice of the Supreme Court, three lawyers elected by the Missouri bar (the organization of all lawyers licensed in this state), and three citizens selected by the governor.

2. An elected official (usually from the executive branch such as the governor) to make appointments from the list submitted by the commission.

3. Subsequent nonpartisan and noncompetitive elections in which incumbent judges run on their records and voters can choose either their retention or dismissal.[7]

The quality of the judiciary is a concern. Although merit plans, screening committees, and popular elections are designed to ensure a competent judiciary, it has often been charged that many judicial appointments are made to pay off political debts or to reward cronies and loyal friends. Also not uncommon are charges that those desiring to be nominated for judgeships are required to make significant political contributions.

Judicial Overload There has been great concern about stress placed on judges by the size of their assigned caseloads. In most states, people appointed to the bench have had little or no training in the role of judge. Others may have held administrative posts and may not have appeared before a court in years. Once they are appointed to the bench, judges are given an overwhelming amount of work that has risen dramatically over the years. The number of civil and criminal filings per state court judge has increased significantly.[8] State court judges deal with far more cases, but federal cases may be more complex and demand more judicial time. In any event, the number of civil and criminal cases, especially in state courts, seems to be outstripping the ability of states to create new judgeships.

THE PROSECUTOR

Depending on the level of government and the jurisdiction in which he or she functions, the prosecutor may be known as a *district attorney, county attorney, state's attorney,* or *U.S. attorney.* Whatever the title, the **prosecutor**

Criminal Justice Now™
Learn more by viewing the "Jackson Media" "In the News" video clip.

Missouri Plan A way of picking judges through nonpartisan elections as a means of ensuring judicial performance standards.

prosecutor Representative of the state (executive branch) in criminal proceedings; advocate for the state's case—the charge—in the adversary trial, for example, the attorney general of the United States, U.S. attorneys, attorneys general of the states, district attorneys, and police prosecutors. The prosecutor participates in investigations both before and after arrest, prepares legal documents, participates in obtaining arrest or search warrants, decides whether to charge a suspect and, if so, with which offense. The prosecutor argues the state's case at trial, advises the police, participates in plea negotiations, and makes sentencing recommendations.

is the people's attorney, who is responsible for representing the public in criminal matters.

Because they are the chief law enforcement officers of a particular jurisdiction, their jurisdiction spans the entire justice system process from the time search and arrest warrants are issued or a grand jury is impaneled to the final sentencing decision and appeal. Some of the general duties of a prosecutor include:

- Provides advice to law enforcement officers during investigation to determine if criminal charges should be filed.

- During the pretrial stage, represents the state in plea negotiations, pretrial motions, evidence, and bail hearings.

- Represents the state at hearings, criminal trials, and appeals.

- Acts as legal advisor to county commissioners and other elected officials.

In addition to these duties, local jurisdictions may create specific programs directed by local prosecutors. For example, career criminal prosecution programs involve identifying dangerous adult and juvenile offenders who commit a high number of crimes, so that prosecutors can target them for swift prosecution. Many jurisdictions have developed protection programs so that victims of domestic violence can obtain temporary court orders (and after a hearing, more permanent court orders) protecting them from an abusive spouse; research indicates that protection orders can reduce the incidence of repeat violence.[9] Some specific program initiatives include:

- Out of concern and realizing the unique vulnerability of seniors, the district attorney in Santa Barbara, California, created the Elder Abuse Unit consisting of attorneys, investigators, and advocates. The elder abuse advocate coordinates with Adult Protective Services, the Long-Term Care Ombudsman Office, and local law enforcement agencies and resources to help victims and families cope with the effects of abuse, neglect, and exploitation. The attorney and investigator identify, review, investigate, and prosecute the cases. All provide services to elder and dependent adults as well as ongoing training programs for local law enforcement and gatekeepers. The purpose of the project is to ensure the safety of the community's elderly citizens and heighten the community's awareness of this form of crime.[10]

- Defendants convicted in Mason County, Washington, are ordered to pay a fee that helps fund a crime victim program with the prosecuting attorney's office. This program assists the attorneys with victims and witnesses for hearings and trials and preparing paperwork for court. Program support includes: direct communication with the victims and witnesses; referrals to other agencies and programs such as the Department of Labor and Industries Crime Victim Compensation program and the crisis clinic; coordinating with the Department of Corrections on case tracking and victim location; and at times, providing transportation for victims and witnesses to court hearings.[11]

Types of Prosecutors

In the federal system, prosecutors are known as U.S. attorneys and are appointed by the president. They are responsible for representing the government in federal district courts. The chief prosecutor is usually an administrator, and assistants normally handle the actual preparation and trial work. Federal prosecutors are professional civil service employees with reasonable salaries and job security.

On the state and county levels, the attorney general and the district attorney, respectively, are the chief prosecutorial officers. Again, the bulk of the criminal prosecution and staff work is performed by scores of full- and part-time attorneys, police investigators, and clerical personnel. Most attorneys who work for prosecutors at the state and county levels are political appointees who earn low salaries, handle many cases, and in some jurisdictions, maintain private law practices. Many young lawyers take these staff positions to gain the trial experience that will qualify them for better opportunities.

In urban jurisdictions, the structure of the district attorney's office is often specialized, with separate divisions for felonies, misdemeanors, and trial and appeal assignments. In rural offices, chief prosecutors handle many of the criminal cases themselves. Where assistant prosecutors are employed, they often work part-time, have limited professional opportunities, and depend on the political patronage of chief prosecutors for their positions.

The personnel practices, organizational structures, and political atmosphere of many prosecutors' offices often restrict the effectiveness of individuals in investigating and prosecuting criminal offenses. For many years, prosecutors have been criticized for bargaining justice away, using their positions as stepping-stones to higher political office, and often failing to investigate or simply dismissing criminal cases. Lately, however, the prosecutor's public image has improved. Violations of federal laws, such as white-collar crime, drug peddling, and corruption, are being more aggressively investigated by the ninety-four U.S. attorneys and the nearly two thousand assistant U.S. attorneys. Aggressive federal prosecutors have also made extraordinary progress in the war against insider trading and security fraud on Wall Street. There have been a number of highly publicized indictments alleging that some corporate managers abused their power to loot company assets.

State crimes ranging from murder to larceny are prosecuted in state courts by district attorneys, who are stepping up their efforts against career criminals, shortening the time it takes to bring serious cases to trial, and addressing the long-neglected problems of victims and witnesses. With such actions, the prosecutor will continue to be one of the most powerful and visible professionals in the justice system.

Today, there are about twenty-four hundred state court prosecutors' offices, which employ about seventy-nine thousand attorneys, investigators, and support staff to handle felony cases in the state trial courts. Prosecution staff members have been increasing and this total represented an increase of 39 percent from 1992 and 13 percent from 1996.[12] Usually, the most active prosecutors are employed in larger counties with populations of over five hundred thousand. Exhibit 8.1 gives a profile of these attorneys.

Exhibit 8.1   Prosecutors in the United States

- Over the past decade, prosecutors' offices nationwide, on average, experienced increases in their staff size, budget for prosecutorial functions, and population served.
- Chief prosecutors are much more likely to serve in a full-time capacity than ten years ago.
- The percentage of prosecutors' offices prosecuting felonies related to domestic violence, child abuse, and bank or thrift fraud has been increasing.
- Each year, more than 40 percent of prosecutors' offices report prosecuting either felony or misdemeanor computer-related crimes under their state's computer statutes.
- About two-thirds of prosecutors' offices today use DNA evidence during plea negotiations or felony trials compared to about half of the offices in 1996.
- About 23 percent of prosecutors' offices assigned prosecutors to handle community-related activities.

Source: Carol J. DeFrances, *Prosecutors in State Courts, 2001* (Washington, D.C.: Bureau of Justice Statistics, 2002).

Criminal Justice ⚖ Now™

*Learn more about **The Prosecution** by exploring the "Domestic Violence Part 3" Role Play activity.*

▌PROSECUTORIAL DISCRETION

One might expect that after the police arrest and bring a suspect to court, the entire criminal court process would be mobilized. This is often not what happens, however. For a variety of reasons, a substantial percentage of defendants are never brought to trial. The prosecutor decides whether to bring a case to trial or to dismiss it outright. Even if the prosecutor decides to pursue a case, the charges may later be dropped if conditions are not favorable for a conviction, in a process called *nolle prosequi*. The courts have protected the prosecutor's right to exercise discretion over legal case processing, maintaining that prosecutorial decision making can be controlled or overturned only if a defendant can prove that the prosecutor let discrimination guide his or her decision making.[13]

Even in felony cases, the prosecutor ordinarily exercises much discretion in deciding whether to charge the accused with a crime.[14] After a police investigation, the prosecutor may be asked to review the sufficiency of the evidence to determine whether a criminal complaint should be filed. In some jurisdictions, this may involve presenting the evidence at a preliminary hearing. In other cases, the prosecutor may decide to seek a criminal complaint through the grand jury or other information procedure.

There is little question that prosecutors exercise a great deal of discretion in even the most serious cases. In one classic study, Barbara Boland examined the flow of felony cases through three jurisdictions in the United States: Golden, Colorado, the borough of Manhattan in New York City, and Salt Lake City, Utah.[15] Although procedures were different in the three districts, prosecutors used their discretion to dismiss a high percentage of the cases before trial. When cases were forwarded for trial, very few defendants were actually acquitted, indicating that the prosecutorial discretion was exercised to screen

Prosecutors have a great deal of discretion to either move forward on cases and bring them to trial or settle them with either a plea or dismissal. Martha Stewart waves to supporters on June 19, 2003, as she leaves a federal courthouse. Stewart was tried on charges that included lying to federal investigators about her trading of ImClone Systems stock. Prosecutors had the choice of seeking an indictment in the case or concluding that Stewart was merely a sharp stock trader who had broken no laws. They could have made her an offer of leniency in exchange for a plea. Instead, they decided to prosecute, and Stewart was convicted and imprisoned.

© Stephen Chenin/Getty Images

out the weakest cases. In addition, of those cases accepted for prosecution, a high percentage ended with the defendant pleading guilty. All the evidence here points to the conclusion that prosecutorial discretion is used to reduce potential trial cases to a minimum.

The prosecutor may also play a limited role in exercising discretion in minor offenses. This role may consist of simply consulting with the police after their investigation results in a complaint being filed against the accused. In such instances, the decision to charge a person with a crime may be left primarily to the discretion of the law enforcement agency. The prosecutor may decide to enter this type of case after an arrest has been made and a complaint has been filed with the court, and she may subsequently determine whether to adjust the matter or proceed to trial.

The power to institute formal charges against the defendant is the key to the prosecutorial function. The ability to initiate or discontinue charges against a defendant is the control and power the prosecutor has over an individual's liberty. Almost seventy years ago, Newman Baker commented on the problems of prosecutorial decision-making:

> "To prosecute or not to prosecute?" is a question which comes to mind of this official scores of times each day. A law has been contravened and the statute says he is bound to commence proceedings. His legal duty is clear. But what will be the result? Will it be a waste of time? Will it be expensive to the state? Will it be unfair to the defendant (the prosecutor applying his own ideas of justice)? Will it serve any good purpose to society in general? Will it have good publicity value? Will it cause a political squabble? Will it prevent the prosecutor from carrying the offender's home precinct when he, the prosecutor, runs for Congress after his term as prosecutor? Was the law violated a foolish piece of legislation? If the offender is a friend, is it the square thing to do to reward friendship by initiating criminal proceedings? These and many similar considerations are bound to come to the mind of the man responsible for setting the wheels of criminal justice in motion.[16]

Factors Influencing Prosecutorial Discretion

Research indicates that widely varied factors influence prosecutorial discretion in invoking criminal sanction. In general they can be divided into legal, extralegal, and resource issues.

Legal Issues Legal issues can include the characteristics of the justice system, crime, the criminal, and the victim. The quality of police work and the amount and relevance of the evidence the police gather is a critical legal variable in deciding whether a prosecutor will bring a case forward to trial.[17] A defendant who is a known drug user, who has a long history of criminal offending, and who causes the victim extensive physical injuries will more likely be prosecuted than one who is a first offender, does not use drugs, and does not seriously injure a victim.[18] Crime seriousness certainly influences discretion. The decision to prosecute federal drug cases is significantly influenced by the amount and type of drug in the suspect's possession.[19]

Victim Issues In some instances, the victim's behavior may influence charging decisions. Some victims may become reluctant to press charges, especially if the offender is a parent or spouse. Domestic violence cases are often difficult to prosecute. Some victims are unlikely to encourage or work with prosecutors even after the police get involved. African-American women are less likely to support prosecution than Caucasian women, perhaps because they have had disappointing experiences with the justice system or lack the resources—such as money to pay babysitters—to vigorously pursue a legal solution to their problems.[20] When Myrna Dawson and Ronit Dinovitzer examined the prosecution of domestic violence cases they found that victim cooperation is a key factor in the decision to prosecute cases: the odds of a case being prosecuted is seven times greater when victims are considered "cooperative." Ironically, Dawson and Dinovitzer found that victim cooperation was linked to prosecutorial sensitivity. Prosecutors were able to gain the cooperation of victims and proceed to trial when they showed interest in the victim's plight—by allowing victims to videotape their statements—or provided victim/witness assistance.[21]

Extralegal Issues Extralegal factors include the offender's race, gender, or ethnic background. Of course, due process considerations demand that these personal characteristics have no bearing on the use of prosecutorial discretion. Nonetheless, their effect on prosecutorial decision-making is uncertain. While some research efforts have found that the race of the offender or victim influences prosecutorial discretion, others show that decisions are relatively unbiased.[22] Proving racial influence is difficult. In order to establish bias, a defendant must produce credible evidence that similarly situated defendants of other races could have been prosecuted, but were not.

Resource Issues Resource issues that influence prosecutorial discretion include the availability of treatment and detention facilities, the size of caseloads, and the number of prosecutors available. In some drug cases, prosecutors may decline to bring the case to trial because it relies on costly forensic analysis, expert witnesses, and forensic accountants in preparing the case for prosecution.[23] Some research efforts have concluded that the availability of resources may be a more critical factor in shaping prosecutorial discretion than either legal or extralegal factors.

Sometimes resources are strained because public interest groups who are interested in curbing behaviors which are of particular concern to them, such as domestic violence or possession of handguns, lobby prosecutors to devote more attention to these social problems. If too successful, lobbying efforts may dilute resources and overextend the prosecutor's office. When prosecutors in Milwaukee substantially increased the prosecution of domestic violence cases, the time taken to process the cases doubled, convictions declined, there was more pretrial crime, and victim satisfaction with the justice process decreased.[24] Prosecutors are politicians and a loss in a key case may hinder their re-election and future political aspirations. And in a world of tight government budgets, a prosecutor's office may be forced to accept plea bargains simply because it lacks the resources and personnel to bring many cases to trial.[25]

The Role of Prosecutorial Discretion

Regardless of its source, the proper exercise of prosecutorial discretion can improve the criminal justice process by preventing the rigid implementation of criminal law. Discretion allows the prosecutor to consider alternative decisions and humanize the operation of the criminal justice system. If prosecutors had little or no discretion, they would be forced to prosecute all cases brought to their attention. Judge Charles Breitel has stated, "If every policeman, every prosecutor, every court, and every postsentence agency performed his or its responsibility in strict accordance with rules of law, precisely and narrowly laid down, the criminal law would be ordered but intolerable."[26]

On the other hand, too much discretion can lead to abuses that result in the abandonment of law. Prosecutors are political creatures. Although they are charged with serving the people, they also must be wary of their reputations; losing too many high-profile cases may jeopardize their chances of re-election. They therefore may be unwilling to prosecute cases where the odds of conviction are low; they are worried about *convictability*.[27]

Prosecutorial Ethics

Although the prosecutor's primary duty is to enforce criminal law, his/her fundamental obligation as an attorney is to seek justice, as well as to convict those who are guilty. If the prosecutor discovers facts suggesting that the accused is innocent, he/she must bring this information to the attention of the court.

In carrying out their stated duties, prosecutors are sometime caught in an ethical conundrum. They are being compelled by their supervisors to do everything possible to obtain a guilty verdict while at the same time acting as concerned public officials to ensure that justice is done. Sometimes this conflict can lead to *prosecutorial misconduct*. According to some legal authorities, unethical prosecutorial behavior is often motivated by the desire to obtain a conviction and by the fact that such misbehavior is rarely punished by the courts.[28] Some prosecutors may conceal evidence or misrepresent it, or influence juries by impugning the character of opposing witnesses. Even where a court may instruct a jury to ignore certain evidence, a prosecutor may attempt to sway the jury or the judge by simply mentioning the tainted evidence. Because appellate courts generally uphold convictions in cases where such misconduct is not considered serious (the *harmless error doctrine*), prosecutors are not penalized for their misbehavior, nor are they personally liable for their conduct. Overzealous, excessive, and even cruel prosecutors, motivated by a desire for political gain or notoriety, produce wrongful convictions, thereby abusing their office and the public trust.[29] According to legal expert Stanley Fisher, prosecutorial excesses appear when the government (1) always seeks the highest charges, (2) interprets the criminal law expansively, (3) wins as many convictions as possible, and (4) obtains the severest penalties.[30]

Curing the Problem Because prosecutorial misconduct is a serious matter, the courts have reviewed such prosecutorial behavior as (1) making disruptive statements in court, (2) failure to adhere to sentence recommendations pursuant to a plea bargain, (3) representing a criminal defendant currently under indictment in a private matter, (4) making public statements harmful to the office of the district attorney that are not constitutionally protected under the First Amendment, and (5) withholding evidence that might exonerate a defendant.

Courts have also been more concerned about prosecutors who use their discretion in a vindictive manner to punish defendants who exercise their legal rights. Three cases illustrate controls placed on "vindictive" prosecutors:

- *North Carolina v. Pearce.* In this case, the U.S. Supreme Court held that a judge in a retrial cannot impose a sentence more severe than that originally imposed. In other words, a prosecutor cannot seek a stricter sentence for a defendant who succeeds in getting her first conviction set aside.[31]

- *Blackledge v. Perry.* The U.S. Supreme Court found that imposing a penalty on a defendant for having successfully pursued a statutory right of appeal is a violation of due process of law and amounts to prosecutorial vindictiveness.[32]

- *Bordenkircher v. Hayes.* In this case, the Court allowed the prosecutor to carry out threats of increased charges made during plea negotiations when the defendant refused to plead guilty to the original charge.[33]

These decisions provide the framework for the "prosecutorial vindictiveness" doctrine: due process of law may be violated if the prosecutor retaliates against a defendant and there is proof of actual vindictiveness. The prosecutor's legitimate exercise of discretion must be balanced against the defendant's legal rights.

Criminal Justice ⚖ Now™

Learn more about The Defense Attorney by exploring the Attorney–Client Privilege Review and Reinforce activity.

THE DEFENSE ATTORNEY

The defense attorney is the counterpart of the prosecuting attorney in the criminal process. The accused has a constitutional right to counsel, and when the defendant cannot afford an attorney, the state must provide one. The accused may obtain counsel from the private bar if he can afford to do so; if the defendant is indigent, private counsel or a **public defender** may be assigned by the court (see the discussion on the defense of the indigent later in this chapter).

The Role of the Criminal Defense Attorney

The defense counsel is an attorney as well as an officer of the court. As an attorney, the defense counsel is obligated to uphold the integrity of the legal profession and to observe the requirements of the ABA's Code of Professional Responsibility in the defense of a client. In the code, the duties of the lawyer to the adversary system of justice are stated as follows:

> Our legal system provides for the adjudication of disputes governed by the rules of substantive, evidentiary, and procedural law. An adversary presentation counters the natural human tendency to judge too swiftly in terms of the familiar that which is not yet fully known; the advocate, by his zealous preparation of facts and law, enables the tribunal to come to the hearing with an open and neutral mind and to render impartial judgments. The duty of a lawyer to his client and his duty to the legal system are the same: to represent his client zealously within the boundaries of the law.[34]

Criminal Justice ⚖ Now™

Learn more about The Defense Attorney by exploring the "Drug Bust Part 3" Role Play activity.

public defender *An attorney generally employed (at no cost to the accused) by the government to represent poor persons accused of a crime.*

adversarial procedure *The procedure used to determine truth in the adjudication of guilt or innocence in which the defense (advocate for the accused) is pitted against the prosecution (advocate for the state), with the judge acting as arbiter of the legal rules. Under the adversary system, the burden is on the state to prove the charges beyond a reasonable doubt. This system of having the two parties publicly debate has proved to be the most effective method of achieving the truth regarding a set of circumstances. (Under the accusatory, or inquisitorial, system, which is used in continental Europe, the charge is evidence of guilt that the accused must disprove; the judge takes an active part in the proceedings.)*

Sixth Amendment *The U.S. constitutional amendment containing various criminal trial rights, such as the right to public trial, right to trial by jury, and the right to confrontation of witnesses.*

indigent *Person who is needy and poor or who lacks the means to hire an attorney.*

Gideon v. Wainwright *The 1963 U.S. Supreme Court case that granted counsel to indigent defendants in felony prosecutions.*

Because of the way the U.S. system of justice operates today, criminal defense attorneys face many role conflicts. They are viewed as the prime movers in what is essentially an **adversarial procedure:** the prosecution and the defense engage in conflict over the facts of the case at hand, with the prosecutor arguing the case for the state and the defense counsel using all the means at his disposal to aid the client.

However, as members of the legal profession, the defense counsel must be aware of their role as officers of the court. As an attorney, the defense counsel is obligated to uphold the integrity of the legal profession and to rely on constitutional ideals of fair play and professional ethics to provide adequate representation for a client.

THE RIGHT TO COUNSEL

The **Sixth Amendment** to the U.S. Constitution allows for provision of counsel at trial. But what about the **indigent** criminal defendant who cannot afford to retain an attorney?

In the 1963 landmark case of ***Gideon v. Wainwright,*** the U.S. Supreme Court took the first major step on the issue of right to counsel by holding that state courts must provide counsel to indigent defendants in felony prosecutions.[35] Almost ten years later, in the 1972 case of *Argersinger v. Hamlin,* the Court extended the obligation to provide counsel to all criminal cases where the penalty includes imprisonment—regardless of whether the offense is a felony or misdemeanor.[36] These two major decisions relate to the Sixth Amendment right to counsel as it applies to the presentation of a defense at the trial stages of the criminal justice system.

In numerous Supreme Court decisions since *Gideon v. Wainwright,* the states have been required to provide counsel for indigent defendants at virtually all other stages of the criminal process, beginning with arrest and concluding with the defendant's release from the system. Today, the Sixth Amendment right to counsel and the Fifth and Fourteenth Amendments guarantee of due process of law have been judicially interpreted together to provide the defendant with counsel by the state in all types of criminal proceedings. The Supreme Court generally requires the states to provide counsel in proceedings that involve the loss of personal liberty, such as criminal trials, juvenile court hearings, and mental health commitments.

Areas still remain in the criminal justice system where the courts have not required assistance of counsel for the accused. These include (1) preindictment lineups, (2) booking procedures, including the taking of fingerprints and other forms of identification, (3) grand jury investigations, (4) appeals beyond the first review, (5) disciplinary proceedings in correctional institutions, and (6) postrelease revocation hearings. Nevertheless, the general rule of thumb is that no person can be deprived of freedom or lose a "liberty interest" without representation by counsel.

Legal Services for the Indigent

To satisfy the constitutional requirements that indigent defendants be provided with the assistance of counsel at various stages of the criminal process, the federal government and the states have had to evaluate and expand criminal defense services. Today, about three thousand state and local agencies are providing indigent legal services in the United States.

Providing legal services for the indigent offender is a huge and costly undertaking. And although most states have a formal set of rules to signify who is an indigent and many require indigents to repay the state for at least part

© 2002 AP/Wide World Photos

The United States Supreme Court has ruled that all criminal defendants facing jail or prison time are entitled to a lawyer. If they cannot afford one, the state must provide counsel free of charge. Most often, that means a public defender. Here, public defender Kathryn Benson talks with Richard Allen Williams following his arraignment in Boone County, Missouri, Circuit Court. Williams, 36, pleaded innocent to ten counts of first-degree murder for allegedly killing patients while working as a nurse at the Truman Memorial Veterans Hospital in Columbia, Missouri. On August 6, 2003, Williams was released after prosecutors admitted that the tests that led to the charges against him were flawed. Without his court-appointed counsel, Williams would still be in prison.

Exhibit	8.2	The forms of indigent defense

- *Public defender.* A salaried staff of full-time or part-time attorneys that renders indigent criminal defense services through a public or private nonprofit organization, or as direct government-paid employees. The first public defender program in the United States opened in 1913 in Los Angeles. Public defenders can be part of a statewide agency, county government, the judiciary, or an independent nonprofit organization or other institution.

- *Assigned counsel.* The appointment is from a list of private bar members who accept cases on a judge-by-judge, court-by-court, or case-by-case basis. This may include an administrative component and a set of rules and guidelines governing the appointment and processing of cases handled by the private bar members. There are two main types of assigned counsel systems. In the first, which makes up about 75 percent of all assigned counsel systems, the presiding judge appoints attorneys on a case-by-case basis; this is referred to as an *ad hoc assigned counsel system.* The second type is referred to as a *coordinated assigned counsel system,* in which an administrator oversees the appointment of counsel and sets up guidelines for the administration of indigent legal services. The fees awarded to assigned counsels can vary widely, ranging from a low of $10 per hour for handling a misdemeanor out of court to over $100 per hour for a serious felony handled in court. Some jurisdictions may establish a maximum allowance per case of $750 for a misdemeanor and $1,500 for a felony. Average rates seem to be between $40 and $80 per hour, depending on the nature of the case. Restructuring the attorney fee system is undoubtedly needed to maintain fair standards for the payment of such legal services.

- *Contract.* Nonsalaried private attorneys, bar associations, law firms, consortiums or groups of attorneys, or nonprofit corporations that contract with a funding source to provide court-appointed representation in a jurisdiction. In some instances, an attorney is given a set amount of money and is required to handle all cases assigned. In other jurisdictions, contract lawyers agree to provide legal representation for a set number of cases at a fixed fee. A third system involves representation at an estimated cost per case until the dollar amount of the contract is reached. At that point, the contract may be renegotiated, but the lawyers are not obligated to take new cases.

Source: Carol J. DeFrances, *State-Funded Indigent Defense Services, 1999* (Washington, D.C.: Bureau of Justice Statistics, 2001).

of their legal services (known as *recoupment*), indigent legal services still cost over $1.5 billion annually.

Programs providing counsel assistance to indigent defendants can be divided into three major categories: public defender systems, **assigned counsel** systems, and **contract systems** (see Exhibit 8.2). In addition, other approaches to the delivery of legal services include the use of mixed systems, such as representation by both the public defender and the private bar, law school clinical programs, and prepaid legal services. Although many jurisdictions have a combination of these programs, statewide public defender programs seem to be on the increase.[37]

These three systems can be used independently or in combination. In Maine the majority of its indigent criminal defense services are through an assigned counsel program; Oregon primarily uses a system of awarded contracts; Minnesota and New Mexico do not have assigned counsel programs but instead rely on statewide public defender programs and contract attorney programs.[38]

In general, the attorney list/assigned counsel system is used in less populated areas, where case flow is minimal and a full-time public defender is not needed. Public defenders are usually found in larger urban areas with high case flow rates. So although a proportionately larger area of the country is served by the assigned counsel system, a significant proportion of criminal defendants receive public defenders.

 Want to read about the mission and organization of a typical public defender's office? To reach the site maintained by the Wisconsin Office of the State Public Defender, go to "Web Links" on your Siegel Essentials of Criminal Justice 5e website: http://cj.wadsworth.com/siegel_ess5e.

assigned counsel A lawyer appointed by the court to represent a defendant in a criminal case because the person is too poor to hire counsel.

contract system (attorney) Providing counsel to indigent offenders by having attorneys under contract to the county handle all (or some) such cases.

The Private Bar

Though most criminal defendants are represented by public supported lawyers, there are also private attorneys who specialize in criminal practice. Since most lawyers are not prepared in law school for criminal work, their skill often results from their experience in the trial courts. While a few nationally known criminal defense attorneys represent defendants for large fees in celebrated and widely publicized case, these are actually relatively few in number.

Besides this limited group of well-known criminal lawyers, some lawyers and law firms serve as house counsel for such professional criminals as narcotics dealers, gamblers, prostitutes, and even big-time burglars. These lawyers, however, constitute a very small percentage of the private bar practicing criminal law.

A large number of criminal defendants are represented by lawyers who often accept many cases for small fees. These lawyers may belong to small law firms or work alone, but a sizable portion of their practice involves representing those accused of crime. Other private practitioners occasionally take on criminal matters as part of their general practice.

Public vs. Private Attorneys Do criminal defendants who hire their own private lawyers do better in court than those who depend on legal representatives provided by the state? While there are some advantages to private counsel, national surveys indicate that state-appointed attorneys do quite well in court. According to data compiled by the federal government:

- Conviction rates for indigent defendants and those with their own lawyers were about the same in federal and state courts. About 90 percent of the federal defendants and 75 percent of the defendants in the most populous counties were found guilty regardless of the type of their attorneys.

- Of those found guilty, however, those represented by publicly financed attorneys were incarcerated at a higher rate than those defendants who paid for their own legal representation—88 percent compared to 77 percent in federal courts and 71 percent compared to 54 percent in the most populous counties.

- On average, sentence lengths for defendants sent to jail or prison were shorter for those with publicly financed attorneys than those who hired counsel. In federal district court those with publicly financed attorneys were given just under five years on average, and those with private attorneys just over five years. In large state courts those with publicly financed attorneys were sentenced to an average of two and a half years, and those with private attorneys to three years.[39]

The data indicates that private counsel may have a slightly better track record in some areas, but that court appointed lawyers acquit themselves quite well.

The Competence of Defense Attorneys

With the Sixth Amendment guarantee of counsel for virtually all defendants, does it require a "competent" attorney be appointed, and if so, how is competency defined?

Inadequacy of counsel may occur in a variety of instances. The attorney may refuse to meet regularly with the client, fail to cross-examine key government witnesses, or fail to investigate the case properly. A defendant's plea of guilty may be based on poor advice, where the attorney may misjudge the admissibility of evidence. When codefendants have separate counsel, conflicts of interest between the defense attorneys may arise. On an appellate level, the lawyer may decline to file a brief, instead relying on a brief submitted for one of the co-appellants.

The concept of attorney competence was defined by the U.S. Supreme Court in the 1984 case of **Strickland v. Washington.**[40] Strickland had been arrested for committing a string of extremely serious crimes, including murder, torture, and kidnapping. Against his lawyer's advice, he pleaded guilty and

Strickland v. Washington *The 1984 U.S. Supreme Court decision upholding that defendants have the right to reasonably effective assistance of counsel (that is, competent representation).*

threw himself on the mercy of the trial judge at a capital sentencing hearing. He also ignored his attorney's recommendation that he exercise his right to have an advisory jury at his sentencing hearing.

In preparing for the hearing, the lawyer spoke with Strickland's wife and mother but did not otherwise seek character witnesses. Nor was a psychiatric examination requested since, in the attorney's opinion, Strickland did not have psychological problems. The attorney also did not ask for a presentence investigation because he felt such a report would contain information damaging to his client.

Although the presiding judge had a reputation for leniency in cases where the defendant confessed, he sentenced Strickland to death. Strickland appealed on the grounds that his attorney had rendered ineffective counsel, citing his failure to seek psychiatric testimony and present character witnesses.

The case eventually went to the Supreme Court, which upheld Strickland's sentence. The Strickland case established the two-pronged test for determining effectiveness of counsel:

1. The defendant must show that the counsel's performance was deficient and that such serious errors were made as to essentially eliminate the presence of counsel guaranteed by the Sixth Amendment.

2. The defendant must also show that the deficient performance prejudiced the case to an extent that the defendant was deprived of a fair trial.

In the case at hand, the Court found insufficient evidence that the attorney had acted beyond the boundaries of professional competence, and upheld Strickland's sentence.

Determining whether defense counsel is ineffective is a subjective decision. The Supreme Court has ruled that an attorney can be effective even when he admits a client's guilt before the trial is over as long as it is part of a reasonable defense strategy, such as gaining sympathy from the jury.[41] For a defense attorney to be considered incompetent, he or she would have to miss filings, fail to follow normal trial procedure, and/or fail to use defense tactics that the average attorney would be sure to follow, such as using expert witnesses or mentioning past behaviors that might mitigate guilt.

Ethical Issues in Criminal Defense and Prosecution

As officers of the court, prosecutors and defense attorneys must obey strict ethical standards of conduct. Because the defense attorney and the prosecutor have different roles, their ethical dilemmas may vary. The defense attorney must maintain confidentiality and advise his client of the constitutional requirements of counsel, the privilege against self-incrimination, and the right to trial. Conversely, the prosecutor represents the public and is not required to abide by such restrictions in the same way. In some cases, the defense

© 2003 AP/Wide World Photos

The prosecution and defense must maintain their professional ethics during the trial process. Sometimes they even have to cooperate in hotly contested and highly publicized murder cases. Here, Assistant District Attorney Freda Black, holding a piece of evidence, looks over shared witness data with District Attorney Jim Hardin, center, and one of Michael Peterson's attorneys, David Rudolf, at Peterson's trial in Durham, North Carolina. The prosecution rested its case against Peterson, who was charged with first-degree murder in the death of his wife, Kathleen. Peterson was found guilty of murder on March 10, 2003, and sentenced to life in prison.

counsel may even be justified in withholding evidence by keeping the defendant from testifying at the trial. In addition, although prosecutors are prohibited from expressing a personal opinion as to the defendant's guilt on summation of the case, defense attorneys are not altogether barred from expressing their belief about a client's innocence. Ethical issues in defense are explored further in the following Policy, Programs, and Issues in Criminal Justice feature.

COURT ADMINISTRATION

In addition to qualified personnel, there is a need for efficient management of the judiciary system. The need for efficient management techniques in an ever-expanding criminal court system has led to the recognition of improved court administration as a way to relieve court congestion. Management goals include improving organization and scheduling of cases, devising methods to allocate court resources efficiently, administering fines and monies due the court, preparing budgets, and overseeing personnel.

The federal courts have led the way in creating and organizing court administration. In 1939, Congress passed the Administrative Office Act, which established the Administrative Office of the United States Courts. Its director was charged with gathering statistics on the work of the federal courts and preparing the judicial budget for approval by the Conference of Senior Circuit Judges. One clause of the act created a judicial council with general supervisory responsibilities for the district and circuit courts.

Unlike the federal government, the states have experienced slow and uneven growth in the development and application of court management principles. The first state to establish an administrative office was North Dakota in 1927. Today, all states employ some form of central administration.

The federal government has encouraged the development of state court management through funding assistance to court managers. In addition, the federal judiciary has provided the philosophical impetus for better and more effective court management.

Using Technology in Court Management

As trial reconvenes, the participants blink into existence on the computer monitors that supply the only commonality applicable to them. Judge, counsel, parties, witnesses, and jury appear in virtual form on each person's monitor. Necessary evidentiary foundations are laid by witnesses with distant counsel's questions; documentary evidence is not seen by the jury until received by the court. A real-time, multimedia record (transcript with digital audio, video, and evidence) is available instantly. Sidebar conferences are accomplished simply by switching the jury out of circuit. During the interim, the jurors can head for their kitchens or for restroom breaks. The public can follow the proceedings on the Internet. Should critical interlocutory motions be argued, the appellate court can directly monitor the proceedings.

This is how court technology expert Fredric I. Lederer foresees the court of the future. His projections may not be too far off. Computers are becoming an important aid in the administration and management of courts. In most jurisdictions today, centralized court administrative services perform numerous functions with the help of sophisticated computers that free the judiciary to fulfill their roles as arbiters of justice. Rapid retrieval and organization of data are now being used for such functions as these:

- Maintaining case histories and statistical reporting
- Monitoring and scheduling cases
- Preparing documents

Criminal Justice ⚖ Now™

Learn more by exploring "Describing the Court System" Vocabulary Check activity.

Policy, Programs, and Issues in Criminal Justice

Ethical Issues in Defense: Should Defense Lawyers Tell the Truth?

One of the most highly publicized criminal cases of the past few years was the Danielle van Dam murder case. The pretty seven-year-old California girl was abducted from her bedroom and later found dead in a wooded area. Suspicion was soon directed at a neighbor, David Westerfield, who was arrested and charged with the crime.

During the trial, Westerfield's defense team, Steven Feldman and Robert Boyce, put on a vigorous defense. They pointed a finger at the lifestyle of the child's parents, Brenda and Damon van Dam, who were forced to admit on the stand that they engaged in partner-swapping and group sex. The defense lawyers told jurors the couple's sex life brought them in contact with sleazy characters who were much more likely to harm Danielle than Westerfield, a neighbor with no felony record. The defense also told jurors that scientific evidence proved Westerfield could not have dumped Danielle's body by a remote roadside. Forensic entomologists testified that the insects in her decaying body indicated her death occurred during a period for which Westerfield could account for his activities. Despite their efforts, physical evidence found in Westerfield's home proved very damaging in court and he was convicted of the murder and sentenced to death.

After the trial was over, the *San Diego Union-Tribune* broke the story that Feldman and Boyce tried to broker a deal before trial in which Westerfield would reveal the location of Danielle's body in exchange for a guarantee that he would not face the death penalty but would receive life without parole. Both sides were about to make the deal when volunteer searchers found Danielle's body. Talk show host Bill O'Reilly (*The O'Reilly Factor*) revealed the contents of the *Union-Tribune* article on national TV. He was disgusted to learn that Westerfield's attorneys Feldman and Boyce knew that their client was guilty before the trial began, yet put on a defense in which they claimed he was innocent:

> Would these two men have allowed Westerfield to walk out of the courtroom a free man if he had been acquitted? Remember, these guys knew he killed Danielle and were willing to lead authorities to her body, according to the *Trib*.

> So forget all the smears they made up. Forget about the fact they consciously misled the jury. Would these two men have allowed Westerfield to walk free, knowing he was a child killer?

O'Reilly added, "No American should ever talk to these two people again—that's how sleazy they are."

He filed a formal complaint with the state bar of California.

While O'Reilly was expressing his disgust, members of the legal community in San Diego defended the trial tactics of Feldman and Boyce. Defense lawyers and former prosecutors pointed out that plea discussions are never admissible during trial and that Feldman and Boyce would have been accused of incompetence if they did not try to raise reasonable doubt in the case. A defense attorney's job isn't to decide whether their client committed the offense but to provide them with a vigorous defense and ensure that their client isn't convicted unless the prosecution can prove its case beyond a reasonable doubt. And it's impossible to make the prosecution meet its burden without aggressively challenging the evidence, even if the defender believes the client committed the crime. One San Diego defense lawyer, Bill Nimmo, defended the lawyers' decision to raise the parents' swinging and the bug evidence. "You [as a defense lawyer] are not personally vouching for everything. You are arguing what the evidence shows, not what you personally know," said Nimmo. "If the evidence is good enough, if the prosecution has strong enough evidence, what do you care what the defense lawyer knows? He'll get convicted." If Westerfield attempted to take the stand and lie about his involvement in the murder, then Feldman and Boyce would be required to tell the judge, but Westerfield did not testify.

Critical Thinking

Do you agree that defense attorneys should put on a vigorous defense, casting doubt on their clients' guilt, even if they know beyond doubt that their client is guilty? If witnesses are not allowed to lie in court, why should attorneys maintain that privilege? An attorney is compelled by professional oath to defend their client to the best of their ability. But does that mean misleading the jury?

InfoTrac College Edition Research

Use *Danielle van Dam* and *David Westerfield* as subject guides on InfoTrac College Edition to learn more about this case.

Sources: Harriet Ryan, "Fox talk show host calls for disbarment of Westerfield lawyers," CourtTV.com website, September 19, 2002, www.courttv.com/trials/westerfield/091902_ctv.html, accessed on August 24, 2005; Alex Roth, "Experts make case for defense attorneys," *San Diego Union-Tribune*, September 22, 2002; Alex Roth, "Story of plea attempt raises ire of many," *San Diego Union-Tribune*, September 18, 2002.

- Indexing cases
- Issuing summonses
- Notifying witnesses, attorneys, and others of required appearances
- Selecting and notifying jurors
- Preparing and administering budgets and payrolls

The federal government has encouraged the states to experiment with computerized information systems. Federal funds were used to begin a fifty-state consortium for the purpose of establishing a standardized crime-reporting system called SEARCH (Systems for the Electronic Analysis and Retrieval of Criminal Histories).

Computer technology is also being applied in the courts in such areas as videotaped testimonies, new court reporting devices, information systems, and data processing systems to handle such functions as court docketing and jury management. In 1968, only ten states had state-level automated information systems; today, all states employ such systems for a mix of tasks and duties. A survey of Georgia courts found that 84 percent used computers for three or more court administration applications.

Other developing areas of court technology include the following.[42]

Communications Court jurisdictions are also cooperating with police departments in the installation of communications gear that allows defendants to be arraigned over closed-circuit television while they are in police custody. Closed-circuit television has been used for judicial conferences and scheduling meetings. Some courts are using voice-activated cameras to record all testimony during trials; these are the sole means of keeping trial records.

Videoconferencing About four hundred courts across the country have videoconferencing capability. It is now being employed for juvenile detention hearings, expert witness, testimony at trial, oral arguments on appeal, and parole hearings. More than one hundred and fifty courts use two-way live, televised remote link-ups for first appearance and arraignment. In the usual arrangement, defendants appear from a special location in the jail where they are able to see and hear and be seen and heard by the presiding magistrate. Such appearances are now being authorized by state statute. Televising appearances minimizes delays in prisoner transfer, effects large cost savings through the elimination of transportation and security costs, and reduces escape and assault risks.

Evidence Presentation High-tech courtrooms are now equipped for real-time transcription and translation, audio-video preservation of the court record, remote witness participation, computer graphics displays, television monitors for jurors, and computers for counsel and judge.

Case Management Case management will soon be upgraded. In the 1970s, municipal courts installed tracking systems, which used databases to manage court data. These older systems were limited and could not process the complex interrelationships of information pertaining to persons, cases, time, and financial matters that occur in court cases.

Contemporary relational databases now provide the flexibility to handle complex case management. To help programmers define the multiplicity of relationships that occur in a court setting, the National Center for State Courts in Williamsburg, Virginia, has developed a methodology for structuring a case management system that tracks a person to the case or cases in which he or she is a defendant, the scheduling of cases to avoid any conflicts, and of increasing importance, the fines that have been levied and the accounts to which the money goes.

Internet Utilization The Internet has begun finding its way into the court system. In the federal system, "J-Net," is the Judiciary's intranet website. It makes it easier for judges and court personnel to find important information in a timely fashion. The federal court's Administrative Office has begun sending official correspondence by e-mail, which provides instantaneous communication of important information. In 1999, an automated library management system was developed, which meant that judges could access a web-based virtual law library. A web-based electronic network providing the public with access to court records and other information via the Internet was also implemented. In 2002, eleven federal courts announced that they would allow Internet access to criminal case files as part of a pilot program adopted by the Judicial Conference of the United States (a panel of twenty-seven federal judges responsible for crafting policy in the federal court system). This was the first time the public could gain access to criminal case files.

Information Sharing Technology has been harnessed to make it easier for courts to share information within and between states. Nebraska, has implemented a statewide automated case management system, known as JUSTICE. The JUSTICE system was designed to reuse data that had already been input by others. The original design included ways to exchange information with the computer systems of other state and local agencies. It eliminated reading and retyping data. This design restructured criminal justice workflow while eliminating unnecessary work.

The computer cannot replace the judge, but it can be used as an ally to help speed the trial process by identifying backlogs and bottlenecks that can be eradicated with intelligent managerial techniques. Just as a manager must know the type and quantity of goods on hand in a warehouse, so an administrative judge must have available information about those entering the judge's domain, what happens to them once they are in it, and how they fare after judgment has been rendered.

SUMMARY

- The U.S. court system is a complex social institution.
- There is no set pattern of court organization. Courts are organized on federal, state, county, and local levels of government.
- Courts of general jurisdiction hear felony cases and larger civil trials.
- Courts of limited jurisdiction hear misdemeanors and more limited civil cases.
- Specialty courts have developed to focus on particular crime problems such as drug abuse.
- Appellate courts review trials if there is a complaint about the process.
- The Supreme Court is the highest court in the land and has final jurisdiction over federal and state cases.
- Courts today hear almost 100 million cases each year, which leads to congestion and delays.

- The judge's duties include approving plea bargains, trying cases, and determining the sentence given the offender.
- Judges can be selected via executive appointment, election, or the Missouri Plan, which combines both activities.
- The prosecutor and the defense attorney are the major officers of justice in the judicial system.
- The prosecutor, who is the people's attorney, has discretion to decide the criminal charge and disposition.
- The prosecutor's daily decisions have a significant impact on police and court operations.
- The prosecutor retains a great deal of discretion in processing cases.
- Political, social, and legal factors all shape the prosecutor's charging decisions.

- The role of the defense attorney in the criminal justice system has grown dramatically during the past few decades.
- Today, providing defense services to the indigent criminal defendant is an everyday practice. Under landmark decisions of the U.S. Supreme Court, particularly *Gideon v. Wainwright* and *Argersinger v. Hamlin,* all defendants who could face imprisonment for any offense must be afforded counsel at trial.
- Methods of providing counsel include assigned counsel systems, where an attorney is selected by the court to represent the accused, and public defender programs, where public employees provide legal services.
- There are many ethical issues facing defense attorneys, such as whether they should keep their clients' statements confidential even though they know they are lying or whether they should defend criminals whom they know are guilty.
- The issue of defense lawyer competence has become an important one for judicial authorities.
- The trial process is undergoing significant change through the introduction of technology and modern court management.
- Caseloads are being more effectively managed and modern communications allow many aspects of the court process to be conducted in cyberspace.
- Some experts believe that we are at the threshold of a new form of trial in which the courthouse of old will be supplanted by the computer, Internet, and wireless communications.

KEY TERMS

state courts of limited jurisdiction 220
court of general jurisdiction 221
appellate court 222
court of last resort 224
writ of certiorari 227

landmark decision 227
jury trial 231
Missouri Plan 233
prosecutor 233
public defender 240
adversarial procedure 240

Sixth Amendment 240
indigent 240
Gideon v. Wainwright 240
assigned counsel 242
contract system (attorney) 242
Strickland v. Washington 243

REVIEW QUESTIONS

1. Should attorneys disclose information given them by their clients concerning participation in an earlier unsolved crime?
2. Should defense attorneys cooperate with a prosecutor if it means that their clients will go to jail?
3. Should a prosecutor have absolute discretion over which cases to proceed on and which to drop?.
4. Should clients be made aware of an attorney's track record in court?
5. Does the assigned counsel system present an inherent conflict of interest, since attorneys are hired and paid by the institution they are to oppose?
6. Do you believe prosecutors have a great deal of discretion? Why or why not?

CHAPTER 9

Pretrial Procedures

© David McNew/Getty Images

R ALPH C. MARTIN II graduated from Brandeis University in 1974, entered the criminal justice program at Northeastern University (where he was one of our students!) before receiving his law degree at Northeastern School of Law in 1978. His career is rather unique. Martin served as the District Attorney of Suffolk County and, in that capacity, was the chief elected law enforcement official for Boston, Chelsea, Revere, and Winthrop from 1992 to 2002. He was appointed in 1992 and won election to the office in 1994 by a margin of almost 20 percent. He ran unopposed in 1998 and became the first African-American and Republican district attorney in Suffolk County's history. As district attorney he oversaw a $15 million budget and an office of 300 people, including 135 prosecutors. Ralph Martin was a highly

Chapter Outline

Chapter Objectives

1. Be able to discuss the advantages of bail
2. Be familiar with the various types of bail systems
3. Be able to discuss the likelihood of making bail
4. Be familiar with the history of bail reform
5. Discuss the difference between preventive detention and release on recognizance
6. Know what is meant by the term *plea bargain*
7. Identify the different types of pleas and how they are used
8. Explain the roles of prosecutor, defense attorney, victim, and judge in the plea negotiation
9. Comment on the success of plea bargain reform
10. Be able to discuss pretrial diversion

respected court officer. He was recognized for his leadership by President Bill Clinton and Attorney General Janet Reno and has traveled across the country to lecture and consult on the business and strategy of managing and reducing crime.

Now a partner at the Bingham McCutchen law firm in Boston, Martin put his more than twenty years experience as a trial lawyer and prosecutor to good use in his practice, which covers the areas of corporate governance and investigations, white collar defense, and general civil litigation. He also leads Bingham McCutchen's Diversity Task Force with the goal of recruitment, retention, and advancement of lawyers from diverse backgrounds.

hether serving as a prosecutor or as a defense attorney, lawyers like Ralph Martin often find themselves engaging in fierce and competitive pretrial negotiations. Many cases, even the most notorious ones, are settled at the pretrial stage of justice which contains a series of decision points that are critical links in the chain of justice. These include arraignments, grand jury investigations, bail hearings, plea bargaining negotiations, and predisposition treatment efforts. These **pretrial procedures** are critically important components of the justice process because the great majority of all criminal cases are resolved informally at this stage and never come before the courts. Although the media like to focus on the elaborate jury trial with its dramatic elements and impressive setting, formal criminal trials are relatively infrequent. Consequently, understanding the events that take place during the pretrial period is essential in grasping the reality of criminal justice policy.

Cases are settled during the pretrial stage in a number of ways. Prosecutors can use their discretion to drop cases before formal charges are filed, because of insufficient evidence, office policy, witness conflicts, or similar problems. Even if charges are filed, the prosecutor can decide not to proceed against the defendant (*nolle prosequi*) because of a change in the circumstances of the case.

In addition, the prosecution and the defense almost always meet to try to arrange a nonjudicial settlement for the case. Plea bargaining, in which the defendant exchanges a guilty plea for some consideration, such as a reduced sentence, is commonly used to terminate the formal processing of the case. The prosecution or the defense may believe that a trial is not in the best interests of the victim, the defendant, or society because of age, mental capacity, or other special circumstances. In this instance, the defendant may have a competency hearing before a judge and be placed in a secure treatment facility until ready to stand trial. Or the prosecutor may waive further action so that the defendant can be placed in a special treatment program, such as a detoxification unit at a local hospital. For example, in a highly publicized 2005 Massachusetts case, a group of students at Milton Academy, an elite prep school, were charged with statutory rape for having sexual relations with a 15-year-old female classmate. Though the boys readily admitted to the sexual encounters with the young woman, prosecutors decided, considering the totality of the circumstances, that the interest of justice would best be served if the boys were treated informally (they agreed to undergo counseling, complete one hundred hours of community service, and serve at least two years of informal probation).[1]

The pretrial stage is one of critical importance in the justice system. In this chapter we look at the various procedures and policies at the center of this critical stage of the justice process.

pretrial procedures *Critical pretrial processes and decisions, including bail, arraignment, and plea negotiation*

bail *The monetary amount for or condition of pretrial release, normally set by a judge at the initial appearance. The purpose of bail is to ensure the return of the accused at subsequent proceedings.*

Criminal Justice ⚖ Now™
Learn more by exploring the Release on Recognizance Review and Reinforce activity.

BAIL

Bail is a cash bond or some other security provided to the court to ensure the appearance of the defendant at every subsequent stage of the criminal justice process, especially trial. Its purpose is to obtain the release from custody of a person charged with a crime. Once the amount of bail is set by the court, the defendant is required to deposit all or a percentage of the entire amount in cash or security (or to pay a professional bonding agent to submit a bond). If the defendant is released on bail but fails to appear in court at the stipulated time, the bail deposit is forfeited. A defendant who fails to make bail is confined in jail until the court appearance.

Bail Today

The most recent national data available indicates that about two-thirds of all defendants make bail and that the remaining third are held in custody prior to trial; of those held in custody 7 percent were denied bail outright (Figure 9.1). Murder defendants (13 percent) were the least likely to be released prior to case disposition, followed by defendants whose most serious arrest charge was robbery (44 percent), motor vehicle theft (46 percent), burglary (49 percent), or rape (56 percent).[2]

How successful is bail? About a third of released defendants were either rearrested for a new offense, failed to appear in court as scheduled, or committed some other violation that resulted in the revocation of their pretrial release. Of these, an estimated 16 percent were rearrested while awaiting disposition of their case; about three-fifths of these new arrests were for a felony.[3] If we assume that courts process about 15 million new cases each year and that 10 million of these cases are given bail, then about 1.6 million people are arrested each year while out on bail, about 10 percent of the total of all arrests.

Criminal Justice ⚖ Now™

*Learn more by exploring the **Pretrial Detention of Felony Defendants** Animated Artwork.*

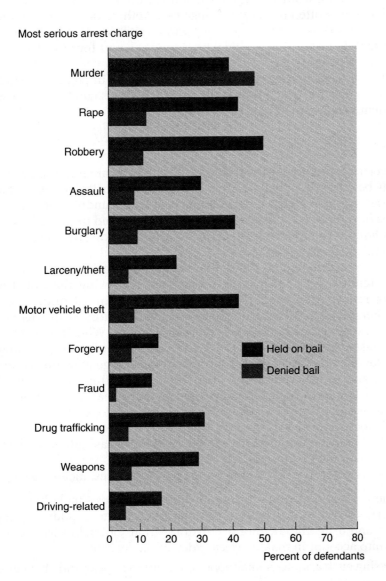

Most serious arrest charge

Figure 9.1
Pretrial detention of felony defendants in the seventy-five largest counties, by most serious arrest charge
Source: Brian A. Reaves, *Felony Defendants in Large Urban Counties, 1998* (Washington, D.C.: Bureau of Justice Statistics, 2001), 16.

■ Held on bail
■ Denied bail

Percent of defendants

Receiving Bail

Whether a defendant can be expected to appear for his or her trial is a key issue in determining bail.[4] Bail cannot be used to punish an accused, nor can it be denied or revoked at the indulgence of the court. Nonetheless, critics argue that money bail is one of the most objectionable aspects of the criminal justice system:

- It is discriminatory because it works against the poor.
- It is costly because the government must pay to detain those offenders who are unable to make bail but who would otherwise remain in the community.
- It is unfair because a higher proportion of detainees receive longer sentences than people released on bail.
- It is dehumanizing because innocent people who cannot make bail suffer in the nation's deteriorated jail system.

There is also the problem of racial and ethnic disparity in the bail process. Some research efforts show that the decision of whether to grant bail may be racially or ethnically biased; black and Latino defendants receive less favorable treatment than whites charged with similar offenses.[5] While these results are troubling, it is often difficult to gauge racial/ethnic differences in the bail process because differences in income, community ties, family support, and criminal record, rather than judicial bias, may account for any observed differences in the bail process.

Despite these drawbacks, the bail system remains in place to ensure that defendants return for trial and that the truly dangerous can be kept in secure confinement pending their court proceedings.

Bail Services

In our overburdened court system it is critical to determine which defendants can safely be released on bail pending trial.[6] In many jurisdictions specialized pretrial services help courts deal with this problem. Hundreds of pretrial bail programs have been established in rural, suburban, and urban jurisdictions, typically housed in probation departments, court offices, and local jails and as independent county contractors.

When first created in the 1960s, they were part of the effort to improve the release/detention decision-making process by improving the breadth and quality of information available to judges at the point of initial decision-making. Personnel gathered information on such factors as the defendant's housing arrangements, family ties, and employment. When the federal government passed the Federal Bail Reform Act of 1966, it encouraged judges to consider factors other than the seriousness of the charge in setting conditions of release and to use conditions other than the setting of a money bond amount, further encouraging the development of pretrial service programs. A "second generation" of pretrial service programs developed during the 1980s and 1990s focused primarily on trying to identify defendants who were unable to make bail but who would be acceptable risks for release either on their own recognizance or under supervision.

These programs provide a number of critical services, including:

- Gathering and verifying information about arrestees—including criminal history, current status in the criminal justice system, address, employment, and drug and alcohol use history—that judicial officers can then take into account in making release/detention decisions.
- Assessing each arrestee's likelihood of failure to appear and chances of being rearrested.

- Monitoring released defendants' compliance with conditions of release designed to minimize pretrial crime, including curfews, orders restricting contact with alleged victims and possible witnesses, home confinement, and drug and alcohol testing.

- Providing direct "intensive" supervision for some categories of defendants by using program staff and collaborating with the police, other agencies, and community organizations.

Virtually all larger jurisdictions in the United States have pretrial release in one form or another. Court-administered programs make up the greatest percentage of pretrial programs, though most newer programs are located within probation departments. The general criteria used to assess eligibility for release center on the defendant's community ties and prior criminal justice involvement. Many jurisdictions have conditional and supervised release and third-party custody release, in addition to release on a person's own recognizance.

Some pretrial services programs are now being aimed at special needs. One type focuses on defendants suffering from mental illness; almost three-quarters of pretrial services programs now inquire about mental health status and treatment as a regular part of their interview, and about one-quarter report having implemented special supervision procedures for defendants with mental illness. Another area of concern is domestic violence. About one-quarter of all pretrial programs have developed special risk-assessment procedures for defendants charged with domestic violence offenses, and about one-third have implemented special procedures to supervise defendants charged with domestic violence offenses. The Policy, Programs, and Issues in Criminal Justice box on the next page describes one state's program in more detail.

pretrial detention Holding an offender in secure confinement before trial.

The Legal Right to Bail

The Eighth Amendment to the U.S. Constitution does not guarantee a right to bail but rather prohibits "excessive bail." Since many state statutes place no precise limit on the amount of bail a judge may impose, many defendants who cannot make bail are placed in detention while awaiting trial. It has become apparent over the years that the bail system is discriminatory because defendants who are financially well-off can make bail, whereas indigent defendants languish in **pretrial detention** in the county jail. In addition, keeping a person in jail imposes serious financial burdens on local and state governments—and, in turn, on taxpayers—who must pay for the cost of confinement. These factors have given rise to bail reform programs that depend on the defendant's personal promise to appear in court for trial (*recognizance*), rather than on financial ability to meet bail.

The Eighth Amendment restriction on excessive bail may also be interpreted to mean that the sole purpose of bail is to ensure that the defendant returns for trial; bail may not be used as a form of punishment, nor may it be used to coerce or threaten a defendant. In most cases, a defendant has the right to be released on reasonable bail. Many jurisdictions also require a bail review hearing by a higher court in cases in which the initial judge set what might be considered excessive bail.

© 2005 AP/Wide World Photos

Not all criminal offenders are entitled to bail. Those who commit capital crimes can be kept in custody prior to their trial or plea. Mark Hacking is escorted out of the courtroom after his pretrial hearing April 15, 2005, in Salt Lake City, Utah. Hacking pleaded guilty to murder in the death of his wife, Lori, in July 2004.

Policy, Programs, and Issues in Criminal Justice

Kentucky's Statewide Pretrial Services Agency

The Kentucky state legislature established the Pretrial Services and Court Security Agency in 1976 to replace the commercial bail bonding system. The new agency immediately assumed responsibility for implementing the pretrial release process, and the enabling act made it a crime to post a bond for profit in Kentucky.

The agency now has more than two hundred staff members located in sixty offices serving a state population of approximately four million. The agency operates within the judicial branch as part of Kentucky's Administrative Office of the Courts. Staff members interview about 180,000 defendants each year, or approximately 84 percent of all arrestees. They conduct interviews around the clock in the state's population centers of Louisville, Lexington, and the Kentucky sector of the Cincinnati metropolitan area. Interviewers are on duty sixteen to twenty hours per day in smaller cities and on call at all times in rural regions. A pretrial officer interviews all arrestees except those who decline to be interviewed or who post bail immediately. The officer's top interview priority is obtaining background information for use by the judge at the defendant's first court appearance. Increasingly, the agency is able to draw on information in its own records system.

Interview information is treated as confidential—only the judge is given access to the report, and neither the interview nor the report can be subpoenaed. The information goes into the agency's records system for future reference in subsequent cases involving the defendant and also may be used by the agency's failure-to-appear unit.

Pretrial officers in Kentucky must be prepared to present information to the judge at the court appearance and to provide—or renew the search for—information the judge may request at that time. Using a point-scoring system that accounts for current charges, prior record, and family and community ties, the agency recommends release on recognizance (ROR) for defendants who score above the cutoff line. Judges are required by law to consider ROR and to identify in writing issues regarding risk of flight or community safety, although this does not always happen in practice. In making the release/detention decision, judges can use a variety of methods in addition to ROR, including placing the defendant in the custody of a person or organization, placing restrictions on the defendant's travel or residence, and requiring the defendant to post a cash bond with the court.

The agency supervises defendants principally through a tracking and notification system, using the system to remind defendants of upcoming court appearances. More intensive supervision is reserved for major felony cases and court requests. Drug testing is done at court request.

The failure to appear (FTA) rate for defendants under the agency's supervision is 8 percent. Most FTAs occur in cases involving minor offenses, such as public intoxication. In most FTA cases, a warrant is issued and the agency's FTA unit draws on all the information the agency has collected to locate and return the defendant. The agency has an active in-service training program and is working to broaden officer skills related to domestic violence, cultural diversity, victim advocacy, and driving while intoxicated.

Critical Thinking

Let's say an effective technology is developed that could be installed in a wearable device that monitors an offender's physical and emotional processes. The device would measure heartbeat, skin conductivity, and so on and alert authorities if the wearer was having an emotional crisis or even contemplating some forbidden activity such as committing crime. Would you be inclined to increase the number of offenders given pretrial release if such a device actually existed?

InfoTrac College Edition Research

What would happen if the jails were so crowded that all arrestees were given immediate pretrial release? To find out, go to InfoTrac College Edition and read Sarah B. Vandenbraak, "Bail, Humbug! Why Criminals Would Rather Be in Philadelphia," *Policy Review,* Summer 1995, 73(4).

Source: Barry Mahoney, Bruce D. Beaudin, John A. Carver III, Daniel B. Ryan, and Richard B. Hoffman, "Pretrial Services Programs: Responsibilities and Potential," *Issues and Practices, A Publication of the National Institute of Justice* (March 2001): 1–122.

In *Stack v. Boyle* the Supreme Court found bail to be a traditional right to freedom before trial that permits unhampered preparation of a defense and prevents the criminal defendant from being punished prior to conviction.[7] The Court held that bail is excessive when it exceeds an amount reasonably calculated to ensure that the defendant will return for trial. To reach this goal, bail should be in the amount that is generally set for similar offenses. Higher bail can be imposed when evidence supporting the increase is presented at a hearing at which the defendant's constitutional rights can be protected. Although *Stack* did not mandate an absolute right to bail, it did set guidelines for state courts to follow: if a crime is bailable, the amount set should not be frivolous, unusual, or beyond a person's ability to pay.

Making Bail

Bail is usually considered at a hearing that is conducted shortly after a person has been taken into custody. At the hearing, such issues as crime type, flight risk, and dangerousness will be considered before a bail amount is set. Some jurisdictions have developed bail schedules to make amounts uniform based on crime and criminal history. As Exhibit 9.1 shows, there are numerous other junctures during which bail is considered.

Because many criminal defendants are indigent, making bail is a financial challenge that if not met can result in a long stay in a county jail. In desperation, indigent defendants may turn to bail bondsmen. For a fee, bonding agents lend money to people who cannot make bail on their own. Typically, they charge a percentage of the bail amount. A person who is asked to put up

Exhibit 9.1 **Pretrial release alternatives**

Stage	Release Mechanism
1. Police	**Field citation release:** An arresting officer releases the arrestee on a written promise to appear in court, made at or near the actual time and location of the arrest. This procedure is commonly used for misdemeanor charges and is similar to issuing a traffic ticket.
2. Police	**Station house citation release:** The determination of an arrestee's eligibility and suitability for release and her actual release are deferred until after she has been removed from the scene of an arrest and brought to the station house or police headquarters.
3. Police/pretrial	**Jail citation release:** The determination of an arrestee's eligibility and suitability for citation release and his actual release are deferred until after he has been delivered by the arresting department to a jail or other pretrial detention facility for screening, booking, and admission.
4. Pretrial/court	**Direct release authority by pretrial program:** To streamline release court processes and reduce the length of stay in detention, courts may authorize pretrial programs to release arrestees without direct judicial involvement. Where court rule delegates such authority, the practice is generally limited to misdemeanor charges, but felony release authority has been granted in some jurisdictions.
5. Police/court	**Bail schedule:** An arrestee can post bail at the station house or jail, according to amounts specified in a bail schedule. The schedule is a list of all bailable charges and a corresponding dollar amount for each. Schedules may vary widely from jurisdiction to jurisdiction.
6. Court	**Judicial release:** Arrestees who have not been released by either the police or the jailer and who have not posted bail appear at the hearing before a judge, magistrate, or bail commissioner within a set period of time. In jurisdictions with pretrial release programs, program staff often interview arrestees detained at the jail prior to the first hearing, verify the background information, and present recommendations to the court at arraignment.

$10,000 will be asked to contribute $2,000 of his own and the bondsman covers the remaining $8,000. After trial, the bondsman keeps the $2,000 as his fee.

Bail Reform

When bailees abscond before trial, bondsmen routinely hire skip tracers, enforcement agents, or bounty hunters to track them down. Each year an estimated 400 full-time bail enforcement agents catch about 25,000 fugitives in the United States.[8] While organizations such as the National Institute of Bail Enforcement attempt to provide training, some untrained and/or unprofessional bounty hunters may use brutal tactics that can end in tragedy. Consequently, efforts have been made to reform and even eliminate money bail and reduce the importance of bonding agents.

Until the early 1960s, the justice system relied primarily on money bonds as the principal form of pretrial release. Many states now allow defendants to be released on their own recognizance without any money bail. **Release on recognizance (ROR)** was pioneered by the Vera Institute of Justice in an experiment called the **Manhattan Bail Project,** which began in 1961 with the cooperation of the New York City criminal courts and local law students.[9] It came about because defendants with financial means were able to post bail to secure pretrial release, while indigent defendants remained in custody. The project found that if the court had sufficient background information about the defendant, it could make a reasonably good judgment about whether the accused would return to court. When release decisions were based on such information as the nature of the offense, family ties, and employment record, most defendants returned to court when released on their own recognizance. The results of the Vera Institute's initial operation showed a default rate of less than 0.7 percent. The bail project's experience suggested that releasing a person on the basis of verified information more effectively guaranteed appearance in court than did money bail. Highly successful ROR projects were set up in major cities around the country, including Philadelphia and San Francisco. By 1980, more than 120 formal programs were in operation, and today they exist in almost every major jurisdiction.[10]

The success of ROR programs in the early 1960s resulted in bail reforms that culminated with the enactment of the federal Bail Reform Act of 1966, the first change in federal bail laws since 1789.[11] This legislation sought to ensure that release would be granted in all non-capital cases in which there was sufficient reason to believe that the defendant would return to court. The law clearly established the presumption of ROR that must be overcome before money bail is required, authorized 10 percent **deposit bail,** introduced the concept of conditional release, and stressed the philosophy that release should be under the least restrictive method necessary to ensure court appearance.

During the 1970s and early 1980s, the pretrial release movement was hampered by public pressure over pretrial increases in crime. As a result, the more recent federal legislation, the **Bail Reform Act of 1984,** mandated that no defendants shall be kept in pretrial detention simply because they cannot afford money bail, established the presumption for ROR in all cases in which a person is bailable, and formalized restrictive preventive detention provisions, which are explained later in this chapter. The 1984 act required that community safety, as well as the risk of flight, be considered in the release decision. Consequently, such criminal justice factors as the seriousness of the charged offense, the weight of the evidence, the sentence that may be imposed upon conviction, court appearance history, and prior convictions are likely to influence the release decisions of the federal court.

release on recognizance (ROR) *A nonmonetary condition for the pretrial release of an accused individual; an alternative to monetary bail that is granted after the court determines that the accused has ties in the community, has no prior record of default, and is likely to appear at subsequent proceedings.*

Manhattan Bail Project The innovative experiment in bail reform that introduced and successfully tested the concept of release on recognizance.

deposit bail The monetary amount set by a judge at a hearing as a condition of pretrial release, ordering a percentage of the total bond required to be paid by the defendant.

Bail Reform Act of 1984 Federal legislation that provides for both greater emphasis on release on recognizance for nondangerous offenders and preventive detention for those who present a menace to the community.

Bail reform is considered one of the most successful programs in the recent history of the criminal justice system. Yet it is not without critics, who suggest that emphasis should be put on controlling the behavior of serious criminals rather than on making sure that nondangerous defendants are released before their trials. Criminal defendants released without bail and those who commit crimes awaiting trial fuel the constant debate over pretrial release versus community protection. Although some experts believe that all people, even non-citizens accused of crimes, enjoy the right to bail, others view it as a license to abscond or commit more crimes.[12]

A number of innovative alternative bail programs are described in Exhibit 9.2. The most often used are personal recognizance, unsecured or personal bond, surety or cash bond, and percentage or deposit bail. As Figure 9.2 shows, most bailees are still released on surety bond; next most common is ROR.

Criminal Justice ⊛ Now™

Learn more by going through **Methods of Pretrial Release** *Vocabulary Check activity.*

Exhibit 9.2 Innovative bail systems

Program	Description
Nonfinancial Release	
Release on recognizance (ROR)	The defendant is released on a promise to appear, without any requirement of money bond. This form of release is unconditional—i.e., without imposition of special conditions, supervision, or specially provided services.
Conditional release	The defendant is released on a promise to fulfill some stated requirements that go beyond those associated with ROR. Four types of conditions are placed on defendants: (1) status quo conditions, such as requiring that the defendant retain residence or employment status; (2) restrictive conditions, such as requiring that the defendant remain in the jurisdiction; (3) contact conditions, such as requiring that the defendant report by telephone or in person to the release program; and (4) problem-oriented conditions, such as requiring that the defendant participate in drug or alcohol treatment programs.
Financial Release	
Unsecured bail	The defendant is released with no immediate requirement of payment. However, if the defendant fails to appear, he or she is liable for the full amount.
Privately secured bail	A private organization or individual posts the bail amount, which is returned when the defendant appears in court.
Property bail	The defendant may post evidence of real property in lieu of money.
Deposit bail	The defendant deposits a percentage of the bail amount, typically 10 percent, with the court. When the defendant appears in court, the deposit is returned, sometimes minus an administrative fee. If the defendant fails to appear, he or she is liable for the full amount of the bail.
Surety bail	The defendant pays a percentage of the bond, usually 10 percent, to a bonding agent who posts the full bail. The fee paid to the bonding agent is not returned to the defendant if he or she appears in court. The bonding agent is liable for the full amount of the bond should the defendant fail to appear. Bonding agents often require posting collateral to cover the full bail amount.
Cash bail	The defendant pays the entire amount of bail set by the judge to secure release. The bail is returned to the defendant when he or she appears in court.

Source: Adapted from Andy Hall, *Pretrial Release Program Options* (Washington, D.C.: National Institute of Justice, 1984), 32–33.

Figure 9.2
Pretrial release of felony defendants in the seventy-five largest counties, by type of release
Source: Gerard Rainville and Brian A. Reaves, *Felony Defendants in Large Urban Counties, 2000* (Washington, D.C.: Bureau of Justice Statistics, 2003), 17.

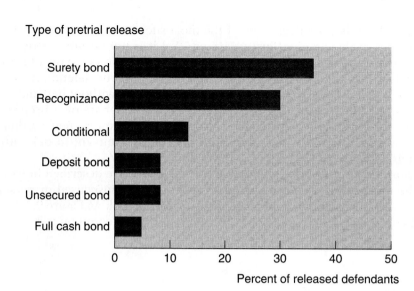

Type of pretrial release

Percent of released defendants

Criminal Justice ⚖ Now™
*Learn more about **Preventive Detention** by exploring the Review and Reinforce activity.*

▮ PREVENTIVE DETENTION

More than half of all violent criminals are now released on bail, including people on trial for committing murder (13 percent). The presumption of bail for felons is challenged by those who believe that releasing dangerous criminals before trial poses a threat to public safety. They point to evidence showing that many people released on bail commit new crimes while at large and often fail to appear for trial. One response to the alleged failure of the bail system to protect citizens is the adoption of **preventive detention** statutes. These laws require that certain dangerous defendants be confined before trial for their own protection and that of the community. Preventive detention is an important manifestation of the crime control perspective on justice, because it favors the use of incapacitation to control the future behavior of suspected criminals. Often, the key question is whether preventive detention is punishment before trial.

The most striking use of preventive detention can be found in the federal Bail Reform Act of 1984.[13] Although the act does contain provisions for ROR, it also allows judges to order preventive detention if they determine "that no condition or combination of conditions will reasonably assure the appearance of the person as required and the safety of any other person and the community."[14]

A number of state jurisdictions have incorporated elements of preventive detention into their bail systems. Although most of the restrictions do not constitute outright preventive detention, they serve to narrow the scope of bail eligibility. These provisions include (1) exclusion of certain crimes from bail eligibility, (2) definition of bail to include appearance in court and community safety, and (3) the limitations on right to bail for those previously convicted. Preventive detention has also been a source of concern for civil libertarians, who believe it violates the due process clause of the U.S. Constitution because it means that a person will be held in custody before proven guilty. In two important cases the U.S. Supreme Court disagreed with this analysis. In *Schall v. Martin,* the Court upheld the application of preventive detention statutes to juvenile defendants on the grounds that such detention is useful to protect the welfare of the minor and society as a whole.[15] In 1987, the Court upheld the Bail Reform Act's provision on preventive detention as it applied to adults in the case of *United States v. Salerno.* Here, the Supreme Court held that the preventive detention act had a legitimate and compelling regulatory purpose and did not violate the Constitution's due process clause. Preventive detention was not designed to punish dangerous individuals but to

preventive detention *The practice of holding dangerous suspects before trial without bail.*

find a solution for the social problem of people committing crimes while on bail; preventing danger to the community is a legitimate societal goal. The Court also stated that society's need for protection can outweigh an individual's liberty interest: under some circumstances, individuals can be held without bail. The act provides that only the most serious criminals can be held and mandates careful procedures to ensure that the judgment of future dangerousness is made after careful deliberation. Finally, the Court found that the Eighth Amendment does not limit the setting (or denial) of bail simply to prohibit defendants' flight to avoid trial and held that considerations of dangerousness are a valid reason to deny pretrial release.[16]

In 2003, the Court applied the preventive detention concept to deportable aliens who commit crime, reasoning their status makes them a special risk and that detention had the legitimate purpose of preventing the aliens from fleeing prior to or during such proceedings.[17]

PRETRIAL DETENTION

The criminal defendant who is not eligible for bail or ROR is subject to pretrial detention in the local county jail. As Figure 9.1 shows, people charged with the most serious offenses such as murder and rape were also the most likely to be detained either because they were denied bail or could not put up the bail amount.

In terms of the number of persons affected each year, pretrial custody accounts for more incarceration in the United States than does imprisonment after sentencing. On any given day in the United States, about three hundred and fifty thousand people were held in more than thirty-five hundred local jails waiting trial; they are *pretrial detainees*.[18] Hundreds of jails are overcrowded, and many are under court orders to reduce their populations and improve conditions. The national jail-crowding crisis has worsened over the years.

Jails are often considered the weakest link in the criminal justice process: they are frequently dangerous, harmful, decrepit, and filled with the poor and friendless. In addition, detainees are often confined with those convicted of crimes and those who have been transferred from other institutions because of overcrowding. Many felons are transferred to jails from state prisons to ease crowding. It is possible to have in close quarters a convicted rapist, a father jailed for nonpayment of child support, and a person awaiting trial for a crime that he did not actually commit. Thus, jails contain a mix of inmates, and this can lead to violence, brutality, and suicide.

The Effects of Detention

What happens to people who do not get bail or who cannot afford to put up bail money? Traditionally, they find themselves more likely to be convicted and then get a longer prison sentence than those who commit similar crimes but

© 2005 AP/Wide World Photos

Prisoners in cell CM-D of the Marion County Lockup in Indianapolis, Indiana, sleep on the floor. Because of rising jail populations many facilities are overcrowded and filled near or beyond their intended capacities. Many jails and detention centers have been using some form of early release to reduce the number of inmates. Despite early releases, crowding continues in some facilities.

who were released on bail; about two-thirds of all defendants granted bail are convicted; in contrast, about three-quarters of all people detained before trial are convicted.[19] Detainees are also more likely to be convicted of a felony offense than releasees, and therefore are eligible for a long prison sentence rather than the much shorter term of incarceration given misdemeanants. People being held in jails are in a less attractive bargaining position than those released on bail, and prosecutors, knowing their predicament, may be less generous in their negotiations.

Criminal Justice ⚖ Now™

Learn more by viewing the "Mexico Bounty Hunters" "In the News" video clip.

CHARGING THE DEFENDANT

Charging a defendant with a crime is a process that varies somewhat, depending on whether it occurs via a *grand jury* or a *preliminary hearing*.

The Indictment Process—The Grand Jury

The grand jury was an early development of the English common law. Under the Magna Carta (1215), no freeman could be seized and imprisoned unless he had been judged by his peers. To determine fairly who was eligible to be tried, a group of freemen from the district where the crime was committed would be brought together to examine the facts of the case and determine whether the charges had merit. Thus, the grand jury was created as a check against arbitrary prosecution by a judge who might be a puppet of the government.

The concept of the grand jury was brought to the American colonies by early settlers and later incorporated into the Fifth Amendment of the U.S. Constitution, which states that "no person shall be held to answer for a capital, or otherwise infamous crime, unless on presentment or indictment of a grand jury." What is the role of the grand jury today? First, the grand jury has the power to act as an independent investigating body. In this capacity, it examines the possibility of criminal activity within its jurisdiction. These investigative efforts may be directed toward general rather than individual criminal conduct—for example, looking at organized crime or insider trading. After an investigation is completed, a report called a **presentment** is issued. The presentment contains not only information concerning the findings of the grand jury but also, usually, a recommendation of indictment.

The grand jury's second and better known role is to act as the community's conscience in determining whether the accusation of the state (the prosecution) justifies a trial. The grand jury relies on the testimony of witnesses called by the prosecution through its subpoena power. After examining the evidence and the testimony of witnesses, the grand jury decides whether probable cause exists for

presentment The report of a grand jury investigation, which usually includes a recommendation of indictment.

© 2003 AP/Wide World Photos

The preliminary hearing is used to determine whether there is sufficient evidence to bind felony defendants over for trial. Maryville, Tennessee, attorney David M. Boyd talks with his client, 20-year-old Aaron Lee Skeen, June 5, 2003, at the Blount County Justice Center in Maryville after his preliminary hearing. Skeen was charged with murder, rape, kidnapping, and burglary in the killing of Sandy Jeffers, whose body was found at the bottom of a 60-foot cliff off the Foothills Parkway in the Great Smoky Mountains. Skeen later plead guilty.

prosecution. If it does, an indictment, or **true bill,** is affirmed. If the grand jury fails to find probable cause, a **no bill** (meaning that the indictment is ignored) is passed. In some states, a prosecutor can present evidence to a different grand jury if a no bill is returned; in other states, this action is prohibited by statute.

Critiquing the Grand Jury The grand jury usually meets at the request of the prosecution, and hearings are closed and secret. Neither the defense attorney, the defendant, nor the general public are allowed to attend. The prosecuting attorney presents the charges and calls witnesses who testify under oath to support the indictment. This process has been criticized as being a "rubber stamp" for the prosecution because the presentation of the evidence is shaped by the district attorney, who is not required by law to reveal information that might exonerate the accused.[20] An alternative is to open the grand jury room to the defense and hold the government to the same types of constitutional safeguards required to protect defendants that are now used at trial.[21]

The Indictment Process—The Preliminary Hearing

The preliminary hearing is used in about half the states as an alternative to the grand jury. Although the purpose of the preliminary hearing and the grand jury hearing is the same—to establish whether probable cause is sufficient to merit a trial—the procedures differ significantly.

The preliminary hearing is conducted before a magistrate or lower court judge, and unlike the grand jury hearing, is open to the public unless the defendant requests otherwise. Present at the preliminary hearing are the prosecuting attorney, the defendant, and the defendant's counsel, if already retained. The prosecution presents its evidence and witnesses to the judge. The defendant or the defense counsel then has the right to cross-examine witnesses and to challenge the prosecutor's evidence.

After hearing the evidence, the judge decides whether there is sufficient probable cause to believe that the defendant committed the alleged crime. If so, the defendant is bound over for trial, and the prosecuting attorney's information (described earlier, similar to an indictment) is filed with the superior court, usually within fifteen days. When the judge does not find sufficient probable cause, the charges are dismissed and the defendant is released from custody.

A unique aspect of the preliminary hearing is the defendant's right to waive the proceeding, a procedure which has advantages (and disadvantages) for both the prosecutor and the defendant. For the prosecutor, waiver helps avoid revealing evidence to the defense before trial. Defense attorneys will waive the preliminary hearing: (1) when the defendant has already decided to plead guilty, (2) in order to speed the criminal justice process, and/or (3) to avoid the negative publicity that might result from the hearing. On the other hand, the preliminary hearing may have some advantage to the defendant who believes that it will result in a dismissal of the charges. In addition, the preliminary hearing gives the defense the opportunity to learn what evidence the prosecution has. Prosecutors may avoid waiver if they want to obtain a record of witness testimony because of the possibility that a witness or witnesses may be unavailable for the trial or unable to remember the facts clearly.

Figure 9.3 outlines the significant differences between the grand jury and the preliminary hearing processes.

Arraignment

After an indictment or information is filed following a grand jury or preliminary hearing, an arraignment takes place before the court that will try the case. At the arraignment, the judge informs the defendant of the charges against her and appoints counsel if one has not yet been retained. According to the Sixth

true bill *The action by a grand jury when it votes to indict an accused suspect.*

no bill *The action by a grand jury when it votes not to indict an accused suspect.*

Figure 9.3
Charging the defendant with a crime

Note the differences between the grand jury and preliminary hearing.

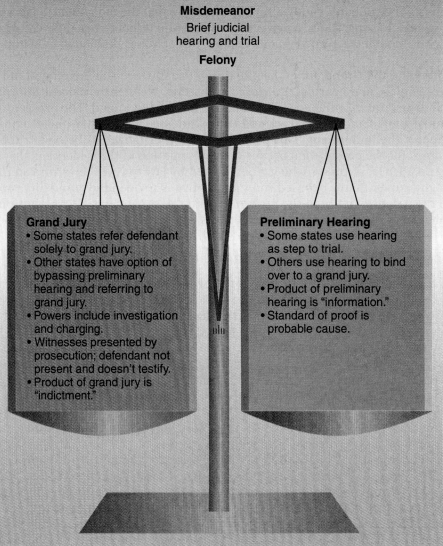

Misdemeanor
Brief judicial hearing and trial
Felony

Grand Jury
• Some states refer defendant solely to grand jury.
• Other states have option of bypassing preliminary hearing and referring to grand jury.
• Powers include investigation and charging.
• Witnesses presented by prosecution; defendant not present and doesn't testify.
• Product of grand jury is "indictment."

Preliminary Hearing
• Some states use hearing as step to trial.
• Others use hearing to bind over to a grand jury.
• Product of preliminary hearing is "information."
• Standard of proof is probable cause.

Amendment of the U.S. Constitution, the accused has the right to be informed of the nature and cause of the accusation; thus, the judge at the arraignment must make sure that the defendant clearly understands the charges.

After the charges are read and explained, the defendant is asked to enter a plea. If a plea of not guilty or not guilty by reason of insanity is entered, a trial date is set. When the defendant pleads guilty or nolo contendere, a date for sentencing is arranged. The magistrate then either sets bail or releases the defendant on personal recognizance.

The Plea

Ordinarily, a defendant in a criminal trial will enter one of three pleas: guilty, not guilty, or nolo contendere.

Guilty More than 90 percent of defendants appearing before the courts plead guilty prior to the trial stage. A guilty plea has several consequences. It functions not only as an admission of guilt but also as a surrender of the entire array of constitutional rights designed to protect a criminal defendant against unjustified conviction, including the right to remain silent, the right to confront witnesses against him or her, the right to a trial by jury, and the right to have an alleged offense proven beyond a reasonable doubt. Once a plea is

Criminal Justice ⊛ Now™

Learn more by viewing the "Presumption of Innocence" "In the News" video clip.

made, it cannot be rescinded or withdrawn after sentencing even if there is a change in the law that might have made conviction more problematic.[22]

As a result, judges must follow certain procedures when accepting a plea of guilty. First, the judge must clearly state to the defendant the constitutional guarantees that are automatically waived by this plea. Second, the judge must believe that the facts of the case establish a basis for the plea and that the plea is made voluntarily. Third, the defendant must be informed of the right to counsel during the pleading process. In many felony cases, the judge will insist on the presence of defense counsel. Finally, the judge must inform the defendant of the possible sentencing outcomes, including the maximum sentence that can be imposed.

After a guilty plea has been entered, a sentencing date is arranged. In a majority of states, a guilty plea may be withdrawn and replaced with a not-guilty plea at any time prior to sentencing if good cause is shown.

Not Guilty At the arraignment or before the trial, a not-guilty plea is entered in one of two ways: (1) it is verbally stated by the defendant or the defense counsel, or (2) it is entered for the defendant by the court when the defendant stands mute before the bench.

Once a plea of not guilty is recorded, a trial date is set. In misdemeanor cases, trials take place in the lower court system, whereas felony cases are normally transferred to the superior court. At this time, a continuance or issuance of bail is once again considered.

Nolo Contendere The plea *nolo contendere* ("no contest") is a plea in which the defendant does not accept or deny responsibility for the charges but agrees to accept punishment. Though it is essentially a plea of guilty, it may not be held against the defendant as proof in a subsequent legal matter such as a civil lawsuit because technically there has been no admission of guilt. This plea is accepted at the discretion of the trial court and must be voluntarily and intelligently made by the defendant.

PLEA BARGAINING

Plea bargaining is one of the most common practices in the criminal justice system today and a cornerstone of the informal justice system. Plea bargaining is actually a relatively recent development, taking hold late in the nineteenth century. Prosecutors wanted to bargain in cases where mandatory sentences were harsher than they considered just or fair, such as mandatory death sentences for certain crimes. At first, judges were reluctant to accept pleas, preferring trials to sharing their power with prosecutors (who make the deal) and entering into an agreement that they believed compromised justice.[23] However, plea bargaining became more attractive at the turn of the twentieth century when the mechanization of manufacture and transportation prompted a flood of complex civil cases; this event persuaded judges that criminal cases had to be settled quickly lest the court system break down.[24]

Today more than 90 percent of criminal convictions are estimated to result from negotiated pleas of guilty. Even in serious felony cases, some jurisdictions will have several plea bargaining arrangements for every trial.

Plea bargaining is the exchange of prosecutorial and judicial concessions for pleas of guilty. Normally, a bargain can be made between the prosecutor and the defense attorney in one of four ways: (1) the initial charges may be reduced to those of a lesser offense, thus automatically reducing the sentence imposed; (2) in cases where many counts are charged, the prosecutor may reduce the number of counts; (3) the prosecutor may promise to recommend a lenient sentence, such as probation; or (4) when the charge imposed has a negative label attached (e.g., child molester), the prosecutor may alter the charge to a more "socially acceptable" one (such as assault) in exchange for a plea of guilty.

Criminal Justice ⚖ Now™

Learn more by going through the **Nolo Contendere** *and* **Plea Bargaining** *Review and Reinforce activities.*

In a jurisdiction where sentencing disparities exist between judges, the prosecutor may even agree to arrange for a defendant to appear before a lenient judge in exchange for a plea; this practice is known as *judge shopping*.

Because of excessive criminal court caseloads and the personal and professional needs of the prosecution and the defense (to get the case over with in the shortest amount of time), plea bargaining has become an essential yet controversial part of the administration of justice. Proponents contend that plea bargaining actually benefits both the state and the defendant in the following ways:

- The overall costs of the criminal prosecution are reduced.
- The administrative efficiency of the courts is greatly improved.
- The prosecution can devote more time to more serious cases.
- The defendant avoids possible detention and an extended trial and may receive a reduced sentence.
- Resources can be devoted more efficiently to cases that need greater attention.[25]

Those who favor plea bargaining believe it is appropriate to enter into plea discussions when the interests of the state in the effective administration of justice will be served.

Opponents of the plea bargaining process believe that the negotiated plea should be eliminated for the following reasons:

- It encourages defendants to waive their constitutional right to trial.
- Plea bargains allow dangerous offenders to receive lenient sentences. Jesse Timmendequas, a previously convicted sex offender, was given a ten-year plea bargained sentence for child rape. Upon his release he raped and killed seven-year-old Megan Kanka in one of the nation's most notorious crimes.[26]
- Plea bargaining also raises the danger that an innocent person will be convicted of a crime if he/she is convinced that the lighter treatment from a guilty plea is preferable to the risk of conviction with a harsher sentence following a formal trial.
- Prosecutors are given a free hand to induce or compel defendants to plea bargain, thus circumventing law.[27]
- It is possible that an innocent person will admit their guilt if they believe that the system is biased and that they have little chance of an acquittal.
- A guilty-plea culture has developed among defense lawyers. Elements of the culture include the belief that most of their clients are dishonest people who committed the crime for which they have been charged and that getting a "sentence discount" for them is the best and only way to go.[28]

Despite these issues, it is unlikely that plea negotiations will be eliminated or severely curtailed in the near future. Supporters of the total abolition of plea bargaining are in the minority. As a result of abuses, however, efforts are being made to improve plea bargaining operations. Such reforms include development of uniform plea practices, representation of counsel during plea negotiations, and establishment of time limits on plea negotiations.

Legal Issues in Plea Bargaining

The U.S. Supreme Court has reviewed the propriety of plea bargaining in several decisions and while imposing limits on the practice has upheld its continued use. The Court has ruled that:

- Defendants are entitled to the effective assistance of counsel to protect them from pressure and influence.[29]

- Pleas must be made voluntarily and without pressure. However, a prosecutor can tell the defendant that he or she may be facing the death penalty if he or she goes to trial.[30]

- A defendant can still plead guilty to gain a lenient sentence even if he or she maintains his or her innocence of the charges.[31]

- Any promise made by the prosecutor during the plea negotiations must be kept after the defendant admits his or her guilt in open court. A prosecutor who promises leniency in private negotiations must stick to that position in court.[32]

- Defendants must also keep their side of the bargain to receive the promised offer of leniency.[33] If, they agree to testify against a co-defendant they must give evidence at trial or forfeit the bargain.

- A defendant's due process rights are not violated when a prosecutor threatens to re-indict the accused on more serious charges, for example as a habitual offender, if the defendant does not plead guilty to a lesser offense.[34]

- Statements made during a plea bargain may be used under some circumstances at trial if the negotiations break down. Statements made during a plea negotiation can be used if the defendant (a) admits to a crime during the bargaining process, but then (b) later testifies in open court that he or she did not do the act and (c) was innocent of the charges.[35]

Plea Bargaining Decision Making

Because the plea bargaining process is largely informal, lacking in guidelines, and discretionary, some effort has been made to determine what kinds of information and how much information is used by the prosecutor to make plea bargaining decisions.

It is possible to view plea bargaining as a form of cost/benefit analysis: the defendant compares the pain of punishment guaranteed by the bargain—for instance, two years in prison—with the punishment associated with a conviction at trial—for instance, twenty years. If they conclude that conviction is inevitable they will be resigned to accept the guaranteed punishment rather than risk trial and harsher treatment. The district attorney uses much the same reasoning process and is less willing to make concessions as the strength of the evidence and the likelihood of conviction increases.

Research on plea negotiation indicates that the process is actually much more complex. Offender, case, and community characteristics weigh heavily on the negotiation process.[36] Such factors as the offense, the defendant's prior record and age, and the type, strength, and admissibility of evidence are considered important in the plea bargaining decision. The attitude of the complainant is also an important factor in the decision-making process; in victimless cases, such as heroin possession, the police attitude is most often considered, whereas in victim-related crimes, such as rape, the attitude of the victim is a primary concern.

There are also intangible factors that shape the bargaining decision:

- The prosecutor's ego and need for self-esteem may shape their negotiations.

- Because they want to win every case, some prosecutors may offer deals the defendant simply cannot refuse.

- Prosecutors seeking publicity for a political run may refuse to bargain so that they may preside over a media trial, such as the Michael Jackson case.

- A bargain may be offered when a prosecutor realizes that sloppy police work and investigation may be exposed by a criminal trial.

- The prosecutor's offices may simply not have sufficient funds to engage in complex and costly trials. An appointed defense counsel may find his or her

Many prosecutors confer with crime victims in their plea bargaining decision and in some cases prosecutors seek approval for the plea from a victim or family member. Here, during his sentencing in Somerset, Kentucky, Jeff Morris turns to the family of slain Pulaski County Sheriff Sam Catron and apologizes for his role in Catron's murder, September 15, 2003. Under a plea bargain, Morris was convicted of murder. Morris, an ex-deputy, was running against Catron in the Republican primary.

© 2003 AP/Wide World Photos

fees are capped by the courts and a plea bargain becomes an economic necessity.[37]

- The defendant retaining a highly respected private attorney with a great trial reputation may encourage prosecutors to offer a favorable bargain: who wants to look bad at trial and lose the case?

- Court-appointed lawyers may want to gain trial experience. They convince their clients not to accept favorable bargains fearing that the case will be settled out of court and they will lose the opportunity to try the case.

- Both the prosecution and defense may be overly optimistic about their abilities and skills. Overconfidence in their abilities may cloud their judgment, causing them to either refuse to offer a bargain in the case of the prosecution or refuse to accept in the case of the defense.

- Some defendants falsely assume they are so charismatic and appealing that a jury will never reach a conviction.[38] Their inflated ego and sense of entitlement inhibit their accepting their own guilt.

The Role of the Defense Counsel

While the prosecutor formulates and offers the deal, the defense counsel—a public defender or a private attorney—is required to play an advisory role in plea negotiations. The defendant's counsel is expected to be aware of the facts of the case and of the law and to advise the defendant of the alternatives available. The defense attorney is basically responsible for making certain that the accused understands the nature of the plea bargaining process and the guilty plea. This means that the defense counsel should explain to the defendant that by pleading guilty, he is waiving certain rights that would be available on going to trial. In addition, the defense attorney has the duty to keep the defendant informed of developments and discussions with the prosecutor regarding plea bargaining. While doing so, the attorney for the accused cannot misrepresent evidence or mislead the client into making a detrimental agreement. The defense counsel is not only ethically but also constitutionally required to communicate all plea bargaining offers to a client even if counsel believes the offers to be unacceptable.[39]

The Role of the Judge

One of the most confusing issues in the plea bargaining process has been the proper role of the judge. Should the judge act only in a supervisory capacity or actually enter into the negotiation process? The leading national legal organization, the ABA, is opposed to judicial participation in plea negotiations.[40] According to ABA standards, judges should not be a party to arrangements for the determination of a sentence, whether as a result of a guilty plea or a finding of guilty based on proof. Furthermore, judicial participation in plea negotiations (1) creates the impression in the mind of the defendant that he/she cannot receive a fair trial, (2) lessens the ability of the judge to make an objective determination of the voluntary nature of the plea, (3) is inconsistent with the theory behind the use of pre-sentence investigation reports, and (4) may induce an innocent defendant to plead guilty because he is afraid to reject the disposition desired by the judge.[41]

In addition to the ABA, the Federal Rules of Criminal Procedure prohibit federal judges from participating in plea negotiations.[42] A few states disallow any form of judicial involvement in plea bargaining, but others permit the judge to participate.

On the other hand, those who suggest that the judge should participate directly in plea bargaining argue that such an approach would make sentencing more uniform and ensure that the plea bargaining process would be fairer and more efficient.

The Role of the Victim

What role should victims play in plea bargaining? Some suggest that the system today is too "victim-driven" and that prosecutors too frequently seek approval for the plea from a victim or family member. Others maintain that the victim plays an almost secondary role in the process.

In reality, the victim is not "empowered" at the pretrial stage of the criminal process. Statutes do not require that the prosecutor defer to the victim's wishes, and there are no legal consequences for ignoring the victim in a plea bargaining decision. Even the ABA's Model Uniform Victims of Crime Act only suggests that the prosecutor "confer" with the victim.[43]

There is no question that the prosecutor should consider the impact that a plea bargain may have on the victim or victim's family. Some victims' groups even suggest that the victim's family have statutory authority to approve or disapprove any plea bargain between the prosecutor and defense attorney in criminal homicide cases. Given the volume of plea bargains, it appears that the victim should have greater control and participation.

Plea Bargaining Reform

Plea bargaining is an inevitable result and essential to the continued functioning of the criminal justice process.[44] Yet, despite its prevalence, its merits are still hotly debated. Those opposed to the widespread use of plea bargaining assert that it is coercive in its inducement of guilty pleas, that it encourages the unequal exercise of prosecutorial discretion, and that it complicates sentencing as well as the job of correctional authorities. Others argue that it is unconstitutional and results in cynicism and disrespect for the entire system.

On the other hand, its proponents contend that the practice ensures the flow of guilty pleas essential to administration efficiency. It allows the system the flexibility to individualize justice and inspires respect for the system because it is associated with certain and prompt punishment.[45]

In recent years, efforts have been made to convert plea bargaining into a more visible, understandable, and fair dispositional process. Safeguards and guidelines have been developed to ensure that innocent defendants do not plead guilty under coercion. Such safeguards include the following: (1) the judge questions the defendant about the facts of the guilty plea before accepting the plea; (2) the defense counsel is present and can advise the defendant of his or her rights; (3) the prosecutor and the defense attorney openly discuss the plea; and (4) full and frank information about the defendant and the offenses is made available at this stage of the process. In addition, judicial supervision ensures that plea bargaining is conducted in a fair manner.

Negotiation Oversight

Some jurisdictions have established guidelines to provide consistency in plea bargaining cases. Guidelines define the kinds and types of cases and offenders that may be suitable for plea bargaining. Guidelines cover such aspects as avoiding over-indictment and controlling unprovable indictments, reducing felonies to misdemeanors, and bargaining with defendants. Other controls might include procedures for internally reviewing decisions by the chief prosecutor and the use of written memorandums to document the need and acceptability for a plea bargain in a given case. Pleas may also be offered on a "take it or leave it" basis. Under this system, a special prosecutor, whose job it is to screen cases, sets the bargaining terms. If the defense counsel cannot accept the agreement, there is no negotiation, and the case must go to trial. Only if complications arise in the case, such as witnesses changing their testimony, can negotiations be reopened.[46]

Banning Plea Bargaining

What would happen if plea bargaining were banned outright, as its critics advocate? Numerous jurisdictions throughout the United States have experimented with bans on plea bargaining. In 1975, Alaska eliminated the practice. Honolulu has also attempted to abolish plea bargaining. Other jurisdictions, including Iowa, Arizona, Delaware, and the District of Columbia, have sought to limit the use of plea bargaining.[47] In theory, eliminating plea bargains means that prosecutors in these jurisdictions give no consideration or concessions to a defendant in exchange for a guilty plea.

In reality, however, in these and most jurisdictions, sentence-related concessions, charge-reduction concessions, and alternative methods for prosecution continue to be used in one fashion or another.[48] Where plea bargaining is limited or abolished, the number of trials may increase, the sentence severity may change, and more questions regarding the right to a speedy trial may arise. Discretion may also be shifted further up the system. Instead of spending countless hours preparing for and conducting a trial, prosecutors may dismiss more cases outright or decide not to prosecute them after initial action has been taken.

Reform can be difficult. Candace McCoy's study of plea reform in California investigated legislative efforts to eliminate the state's plea bargaining process. Instead of achieving a ban on plea bargaining, the process shifted from the superior to the municipal courts. McCoy found that the majority of defendants pled guilty after some negotiations and that the new law actually accelerated the guilty plea process. McCoy's alternative model of plea bargaining reform includes emphasizing public scrutiny of plea bargaining, adhering to standards of professionalism, and making a greater commitment to due process procedures.[49]

In sum, plea bargaining is a complex process. It involves such issues as trial costs; attorney competence, compensation, and workloads; sentencing and bail rules; witness availability; and estimations of trial outcomes among a myriad of other factors.[50] While heavily criticized, it remains a mainstay of the justice process.

PRETRIAL DIVERSION

Another important feature in the early court process is placing offenders into noncriminal **diversion** programs before their formal trial or conviction. The first pretrial diversion programs were established more than forty years ago to reduce the stigma created by the formal trial process. To avoid stigma and labeling, diversion programs suspend criminal proceedings so that the accused can participate in a community treatment program under court supervision. Diversion programs give the client an opportunity to:

- Avoid the stigma of a criminal record
- Continue to work and support his or her family
- Continue educational goals
- Access rehabilitation services, such as anger management, while remaining in the community
- When needed, make restitution to the victim of crime or pay back the community through volunteer services

Diversion also enables the justice system to reduce costs and alleviate prison crowding. Exhibit 9.3 illustrates the steps and procedures in a pretrial program used in and run by a district attorney's office.

Criminal Justice Now™
Learn more about Careers in Criminal Justice by exploring the "On the Job" features Detention Enforcement Officer and Pretrial Release Officer.

diversion A noncriminal alternative to trial, usually featuring counseling, job training, and educational opportunities.

Exhibit 9.3	Pretrial Diversion Program, Iberville, West Baton Rouge, and Pointe Coupee parishes in Louisiana

1. Transfer agency submits offense report to the district attorney.
2. District attorney determines if the case appears to be suitable for pretrial intervention.
3. Case is forwarded to the director of the pretrial program.
4. Director schedules a screening appointment, at which time the following procedures are performed:
   - Candidate is notified that this program is strictly voluntary and upon completion of the program, charges are dismissed.
   - Criminal history is obtained.
   - Victim is contacted (if required).
   - Arresting officer is contacted (if necessary).
5. If the individual is considered a candidate for the program, he is placed on probation for up to two years. Conditions of probation may include community service, counseling (i.e., anger management, alcohol, drug counseling, MADD, etc.), and/or restitution.
6. Only first offense simple possession of marijuana may be eligible for pretrial diversion.
7. If the individual is declined, the case is returned to the district attorney along with an explanation for being declined.

Source: Pretrial Diversion Program, www.rickywardda.com/pretrial.htm, accessed on July 27, 2005.

Diversion programs can take many forms. Some are separate, independent agencies that were originally set up with federal funds but are now being continued with county or state assistance. Others are organized as part of a police, prosecutor, or probation department's internal structure. Still others are a joint venture between the county government and a private, nonprofit organization that actually carries out the treatment process.

First viewed as a panacea that could reduce court congestion and help treat minor offenders, diversion programs soon came under fire when national evaluations concluded that they are no more successful at avoiding stigma and reducing recidivism than traditional justice processing.[51] There was also the suspicion that diversion may *widen the net of the justice system.* By this, critics meant that the people placed in diversion programs are the ones most likely to have otherwise been dismissed after a brief hearing with a warning or small fine.[52] Now they were receiving more treatment than they would have had the program not been in place. Those who would have ordinarily received a more serious sentence were not eligible for diversion anyway. Thus, rather than limiting contact with the system, the diversion programs actually increase its grasp.

Of course, not all justice experts agree with this charge and some programs have shown great promise. Recent evaluations (2005) indicate that given the proper treatment, some types of offenders, such as drug offenders, who are offered a place in pretrial programs can significantly lower their rates of recidivism.[53]

SUMMARY

- Many important decisions about what happens to a defendant are made prior to trial.

- Hearings, such as before the grand jury and the preliminary hearing, are held to determine if probable cause exists to charge the accused with a crime. If so, the defendant is arraigned, enters a plea, is informed of his constitutional rights, particularly the right to the assistance of counsel, and is considered for pretrial diversion.

- The use of money bail and other alternatives, such as release on recognizance, allows most defendants to be free pending their trial.

- Bail reform has resulted in the use of release on recognizance (ROR) to replace money bail for non-dangerous offenders.

- Preventive detention has been implemented because many believe that significant numbers of criminals violate their bail and commit further crimes while on pretrial release and to prevent dangerous offenders from getting bail.

- Research indicates that most cases never go to trial but are bargained out of the system.

- Bargains can be made for a plea of guilty in exchange for a reduced sentence, dropping charges, lowering the charge, or substituting a more socially acceptable charge for one with negative connotations.

- People who plead guilty generally get lower sentences than those who go to trial.

- The Supreme Court has shaped the legal contours of the plea system. It has ruled that bargains must be kept by both the prosecution and defense.

- Although plea bargaining has been criticized, efforts to control it have not met with success.

- Diversion programs that offer a criminal defendant the ability to enter a treatment program rather than undergo a criminal trial continue to be used throughout the United States.

KEY TERMS

pretrial procedures 252
bail 252
pretrial detention 255
release on recognizance (ROR)
  258

Manhattan Bail Project 258
deposit bail 258
Bail Reform Act of 1984 258
preventive detention 260
presentment 262

true bill 263
no bill 263
diversion 271

REVIEW QUESTIONS

1. Should criminal defendants be allowed to bargain for a reduced sentence in exchange for a guilty plea? Should the victim always be included in the plea bargaining process?

2. Should those accused of violent acts be subjected to preventive detention instead of bail, even though they have not been convicted of a crime? Is it fair to the victim to have his alleged attacker running around loose?

3. What purpose does a grand jury or preliminary hearing serve in adjudicating felony offenses? Should one of these methods be abandoned and if so, which one?

4. Why should we provide pretrial services for defendants?

5. Should suspects in a terrorist case be allowed bail? If so, wouldn't that give them a license to carry out their plot?

CHAPTER 10

The Criminal Trial

© 2005 AP/Wide World Photos

DR. WADE SCHINDLER has an unusual career in criminal justice: he is a professional expert, trainer, and security consultant. In the past twenty-two years, Schindler, the author of several books, has testified on numerous court cases involving security and law enforcement. He is one of a small cadre of experts who testify in court cases involving such topics as

- Police use of deadly force
- Police failure to protect
- Police and security officer training

Schindler got his start as a police officer in the New Orleans Police Department where he worked as a patrol officer, desk sergeant, homicide detective, and had undercover assignments. His experience, along

Chapter Outline

Chapter Objectives

1. Be familiar with the concept of the jury trial
2. Know what it means to confront witnesses
3. Understand the term "speedy trial"
4. Be familiar with concept of the pro se defense
5. Be able to discuss what a fair trial actually means
6. Discuss the right of the press to attend trials
7. Discuss the issues surrounding the broadcast of criminal trials
8. Know the difference between a challenge for cause and a peremptory challenge
9. Identify the different ways evidence is presented in criminal trials
10. Explain the concept of proof beyond a reasonable doubt

with a Ph.D. in criminal justice, qualifies him to assist and advise public agencies, business owners, and institutions, as well as insurance companies when they are hit with liability claims by people who maintain they were injured due to employer negligence. His education also allows him to conduct scientific inquiries, and he is qualified to discuss and testify about the likelihood of crime occurring at a given site and whether the employer should have been aware of potential danger. Schindler also conducts on-site examinations and analysis of a facility, business, home, or public or private institution to ascertain the present security status, identify deficiencies or excesses, determine protection needs, and make recommendations to improve overall security. He is then qualified to testify that his employer did everything possible to protect their clients.

Expert witnesses such as Wade Schindler play an important role in the criminal trial, an open and public hearing designed to examine the facts of the case brought by the state against the accused. Though trials are relatively rare events and most cases are settled by a plea bargain, the trial is an important and enduring fixture in the criminal justice system. By its very nature, it is a symbol of the moral authority of the state. The criminal trial is the symbol of the administration of objective and impartial justice. Regardless of the issues involved, the defendant's presence in a courtroom is designed to guarantee that she will have a hearing conducted under rules of procedure in an atmosphere of fair play and objectivity and that the outcome of the hearing will be clear and definitive. If the defendant believes that her constitutional rights and privileges have been violated, she may appeal the case to a higher court, where the procedures of the original trial will be examined. If after examining the trial transcript, the appellate court rules that the original trial employed improper and unconstitutional procedures, it may order a new hearing be held or even that the charges against the defendant be dismissed.

Most formal trials are heard by a jury, though some defendants waive their constitutional right to a jury trial and request a **bench trial,** in which the judge alone renders a **verdict.** In this situation, which occurs daily in the lower criminal courts, the judge may initiate a number of formal or informal dispositions, including dismissing the case, finding the defendant not guilty, finding the defendant guilty and imposing a sentence, or even continuing the case indefinitely. The decision the judge makes often depends on the seriousness of the offense, the background and previous record of the defendant, and the judgment of the court about whether the case can be properly dealt with in the criminal process. The judge may simply continue the case without a finding, in which case the verdict is withheld without a finding of guilt to induce the accused to improve her behavior in the community; if the defendant's behavior does improve, the case is ordinarily closed within a specific amount of time.

This chapter reviews some of the institutions and processes involved in **adjudication** and trial. We begin with a discussion of the legal rights that structure the trial process.

Criminal Justice ⚖ Now™

Learn more about exploring the "Beyond a Reasonable Doubt" Review and Reinforce activity.

bench trial *The trial of a criminal matter by a judge only. The accused waives any constitutional right to trial by jury.*

verdict *A finding of a jury or a judge on questions of fact at a trial.*

adjudication *The determination of guilt or innocence; a judgment concerning criminal charges. The majority of offenders charged plead guilty; of the remainder, some cases are adjudicated by a judge and a jury, some are adjudicated by a judge without a jury, and others are dismissed.*

▌CIVIL RIGHTS DURING TRIAL

Underlying every trial are constitutional principles, complex legal procedures, rules of court, and interpretations of statutes, all designed to ensure that the accused will receive a fair trial. Every person charged with a crime has a fundamental right to a fair trial that takes place before an impartial judge and jury, in an environment of judicial restraint, orderliness, and fair decision-making. While there is no strict definition of what constitutes a "fair trial," for obvious reasons it cannot take place in a hostile courtroom, be conducted by a prejudiced judge, or decided by a biased jury. Any behavior that produces prejudice toward the accused can preclude a fair trial. A defendant cannot be required to go to trial in prison clothing or walk into the courtroom while shackled.[1]

In the following sections, some of the principles that guide fair trials are discussed in some detail.

The Right to Be Competent at Trial

In order for a trial to be considered fair, a criminal defendant must be mentally competent to understand the nature and extent of the legal proceedings. If a defendant is mentally incompetent the trial must be postponed until treatment renders the defendant capable of participating in his or her own defense. Can state authorities force a mentally unfit defendant to be psychologically treated so that the defendant can be tried? Yes, if the treatment (1) is medically appropriate and (2) essential for the defendant's own safety or the safety of others.[2] In a 2003 case, *Sell v. United States,* the Court set out four rules which guide the use of forced medication:[3]

- A court must find that *important* governmental interests are at stake. For example, medication may be approved if a dangerous defendant would otherwise be released.

- The court must conclude that forced medication will *significantly further* state interests. It must find that medication is substantially likely to render the defendant competent to stand trial and substantially unlikely to have side effects that will interfere significantly with the defendant's ability to assist counsel in conducting a defense.

- The court must conclude that involuntary medication is *necessary* to further state interests and find that alternative, less intrusive treatments are unlikely to achieve substantially the same results.

- The court must conclude that administering the drugs is *medically appropriate.*

If these four conditions are met, then a court can order a mentally incompetent criminal defendant to be treated so he or she can stand trial.

The Right to Confront Witnesses

The Sixth Amendment gives criminal defendants the right to confront witnesses who testify against them at trial. The **confrontation clause** is essential to a fair criminal trial because it restricts and controls the admissibility of secondhand evidence. This means that under normal circumstances, evidence can only be presented by witnesses who are present in court and able to testify under oath. During their testimony, witnesses must attest to their personal knowledge of the crime and not repeat what others told them, known as **hearsay evidence.** Let's say that Joe hears from Steve about an incident in which someone was injured. Steve witnessed it, but Joe did not. If Joe attempts to repeat Steve's version in court, the testimony would be objected to as hearsay. A witness is, however, permitted to repeat a rumor or testify that someone told her a story. Under the hearsay rule, the testimony would not be evidence of the actual facts of the story, but only that this person heard those words spoken by others.

Under the confrontation clause, the accused has the right to confront the witnesses and challenge their assertions and perceptions: Did they really see what they believe? Are they biased? Can they be trusted? What about the veracity of their testimony? The confrontation clause also applies to documents that someone wrote implicating a defendant, or even a taped confession given by an accomplice to police that contains some statements

© 2005 AP/Wide World Photos

The Sixth Amendment requires that all criminal defendants have a right to see and confront witnesses who present evidence during their trial. The confrontation clause allows defendants to hear what is being said and present a rebuttal if they believe the evidence is false or inaccurate. Giselle Abreu points to a monitor to show where she says she saw her boyfriend Michael Colono and defendant Alexander Pring-Wilson fighting in a parking lot, during her testimony in Cambridge Superior Court in Cambridge, Massachusetts, September 20, 2004. Pring-Wilson, a Harvard graduate student, was convicted of killing the 18-year-old cook after a chance encounter led to a brawl.

 www To read more about *Maryland v. Craig* and similar cases, go to "Web Links" on your Siegel Essentials of Criminal Justice 5e website: http://cj.wadsworth.com/siegel_ess5e.

confrontation clause *The constitutional right of a criminal defendant to see and cross-examine all the witnesses against him or her.*

hearsay evidence *Testimony that is not firsthand but related information told by a second party.*

implicating the accused. The author of the documents or confession must be in court to testify to their accuracy.[4]

The right of confrontation and cross-examination is an essential requirement for a fair trial.[5] In a significant exception to the rule, the Supreme Court in *Maryland v. Craig* (1990) held that in cases of child abuse it is permissible to cross-examine young victims via closed-circuit TV. This procedure can be employed if the judge believes that their being in the presence of their attackers would simply be too traumatic.[6] *Maryland v. Craig* is important because it shows that the confrontation clause may be waived to further an important public policy, such as protecting a child from trauma in a criminal trial.

The Right to a Jury Trial

The Sixth Amendment to the U.S. Constitution guarantees the right to a jury trial; however, the Constitution is silent on whether all offenders, both misdemeanants and felons, have an absolute right to a jury trial. This right has been extended in a series of legal cases:

- *Duncan v. Louisiana* (1968). The Sixth Amendment right to a jury trial applies to all defendants accused of serious crimes.[7]
- *Baldwin v. New York* (1970). A defendant has a constitutional right to a jury trial when facing a prison sentence of six months or more, regardless of whether the crime committed was a felony or a misdemeanor.[8]
- *Blanton v. North Las Vegas* (1989). There is no right to jury trials for crimes defined as petty offenses with punishments of less than six months.[9]
- *Lewis v. United States* (1996). There is no right to a jury trial if the defendant is charged with a string of petty offenses tried together, even where the potential aggregate sentence could exceed six months.[10] This decision gives the prosecutor the right to exercise discretion to join different offenses in one trial without requiring that a jury hear the case.

The Right to a Twelve-Person Jury

Can a defendant be tried and convicted of a crime by a jury of fewer than twelve persons? Traditionally, twelve jurors have deliberated as the triers of fact in criminal cases involving misdemeanors or felonies. However, the U.S. Constitution does not specifically require a jury of twelve persons. As a result, in *Williams v. Florida* in 1970, the U.S. Supreme Court held that a **six-person jury** in a criminal trial does not deprive a defendant of the constitutional right to a jury trial.[11] The Court made clear that the twelve-person panel is not a necessary ingredient of a trial by jury, and it upheld a Florida statute permitting the use of a six-person jury in a robbery trial.

Williams v. Florida has offered a welcome measure of relief to an overburdened crime control system.[12] Today, jury size may be reduced for all but the most serious criminal cases.

 To access a site with links to **famous trials in world history,** from Joan of Arc to O. J., go to "Web Links" on your Siegel Essentials of Criminal Justice 5e website: http://cj.wadsworth.com/siegel_ess5e.

The Right to a Unanimous Jury Verdict

Besides the convention of twelve-person juries in criminal trials, tradition also had been that the jurors' decision must be unanimous. However, in the 1972 case of *Apodica v. Oregon,* the U.S. Supreme Court held that the Sixth and Fourteenth Amendments do not prohibit criminal convictions by less than unanimous jury verdicts in non-capital (murder) cases.[13] In the *Apodica* case, the Court upheld an Oregon statute requiring only ten of twelve jurors to convict the defendant of assault with a deadly weapon, burglary, and grand

six-person jury The criminal trial of a defendant before a jury of six persons as opposed to a traditional jury of twelve persons.

larceny. Such verdicts are not unusual in civil matters, but much controversy remains regarding their place in the criminal process.

The Right to Counsel at Trial

Recall from previous chapters that the defendant has a right to counsel at numerous points in the criminal justice process. Today, state courts must provide counsel at trial to indigent defendants who face even the possibility of incarceration.[14] The threat of incarceration need not be immediate. Even if the defendant is sentenced to probation in which a prison or jail term is suspended, or any other type of sentence containing a threat of future incarceration, they are afforded the right to counsel at trial.[15]

The Right to Self-Representation

Do criminal defendants have the right to act as their own lawyers? In the case of *Faretta v. California*, the Supreme Court ruled that defendants in most state courts and in the federal system have the right to proceed **pro se**, or for themselves.[16] This permits defendants to choose between hiring counsel or conducting their own defense. However, in *Faretta*, the Court recognized the right to proceed pro se, but made it conditional on a showing that the defendant could competently, knowingly, and intelligently waive his right to counsel. The Court's decision was based on the belief that while the right of self-representation is supported by the Sixth Amendment, as well as in English and colonial jurisprudence from which the amendment emerged, a defendant who is not competent to conduct a criminal defense can be forced or required to use the services of a court appointed attorney. Similarly, in *Martinez v. Court of Appeal of California* (2000), the Court limited the pro se rule to trials; there is no right to self-representation in appeals. A state may require that an appellant be represented by counsel in the legally complex appeal process.[17]

 Does self-representation ever make sense? To find out, go to "Web Links" on your Siegel Essentials of Criminal Justice 5e website: http://cj.wadsworth.com/siegel_ess5e.

The Right to a Speedy Trial

The tactics employed by wary defense attorneys (pretrial motions, complex plea negotiations, delay tactics during trial) along with inefficiencies in the court process (such as the frequent granting of continuances, poor scheduling procedures, and the abuse of time by court personnel) has made delay in criminal cases a serious and constitutional issue. As the American Bar Association states in the *Standards Relating to Speedy Trial*: "Congestion in the trial courts of this country, particularly in urban centers, is currently one of the major problems of judicial administration."[18] Delays in the trial process conflict with the Sixth Amendment's guarantee of a right to a speedy trial.[19]

The Supreme Court has called the right to a speedy trial "as fundamental as any of the rights secured by the Sixth Amendment."[20] Its primary purposes are to:

- Improve the credibility of the trial by having witnesses available for testimony as early as possible.
- Help criminal defendants avoid lengthy pretrial detention.
- Avoid extensive pretrial publicity and questionable conduct of public officials that may influence the defendant's right to a fair trial.
- Avoid any delay that could affect the defendant's ability to defend him- or herself against charges.

pro se The right of self-representation.

To access the Federal Criminal Code rules on speedy trial, go to "Web Links" on your Siegel Essentials of Criminal Justice 5e website: http://cj.wadsworth.com/ siegel_ess5e.

There is no set time that defines speedy trial. In *Doggett v. United States,* the Court found that a delay of eight and a half years between indictment and arrest was prejudicial to the defendant and required a dismissal of the charges against the defendant.[21] But this is an extreme case. Typically when a defendant invokes the speedy trial clause, the appellate court will evaluate the length of delay, the reason for the delay, when the defendant made the claim, and what damage the delay caused. If the prosecution deliberately slows the case down, that may have a greater effect on the appeal process than if the case was delayed because a witness could not be located. And if the defendant agreed to the delay or caused the delay, the speedy-trial right may be lost.

The Right to a Public Trial

The familiar language of the Sixth Amendment clearly states that "the accused shall enjoy the right to a speedy and public trial." Underlying this provision is the belief that a trial in the criminal justice system must be a public activity. The amendment is rooted in the principle that justice cannot survive behind walls of silence.[22] Secret hearings that bar the public are not permitted in our free society.[23]

Not only does the public have the right to attend trials, so too does the press. However, the Court has tried to shape the extent of press coverage in a number of important rulings, some which control pretrial publicity and others the trial process itself.

Pretrial Publicity Adverse pretrial publicity can prevent a defendant from getting a fair trial. The release of premature evidence by the prosecutor, extensive and critical reporting by the news media, and vivid and uncalled-for details in indictments can all prejudice a defendant's case. Press coverage can begin early in a criminal case and help bias the outcome.

Judges involved in newsworthy criminal cases have attempted to place restraints on pretrial media coverage to preserve the defendant's right to a fair trial. The Supreme Court has shaped pretrial publicity in three significant cases:

• *Nebraska Press Association v. Stuart* (1976). It is unconstitutional for a trial judge to prohibit the press from reporting on details of the crime.[24]

News photographers take pictures of reputed Ku Klux Klan member Edgar Ray Killen of Union, Mississippi, as he sits in a Neshoba County Courthouse, in Philadelphia, Mississippi, January 7, 2005. Killen was indicted on murder charges in the 1964 slayings of three civil rights workers. The criminal proceedings garnered national attention, including extensive coverage in the courtroom. The state Supreme Court ruled on January 20, 2005, that before cameras can be barred from Mississippi courtrooms, a judge must provide a detailed ruling on why he believes a defendant might be deprived of a fair trial. A 5–3 majority of the court ruled that without such specific findings, cameras cannot be barred.

"Prior restraints on speech and publication," they state, "are the most serious and least tolerable infringement on First Amendment rights."[25]

- *Gannett Co. v. DePasquale* (1979). The press corps' right to attend pretrial judicial hearings can be outweighed by the defendant's right to due process.[26] The interest of justice requires that the defendant's case not be jeopardized by press coverage.

- *Press-Enterprise Co. v. Superior Court* (1986). Closing a hearing is permissible under the First Amendment only if there is substantial probability that the defendant's right to a fair trial would be prejudiced by publicity.[27]

So, as a general rule, pretrial publicity and reporting cannot be controlled. However, judges may bar the press from some pretrial legal proceedings and hearings, such as preliminary hearings, when police officers make an arrest, or when a warrant is being served, if their presence will harm the defendant's right to a fair trial.[28]

Press Coverage During Trials In the landmark case *Richmond Newspapers, Inc. v. Virginia* (1980), the Supreme Court clearly established that criminal trials must remain open to the press.[29] The Court extended the right of the press to attend trials involving even highly sensitive, sexually related matters in which the victim is under eighteen years of age.[30]

More recently the issue of press coverage has focused on bringing TV cameras into the courtroom. Because of the public interest in high-profile criminal cases, whether jury trials should be televised is one of the most controversial questions in the criminal justice system. The legal community is divided over the use of TV cameras in the courtroom. Today, many state courts permit such coverage, often at the judge's discretion, but federal courts prohibit TV coverage altogether. In 1981, the U.S. Supreme Court in *Chandler v. Florida* removed any constitutional obstacles to the use of electronic media coverage and still photography of public criminal proceedings over the objections of a criminal defendant.[31] To be certain, the defendant has a constitutional right to a public trial, but it is equally imperative that the media be allowed to exercise its **First Amendment** rights.

In sum, the defendant's right to an impartial trial and jury under the Fifth and Sixth Amendments often runs into direct conflict with the First Amendment's guarantee of freedom of the press and public access.

WWW To find information on **Court TV,** go to "Web Links" on your Siegel *Essentials of Criminal Justice 5e* website: http://cj.wadsworth.com/ siegel_ess5e.

The Right to Be Convicted by Proof Beyond a Reasonable Doubt

Proof beyond a reasonable doubt is the standard required to convict a defendant charged with a crime at the adjudicatory stage of the criminal process. This requirement dates back to early American history and over the years has become the accepted measure of persuasion needed by the prosecutor to convince the judge or jury of the defendant's guilt. Many twentieth-century U.S. Supreme Court decisions have reinforced this standard by making "beyond a reasonable doubt a due process and constitutional requirement."[32] In *Brinegar v. United States* (1949), for instance, the Supreme Court stated:

> Guilt in a criminal case must be proven beyond a reasonable doubt and by evidence confined to that which long experience in the common-law tradition, to some extent embodied in the Constitution, has crystallized into rules of evidence consistent with that standard. These rules are historically grounded rights of our system, developed to safeguard men from dubious and unjust convictions with resulting forfeitures of life, liberty, and property.[33]

The reasonable doubt standard is an essential ingredient of the criminal justice process. It is the prime instrument for reducing the risk of convictions

First Amendment The U.S. constitutional amendment that guarantees freedom of speech, religion, press, and assembly, and the right of the people to petition the government for a redress of grievances.

proof beyond a reasonable doubt The standard of proof needed to convict in a criminal case. The evidence offered in court does not have to amount to absolute certainty, but it should leave no reasonable doubt that the defendant committed the alleged crime.

Exhibit 10.1	Evidentiary standards of proof: Degrees of certainty	
Standard	**Definition**	**Ruling**
Absolute certainty	No possibility of error; 100% certainty	Not used in civil or criminal law
Beyond reasonable doubt; moral certainty	Conclusive and complete proof, without leaving any reasonable doubt about the innocence or guilt of the defendant; allows the defendant the benefit of any possibility of innocence	Criminal trial
Clear and convincing	Prevailing and persuasive to the trier of fact	Civil commitments, insanity defense evidence
Preponderance of evidence	Greater weight of evidence in terms of credibility; more convincing than an opposite point of view	Civil trial
Probable cause	U.S. constitutional standard for arrest and search warrants, requiring existence of facts sufficient to warrant that a crime has been committed	Arrest, preliminary hearing, motions
Sufficient evidence	Adequate evidence to reverse a trial court	Appellate review
Reasonable suspicion	Rational, reasonable belief that facts warrant investigations of a crime on less than probable cause	Police investigations
Less than probable cause	Mere suspicion; less than reasonable belief to conclude criminal activity exists	Prudent police investigation where safety of an officer or others is endangered

based on factual errors.[34] The underlying premise of this standard is that it is better to release a guilty person than to convict someone who is innocent. Since the defendant is presumed innocent until proven guilty, this standard forces the prosecution to overcome this presumption with the highest standard of proof. Unlike the civil law, where a mere **preponderance of the evidence** is the standard, the criminal process requires proof beyond a reasonable doubt for each element of the offense.[35] The various evidentiary standards of proof are analyzed and compared in Exhibit 10.1.

Criminal Justice ⚖ Now™
Learn more about Trials by going through the Learning Module.

THE TRIAL PROCESS

The trial of a criminal case is a formal process conducted in a specific and orderly fashion in accordance with rules of criminal law, procedure, and evidence. Unlike what transpires in popular TV programs involving lawyers— where witnesses are often asked leading and prejudicial questions and where judges go far beyond their supervisory role—the modern criminal trial is a complicated and often time-consuming, technical affair. It is a structured adversary proceeding in which both the prosecution and defense follow specific procedures and argue the merits of their cases before the judge and jury. Each side seeks to present its case in the most favorable light. When possible, the prosecutor and the defense attorney will object to evidence they

preponderance of the evidence
The level of proof in civil cases; more than half the evidence supports the allegations of one side.

consider damaging to their positions. The prosecutor will use direct testimony, physical evidence, and a confession, if available, to convince the jury that the accused is guilty beyond a reasonable doubt. The defense attorney will rebut the government's case with her own evidence, make certain that the rights of the criminal defendant under the federal and state constitutions are considered during all phases of the trial, and determine whether an appeal is appropriate if the client is found guilty.

Although each jurisdiction in the United States has its own trial procedures, all jurisdictions conduct criminal trials in a generally similar fashion. The basic steps of the criminal trial, which proceed in an established order, are described in this section and outlined in Figure 10.1.

Jury Selection

In both civil and criminal cases, jurors are selected randomly from licensing or voter registration lists within each court's jurisdiction. Few states impose qualifications on those called for jury service, though most mandate a residency requirement.[36] There is also little uniformity in the amount of time served by jurors, with the term ranging from one day to months, depending on the nature of the trial. In addition, most jurisdictions prohibit convicted felons from serving on juries, as well as others exempted by statute, such as public officials, physicians, and attorneys.

The initial list of persons chosen, which is called **venire,** or jury array, provides the state with a group of potentially capable citizens able to serve on a jury. Many states, by rule of law, review the venire to eliminate unqualified persons and to exempt those who by reason of their professions are not allowed to be jurors. The actual jury selection process begins with those remaining on the list.

The court clerk, who handles the administrative affairs of the trial—including the processing of the complaint, evidence, and other documents—randomly selects enough names to fill what she believes will be the required number of places on the jury. After reporting to a courtroom, the prospective jurors are first required to swear that they will truthfully answer all questions asked about their qualifications to serve. A group of twelve will be asked to sit in the jury box while the remaining group stands by.

Voir Dire Once twelve prospective jurors are chosen, the lengthy process of **voir dire** (from the French for "to tell the truth") starts. To determine their appropriateness to sit on the jury, prospective jurors are examined under oath by the government, the defense, and sometimes the judge, about their backgrounds, occupations, residences, and possible knowledge of or interest in the case. A juror who acknowledges any bias for or prejudice against the defendant—if the defendant is a friend or relative, or if the juror has already formed an opinion about the case—may be removed by either the prosecution or defense with a **challenge for cause** asking the judge to dismiss the biased juror. If the judge accepts the challenge, the juror is removed for cause and replaced with another from the remaining panel. Because normally no limit is placed on the number of challenges for cause that can be exercised, it often takes considerable time to select a jury for controversial and highly publicized criminal cases.

Peremptory Challenges Besides challenges for cause, both the prosecution and the defense are allowed **peremptory challenges,** which enable the attorneys to excuse jurors for no particular reason or for undisclosed reasons. A prosecutor might not want a bartender as a juror in a drunk-driving case, believing that a person with that occupation would be sympathetic to the accused. Or the defense attorney might excuse a prospective male juror because

Criminal Justice ⊛ Now™
Learn more by viewing the "BTK Killer Pleads Guilty" "In the News" video clip.

venire The group called for jury duty from which jury panels are selected.

voir dire The process in which a potential jury panel is questioned by the prosecution and the defense in order to select jurors who are unbiased and objective.

challenge for cause Removing a juror because he or she is biased or has prior knowledge about a case, or for other reasons that demonstrate the individual's inability to render a fair and impartial judgment in a case.

peremptory challenge The dismissal of a potential juror by either the prosecution or the defense for unexplained, discretionary reasons.

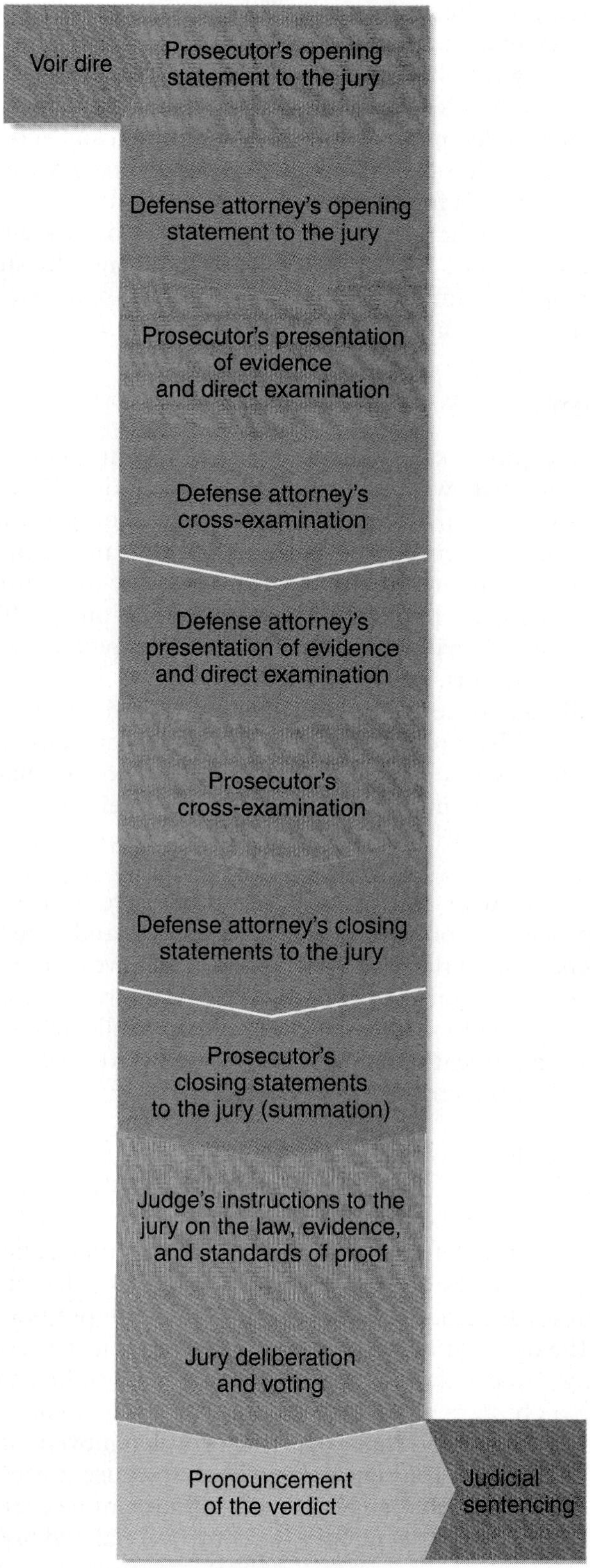

Figure 10.1 The steps in a jury trial

Source: Marvin Zalman and Larry Siegel, *Criminal Procedure: Constitution and Society* (St. Paul, Minn.: West, 1991), 655.

the attorney prefers to have a predominantly female jury. The number of peremptory challenges given to the prosecution and defense is limited by state statute and often varies by case and jurisdiction.

The peremptory challenge has been criticized by legal experts who question the fairness and propriety with which it has been used.[37] Historically, the most significant criticism was that it was used by the prosecution to exclude African Americans from serving on juries in which the defendant was also African American, a policy that seemed to allow legally condoned discrimination against minority group members. In the landmark 1986 case *Batson v. Kentucky,* the Supreme Court held that the use of peremptory challenges against potential jurors by prosecutors in criminal cases violated the U.S. Constitution if the challenges were based solely on race.[38] Since that decision, the issue of race discrimination in the use of peremptory challenges has been raised by defendants in numerous cases. In the 1991 case of *Powers v. Ohio,* the Supreme Court held that it is unconstitutional to exclude juries based on race even if they are not the same race as the defendant. In other words, the equal protection clause prohibits a prosecutor from using the peremptory challenge to exclude qualified and unbiased persons from a jury solely by reason of race, regardless of the race of the parties involved.[39] In 1994, the Court applied the *Batson* doctrine to gender-based peremptory challenges, ruling that attorneys must provide a nondiscriminatory reason for removing a large number of prospective male or female jurors (*J.E.B. v. Alabama*).[40] Exhibit 10.2 summarizes these decisions.

Batson strikes down a legal procedure that was out of sync with modern ideas of justice and fairness. It prevents an element of racial discrimination from entering into the trial stage of justice, which is one of the cornerstones of American freedom. Yet it preserves, under controlled circumstances, the use of the peremptory challenge, which is an integral part of the jury selection process.

Criminal Justice Now™

*Learn more by exploring the **Steps in a Jury Trial** Animated Artwork and the **Order of Events in a Trial** Review and Reinforce activity.*

WWW To read about juror selection in California, go to "Web Links" on your Siegel Essentials of Criminal Justice 5e website: http://cj.wadsworth.com/siegel_ess5e.

Exhibit 10.2	Evolution of *Batson v. Kentucky* and its progeny
Case	**Ruling**
Batson v. Kentucky (1986)	Under the Fourteenth Amendment, the Supreme Court ruled that prosecutors were barred from using peremptory challenges to remove black jurors because of their race.
Powers v. Ohio (1991)	The Court concluded that a defendant has the standing to object to the race-based exclusion by the use of peremptory challenges of jurors on the grounds of equal protection, even if they were not of the same race as the challenged jurors.
Edmonson v. Leesville Concrete Co. (1991)	The *Batson* ruling applies to attorneys in civil lawsuits. In other words, a private party in a civil action may not raise peremptory challenges to exclude jurors on the basis of race.
Georgia v. McCollum (1992)	On the basis of *Batson,* the *McCollum* decision prohibited the exercise of peremptory challenges on the basis of race by defense attorneys in criminal cases.
J.E.B. v. Alabama (1994)	The Court held that the equal protection clause of the Fourteenth Amendment bars discrimination in jury selection on the basis of sex. Discrimination in jury selection, whether based on race or gender, causes harm to the litigants, the community, and the individual jurors who are wrongfully excluded from participation in the judicial process.

Opening Statements

Once the jury has been selected and the criminal complaint has been read to the jurors by the court clerk, the prosecutor and the defense attorney may each make an opening statement about the case. The purpose of the prosecutor's statement is to introduce the judge and the jury to the particular criminal charges, to outline the facts, and to describe how the government will prove the defendant guilty beyond a reasonable doubt. The defense attorney reviews the case and indicates how the defense intends to show that the accused is not guilty.

Typically, current rules dictate that the prosecutor is entitled to offer an opening statement first followed by the defense statement. The opening statement gives the jury a concise overview of the evidence that is to follow. Neither attorney is allowed to make prejudicial remarks or inflammatory statements or mention irrelevant facts. Both are free, however, to identify what they will eventually prove by way of evidence, which includes witnesses, physical evidence, and the use of expert testimony. As a general rule, the opening statements used in jury trials are important because they provide the fact finders (i.e., the jury) with an initial summary of the case. They are infrequently used and less effective in bench trials, however, where juries are not used. Most lower-court judges have handled hundreds of similar cases and do not need the benefit of an opening statement.

Witness Testimony

Following the opening statements, the government begins its case by presenting evidence to the court through its witnesses. Those called as witnesses—such as police officers, victims, or experts—provide testimony via **direct examination.** During direct examination, the prosecutor questions the witness to reveal the facts believed pertinent to the government's case. Testimony involves what the witness actually saw, heard, or touched, and does not include opinions. However, a witness's opinion can be given in certain situations, such as when describing the motion of a vehicle or indicating whether a defendant appeared to act intoxicated or insane. Witnesses may also qualify

direct examination The questioning of one's own (prosecution or defense) witness during a trial.

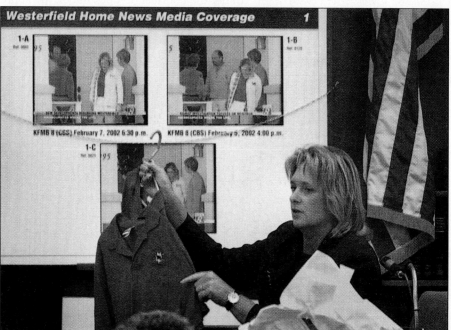

The prosecutor calls witnesses in order to present a sufficient level of evidence to gain a conviction. Here, a San Diego police detective testifies during the trial of David Westerfield, who was accused of killing Danielle van Dam. The physical evidence presented at trial was sufficient to gain a conviction on murder charges.

© 2003 AP/Wide World Photos

to give opinions because they are experts on a particular subject relevant to the case; for example, a psychiatrist may testify about a defendant's mental capacity at the time of the crime.

Upon completion of the prosecutor's questioning, the defense usually conducts a **cross-examination** of the witness. During this exchange, the defense attorney may challenge elements of the testimony, such as the accuracy in reporting what was seen or heard. The right to cross-examine witnesses is an essential part of a trial, and unless extremely unusual circumstances exist (such as a person's being hospitalized), witness statements will not be considered unless they are made in court and open for question. If desired, the prosecutor may seek a second direct examination after the defense attorney has completed cross-examination; this allows the prosecutor to ask additional questions about information brought out during cross-examination. Finally, the defense attorney may then question, or re-cross-examine, the witness once again. All witnesses for the trial are sworn in and questioned in the same basic manner.

Presentation of Evidence at a Criminal Trial

The central purpose of the cross-examination process is to introduce evidence upon which the jury can decide the case. There are numerous types of evidence presented at trial. These include:

- *Testimonial evidence.* Given by police officers, citizens, and experts, this is the most basic form of evidence. The witness must state, under oath, what they heard, saw, or experienced.

- *Real evidence.* **Real evidence** consists of the exhibits that can be taken into the jury room for review by the jury. A revolver that may have been in the defendant's control at the time of a murder, tools in the possession of a suspect charged with a burglary, and a bottle allegedly holding narcotics are all examples of real, or physical, evidence. Photographs, maps, diagrams, and crime scene displays are further types of real evidence.

- *Documentary evidence.* This type of evidence includes writings, government reports, public records, business or hospital records, fingerprint identification, and DNA profiling.

- *Circumstantial evidence.* **Circumstantial (indirect) evidence** is also often used in trial proceedings. Such evidence is often inferred or indirectly used to prove a fact in question. For example, in a murder case, evidence that carpet fibers found on the body match the carpet in the defendant's home may be used at trial to link the two, even though they do not provide direct evidence that the suspect actually killed the victim.

In general, the primary test for the admissibility of evidence in a criminal proceeding is its relevance; that is, the court must consider whether the gun, tool, or bottle has relevant evidentiary value in determining the issues in the case. Ordinarily, evidence that establishes an element of the crime is acceptable to the court. In a prosecution for possession of drugs, evidence that shows the defendant to be a known drug user might be relevant. In a prosecution for bribery, photos of the defendant receiving a package from a co-conspirator would clearly be found relevant to the case.

Motion for a Directed Verdict

Once the prosecution has provided all the government's evidence against a defendant, it will inform the court that it rests the people's case. The defense attorney at this point may enter a motion for a **directed verdict.** This is a procedural device in which the defense attorney asks the judge to order the jury to return a verdict of not guilty. Depending on the weight of the prosecution's

Criminal Justice ⚖ Now™

Learn more by exploring the Adversary System, Peremptory Challenge, and Circumstantial Evidence Review and Reinforce activities.

cross-examination *The process in which the defense and the prosecution interrogate witnesses during a trial.*

real evidence *Any object produced for inspection at the trial (such as a weapon or photograph).*

circumstantial (indirect) evidence *Evidence not bearing on the fact in dispute but on various indirect circumstances from which the judge or jury might infer the existence of the fact (for example, if the defendant was seen in the house with wet clothing, that is circumstantial evidence that the person had walked in the rain).*

directed verdict *The right of a judge to direct a jury to acquit a defendant because the state has not proven the elements of the crime or otherwise has not established guilt according to law.*

case, the judge may either sustain it or overrule the motion. In essence, the defense attorney argues in the directed verdict that the prosecutor's case against the defendant is insufficient to support the legal elements needed to prove the defendant guilty beyond a reasonable doubt. If the motion is sustained, the trial is terminated. If it is rejected by the court, the case continues with the defense portion of the trial.

Presentation of the Defense Attorney's Evidence

The defense attorney has the option of presenting many, some, or no witnesses on behalf of the defendant. The burden of guilt is on the prosecution, and if the defense team believes that the burden has not been met they may feel there is no need to present witnesses of their own. In addition, the defense attorney must decide whether the defendant should take the stand and testify in his own behalf. In a criminal trial, the defendant is protected by the Fifth Amendment right to be free from self-incrimination, which means that a person cannot be forced by the state to testify against himself. However, defendants who choose voluntarily to tell their side of the story can be subject to cross-examination by the prosecutor.

The defense attorney is charged with putting on a vigorous defense in the adversary system of justice. They present their own witnesses and introduce evidence to refute the prosecution's allegations. After the defense concludes its case, the government may then present rebuttal evidence. If the judge grants permission, this involves bringing evidence forward used to refute, counteract, or disprove evidence introduced by the defense. A prosecutor may not go into new matters or present evidence that further supports or reinforces her own case. At the end of rebuttal, the defense may be allowed *surrebuttal*, that is, presenting witnesses to respond to issues that were raised for the first time in the prosecutor's rebuttal case. The defense cannot restate its case or introduce new issues during surrebuttal evidence.

After all evidence has been presented to the court, the defense attorney may again submit a motion for a directed verdict. If the motion is denied, both the prosecution and the defense prepare to make closing arguments, and the case on the evidence is ready for consideration by the jury.

Closing Arguments

Closing arguments are used by the attorneys to review the facts and evidence of the case in a manner favorable to each of their positions. At this stage of the trial, both prosecution and defense are permitted to draw reasonable inferences and to show how the facts prove or refute the defendant's guilt. Often both attorneys have a free hand in arguing about the facts, issues, and evidence, including the applicable law. They cannot comment on matters not in evidence, however, or on the defendant's failure to testify in a criminal case. Normally, the defense attorney will make a closing statement first, followed by the prosecutor. Either party can elect to forgo the right to make a final summation to the jury.

Instructions to the Jury

In a criminal trial, the judge will instruct, or **charge,** the jury members on the principles of law that ought to guide and control their decision on the defendant's innocence or guilt. Included in the charge will be information about the elements of the alleged offense, the type of evidence needed to prove each element, and the burden of proof required to obtain a guilty verdict. Although the judge commonly provides the instruction, he or she may ask the prosecutor and the defense attorney to submit instructions for consideration; the judge will then use discretion in determining whether to use any of their instructions. The instructions that cover the law applicable to the case are extremely important

charge In a criminal case, the judge's instruction to the jurors before deliberation.

because they may serve as the basis for a subsequent appeal. Procedurally, in highly publicized and celebrated cases, the judge may have sequestered the jury overnight to prevent them from having contact with the outside world. This process, called *sequestration*, is discretionary, and most judges believe that sequestering or "locking up a jury" is needed only in sensational cases.

Criminal Justice ⚖ Now™

*Learn more about **Careers in Criminal Justice** by exploring the "On the Job" feature **Court Reporter**.*

The Verdict

Once the charge is given to the jury members, they retire to deliberate on a verdict. As previously mentioned, the verdict in a criminal case—regardless of whether the trial involves a six- or twelve-person jury—is usually required to be unanimous. Unanimity of twelve is not required by the U.S. Constitution in state cases but is the rule in federal criminal trials. Unanimity is required with six-person juries. A review of the case by the jury may take hours or even days. The jurors always meet privately during their deliberations, and in certain lengthy and highly publicized cases, they are kept overnight in a hotel until the verdict is reached. In less sensational cases, the jurors may be allowed to go home, but they are cautioned not to discuss the case with anyone.

If a verdict cannot be reached, the trial may result in a *hung jury*, after which the prosecutor must bring the defendant to trial again if the prosecution desires a conviction. If found not guilty, the defendant is released from the criminal process. If the defendant is convicted, the judge will normally order a pre-sentence investigation by the probation department before imposing a sentence. Before sentencing, the defense attorney will probably submit a motion for a new trial, alleging that legal errors occurred in the trial proceedings. The judge may deny the motion and impose a sentence immediately, a practice quite common in most misdemeanor offenses. In felony cases, however, the judge will set a date for sentencing, and the defendant will either be placed on bail or held in custody until that time.

The Sentence

The imposition of the criminal sentence is normally the responsibility of the trial judge. In some jurisdictions, the jury may determine the sentence or make recommendations involving leniency for certain offenses. Often, the sentencing decision is based on information and recommendations given to the court by the probation department after a pre-sentence investigation of the defendant. The sentence itself is determined by the statutory requirements for the particular crime as established by the legislature; in addition, the judge ordinarily has

© 2005 Nick Ut/Reuters/POOL/Corbis

Actor Robert Blake weeps as the verdict is read at his murder trial in Los Angeles, March 16, 2005. Blake was found not guilty of first-degree murder in the May 2001 shooting death of his estranged wife of six months, Bonny Lee Bakley. Jurors, who reached their verdict on the eighth day of deliberations, also found the 71-year-old former star of the 1970s cop show *Baretta* not guilty of one count of soliciting someone else to kill his spouse.

a great deal of discretion in reaching a sentencing decision. The different criminal sanctions available include fines, probation, imprisonment, and even commitment to a state hospital. The sentence may be a combination of all these.

The Appeal

Defendants have as many as three possible avenues of appeal: *the direct appeal, postconviction remedy,* and *federal court review.* Both the direct appeal and federal court review provide the convicted person with the opportunity to appeal to a higher state or federal court on the basis of an error that affected the conviction in the trial court. Extraordinary trial court errors, such as the denial of the right to counsel or the inability to provide a fair trial, are subject to the plain error rule of the federal courts.[41] Harmless errors, such as the use of innocuous identification procedures or the denial of counsel at a noncritical stage of the proceeding, would not necessarily result in the overturning of a criminal conviction. A postconviction appeal (or remedy), on the other hand, or what is often referred to as *collateral attack,* takes the form of a legal petition, such as habeas corpus, and is the primary means by which state prisoners have their convictions or sentences reviewed in the federal court. A **writ of habeas corpus** (meaning "you have the body") seeks to determine the validity of a detention by asking the court to release the person or give legal reasons for the incarceration.

In most jurisdictions, direct criminal appeal to an appellate court is a matter of right. This means that the defendant has an automatic right to appeal a conviction based on errors that may have occurred during the trial proceedings. A substantial number of criminal appeals are the result of disputes over points of law, such as the introduction at the trial of illegal evidence detrimental to the defendant or statements made during the trial that were prejudicial to the defendant. Through objections made at the pretrial and trial stages of the criminal process, the defense counsel will reserve specific legal issues on the record as the basis for appeal. A copy of the transcript of these proceedings will serve as the basis on which the appellate court will review any errors that may have occurred during the lower-court proceedings.

Because an appeal is an expensive, time-consuming, and technical process involving a review of the lower-court record, the research and drafting of briefs, and the presentation of oral arguments to the appellate court, the defendant has been granted the right to counsel at this stage of the criminal process. In the 1963 case of *Douglas v. California,* the U.S. Supreme Court held that an indigent defendant has a constitutional right to the assistance of counsel on a direct first appeal.[42] If the defendant appeals to a higher court, the defendant must have private counsel or apply for permission to proceed **in forma pauperis** (meaning "in the manner of a pauper")—that is, the defendant may be granted counsel at public expense if the court believes the appeal has merit. There is no constitutional right to free counsel beyond the first appeal.[43]

After an appeal has been fully heard, the appeals court renders an opinion on the procedures used in the case. If an error of law is found—such as an improper introduction of evidence or an improper statement by the prosecutor that was prejudicial to the defendant—the appeals court may reverse the decision of the trial court and order a new trial. If the lower-court decision is upheld, the case is finished, unless the defendant seeks a discretionary appeal to a higher state or federal court.

Over the last decade, criminal appeals have increased significantly in almost every state and the federal courts. Criminal case appeals make up close to 50 percent of the state appellate caseload and over 35 percent of the total federal caseload, which includes prisoner petitions and ordinary criminal appeals. Today, a substantial number of these appeals involve drug-related cases and appeals of sentences where the offender was institutionalized. Most appeals occur after final trial court decisions on convictions and sentencing of the defendant.

writ of habeas corpus *A judicial order requesting that a person detaining another produce the body of the prisoner and give reasons for his or her capture and detention. Habeas corpus is a legal device used to request that a judicial body review the reasons for a person's confinement and the conditions of confinement. Habeas corpus is known as "the great writ."*

in forma pauperis *"In the manner of a pauper." A criminal defendant granted permission to proceed in forma pauperis is entitled to assistance of counsel at state expense.*

SUMMARY

- The number of cases disposed of by trials is relatively small in comparison with the total number that enter the criminal justice system. Nevertheless, the criminal trial provides the defendant with an important option.

- Unlike other steps in the system, the U.S. criminal trial allows the accused to assert the right to a day in court. The defendant may choose between a trial before a judge alone or a trial by jury.

- The purpose of the trial is to adjudicate the facts, ascertain the truth, and determine the guilt or innocence of the accused.

- Criminal trials represent the adversary system at work. The state uses its authority to seek a conviction, and the defendant is protected by constitutional rights, particularly those under the Fifth and Sixth Amendments.

- When they involve serious crimes, criminal trials are complex legal affairs. Each jurisdiction relies on rules and procedures that have developed over many years to resolve legal issues.

- As the U.S. Supreme Court has extended the rights of the accused, the procedures have undoubtedly contributed to the system's complexities and delays.

- Some solutions have included smaller juries, more efficient control of police misconduct, and reduced time delays between arrest, indictment, and trial. But the right to a fair trial, trial by jury, and the due process rights to counsel and confrontation also need to be guarded and protected in the twenty-first century.

- An established order of steps is followed throughout a criminal trial, beginning with the selection of a jury, proceeding through opening statements and the introduction of evidence, and concluding with closing arguments and a verdict.

- The criminal trial serves both a symbolic and a pragmatic function for defendants who require a forum of last resort to adjudicate their differences with the state.

- The trial is the central test of the facts and law involved in a criminal case.

KEY TERMS

bench trial 276
verdict 276
adjudication 276
confrontation clause 277
hearsay evidence 277
six-person jury 278
pro se 279
First Amendment 281

proof beyond a reasonable
doubt 281
preponderance of the evidence 282
venire 283
voir dire 283
challenge for cause 283
peremptory challenge 283

direct examination 286
cross-examination 287
real evidence 287
circumstantial (indirect)
evidence 287
directed verdict 287
charge 288
writ of habeas corpus 290
in forma pauperis 290

REVIEW QUESTIONS

1. What are the steps involved in the criminal trial?
2. What are the pros and cons of a jury trial versus a bench trial?
3. What are the legal rights of the defendant in a trial process?
4. Should people be denied the right to serve as jurors without explanation or cause? In other words, should the peremptory challenge be maintained?

5. "In the adversary system of criminal justice, the burden of proof in a criminal trial to show that the defendant is guilty beyond a reasonable doubt is on the government." Explain the meaning of this statement.

CHAPTER 11

Punishment and Sentencing

© Shepard Sherbell/Corbis

TIM KENNY received his B.A. from the University of Michigan. In his junior year in college, he began thinking about a legal career, his interest piqued by attending several court proceedings. He applied to the University of Michigan Law School, where he graduated with his J.D. degree. Because he found the practice of criminal law exciting and derived satisfaction from helping to represent crime victims, Kenny spent twenty years as an assistant prosecutor in Detroit. Among his posts, he spent more than three years prosecuting homicide cases, six years as a career criminal prosecutor, and more than four years prosecuting major narcotics-trafficking organizations. As a result of these efforts, Kenny received an award in 1991 from the Federal Bar Association for excellence in the practice of criminal law.

Tim Kenny is now a judge in the Criminal Division of the largest circuit court in the state of Michigan. His bench disposes of approximately thirteen thousand felony cases each year. His days are varied and complex. He might see three or four defendants who are part of the Drug Court program to evaluate their progress in living a drug-free lifestyle. Then he

Chapter Outline

Chapter Objectives

1. Understand the concept of criminal punishment
2. Know the different types of punishment used throughout history
3. Recognize the differences between concurrent and consecutive sentences
4. Be familiar with the various reasons for applying criminal sanctions
5. Be able to discuss the concept of indeterminate sentencing
6. Recognize why determinate sentencing was instituted
7. Know what is meant by the term "three-strikes-and-you're-out"
8. Understand the concept of mandatory sentencing
9. Know the arguments for and against capital punishment
10. Be able to discuss the issue of whether the death penalty deters murder

might handle several felony sentencing hearings and probation violation hearings. After these matters are resolved, the rest of the day is spent doing felony trial work (approximately 65–70 cases per year).

Although being a judge is always challenging, some parts of the job are particularly demanding:

- Finding appropriate facilities for the mentally ill who come through the criminal courts
- Finding quality rehabilitative facilities for those with substance-abuse issues
- Resolving domestic violence cases
- Dealing with jail overcrowding

These issues demand that a judge be in constant contact with community resources so there can be a balance between rehabilitation and protection for the community.

Historically, people who violated the law were considered morally corrupt and in need of strong discipline. If punishment was harsh enough, it was assumed, they would never repeat their mistakes. Punishment was also viewed as a spectacle that taught a moral lesson. The more gruesome and public the sentence, the greater the impact it would have on the local populace.[1] Harsh physical punishments would control any thoughts of rebellion and dissent against the central government and those who held political and economic control. During the Middle Ages, the philosophy of punishment was to "torment the body for the sins of the soul."[2] People found guilty of crime faced a wide range of punishment, including physical torture, branding, whipping, and for most felony offenses, death. Such barbaric use of state power is, of course, not tolerated in the United States today.

The controversy over punishment involves both its nature and extent: Is contemporary punishment too harsh or too lenient? Do people get widely different sentences for very similar crimes?[3] Is there discrimination in sentencing based on race, gender, or social class?[4] These are but a few of the most significant issues in the sentencing process.

This chapter first examines the history of punishment and then focuses on incarceration and capital punishment, the two most traditional and punitive forms of criminal sanctions used today. Chapter 12 reviews alternative sentences that have been developed to reduce the strain on the overburdened correctional system; these sentences provide intermediate sanctions designed to control people whose behavior and personality make incarceration unnecessary. Such sanctions include probation and other forms of community correction.

Criminal Justice ⊛ Now™

Learn more by exploring the Role Play activities for this chapter: Drug Bust Part 4; Burglary Part 4; and Domestic Violence Part 4.

▌THE HISTORY OF PUNISHMENT

The punishment and correction of criminals has changed considerably through the ages, reflecting custom, economic conditions, and religious and political ideals.[5]

From Exile to Fines, Torture to Forfeiture

In early Greece and Rome, the most common state-administered punishment was banishment, or exile. Only slaves were commonly subjected to harsh physical punishment for their misdeeds. Interpersonal violence, even attacks that resulted in death, were viewed as a private matter. These ancient peoples typically used economic punishments, such as fines, for such crimes as assault on a slave, arson, or housebreaking.

During the Middle Ages (the fifth to fifteenth centuries), there was little law or governmental control. Offenses were settled by blood feuds carried out by the families of the injured parties. When possible, the Roman custom of settling disputes by fine or an exchange of property was adopted as a means of resolving interpersonal conflicts with a minimum of bloodshed. After the eleventh century, during the feudal period, forfeiture of land and property was common punishment for persons who violated law and custom or who failed to fulfill their feudal obligations to their lord. The word *felony* actually has its origins in the twelfth century, when the term *felonia* referred to a breach of faith with one's feudal lord.

During this period the main emphasis of criminal law and punishment was on maintaining public order. If in the heat of passion or while intoxicated a person severely injured or killed his neighbor, freemen in the area would gather to pronounce a judgment and make the culprit do penance or pay compensation called **wergild.** The purpose of the fine was to pacify the injured party and ensure that the conflict would not develop into a blood feud and an-

wergild *Under medieval law, the money paid by the offender to compensate the victim and the state for a criminal offense.*

In earlier times, punishment was quite severe. Even kings, such as Charles I of England, were not immune from death by beheading.

The Granger Collection, New York

archy. The inability of the peasantry to pay a fine led to the use of corporal punishment, such as whipping or branding, as a substitute penalty.

The development of the common law in the eleventh century brought some standardization to penal practices. However, corrections remained an amalgam of fines and brutal physical punishments. The criminal wealthy could buy their way out of punishment and into exile, but capital and corporal punishment were used to control the criminal poor, who were executed and mutilated at ever-increasing rates. Execution, banishment, mutilation, branding, and flogging were used on a whole range of offenders, from murderers and robbers to vagrants and Gypsies. Punishments became unmatched in their cruelty, featuring a gruesome variety of physical tortures, often part of a public spectacle, presumably so that the sadistic sanctions would act as deterrents. But the variety and imagination of the tortures inflicted on even minor criminals before their death suggest that retribution, sadism, and spectacle were more important than any presumed deterrent effect.

Public Work and Transportation to the Colonies

By the end of the sixteenth century, the rise of the city and overseas colonization provided tremendous markets for manufactured goods and spurred the need for labor. Punishment of criminals changed to meet the demands created by these social conditions. Instead of being tortured or executed, many offenders were made to do hard labor for their crimes. *Poor laws,* developed at the end of the sixteenth century, required that the poor, vagrants, and vagabonds be put to work in public or private enterprises. Houses of correction were developed to make it convenient to assign petty law violators to work details. In London a workhouse was developed at Brideswell in 1557; its use became so popular that by 1576 Parliament ordered a Brideswell-type workhouse to be built in every county in England. Many convicted offenders were pressed into sea duty as galley slaves. Galley slavery was considered a fate so loathsome that many convicts mutilated themselves rather than submit to servitude on the high seas.

The constant shortage of labor in the European colonies also prompted authorities to transport convicts overseas. In England, an Order in Council of 1617 granted a reprieve and stay of execution to people convicted of robbery and other felonies who were strong enough to be employed overseas. Similar measures were used in France and Italy to recruit galley slaves and workers.

Transporting convicts to the colonies became popular: it supplied labor, cost little, and was actually profitable for the government, since manufacturers and plantation owners paid for the convicts' services. The Old Bailey Court in London supplied at least ten thousand convicts between 1717 and 1775. Convicts would serve a period as workers and then become free again.

The American Revolution ended the transportation of felons to North America, but it continued in Australia and New Zealand. Between 1787 and 1875, when the practice was finally abandoned, over 135,000 felons were transported to Australia.

Although transportation in lieu of a death sentence may at first glance seem advantageous, transported prisoners endured enormous hardships. Those who were sent to Australia suffered incredible physical abuse, including severe whippings and mutilation. Many of the British prison officials placed in charge of the Australian penal colonies could best be described as sociopaths or sadists.

The Rise of the Prison

Between the American Revolution in 1776 and the first decades of the nineteenth century, the European and U.S. populations increased rapidly. Transportation of convicts to North America was no longer an option. The increased use of machinery made industry capital-intensive, not labor-intensive. As a result, there was less need for unskilled laborers in England, and many workers could not find suitable employment.

The gulf between poor workers and wealthy landowners and merchants widened. The crime rate rose significantly, prompting a return to physical punishment and increased use of the death penalty. During the later part of the eighteenth century, 350 types of crime in England were punishable by death. Although many people sentenced to death for trivial offenses were spared the gallows, the use of capital punishment was extremely common in England during the mid-eighteenth century. Prompted by the excessive use of physical and capital punishment, legal philosophers argued that physical punishment should be replaced by periods of confinement and incapacitation. Jails and workhouses were thus used to hold petty offenders, vagabonds, the homeless, and debtors. However, these institutions were not meant for hard-core criminals. One solution to imprisoning a growing criminal population was to keep prisoners in abandoned ships anchored in rivers and harbors throughout England. In 1777, the degradation under which prisoners lived in these ships inspired John Howard, the sheriff of Bedfordshire, to write *The State of the Prisons in England and Wales*, which led to Parliament's passage of legislation mandating the construction of secure and sanitary structures to house prisoners.

By 1820, long periods of incarceration in walled institutions called reformatories or **penitentiaries** began to replace physical punishment in England and the United States. These institutions were considered liberal reforms during a time when harsh physical punishment and incarceration in filthy holding facilities were the norm. The history of correctional institutions will be discussed further in chapter 12. Incarceration has remained the primary mode of punishment for serious offenses in the United States since it was introduced in the early nineteenth century. Ironically in our high-tech society, some of the institutions developed soon after the Revolutionary War are still

penitentiary *A state or federal correctional institution for incarceration of felony offenders for terms of one year or more.*

in use today. In contemporary society, prison as a method of punishment has been supplemented by a sentence to community supervision for less serious offenders, and the death penalty is reserved for those considered to be the most serious and dangerous.

THE GOALS OF MODERN SENTENCING

When we hear about a notorious criminal—such as serial killer Jeffrey Dahmer and Oklahoma City bomber Tim McVeigh—receiving a long prison sentence or the death penalty for a particularly heinous crime, each of us has a distinct reaction. Some of us are gratified that a truly evil person "got just what he deserved"; many people feel safer because a dangerous person is now "where he can't harm any other innocent victims"; others hope the punishment serves as a warning to potential criminals that "everyone gets caught in the end"; some may actually feel sorry for the defendant—"he got a raw deal, he needs help, not punishment"—and still others hope that "when he gets out, he'll have learned his lesson." And when an offender is forced to pay a large fine, we say, "What goes around comes around."

Each of these sentiments may be at work when criminal sentences are formulated. After all, sentences are devised and implemented by judges, many of whom are elected officials and share the general public's sentiments and fears. The objectives of criminal sentencing today can usually be grouped into six distinct areas: *general deterrence, incapacitation, specific deterrence, retribution/just desert, rehabilitation,* and *equity/restitution.*

General Deterrence

According to the concept of **general deterrence,** harsh sentences will convince those contemplating violating the law that crime does not pay. By punishing an offender severely, the state can demonstrate its determination to control crime and deter potential offenders.

Punishing one person to control the behavior of another is a tricky task. Too lenient a sentence may encourage criminal conduct; too severe a sentence may reduce the system's ability to dispense fair and impartial justice and actually encourage criminality. If, for example, the crime of rape were punished by death, rapists might be encouraged to kill their victims to dispose of the one person who could identify them at trial. Since they would already be facing the death penalty for rape, they would have nothing more to lose. Maintaining a balance between fear and justice is an ongoing quest in the justice system.

Some justice experts believe that the recent decline in the crime rate is a result of toughening criminal penalties. Once arrested, people have a greater chance of being convicted today than they did in the past. This phenomenon is referred to as "expected punishment," defined as the number of days in prison a typical criminal can expect to serve per crime. Expected punishment increases as the probability of being apprehended, prosecuted, convicted, and going to prison rises.[6] While expected punishment rates have risen during the past decade, they are actually still quite low because (1) crime clearance rates remain under 50 percent, (2) many cases are dropped at the pretrial and trial stages (nolle prosequi), and (3) about one-third of convicted felons are given probationary rather than prison sentences.[7]

Take burglary for instance: victims experience about 3.3 million burglaries each year and report about two-thirds of these to the police (2.1 million). The burglary clearance rate is only 13 percent or 270,000 arrests; of those caught, about 72,000 are convicted and sent to prison. So about 70,000 people are sent

Criminal Justice ⚖ Now ™

*Learn more about **Philosophies of Punishment** by going through the Learning Module.*

Criminal Justice ⚖ Now ™

*Learn more by exploring the **Deterrence** Review and Reinforce activity.*

general deterrence A crime control policy that depends on the fear of criminal penalties. General deterrence measures, such as long prison sentences for violent crimes, are aimed at convincing the potential law violator that the pains associated with the crime outweigh the benefits.

to prison for 3.3 million burglaries. The odds of becoming a successful burglar seem pretty good. (Keep in mind that some burglars commit many crimes per year, so we are not talking about 3.3 million individual burglars!)

Because the justice system is still inefficient, the general deterrent effect of punishment is less than desired. In addition, some people may be too desperate or psychologically impaired by drugs or alcohol to be deterred by the threat of criminal punishments. Others face economic circumstances so difficult that the threat of punishment cannot negate their need to violate the law in order to survive.

While achieving crime reductions through deterrence strategies may prove difficult, some experts still believe that get-tough policies featuring long, mandatory prison sentences with little chance for early release can produce results.[8]

Incapacitation

Because criminals will not be able to repeat their criminal acts while they are under state control, **incapacitation** of criminals is another goal of sentencing. For some offenders, this means a period in a high-security state prison where behavior is closely monitored. By keeping dangerous criminals behind bars they will not be able to repeat their illegal activities.

Does incapacitating criminals help reduce the crime rate? The evidence is mixed. There have been periods, such as between 1980 and 1990, when the prison population increased and so too did the crime rate.

However, those who favor an incapacitation policy claim that the crime-reducing effect of putting people behind bars will eventually work if enough dangerous people are incapacitated.[9] The number and percentage of the general population behind bars escalated rapidly between 1990 and 2004, and the crime rate fell. To incapacitation advocates, this correlation is not a mere coincidence but a true effect; they believe that incapacitating dangerous criminals is a valid goal of sentencing.

Specific Deterrence

Another goal of punishment is to convince offenders that the pains of punishment are greater than the benefits of crime, hence they will not repeat their criminal offending; the experience of suffering punishment should inhibit future law violations.

Does a **specific deterrence** strategy reduce crime rates? A few research efforts have found that experiencing punishment can have significant specific deterrence on future criminality, but they are balanced by research that has failed to find specific deterrence effects. For example, Lawrence Sherman and Richard Berk found that the more severe the punishment they experience the less likely spousal abusers will re-offend.[10] While Sherman's findings were very influential, subsequent research failed to find a similar outcome.[11] Robert Davis and his associates found little association between severity of punishment for past spousal abuse and re-arrest on subsequent charges. Men were just as likely to **recidivate** if their case was dismissed, if they were given probation, or even if they were sent to jail.[12]

Claims for a specific deterrent effect are further weakened by data showing that most inmates (more than 80 percent) who are released from prison have had prior convictions, and the great majority (68 percent) will re-offend soon after their release. A prison stay seems to have little effect on re-offending.[13]

Despite these sketchy results, the goal of specific deterrence remains a fundamental part of sentencing. Some judges and policymakers maintain that a "taste of the bars" should reduce the desire for repeat offending.[14]

incapacitation The policy of keeping dangerous criminals in confinement to eliminate the risk of their repeating their offense in society.

specific deterrence A crime control policy suggesting that punishment should be severe enough to convince convicted offenders never to repeat their criminal activity.

recidivism Repetition of criminal behavior; habitual criminality. Recidivism is measured by (1) criminal acts that resulted in conviction by a court when committed by individuals who are under correctional supervision or who had been released from correctional supervision within the previous three years and (2) technical violations of probation or parole in which a sentencing or paroling authority took action that resulted in an adverse change in the offender's legal status.

Retribution/Just Desert

According to the retributive goal of sentencing, the essential purpose of the criminal process is to punish offenders—fairly and justly—in a manner that is proportionate to the gravity of their crimes.[15]

Offenders are punished simply and solely because they *deserve* to be disciplined for what they have done; "the punishment should fit the crime."[16] It would be wrong to punish people to set an example for others or to deter would-be criminals, as the general deterrence goal demands. Punishment should be no more or less than the offender's actions deserve; it must be based on how **blameworthy** the person is. This is referred to as the concept of **just desert**.[17]

According to this view, punishments must be equally and fairly distributed to all people who commit similar illegal acts. Determining just punishments can be difficult because there is generally little consensus about the treatment of criminals, the seriousness of crimes, and the proper response to criminal acts. Nonetheless, there has been an ongoing effort to calculate fair and just sentences by creating guidelines to control judicial decision making. This effort will be discussed in greater detail later in the chapter.

Rehabilitation

Some sentences are based on the need to treat and/or rehabilitate criminal offenders. Because society has failed them, many offenders have been forced to grow up in disorganized neighborhoods, have been the target of biased police officers, and are disadvantaged at home, at school, and in the job market. To compensate for these deprivations, the justice system is obligated to help these unfortunate people and not simply punish them for their misdeeds.[18] Rehabilitation advocates believe that if the proper treatment is applied, an offender will present no further threat to society.[19] It is not surprising then that the general public supports the treatment goal of sentencing and prefers it over policies based on punishment and incarceration.[20]

Equity/Restitution

Because criminals gain from their misdeeds, it seems both fair and just to demand that they reimburse society for its loss caused by their crimes. In the early common law, wergild and fines represented the concept of creating an equitable solution to crime by requiring the convicted offender to make restitution to both the victim and the state. Today, judges continue to require that offenders pay victims for their losses.

The **equity** goal of punishment means that convicted criminals must pay back their victims for their loss, the justice system for the costs of processing their case, and society for any disruption they may have caused. In a so-called victimless crime such as drug trafficking, the social costs might include the expense of drug enforcement efforts, drug treatment centers, and care for infants born to drug-addicted mothers. In predatory crimes, the costs might include the services of emergency room doctors, lost workdays and productivity, and treatment for long-term psychological problems. To help defray these costs, convicted offenders might be required to pay a fine, forfeit the property they acquired through illegal gain, do community service work, make financial restitution to their victim, and reimburse the state for the costs of the criminal process. Because the criminals' actions helped expand their personal gains, rights, and privileges at society's expense, justice demands that they lose rights and privileges to restore the social balance.

Each factor that influences sentencing decisions is illustrated in Figure 11.1.

Criminal Justice ⚖ Now™
*Learn more by exploring the **Just Deserts** Review and Reinforce activity.*

blameworthy *The culpability or guilt a person maintains for participating in a particular criminal offense.*

just desert *The philosophy of justice asserting that those who violate the rights of others deserve to be punished. The severity of punishment should be commensurate with the seriousness of the crime.*

equity *The action or practice of awarding each person his or her just due; sanctions based on equity seek to compensate individual victims and the general society for their losses due to crime.*

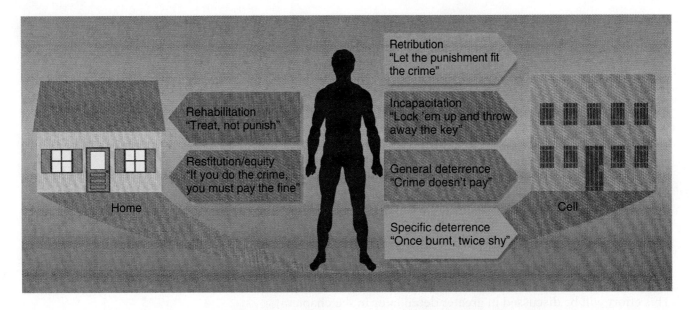

Figure 11.1 The goals behind sentencing decisions

Criminal Justice Now™

Learn more by going through the Sentencing Learning Module.

IMPOSING THE SENTENCE

In most felony cases, except where the law provides for mandatory prison terms, sentencing is usually based on a variety of information available to the judge. Some jurisdictions allow victims to make impact statements that are considered at sentencing hearings. Most judges also consider a pre-sentence investigation report by the probation department in making a sentencing decision. This report is a social and personal history, as well as an evaluation of the defendant's chances for rehabilitation within the community.

Criminal Justice Now™

Learn more by exploring the Consecutive vs Concurrent Sentences Animated Artwork and the Sentencing Disparity Review and Reinforce activity.

Concurrent vs. Consecutive Sentences

In some instances, when an accused is convicted of two or more charges, the judge must decide whether to impose consecutive or **concurrent sentences.** If the sentences are concurrent, they begin the same day and are completed when the longest term has been served. For example, a defendant is convicted of burglarizing an apartment and assaulting its occupant; he is sentenced to three years on a charge of assault and ten years for burglary, with the sentences to be served concurrently. After ten years in prison, the sentences would be completed.

In contrast, receiving a **consecutive sentence** means that on completion of the sentence for one crime the offender begins serving time for the second of multiple crimes. If the defendant in the previous example had been sentenced consecutively, he would serve three years on the assault charge and then ten years for the burglary. Therefore, the total term on the two charges would be thirteen years. Concurrent sentences are the norm; consecutive sentences are requested for the most serious criminals and for those who are unwilling to cooperate with authorities. Figure 11.2 shows the difference between a consecutive and concurrent sentence.

The Effect of Good Time

When judges impost an incarceration sentence, they know and take into account the fact that the amount of time spent in prison is reduced by the implementation of "time off for good behavior." This concept was first used in

concurrent sentences Prison sentences for two or more criminal acts, served simultaneously and run together.

consecutive sentences Prison sentences for two or more criminal acts, served one after the other.

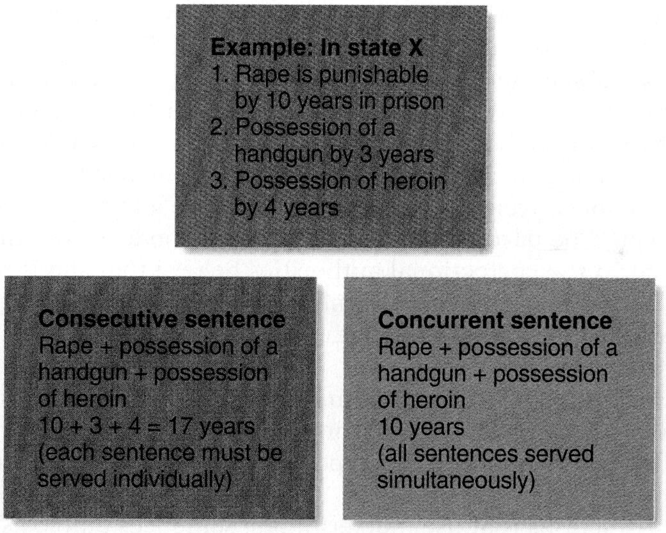

Example: In state X
1. Rape is punishable by 10 years in prison
2. Possession of a handgun by 3 years
3. Possession of heroin by 4 years

Consecutive sentence
Rape + possession of a handgun + possession of heroin
10 + 3 + 4 = 17 years
(each sentence must be served individually)

Concurrent sentence
Rape + possession of a handgun + possession of heroin
10 years
(all sentences served simultaneously)

Figure 11.2 Consecutive versus concurrent sentences

1817 in New York, and it was quickly adopted in most other jurisdictions. Good time is still in use today; inmates can accrue *standard good time* at a rate ranging from ten to fifteen days per month. In addition, some correctional authorities grant *earned sentence reductions* to inmates who participate in treatment programs, such as educational and vocational training, or who volunteer for experimental medical testing programs. In some jurisdictions more than half of a determinate sentence can be erased by accumulating both standard and earned good time.

Good-time laws allow inmates to calculate their release date at the time they enter prison by subtracting the expected good time from their sentence. However, good time can be lost if inmates break prison rules, get into fights, or disobey correctional officers. In some jurisdictions, former inmates can be returned to prison to serve the balance of their unexpired sentence when their good time is revoked for failing to conform to conditions set down for their release (for example, not reporting to a postrelease supervisor or abusing drugs).

SENTENCING MODELS

When a convicted offender is sentenced to prison, the statutes of the jurisdiction in which the crime was committed determine the penalties that may be imposed by the court. Over the years, a variety of sentencing structures have been used in the United States. They include indeterminate sentences, determinate sentences, and mandatory sentences.

Indeterminate Sentences

In the 1870s, prison reformers such as Enoch Wines and Zebulon Brockway, called for creation of **indeterminate sentences,** tailored to fit individual needs. Offenders, the argument went, should only be placed in confinement until they are rehabilitated and then released on parole. Criminals were believed to be "sick" rather than bad; they could be successfully treated in prison. Rather than holding that "the punishment should fit the crime," reformers believed "the treatment should fit the offender."

The indeterminate sentence is still the most widely used type of sentence in the United States. Convicted offenders are typically given a "light"

Criminal Justice Now™

Learn more by viewing the "Martha Sentence" "In the News" video clip.

indeterminate sentence A term of incarceration with a stated minimum and maximum length, such as a sentence to prison for a period of from three to ten years. The prisoner would be eligible for parole after the minimum sentence has been served. Based on the belief that sentences should fit the criminal, indeterminate sentences allow individualized sentences and provide for sentencing flexibility. Judges can set a high minimum to override the purpose of the indeterminate sentence.

minimum sentence that must be served and a lengthy maximum sentence that is the outer boundary of the time that can be served. For example, the legislature might set a sentence of a minimum of two years and a maximum of twenty years for burglary; the convicted offender must be sentenced to no less than two years but no more than twenty years in prison. Under this scheme, the actual length of time served by the offender is controlled by both the judge and the correctional agency. A judge could sentence a burglar to 5–15; the inmate then would be paroled from confinement soon after serving the minimum sentence if the correctional authorities believe that she is ready to live in the community. If the inmate accumulates good time, she could be released in as little as thirty months; a troublesome inmate would be forced to do all fifteen years.

The basic purpose of the indeterminate sentence is to individualize each sentence in the interests of rehabilitating the offender. This type of sentencing allows for flexibility not only in the type of sentence to be imposed but also in the length of time to be served.

Most jurisdictions that use indeterminate sentences employ statutes that specify minimum and maximum terms but allow judicial discretion to fix the actual sentence within those limits. The typical minimum sentence is at least one year; a few state jurisdictions require at least a two-year minimum sentence for felons.[21]

Determinate Sentences

Dissatisfaction with the disparity and uncertainty of indeterminate sentencing has prompted some states and the federal government to abandon it in favor of *determinate sentencing models* or *structured sentencing models* (discussed in the next section) which are aimed at curbing judicial discretion.

Determinate sentences offer a fixed term of years, the maximum set in law by the legislature, to be served by the offender sentenced to prison for a particular crime. For example, if the law provided for a sentence of up to twenty years for robbery, the judge might sentence a repeat offender to a fifteen-year term; another less-experienced felon might receive a more lenient sentence of five years.

In order to regulate the length of determinate sentences and curb judicial discretion, most jurisdictions that employ them have developed methods to structure and control the sentencing process and make it more rational. To accomplish this task, **sentencing guidelines** have been implemented by determinate sentencing states and the federal government. Guidelines give judges a recommended sentence based on the seriousness of a crime and the background of an offender: The more serious the crime and the more extensive the offender's criminal background, the longer the prison term recommended by the guidelines. For example, guidelines might recommend a sentence of five years for robbery if the offender had no prior offense record and did not use excessive force or violence. For a second offense, the recommended sentence would increase to seven years; those who used force and had a prior record will have three years added to their sentence, and so on. By eliminating judicial discretion, guidelines are designed to reduce racial and gender disparity.[22] Exhibit 11.1 lists some of the goals of sentencing guidelines.

How Are Guidelines Used? Today, about eighteen states use some form of structured sentencing. Until recently some states used *voluntary/advisory sentencing guidelines* (sometimes called descriptive guidelines), which merely suggest rather than mandate sentences, while others were *presumptive sentencing guidelines* (sometimes called prescriptive guidelines) which required judges to use the guidelines to shape their sentencing decisions[23]

| Exhibit | 11.1 | The goals of sentencing guidelines |

- Reduce judicial disparity in sentencing.
- Promote more uniform and consistent sentencing.
- Project the amount of correctional resources needed.
- Prioritize and allocate correctional resources.
- Increase punishments for certain categories of offenders and offenses.
- Decrease punishment for certain categories of offenders and offenses.
- Establish truth in sentencing.
- Make the sentencing process more open and understandable.
- Encourage the use of particular sanctions for particular categories of offenders.
- Encourage increased use of nonincarceration sanctions (intermediate and community-based).
- Reduce prison crowding.
- Provide a rational basis for sentencing.
- Increase judicial accountability.

Source: Robin Lubitz and Thomas Ross, *Sentencing Guidelines: Reflections on the Future* (Washington, D.C.: National Institute of Justice, June 2001).

However, two recent Supreme Court cases have put a moratorium on the use of presumptive guidelines and placed their future in doubt. First, in *Blakely v. Washington*, the Court found that Washington State's sentencing guidelines were a violation of a defendant's Sixth Amendment rights because they allow a judge to consider aggravating factors that would enhance the sentence.[24] The Court ruled that this amounts to a finding of fact without the benefit of a jury trial or personal admission. In *Blakely*, the sentencing judge, acting alone, decided that the offense involved "deliberate cruelty" and enhanced Blakely's sentence. Proving a state of mind such as "deliberate cruelty" must be determined by a jury "beyond a reasonable doubt" and not by a judge applying guidelines. Then in *United States v. Booker*, the Court ruled that the federal guidelines were unconstitutional, allowing that judges should consider the guideline ranges but must also be permitted the right to alter sentences in consideration of other factors; sentences could then be subject to appellate review if they were unreasonable.[25] Since these cases were decided, guidelines have been used in an advisory capacity alone.

Even before *Blakely* and *Booker* limited their use, presumptive guidelines had been criticized as being rigid, harsh, overly complex, and disliked by the judiciary.[26] They substantially increased correctional populations, especially when they were used in a haphazard fashion and not tied to the availability of correctional resources.[27]

There have been charges that guidelines are racially biased despite their stated goal of removing discrimination from the sentencing process. For example, the federal guidelines recommend that possession of crack cocaine be punished far more severely than possession of powdered cocaine. Critics charge that this amounts to racial bias because African Americans are much more likely to possess crack cocaine, whereas white offenders usually possess powdered cocaine.[28] Some jurisdictions give enhanced sentences if defendants have a prior juvenile conviction or if they were on juvenile probation or parole at the time of an arrest. African-American offenders are more likely than white offenders to have a prior record as a juvenile and therefore receive harsher sentences for their current crime.[29]

In the aftermath of *Blakely* and *Booker* the future of guidelines is hazy. It is possible that they will only be employed in an advisory fashion or that their use will be strictly curtailed, modified, or even discontinued.

Mandatory Sentences

Another effort to limit judicial discretion and at the same time get tough on crime has been the development of the **mandatory sentence.** Some states have passed legislation prohibiting people convicted of certain offenses, such as violent crimes or drug trafficking from being placed on probation; they must serve at least some time in prison. Other statutes are aimed at chronic recidivists. Mandatory sentencing legislation may impose minimum and maximum terms, but usually it requires a fixed prison sentence.

Mandatory sentencing generally limits the judge's discretionary power to impose any disposition but that authorized by the legislature; as a result, it limits individualized sentencing and restricts sentencing disparity. More than thirty-five states have already replaced discretionary sentencing with fixed-term mandatory sentences for such crimes as the sale of hard drugs, kidnapping, gun possession, and arson. The results have been mixed. Mandatory sentences have helped increase the size of the correctional population to record levels. Because of mandatory sentences, many offenders who in the past might have received probation are being incarcerated. They have also failed to eliminate racial disparity from the sentencing process.[30]

Three-Strikes Laws

Three-strikes (and-you're-out) laws provide lengthy terms for any person convicted of three felony offenses, even if the third crime is relatively trivial. California's three-strikes law is aimed at getting habitual criminals off the street. Anyone convicted of a third felony must do a minimum term of twenty-five years to life; the third felony does not have to be serious or violent. The Federal Crime Act of 1994 also adopted a three-strikes provision, requiring a mandatory life sentence for any offender convicted of three felony offenses; twenty-six states have so far followed suit and passed some form of the three-strikes law.

Although welcomed by conservatives looking for a remedy for violent crime, the three-strikes policy is controversial because a person convicted of a minor felony can receive a life sentence.

Three-strikes laws have undeniable political appeal to legislators being pressured by their constituents to "do something about crime." Yet even if possibly effective against crime, any effort to deter criminal behavior through tough laws is not without costs. Criminologist Marc Mauer, a leading opponent of the three-strikes law, finds that the approach may satisfy the public's hunger for retribution but makes little practical sense. First, many "three-time losers" are on the brink of aging out of crime; locking them up for life should have little effect on the crime rate. In addition, current sentences for chronic violent offenders are already severe, yet their punishment seems to have had little influence on reducing national violence rates. A three-strikes policy also suffers because criminals typically underestimate their risk of apprehension while overestimating the rewards of crime. Given their inflated view of the benefits of crime, coupled with a seeming disregard of the risks of apprehension and punishment, it is unlikely a three-strikes policy can have a measurable deterrent effect on the crime rate.

Even if such a policy could reduce the number of career offenders on the street, the drain in economic resources that might have gone for education and social welfare ensures that a new generation of young criminals will fill the offending shoes of their incarcerated brethren. Mauer also suggests that a three strikes policy will enlarge an already overburdened prison system, driving up costs, and, presumably, reducing resources available to house non-three-strikes inmates. Mauer warns too that African Americans face an increased risk of being sentenced under three-strikes statutes, expanding the racial disparity in sentencing. More ominous is the fact that police officers

mandatory sentence *A statutory requirement that a certain penalty shall be set and carried out in all cases on conviction for a specified offense or series of offenses.*

may be put at risk because two-time offenders would violently resist arrest, knowing that they face a life sentence.

Legal Controls Because of its use with petty offenders, there are ongoing legal challenges to the use of three-strikes laws, and their future is still uncertain. However, on March 6, 2003, the U.S. Supreme Court in *Lockyer v. Andrade* upheld the three-strike sentence of Leandro Andrade, a man sentenced to prison in California for fifty years for stealing $153 worth of videotapes. It also upheld the conviction of Gary Ewing, who appealed a prior twenty-five-year sentence for stealing a set of golf clubs (*Ewing v. California*, 2002). In both cases the Court ruled that the challenged sentences were not so grossly disproportionate as to violate the Eighth Amendment's prohibition against cruel and unusual punishment. In her majority decision, Justice Sandra Day O'Connor added that any criticism of the law "is appropriately directed at the legislature" and was not a judicial matter. Four judges dissented in the case arguing that the Court's test for sentence disproportionality had been met. Writing in the *Andrade* case, Justice Souter said, "If Andrade's sentence is not grossly disproportionate, the principle has no meaning."

Truth in Sentencing

Truth-in-sentencing laws, another get-tough measure designed to fight a rising crime rate, require offenders to serve a substantial portion of their prison sentence behind bars.[31] Parole eligibility and good-time credits are restricted or eliminated. The movement was encouraged by the Violent Offender Incarceration and Truth-in-Sentencing Incentive Grants Program, part of the federal government's 1994 crime act, which offered funds to support the state costs involved with creating longer sentences. To qualify for federal funds, states must require persons convicted of a violent felony crime to serve not less than 85 percent of the prison sentence. The provision is already having an effect: violent offenders released from prison in 1996 served slightly more than half of their prison sentence, or forty-five months. Under truth-in-sentencing laws, violent inmates entering prison today will serve an average of eighty-eight months behind bars. Today, more than half the states and the District of Columbia met the federal Truth-in-Sentencing Incentive Grants Program eligibility criteria and another thirteen have adopted some form of truth-in-sentencing program.

■ HOW PEOPLE ARE SENTENCED

The federal government conducts surveys on sentencing practices in state and federal courts.[32] In their most recent effort they found that more than one million adults are convicted of felonies in a single year (2002). What happens after convictions? About two-thirds (69 percent) of all felons convicted in state courts were sentenced to a period of confinement—41 percent to state prisons and 28 percent to local jails. The remaining third were sentenced to straight probation with no jail or prison time to serve. Felons sentenced to a state prison had an average sentence of four and a half years, but were likely to serve 51 percent of that sentence—or just two and a quarter years—before release. Besides being sentenced to incarceration or probation, 36 percent or more of convicted felons also were ordered to pay a fine, pay victim restitution, receive treatment, perform community service, or comply with some other additional penalty. A fine was imposed on at least 25 percent of convicted felons. As Table 11.1 shows, violent offenders who are given an incarceration sentence average about five years, while property offenders are typically sentenced to about two years.

Criminal Justice ⚖ Now™
Learn more by exploring the Sentencing Discrimination Review and Reinforce activity.

truth in sentencing A new sentencing scheme which requires that offenders serve at least 85 percent of their original sentence before being eligible for parole or other forms of early release.

Table 11.1	Average length of felony sentences imposed by state courts			
Average maximum sentence length (in months) for felons sentenced to incarceration				
Most serious conviction offense	**Total**	**Prison**	**Jail**	**Probation**
All offenses	36	53	7	38
Violent offenses	62	84	8	43
Property offenses	28	41	7	37
Drug offenses	32	48	6	36
Weapons offenses	28	38	7	35
Other offenses	23	38	6	37

© 2003 AP/Wide World Photos

Leandro Andrade was sentenced to fifty years in prison for stealing four videotapes from a Wal-Mart in 1995 under California's three-strikes-and-you're-out law. The Supreme Court ruled that his sentence was not excessive.

As Figure 11.3 shows, while the number of convicted offenders being sent to prison is slightly lower than in 1988, the incarceration rate has remained relatively stable for the past fifteen years.

What Factors Affect Sentencing?

What factors influence judges when they decide on criminal sentences? As already mentioned, crime seriousness and the offender's prior record are certainly considered. State sentencing codes usually include various factors that can legitimately influence the length of prison sentences, including the following:

- The severity of the offense
- The offender's prior criminal record
- Whether the offender used violence
- Whether the offender used weapons
- Whether the crime was committed for money

Research does in fact show a strong correlation between these legal variables and the type and length of sentence received. Judges seem less willing to use discretion in cases involving the most serious criminal charges such as terrorism, while employing greater control in low-severity cases.[33]

Besides these legally appropriate factors, sentencing experts suspect that judges may also be influenced by the defendant's age, race, gender, and income. Considerations of such variables would be a direct violation of constitutional due process and equal protection, as well as of federal statutes, such as the Civil Rights Act. Limiting judicial bias is one of the reasons why states have adopted determinate and mandatory sentencing statutes. Do extralegal factors actually influence judges when they make sentencing decisions?

Social Class Evidence supports an association between social class and sentencing outcomes: members of the lower class may expect to get longer prison sentences than more affluent defendants. One reason is that poor defendants may be unable to obtain quality legal representation or to make

Percent

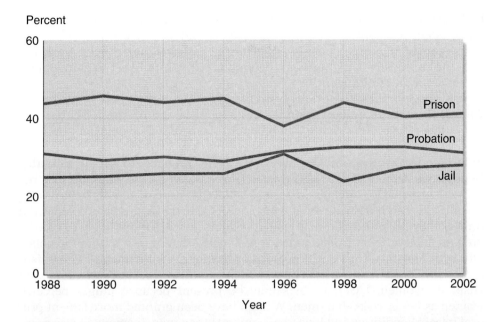

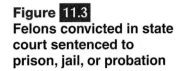

© 2005 AP/Wide World Photos

The circumstances of the case often influence sentencing discretion. Former America West pilots Thomas Cloyd, second from left, and Christopher Hughes, second from right, stand with their attorneys as the verdict is read June 8, 2005, convicting them of operating an aircraft while drunk in the cockpit after an all-night drinking binge. A Florida judge sentenced Cloyd to five years in prison and co-pilot Hughes to two and a half years. At their sentencing, Judge David Young told Cloyd, citing his prior clashes with the law involving alcohol, "Frankly, sir, I have no sympathy and sentence you to five years in prison." Young sentenced Hughes to less time because he had no prior criminal record, telling him, "You're very lucky that one day you will go home to your children. If you don't stop drinking, you won't be allowed to see them, because you will die." Should both pilots be given the same sentence or should their background and past behavior influence the sentence?

bail, factors that influence sentencing.[34] Not all research efforts have found a consistent relationship between social class and sentence length. The relationship may be more robust for some crime patterns than others. Nonetheless, the consensus is that affluent defendants are more likely to gain lenient sentences than the indigent.[35]

Gender Does a defendant's gender influence how he or she is sentenced? Some theorists believe that women benefit from sentence disparity because the criminal justice system is dominated by men who have a paternalistic or protective attitude toward women; this is referred to as the **chivalry hypothesis.** Others argue that female criminals can be the victim of bias because their behavior violates what men believe is "proper" female behavior.[36]

Most research indicates that women receive more favorable outcomes the further they go in the criminal justice system: they are more likely to receive preferential treatment from a judge at sentencing than they are from the police officer making the arrest or the prosecutor seeking the indictment.[37] Favoritism crosses both racial and ethnic lines, benefiting African American, white, and Hispanic women.[38] Gender bias may be present because judges perceive women as better risks than men. Women have been granted more lenient pretrial release conditions and lower bail amounts than men; women are also more likely to spend less time in pretrial detention.[39] Ironically, mandatory and structured sentences, designed originally to limit bias and discretion, have resulted in harsher sentences for women. Because they are "gender neutral" they reverse any advantage women may have had in sentencing decisions. Some women who are peripherally involved in drug trafficking through association with boyfriends and husbands have received very long sentences.[40]

Age Another extralegal factor that may play a role in sentencing is age. Judges may be more lenient with elderly defendants and more punitive toward younger ones.[41] Although sentencing leniency may be a result of judges' perception that the elderly pose little risk to society, such practices are a violation of the civil rights of younger defendants.[42] On the other hand, judges may also wish to protect the youngest defendants, sparing them the pains of a prison experience.[43]

Victim Characteristics Victim characteristics may also influence sentencing. Victims may be asked or allowed to make a **victim impact statement** before the sentencing judge giving them the opportunity to tell of their experiences and describe their ordeal. In a murder case, the surviving family can recount the effect the crime has had on their lives and well being.[44] The effect of victim and witness statements on sentencing has been the topic of some debate. Some research finds that victim statements result in a higher rate of incarceration, but other efforts find that the effects of victim and witness statements are insignificant.[45]

A victim's personal characteristics may influence sentencing. Sentences may be reduced when victims have "negative" personal characteristics or qualities. For example, people convicted of raping prostitutes or substance abusers receive much shorter sentences than those who assault women without these negative characteristics.[46]

chivalry hypothesis *The view that the low female crime and delinquency rates are a reflection of the leniency with which police treat female offenders.*

victim impact statement *A post-conviction statement by the victim of crime that may be used to guide sentencing decisions.*

Race No issue concerning personal factors in sentencing is more important than the suspicion that race influences sentencing outcomes. Racial disparity in sentencing has been suspected because a disproportionate number of African-American inmates are in state prisons and on death row. Minorities seem to receive longer sentences than Caucasians, especially those that are indigent or unemployed.[47] Young black men are more likely to be imprisoned for drug offenses, a practice (says sentencing expert Michael Tonry) that places the entire cohort of young African-American males in jeopardy.[48] Because this issue is so important, it is the focus of the following Race, Culture, and Gender in Criminal Justice feature.

■ CAPITAL PUNISHMENT

The most severe sentence used in the United States is capital punishment, or execution. More than 14,500 confirmed executions have been carried out in America under civil authority, starting with the execution of Captain George Kendall in 1608. Most of these executions have been for murder and rape. However, federal, state, and military laws have conferred the death penalty for other crimes, including robbery, kidnapping, treason (offenses against the federal government), espionage, and desertion from military service.

In recent years, the U.S. Supreme Court has limited the death penalty to first-degree murder and only then when aggravating circumstances, such as murder for profit or murder using extreme cruelty, are present.[49] The federal government still has provisions for granting the death penalty for espionage by a member of the armed forces, treason, and killing during a criminal conspiracy, such as drug trafficking. Some states have laws assessing capital punishment for such crimes as aircraft piracy, ransom kidnapping, and the aggravated rape of a child, but it remains to be seen whether the courts will allow criminals to be executed today for any crime less than aggravated first-degree murder.

Today, the death penalty for murder is used in thirty-seven states and by the federal government. Of the thirty-five hundred people under sentence of death, slightly more than half are white, about 40 percent African American and the remainder other races; more than forty women are on death row. As Figure 11.4 on page 312 shows, in 2004, fifty-nine inmates were executed, six fewer than in 2003.

Lethal injection is the predominant method of death, though a number of states maintain the gas chamber and the electric chair. Although the death penalty is generally approved of in the United States, it fares less well abroad; see the Race, Culture, and Gender in Criminal Justice feature on page 313.

Despite its continued use and public acceptance, there seems to be growing unease with the administration of the death penalty, and the recent use of scientific evidence based on DNA has resulted in numerous exonerations of death row inmates. On January 11, 2003, Illinois Governor George Ryan announced a decision to commute all Illinois death sentences—a gesture that spared the lives of 163 men and 4 women who have served a collective two thousand years for the murders of more than 250 people. In the case of *People v. Stephen LaValle* (2004), a New York appellate court declared the state's capital punishment law unconstitutional, placing a moratorium on its use for the near term.[50] As Figure 11.5 on page 312 shows, this growing uneasiness has had an effect on the use of capital punishment. The number of inmates on death row has peaked and now is declining.

No issue in the criminal justice system is more controversial or emotional than the implementation of the death penalty. Opponents and proponents have formulated a number of powerful arguments in support of their positions; these arguments are reviewed in the following sections.

Arguments for the Death Penalty

The death penalty has long been one of the most controversial aspects of the justice system, and it likely will continue to be a source of significant debate.[51] What are the views supporting and rejecting the death penalty?

Criminal Justice ⚖ Now™

*Learn more about **Careers in Criminal Justice** by exploring the "On the job" feature "Judge."*

Race, Culture, and Gender in Criminal Justice

Race and Sentencing

Racial bias in sentencing has long been suspected. A number of studies find that minorities receive significantly longer sentences than Caucasians. For example, when Shawn Bushway and Anne Morrison Piehl studied sentencing outcomes in Maryland, they found that on average African Americans have 20 percent longer sentences than whites, even when holding constant age, gender, and recommended sentence length. Tracy Nobiling, Cassia Spohn, and Miriam DeLone also found that racial status influences sentencing partially because minority group members have a lower income than Caucasians and are more likely to be unemployed. Some judges may view young, minority males as "social dynamite," considering them more dangerous and likely to recidivate than white offenders.

Patterns of Racial Disparity
What causes racial disparity in sentencing? Minority defendants suffer discrimination in a variety of court actions that influence case outcome: they are more likely to be detained before trial than whites and, upon conviction, are more likely to receive jail sentences rather than fines. Prosecutors are less likely to divert minorities from the legal system than whites who commit the same crimes; minorities are less likely to win appeals than white appellants.

Race may impact on sentencing because some race-specific crimes are punished more harshly than others. African-Americans receive longer sentences for drug crimes than Anglos because (1) they are more likely to be arrested for crack possession and sales and (2) crack dealing is more severely punished by state and federal laws than other drug crimes.

Because Caucasians are more likely to use marijuana and methamphetamines, prosecutors are more willing to plea bargain and offer shorter jail terms.

Racial bias in sentencing has also been linked to the victim/offender status. Judges may base sentencing decisions on the race of the victim and not the race of the defendant. For example, Charles Crawford, Ted Chiricos, and Gary Kleck found that African-American defendants are more likely to be prosecuted under habitual offender statutes if they commit crimes where there is a greater likelihood of a white victim, as with larceny and burglary, than if they commit violent crimes that are largely intra-racial. Where there is a perceived "racial threat," punishments are enhanced.

System Effects
Sentencing disparity may also reflect race-based differences in criminal justice practices and policies associated with sentencing outcome. Probation presentence reports may favor white over minority defendants, causing judges to award whites probation more often than minorities.

Defendants who can afford bail receive more lenient sentences than those who remain in pretrial detention; minority defendants are less likely to make bail because they suffer a higher degree of income inequality. That is, minorities earn less on average and therefore are less likely to be able to make bail.

Sentencing outcome is also affected by the defendant's ability to afford a private attorney and put on a vigorous legal defense that makes use of high-paid expert witnesses. These factors place the poor and

Incapacitation Supporters argue that death is the "ultimate incapacitation" and the only one that can ensure that convicted killers can never be pardoned, be paroled, or escape. Most states that do not have capital punishment provide the sentence of "life in prison without the chance of parole." However, forty-eight states grant their chief executive the right to grant clemency and commute a life sentence and may give "lifers" eligibility for various furlough and release programs.

Death penalty advocates believe that the potential for recidivism is a serious enough threat to require that murderers be denied further access to the public.[52] More than 250 inmates on death row today had prior homicide convictions; if they had been executed for their first offense, 250 innocent people would still be alive.[53]

minority-group members at a disadvantage in the sentencing process and result in sentencing disparity. And while considerations of prior record may be legitimate in forming sentencing decisions, there is evidence that minorities are more likely to have prior records because of organizational and individual bias on the part of police.

Are Sentencing Practices Changing?

If in fact racial discrepancies exist, new sentencing laws featuring determinate and mandatory sentences may be helping to reduce disparity. Jon'a Meyer and Tara Gray found that jurisdictions in California that use mandatory sentences for crimes such as drunk driving also show little racial disparity in sentencing outcomes. Similarly, a national survey of sentencing practices conducted by the Bureau of Justice Statistics found that while white defendants are somewhat more likely to receive probation and other non-incarceration sentences than black defendants (34 percent versus 31 percent), there was little racial disparity in the length of prison sentences.

While these results are encouraging it is also possible that some studies miss a racial effect because they combine Anglo and Hispanic cases into a single category of "white" defendants and then compare them with the sentencing of black defendants. Darrell Steffensmeier and Stephen Demuth's analysis of sentencing in Pennsylvania found that Hispanics are punished considerably more severely than non-Hispanic Caucasians and that combining the two groups masks the ethnic differences in sentencing.

Critical Thinking

1. If race does influence sentencing, can anything be done to reduce its impact?

2. Should a person's race, personal experiences, and background be taken into account when a sentence is pronounced? When a young man is being sentenced on a burglary charge, should the sentencing judge consider the fact that he has had a difficult childhood, lives in a racially segregated neighborhood, and attends substandard schools?

InfoTrac College Edition Research

Use the terms *race* and *sentencing* as key terms on InfoTrac College Edition to find out more about the relationship between these two factors.

Sources: Shawn Bushway and Anne Morrison Piehl, "Judging Judicial Discretion: Legal Factors and Racial Discrimination in Sentencing," *Law & Society Review* 35 (2001): 733–765; Barbara Koons-Witt, "The Effect of Gender on the Decision to Incarcerate Before and After the Introduction of Sentencing Guidelines," *Criminology* 40 (2002): 97–129; Marian R. Williams and Jefferson E. Holcomb, "Racial Disparity and Death Sentences in Ohio" *Journal of Criminal Justice* 29 (2001): 207–218; Rodney Engen and Randy Gainey, "Modeling the Effects of Legally Relevant and Extra-legal Factors Under Sentencing Guidelines: The Rules Have Changed," *Criminology* 38 (2000): 1207–1230; Darrell Steffensmeier and Stephen Demuth, "Ethnicity and Judges' Sentencing Decisions: Hispanic-Black-White Comparisons," *Criminology* 39 (2001): 145–178; Tracy Nobiling, Cassia Spohn, and Miriam DeLone, "A Tale of Two Counties: Unemployment and Sentence Severity," *Justice Quarterly* 15 (1998): 459–486; Travis Pratt, "Race and Sentencing: A Meta-Analysis of Conflicting Empirical Research Results," *Journal of Criminal Justice* 26 (1998): 513–525; Charles Crawford, Ted Chiricos, and Gary Kleck, "Race, Racial Threat, and Sentencing of Habitual Offenders," *Criminology* 36 (1998): 481–511; Jon'a Meyer and Tara Gray, "Drunk Drivers in the Courts: Legal and Extra-Legal Factors Affecting Pleas and Sentences," *Journal of Criminal Justice* 25 (1997): 155–163; Alexander Alvarez and Ronet Bachman, "American Indians and Sentencing Disparity: An Arizona Test," *Journal of Criminal Justice* 24 (1996): 549–561; Carole Wolff Barnes and Rodney Kingsnorth "Race, Drug, and Criminal Sentencing: Hidden Effects of the Criminal Law," *Journal of Criminal Justice* 24 (1996): 39–55; Samuel Walker, Cassia Spohn, and Miriam DeLone, *The Color of Justice, Race, Ethnicity and Crime in America* (Belmont, Calif.: Wadsworth, 1996), 145–146.

Deterrence Proponents of capital punishment argue that executions serve as a strong deterrent for serious crimes. Although capital punishment would probably not deter the few mentally unstable criminals, it could have an effect on the cold, calculating murderer, such as the hired killer or someone who kills for profit. The fear of death may also convince felons not to risk using handguns during armed robberies.

Proponents argue that the deterrent effect of an execution can produce a substantial decline in the murder rate.[54] They argue, for example, that homicide rates *increased* dramatically in the 1960s and 1970s when executions were halted by the courts and death penalty laws were subsequently abolished. It is not a coincidence that murder rates have dropped since the death penalty was reinstated; murder rates would actually be much higher if capital punishment

Figure 11.4
Executions, 1930–2004

Source: Bureau of Justice Statistics, *Capital Punishment, 2003,* www.ojp.usdoj.gov/bjs/glance/exe.htm, accessed on September 26, 2005.

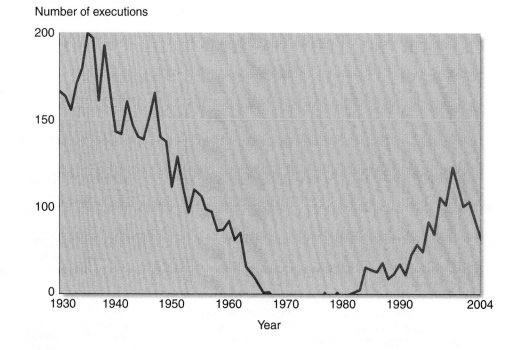

Number of executions

Year

was not being used.[55] The death penalty scares would-be criminals and, not surprisingly, homicide rates drop after a well-publicized execution.[56]

Morally Correct This argument contends that the death penalty is morally correct: it is mentioned in the Bible and other religious works. Although the U.S. Constitution forbids "cruel and unusual punishments," this prohibition does not include the death penalty since capital punishment was widely used at the time the Constitution was drafted. The "original intent" of the founding fathers was to allow the states to use the death penalty; capital punishment may be cruel, but it is not unusual.

The death penalty is morally correct because it provides the greatest justice for the victim and helps alleviate the psychic pain of the victim's family and friends. The death penalty makes a moral statement: There is behavior that is so unacceptable to a community of human beings that one who engages in such behavior forfeits his right to live.[57]

Figure 11.5
Prisoners on death row, 1953–2003

Source: Bureau of Justice Statistics, *Capital Punishment, 2003,* www.ojp.usdoj.gov/bjs/glance/dr.htm, accessed on September 26, 2005.

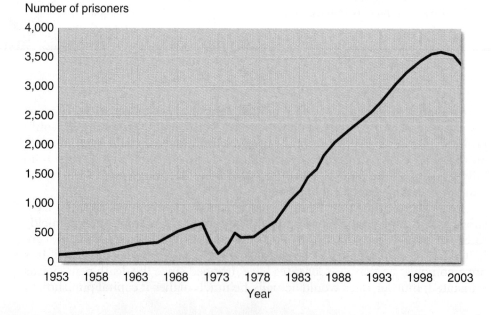

Number of prisoners

Year

Race, Culture, and Gender in Criminal Justice

The Death Penalty Abroad

The United States is not alone in using the death penalty, though the trend has been to abolish its usage. According to the latest data from watchdog group Amnesty International:

- 85 countries and territories have abolished the death penalty for all crimes.
- 11 countries have abolished the death penalty for all but exceptional crimes, such as wartime crimes.
- 24 countries can be considered abolitionist in practice: they retain the death penalty in law but have not carried out any executions for the past ten years or more and are believed to have a policy or established practice of not carrying out executions.
- This makes a total of 120 countries that have abolished the death penalty in law or practice.
- 76 other countries and territories retain and use the death penalty, but the number of countries that actually execute prisoners in any one year is much smaller.

According to Amnesty International, almost 4,000 people were executed in 25 countries in 2004, and about 7,000 people were sentenced to death in 64 countries. In 2004, 97 percent of all known executions took place in China, Iran, Vietnam, and the U.S. China executed at least 3,400 people, but the actual number may be as a high as 10,000. Iran executed at least 159 people, and Vietnam at least 64. In addition to violent crimes, executions were carried out for crimes such as stealing gasoline, bribery, pimping, embezzlement, tax fraud, drug offenses, and selling harmful foodstuffs.

While opposition to executions is growing in many areas, there are some nations in which the public still demands the use of the death penalty. The governments of Jamaica, Guyana, and Barbados have all expressed interest in speeding the use of the death penalty, and more than 250 prisoners are currently on death row across the English-speaking Caribbean. Japan, a nation that prides itself on nonviolence, routinely uses the death penalty.

Executions of Juveniles

International human rights treaties prohibit anyone under 18 years old at the time of the crime being sentenced to death. The International Covenant on Civil and Political Rights, the American Convention on Human Rights, and the UN Convention on the Rights of the Child all have provisions to this effect. More than one hundred countries have laws specifically excluding the execution of juvenile offenders or may be presumed to exclude such executions by being parties to one or another of the above treaties. A small number of countries, however, continue to execute juvenile offenders. Seven countries since 1990 are known to have executed prisoners who were under 18 years old at the time of the crime: Iran, Nigeria, Pakistan, Congo, Saudi Arabia, the U.S., and Yemen. Since 1994 there have been twenty executions of juvenile offenders, including thirteen in the United States (before the practice was prohibited).

Critical Thinking

1. The movement toward abolition in the United States is encouraged by the fact that so many nations have abandoned the death penalty. Should we model our own system of punishments after other nations or is our crime problem so unique that it requires the use of capital punishment?
2. Do you believe that someone who joins a terrorist group and trains to kill Americans deserves the death penalty even if they have never actually killed anyone?

InfoTrac College Edition Research

Are there really innocent people on death row? To find out, read Peter Vilbig, "Innocent on Death Row," *New York Times Upfront*, September 18, 2000, 10.

The death penalty remains a controversial issue around the world. To learn more, read Stefanie Grant, "A Dialogue of the Deaf? New International Attitudes and the Death Penalty in America," *Criminal Justice Ethics 17* (1998): 19.

Sources: Amnesty International's most recent data on the death penalty can be read at http://web.amnesty.org/pages/deathpenalty-index-eng, accessed on July 29, 2005; "Nigeria: Stoning Sentence Stands," *New York Times*, September 10, 2002, Late Edition, A6; Death Penalty News, "Saudi Arabia Executes Man for Sorcery," Amnesty International, March 2000; "USA Set to Break a Global Consensus—Execution of Child Offender Due," Amnesty International News Release, October 22, 2001; "China 'Striking Harder' than Ever Before," Amnesty International News Release, June 7, 2001; Associated Press, "Saudi Brothers Beheaded for Raping," *New York Times*, July 20, 2001, 3; Larry Rohter, "In Caribbean, Support Growing for Death Penalty," *New York Times*, October 4, 1998; Associated Press, "Chechen Pair Executed in Public," *Boston Globe*, September 19, 1997, 9; Reuters, "Saudi Beheadings over 100 for 1997," *Boston Globe*, September 28, 1997, A29.

Proportional to the Crime Putting dangerous criminals to death also conforms to the requirement that the punishment must be proportional to the seriousness of the crime. Since we use a system of escalating punishments, it follows that the most serious punishment should be used to sanction the most serious crime. Before the brutality of the death penalty is considered, the cruelty with which the victim was treated should not be forgotten.

Reflects Public Opinion The death penalty is justified because it represents the will of the people. A majority of the general public believes that criminals who kill innocent victims should forfeit their own lives. Public opinion polls show that Americans favor the use of the death penalty by a wide majority.[58] Public approval rests on the belief that the death penalty is an important instrument of social control, can deter crime, and is less costly than maintaining a murderer in prison for life.[59] Research by Alexis Durham and his associates found that almost everyone (95 percent) would give criminals the death penalty under some circumstances, and the most heinous crimes are those for which the public is most likely to approve capital punishment.[60]

Unlikely Chance of Error The many legal controls and appeals currently in use make it almost impossible for an innocent person to be executed or for the death penalty to be used in a racist or capricious manner. Although some unfortunate mistakes may have been made in the past, the current system makes it virtually impossible to execute an innocent person. Federal courts closely scrutinize all death penalty cases and rule for the defendant in an estimated 60 to 70 percent of the appeals. Such judicial care should ensure that only those who are both truly guilty and deserving of death are executed.

In sum, those who favor the death penalty find it to be traditional punishment for serious crimes and one that can help prevent criminality; in keeping with the traditional moral values of fairness and equity; and highly favored by the public.

Arguments Against the Death Penalty

Arguments for the death penalty are matched by those that support its abolition.

Possibility of Error Critics of the death penalty believe capital punishment has no place in a mature democratic society.[61] They point to the finality of the act and the real possibility that innocent persons can be executed. Examples of people wrongfully convicted of murder abound. According to classic research by Michael Radelet and Hugo Bedeau, there have been about 350 wrongful murder convictions this century, of which 23 led to executions. They estimate that about three death sentences are returned every two years in cases where the defendant has been falsely accused. More than half the errors stem from perjured testimony, false identifications, coerced confessions, and suppression of evidence. In addition to the 23 who were executed, 128 of the falsely convicted served more than six years in prison, 39 served more than sixteen years in confinement, and 8 died while serving their sentence.[62]

A congressional report cited forty-eight cases in the past two decades in which people who served time on death row were released because of new evidence proving their innocence; one Maryland man served nine years on death row before DNA testing proved that he could not have committed the crime.[63] These findings show that even with the best intentions there is grave risk that an innocent person can be executed.[64]

Because of the chances of error, a number of states have placed a moratorium on executions until the issue of errors in the process can be adequately addressed.[65] Because these errors may occur, some commentators have

Those who oppose the death penalty argue that it is possible that mistakes can be made and innocent people executed. Juan Melendez, left, spent eighteen years on death row before being exonerated. DNA testing and other modern technologies have been used to overturn the convictions of many death row inmates. Considering the chance of error, would you advocate a moratorium being placed on executions until more precise guidelines for its use are formulated?

called for a new evidentiary standard of "absolute certainty" to replace "beyond a reasonable doubt" in death penalty cases (others argue that standard would end guilty verdicts because at least one juror would always have some uncertainty).[66]

Unfair Use of Discretion Critics also frown on the tremendous discretion used in seeking the death penalty and the arbitrary manner in which it is imposed. Of the approximately 10,000 persons convicted each year on homicide charges, only 250 to 300 are sentenced to death, while an equal number receive a sentence of probation or community supervision only. It is true that many convicted murderers do not commit first-degree murder and therefore are ineligible for execution, but it is also likely that many serious criminals who could have received the death penalty are not sentenced to death because of prosecutorial discretion. Some escape death by cooperating or giving testimony against their partners in the crime. A person who commits a particularly heinous crime and knows full well that he will receive the death penalty if convicted may be the one most likely to plea bargain to avoid capital punishment. Is it fair to spare the life of a dangerous killer who cooperates with the prosecutor while executing another who does not?

Abolitionists also argue that juries use inappropriate discretion when they make capital punishment recommendations. The ongoing Capital Jury Project has been interviewing members of juries involved in making death penalty decisions and finds that many are motivated by ignorance and error (see Exhibit 11.2).

Exhibit	11.2	The Capital Jury Project (CJP)

The Capital Jury Project (CJP), begun by sociologist William Bowers in 1990, has sent research teams to fifteen states to interview jurors in death penalty cases. The three-hour-plus interviews are taped and coded for analysis.

CJP findings show that the decision-making in capital cases often strays from legal and moral guidelines. Some express overwhelming racial prejudice in making their decisions. Others say that they have decided on the punishment before the trial is completed and the defendant found guilty!

Others are confused about the law and influenced by factual misconceptions. For example, many believe that prison terms are far shorter than they really are and many underestimate the time served for murder by ten years or more. Many jurors mistakenly believe that the death penalty is mandatory in cases when it is not, while others reject capital punishment in situations in which the law clearly mandates its use. The greater the factual errors, the more likely the juror will vote for death.

Many capital jurors are unwilling to accept primary responsibility for their punishment decisions. They vote for the death penalty in the mistaken belief that most defendants will never be executed, absolving them of responsibility. They often place responsibility for the defendant's punishment elsewhere, such as with the judge or other jurors. For example, one female juror who had recommended death told CJP interviewers that she had voted only to go along with the other jurors and that she had never believed the man should be executed. "I really had no thought about it," she said. "It wasn't my choice to make. It was a judgment call. It really doesn't mean a whole lot what I say because it's ultimately up to the judge." These feelings were most often expressed in states where the law allows judges to override a jury's decisions and either impose or reject a capital sentence.

The CJP findings indicate that jurors often rely on faulty information and use extralegal criteria in making a decision that is truly "life or death."

Sources: William J. Bowers, "The Capital Jury Project: Rationale, Design, and Preview of Early Findings," *Indiana Law Journal 70* (1995): 1043–1102; William J. Bowers, Marla Sandys, and Benjamin Steiner, "Foreclosed Impartiality in Capital Sentencing: Jurors' Predispositions, Trial Experience, and Premature Decision Making," *Cornell Law Review 83* (1998): 1476–1556; Margaret Vandiver, "Race in the Jury Room: A Preliminary Analysis of Cases from the Capital Jury Project," unpublished paper presented to the American Academy of Criminal Justice Sciences, March 1997.

Those who abhor the use of discretion in capital cases also point to instances where offenders who killed in the spur of the moment are executed while truly vicious criminals who grievously injure victims during murder attempts are spared the death penalty. Some particularly heinous crimes are not punished with death simply because a physician's skill saved the victim. Some notable cases come to mind. Lawrence Singleton used an axe to cut off the arms of a woman he raped, yet he served only eight years in prison because the victim's life was saved by prompt medical care (after being released from prison, Singleton killed a female companion in 1997). "David," a boy severely burned in a murder attempt, lives in fear because his assailant—his father, Charles Rothenberg—was paroled from prison after serving a short sentence.[67] Although these horrific crimes received national attention and the intent to kill the victim was present, the death penalty could not be applied because of the availability of effective medical treatment. Areas that have superior medical resources actually have lower murder rates than less well-equipped areas; for example, ambulance response time can reduce the death rate by expeditiously transporting victims to an appropriate treatment center.[68] It makes little sense to punish someone for an impulsive murder while sparing the life of those who intentionally maim and torture victims who happen by chance to live because of prompt medical care.

Misplaced Vengeance   Although critics acknowledge that the general public approves of the death penalty, they maintain that prevailing attitudes reflect a primitive desire for revenge and not "just desert." Public acceptance of capital punishment has been compared to the approval of human sacrifices practiced by the Aztecs in Mexico five hundred years ago.[69] It is ironic that many death penalty advocates also oppose abortion on the grounds that it is the taking of human life.[70] The desire to be vengeful and punitive outweighs their concern about taking life.

At least thirty states now have a sentence of life in prison without parole, and this can more than make up for an execution. Being locked up in a hellish prison without any chance of release (barring a rare executive reprieve) may be a worse punishment than a painless death by lethal injection. If vengeance is the goal, life without parole may eliminate the need for capital punishment.

Weak Public Support Though death penalty backers claim that a majority of the public supports the death penalty, approval ratings have been in decline for the past decade; public support has declined from the 80 percent level in 1995 to less than 66 percent a decade later.[71] When surveys give respondents a choice of punishments, such as life without parole, support for the death penalty declines to the 50 percent level.[72] Well-publicized incidents of innocent people being sentenced to death has helped erode support for capital punishment.[73] So while a majority of the public still supports the death penalty in principle, a substantial proportion lack confidence in its use and believe that executions should be halted until the system can be made foolproof.[74]

Public opinion for the death penalty is not solid and may be influenced by such factors as the personal characteristics of the offender and the circumstances of the offense.[75] People who generally support the death penalty may not want to see it used with juveniles, the mentally challenged, or the mentally ill.[76] It is possible that politicians favor the death penalty in the mistaken belief that the public favors such harsh punishment for criminal offenders.[77]

Little Deterrent Effect Those opposed to the death penalty also find little merit in the argument that capital punishment deters crime. They charge that there is little hard evidence that the threat of a death sentence can convince potential murderers to forgo their criminal activity. Most murders involve people who knew each other, very often friends and family members. Since murderers are often under the influence of alcohol or drugs or are suffering severe psychological turmoil, no penalty will likely be a deterrent. Most research concludes that the death penalty is not an effective deterrent.[78] Homicides rates in counties that routinely employ the death penalty are no higher than rates in counties which rarely if ever use capital punishment. There is little empirical evidence that the threat or the reality of the death penalty can reduce murder rates.[80]

No Hope of Rehabilitation The death sentence rules out any hope of offender rehabilitation. There is evidence that convicted killers often make good parole risks; convicted murderers are often model inmates, and once released, commit fewer crimes than other parolees. It is possible that the general public, including people who sit on juries, overestimate the dangerousness of people who commit murder. In reality, those people given a life sentence for capital murder have a *less than 1 percent* (0.2 percent) chance of committing another homicide over a forty-year term; the risk of their committing an assault is about 16 percent.[81]

Race, Gender, and Other Bias Capital punishment may be tarnished by gender, racial, and ethnic and other biases. More people are sentenced to death and the death penalty is used more often in nations when there is a large minority population; this is referred to as the *minority group-threat hypothesis* (in other words, use of extreme punishment is related to the regulation of groups that are racially, culturally, or ethnically different).[82]

- There is evidence that homicides with male offenders and female victims are more likely to result in a death sentence than homicides involving female offenders and male victims.[83]

- Homicides involving strangers are more likely to result in a death sentence than homicides involving nonstrangers or acquaintances.

- Prosecutors are more likely to recommend the death sentence for people who kill white victims than they are in any other racial combination of victim and criminal—e.g., whites who kill blacks.[84] Killing a white female is more likely to result in the death penalty than any other combination of race/gender.[85]

It is not surprising considering these patterns that since the death penalty was first instituted in the United States, disproportionate numbers of minorities have been executed. Charges of racial bias are supported by the disproportionate numbers of African Americans who have received the death sentence, are currently on death row, and who have been executed (53.5 percent of all executions). Racism was particularly blatant when the death penalty was invoked in rape cases: of those receiving the death penalty for rape, 90 percent in the South and 63 percent in the North and West were African American.[86] Today, about 40 percent of the inmates on death row are African American, a number disproportionate to the minority representation in the population. When a black criminal kills a white victim (14 percent) the likelihood of the death penalty being invoked is far greater than when a white kills a black victim.[87] In contrast, since 1976 only two white criminals have been executed for murdering a black victim, the most recent being Kermit Smith, who was executed on January 24, 1995, in North Carolina for the kidnap, rape, and murder of a twenty-year-old college cheerleader.[88]

Causes More Crime Than It Deters Some critics fear that the introduction of capital punishment will encourage criminals to escalate their violent behavior, consequently putting police officers at risk. A suspect who kills someone during a botched robbery may be inclined to "fire away" upon encountering police rather than surrender peacefully; the killer faces the death penalty already, what does he have to lose? Geoffrey Rapp studied the effect of capital punishment on the killings of police and found that, all other things being equal, the greater the number of new inmates on death row, the greater the number of police officers killed by citizens.[89] Rapp concluded that what the death penalty seems to do is create an extremely dangerous environment for law enforcement officers because it does not deter criminals and may lull officers into a false sense of security, because officers believe that the death penalty will deter violence directed against them and will cause them to let their guard down.

It Is Brutal Abolitionists believe that executions are unnecessarily cruel and inhuman and come at a high moral and social cost. Our society does not punish criminals by subjecting them to the same acts they themselves committed. Rapists are not sexually assaulted, and arsonists do not have their houses burned down; why, then, should murderers be killed?

Robert Johnson has described the execution process as a form of torture in which the condemned are first tormented psychologically by being made to feel powerless and alone while on death row; suicide is a constant problem among those on death row.[90] The execution itself is a barbaric affair marked by the smell of burning flesh and stiffened bodies. The executioners suffer from delayed stress reactions, including anxiety and a dehumanized personal identity.

The brutality of the death penalty may actually produce more violence than it prevents—the so-called **brutalization effect**.[91] Executions may increase murder rates because they raise the general violence level in society and because violence-prone people actually identify with the executioner, not with the target of the death penalty. When someone gets in a conflict with such violence-prone individuals or challenges their authority, these indi-

brutalization effect The belief that capital punishment creates an atmosphere of brutality that enhances, rather than deters, the level of violence in society. The death penalty reinforces the view that violence is an appropriate response to provocation.

viduals may execute them in the same manner the state executes people who violate its rules.[92] There is evidence that the brutalization effect does influence murder rates: stranger homicides increase after an execution.[93] People may be more inclined to settle conflicts with violence after a state executes a criminal—"If they can do it, why can't I?"[94]

Because of its brutality, many enlightened countries, including Denmark and Sweden, have long since abandoned the death penalty, and 40 percent of the countries with a death penalty have active abolitionist movements.[95] It is ironic that citizens of countries that have eliminated the death penalty sometimes find themselves on death row in the United States.

It Is Expensive Some people complain that they do not want to support "some killer in prison for thirty years." Abolitionists counter that legal appeals drive the cost of executions far higher than the cost of years of incarceration. If the money spent on the judicial process were invested, the interest would more than pay for the lifetime upkeep of death row inmates. Because of numerous appeals, the median time between conviction by a jury, sentencing by a judge, and execution averaged fourteen years in California; the state spends more than $5 million per year on death row appeals.[96]

Morally Wrong The death penalty is brutal and demeaning. Even if the general public voices approval of the death penalty, abolitionists argue that "social vengeance by death is a primitive way of revenge which stands in the way of moral progress."[97] And while early religious leaders accepted the death penalty, today others such as the Catholic Church condemn the practice.[98] In his recent book, *The Contradictions of American Capital Punishment*, Franklin Zimring links America's obsession with the death penalty—unique among westernized nations—with its vigilante tradition, in which people on the frontier took justice in their own hands, assuming that their targets were always guilty as charged.[99] The death penalty was widely practiced against slaves, and at one time mass executions were a brutal and common practice to stifle any thought of escapes and/or revolts.[100]

While the debate continues onward, there seems to be little question that the public's support for the death penalty has weakened and, concomitantly, the number of death sentences being handed down is in sharp decline (see Figure 11.6).[101] Whether these developments are harbingers of the demise of capital punishment remains to be seen.

Legal Issues in Capital Punishment

The constitutionality of the death penalty has been a major concern to both the nation's courts and its social scientists. In 1972, the U.S. Supreme Court in *Furman v. Georgia*[102] decided that the discretionary imposition of the death penalty was cruel and unusual punishment under the Eighth and Fourteenth Amendments of the U.S. Constitution. The Supreme Court did not completely rule out the use of capital punishment as a penalty; rather, it objected to the arbitrary and capricious manner in which it was imposed. After *Furman*, many states changed statutes that had allowed jury discretion in imposing the death penalty. Then, in July 1976, the Supreme Court ruled on the constitutionality of five state death penalty statutes. In the first case, *Gregg v. Georgia*,[103] the Court found valid the Georgia statute holding that a finding by the jury of at least one "aggravating circumstance" out of ten is required in pronouncing the death penalty in murder cases. In the *Gregg* case, the jury imposed the death penalty after finding beyond a reasonable doubt two aggravating circumstances: (1) the offender was engaged in the commission of two other capital felonies, and (2) the offender committed the offense of murder for the purpose of receiving money and other financial gains (i.e., an automo-

Figure 11.6
Decline of death sentences since 1998

Source: Death Penalty Information Center, www.deathpenaltyinfo.org/index.php, accessed on September 26, 2005.

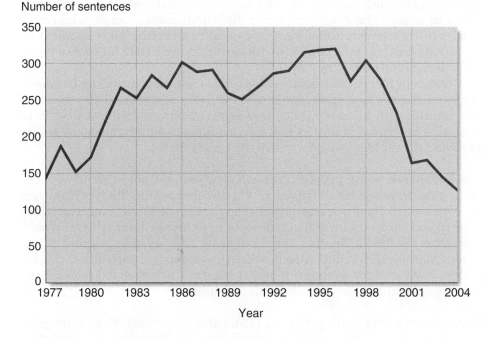

Number of sentences

Year

bile).[104] The *Gregg* case signaled the return of capital punishment as a sentencing option.

Although the Court has generally supported the death penalty, it has also placed some limitations on its use. Rulings have promoted procedural fairness in the capital sentencing process. In *Ring v. Arizona,* the Court found that juries, not judges, must make the critical findings that send convicted killers to death row. The Court reasoned that the Sixth Amendment's right to a jury trial would be "senselessly diminished" if it did not allow jurors to decide whether a person deserves the death penalty.[105] The Court has also limited who may be eligible for death:

- The Court has limited the crimes for which the death penalty can be employed by ruling that it is not permissible to punish rapists with death.[106] Only people who commit intentional or felony murder may be executed.

- People who are mentally ill may not be executed.[107] In a 2002 case, *Atkins v. Virginia,* the Court ruled that execution of mentally retarded criminals is "cruel and unusual punishment" prohibited by the Eighth Amendment.[108]

- In *Roper vs. Simmons* (2005), the Court set a limit of eighteen years as the age of defendants who could be sentenced to death.[109] The Court said that executing young teens violates "the evolving standards of decency that mark the progress of a maturing society," and that American society regards juveniles as less responsible than adult criminals. Although nineteen states had allowed the execution of juvenile murderers prior to *Simmons,* only Texas, Virginia, and Oklahoma have executed any in the past decade.

Does the Death Penalty Deter Murder?

The key issue in the capital punishment debate is whether it can actually lower the murder rate and save lives. Despite its inherent cruelty, capital punishment might be justified if it proved to be an effective crime deterrent that could save many innocent lives. Abolitionists claim it has no real deterrent value; advocates claim it does. Who is correct?

Timothy Ring, shown here, a former state corrections officer, was sentenced by a judge to death for killing a guard in an armored truck robbery in 1994. He appealed his sentence and in a 2002 ruling, *Ring v. Arizona,* the U.S. Supreme Court ruled that juries, not judges, must make the critical findings that send convicted killers to death row. In a 7–2 decision, the Court held that a death sentence where the necessary aggravating factors are determined by a judge violates a defendant's constitutional right to a trial by jury. On June 24, 2004, in *Summerlin v. Stewart*, the Court held that *Ring* was not retroactive, thereby denying new sentencing hearings for dozens of death row inmates in Arizona, Idaho, Montana, and Nebraska whose sentences were originally handed down by judges.

Considerable empirical research has been carried out on the effectiveness of capital punishment as a deterrent. In particular, studies have tried to discover whether the death sentence serves as a more effective deterrent than life imprisonment for capital crimes such as homicide. Three methods have been used:

- *Immediate-impact studies,* which calculate the effect a well-publicized execution has on the short-term murder rate
- *Time-series analysis,* which compares long-term trends in murder and capital punishment rates
- *Contiguous-state analysis,* which compares murder rates in states that have the death penalty with a similar state that has abolished capital punishment

Using these three methods over a sixty-year period, most researchers have failed to show any deterrent effect of capital punishment.[110] These studies show that murder rates do not seem to rise when a state abolishes capital punishment any more so than they decrease when the death penalty is adopted. The murder rate is also quite similar both in states that use the death penalty and neighboring states that have abolished capital punishment. Finally, little evidence shows that executions can lower the murder rate. One test of the deterrent effect of the death penalty in Texas found no association between the frequency of execution during the years 1984 to 1997 and murder rates.[111]

A few studies have found that the long-term application of capital punishment may actually reduce the murder rate.[112] However, these have been disputed by researchers who have questioned the methodology used and indicate that the deterrent effects the studies uncovered are an artifact of the statistical techniques used in the research.[113]

The general consensus among death penalty researchers today is that the threat of capital punishment has little effect on murder rates. It is still unknown why capital punishment fails as a deterrent, but the cause may lie in the nature of homicide. As noted earlier, murder is often a crime of passion involving people who know each other, and many murders are committed by people under the influence of drugs and alcohol—more than 50 percent of all people arrested for murder test positively for drug use. People involved in interpersonal conflict with friends, acquaintances, and family members and who may be under the influence of drugs and alcohol are not likely to be capable of considering the threat of the death penalty.

Murder rates have also been linked to the burdens of poverty and income inequality. Desperate adolescents who get caught up in the cycle of urban violence and become members of criminal groups and gangs may find that their life situation gives them little choice except to engage in violent and deadly behavior; they have few chances to ponder the deterrent impact of the death penalty.

The failure of the "ultimate deterrent" to deter the "ultimate crime" has been used by critics to question the value of capital punishment.

Despite the less-than-conclusive empirical evidence, many people still hold to the efficacy of the death penalty as a crime deterrent, and recent U.S. Supreme Court decisions seem to justify its use. Of course, even if the death penalty were no greater a deterrent than a life sentence, some people would still advocate its use on the grounds that it is the only way to permanently rid society of dangerous criminals who deserve to die.

SUMMARY

- Punishment and sentencing have gone through various phases throughout the history of Western civilization.

- Initially, punishment was characterized by retribution and the need to fix sentences for convicted offenders. The prison developed as a place of reform.

- At the tail end of the nineteenth century, individualized sentencing was created and became widely accepted. The concept of rehabilitation was used to guide sentencing.

- During the 1970s, experts began to become disenchanted with rehabilitation and concepts related to treating the individual offender. There was less emphasis on treatment and more on the legal rights of offenders. A number of states returned to the concept of punishment in terms of mandatory and fixed sentences.

- The philosophy of sentencing has thus changed from a concentration on rehabilitation to a focus on incapacitation and deterrence, where the goal is to achieve equality of punishment and justice in the law and to lock up dangerous criminals for as long as possible.

- Sentencing in today's criminal justice system is primarily based on deterrence, incapacitation, retribution, and rehabilitation. Traditional dispositions include fines, probation, and incarceration, with probation being the most common choice.

- Though sentences are getting shorter and fewer people are sent to prison per crime, people are serving a greater proportion of their sentence than they did a decade ago. Consequently, prison populations are not dropping despite a drop in the crime rate.

- Most states use indeterminate sentences, which give convicted offenders a short minimum sentence after which they can be released on parole if they are considered rehabilitated.

- A number of states have developed determinate sentences that eliminate parole and attempt to restrict judicial discretion so that convicted criminals are given a single sentence that they must serve without parole.

- Efforts have been made to control judicial discretion and to reduce sentencing disparity. Methods for making dispositions more uniform include sentencing guidelines that create uniform sentences based on offender background and crime characteristics.

- Jurisdictions that use either determinate or indeterminate sentences also allow inmates to be released early on good behavior.

- Social and personal factors continue to influence sentencing. Some evidence suggests that young males, especially if they are members of a minority group, are more likely to receive longer sentences than older, Caucasian females.

- The death penalty continues to be the most controversial sentence, with over half the states reinstituting capital punishment laws since the 1972 *Furman v. Georgia* decision.

- Although little evidence exists that the death penalty deters murder, supporters still view it as necessary in terms of incapacitation and retribution and cite the public's support for the death penalty and the low chance of error in its application.

- Opponents point out that mistakes can be made, that capital sentences are apportioned in a racially biased manner, and that the practice is cruel and barbaric.

- Federal courts have generally supported the legality of capital punishment.

- The death penalty is used abroad, though it has been abolished in many nations. The United States leads the world in the execution of juveniles.

- Because of the danger of executing an innocent person, some states have put a moratorium on capital punishment. The number of people on death row seems to have peaked.

KEY TERMS

wergild 294
penitentiary 296
general deterrence 297
incapacitation 298
specific deterrence 298
recidivism 298
blameworthy 299

just desert 299
equity 299
concurrent sentences 300
consecutive sentences 300
indeterminate sentence 301
determinate sentence 302
sentencing guidelines 302

mandatory sentence 304
truth in sentencing 305
chivalry hypothesis 308
victim impact statement 308
brutalization effect 318

REVIEW QUESTIONS

1. Discuss the sentencing dispositions in your jurisdiction. What are the pros and cons of each?

2. Compare the various types of incarceration sentences. What are the similarities and differences? Why are many jurisdictions considering the passage of mandatory sentencing laws?

3. Discuss the issue of capital punishment. In your opinion, does it serve as a deterrent? What new rulings has the U.S. Supreme Court made on the legality of the death penalty?

4. Why does the problem of sentencing disparity exist? Do programs exist that can reduce disparate sentences? If so, what are they? Should all people who commit the same crime receive the same sentence? Explain.

5. Should convicted criminals be released from prison when correctional authorities are convinced they are rehabilitated? Why or why not?

PART 4

Corrections and Alternative Sanctions

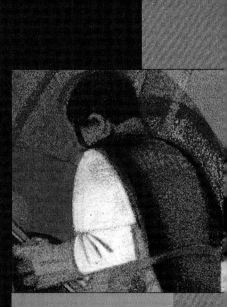

Kathy Boudin, onetime member of the radical Weather Underground, was convicted of murder and robbery in connection with a 1981 Brink's armored car heist in New York in which a security guard and two police officers were killed. Serving a sentence of twenty to life, she was repeatedly denied parole. Even though she was a model prisoner, New York State parole board officials repeatedly said that her release would "undermine respect for the law."

Boudin was part of the getaway team for six armed radicals who robbed the Brink's truck of $1.6 million. After one parole review, her lawyer said, "It's a sad day for Kathy. She was sentenced to twenty years by a judge who sat on her case for two and a half years and knew all the facts, and she did her twenty years with honor. For the system now not to keep its promise to someone who has been on exemplary behavior for two decades under- mines respect for the law." Supporters of Boudin argued that she had turned her life around while in prison, working to help inmates with AIDS and earning a master's degree in adult education while behind bars. A mother, Boudin also developed a program on parenting behind bars and helped write a handbook for inmates whose children are in foster care. Al- though the parole board continually noted her good behavior in prison, they also said that, "due to the violent nature and circumstances" of her crime, "your release at this time would be incompatible with the welfare of society and would serve to deprecate the seriousness of the criminal behavior." Fi- nally, on August 20, 2003, Kathy Boudin was released on parole.

The Boudin case is notorious, but it is by no means unusual. The correc- tional system not only must house the nation's most dangerous people but also must decide when they are rehabilitated and ready to return to society. Do you believe it was correct to keep Kathy Boudin in prison longer because she did in fact participate in a robbery which left three people dead, or does her exemplary behavior in prison warrant early re- lease? Can people be rehabilitated behind bars, and, if so, should they be granted early release as was Boudin?

The following three chapters explore the correctional system and process. The first focuses on community corrections and the expanding field of restorative justice; the subsequent two focus on institutional corrections. ■

CHAPTER 12

Community Sentences: Probation, Intermediate Sanctions, and Restorative Justice

DR. DEBRA HEATH-THORNTON holds an Associate's Degree in Criminal Justice from Genesee Community College, a Bachelor's Degree in Criminal Justice from Rochester Institute of Technology, a Master's Degree in Criminal Justice from Buffalo State College, a Master's Degree in Education from Buffalo State College, and a Doctor of Education Degree with a focus in Educational Leadership! She has held numerous positions in criminal justice, including crime victim advocate, caseworker with a pretrial diversion program, and criminal justice planner. She witnessed firsthand both the pain that crime victims suffered and the

Chapter Outline

Chapter Objectives

1. Be familiar with concept of community sentencing
2. Know the history of community sentences
3. Recognize the different types of probation sentences
4. Be familiar with the rules of probation
5. Be able to discuss the legal issues in probation
6. Discuss the effectiveness of probation
7. Understand the concept of alternative sanctions
8. Know the various alternative sanctions, from fines to community incarceration
9. Explain the principles of restorative justice
10. Understand the concept of "reintegrative shaming"

remorse that offenders who caused the pain were forced to endure. She also became engaged with the communities that loved these broken people. In her work as a county criminal justice director, she was introduced to restorative justice, a perspective of crime and criminal justice that takes all of these parties into account—victims, offenders, and communities. Her role placed her in a position where she was constantly faced with the plight of offenders and yet ever mindful of victims and communities as well.

What does she see as the greatest challenges facing the justice system? Number one is getting the public to regard crime as *everybody's* problem. While the physical harm to victims is often easy to comprehend, crime also imposes financial and emotional losses on the community. It causes insurance rates to increase and decreases the ability to feel secure in their own neighborhoods. These problems can only be dealt with through community involvement, which requires enlisting support for the victims of crime, promoting effective reintegration programs for criminal offenders, and developing education and public information programs to help neighbors understand the impact of crime.

Dr. Debra Heath-Thornton's values reflect the core of community sentencing—probation, alternative sanction, and restorative justice. Many of those convicted in criminal courts are deserving of a second chance; most present little threat to society. If they can be reintegrated into the community and given the proper treatment they are unlikely to recidivate. Considering these circumstances, it seems foolish to incarcerate them in an overcrowded and dangerous prison system, which can damage younger inmates and lock them into a life of crime. It may be both more effective and less costly to have them remain in the community under the supervision of a trained court officer, where they can receive treatment that will help them turn around their lives. Rehabilitation would be aided immensely if those who commit crime could be made to understand the problems their actions cause their family, friends, and community.

Considering the potential benefits and cost-effectiveness of a community sentence, it is not surprising that their number is at an all-time high. There are now a great variety of community sentences, ranging from traditional probation to house arrest and placement in community correctional centers.

Both traditional probation and the newer forms of community sentences have the potential to become reasonable alternatives to many of the economic and social problems faced by correctional administrators:

- They are less costly than jail or prison sentences.
- They help the offender maintain family and community ties.
- They can be structured to maximize security and maintain public safety.
- They can be scaled in severity to correspond to the seriousness of the crime.
- They can feature restoration and reintegration rather than punishment and ostracism.

This chapter reviews these criminal sanctions. It begins with a brief history of community sentencing. It then turns to traditional probation and discusses its role as a community-based correctional practice. Then it focuses on so-called alternative or intermediate sanctions such as intensive supervision, house arrest, and electronic monitoring. Finally, the chapter turns to a discussion of the concept of restorative justice and programs based on its principles.

probation A sentence entailing the conditional release of a convicted offender into the community under the supervision of the court (in the form of a probation officer), subject to certain conditions for a specified time. The conditions are usually similar to those of parole. (Note: Probation is a sentence, an alternative to incarceration; parole is administrative release from incarceration.) Violation of the conditions of probation may result in revocation of probation.

▌PROBATION

Probation is a criminal sentence that suspends or delays a correctional term in a prison or jail. The offender who is on probation has been convicted of a crime, but instead of being incarcerated the offender is returned to the community for a period in which he or she will have to abide to certain conditions set forth by the court under the supervision of a probation officer.

The philosophy of probation today rests on the assumption that the typical offender is not actually a dangerous criminal or a menace to society but someone who has the ability and potential to reform. If the offender is institutionalized instead of being granted community release, the prison community becomes the new reference point. The offender is forced to interact with hardened criminals, and the "ex-con" label prohibits him from making successful adjustments to society. Probation provides offenders with the opportunity to prove themselves, gives them a second chance, and allows them to be closely supervised by trained personnel who can help them reestablish proper forms of behavior in the community. Even dangerous offenders who might normally be sent to a penal institution can be successfully rehabilitated in the community if given the proper balance of supervision, treatment, and control.

There are now approximately two thousand adult probation agencies in the United States. Slightly more than half are associated with a state-level agency, while the remainder are organized at the county or municipal level of government. About thirty states combine probation and parole supervision into a single agency.

About 4 million people are currently on probation. The adult parole population has grown about 2 percent per year since 1995 and, as Figure 12.1 shows, the number of people on probation has far outstripped those in other forms of correction. Without probation, the correctional system would rapidly become even more overcrowded, overly expensive, and unmanageable.

The History of Community Sentencing

How did this idea of community supervision and control begin? The roots of probation can be traced back to the traditions of the English common law. During the Middle Ages, judges wishing to spare deserving offenders from the pains of the then commonly used punishments of torture, mutilation, and death used their power to grant clemency and stays of execution. The common-law practice of **judicial reprieve** allowed judges to suspend punishment so that convicted offenders could seek a pardon, gather new evidence, or demonstrate that they had reformed their behavior. Similarly, the practice of **recognizance** enabled convicted offenders to remain free if they agreed to enter into a debt obligation with the state. The debt would have to be paid only if the offender was caught engaging in further criminal behavior. Sometimes **sureties** were required—these were people who made themselves responsible for the behavior of an offender after he was released.

Criminal Justice ⚖ Now™

Learn more about **Probation** *by exploring the* **Probation and Parole** *Learning Module.*

The most **recent data on the extent of probation** is provided by the Bureau of Justice Statistics. To reach this site go to "Web Links" on your Siegel Essentials of Criminal Justice 5e website: http://cj.wadsworth.com/siegel_ess5e.

judicial reprieve The common-law practice that allowed judges to suspend punishment so that convicted offenders could seek a pardon, gather new evidence, or demonstrate that they had reformed their behavior.

recognizance During the Middle Ages, the practice of letting convicted offenders remain free if they agreed to enter a debt relation with the state to pay for their crimes.

sureties During the Middle Ages, people who made themselves responsible for the behavior of offenders released in their care.

Number of prisoners

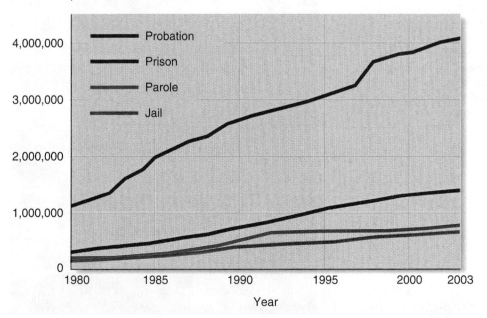

Figure 12.1
Adult correctional populations, 1980–2003
Sources: Bureau of Justice Statistics Correctional Surveys (The Annual Probation Survey, National Prisoner Statistics, Survey of Jails, and The Annual Parole Survey), www.ojp.usdoj.gov/bjs/glance/corr2.htm, accessed September 28, 2005.

John Augustus Early U.S. courts continued the practice of indefinitely suspending sentences of criminals who seemed deserving of a second chance, but it was John Augustus of Boston who is usually credited with originating the modern probation concept.[1] As a private citizen, Augustus began in 1841 to supervise offenders released to his custody by a Boston judge. Over an eighteen-year period, Augustus supervised close to two thousand probationers and helped them get jobs and establish themselves in the community. Augustus had an amazingly high success rate, and few of his charges became involved in crime again.

In 1878, Augustus's work inspired the Massachusetts's legislature to pass a law authorizing the appointment of a paid probation officer for the city of Boston. In 1880, probation was extended to other jurisdictions in Massachusetts, and by 1898 the probation movement had spread to the superior (felony) courts.[2] The Massachusetts experience was copied by Missouri (1887) and Vermont (1898), and soon after by most other states. In 1925, the federal government established a probation system for the U.S. district courts. The probation concept soon became the most widely used correctional mechanism in the United States.[3]

The Concept of Probation

Although the term today has many meanings, probation usually indicates a nonpunitive form of sentencing for convicted criminal offenders and delinquent youth, emphasizing maintenance in the community and treatment without institutionalization or other forms of punishment.[4] Once on probation, the offender is subject to certain rules and conditions that must be followed in order to remain in the community.

Most probation orders involve a contract between the court and the offender in which a prison or jail term is suspended and the probationer promises to obey a set of **probation rules** or conditions mandated by the court. If the rules are violated, or if the probationer commits another criminal offense, pro-

probation rules Conditions or restrictions mandated by the court which must be obeyed by a probationer.

A probation sentence may be combined with a variety of other sentencing alternatives. Here, former county clerk Juanita Wright is comforted by her daughter Paula Hughes prior to her sentencing on embezzlement charges, May 17, 2000, in Ashland County Common Pleas Court in Ashland, Ohio. The 78-year-old grandmother pleaded guilty to embezzling $178,000 in county funds over a ten-year period. She received thirty days in jail, eleven months house arrest, four hundred hours of community service, five years probation, and a $5,000 fine and repayment of the embezzled funds out of her retirement account. In addition, she has to undergo treatment for a gambling addiction, take financial management classes, and get a job.

© 2003 AP/Wide World Photos

bation may be revoked. **Revocation** means that the community sentence is terminated and the original sentence of incarceration is enforced. If an offender on probation commits a second offense that is more serious than the first, he or she may also be indicted, tried, and sentenced on the second offense. However, probation may be revoked simply because the rules and conditions of probation have not been met; it is not necessary for an offender to commit another crime.

Awarding Probation

Probationary sentences may be granted by state and federal district courts and state superior (felony) courts. In some states, juries may recommend probation if the case meets certain legally regulated criteria (for example, if it falls within a certain class of offenses as determined by statute). Even in those jurisdictions that allow juries to recommend probation, judges have the final say in the matter and may grant probation at their discretion. In non-jury trials, probation is granted solely by judicial mandate. Some states have attempted to shape judicial discretion by creating guidelines for granting probation (see chapter 10). For example, California's probation statute directs judges to use the criteria set out in Exhibit 12.1 in making the decision to award probation.

revocation An administrative act performed by a parole authority that removes a person from parole, or a judicial order by a court removing a person from parole or probation, in response to a violation on the part of the parolee or probationer.

Exhibit 12.1	2005 California Rules of Court: Probation

Rule 4.414. Criteria affecting probation

Criteria affecting the decision to grant or deny probation include:

(a) Facts relating to the crime, including:
(1) The nature, seriousness, and circumstances of the crime as compared to other instances of the same crime.
(2) Whether the defendant was armed with or used a weapon.
(3) The vulnerability of the victim.
(4) Whether the defendant inflicted physical or emotional injury.
(5) The degree of monetary loss to the victim.
(6) Whether the defendant was an active or passive participant.
(7) Whether the crime was committed because of an unusual circumstance, such as great provocation, which is unlikely to recur.
(8) Whether the manner in which the crime was carried out demonstrated criminal sophistication or professionalism on the part of the defendant.
(9) Whether the defendant took advantage of a position of trust or confidence to commit the crime.

Rule 4.413. Probation eligibility when probation is limited

In cases where probation is limited by statute, a judge may grant community supervision if the following circumstances exist:

(2) A fact or circumstance not amounting to a defense, but reducing the defendant's culpability for the offense, including:
(i) The defendant participated in the crime under circumstances of great provocation, coercion, or duress not amounting to a defense, and the defendant has no recent record of committing crimes of violence.
(ii) The crime was committed because of a mental condition not amounting to a defense, and there is a high likelihood that the defendant would respond favorably to mental health care and treatment that would be required as a condition of probation.
(iii) The defendant is youthful or aged, and has no significant record of prior criminal offenses.

Sources: 2005 California Rules of Court Rule 4.413 and 4.414, amended effective July 1, 2003; adopted effective July 1, 1977; former rule 414 amended and relettered effective January 1, 1991; previously renumbered effective January 1, 2001; www.courtinfo.ca.gov/rules/titlefour/title4-48.htm and www.courtinfo.ca.gov/rules/titlefour/title4-47.htm, accessed on September 28, 2005.

About one-half of all cases involve a direct sentence to probation without the possibility of a prison term if probation rules are violated. However, the offender may realize that further criminal activity will result in a harsher sentence being imposed. In about 30 percent of probation sentences, judge will formulate a prison sentence and then suspend it if the offender agrees to obey the rules of probation while living in the community (a **suspended sentence**).[5] Some offenders (about 9 percent) receive some form of split sentence in which they must first serve a jail term before being released on probation.

The term of a probationary sentence may simply extend to the limit of the suspended prison term, but in most cases the judge will devise a specific probationary period. For misdemeanors, probation usually extends for the entire period of the jail sentence, whereas felonies are more likely to warrant probationary periods that are actually shorter than the suspended prison sentences.

Probation Eligibility

Although originally conceived as a way to provide a second chance for young offenders who committed non-serious crimes, probation today is also a means of reducing the population overload in an overcrowded and underfunded correctional system. Many serious criminal offenders are therefore given probation sentences, including people convicted of homicide (about 5 percent), sexual assault (about 18 percent), robbery (14 percent), and aggravated assault (29 percent) charges.[6]

So there are two distinct sides to probation, one involving the treatment and rehabilitation of non-dangerous offenders deserving of a "second chance" and the other the supervision and control of criminals who might otherwise be incarcerated.

Conditions of Probation

When granting probation, the court sets down certain conditions or rules of behavior which the probationer is bound to obey. Some conditions are standard and are applied in every probation case (e.g., "do not leave the jurisdiction"), but the sentencing judge usually has broad discretion to set specific conditions on a case-by-case basis. Sometimes an individual probationer is given specific rules that relate to his or her particular circumstances, such as the requirement to enroll in an anger management or drug treatment program, make a personal apology to the victim, or have no contact with his or her ex-spouse.[7] A presiding judge may not impose capricious or cruel conditions, of course, such as requiring an offender to make restitution out of proportion to the seriousness of the criminal act.[8] Judges may, however, legally impose restrictions tailored to fit the probationer's individual needs and/or to protect society from additional harm. In one 2003 case, Albert Lee—who had pled guilty to transporting child pornography via computer and enticing a minor by computer to engage in sex—was given a probation sentence with conditions that required him to (1) register as a sex offender, (2) not be allowed contact with his victims, (3) have no contact with persons under the age of 18, (4) not own or operate a personal computer or other device that allows Internet access, (5) not be housed in an area where minors congregate, (6) not hire any minors to perform household chores or yard work, and (7) allow random searches of his residence to be conducted for the presence of sexual risk factors. He was also required to submit to periodic polygraph questioning about his activities to see if he had violated any of these conditions. Lee sued, saying this final condition was a violation of his Fifth Amendment right against self-incrimination. However, the Third U.S. Circuit Court of Appeals ruled that the conditions of Lee's probation were appropriate for his crime and that the use of a polygraph did not violate his

suspended sentence A prison term that is delayed while the defendant undergoes a period of community treatment. If the treatment is successful, the prison sentence is terminated.

constitutional rights as long as his probation would not be revoked simply because he refused to answer a question.[9]

Probationers' community supervision may be revoked if they fail to comply with these conditions and to obey the reasonable requests of the probation staff to meet their treatment obligations.[10]

Exhibit 12.2 lists suggested rules for convicted sex offenders.

Administration of Probation Services

Probation services are organized in a variety of ways, depending on the state and the jurisdiction in which they are located. Some states have a statewide probation service, but each court jurisdiction actually controls its local department. Other states maintain a strong statewide authority with centralized control and administration. Thirty states combine probation and parole services in a single unit; some combine juvenile and adult probation departments, whereas others maintain these departments separately.

The typical probation department is situated in a single court district, such as juvenile, superior, district, or municipal court. The relationship between the department and court personnel (especially the judge) is extremely close.

© 2003 AP/Wide World Photos

A judge may impose special conditions of probation depending on the circumstances of the case. Kevin Kelly looks back toward his family as he waits for his sentencing hearing to begin February 21, 2003, at the Prince William County Courthouse in Manassas, Virginia. Kelly, a father of thirteen who allowed his youngest daughter to die in a sweltering van, was given probation, but will spend one night in jail every February 21st for the next seven years. Kelly, convicted of involuntary manslaughter and reckless endangerment for allowing his daughter to die in a sweltering van, was given probation, but will spend one night in jail every February 21st for the next seven years. Passersby found Frances Kelly, at 21 months, the youngest of Kelly's 13 children, strapped into her car seat inside the family's van, which was parked at their Manassas home.

Exhibit 12.2	Special probation rules suggested for convicted sex offenders

- Your employment must be approved by the probation agency.
- You shall participate in treatment with a therapist approved by the probation department.
- You shall participate in periodic polygraph examinations.
- You shall not have contact with children under age 18.
- You shall not frequent places where children congregate, such as schoolyards, parks, playgrounds, and arcades.
- You shall maintain a driving log (mileage; time of departure, arrival, return; routes traveled and with whom, etc.).
- You shall not drive a motor vehicle alone without prior permission of your supervising officer.
- You shall not possess any pornographic, sexually oriented, or sexually stimulating visual, auditory, telephonic, or electronic media and computer programs or services that are relevant to your deviant behavior pattern.
- You shall reside at a place approved by the supervising officer, including supervised living quarters.
- You shall abide by a curfew imposed by the supervising officer and comply with electronic monitoring, if so ordered.
- You shall not have contact, directly or through third parties, with your victims.
- You shall abstain from alcoholic beverages and participate in periodic drug testing.

Source: Adapted from Kim English, Suzanne Pullen, and Linda Jones, *Managing Adult Sex Offenders in the Community—A Containment Approach* (Washington, D.C.: National Institute of Justice, 1997), 5.

In the typical department, the chief probation officer (CPO) sets policy, supervises hiring, determines training needs, and may personally discuss with or recommend sentencing to the judge. In state-controlled departments, some of the CPO's duties are mandated by the central office; training guidelines, for example, may be determined at the state level. If, on the other hand, the department is locally controlled, the CPO is invested with great discretion in the management of the department.

The line staff, or the probation officers (POs), may be in direct and personal contact with the entire supervisory staff, or they may be independent of the CPO and answer mainly to the assistant chiefs. Line staff perform the following major functions:

- Supervise or monitor cases assigned to them to ensure that the rules of probation are followed.
- Attempt to rehabilitate their cases through specialized treatment techniques.
- Investigate the lives of convicted offenders to enable the court to make intelligent sentencing decisions.
- Occasionally collect fines due the court or oversee the collection of delinquent payments, such as child support.
- Interview complainants and defendants to determine whether criminal action should be taken, whether cases can be decided informally, whether diversion should be advocated, and so on. This last procedure, called *intake,* is common in juvenile probation.

How probation officers carry out these tasks may be a function of their self-image and professional orientation. Some POs view themselves as "social workers" and maintain a treatment orientation; their goal is to help offenders adjust in the community. Others are "law enforcers" who are more concerned with supervision, control, and public safety. An officer's style is influenced by both personal values and the department's general policies and orientation toward the goals of probation.[11] New York City probation officers are now authorized to carry handguns under a new departmental policy intended to enhance the supervision of their clients, the majority of whom are felons. Arming the officers became necessary when the department began to require officers to spend more time visiting their clients in their neighborhoods and homes. Other departments have armed their officers as the number of probationers increase and duties become more dangerous.[12]

Duties of Probation Officers

Staff officers in probation departments are usually charged with five primary tasks: investigation, intake, diagnosis, treatment supervision, and risk classification.

Investigation In the investigative stage, the supervising probation officer accumulates important information on the background and activities of the offender who is being considered for probation. This **pre-sentence investigation** serves the basis for sentencing and controls whether the convicted defendant will be granted community release or sentenced to secure confinement. In the event that the offender is placed on probation, the investigation becomes useful as a tool to shape treatment and supervision efforts.

The style and content of pre-sentence investigations may vary among jurisdictions and also among individual POs within the same jurisdiction. Some departments require voluminous reports covering every aspect of the defendant's life; other departments, which may be rule oriented, require that

pre-sentence investigation An investigation performed by a probation officer attached to a trial court after the conviction of a defendant. The report contains information about the defendant's background, education, previous employment, and family; his or her own statement concerning the offense; prior criminal record; interviews with neighbors or acquaintances; and his or her mental and physical condition (that is, information that would not be made public record in the case of guilty plea or that would be inadmissible as evidence at a trial but could be influential and important at the sentencing stage).

officers stick to the basic facts, such as the defendant's age, race, sex, and previous offense record. Each department also has its own standards for pre-sentence investigations.

At the conclusion of most pre-sentence investigations, a recommendation is made to the presiding judge that reflects the department's sentencing posture on the case at hand. This is a crucial aspect of the report, because the probation department's recommendation is followed by the sentencing judge in most cases.

Intake Probation officers who conduct **intake** interviews may be looking to settle the case without the necessity of a court hearing. The probation officer will work with all parties involved in the case—offender, victim, police officer, and so on—to design an equitable resolution of the case. If the intake process is successful, the probation officer may settle the case without further court action, recommend restitution or other compensation, or recommend unofficial or informal probation. If an equitable solution cannot be found, the case would be filed for a court hearing.

Diagnosis In order to select appropriate treatment modes, probation officers—using their training in counseling, social work, or psychology—analyze the probationer's character, attitudes, and behavior. The goal of diagnosis is to develop a personality profile that may be helpful in treating the offender. An effective diagnosis integrates all that has been learned about the individual, organized in such a way as to provide a means for the establishment of future treatment goals.[13]

Treatment Supervision After the diagnosis has been completed, the probation staff is asked to carry out the treatment supervision, a program of therapy designed to help the client to deal with the problems that resulted in their antisocial behavior. In years past, the probation staff had primary responsibility for supervision and treatment, but today's large caseloads limit opportunities for hands-on treatment; most probation treatment efforts rely on community resources.

intake The process in which a probation officer settles cases at the initial appearance before the onset of formal criminal proceedings; also, process in which a juvenile referral is received and a decision is made to file a petition in the juvenile court, release the juvenile, or refer the juvenile elsewhere.

Supervising clients in the community and making sure they obey probation rules is a critical element of a probation officer's professional responsibility. In some instances this means going to their home for on-site substance abuse testing. Olmsted County probation officer Bernie Sizer, right, tests Kevin Rood for alcohol during a visit to Rood's apartment in Rochester, Minnesota, April 25, 2005. Sizer and fellow officer Holly Busby monitor about fifty people convicted of crimes such as child molestation, incest, and statutory rape.

© 2005 AP/Wide World Photos

A PO who discovers that a client has a drinking problem may place the client in a detoxification program. A spousal abuser may be required to enroll in an anger management or drug treatment program, make a personal apology to the victim, or have no contact with his or her ex-spouse.[14] In the case of juvenile delinquency, a PO may work with teachers and other school officials to help a young offender stay in school. The need for treatment is critical and the vast size of probation caseloads, especially the large numbers of narcotics abusers, can provide a formidable challenge to community-based substance abuse programs.[15]

Effective supervision is critical for another reason: it protects the probation department from civil liability. Failure to supervise probationers adequately and determine whether they are obeying the rules of probation can result in the officer and the department being held legally liable for civil damages. For example, if a probationer with a history of child molestation attacks a child while working as a school custodian, the probationer's case supervisor could be held legally responsible for failing to check on the probationer's employment activities.[16]

Risk Classification Probationers typically receive a **risk classification** that assigns them classified to a level and type of supervision on the basis of their particular needs and the risks they present to the community. Some clients may receive frequent (intensive) supervision in which they are contacted by their supervising probation officer almost every day, whereas other minor offenders are assigned to minimum monitoring by a PO.

A number of risk assessment classification approaches are used, but most employ such objective measures as the offender's age, employment status, drug abuse history, prior felony convictions, and number of address changes in the year prior to sentencing. Efforts are underway to create more effective instruments using subjective information obtained through face-to-face interviews and encounters.[17]

Does classification make a dramatic difference in the success of probation? Though there is little clear-cut evidence that classification has a substantial impact on reducing recidivism, its use has become commonplace and administrators believe that it may be a useful tool in case management and treatment delivery.[18] The classification of offenders aids the most important goal of supervision: reducing the risk the probationer presents to the community. In addition, classification ensures that the most serious cases get the most intensive supervision and that resources are not wasted on cases with relatively few treatment needs.[19]

Legal Rights of Probationers

What are the legal rights of probationers? How has the Court set limits on the probation process? A number of important legal issues surround probation, one set involving the civil rights of probationers and another involving the rights of probationers during the revocation process:

Civil Rights The U.S. Supreme Court has ruled that probationers have a unique status and therefore are entitled to fewer constitutional protections than other citizens.

- *Minnesota v. Murphy* (1984).[20] In *Murphy*, the Supreme Court ruled that the probation officer/client relationship is not confidential, as physician/patient or attorney/client relationships are. If a probationer admits to committing a crime to his or her probation supervisor, the information can be passed on to the police or district attorney. Furthermore, the *Murphy* decision held that a probation officer could even use trickery or psychological pressure to get information and turn it over to the police.

risk classification Classifying probationers so that they may receive an appropriate level of treatment and control.

- *Griffin v. Wisconsin* (1987).[21] In *Griffin*, the Supreme Court held that a probationer's home may be searched without a warrant on the grounds that probation departments "have in mind the welfare of the probationer" and must "respond quickly to evidence of misconduct."

- *United States v. Knights* (2001).[22] In *Knights*, the Supreme Court upheld the legality of a warrantless search of a probationer's home for the purposes of gathering criminal evidence. In *Knights*, the Court ruled that the home of a probationer who is suspected of a crime can be searched without a warrant if the search was based on (1) reasonable suspicion that he had committed another crime while on probation and (2) that a condition of his previous probation was that he would submit to searches. The Court reasoned that the government's interest in preventing crime, combined with Knights's diminished expectation of privacy, required only a *reasonable suspicion* to make the search fit within the protections of the Fourth Amendment.

Revocation Rights During the course of a probationary term, a violation of the rules or terms of probation or the commitment of a new crime can result in probation being revoked, at which time the offender may be placed in an institution. Revocation is not often an easy decision, since it conflicts with the treatment philosophy of many probation departments.

When revocation is chosen, the offender is notified, and a formal hearing is scheduled. If the charges against the probationer are upheld, the offender can then be placed in an institution to serve the remainder of the sentence. Most departments will not revoke probation unless the offender commits another crime or seriously violates the rules of probation.

Because placing a person on probation implies that probation will continue unless the probationer commits some major violation, the defendant has been given certain procedural due process rights at this stage of the criminal process. In some significant decisions, the U.S. Supreme Court provided procedural safeguards to apply at proceedings to revoke probation (and parole):

- *Mempa v. Rhay* (1967). The Court unanimously held that a probationer was constitutionally entitled to counsel in a revocation-of-probation proceeding where the imposition of sentence had been suspended.[23]

- *Morrissey v. Brewer* (1972). In *Morrissey*, the Supreme Court required an informal inquiry to determine whether there was probable cause to believe the arrested parolee had violated the conditions of parole, as well as a formal revocation hearing with minimum due process requirements. Because the revocations of probation and parole are similar, the standards in the *Morrissey* case affected the probation process as well.[24]

- *Gagnon v. Scarpelli* (1973). In *Gagnon*, the Supreme Court held that both probationers and parolees have a constitutionally limited right to counsel in revocation proceedings.[25] This means that during a probation revocation hearing, the defendant must be given counsel if it is required for an effective defense. A judge may deny counsel under some circumstances, such as when probation will be continued despite the violation. The *Gagnon* case can be viewed as a step forward in the application of constitutional safeguards to the correctional process. The provision of counsel helped give control over the unlimited discretion exercised in the past by probation and parole personnel in revocation proceedings.

- *United States v. Granderson* (1994). In *Granderson*, the Supreme Court helped clarify what can happen to a probationer whose community sentence is revoked. Granderson was eligible for a six-month prison sentence but instead was given sixty months of probation. When he tested positive for drugs, his probation was revoked. The statute he was sentenced under required that he serve one-third of his original sentence in prison. When the trial court sentenced him to twenty months, he appealed. Was his original sentence six months or sixty months? The Supreme Court found that it would be unfair to force a probationer to serve more time in prison than he would have if originally incarcerated and ruled that the proper term should have been one-third of the six months, or two months.[26]

How Successful Is Probation?

Probation is the most commonly used alternative sentence for a number of reasons: it is humane, it helps offenders maintain community and family ties, and it is cost-effective. Incarcerating an inmate typically costs over $25,000 per year, whereas probation costs about $2,000 per year.

Although unquestionably inexpensive, is probation successful? If most probation orders fail, the costs of repeated criminality would certainly outweigh the cost savings of a probation sentence. National data indicate that about 60 percent of probationers successfully complete their probationary sentence while about 40 percent are rearrested, violate probation rules, or abscond.[27] Most revocations occur for technical violations that occur during the first three months of the probation sentence.[28] Studies of federal probationers show even better results (30 percent failure rate).[29] Although a 30–40 percent failure rate may seem high, even the most serious criminals who receive probation are less likely to recidivate than those who are sent to prison for committing similar crimes.[30]

How Successful Is Felony Probation?

Are probationers convicted of serious felonies more likely to recidivate than minor offenders? Does their lenient sentence present a threat to the community? Tracking the outcome of felony probation was the goal of Joan Petersilia and her colleagues at the RAND Corporation, a private think tank, when they traced 1,672 men convicted of felonies who had been granted probation in Los Angeles and Alameda counties in California.[31] In this now-classic study, Petersilia found that 1,087 (65 percent) were rearrested; of those rearrested, 853 (51 percent) were convicted; and of those convicted, 568 (34 percent) were sentenced to jail or prison. Of the probationers who had new charges filed against them, 75 percent were charged with burglary, theft, robbery, and other predatory crimes; 18 percent were convicted of serious, violent crimes.

The RAND researchers found that probation is by far the most common sentencing alternative to prison, used in about 60 to 80 percent of all criminal convictions. However, the crimes and criminal records of about 25 percent of all probationers are indistinguishable from those of offenders who go to prison. This data indicates that many people given prison sentences could have been granted community sentences and vice versa. This is a disturbing finding when so many felons granted community sentences fail to complete their probationary period.

While the failure rate found by Petersilia seems disturbingly high, even the most serious criminals who receive probation are less likely to recidivate than those who are sent to prison for committing similar crimes.[32]

Criminal Justice ⊛ Now™

*Learn more by exploring **Recidivism** and **Conditions of Parole** Review and Reinforce activities.*

Who Fails on Probation and Why?

Who is most likely to fail on probation? Young males who are unemployed or who have a very low income, a prior criminal record, and a history of instability are most likely to be rearrested. In contrast, probationers who are married with children, have lived in the area for two or more years, and are adequately employed are the most likely to be successful on probation.[33] Recent research (2005) shows, surprisingly, that males convicted on sexual offenses seem to do quite well on probation.[34] Among female probationers, those who have stable marriages, are better educated, and are employed full- or part-time are more likely to complete probation orders successfully than male or female probationers who are single, less educated, and unemployed. Prior record is also related to probation success: clients who have a history of criminal behavior, prior probation, and previous incarceration are the most likely to fail.[35]

Probationers bring with them a lot of emotional baggage that may reduce their chances of successful rehabilitation. Many are felons who have long histories of offending; more than 75 percent of all probationers have had prior convictions. Others suffer from a variety of social and psychological disabilities. Surveys indicate that almost 20 percent suffer from mental illness.[36] Whether mentally ill or mentally sound, probationers are likely to have grown up in households in which family members were incarcerated, and so have lived part of their lives in foster homes or state institutions. Many had parents or guardians who abused drugs; they also suffered high rates of physical and sexual abuse. They are now unemployed or underemployed, and almost half are substance abusers. Considering their harsh and abusive backgrounds and their current economic distress and psychological stresses and strains, it comes as no surprise that many find it difficult to comply with the rules of probation and forgo criminal activity.

The Future of Probation

A number of initiatives are now ongoing or being suggested that may help shape the future of probation:

- *Making probationers pay.* At least twenty-five states now impose some form of fee on probationers to defray the cost of community corrections. Massachusetts initiated **day fees,** which are based on the probationer's wages (the usual fee is between one and three days' wages each month).[37] Texas requires judges to impose supervision fees unless the offender is truly unable to pay; fees make up more than half the probation department's annual budget.[38]

- *HotSpot probation.* Maryland's HotSpot probation initiative involves police officers, probation agents, neighbors, and social service professionals to form community probation supervision teams. Using a team approach, they provide increased monitoring of offenders through home visits and drug testing. They also work with the offenders to ease re-entry through offender creation of work crews which aid in community clean-ups, work on vacant houses, and participate in other projects. Evaluations find that the recidivism rates of HotSpot probationers was not significantly different from that of traditional probation, but the initiative seems to have a great deal of utility and warrants further study.[39]

- *Area needs.* Some experts suggest that probation caseloads be organized around area rather than client needs. Research shows that probationers' residences are concentrated in certain locations. In the future, probation officers may be assigned cases based on where they live in order to develop a working knowledge of community issues and develop expertise on how to best serve their clients' interests and needs.[40]

Probation is unquestionably undergoing dramatic changes. In many jurisdictions, traditional probation is being supplemented by **intermediate sanctions,** which are penalties that fall between traditional community supervision and confinement in jail or prison. These new correctional services are discussed in the following section.

day fees *A program requiring probationers to pay in part for the costs of their treatment.*

intermediate sanctions *The group of punishments falling between probation and prison ("probation plus"). Community-based sanctions, including house arrest and intensive supervision, serve as alternatives to incarceration.*

▌INTERMEDIATE SANCTIONS

In 2005, Jennifer Wilbanks became notorious for running away just before her wedding and claiming to have been abducted. When the truth was revealed, she pled guilty to charges of filing a false police report. At her hearing she told the court, "I'm truly sorry for my actions and I just want to thank Gwinnett County and the city of Duluth." The judge, Ronnie Batchelor, then sentenced her to two years of probation and 120 hours of community service. He also ordered her to continue mental health treatment and pay the sheriff's office $2,550 in addition to the $13,250 she previously agreed to pay the city of Duluth, Georgia, to help cover the overtime costs incurred in searching for her.[41]

Wilbanks's sentence reflects the growing trend to add additional sanctions to traditional probation sentences; in her case it was monetary fines and community service. These programs can be viewed as "probation plus," since they add restrictive penalties and conditions to traditional community service orders, which featured treatment and rehabilitation over control and restraint.[42]

Intermediate sanctions include programs that are usually administered by probation departments: intensive probation supervision, house arrest, electronic monitoring, restitution orders, shock probation or split sentences, and residential community corrections.[43] Some experts also include high-impact shock incarceration, or boot camp experiences, within the definition of intermediate sanctions, but these programs are usually operated by correctional departments and are therefore discussed separately in chapter 13. Intermediate sanctions also involve sentences administered independently of probation staffs: fines and forfeiture, pretrial programs, and pretrial and posttrial residential programs. Intermediate sanctions therefore range from the barely intrusive, such as restitution orders, to the highly restrictive, such as house arrest accompanied by electronic monitoring and a stay in a community correctional center.

© 2005 AP/Wide World Photos

Intermediate sanctions have been employed in some high-profile cases. A billboard with the likeness of runaway bride Jennifer Wilbanks is shown in Duluth, Georgia, May 3, 2005. Wilbanks, who had vanished April 26 after saying she was going out jogging, initially told authorities she was abducted. But she later admitted she took a cross-country bus trip to Albuquerque, New Mexico, to avoid her lavish, six-hundred-guest wedding, which was to have taken place that Saturday. Charged with making false statements, she pleaded guilty and was sentenced to two years' probation and 120 hours of community service (including mowing lawns and cleaning toilets in government buildings) and was ordered to pay $2,250 in restitution to the Gwinnett County Sheriff's Department.

Advantages of Intermediate Sanctions

What are the advantages of creating a system of intermediate sanctions? Advocates point to a number of benefits that these programs can provide. Intermediate sanctions offer effective alternatives to prisons and jails. Penal institutions have proven to be costly, ineffective, and injurious. Little evidence exists that incapacitation prevents future criminality; most inmates recidivate soon after serving their release from prison. Some correctional systems have become inundated with new inmates even as crime rates have fallen. Harsh sentencing policies mean more people are behind bars than ever before.

Intermediate sanctions also have the potential to save money. Although they are more expensive than traditional probation, they are far less costly than incarceration. If those offenders given alternative sanctions would have otherwise been incarcerated, the extra cost would be significant. In addition, offenders given intermediate sanctions generate income, pay taxes, reimburse victims, perform community service, and provide other cost savings that would be nonexistent had they been incarcerated. Also, intermediate sanctions may reduce the need for future prison and jail construction. Intermediate sanctions also help meet the need for developing community sentences that are fair, equitable, and proportional.[44] It seems unfair to treat both a rapist and a shoplifter with the same type of probationary sentence, considering the differences in their crimes. As Figure 12.2 illustrates, intermediate sanctions can form the successive steps of a meaningful "ladder" of scaled punishments outside of prison, thereby restoring fairness and equity to nonincarceration sentences.[45] Forgers may be ordered to make restitution to their victims, and rapists can be placed in a community facility and receive counseling at a local clinic. This feature of intermediate sanctions allows judges to fit the punishment to the crime without resorting to a prison sentence. Among their benefits are included:

- Intermediate sentences can be designed to increase control over probationers whose serious or repeat crimes make a straight probation sentence inappropriate, yet for whom a prison sentence would be unduly harsh and counterproductive.[46] Some forms, such as electronic monitoring, also provide increased surveillance for probationers who might otherwise continue to commit crimes while in the community. Self-report surveys suggest that about half of probationers commit at least one offence during the time they are on probation and that about a third report committing more than four offences during this same time.[47] Intermediate sanctions may help reduce this hidden recidivism.

- Intermediate sanctions can serve the needs of a number of offender groups. The most likely candidates are convicted criminals who would normally be sent to prison but who pose either a low risk of recidivism or who are of little threat to society (such as nonviolent property offenders). Used in this sense, intermediate sanctions are a viable solution to the critical problem of prison overcrowding.

- Intermediate sanctions can also reduce overcrowding in jails by providing alternatives to incarceration for misdemeanants and cut the number of pretrial detainees who currently make up about half the inmate population.[48] Some forms of bail already require conditions that are a form of intermediate sanctions, such as supervision by court officers and periods of home confinement (conditional bail).

- Intermediate sanctions can also potentially be used as halfway-back strategies for probation and parole violators. Probationers who violate the conditions of their community release could be placed under increasingly more intensive supervision before actual incarceration is required. Parolees who pose the greatest risk of recidivism might receive conditions that require close monitoring, or home confinement. Parole violators could be returned to a community correctional center rather than a walled institution.

In the following sections, the forms of intermediate sanctions currently in use are more thoroughly discussed.

Fines

Fines are monetary payments imposed on offenders as an intermediate punishment for their criminal acts. They are a direct offshoot of the early common law practice of requiring that compensation be paid to the victim and the state (wergild) for criminal acts. Fines are still commonly used in Europe, where they are often the sole penalty, even in cases involving chronic offenders who commit fairly serious crimes.[49]

fine Levying a money payment on offenders to compensate society for their misdeeds.

Figure 12.2
The punishment ladder

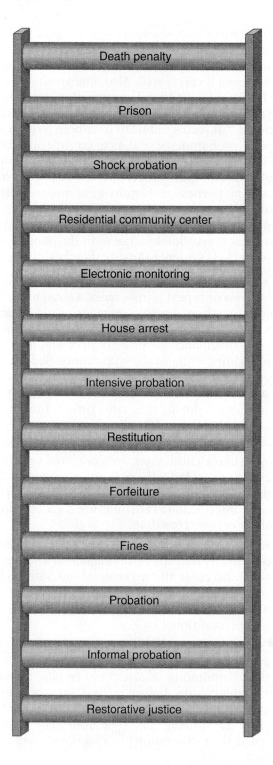

In the United States, fines are most commonly used in cases involving misdemeanors and lesser offenses. Fines are also frequently used in felony cases where the offender benefited financially.

Fines may be used as a sole sanction but are typically combined with other punishments such as probation. Judges commonly levy other monetary sanctions along with fines, such as court costs, public defender fees, probation and treatment fees, and victim restitution, to increase the force of the financial punishment. However, there is evidence that many offenders

© 2005 AP/Wide World Photos

Fines are the most common criminal sentence and may be used in conjunction with other sanctions. Here Ohio Supreme Court Justice Alice Robie Resnick and her husband, Melvin Resnick, leave Bowling Green Municipal Court, February 7, 2005, in Bowling Green, Ohio, where she pleaded guilty to drunken driving. Resnick's license was suspended and she was ordered to complete a three-day alcohol rehabilitation program. If Resnick does not complete the program, she could be jailed for up to thirty days. She also was fined $500 and another $100 for a separate traffic offense of driving outside marked lanes.

fail to pay fines and that courts are negligent in their efforts to collect unpaid fees.[50]

In most jurisdictions, little guidance is given to the sentencing judge directing the imposition of the fine. Judges often have inadequate information on the offender's ability to pay, resulting in defaults and contempt charges. Because the standard sanction for nonpayment is incarceration, many offenders held in local jails are confined for nonpayment of criminal fines. Although the U.S. Supreme Court in *Tate v. Short* (1971) recognized that incarcerating a person who is financially unable to pay a fine discriminates against the poor, many judges continue to incarcerate offenders for noncompliance with financial orders.[51]

Day Fines   Because judges rely so heavily on offense seriousness to fix the level of fines, financial penalties may have a negative impact on success rates. The more serious the offense and the higher the fine, the greater the chances that the offender will fail to pay the fine and risk probation revocation. To overcome this sort of problem, some jurisdictions began experimenting with **day fines.** The first day fines pilot program in the U.S. was designed and operated by the Vera Institute of Justice in Staten Island, New York, between 1987 and 1989. Since then, similar structured fine systems have been tried experimentally in Arizona, Connecticut, Iowa, and Oregon.[52]

A concept that originated in Europe, day fines are geared to an offender's net daily income. In an effort to make them equitable and fairly distributed, fines are based on the severity of the crime, weighted by a daily-income value taken from a chart similar to an income tax table; the number of the offender's dependents is also taken into account. The day fine concept means that the severity of punishment is geared to the offender's ability to pay.

Day fines hold the promise of becoming an equitable solution to the problem of setting the amount of a fine according to the offender's ability to pay. However, there is little conclusive evidence whether the day fine program actually works as intended.[53]

day fine *A fine geared to the average daily income of the convicted offender in an effort to bring equity to the sentencing process.*

Forfeiture

Another intermediate sanction with a financial basis is criminal (*in personam*) and civil (*in rem*) **forfeiture.** Both involve the seizure of goods and instrumentalities related to the commission or outcome of a criminal act. The difference is that criminal forfeiture proceedings target criminal defendants and can only follow a criminal conviction. In contrast, civil forfeiture proceedings target property used in a crime and do not require that formal criminal proceedings be initiated against a person or that the person be proven guilty of a crime.[54] For example, federal law provides that after arresting drug traffickers, the government may seize the boats they used to import the narcotics, the cars they used to carry the drugs overland, the warehouses in which the drugs were stored, and the homes paid for with the drug profits; on conviction, the drug dealers lose permanent ownership of these "instrumentalities" of crime.

Forfeiture is not a new sanction. During the Middle Ages, "forfeiture of estate" was a mandatory result of most felony convictions. The Crown could seize all of a felon's real and personal property. Forfeiture derived from the common law concept of "corruption of blood" or "attaint," which prohibited a felon's family from inheriting or receiving his property or estate. The common law mandated that descendants could not inherit property from a relative who may have attained the property illegally: "[T]he Corruption of Blood stops the Course of Regular Descent, as to Estates, over which the Criminal could have no Power, because he never enjoyed them."[55]

Forfeiture was reintroduced to U.S. law with the passage of the Racketeer Influenced and Corrupt Organization (RICO) Act and the Continuing Criminal Enterprises Act, both of which allow the seizure of any property derived from illegal enterprises or conspiracies. Although these acts were designed to apply to ongoing criminal conspiracies, such as drug or pornography rings, they are now being applied to a far-ranging series of criminal acts, including white-collar crimes. More than one hundred federal statutes use forfeiture of property as a punishment.

Although law enforcement officials at first applauded the use of forfeiture as a hard-hitting way of seizing the illegal profits of drug law violators, the practice has been criticized because the government has often been overzealous in its application. For example, million-dollar yachts have been seized because someone aboard possessed a small amount of marijuana; this confiscatory practice is referred to as **zero tolerance.** This strict interpretation of the forfeiture statutes has come under fire because it is often used capriciously, the penalty is sometimes disproportionate to the crime involved, and it makes the government a "partner in crime."[56] It is also alleged that forfeiture unfairly targets a narrow range of offenders. For example, it is common for government employees involved in corruption to forfeit their pensions; employees of public companies are exempt from such punishment.[57] There is also the issue of conflict of interest: because law enforcement agencies can use forfeited assets to supplement their budgets they may direct their efforts to cases that promise the greatest "payoff" rather than ones that have the highest law enforcement priority.[58]

Restitution

Another popular intermediate sanction is **restitution,** which can take the form of requiring offenders either to pay back the victims of crime (**monetary restitution**) or serve the community to compensate for their criminal acts (**community service restitution**).[59] Restitution programs offer offenders a chance to avoid a jail or prison sentence or a lengthier probation period. It may help them develop a sense of allegiance to society, better work habits,

Criminal Justice ⚖ Now™

Learn more by exploring the ***Types of Sanctions*** *Vocabulary Check activity.*

forfeiture *The seizure of personal property by the state as a civil or criminal penalty.*

zero tolerance *The practice of seizing all instrumentalities of a crime, including homes, boats, and cars. It is an extreme example of the law of forfeiture.*

restitution *A condition of probation in which the offender repays society or the victim of crime for the trouble the offender caused.*

monetary restitution *A sanction that requires that convicted offenders compensate crime victims by reimbursing them for out-of-pocket losses caused by the crime. Losses can include property damage, lost wages, and medical costs.*

community service restitution *An alternative sanction that requires an offender to work in the community at such tasks as cleaning public parks or working with disabled children in lieu of an incarceration sentence.*

and some degree of gratitude for being given a second chance. Restitution serves many other purposes, including giving the community something of value without asking it to foot the bill for an incarceration stay and helping victims regain lost property and income.

If a defendant is sentenced to pay monetary restitution as part of their probation order, a determination of victim loss is made and a plan for paying fair compensation developed. To avoid the situation in which a wealthy offender can fill a restitution order by merely writing a check, judges will sometimes order that compensation be paid out of income derived from a low-paid social service or public works job.

Community service orders usually require duty in a public nursing home, shelter, hospital, drug treatment unit, or works program; some young vandals may find that they must clean up the damage they caused to the school or the park. Judges and probation officers have embraced the concept of restitution because it appears to benefit the victim, the offender, the criminal justice system, and society.[60] Financial restitution is inexpensive to administer, helps avoid stigma, and provides compensation for victims of crime. Offenders ordered to do community service work have been placed in schools, hospitals, and nursing homes. Helping them avoid a jail sentence can mean saving the public thousands of dollars that would have gone to maintaining them in a secure institution, frees up needed resources, and gives the community the feeling that equity has been returned to the justice system.

Does restitution work? Most reviews rate it as a qualified success. A recent (2005) evaluation of community service in Texas found that nearly three-fourths of offenders with community service orders met their obligations and completed community service work.[61] The Texas experience is not atypical; most restitution clients successfully complete their orders and have no subsequent contact with the justice system.[62]

Shock Probation and Split Sentencing

Shock probation and **split sentences** are alternative sanctions designed to allow judges to grant offenders community release only after they have sampled prison life. These sanctions are based on the premise that if offenders are given a taste of incarceration sufficient to shock them into law-abiding behavior, they will be reluctant to violate the rules of probation or commit another crime.

In a number of states and in the Federal Criminal Code, a jail term can actually be a condition of probation, known as *split sentencing*. About 10 percent of probationers are now given split sentences. The shock probation approach involves resentencing an offender to probation after a short prison stay. The shock comes because the offender originally received a long maximum sentence but is then eligible for release to community supervision at the discretion of the judge (usually within ninety days of incarceration).

Some states have linked the short prison stay with a boot camp experience, referred to as *shock incarceration*, in which young inmates undergo a brief but intense period of military-like training and hard labor designed to impress them with the rigors of prison life.[63] (Boot camp programs are discussed in greater detail in chapter 13.) Shock probation and split sentencing have been praised as ways to limit prison time, reintegrate the client quickly into the community, maintain family ties, and reduce prison populations and the costs of corrections.[64] An initial jail sentence probably makes offenders more receptive to the conditions of probation, because it amply illustrates the problems they will face if probation is violated.

But split sentences and shock probation programs have been criticized by those who believe that even a brief period of incarceration can interfere with the purpose of probation, which is to provide the offender with nonstigmatizing,

shock probation *A sentence in which offenders serve a short prison term before they begin probation, to impress them with the pains of imprisonment.*

split sentence *A practice that requires convicted criminals to spend a portion of their sentence behind bars and the remainder in the community.*

community-based treatment. Even a short-term commitment subjects probationers to the destructive effects of institutionalization, disrupts their life in the community, and stigmatizes them for having been in jail.

Intensive Probation Supervision

Intensive probation supervision (IPS) programs, also referred to as *intensive supervision programs,* have been implemented in some form in about forty states and today include about one hundred thousand clients. IPS programs involve small caseloads of fifteen to forty clients who are kept under close watch by probation officers.[65] IPS programs typically have three primary goals:

- *Decarceration.* Without intensive supervision, clients would normally be sent to already overcrowded prisons or jails.
- *Control.* High-risk offenders can be maintained in the community under much closer security than traditional probation efforts can provide.
- *Reintegration.* Offenders can maintain community ties and be reoriented toward a more productive life while avoiding the pains of imprisonment.

In general, IPS programs rely on a great degree of client contact to achieve the goals of decarceration, control, and reintegration. Most programs have admissions criteria based on the nature of the offense and the offender's criminal background. Some programs exclude violent offenders; others will not take substance abusers. In contrast, some jurisdictions do not exclude offenders based on their prior criminal history.

IPS programs are used in several ways. In some states, IPS is a direct sentence imposed by a judge; in others, it is a postsentencing alternative used to divert offenders from the correctional system. A third practice is to use IPS as a case management tool to give the local probation staff flexibility in dealing with clients. Other jurisdictions use IPS in all three ways, in addition to applying it to probation violators to bring them halfway back into the community without resorting to a prison term.

The Effectiveness of IPS Indications exist that the failure rate in IPS caseloads is high, in some cases approaching 50 percent; IPS clients have a higher rearrest rate than other probationers.[66] It should come as no surprise that IPS clients fail more often because, after all, they are more serious criminals who might otherwise have been incarcerated and are now being watched and supervised more closely than probationers. Probation officers may also be more willing to revoke the probation of IPS clients because they believe the clients are a risk to the community and, under normal circumstances, would have been incarcerated. Why risk the program to save a few "bad apples"?

While national evaluations of the program have not been encouraging, IPS seems to work better for some offenders than with others. Those with good employment records seem to do better than the underemployed or unemployed.[67] Younger offenders who commit petty crimes are the most likely to fail on IPS; ironically, people with these characteristics are the ones most likely to be included in IPS programs.[68]

IPS may also be more effective if it is combined with particular treatment modalities such as cognitive-behavioral treatment, which stresses such life skills as problem solving, social skills, negotiation skills, management of emotion, and values enhancement.[69]

House Arrest

When Martha Stewart was released from prison in 2005 she was required to serve a five-month term of house arrest in which she could not leave home for more than 48 hours at a time and had to wear an electronic tracking device. Her

Criminal Justice ⚖ Now™

Learn more by viewing the "Martha Sentence" "In the News" video clip.

intensive probation supervision (IPS) A type of intermediate sanction involving small probation caseloads and strict monitoring on a daily or weekly basis.

sentence was not unique except for the fact that Martha's estate was so big that walking to the edges of her property put her out of range of her tracking device.

The **house arrest** concept requires convicted offenders to spend extended periods of time in their own home as an alternative to an incarceration sentence. For example, persons convicted on a drunk-driving charge might be sentenced to spend between 6 P.M. Friday and 8 A.M. Monday and every weekday after 5:30 P.M. in their home for six months. According to current estimates, more than ten thousand people are under house arrest.

As with IPS programs, there is a great deal of variation in house arrest initiatives: some are administered by probation departments, while others are simply judicial sentences monitored by surveillance officers. Some check clients twenty or more times a month while others do only a few curfew checks. Some use twenty-four-hour confinement, while others allow offenders to attend work or school.

No definitive data exists indicating that house arrest is an effective crime deterrent, nor is there sufficient evidence to conclude that it has utility as a device to lower the recidivism rate. One evaluation found that nearly 10 percent of the house arrest sample had their probation revoked for technical violations within eighteen months of their sentencing.[70] Another found that recidivism rates were almost identical to a matched sample of inmates released from secure correctional facilities; four out of five offenders in both forms of correction recidivated within five years.[71] Although these findings are troublesome, the advantages of house arrest in reducing costs and overcrowding in the correctional system probably make further experimentation inevitable.

Electronic Monitoring

For house arrest to work, sentencing authorities must be assured that arrestees are actually at home during their assigned times. Random calls and visits are one way to check on compliance with house arrest orders. However, one of the more interesting developments in the criminal justice system has been the introduction of **electronic monitoring (EM)** devices to manage offender obedience to home confinement orders.[72]

Electronically monitored offenders wear devices that send signals to a control office; the devices are worn around their ankles, wrists, or necks. Two

house arrest A form of intermediate sanction that requires that the convicted offender spend a designated amount of time per week in his or her own home—for example, from 5 P.M. Friday until 8 A.M. Monday.

electronic monitoring (EM) Requiring a convicted offender to wear a monitoring device as part of his or her community sentence. Electronic monitoring is typically part of a house arrest order and enables the probation department to ensure that the offender is complying with court-ordered limitations on his or her freedom.

© 2005 AP/Wide World Photos

Electronic monitoring devices hold the promise of being a low-cost means of keeping tabs on probationers and other offenders serving their time in the community. Steven Wesley, regional manager for the State of Delaware Juvenile Probation and Aftercare, a division of Youth Rehabilitation Services, holds a global positioning systems transmitter that can be worn on the wrist or on the ankle. With the help of a federal grant, Youth Rehabilitation Services is expanding a pilot program that uses global positioning systems to track the movements of juvenile delinquents under house arrest.

basic types of systems are used: active and passive. *Active systems* constantly monitor offenders by continuously sending a signal to the central office. If offenders leave their home at an unauthorized time, the signal is broken, and the "failure" is recorded. In some cases, the control officer is automatically notified electronically through a beeper. In contrast, *passive systems* usually involve random phone calls generated by computers to which the offenders have to respond within a particular time (such as thirty seconds). In addition to probationers, EM can be used at the front end of the system with bailees and at the back end with parolees.

The various kinds of EM devices are described in Exhibit 12.3.

Electronic monitoring supporters claim the EM has the benefits of relatively low cost and high security, while helping offenders avoid the pains of imprisonment in overcrowded, dangerous state facilities. Electronic monitoring is capital-intensive rather than labor-intensive. Since offenders are monitored by computers, an initial investment in hardware rules out the need for hiring many more supervisory officers to handle large numbers of clients.

There are some indications that EM can be an effective addition to the galaxy of intermediate sanctions, providing the judiciary with an enhanced supervision tool.[73] EM can be used as part of a pretrial diversionary program, to

| Exhibit 12.3 | **Available electronic monitoring systems** |

- *Identity verification devices* range from personal identification numbers to biometric verification that recognizes different parts of the human body to ensure the reporting person is the intended offender.
- *Remote alcohol detection devices* require users to blow into the device, which is usually in the offender's home, to measure blood alcohol content. The results are recorded by a computer to determine compliance with conditions of alcohol consumption.
- *Ignition interlock devices* are linked to the electrical systems of automobiles. The driver must expel deep lung air into the device to operate the vehicle. If the driver's blood alcohol content registers above a predetermined level deemed unsafe to drive, the vehicle will not start.
- *Programmed contact systems* are used to contact and verify the location of offenders in their homes or elsewhere. They utilize a central computer that either receives telephone calls from or makes calls to offenders in one or more locations.
- *Continuous signaling devices* are battery-powered and transmit a radio signal two or more times per minute. These are placed on the offender's wrist or ankle with a tamper-resistant strap, and must be worn at all times. A receiver detects the transmitter's signals and conveys a message via telephone report to a central computer when it either stops receiving the radio frequency or the signal resumes. Receivers can detect transmitter signals from a range of up to, and in some cases, exceeding, 150 feet when installed in a typical home environment.
- *Victim notification systems* alert the victim when the offender is approaching that person's residence. A transmitter is worn by both the offender and the victim, and a receiver is placed at both residences.
- *Field monitoring devices,* or "drive-by" units, are another type of continuous signaling technology. Probation or parole officers or other authorities use a portable device that can be handheld or used in a vehicle with a roof-mounted antenna. When within two hundred to eight hundred feet of an offender's ankle or wrist transmitter, the portable device can detect the radio signals of the offender's transmitter.
- *Group monitoring units* allow supervisors to monitor several offenders in the same location, such as for verifying attendance of multiple offenders in a day-reporting program or monitoring offenders confined in a residential group setting.
- *Location tracking systems,* also known as global positioning systems, offer yet another way to monitor offenders. Receivers detect satellite signals that include the exact time the signal is sent and the identity of the satellite sending the signal. This information is processed to determine the person's location. This more expensive technology usually is used for high-risk offenders. It can determine when an offender leaves an area where he or she is supposed to be (inclusion zone) or enters an area where he or she is not allowed to be (exclusion zone)

Source: Ann Crowe, "Electronic Supervision: From Decision Making to Implementation," *Corrections Today 64* (2002): 131–132.

enhance probation, or as a post-incarceration security measure.[74] The public supports EM as a cost-effective alternative to prison sentences that have proven ineffective.[75] Surveys of offenders find that they find EM preferable to incarceration.[76] Programs have been found to save money and avoid new construction costs without widening the net of social control.[77] However, not all evaluations have been successful, and some find that offenders monitored on EM misunderstand its purpose and are as likely to recidivate as those released without such supervision.[78]

Residential Community Corrections

The most secure intermediate sanction is a sentence to a **residential community corrections (RCC)** facility. Such a facility has been defined as "a freestanding nonsecure building that is not part of a prison or jail and houses pretrial and adjudicated adults. The residents regularly depart to work, to attend school, and/or participate in treatment activities and programs."[79]

Traditionally, the role of community corrections was supplied by the nonsecure halfway house, which was designed to reintegrate soon-to-be-paroled prison inmates back into the community. Inmates spend the last few months in the halfway house, acquiring suitable employment, building up cash reserves, obtaining an apartment, and developing a job-related wardrobe.

The traditional concept of community corrections has expanded. Today, the community correctional facility is a vehicle to provide intermediate sanctions as well as a pre-release center for those about to be paroled from the prison system. RCC has been used as a direct sentencing option for judges who believe particular offenders need a correctional alternative halfway between traditional probation and a stay in prison. Placement in an RCC center can be used as a condition of probation for offenders who need a nonsecure community facility that provides a more structured treatment environment than traditional probation. It is commonly used in the juvenile justice system for youths who need a more secure environment than can be provided by traditional probation yet who are not deemed a threat to the community and do not require a secure placement.

Probation departments and other correctional authorities have been charged with running RCC centers that serve as a pre-prison sentencing alternative. In addition, some RCC centers are operated by private, nonprofit groups that receive referrals from the county or district courts and from probation or parole departments. Portland House, a private residential center in Minneapolis, operates as an alternative to incarceration for young adult offenders. The twenty-five residents regularly receive group therapy and financial, vocational, educational, family, and personal counseling. Residents may work to earn a high school equivalency degree. With funds withheld from their earnings at work-release employment, residents pay room and board, family and self-support, and income taxes. Portland House appears to be successful. It is significantly cheaper to run than a state institution, and the recidivism rate of clients is much lower than that of those who have gone through traditional correctional programs.[80]

Besides acting as sole sentences and halfway houses, RCC facilities have also been residential pretrial release centers for offenders who are in immediate need of social services before their trial and as halfway-back alternatives for both parole and probation violators who might otherwise have to be imprisoned. In this capacity, RCC programs serve as a base from which offenders can be placed in outpatient psychiatric facilities, drug and alcohol treatment programs, job training, and so on. Some programs make use of both inpatient and outpatient programs to provide clients with specialized treatment, such as substance abuse management.[81]

residential community corrections (RCC) A nonsecure facility, located in the community, that houses probationers who need a more secure environment. Typically, residents are free during the day to go to work, school, or treatment, and return in the evening for counseling sessions and meals.

One recent development has been the use of RCC facilities as **day reporting centers (DRCs).**[82] Day reporting centers provide a single location to which a variety of clients can report for supervision and treatment. Used in Georgia, Delaware, Utah, and other jurisdictions, DRCs utilize existing RCC facilities to service nonresidential clients. They can be used as a step up in security for probationers who have failed in the community and a step down in security for jail or prison inmates.[83] The Atlanta Day Reporting Center, opened in June 2001, was developed as a joint project by the Georgia Parole Board and the Department of Corrections. It provides 125 probationers and parolees with structured daily programs in GED preparation, substance abuse recovery, and cognitive skills training. Although offenders return to their homes at night, the center intensifies training and support and therefore affords many of the well-documented benefits of traditional halfway houses.[84]

More than two thousand state-run community-based facilities are in use today. In addition, up to twenty-five hundred private, nonprofit RCC programs operate in the United States. About half also house inmates who have been released from prison (halfway houses) and use the RCC placement as a method to ease back into society. The remainder are true intermediate sanctions, including about four hundred federally sponsored programs.

Despite the thousands of traditional and innovative RCC programs in operation around the United States, relatively few efforts have been made to evaluate their effectiveness. Those evaluations that do exist suggest that many residents do not complete their treatment regimen in RCC facilities, violating the rules or committing new offenses.[85]

For example, California's Substance Abuse and Crime Prevention Act (SACPA), allows adults convicted of nonviolent drug possession offenses to participate in community-based drug treatment programs. A recent evaluation of the program (2004) found that SACPA clients were likely to be rearrested for drug crimes, undercutting the effectiveness of the treatment initiative.[86] One reason for the failure may have been that the sudden influx of offenders simply overwhelmed the treatment resources of an already strained community treatment system; many clients were simply "under-treated."

It is possible that rather than being used as a "last resort" community alternative before sentence to a jail or prison, RCC placement might actually work better with first-time offenders who have relatively little experience with the criminal or juvenile justice systems.[87]

Criminal Justice ⚖ Now™

Learn more by exploring the **Restorative Justice** *Review and Reinforce activity.*

day reporting center (DRC) *A nonresidential community-based treatment program.*

restorative justice *A view of criminal justice that focuses on crime as an act against the community rather than the state. Justice should involve all parties who are affected by crime—victims, criminals, law enforcement, and the community.*

RESTORATIVE JUSTICE

Some crime experts believe that, ironically, rather than reducing crime and recidivism, policies based on getting "tough on crime," even intermediate sanctions, can cause crime rates to fluctuate higher and offenders to commit more crime. Punishment does not work because it destroys the offender's dignity and piece of mind. Traditional community-based correctional models such as probation have proven ineffective. And when they are supplemented by the new alternative/intermediate sanctions the effect is to add a punitive aspect that can further hinder rehabilitation efforts. Instead, **restorative justice** advocates suggest a policy based on (1) restoring the damage caused by crime and (2) creating a system of justice that includes all the parties harmed by the criminal act: the victim, the offender, the community, and society.[88]

Restorative justice models jibe with the thoughts of Australian justice expert John Braithwaite, who argues that crime control today involves shaming and stigmatizing offenders. This helps set them apart from normative society and hurts their potential for change. Instead he calls for a policy of *reintegrative shaming*. Here disapproval is limited to the offender's evil deeds, and not to the offender himself. Law violators must be made to realize that while their actions have caused harm, they are still valuable people—people who can be reaccepted by society. A critical element of reintegrative shaming occurs when the offenders begin to understand and recognize their wrongdoing and shame themselves. To be reintegrative, shaming must be brief and controlled and then followed by ceremonies of forgiveness, apology, and repentance.[89] Braithwaite's work is at the core of the restorative justice movement.

The Concept of Restoration

According to the restorative view, crimes can seem quite different, ranging from a violent assault to a white-collar fraud scheme. Nonetheless, they all share one common trait: they bring harm to the community in which they occur. The traditional justice system has done little to involve the community in the justice process. What has developed is a system of coercive punishments administered by bureaucrats that is inherently harmful to offenders and reduces the likelihood they will ever again become productive members of society. This system relies on punishment, stigma, and disgrace. What is needed instead is a justice policy that repairs the harm caused by crime and includes all parties that have suffered from that harm, including the victim, the community, and the offender. Exhibit 12.4 sets out the principles of the restorative justice approach.

An important aspect of achieving these goals is that offenders accept accountability for their actions and responsibility for the harm their actions caused. Only then can they be restored as productive members of their community. Restoration involves turning the justice system into a "healing" process rather than a distributor of retribution and revenge.

Most people involved in offender/victim relationships actually know one another or were related in some way before the criminal incident took place. Instead of treating one of the involved parties as a victim deserving sympathy and the other as a criminal deserving punishment, it is more productive to address the issues that produced the conflict between these people. Rather than take sides and choose whom to isolate and punish, society should try to reconcile the parties involved in conflict.[90] The effectiveness of justice ultimately depends on the stake a person has in the community (or a particular social group). If a person does not value her membership in the group, she will be unlikely to accept responsibility, show remorse, or repair the injuries caused by her actions.

Exhibit 12.4   The basic principles of restorative justice

- Crime is an offense against human relationships.
- Victims and the community are central to justice processes.
- The first priority of justice processes is to assist victims.
- The second priority is to restore the community, to the degree possible.
- The offender has a personal responsibility to victims and to the community for crimes committed.
- The offender will develop improved competency and understanding as a result of the restorative justice experience.
- Stakeholders share responsibilities for restorative justice through partnerships for action.

Source: Anne Seymour, "Restorative Justice/Community Justice," in the *National Victim Assistance Academy* textbook (Washington, D.C.: National Victim Assistance Academy, 2001, updated July 2002).

Restoration Programs

Restoration programs try to involve all the parties involved in a criminal act: the victim, the offender, and the community. Although processes differ in structure and style, they generally include the following:

- Recognition by offenders that they have caused injury to personal and social relations, and a determination and acceptance of responsibility (ideally accompanied by a statement of remorse)

- A commitment to both material (e.g., monetary restitution) and symbolic reparation (e.g., an apology)

- A determination of community support and assistance for both victim and offender

The intended result of the process is to repair injuries suffered by the victim and the community while assuring reintegration of the offender.

Negotiation, mediation, consensus building, and peacemaking have been part of the dispute resolution process in European and Asian communities for centuries.[91] Native American and Native Canadian people have long used the type of community participation in the adjudication process (for example, sentencing circles, sentencing panels, elders panels) that restorative justice advocates are now embracing.[92]

In some Native American communities, people accused of breaking the law meet with community members, victims if any, village elders, and agents of the justice system in a **sentencing circle.** All members of the circle express their feelings about the act that was committed and raise questions or concerns. The accused can express regret about his or her actions and a desire to change the harmful behavior. People may suggest ways the offender can make things up to the community and those who were harmed. A treatment program, such as Alcoholics Anonymous, may be suggested, if appropriate.

Restoration in Practice

Restorative justice policies and practices are now being adapted around the world. Legislation in nineteen states includes reference to the use of victim/offender mediation. There are more than fourteen hundred victim/offender mediation programs in North America and Europe.[93] Restorative justice is being embraced on many levels in the justice system.

Schools Some schools have employed restorative justice practices in order to deal with students who are involved in drug and alcohol abuse without having to resort to more punitive measures such as expulsion. Schools in Minnesota, Colorado, and elsewhere are now trying to involve students in "relational rehabilitation" programs, which strive to improve offenders' relationships with key figures in the community who may have been harmed by their actions.[94]

Police Restorative justice has also been implemented when crime is first encountered by police. The new community policing models can be viewed as an attempt to bring restorative concepts into law enforcement. Restorative justice relies on criminal justice policymakers listening to and responding to the needs of those who will be affected by their actions, and community policing relies on policies established with input and exchanges between officers and citizens.[95]

Courts In the court system, restorative programs usually involve diverting the formal court process. Instead, these programs encourage meeting and reconciling the conflicts between offenders and victims via victim advocacy, mediation programs, and sentencing circles, in which crime victims and their families are

sentencing circles A type of sentencing in which victims, family members, community members, and the offender participate in an effort to devise fair and reasonable sanctions that are ultimately aimed at reintegrating the offender back into the community.

Race, Culture, and Gender in Criminal Justice

Conferencing in Australia

The aim of conferencing is to divert offenders from the justice system by offering them the opportunity to attend a conference to discuss and resolve the offence instead of being charged and appearing in court. Conferencing was introduced into the Australian juvenile and criminal justice systems in the early 1990s by police in the city of Wagga Wagga, New South Wales. Other police services experimented with the idea, and during 1992–1995, police-run conferences were established in the Australian Capital Territory (ACT) and were tried on a pilot basis in Western Australia, the Northern Territory, Queensland, and Tasmania. Other applications of the conferencing idea have been tried in schools and workplaces in New South Wales and Queensland beginning in 1994, and these continue to operate.

Conferencing is not offered where offenders wish to contest their guilt. Those that do not are referred to the conference, which normally lasts one to two hours and is attended by the victims and their supporters, the offenders and their supporters, and other relevant parties. The conference coordinator focuses the discussion on condemning the act, without condemning the character of the actor. Offenders are asked to explain what happened, how they have felt about the crime, and what they think should be done. The victims and others are asked to describe the physical, financial, and emotional consequences of the crime. This discussion may lead the offenders, their families, and friends to experience the shame of the act, prompting an apology to the victim. A plan of action is developed and signed by key participants. The plan may include the offender paying compensation to the victim, doing work for the victim or the community, or any other undertaking the participants may agree upon. It is the responsibility of the conference participants to determine the outcomes that are most appropriate for these particular victims and these particular offenders.

Critical Thinking

1. How can this essentially humanistic approach be sold to the general public that now supports more punitive sanctions? For example, would it be feasible to claim that using restorative justice with nonviolent offenders frees up resources for the relatively few dangerous people in the criminal population?

2. Would a method that works in Australia also have utility in the U.S. with its more heterogeneous population, greater social problems, and more violent crime?

InfoTrac College Edition Research

To read more about conferencing in Australia, go to Hayes Hennessey, "Assessing Reoffending in Restorative Justice Conferences," *Australian and New Zealand Journal of Criminology* 38 (2005): 77–101.

Source: Australian Institute of Criminology, "Restorative Justice: An Australian Perspective," www.aic.gov.au/rjustice/australia.html, accessed on August 1, 2005.

brought together with offenders and their families in an effort to formulate a sanction that addresses the needs of each party. Victims are given a chance to voice their stories, and offenders can help compensate them financially or provide some service (for example, fix damaged property).[96] Again, the goal is to enable offenders to appreciate the damage they have caused, to make amends, and to be reintegrated back into society. The Race, Culture, and Gender in Criminal Justice feature that follows discusses restorative justice in Australia.

The Challenge of Restorative Justice

Although restorative justice holds great promise, there are also some concerns.[97] Research indicates that entry into programs may be tilted towards white offenders and more restrictive to minorities, a condition which negates the purpose of the restorative movement.[98] Restorative programs must also be wary of the cultural and social differences that can be found throughout our heterogeneous society. What may be considered "restorative" in one subculture may be considered insulting and damaging in another.[99] Similarly, so many diverse programs call themselves "restorative" that it is difficult to evaluate them, because each one may be pursuing a unique objective. In other words, there is still no single definition of what restorative justice is and only sketchy data on whether it is effective.[100] The following Race, Culture and Gender box looks at the evaluation of one program in England:

Race, Culture, and Gender in Criminal Justice

Restorative Cautioning in England

After an arrest is made, police in England and Wales have four alternative procedures they may follow: (1) take no further action, (2) give an informal warning, (3) administer a formal police caution, or (4) decide to prosecute by sending the case to the Crown Prosecution Service. If the officer in charge decides to formally caution the suspect, the case will terminate at the police level. The formal caution, usually given by a senior officer, involves forcefully reminding the offender not to reoffend. Although the formal caution results in termination of the case, it is recorded in the National Police Computer and can be disclosed to courts in subsequent criminal cases.

English police forces are now experimenting with a form of restorative cautioning. This uses a trained police facilitator with a script to encourage an offender to take responsibility for repairing the harm caused by the offence. Sometimes the victim is present, in which case the meeting is called a restorative conference; usually, however, the victim is not present. Traditional cautioning, on the other hand, lasts only a few minutes, requires no special training, and focuses on the officer explaining the possible consequences of future offending.

In 2004, the U.K. Home Office conducted a study that attempted to evaluate the effectiveness of restorative cautioning. They compared resanctioning rates from the Thames Valley police force, where restorative cautioning is standard policy, with rates from two police forces in similar jurisdictions—Sussex and Warwickshire—where traditional cautioning is used. Resanctioning is defined as an offender receiving either a conviction or a police disposition.

In order to test the impact of restorative cautioning, the study looked at resanctioning rates over a two-year period using the records of twenty-nine thousand offenders from the three police forces. The study showed that resanctioning rates in Thames Valley were statistically significantly lower than in the other two jurisdictions. However, resanctioning rates declined in all three jurisdictions. Thames Valley had significantly lower rates than Sussex for all three years as well as significantly lower rates than Warwickshire for the first two years of the study. Restorative cautioning also seemed to provide many positive outcomes for both victims and offenders regardless of their impact on resanctioning:

- Helps offenders understand the impact of crime
- Provides symbolic and material reparation to victims
- Provides a sense of resolution in the case

Critical Thinking

1. How would the cautioning system work in the United States? Is it too lenient, too formal, or would it be an effective program?

2. Would restorative justice measures work with felony offenders such as rapists and drug abusers? Can we really forgive their misdeeds? Should they be given the privilege of remaining in the community while they receive treatment? Should they not be punished for their criminal activity and not merely restored to the community?

InfoTrac College Edition Research

To learn more about *policing in England*, use it in a keyword search on InfoTrac College Edition.

Sources: Aidan Wilcox, Richard Young, and Carolyn Hoyle, "Two-year resanctioning study: a comparison of restorative and traditional cautions" (British Home Office, 2004) www.homeoffice.gov.uk/rds/pdfs04/rdsolr5704.pdf, accessed August 1, 2005; Lynette Parker, "Evaluating Restorative Programmes: Reports from Two Countries" (Restorative Justice.org, June 2005), www.restorativejustice.org/editions/2005/june05/evaluations/, accessed on September 15, 2005.

Exhibit	12.5	Victim concerns about restorative justice

- Restorative justice processes can cast victims as little more than props in a psychodrama focused on the offender, to restore him and thereby render him less likely to offend again.
- A victim, supported by family and intimates while engaged in restorative conferencing, and feeling genuinely free to speak directly to the offender, may press a blaming rather than restorative shaming agenda.
- The victims' movement has focused for years on a perceived imbalance of "rights." Criminal defendants enjoy the presumption of innocence, the right to proof beyond a reasonable doubt, the right not to have to testify, and lenient treatment when found guilty of crime. Victims were extended no rights at all in the legal process. Is restorative justice another legal giveaway to criminals?
- Victims' rights are threatened by some features of the restorative justice process, such as respectful listening to the offender's story and consensual dispositions. These features seem affronts to a victim's claim of the right to be seen as a victim, to insist on the offender being branded a criminal, to blame the offender, and not to be "victimized all over again by the process."
- Many victims do want an apology, if it is heartfelt and easy to get, but some want, even more, to put the traumatic incident behind them; to retrieve stolen property being held for use at trial; to be assured that the offender will receive treatment he is thought to need if he is not to victimize someone else. For victims such as these, restorative justice processes can seem unnecessary at best.
- Restorative processes depend, case by case, on victims' active participation, in a role more emotionally demanding than that of complaining witness in a conventional criminal prosecution; this is itself a role avoided by many, and perhaps most, victims.

Source: Michael E. Smith, *What Future for "Public Safety" and "Restorative Justice" in Community Corrections?* (Washington, D.C.: National Institute of Justice, 2001).

Possibly the greatest challenge in carrying out the goals of restorative justice is the difficult task of balancing the needs of offenders with those of their victims. If programs focus solely on the victim's needs they may risk ignoring the offender's needs and increasing the likelihood of re-offending. Restorative justice advocates may falsely assume that relatively brief interludes of public shaming will change deeply rooted criminal predispositions.[101] In contrast, programs that focus on the offender may turn off victims and their advocates. Some victim advocacy groups have voiced concerns about the focus of restorative justice programs (see Exhibit 12.5).

These are a few of the obstacles that restorative justice programs must overcome in order to be successful and productive. Yet, because the method holds so much promise, criminologists are now conducting numerous demonstration projects testing restorative concepts. Some evaluations indicate that programs can reduce recidivism rates.[102] A recent evaluation of Vermont's Reparative Probation Program found that the program was largely successful in meeting its program goals, gaining community involvement, repairing harm, and reintegrating offenders.[103]

Criminal Justice ⊕ Now™

*Learn more about **Careers in Criminal Justice** by exploring the "On the Job" feature "Regional Parole Administrator."*

SUMMARY

- Community sentences can be traced to the common law practice of granting clemency to deserving offenders.
- The modern probation concept was developed by John Augustus of Boston, who personally sponsored two thousand convicted inmates over an eighteen-year period.
- Today, probation is the community supervision of convicted offenders by order of the court. It is a sentence reserved for defendants whom the

magistrate views as having potential for rehabilitation without needing to serve prison or jail terms.
- Probation is practiced in every state and by the federal government and includes both adult and juvenile offenders.
- In the decision to grant probation, most judges are influenced by their personal views and the presentence reports of the probation staff. Some states have set up guidelines for granting probation.

- Once on probation, the offender must follow a set of rules or conditions, the violation of which may lead to revocation of probation and reinstatement of a prison sentence.
- Probation rules vary from case to case but usually involve such demands as refraining from using alcohol or drugs, obeying curfews, and terminating past criminal associations.
- Probation officers are usually organized into countywide departments, although some agencies are statewide and others are combined parole-probation departments.
- In recent years, the U.S. Supreme Court has granted probationers greater due process rights. Today, when the state wishes to revoke probation, it must conduct a full hearing on the matter and provide the probationer with an attorney when that assistance is warranted.
- To supplement probation, a whole new family of intermediate sanctions has been developed. These range from pretrial diversion to residential community corrections. Other widely used intermediate sanctions include fines and forfeiture, house arrest, and intensive probation supervision.
- Electronic monitoring (EM) involves a device worn by an offender under home confinement. While some critics complain that EM smacks of a "Big Brother Is Watching You" mentality, it would seem an attractive alternative to a stay in a dangerous, deteriorated, secure correctional facility.
- A stay in a community correctional center is one of the most intrusive alternative sentencing op-

tions. Residents may be eligible for work and educational release during the day while attending group sessions in the evening. Residential community correction is less costly than more secure institutions, while being equally effective.
- It is too soon to determine whether alternative sanction programs are successful. There is little evidence they can lower recidivism rates. They do provide a hope of being low-cost, high-security alternatives to traditional corrections.
- Alternative sentences can help reduce overcrowding in the prison system and spare nonviolent offenders the pains of a prison experience. Although alternatives may not be much more effective than a prison sentence in reducing recidivism rates, they are far less costly and can free up needed space for more violent offenders.
- A promising approach to community sentencing is the use of restorative justice programs. These are being used in the U.S. and abroad.
- Restorative programs stress healing and redemption rather than punishment and deterrence.
- Restoration means that the offender accepts accountability for her actions and accepts the responsibility for the harm her actions caused. Restoration involves turning the justice system into a "healing" process rather than being a distributor of retribution and revenge.
- Restoration programs are now being used around the nation and involve mediation, sentencing circles, and the like.

KEY TERMS

probation 328
judicial reprieve 329
recognizance 329
sureties 329
probation rules 331
revocation 331
suspended sentence 332
pre-sentence investigation 334
intake 335
risk classification 336
day fees 339

intermediate sanctions 339
fine 341
day fine 343
forfeiture 344
zero tolerance 344
restitution 344
monetary restitution 344
community service restitution 344
shock probation 345
split sentence 345

intensive probation supervision (IPS) 346
house arrest 347
electronic monitoring (EM) 347
residential community corrections (RCC) 349
day reporting center (DRC) 350
restorative justice 350
sentencing circles 352

REVIEW QUESTIONS

1. What is the purpose of probation? Identify some conditions of probation and discuss the responsibilities of the probation officer.

2. Discuss the procedures involved in probation revocation. What are the rights of the probationer? Is probation a privilege or a right? Explain.

3. Should a convicted criminal make restitution to the victim? Why or why not? When is restitution inappropriate?

4. Should offenders be fined based on the severity of what they did or according to their ability to pay? Is it fair to base day fines on wages? Why or why not? Should offenders be punished more severely because they are financially successful? Explain.

5. Does house arrest involve a violation of personal freedom? Does wearing an ankle bracelet smack of "Big Brother"? Would you want the government monitoring your daily activities? Could this be expanded, for example, to monitor the whereabouts of AIDS patients? Explain.

6. Do you agree that criminals can be restored through community interaction? Considering the fact that recidivism rates are so high, are traditional sanctions a waste of time and restorative ones the wave of the future?

CHAPTER 13

Corrections: History, Institutions, and Populations

© 2005 AP/Wide World Photos

DEBRA RASOULYIAN holds a B.S. in Business Administration from Auburn University at Montgomery, an M.S. in Counseling and Human Development from Troy State University, and an Ed.S. in Community Counseling from Georgia State University. In 1996 she was recruited to work in the Atlanta Detention Center as an inmate counselor. In 1999, the City Council asked that an in-custody program for prostitutes with drug-related charges be created. Rasoulyian became the director of the Women for Women (W4W) program, established as an intensive in-custody substance abuse treatment program using a therapeutic community (TC) model. The Women for Women program provided clients with intensive cognitive restructuring therapy, substance abuse treatment, HIV/AIDS education, life skills, spirituality, parenting courses, career counseling, yoga, music therapy, and individual and group counseling. After graduation from the program, the women were sent to

Chapter Outline

Chapter Objectives

1. Be familiar with the history of penal institutions
2. Know the differences between the Auburn (congregate) and Pennsylvania (isolate) systems
3. Understand the history of penal reform
4. Be familiar with the concept of the jail
5. Be able to discuss the issue of the new generation jails
6. Describe the different levels of prison security
7. Discuss the super-maximum-security prison
8. Know the current trends in prison security
9. Discuss the benefits and drawbacks of boot camps and private prisons
10. Explain the current trends in the prison population

residential treatment in the community for several months, and then given housing. Aftercare was a major component to the program's success, as almost 75 percent of the women were homeless when they entered the program. Despite the fact that most clients had multiple social problems ranging from addiction to mental illness, the program proved highly successful. Graduates of the program are now program managers in substance abuse centers, certified addiction counselors, working mothers, wives, retail managers, choir directors, administrators, domestic violence counselors, members of boards . . . the list is endless. When the program was closed due to budget constraints, Debra Rasoulyian became a founding member of the Restorative Justice Center Foundation, which is presently raising money to reinstitute the program and continue efforts to stop the revolving door of recidivism.

Rasoulyian's career represents the ideal for people wanting to become part of the contemporary correctional system. This vast organization has branches in the federal, state, and county levels of government. Felons may be placed in state or federal penitentiaries (prisons), which are usually isolated, high-security structures. Misdemeanants are housed in county jails, sometimes called reformatories or houses of correction. Juvenile offenders have their own institutions, sometimes euphemistically called schools, camps, ranches, or homes. Usually, the latter are nonsecure facilities, often located in rural areas, and provide both confinement and rehabilitative services for young offenders.

Other types of correctional institutions include ranches and farms for adult offenders and community correctional settings, such as halfway houses, for inmates who are about to return to society. Today's correctional facilities encompass a wide range, from super-maximum-security institutions, such as the federal prison in Florence, Colorado, where the nation's most dangerous felons are confined, to low-security camps that house white-collar criminals convicted of such crimes as insider trading and mail fraud.

One of the great tragedies of our time is that correctional institutions—whatever form they may take—do not seem to correct. They are, in most instances, overcrowded, understaffed, outdated warehouses for social outcasts. Overcrowding is the most significant crisis faced by the corrections system today, which holds about two million inmates. Prisons and jails are more suited to control, punishment, and security than to rehabilitation and treatment. It is a sad but unfortunately accurate observation that today's correctional institution has become a revolving door, and all too many of its residents return time and again. Although no completely accurate statement of the recidivism rate is available, it is estimated that more than half of all inmates will be back in prison within six years of their release.

Even though the penal institutions seem unsuccessful, great debate continues over the direction of their future operations. Some penal experts maintain that **prisons** and **jails** are not really places for rehabilitation and treatment, but should be used to keep dangerous offenders apart from society and give them the "just deserts" for their crimes.[1] In this sense, prison success would be measured by such factors as physical security, length of incapacitation, relationship between the crime rate and the number of incarcerated felons, and inmates' perceptions that their treatment is fair and proportionate. The dominance of this correctional philosophy is illustrated by the fact that the number of people under lock and key has risen during the past decade even though the crime rate has declined. All too often, building prisons and putting people behind bars is used to energize political campaigns and not to provide effective and efficient treatment. Political candidates who advocate inmate rehabilitation soon find themselves on the defensive among voters.[2]

While punishment has its political appeal, many penal experts maintain that if properly funded and effectively directed, correctional facilities can provide successful offender rehabilitation.[3] Many examples of the treatment philosophy flourish in prisons: educational programs allow inmates to get college credits; vocational training has become more sophisticated; counseling and substance abuse programs are almost universal; and every state maintains some type of early-release and community correctional programs.

In this chapter, we explore the correctional system, beginning with the history and nature of correctional institutions. Then in chapter 14 we examine institutional life in some detail.

 The American Correctional Association is a multidisciplinary organization of professionals representing all facets of corrections and criminal justice, including federal, state, and military correctional facilities and prisons, county jails and detention centers, probation/parole agencies, and community corrections/halfway houses. It has more than twenty thousand members. To learn about what the group does, go to "Web Links" on your Siegel Essentials of Criminal Justice 5e website: http://cj.wadsworth.com/siegel_ess5e.

Criminal Justice ⚖ Now™
*Learn more by exploring the **Development of Corrections in America** Vocabulary Check activity.*

prison *A state or federal correctional institution for incarceration of felony offenders for terms of one year or more.*

jail *A place to detain people awaiting trial, to serve as a lockup for drunks and disorderly individuals, and to confine convicted misdemeanants serving sentences of less than one year.*

THE HISTORY OF CORRECTIONAL INSTITUTIONS

Although the routine use of incarceration as a criminal punishment began in the later eighteenth and early nineteenth centuries, some early European institutions were created specifically to detain and punish criminal offenders.[4]

Penal institutions were constructed in England during the tenth century to hold pretrial detainees and those waiting for their sentence to be carried out.[5] During the twelfth century, King Henry II of England constructed a series of county jails to hold thieves and vagrants prior to the disposition of their sentence.

There are a number of examples of early correctional facilities. Le Stinche, a prison in Florence, Italy, was used to punish offenders as early as 1301.[6] In 1557 the workhouse in Brideswell, England, was built to hold people convicted of relatively minor offenses who would work to pay off their debt to society; those committing more serious offenses were held there prior to their execution. The first penal institutions were foul places devoid of proper care, food, and medical treatment. The jailer, usually a shire reeve (sheriff)—an official appointed by king or noble landholder as chief law enforcement official of a county—ran the jail under the "fee system." This required inmates to pay for their own food and services. Those who could not pay were fed scraps until they literally starved to death:

> In 1748 the admission to Southwark Prison was eleven shillings and fourpence. Having got in, the prisoner had to pay for having himself put in irons, for his bed, of whatever sort, for his room if he was able to afford a separate room. He had to pay for his food, and when he had paid his debts and was ready to go out, he had to pay for having his irons struck off, and a discharge fee. . . . The gaolers

"Prisoners Exercising," by Vincent van Gogh. Painted in 1890, this work captures the despair of the nineteenth-century penal institution. The face of the prisoner near the center of the picture looking at the viewer is van Gogh's.

[jailers] were usually "low bred, mercenary and oppressive, barbarous fellows, who [thought] of nothing but enriching themselves by the most cruel extortion, and [had] less regard for the life of a poor prisoner than for the life of a brute."[7]

From 1776 to 1785, a growing inmate population forced the English to house prisoners on **hulks,** abandoned ships anchored in harbors. The hulks became infamous for their degrading conditions and brutal punishments, but were not totally abandoned until 1858. The writings of John Howard, the reform-oriented sheriff of Bedfordshire, drew attention to the squalid conditions in British penal institutions. His famous book, *The State of the Prisons in England and Wales* (1777), condemned the lack of basic care given English inmates awaiting trial or serving sentences.[8] Howard's efforts to create humane standards in the British penal system resulted in the Penitentiary Act, by which Parliament established a more orderly penal system, with periodic inspections, elimination of the fee system, and greater consideration for inmates.

American Developments

Although Europe had jails and a variety of other penal facilities, it was in the United States that correctional reform was instituted. The first American jail was built in James City in the Virginia colonies in the early seventeenth century. However, the "modern" American correctional system had its origins in Pennsylvania under the leadership of William Penn, who ordered that a new type of institution be built to replace the then widely used public forms of punishment: stocks, pillories, gallows, and branding irons. Each county was instructed to build a house of corrections similar to today's jails. County trustees or commissioners were responsible for raising money to build the jails and providing for their maintenance, although they were operated by the local sheriff. Penn's reforms remained in effect until his death in 1718, when the criminal penal code was changed back to open public punishment and brutality. Other early correctional institutions include Connecticut's Newgate Prison, which opened in 1773 on the site of an abandoned copper mine,[9] and Castle Island Prison, which was opened in Massachusetts in 1785 and operated for about fifteen years.

The Quaker Influence The origin of the modern correctional system is usually traced to eighteenth-century developments in Pennsylvania. In 1776, postrevolutionary Pennsylvania again adopted William Penn's code and in 1787, a group of Quakers led by Benjamin Rush formed the Philadelphia Society for Alleviating the Miseries of Public Prisons. The aim of the society was to bring some degree of humane and orderly treatment to the growing penal system. The Quakers' influence on the legislature resulted in limiting the use of the death penalty to cases involving treason, murder, rape, and arson. Their next step was to reform the institutional system so that the prison could serve as a suitable alternative to physical punishment.

The only models of custodial institutions at that time were the local county jails that Penn had established. The Pennsylvania jails placed men, women, and children of all ages indiscriminately in one room. Liquor was often freely sold.

Under pressure from the Quakers to improve these conditions, the Pennsylvania state legislature in 1790 called for the renovation of the prison system. The ultimate result was the creation of a separate wing of Philadelphia's **Walnut Street Jail,** which had been in operation since 1776 as a local facility, to house convicted felons, except those sentenced to death. The legislation creating a state **"penitentiary house"** ushered in ten years of reform and attracted worldwide notice. Some prisoners were placed in solitary cells, where they remained in isolation and did not have the right to work; the majority of the several hundred inmates lived together in large common rooms.[10]

Eastern State Penitentiary became the most expensive and most copied building of its time. It is estimated that more than three hundred prisons worldwide are based on the penitentiary's wagon-wheel or radial floor plan. Some of America's most notorious criminals were held in its vaulted, sky-lit cells, including Al Capone. After 142 years of consecutive use, Eastern State Penitentiary was abandoned in 1971. To reach this site, go to "Web Links" on your Siegel Essentials of Criminal Justice 5e website: http://cj.wadsworth.com/siegel_ess5e.

hulk *A mothballed ship that was used to house prisoners in eighteenth-century England.*

Walnut Street Jail *In 1790, a separate wing of Philadelphia's Walnut Street Jail was built to house convicted felons. This was the forerunner of the secure correctional system in the United States.*

penitentiary house *A secure correctional facility, based on the Quaker concept that incarcerated criminals should experience penitence.*

The Walnut Street Jail was not a total success. Overcrowding undermined the goal of solitary confinement of serious offenders, and soon more than one inmate was placed in each cell. The isolation had a terrible psychological effect on inmates, and eventually inmates were given in-cell piecework on which they worked up to eight hours a day. Despite these difficulties, similar institutions were constructed in New York (Newgate in 1791) and New Jersey (Trenton in 1798).

The Auburn System As the nineteenth century got underway, both the Pennsylvania and the New York prison systems were experiencing difficulties maintaining the ever-increasing numbers of convicted criminals. Initially, administrators dealt with the problem by increasing the use of pardons, relaxing prison discipline, and limiting supervision.

In 1816, New York built a new prison at Auburn, hoping to alleviate some of the overcrowding at Newgate. The Auburn Prison design became known as the **tier system** because cells were built vertically on five floors of the structure. It was also referred to as the **congregate system** since most prisoners ate and worked in groups. Later, in 1819, construction was started on a wing of solitary cells to house unruly prisoners. Three classes of prisoners were then created: one group remained continually in solitary confinement as a result of breaches of prison discipline; the second group was allowed labor as an occasional form of recreation; and members of the third and largest class worked and ate together during the day and were separated only at night.

The philosophy of the **Auburn system** was crime prevention through fear of punishment and silent confinement. The worst felons were to be cut off from all contact with other prisoners, and although they were treated and fed relatively well, they had no hope of pardon to relieve their solitude or isolation. For a time, some of the worst convicts were forced to remain totally alone and silent during the entire day; this practice caused many prisoners to have mental breakdowns, resulting in many suicides and self-mutilations. This practice was abolished in 1823.

The combination of silence and solitude as a method of punishment was not abandoned easily. Prison officials sought to overcome the side effects of total isolation while maintaining the penitentiary system. The solution adopted at Auburn was to keep convicts in separate cells at night but allow them to work together during the day under enforced silence. Hard work and silence became the foundation of the Auburn system wherever it was adopted. Silence was the key to prison discipline; it prohibited the formulation of escape plans, it prevented plots and riots, and it allowed prisoners to contemplate their infractions. Regimentation became the standard mode of prison life. Convicts did not simply walk from place to place; rather, they went in close order and single file, each looking over the shoulder of the preceding person, faces inclined to the right, feet moving in unison.[11]

When discipline was breached in the Auburn system, punishment was applied in the form of a rawhide whip on the inmate's back. Immediate and effective, Auburn discipline was so successful that when one hundred inmates were used to build the famous Sing Sing Prison in 1825, not one dared try to escape, although they were housed in an open field with only minimal supervision.[12]

The Pennsylvania System Pennsylvania took the radical step of establishing a prison that placed each inmate in a single cell for the duration of his sentence. Classifications were abolished because each cell was intended as a miniature prison that would prevent the inmates from contaminating one another.

The new Pennsylvania state prison opened in 1826. Called the Western Penitentiary, it had an unusual architectural design. It was built in a circle,

www The penitentiary movement spread around the world. In Australia, Fremantle Prison was built by convicts between 1850 and 1860. Convicts were brought to western Australia to help in the building of roads, bridges, port facilities, and public buildings. To read about the history of the institution and to get a virtual tour, go to "Web Links" on your Siegel Essentials of Criminal Justice 5e website: http://cj.wadsworth.com/siegel_ess5e.

tier system The structure of early prisons having numerous floors or wings that stacked cells one over another.

congregate system The Auburn Prison, one of the nation's first correctional facilities, was a congregate system, since most prisoners ate and worked in groups.

Auburn system The prison system developed in New York during the nineteenth century that stressed congregate working conditions.

with the cells positioned along its circumference. Built back to back, some cells faced the boundary wall while others faced the internal area of the circle. Its inmates were kept in solitary confinement almost constantly, being allowed out for about an hour a day for exercise. In 1821, construction began on a second, similar penitentiary using the isolate system in Philadelphia: this was the Eastern State Penitentiary, which opened in 1829.

Supporters of the **Pennsylvania system** believed that the *penitentiary* was truly a place to experience penitence. By advocating totally removing the sinner from society and allowing the prisoner a period of isolation during which to reflect alone on the evils of crime, the supporters of the Pennsylvania system reflected the influence of religion and religious philosophy on corrections. Solitary confinement (with in-cell labor) was believed to make work so attractive that upon release the inmate would be well-suited to resume a productive existence in society.

Pennsylvania vs. New York: Isolate vs. Congregate

Many fiery debates occurred between advocates of the Pennsylvania system and adherents of the Auburn system. Those supporting the latter boasted of its supposed advantages; it was the cheapest and most productive way to reform prisoners. They criticized the Pennsylvania system as cruel and inhumane, suggesting that solitary confinement was both physically and mentally damaging. The Pennsylvania system's devotees, on the other hand, argued that their system was quiet, efficient, humane, and well-ordered and provided the ultimate correctional facility.[13] They chided the Auburn system for tempting inmates to talk by putting them together for meals and work and then punishing them when they did talk. Finally, the Auburn system was accused of becoming a breeding place for criminal associations by allowing inmates to get to know one another.

The Auburn system eventually prevailed and spread throughout the United States; many of its features are still used today. Its innovations included congregate working conditions, the use of solitary confinement to punish unruly inmates, military regimentation, and discipline. In Auburn-style institutions, prisoners were marched from place to place; their time was regulated by bells telling them to wake up, sleep, and work. The system was so like the military that many of its early administrators were recruited from the armed services.

Although the prison was viewed as an improvement over capital and corporal punishment, it quickly became the scene of depressed conditions; inmates were treated harshly and were routinely whipped and tortured. Prison brutality flourished in these institutions, which had originally been devised as a more humane correctional alternative. In these early penal institutions, brutal corporal punishment took place indoors, where, hidden from public view, it could become even more savage.[14]

Prisons at the Turn of the Twentieth Century

The prison of the late nineteenth century was remarkably similar to that of today. The congregate system was adopted in all states except Pennsylvania. Prisons were overcrowded, and the single-cell principle was often ignored. The prison, like the police department, became the scene of political intrigue and efforts by political administrators to control the hiring of personnel and dispensing of patronage.

Prison industry developed and became the predominant theme around which institutions were organized. Some prisons used the **contract system,** in which officials sold the labor of inmates to private businesses, which then

Pennsylvania system *The prison system developed during the nineteenth century that stressed total isolation and individual penitence as a means of reform.*

contract system (convict) *The system used early in the twentieth century by which private industry contracted with prison officials for convict labor and set up shops on prison grounds for them to work.*

Inmates in a nineteenth-century prison return from a work detail in lockstep.

Stock Montage, Inc.

set up shops and supervised the inmates inside the prison itself. Under the **convict-lease system,** the state leased its prisoners to a business outside the prison walls for a fixed annual fee and gave up supervision and control. Finally, some institutions had prisoners produce goods for the prison's own use.[15]

The development of prison industry quickly led to the abuse of inmates, who were forced to work for almost no wages, and to profiteering by dishonest administrators and businessmen. During the Civil War era, prisons were major manufacturers of clothes, shoes, boots, furniture, and the like. Beginning in the 1870s, opposition by trade unions sparked restrictions on interstate commerce in prison goods.

Reform Movements Prison operations were also reformed. The National Congress of Penitentiary and Reformatory Discipline, held in Cincinnati in 1870, heralded a new era of prison reform. Organized by penologists Enoch Wines and Theodore Dwight, the congress provided a forum for corrections experts from around the nation to call for the treatment, education, and training of inmates.

One of the most famous people to attend the congress, Zebulon R. Brockway, warden at the Elmira Reformatory in New York, advocated individualized treatment, the indeterminate sentence, and parole. The reformatory program initiated by Brockway included elementary education for illiterates, designated library hours, lectures by faculty members of the local Elmira College, and a group of vocational training shops. From 1888 to 1920, Elmira administrators used military-like training to discipline the inmates and organize the institution. The military organization could be seen in every aspect of the institution: schooling, manual training, sports, supervision of inmates, and even parole decisions.[16] The cost to the state of the institution's operations was to be held to a minimum.

Although Brockway proclaimed Elmira to be an ideal reformatory, his actual achievements were limited. The greatest significance of his contribution was the injection of a degree of humanitarianism into the industrial prisons of that day.[17] Although many institutions were constructed across the nation and labeled reformatories based on the Elmira model, most of them continued to be industrially oriented.[18]

convict-lease system The system whereby the state leased its prisoners to a business for a fixed annual fee and gave up supervision and control.

Creation of Parole The forerunner of parole began in Ireland in the 1850s, when Sir Walter Crofton, Ireland's prison director, set up a system whereby penitentiary inmates spent the last portion of their sentences living in an intermediate institution and working in the outside community. Crofton's methods proved so popular that under Quaker influence, New York City opened the Isaac T. Hopper Home in 1845 as a shelter for released inmates. The Hopper home was followed by a shelter for women released from the Detroit House of Correction, opened by Zebulon Brockway in 1868; the Philadelphia House of Industry, opened in 1889; and Hope Hall, a refuge for ex-inmates in New York, opened by Maud Ballington Booth in the 1890s.[19]

Prisons in the Twentieth Century The early twentieth century was a time of contrasts in the prison system of the United States.[20] At one extreme were those who advocated reform, such as the Mutual Welfare League led by Thomas Mott Osborne. Prison reform groups proposed better treatment for inmates, an end to harsh corporal punishment, the creation of meaningful prison industries, and educational programs. Reformers argued that prisoners should not be isolated from society and that the best elements of society—education, religion, meaningful work, self-governance—should be brought to the prison. Osborne went so far as to spend one week in New York's notorious Sing Sing Prison to learn firsthand about its conditions.

Opposed to the reformers were conservative prison administrators and state officials who believed that stern disciplinary measures were needed to control dangerous prison inmates. They continued the time-honored system of regimentation and discipline. Although the whip and the lash were eventually abolished, solitary confinement in dark, bare cells became a common penal practice.

In time, some of the more rigid prison rules gave way to liberal reform. By the mid-1930s, few prisons required inmates to wear the red-and-white-striped convict suit and substituted nondescript gray uniforms. The code of silence ended, as did the lockstep shuffle. Prisoners were allowed "the freedom of the yard" to mingle and exercise an hour or two each day.[21] Movies and radio appeared in the 1930s. Visiting policies and mail privileges were liberalized.

A more important trend was the development of specialized prisons designed to treat particular types of offenders. For example, in New York the prisons at Clinton and Auburn were viewed as industrial facilities for hardcore inmates; Great Meadow was an agricultural center to house nondangerous offenders; and Dannemora was a facility for the criminally insane. In California, San Quentin housed inmates considered salvageable by correctional authorities, whereas Folsom was reserved for hard-core offenders.[22]

Prison Industry Prison industry also evolved. Opposition by organized labor helped put an end to the convict-lease system and forced inmate labor. By 1900, a number of states had restricted the sale of prisoner-made goods on the open market. The worldwide Great Depression that began in 1929 prompted industry and union leaders to pressure state legislators further to reduce competition from prison industries. A series of ever-more restrictive federal legislative initiatives led to the Sumners-Ashurst Act (1940), which made it a federal offense to transport out of state goods made in prison for private use, regardless of the laws of the state receiving the goods.[23] The restrictions imposed by the federal government helped to curtail prison industry severely for forty years. Private entrepreneurs shunned prison investments because they were no longer profitable; the result was inmate idleness and make-work jobs.[24]

Despite some changes and reforms, the prison in the mid-twentieth century remained a destructive penal institution. Although some aspects of inmate life improved, severe discipline, harsh rules, and solitary confinement were the way of life.

Contemporary Correctional Trends

During the past fifty years, the correctional system has undergone a long period of change and turmoil. Three trends stand out. First, between 1960 and 1980, during what is referred to as the *prisoners' rights movement,* inmates demanded and received civil rights through the court process. After many years of indifference (a policy referred to as the *hands-off doctrine*), state and federal courts ruled in a series of cases that institutionalized inmates had rights to freedom of religion and speech, medical care, procedural due process, and proper living conditions. Since 1980, an increasingly conservative judiciary has curtailed the expansion of inmate rights.

Second, well-publicized riots at New York's Attica Prison and the New Mexico State Penitentiary drew attention to the potential for death and destruction that lurks in every prison. Prison rapes and killings have become commonplace. The locus of control in many prisons shifted from the correctional staff to violent inmate gangs. In reaction, some administrators have tried to improve conditions and provide innovative programs that give inmates a voice in running the institution. Another reaction was to tighten discipline and build new super-maximum-security prisons to control the most dangerous offenders. The problem of prison overcrowding made attempts to improve conditions extremely difficult.

Third, the role of the prison and the correctional experience began to be reexamined. Between 1960 and 1980, it was common for correctional administrators to cling to the **medical model,** which viewed inmates as "sick people" who were suffering from some social malady that prevented them from adjusting to society. Correctional treatment could help "cure" them and enable them to live productive lives once they returned to the community. In the 1970s, efforts were also made to help offenders become reintegrated into society by providing them with new career opportunities that relied on work-release programs. Inmates were allowed to work outside the institution during the day and return in the evening; some were given extended furloughs in the community. Work release became a political issue when Willie Horton, a furloughed inmate in Massachusetts, raped a young woman. Criticism of its "liberal" furlough program helped George Bush defeat Governor Michael Dukakis of Massachusetts for the U.S. presidency in 1988; in the aftermath of the Horton case, a number of states, including Massachusetts, restricted their furlough policies.

As the nation moved toward a more conservative political outlook, prisons have come to be viewed as places for control, incapacitation, and punishment, rather than as sites for rehabilitation and reform. Advocates of the *no frills,* or **penal harm,** movement believe that if prison is a punishing experience, criminals will be deterred from crime and current inmates will be encouraged to go straight. Besides, why should people who have engaged in antisocial activities receive benefits behind bars that are sometimes unavailable to the honest and law-abiding, such as higher education courses. Nonetheless, efforts to use correctional institutions as treatment facilities have not ended, and while public support for rehabilitation has declined, most people continue to view treatment as a legitimate correctional objective, especially for juvenile and nonviolent offenders.[25]

The alleged failure of correctional treatment, coupled with constantly increasing correctional costs, has prompted the development of alternatives to incarceration, such as intensive probation supervision, house arrest, and electronic monitoring (see chapter 12). What has developed is a dual correctional policy: keep as many nonviolent offenders out of the correctional system as possible by means of community-based programs; incarcerate dangerous, violent offenders for long periods of time.[26] These efforts have been compromised by a growing get-tough stance in judicial and legislative sentencing policy, accented by mandatory minimum sentences for gun crimes and drug

Criminal Justice ⚖ Now™
Learn more by going through Corrections Learning Module.

medical model A view of corrections holding that convicted offenders are victims of their environment who need care and treatment to transform them into valuable members of society.

penal harm The view that prison should be a punishing experience and that criminals will be deterred from crime and current inmates will be encouraged to go straight.

trafficking. Despite the development of alternatives to incarceration, the number of people under lock and key has skyrocketed.

In the following sections, we review the most prominent types of correctional facilities in operation today.

JAILS

The nation's jails are institutional facilities with five primary purposes:

- They detain accused offenders who cannot make or are not eligible for bail prior to trial.
- They hold convicted offenders awaiting sentence.
- They serve as the principal institution of secure confinement for offenders convicted of misdemeanors.
- They hold probationers and parolees picked up for violations and waiting for a hearing.
- They house felons when state prisons are overcrowded.

A number of formats are used to jail offenders. About fifteen thousand local jurisdictions maintain short-term police or municipal lockups that house offenders for no more than forty-eight hours before a bail hearing can be held; thereafter, detainees are kept in the county jail. In some jurisdictions, such as New Hampshire and Massachusetts, a house of corrections holds convicted misdemeanants, and a county jail holds pretrial detainees. Today, the jail is a multipurpose correctional institution whose other main functions are set out in Exhibit 13.1.

Jail Populations

As Figure 13.1 shows, more than 700,000 people are being held in jails today and the number has risen significantly since 1990 though the crime rate has trended downward. Almost nine out of every ten jail inmates are adult males. However, the number of adult females in jail has been increasing faster than males. The number of juveniles held in adult facilities declined from 1999 to 2004, a result of ongoing government initiatives to remove juveniles from adult facilities; about 7,000 minors are still being held in adult jails.

Characteristics of jail inmates tend to reflect arrest data: men, the poor, racial and ethnic minorities are over-represented. The overwhelming number of jail inmates, almost 90 percent, are males. Nearly six in ten persons in local

Exhibit 13.1   Jail functions and services

- Receive individuals pending arraignment and hold them awaiting trial, conviction, or sentencing
- Readmit probation, parole, and bail-bond violators and absconders
- Temporarily detain juveniles pending transfer to juvenile authorities
- Hold mentally ill persons pending their movement to appropriate health facilities
- Hold individuals for the military, for protective custody, for contempt, and for the courts as witnesses
- Release convicted inmates to the community upon completion of sentence
- Transfer inmates to federal, state, or other authorities
- House inmates for federal, state, or other authorities because of crowding of their facilities
- Sometimes operate community-based programs as alternatives to incarceration
- Hold inmates sentenced to short terms (generally under one year)

Source: Paige M. Harrison and Allen J. Beck, *Prison and Jail Inmates at Midyear 2004* (Washington, D.C.: Bureau of Justice Statistics, 2005).

Number of jail inmates (one-day count)

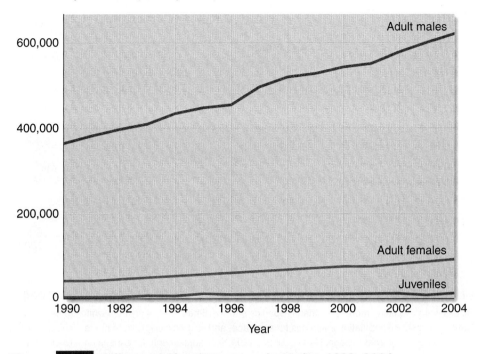

Figure 13.1 Jail population by age and gender, 1990–2004
Source: Bureau of Justice Statistics Correctional Surveys (the National Probation Data Survey,
National Prisoner Statistics, Survey of Jails, and the National Parole Data Survey),
www.ojp.usdoj.gov/bjs/glance/jailag.htm, accessed on September 27, 2005.

jails are racial or ethnic minorities. Whites make up 45 percent of the jail population; blacks, 39 percent; Hispanics, 15 percent; and other races (Asians, American Indians, Alaska Natives, Native Hawaiians, and other Pacific Islanders) the rest. As Figure 13.2 shows, there is a disproportionate number of ethnic and racial minorities in the jail population, presumably reflecting such factors as over-representation in the arrest statistics, failure to secure bail, inferior legal representation, and racial/ethnic bias in the justice system.

Jail Conditions

Jails are usually a low-priority item in the criminal justice system. Because they are often administered on a county level, jail services have not been sufficiently regulated, nor has a unified national policy been developed to mandate what constitutes adequate jail conditions. Consequently, many jails have developed into squalid, crumbling holding pens holding dangerous and or troubled people, many of whom suffer emotional problems which remain untreated. Many inmates have been the victim of prior physical and sexual abuse: about 13 percent of males and 47 percent of female inmates report having experienced either physical or sexual abuse.[27] It is not surprising then that about 16 percent of those in local jails report either having a mental condition or an overnight stay in a mental hospital at least once in their lives.[28] Being warehoused in local jails does little to alleviate their problems.

A national effort has been made to remove as many people from local jails as possible through the adoption of both bail reform measures and pretrial diversion. Considering these measures and the declining crime rate, why do jail populations continue to increase? There are a number of reasons for this phenomenon. As prisons become more overcrowded, prison correctional officials use local jails to house inmates for whom there is no room in state prisons.

Number of jail inmates per 100,000

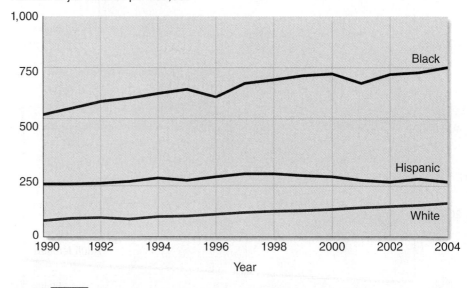

Figure 13.2 **Jail incarceration rates by race and ethnicity, 1990–2004**
Blacks were two times more likely than Hispanics and five times more likely than whites to be in jail.
Note: U.S. resident population estimates for sex, race, and Hispanic origin were made using a U.S. Census Bureau Internet release, December 23, 1999, with adjustments for census undercount. Estimates for 2000–2004 are based on the 2000 Census and then estimated for July 1 of each year.
Source: Bureau of Justice Statistics Correctional Surveys (the National Probation Data Survey, National Prisoner Statistics, Survey of Jails, and the National Parole Data Survey), www.ojp.usdoj.gov/bjs/glance/jailrair.htm, accessed on September 27, 2005.

Jail populations also respond to the efforts being made to reduce or control particular crime problems, including substance abuse, spousal abuse, and driving while intoxicated (DWI). Some jurisdictions have passed legislation requiring that people arrested on suspicion of domestic violence be held in confinement for a number of hours to "cool off" before becoming eligible for bail. Other jurisdictions have attempted to deter drunk driving by passing mandatory jail sentences for people convicted of DWI; such legislation can quickly result in overcrowded jails.[29]

New-Generation Jails

To relieve overcrowding and improve effectiveness, a jail-building boom has been under way. Many of the new jails are using modern designs to improve effectiveness; these are referred to as *new-generation jails*.[30] Traditional jails are constructed and use what is referred to as the *linear/intermittent surveillance model*. Jails using this design are rectangular, with corridors leading to either single- or multiple-occupancy cells arranged at right angles to the corridor. Correctional officers must patrol to see into cells or housing areas, and when they are in a position to observe one cell they cannot observe others; unobserved inmates are essentially unsupervised.

In contrast, new-generation jails allow for continuous observation of residents. There are two types: direct and indirect supervision jails. *Direct supervision jails* contain a cluster of cells surrounding a living area or "pod," which contains tables, chairs, televisions, and other material. A correctional officer is stationed within the pod. The officer has visual observation of inmates and maintains the ability to relate to them on a personal level. By placing the officer in the pod, there is an increased awareness of the behaviors and needs of the inmates. This results in a safer environment for both staff and inmates. Since interaction between inmates is constantly and closely monitored, dissension can be quickly detected before it escalates. During the day, inmates stay in the open area (dayroom) and typically are not permitted to go into their rooms except with permission of the officer in charge. The officer controls door locks to cells from the control panel. In case of trouble or if the officer leaves the station for an extended period of time, command of this panel can be switched to a panel at a remote location, known as *central control*. The officer usually wears a device that permits immediate communication with central control in case of trouble, and the area is also covered by a video camera monitored by an officer in the central control room. *Indirect supervision jails* use similar construction; however, the correctional officer's station is located inside a secure room. Microphones and speakers inside the living unit permit the officer to hear and communicate with inmates. Although these institutions have not yet undergone extensive evaluation, research shows that they may help reduce postrelease offending in some situations.[31]

PRISONS

The federal Bureau of Prisons and every state government maintain closed correctional facilities, also called prisons, penitentiaries, or reformatories. The most recent government figures show that state prisons cost taxpayers about $30 billion each year, increasing from about $12 billion in 1986; this amounts to an annual cost of $100 for every American citizen.[32]

The prison is the final repository for the most troubled criminal offenders. Many come from distressed backgrounds and have little hope or opportunity; all too many have emotional problems and grew up in abusive households. A majority are alcohol- and drug-dependent at the time of their arrest. Those considered both dangerous and incorrigible may find themselves in super-maximum-security prisons, where they spend most of their days confined to their cells.

Types of Prisons

There are more than fifteen hundred public and private adult correctional facilities housing state prisoners. In addition, there were eighty-four federal facilities and twenty-six private facilities that house federal inmates. Usually, prisons are organized or classified on three levels—maximum, medium, and minimum security—and each has distinct characteristics.

Maximum-Security Prisons Housing the most notorious criminals and the subject of films and stories, **maximum-security prisons** are probably the institutions most familiar to the public. Famous "max prisons" have included Sing Sing, Joliet, Attica, Walpole, and the most fearsome prison of all, the now-closed federal facility on Alcatraz Island known as The Rock.

A typical maximum-security facility is fortress-like, surrounded by stone walls with guard towers at strategic places. These walls may be twenty-five feet high, and sometimes inner and outer walls divide the prison into courtyards. Barbed wire or electrified fences are used to discourage escapes. High security, armed guards, and stone walls give the inmate the sense that the facility is impregnable and reassure the citizens outside that convicts will be completely incapacitated. Because they fear that violence may flair up at any minute, prison administrators have been quick to adapt the latest high-tech security

maximum-security prison A correctional institution that houses dangerous felons and maintains strict security measures, high walls, and limited contact with the outside world.

Maximum-security prisons are used to house the state's most dangerous violent criminals. Security is generally strict and inmates monitored closely. The prison facility itself is designed with high security in mind: hidden corners where people can congregate are eliminated and passages are constructed so they can be easily blocked off to quell disturbances.

© 2001 AP/Wide World Photos

measure. It is possible that in the future prison officials may lean on technology to control the prison environment. This issue is discussed in the following Criminal Justice and Technology box.

Inmates live in interior, metal-barred cells that contain their own plumbing and sanitary facilities and are locked securely either by key or electronic device. Cells are organized in sections called *blocks,* and in large prisons, a number of cell blocks make up a wing. During the day, the inmates engage in closely controlled activities: meals, workshops, education, and so on. Rule violators may be confined to their cells, and working and other shared recreational activities are viewed as privileges.

The byword of the maximum-security prison is *security*. Correctional workers are made aware that each inmate may be a dangerous criminal or violent, and that as a result, the utmost security must be maintained. These prisons are designed to eliminate hidden corners where people can congregate, and passages are constructed so that they can be easily blocked off to quell disturbances.

The **federal Bureau of Prisons** maintains a website. To reach this site go to "Web Links" on your Siegel Essentials of Criminal Justice 5e website: http://cj.wadsworth.com/siegel_ess5e.

super-maximum-security prison The newest form of a maximum-security prison that uses high-level security measures to incapacitate the nation's most dangerous criminals. Most inmates are in twenty-three hours per day lockdown.

medium-security prison A less secure institution that houses nonviolent offenders and provides more opportunities for contact with the outside world.

Super-Maximum-Security Prisons Some states have constructed **super-maximum-security prisons** (supermax prisons) to house the most predatory criminals. These high-security institutions can be independent correctional centers or locked wings of existing prisons.[33] Some supermax prisons lock inmates in their cells twenty-two to twenty-four hours a day, never allowing them out unless they are shackled.[34] The Policy, Programs, and Issues in Criminal Justice box on page 376 covers supermax prisons in greater detail.

Medium-Security Prisons Similar in appearance to maximum-security prisons, in **medium-security prisons** the security and atmosphere are neither so tense nor so vigilant. Medium-security prisons are also surrounded by walls, but there may be fewer guard towers or other security precautions; visitations with personal contact may be allowed, Although most prisoners are housed in cells, individual honor rooms in medium-security prisons are used to reward those who make exemplary rehabilitation efforts. Finally, medium-security prisons promote greater treatment efforts, and the relaxed atmosphere allows freedom of movement for rehabilitation workers and other therapeutic personnel.

Criminal Justice and Technology

Technocorrections: Contemporary Correctional Technology

A correctional establishment that takes advantage of all the potential offered by the new technologies to reduce the costs of supervising criminal offenders and minimize the risk they pose to society defines the field of technocorrections. What are some of the recent developments in this area of correctional security?

Ground-Penetrating Radar

Special Technologies Laboratories (STL) of Santa Barbara, California, has developed a new technology called ground-penetrating radar (GPR), which is able to locate tunnels inmates use to escape. GPR works almost like an old-fashioned Geiger counter, held in the hand and swept across the ground by an operator. Instead of detecting metal, however, the GPR system detects changes in ground composition, including voids such as those created by a tunnel.

Heartbeat Monitoring

The weakest security link in any prison has always been the *sally port*, where trucks unload their supplies and where trash and laundry are taken out of the facility. Over the years, inmates have hidden in loads of trash, old produce, laundry—any possible container that might be exiting the facility. Now it is possible to prevent escapes by monitoring inmates' heartbeats! The Advanced Vehicle Interrogation and Notification System (AVIAN) works by identifying the shock wave generated by the beating heart, which couples to any surface the body touches. The system takes in all the frequencies of movement, such as the expansion and contraction of the engine or rain hitting the roof, and determines if there is a pattern similar to a human heartbeat.

Nonlethal Electrified Fences

Similar in concept to the handheld stun guns used by law enforcement agencies throughout the United States, nonlethal electrified containment fences stop inmates without causing severe harm or death. If an inmate tries to climb or cut through the perimeter fence, he or she will receive a nonlethal jolt of electricity, which causes temporary immobilization. At the same time, the system initiates an alarm to prison staff that an attempt has occurred and identifies its location

Satellite Monitoring

Systems are now being developed to monitor offenders by satellite using cellular technology combined with the federal government's global positioning system of satellites. While in the community, each offender wears an ankle bracelet and carries a three-pound portable tracking device (a so-called smart box), programmed with information on his or her geographical restrictions. For instance, a sex offender may be forbidden to come within five miles of his victim's home or workplace, or a pedophile may be barred from getting close to a school. A satellite monitors the geographic movements of the offender, either in real time or by transmitting the information to the smart box for later retrieval. The smart box and the ankle bracelet sound an alarm when boundaries are breached, alerting potential victims.

Sticky Shocker

This is a less-than-lethal projectile that uses stun-gun technology to temporarily incapacitate a person at standoff range. The Sticky Shocker is a low-impact, wireless projectile fired from compressed gas or powder launchers and is accurate to within ten meters.

Backscatter Imaging System for Concealed Weapons

This system utilizes a backscatter imager to detect weapons and contraband. The primary advantage of this device over current walk-through portals is that it can detect nonmetallic as well as metallic weapons. It uses low-power X-rays equal to about five minutes of exposure to the sun at sea level. Although these X-rays penetrate clothing, they do not penetrate the body.

Body-Scanning Screening System

This is a stationary screening system to detect non-metallic weapons and contraband in the lower body cavities. It uses simplified magnetic resonance imaging (MRI) as a noninvasive alternative to X-ray and physical body cavity searches. The stationary screening system makes use of first-generation medical MRI.

Transmitter Wristbands

These wristbands broadcast a unique serial number via radio frequency every two seconds so that antennas throughout the prison can pick up the signals and pass the data via a local area network to a central monitoring station PC. The wristbands can sound an alert when a prisoner gets close to the perimeter fence or when an inmate doesn't return from a furlough on time; they can even tag gang members and notify guards when rivals get into contact with each other.

(continued)

Criminal Justice and Technology *(continued)*

Personal Health Status Monitor

It may be getting easier to monitor inmates who are at risk of committing suicide. Correctional authorities are now developing a personal health status monitor that uses acoustics to track the heartbeat and respiration of a person in a cell. The monitor does not actually need to be located on the person; because it is the size of two packs of cigarettes, it can be placed on the ceiling or just outside a cell. The device is similar to ones that are installed inside infant cribs in hospitals.

More advanced health status monitors are now being developed that can monitor five or more vital signs at once, and based on the combination of findings, can produce an assessment of an inmate's state of health. This more advanced version of the personal health status monitor may take another decade to develop, but the current version may already help save lives that would otherwise be lost to suicide.

All-in-One Drug Detection Spray

Drug detection sprays detect if someone possesses marijuana, methamphetamines, heroin, or cocaine. A specially made piece of paper is wiped on a surface; when sprayed with one of the aerosol sprays, it changes color within fifteen seconds if as little as four to twenty micrograms of the drug is present. A new detection device is now being developed that uses a single spray that will test for all drugs at once. The test paper will turn different colors depending on which drugs the spray contacts, and several positive results will be possible with a single use of the spray.

Radar Vital Signs Monitor/Radar Flashlight

Researchers at Georgia Tech have developed a hand-held radar flashlight that can detect the respiration of a human in a cell from behind a twenty-centimeter hollow-core concrete wall or an eight-inch cinder block wall. It instantly gives the user a bar-graph readout that is viewed on the apparatus itself. Other miniature radar detectors give users heartbeat and respiration readings. The equipment is expected to be a useful tool in searches for people who are hiding, because the only thing that successfully blocks its functioning is a wall made of metal or conductive material. The radar detectors can also be used in telemedicine and for individuals on whom electrodes would be difficult to apply. Future applications for this technology include advanced lie detectors and using the human heartbeat as a biometric for personnel identification.

Personal Alarm Location System

It is now possible for prison employees to carry a tiny transmitter linking them with a computer in a central control room. In an emergency, they can hit an alarm button and transmit to a computer that automatically records whose distress button has been pushed. An architectural map of the facility instantly appears on-screen, showing the exact location of the unfortunate staff member. Although sensors are only placed inside the prison, the Personal Alarm Location System (PALS) works up to three hundred feet outside prison walls. It locates within a range of four meters inside the room where the duress button is pushed, and also locates signals in between floors. The PALS system also

Minimum-Security Prisons Operating without armed guards or perimeter walls, **minimum-security prisons** usually house the most trustworthy and least violent offenders; white-collar criminals may be their most common occupants. Inmates are allowed a great deal of personal freedom. Instead of being marched to activities by guards, they are summoned by bells or loudspeaker announcements and they assemble on their own. Work furloughs and educational releases are encouraged, and vocational training is of the highest level. Dress codes are lax, and inmates are allowed to grow beards or mustaches or demonstrate other individual characteristics.

Minimum-security facilities may have dormitories or small private rooms for inmates. Prisoners are allowed to own personal possessions that might be deemed dangerous in a maximum-security prison, such as radios.

Minimum-security prisons have been criticized for being like "country clubs"; some federal facilities for white-collar criminals even have tennis courts and pools (they are called derisively "Club Fed"). Yet they remain prisons, and the isolation and loneliness of prison life deeply affect the inmates.

minimum-security prison The least secure institution that houses white-collar and nonviolent offenders, maintains few security measures, and has liberal furlough and visitation policies.

has an option that tracks the movement of employees who have pressed their duress buttons. If an officer moves after hitting the duress button, the red dot that represents him or her on the computer screen will move as well. The PALS system, now being used in six correctional institutions in the United States and Canada, is scheduled to be adopted in others.

Under-Vehicle Surveillance System

An under-vehicle surveillance system utilizes a drive-over camera that records a video image of the license plate and the underside of any vehicle entering or leaving the secure perimeter of the prison. This system allows prison staff to check each vehicle for possible escape attempts and keeps a digital recording of every vehicle that enters or exits the prison.

Biometric Recognition

A new biometric system, the facial recognition system, utilizes facial recognition by matching more than two hundred individual points on the human face with a digitally stored image. The system is used to control access in buildings and rooms inside buildings, and is now available and will become much more common in the near future.

Future Technology

Not yet employed but in the planning stage are the following technological breakthroughs:

- *The angel chip.* This microchip would be implanted underneath the skin of the user and would contain vital and identifying information.

- *Noninvasive drug detection.* A swab or patch being developed; when placed on the skin, it absorbs perspiration and detects the presence of illegal drugs.

Critical Thinking

1. Some elements of technocorrections intrude on the privacy of inmates. Should the need for security outweigh an inmate's right to privacy?
2. Should probationers and parolees be monitored with modern technology? Do they deserve more privacy than incarcerated inmates?

InfoTrac College Edition Research

To read a commentary on correctional technology and its applications, go to Debbie Mahaffey, "Security and Technology: The Human Side," *Corrections Today* 66 (2004): 8. To learn about a technological application that seems to be highly effective, go to Frank Lu and Laurence Wolfe, "Automated Record Tracking (SMART) Application," *Corrections Today* 66 (2004): 78–81.

Sources: Gary Burdett and Mike Retford, "Technology Improves Security and Reduces Staff in Two Illinois Prisons," *Corrections Today* 65 (2003): 109–110; Mark Robert, "Big Brother Goes Behind Bars," *Fortune* 146 (September 30, 2002): 44; Tony Fabelo, *Technocorrections: The Promises, the Uncertain Threats, Sentencing & Corrections: Issues for the 21st Century Series* (Washington, D.C.: National Institute of Justice, 2000); Irwin Soonachan, "The Future of Corrections: Technological Developments Are Turning Science Fiction into Science Fact," *Corrections Today* 62 (2000): 64–66; Steve Morrison, "How Technology Can Make Your Job Safer," *Corrections Today* 62 (2000): 58–60; Gabrielle deGroot, "Hot New Technologies," *Corrections Today* 59 (1997): 60–63.

▌ALTERNATIVE CORRECTIONAL INSTITUTIONS

Criminal Justice ⚖ Now™
Learn more by viewing the "Peru Trial" "In the News" video clip.

In addition to prisons and jails, a number of other correctional institutions are operating within the United States. Some have been in use for quite some time, whereas others have been developed as part of innovative or experimental programs.

Prison Farms and Camps

Prison farms and camps are used to detain offenders. These types of facilities are found primarily in the South and the West and have been in operation since the nineteenth century. Today, about forty farms, forty forest camps, eighty road camps, and more than sixty similar facilities (vocational training centers, ranches, and so on) exist in the nation. Prisoners on farms produce dairy products, grain, and vegetable crops that are used in the state correctional system and other governmental facilities, such as hospitals and schools.

Policy, Programs, and Issues in Criminal Justice

Ultra-Maximum-Security Prisons

More than thirty states now operate super-maximum-security or ultra-maximum-security prisons or units, also known as super-max prisons. These high-security institutions can be independent correctional centers or locked wings of existing prisons operating under such names as the "secure housing unit" or "maximum control unit."

The first federal supermax prison was located in Marion, Illinois; it was infamous for its tight security and isolate conditions. Marion has been succeeded by a new facility in Florence, Colorado, which has the most sophisticated security measures in the United States, including 168 video cameras and 1,400 electronically controlled gates. Inside the cells all furniture is unmovable: the desk, bed, and TV stand are made of cement. All potential weapons, including soap dishes, toilet seats, and toilet handles, have been removed. The cement walls are five-thousand-pound quality, and steel bars are placed so they crisscross every eight inches inside the walls. Cells are angled so that inmates cannot see each other or the outside scenery. This cuts down on communication and denies inmates a sense of location, in order to prevent escapes.

Getting out of the prison seems impossible. There are six guard towers at different heights to prevent air attacks. To get out, the inmates would have to pass through seven three-inch-thick steel doors, each of which can be opened only after the previous one has closed. If a guard tower is ever seized, all controls are switched to the next station. If the whole prison is seized, it can be controlled from the outside.

A national survey of supermax prisons conducted by the American Correctional Association found that although the cost of running these institutions is generally higher than in less secure facilities they tend to be popular with correctional administrators, who believe that isolating troublemakers helps them maintain order. However, these institutions contain only minimal correctional treatment programs, limited to television and video programming and other relatively limited methods. Transitional programming is available only in some jurisdictions.

Critiquing the Supermax Prison

Threat of transfer to a supermax institution is used to deter inmate misbehavior in less restrictive institutions. Civil rights watchdog groups charge that these prisons violate United Nations standards for the treatment of inmates. They are usually located in rural areas, which makes staffing difficult in the professional areas of dentistry, medicine, and counseling. Senior officers would rather not work in these institutions, leaving the most difficult inmates in the hands of the most inexperienced correctional officers.

A recent survey by Leena Kurki and Norval Morris found that although conditions vary from state to

---

Forestry camp inmates maintain state parks, fight forest fires, and do reforestation work. Ranches, primarily a western phenomenon, employ inmates in cattle raising and horse breeding, among other activities. Road gangs repair roads and state highways.

Shock Incarceration in Boot Camps

Another correctional innovation that gained popularity in the 1980s–1990s, the **boot camp** involves youthful, first-time offenders in military discipline and physical training. The concept is that short periods (90 to 180 days) of high-intensity exercise and work will "shock" the inmate into going straight. Tough physical training is designed to promote responsibility and improve decision-making skills, build self-confidence, and teach socialization skills. Inmates are treated with rough intensity by drillmasters who may call them names and punish the entire group for the failure of one member.[35]

Some programs also include educational and training components, counseling sessions, and treatment for special-needs populations, whereas others

boot camp *A short-term militaristic correctional facility in which inmates undergo intensive physical conditioning and discipline.*

state, many supermaxes subject inmates to nearly complete isolation and deprivation of sensory stimuli. Although the long-term effects of such conditions are still uncertain, Kurki and Morris believe that they are likely to be extremely harmful, especially for those who suffer from preexisting mental illness or those with subnormal intelligence.

The development of the ultramax prison represents a shift from previous correctional policy, which favored dispersing the most troublesome inmates to different prisons in order to prevent them from joining forces or planning escapes. The supermax model finds that housing the most dangerous inmates in an ultra-secure facility eases their control while reducing violence levels in the general prison population. Kurki and Morris, however, argue that while the supermax prison is considered the ultimate control mechanism for disruptive inmates, individuals are actually less to blame for prison violence and disruption than are dysfunctional prison regimes and misguided prison administrators, which make prisons the violent institutions they are. And, ironically, when anthropologist Lorna Rhodes conducted research in a supermax prison in Washington State, she found that total security units tend to create the very things they were designed to eliminate: the tighter the control and the more extreme the isolation, the more discipline and mental health problems they generate. Rhodes found that many inmates who were not mentally ill when they entered the prison become psychotic under the strain of isolation. Filled with fear, angry at the system that renders them less than human, they strike back with the only weapons they have: they smear feces on cell walls or on themselves; they store their body wastes and blood, and throw them at guards. They get pleasure when the guards are terrified about contracting AIDS or hepatitis. As inmates become more unruly, prison administrators strike back with more security and restraint in a never-ending cycle.

Critical Thinking

1. Ultramax prisons are reminiscent of the old Pennsylvania system, which made use of solitary confinement and high security. Is this inhumane in our more enlightened age? Why or why not?

2. Should all convicted terrorists be kept in supermax prisons, or should these facilities be reserved only for those proven to be violent and dangerous to other inmates?

InfoTrac College Edition Research

To read about the conditions in the new supermaximum-security prisons, go to InfoTrac College Edition and read "Cruel and Unusual Punishment," *Harper's Magazine*, July 2001 v303 i1814 p92.

Sources: Lorna A. Rhodes, *Total Confinement: Madness and Reason in the Maximum Security Prison* (California: University of California Press, 2004); Leena Kurki and Norval Morris, "The Purpose, Practices, and Problems of Supermax Prisons," in Michael Tonry, ed., *Crime and Justice: An Annual Edition* (Chicago: University of Chicago Press, 2001), 385–422; Richard H. Franklin, "Assessing Supermax Operations," *Corrections Today 60* (1998): 126–128.

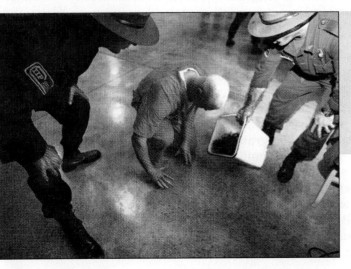

© Jacksonville Courier/Zuzana Killiam/The Image Works

Boot camps use strict discipline regimes, which some critics find demeaning to inmates. Here, at the Prison Boot Camp in Illinois, one correctional officer bangs a metal wastebasket against the cement floor. Two officers yell insults at a new inmate, demanding that he hurry and gather his newly cut hair into the basket. Critics have questioned the effectiveness of boot camps, and some jurisdictions are now phasing them out.

devote little or no time to therapeutic activities. Some receive program participants directly from court sentencing, whereas others choose potential candidates from the general inmate population. Some allow voluntary participation and others voluntary termination.[36]

Is **shock incarceration** a correctional panacea or another fad doomed to failure? Those who advocate shock incarceration portray it as a lower-cost alternative to overcrowded prisons. Both staff and inmates report benefiting from the experience.[37] While the costs of boot camps are no lower than those of traditional prisons on a daily basis, because sentences are shorter they provide long-term savings. A number of states, including Georgia and New York, make extensive use of shock incarceration facilities.

Despite such support, empirical research by Doris Layton Mackenzie, a criminologist who has been involved in many evaluations of boot camp, has yielded disappointing results. She finds that clients leaving boot camps often have higher rates of technical violations and revocations than traditional probationers and parolees.[38] Mackenzie's extensive evaluations of the boot camp experience generate little evidence that they can significantly lower recidivism rates. Those few programs that seem to work best stress treatment and therapeutic activities, are voluntary, and are longer in duration.[39] Because of these sketchy results, the future of the boot camp approach is clouded. Recently (2005), the federal government announced the closing of its boot camp program.[40]

Community Correctional Facilities

One of the goals of correctional treatment is to help reintegrate the offender back into society. Placing offenders in a prison makes them more likely to adapt an inmate lifestyle than to reassimilate conventional social norms. As a result, the **community treatment** concept began to take off in the 1960s. State and federal correctional systems created community-based correctional models as an alternative to closed institutions. Many are **halfway houses** to which inmates are transferred just before their release into the community. These facilities are designed to bridge the gap between institutional living and the community. Specialized treatment may be offered, and the residents use the experience to cushion the shock of reentering society.

As you may recall, commitment to a community correctional center may also be used as an intermediate sanction and sole mode of treatment. An offender may be assigned to a community treatment center operated by the state department of corrections or to probation. Alternatively, the corrections department can contract with a private community center. This practice is common in the treatment of drug abusers and other nonviolent offenders whose special needs can be met in a self-contained community setting that specializes in specific types of treatment.

Halfway houses and community correctional centers can look like residential homes and in many instances were originally residences; in urban centers, older apartment buildings can be adapted for the purpose. Usually, these facilities have a central treatment theme—such as group therapy or reality therapy—that is used to rehabilitate and reintegrate clients.

Despite the encouraging philosophical concept presented by the halfway house, evaluation of specific programs has not led to a definite endorsement of this type of treatment.[41] One significant problem has been a lack of support from community residents, who fear the establishment of an institution housing "dangerous offenders" in their neighborhood. Court actions and zoning restrictions have been brought in some areas to foil efforts to create halfway houses.[42] As a result, many halfway houses are located in decrepit neighborhoods in the worst areas of town—certainly a condition that must influence

shock incarceration A short prison sentence served in boot camp–type facilities.

community treatment The attempt by correctional agencies to maintain convicted offenders in the community instead of a secure facility; it includes probation, parole, and residential programs.

halfway house A community-based correctional facility that houses inmates before their outright release so that they can become gradually acclimated to conventional society.

the attitudes and behavior of the inmates. Furthermore, the climate of control exercised in most halfway houses, where rule violation can be met with a quick return to the institution, may not be one that the average inmate can distinguish from his former high-security penal institution.

Despite these problems, the promise held by community correctional centers, coupled with their low cost of operations, has led to their continued use into the new millennium.

Private Prisons

Correctional facilities are now being run by private firms as business enterprises. In some instances, a private corporation will finance and build an institution and then contract with correctional authorities to provide services for convicted criminals. Sometimes the private concern will finance and build the institution and then lease it outright to the government. This model has the advantage of allowing the government to circumvent the usually difficult process of getting voters to approve a bond issue and raising funds for prison construction. Another common method of private involvement is with specific service contracts; for example, a private concern might be hired to manage the prison health-care system, food services, or staff training.

On January 6, 1986, the U.S. Corrections Corporation opened the first private state prison in Marion, Kentucky—a three-hundred-bed minimum-security facility for inmates who are within three years of parole. Today, more than twenty companies are trying to enter the private prison market, five states are contracting with private companies to operate facilities, and more than ten others—including Oregon, New Mexico, and Florida—have recently passed laws authorizing or expanding the use of private prison contractors.[43]

Do Private Prisons Work? Some evaluations of recidivism among inmates released from private and public facilities find that recidivism rates are equal and/or lower among the private prison group than the state prison inmates.[44] Inmates released from private prisons who re-offend commit less serious offenses than those released from public institutions. Private and state institutions cost about the same to operate, but private prisons seem cheaper to construct.[45]

These findings help support the concept of the private correctional institution. Nonetheless, some experts question reliance on private prisons, believing that their use raises a number of vexing problems. For example, will private providers be able to evaluate programs effectively knowing that a negative evaluation might cause them to lose their contract? Will they skimp on services and programs in order to reduce costs? Might they not skim off the "easy" cases and leave the hard-core inmate to the state's care? And will the need to keep business booming require widening the net to fill empty cells? Must they maintain state-mandated liability insurance to cover inmate claims?[46] Some private service providers have been sued because their services were inadequate, causing harm to inmates.[47]

Private corrections firms also run into opposition from existing state correctional staff and management, who fear the loss of jobs and autonomy. Moreover, the public may be skeptical about an untested private concern's ability to provide security and protection. Private corrections also face administrative problems. How will program quality be controlled? To compete on price, a private facility may have to cut corners to beat the competition. Determining accountability for problems and mishaps will be difficult when dealing with a corporation whose managers and officers are protected legally from personal responsibility for their actions.

Criminal Justice Now™
Learn more by exploring the "Privatization" Review and Reinforce activity.

Legal Issues There are also unresolved legal problems: Can privately employed guards patrol the perimeter and use deadly force to stop escape attempts? Do private correctional officers have less immunity from lawsuits than state employees? The case of *Correctional Services Corp. v. Malesko* helps define the rights and protections of inmates in private correctional facilities. Malesko had a heart condition but was forced to walk up stairs rather than take an elevator. When he suffered a heart attack he sued the Correctional Services Corp. (CSC), which was operating the prison, under the federal Civil Rights Act, alleging that the denial of proper medical care violated his civil rights. Citizens are generally allowed to seek damages against federal agents who violate their civil rights. However, the U.S. Supreme Court ruled that although Malesko could sue an individual employee of the private correctional corporation for allegedly violating his constitutional rights, he could not sue the correctional corporation itself. This decision shields the private prison corporation from suits brought under the federal civil rights statute. The *Malesko* decision upholds the concerns of some critics, who view the private prison as an insidious expansion of state control over citizens: a state-supported entity that actually has more freedom to exert control than the state itself.[48]

In the abstract, a private correctional enterprise may be an attractive alternative to a costly correctional system, but these legal, administrative, and cost issues need to be resolved before private prisons can become widespread.[49] A balance must be reached between the need for a private business to make a profit and the integrity of a prison administration that must be concerned with such complex issues as security, rehabilitation, and dealing with highly dangerous people in a closed environment.[50]

Criminal Justice Now™
Learn more by exploring the "Pretrial Detainees" Review and Reinforce activity.

INMATE POPULATIONS

This vast correctional system, with more than 1,600 institutions, now contains over 1.4 million people. Like the jail population, the background and characteristics of inmates reflect arrest data: disproportionately young, male, minority, and poor. While the number of women under the jurisdiction of state or federal prison authorities is increasing at a faster rate than the number of males, females still make up less than 10 percent of the total prison population. In both jails and prisons, there were 123 female inmates per 100,000 women in the United States, compared to 1,348 male inmates per 100,000 men. Similarly, the rate of minority incarceration far outstrips the rate for whites:

- 4,919 black male prison and jail inmates per 100,000 black males
- 1,717 Hispanic male inmates per 100,000 Hispanic males
- 717 white male inmates per 100,000 white males[51]

Many inmates suffer from multiple social problems. Inmates are undereducated and underemployed; a significant number have been socialized in abusive homes. About 68 percent of prison inmates did not receive a high school diploma compared to 18 percent of the general population.[52]

It is not surprising then that surveys show that inmates, both in the United States and abroad, suffer from serious psychological and emotional problems. Almost 4 percent of male inmates suffer from psychotic illnesses, 10 percent were diagnosed with major depression, and 65 percent had a personality disorder, including 47 percent with antisocial personality disorder. Prisoners were several times more likely to have psychosis and major depression, and about ten times more likely to have antisocial personality disorder, than the general population.[53]

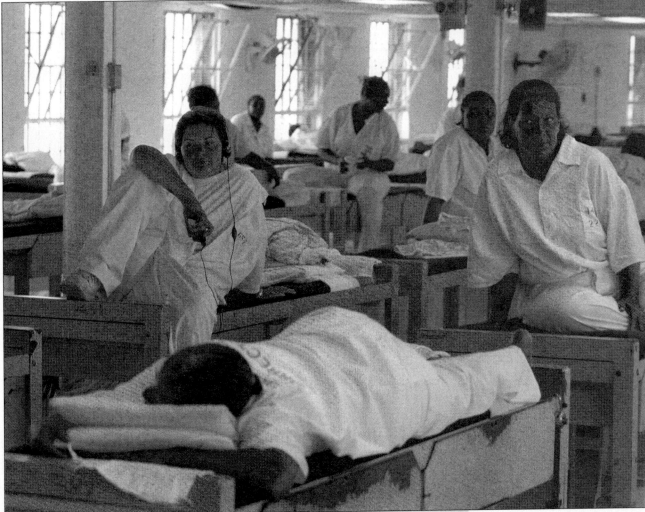

Despite a "drop-off" in the crime rate, prison and jail populations are still rising. Some institutions are quite overcrowded. With windows open and no air conditioning, a dorm holds 250 women inmates at Tutwiler Women's Prison, Montgomery, Alabama. District Court Judge Myron Thompson issued a permanent injunction in August 2004 ordering comprehensive improvements to provide relief from overcrowded conditions and inadequate medical care at the facility.

Growth Trends

As Figure 13.3 shows, the inmate population has continued to increase despite a decade long crime drop. How is this possible? As we shall see below, inmates are now serving a greater percentage of their sentences behind bars before being eligible for parole or release.

Because of this increase, inmates are routinely housed two and three to a cell or in large dormitory-like rooms that hold more than fifty people. Military bases and even tents have been used to house overflow inmates. In addition to detainees and misdemeanants, thousands of people convicted of felonies are being held in local jails because of prison crowding.

State correctional authorities have attempted to deal with the overcrowding problem by building new facilities, using construction techniques that limit expenditures, such as modular and preassembled units. Precast concrete cells are fabricated as fully finished units and can be installed quickly.

Number of inmates in state prisons

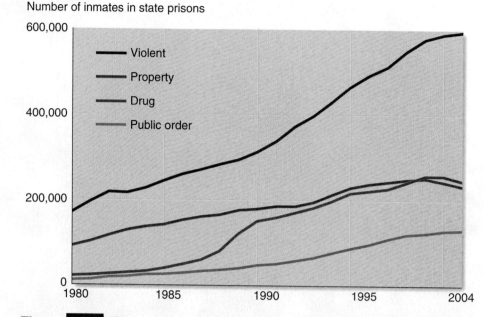

Figure 13.3 State prison population by offense type, 1980–2004

Sources: *Correctional Populations in the United States, Annual* (Washington, D.C.: Bureau of Justice Statistics, 2002); Paige Harrison and Allen Beck, *Prisoners in 2001* (Washington, D.C.: Bureau of Justice Statistics, 2002), updated.

Explaining Prison Population Trends

Why did the prison population grow so rapidly over the past decade even though the crime rate fell? One reason may be that public concern about drugs and violent crime has not been lost on state lawmakers. Tough new criminal legislation, including mandatory sentencing laws, increase the chances a convicted offender will be incarcerated and limit the availability for early release via parole. Although probation and community sentences still predominate, structural changes in criminal codes and crime rates helped produce an expanding correctional population. The amount of time served in prison has increased because of such developments as truth-in-sentencing laws that require inmates to serve at least 85 percent of their sentences behind bars.[54] In addition, get-tough policies have helped curtail the use of parole and have reduced judicial discretion to impose nonincarceration sentences.[55]

So many people are now going to prison that the federal government estimates that a significant portion of the nation's population will at one time or another be behind prison gates. About 5 percent of the population, or more than thirteen million people, will serve a prison sentence some time during their lives. Men are over eight times more likely than women to be incarcerated in prison at least once during their lives. Among men, African Americans (28.5 percent) are about twice as likely as Hispanics (16.0 percent) and six times more likely than whites (4.4 percent) to be admitted to prison during their lives. Among women, 3.6 percent of African Americans, 1.5 percent of Hispanics, and 0.5 percent of whites will enter prison at least once.[56]

As more people go to prison and are forced to serve more of their sentence, the prison population will age, bringing additional costs in terms of health care and special programming. This trend is the subject of the following Policy, Programs, and Issues in Criminal Justice feature, called "The Problem of Elderly Inmates."

Policy, Programs, and Issues in Criminal Justice

The Problem of Elderly Inmates

Restrictive crime control policies such as three strikes and truth in sentencing have increased the time people spend behind bars. The result: a growing number of elderly inmates who require health care, diets, and work and recreational opportunities that are different from those of the general population. Because they have specific problems, such as lack of mobility and incontinence, they may feel alienated and vulnerable. Not surprisingly, it is quite costly to care for their needs: it is estimated that the cost of keeping an elderly prisoner in jail is roughly three-and-a-half times that of keeping a younger prisoner.

There are about 40,000 inmates age 55 and over in the correctional system today. In 1990, there were 49 people over 55 for every 100,000 residents; by 1996 the number had jumped to 69, and today it is more than 141. If current trends persist, some states such as California will see their elderly inmate population increase significantly in the next decade.

Research indicates that older prisoners tend to be loners who may experience symptoms of depression or anxiety. They suffer from an assortment of physical and health problems associated with aging, including arthritis, ulcers, prostate problems, hypertension, and emphysema. Because they may have had a long-term history with smoking and alcohol consumption, they may suffer incontinence as well as heart, respiratory, and degenerative diseases. After reviewing available evidence, one study found:

- The proportion of state and federal inmates 55 years of age and older is steadily increasing. The number of inmates older than 75 will continue to increase in the future if current sentencing practices remain in place.

- The older inmate is most likely an unmarried white man with children, and did not graduate from high school.
- Older offenders are most likely to be incarcerated for violent crimes, often perpetrated against family members in the home.
- Older inmates are likely to report one or more chronic health problems. Cigarette and alcohol use is common.
- Most states and the federal Bureau of Prisons have implemented limited provisions to accommodate older inmates with special needs.

Critical Thinking

1. Is it practical to keep the elderly in prison or should they be moved to less secure nursing homes?
2. How much medical care would you provide aging inmates? State of the art? Life maintaining? Minimum possible under law?

InfoTrac College Edition Research

To read about homes for elderly inmates, go to Vince Beiser, "Pensioners or Prisoners?" *The Nation 268* (1999): 28.

Sources: Ronald Aday, *Aging Prisoners: Crisis in American Corrections* (Westport, Conn.: Praeger, 2003); James Morton, "The Elderly in Prison," *Journal of Criminal Law 69* (2005): 189–191; Paige M. Harrison and Allen Beck, *Prisoners in 2002* (Washington, D.C.: Bureau of Justice Statistics, 2003); Kathleen Auerhahn, "Selective Incapacitation, Three Strikes, and the Problem of Aging Prison Populations," *Criminology and Public Policy 1* (2002): 353–387; Catherine Lemieux, Timothy Dyeson, and Brandi Castiglione, "Revisiting the Literature on Prisoners Who Are Older: Are We Wiser?" *Prison Journal 82* (2002): 432–456.

Future Trends

Despite such ominous signs, the nation's prison population may be "maxing out." Budget cutbacks and belt tightening may halt the expansion of prison construction and the housing of ever more prisoners in already crowded prison facilities. Although new modular construction techniques and double- and triple-bunking of inmates make existing prisons expandable, the secure population probably cannot expand endlessly. As costs skyrocket, some states are now spending more on prisons than on higher education. The public may begin to question the wisdom of a strict incarceration policy. There may also be fewer criminals to incarcerate. The waning of the crack cocaine epidemic

Criminal Justice ⚖ Now™

*Learn more about **Careers in Criminal Justice** by exploring the "On the Job" features **Warden** and **Correctional Officer.***

in large cities may hasten this decline, because street crimes will decline and fewer offenders will be eligible for the long penalties associated with the possession of crack.[57] As noted earlier, fewer people are now receiving a prison sentence than five years ago, and if this trend holds the prison population will eventually decline.

In the final analysis, change in the correctional population may depend on the faith judges and legislators place in incarceration as a crime control policy. As long as policymakers believe that incarcerating predatory criminals can bring down crime rates, then the likelihood of a significant decrease in the institutional population seems remote. If there is little evidence that this costly system does lower crime rates, then less costly and equally effective alternatives may be sought.

SUMMARY

- Today's correctional institutions can trace their development from European origins.
- Punishment methods developed in Europe were modified and improved by American colonists, most notably William Penn. He replaced the whip and other methods of physical punishment with confinement in county institutions or penitentiaries.
- Later, as needs grew, the newly formed states created their own large facilities. Discipline was harsh within them, and most enforced a code of total and absolute silence.
- Auburn Prison in New York developed the system of congregate working conditions during the day and isolation at night.
- Pennsylvania adopted an isolate system which required inmates be locked into their cells for the duration of their sentence. While secure, it drove many inmates mad.
- The congregate system, developed in New York, has been adopted in our present penal system.
- Correctional rehabilitation programs began to develop in the late nineteenth century.
- Parole developed abroad but was imported to the U.S. and became the predominant type of prison release.
- Over the centuries there have been a number of correctional reforms, including the development of specialized prisons.

- A number of institutions currently house convicted offenders. Jails are used for misdemeanants and minor felons. Because conditions are so poor in jails, they have become a major trouble spot for the criminal justice system.
- New-generation jails have improved security and reduced violence.
- Federal and state prisons—classified as minimum, medium, and maximum security—house most of the nation's incarcerated felons.
- Their poor track record has spurred the development of new correctional models, specifically the boot camp, the halfway house, and the community correctional center.
- The success of these institutions has been challenged by research efforts indicating that their recidivism rates are equal to or higher than those of state prisons.
- One recent development has been the privately run correctional institution operated by private companies, which receive a fee for their services.
- The prison population has skyrocketed in the past few years.
- People are spending a greater portion of their sentence behind bars, creating the problem of elderly prisoners.
- A significant percentage of the American public will serve a prison sentence during their lifetime. There are significant racial discrepancies in the likelihood of going to prison.

KEY TERMS

prison 360
jail 360
hulk 362
Walnut Street Jail 362
penitentiary house 362
tier system 363
congregate system 363
Auburn system 363

Pennsylvania system 364
contract system (convict) 364
convict-lease system 365
medical model 367
penal harm 367
maximum-security prison 371
super-maximum-security
   prison 372

medium-security prison 372
minimum-security prison 374
boot camp 376
shock incarceration 378
community treatment 378
halfway house 378

REVIEW QUESTIONS

1. Would you allow a community correctional center to be built in your neighborhood? Why or why not?

2. Should pretrial detainees and convicted offenders be kept in the same institution? Explain.

3. What can be done to reduce correctional overcrowding?

4. Should private companies be allowed to run correctional institutions? Why or why not?

5. What are the drawbacks to shock incarceration?

CHAPTER **14**

Prison Life: Living in and Leaving Prison

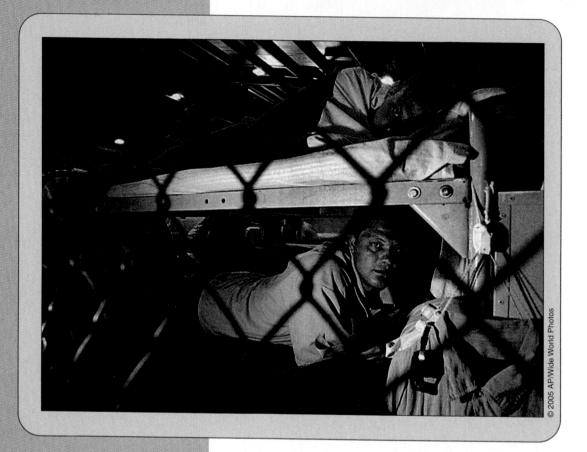

© 2005 AP/Wide World Photos

RACHEL ANITA JUNG is a training officer in the Arizona Department of Corrections. After receiving her B.A. degree in Criminal Justice from California State University, San Bernardino, she went on to earn an M.S. degree in Criminal Justice from the University of Alabama, Tuscaloosa.

Jung always knew she would be in a helping/public service profession. She had a basic curiosity about human behavior, which is why she took courses in both law enforcement and psychology while she was in college. She joined professional associations prior to her first job in the criminal justice field to stay current on issues concerning corrections and law enforcement. Jung has held a variety of positions including jail screener, case manager for a treatment and referral program for substance abusers, and adult probation officer. She is particularly interested in applying restorative justice to corrections.

Chapter Outline

Chapter Objectives

1. Understand the experience of living in prison
2. Be familiar with the various elements of the inmate social code
3. Recognize the differences between the prison culture today and at mid-century
4. Know what is meant by the "make-believe family"
5. Be able to discuss the problems of women in prison
6. Recognize the recent changes in correctional law
7. Describe the role of the prison rehabilitation efforts
8. Know about the problems faced by correctional officers
9. Understand the different forms of parole
10. Show how the problem of re-entry has influenced the correctional system

As training officer for the Arizona Department of Corrections, her position has evolved from coordinating training programs for all institutional personnel (officers, support staff, administration, maintenance, health services, and criminal investigations) to development of statewide curriculum. Jung delivers training programs periodically in the pre-service academy as well as at various institutions throughout the state. Most recently, she has managed executive development for the corrections staff.

While the job has challenges, Jung is highly motivated. The restorative justice movement she favors seems to be having a great impact on corrections. Jung believes her job can help her influence some of the key players in the correctional system—correctional staff, the public, victims, and offenders.

People like Rachel Jung are the backbone of the correctional system. Today there are more than 1,600 adult correctional facilities in the United States—including prisons, prison hospitals, prison farms, boot camps; centers for reception, classification, or alcohol and drug treatment; and community-based facilities such as halfway houses, group homes, and work release centers.[1] A significant number of facilities are old, decrepit, archaic structures: of the prisons in this country, 25 were built before 1875, 79 between 1875 and 1924, and 141 between 1925 and 1949. In fact, some of the first prisons ever constructed, such as the Concord Reformatory in Massachusetts, are still in operation.

Although most prisons are classified as medium security, more than half of all inmates are held in large, maximum-security institutions. Despite the continuous outcry by penologists against the use of fortress-like prisons, institutions holding a thousand or more inmates still predominate. Prison overcrowding is a significant problem. The prison system now holds about 1.5 million people. Many institutions are operating above stated capacity. Recreation and workshop space has been turned into dormitories housing thirty or more inmates in a single room. Most prison experts agree that a minimum of sixty square feet is needed for each inmate, but many prisons fail to reach this standard.

This giant system, designed to reform and rehabilitate offenders, is instead undergoing a crisis of massive proportions. Institutions are so overcrowded that meaningful treatment efforts are often a matter of wishful thinking; recidivism rates are shockingly high. Inmates are resentful of the deteriorated conditions, and correctional officers fear that the institution is ready to explode. Rather than deter people from future criminality, a prison stay may actually reinforce and/or encourage their criminal offending.[2] This lack of success is not lost on the general public. Though it might surprise some "get tough" politicians, the general public is not ready to embrace a prison building boom at the expense of rehabilitation efforts.[3]

This chapter presents a brief review of some of the most important issues confronting the nation's troubled correctional system.

▮ MEN IMPRISONED

According to prevailing wisdom, prisons in the United States are **total institutions.** This means that inmates locked within their walls are segregated from the outside world, kept under constant scrutiny and surveillance, and forced to obey strict official rules to avoid facing formal sanctions. Their personal possessions are taken from them, and they must conform to institutional dress and personal appearance norms. Many human functions are strictly curtailed—heterosexual sex, friendships, family relationships, education, and participation in groups become privileges of the past. Some institutions employ a **no-frills policy,** which means that inmates will receive the bare minimum of food, services, and medical care required by law. The purpose: convince them that prison is no place to be and they'd better not return.

Inmates quickly learn what the term *total institution* really means. When they arrive at prison, they are stripped, searched, shorn, and assigned living quarters. Before they get there, though, their first experience occurs in a classification or reception center, where they are given a series of psychological and other tests and evaluated on the basis of their personality, background, offense history, and treatment needs. Based on the classification they are given, they will be assigned to a permanent facility. Hard-core, repeat, and violent offenders will go to the maximum-security unit; offenders with learning disabilities may be assigned to an institution that specializes in educational services; mentally disordered offenders will be held in a facility that can

total institution *A regimented, dehumanizing institution such as a prison in which like-situated people are kept in social isolation, cut off from the world at large.*

no-frills policy *A correctional policy that stipulates that prisons are aimed at punishing and not coddling inmates. A "no-frills" orientation usually means a strict regimen of work and discipline, and reduced opportunities for recreation and education.*

provide psychiatric care; and so on. Some states have instituted rigorous classification instruments designed to maximize the effectiveness of placements thereby cutting down on the cost of incarceration. If classification can be conducted in an efficient and effective manner, non-dangerous offenders will not needlessly be kept in expensive high security facilities.[4]

All previous concepts of personal privacy and dignity are soon forgotten. Personal losses include the deprivation of liberty, goods and services, heterosexual relationships, autonomy, and security.[5] Inmates may be subject to verbal and physical attack and threats, with little chance of legal redress. Although criminal law applies to inmates as to any other citizen, it is rarely enforced within prison walls.[6] Therefore, part of living in prison involves learning to protect yourself and developing survival instincts.

Inmates in large, inaccessible prisons may find themselves physically cut off from families, friends, and associates. Visitors may find it difficult to travel great distances to see them; mail is censored and sometimes destroyed.

Adjusting to Prison

Inmates go through a variety of attitude and behavior changes, or cycles, as their sentence unfolds. During the early part of their prison stay, inmates may become easily depressed while considering the long duration of the sentence and the loneliness and dangers of prison life. They must learn the ins and outs of survival in the institution: Which persons can be befriended, and which are best avoided? Who will grant favors and for what repayment? Some inmates will request that regular payments be made to them in exchange for protection from homosexual rape and beatings. To avoid victimization, inmates must learn to adopt a lifestyle that shields them from victimization.[7] They must discover areas of safety and danger. Some learn how to fight back to prove they are not people who can be taken advantage of. While some kill their attackers and get even longer sentences, others join cliques that provide protection and the ability to acquire power within the institution.

Inmates may find that some prisoners have formed cliques, or groups, based on ethnic backgrounds or personal interests; they are also likely to encounter Mafia-like or racial terror groups that must be dealt with. Inmates may find that power in the prison is shared by correctional officers and

Some inmates find it very difficult to adjust to life behind bars, and organizations have been created to ease the transition. Johnny Ellis reads an essay to fellow inmates at the San Francisco County Jail in San Bruno, California, on August 19, 2004. The group was participating in Roads to Recovery, a class designed to help substance-abusing inmates get rid of their dependencies. The class is funded by the Inmate Welfare Fund.

© 2004 AP/Wide World Photos

inmate gangs; the only way to avoid being beaten and raped may be to learn how to beat and rape.[8] If they are weak and unable to defend themselves, new inmates may find that they are considered "punks"; if they ask a guard for help, they are labeled a "snitch." Younger inmates who may not be able to defend themselves, gay men, and bisexual men are selected most often to be targets of sexual assaults.[9] After that, they may spend the rest of their sentence in protective custody, sacrificing the "freedom of the yard" and rehabilitation services for personal protection.[10]

Despite all these hardships, many inmates learn to adapt to the prison routine. Each prisoner has his own method of coping. He may stay alone, become friends with another inmate, join a group, or seek the advice of treatment personnel. Inmates soon learn that their lifestyle and activities can contribute to their being victimized by more aggressive inmates. The more time they spend in closely guarded activities, the less likely they are to become the victims of violence. The more they isolate themselves from others who might protect them, the greater their vulnerability to attack. The more visitors they receive, the more likely they are to be attacked by fellow inmates jealous of their relationships with the outside world.[11]

Of course, not all inmates learn to cope. Some inmates repeatedly violate institutional rules. Predicting who will become an institutional troublemaker is difficult, but rule-breaking behavior has been associated with being a younger inmate with a low IQ, possessing numerous juvenile convictions, being a repeat offender, and having victimized a stranger. Inmates who have limited intelligence and little self-control may not be able to form adaptive coping mechanisms and manage the stress of being in prison.[12]

The Inmate Social Code

For many years, criminal justice experts maintained that inmates formed their own world with a unique set of norms and rules, known as the **inmate subculture.**[13] A significant aspect of the inmate subculture was a unique **inmate social code,** unwritten guidelines that expressed the values, attitudes, and type of behavior that older inmates demanded of young ones. Passed on from one generation of inmates to another, the inmate social code represented the values of interpersonal relations in the prison.

National attention was first drawn to the inmate social code and subculture by Donald Clemmer's classic book *The Prison Community,* in which he presented a detailed sociological study of life in a maximum-security prison.[14] Clemmer was able to identify a unique language, or *argot,* that prisoners use. He found that prisoners tend to group themselves into cliques on the basis of such personal criteria as sexual preference, political beliefs, and offense history. He found complex sexual relationships in prison and concluded that many heterosexual men will turn to homosexual relationships when faced with long sentences and the loneliness of prison life.

Clemmer's most important contribution may have been his identification of the **prisonization** process. This he defined as the inmate's assimilation into the existing prison culture through acceptance of its language, sexual code, and norms of behavior. Those who become the most "prisonized" will be the least likely to reform on the outside.

Using Clemmer's work as a jumping-off point, a number of prominent sociologists have set out to explore more fully the various roles in the prison community. The most important principles of the dominant inmate culture are listed in Exhibit 14.1.

Although some inmates violate the code and exploit their peers, the "right guy" is someone who uses the inmate social code as his personal behavior guide. He is always loyal to his fellow prisoners, keeps his promises, is dependable and trustworthy, and never interferes with inmates who are

inmate subculture The loosely defined culture that pervades prisons and has its own norms, rules, and language.

inmate social code An unwritten code of behavior, passed from older inmates to younger ones, which serves as guidelines for appropriate inmate behavior within the correctional institution.

prisonization Assimilation into the separate culture in the prison that has its own set of rewards and behaviors. This loosely defined culture that pervades prisons has its own norms, rules, and language. The traditional culture is now being replaced by a violent gang culture.

| **Exhibit 14.1** | **Elements of the inmate social code** |

1. *Don't interfere with inmates' interests.* Within this area of the code are maxims concerning serving the least amount of time in the greatest possible comfort. For example, inmates are warned never to betray another inmate to authorities; in other words, grievances must be handled personally. Other aspects of the noninterference doctrine include "Don't be nosy," "Don't have a loose lip," "Keep off the other inmates' backs," and "Don't put another inmate on the spot."

2. *Don't lose your head.* Inmates are also cautioned to refrain from arguing, quarreling, or engaging in other emotional displays with fellow inmates. The novice may hear such warnings as "Play it cool," and "Do your own time."

3. *Don't exploit inmates.* Prisoners are warned not to take advantage of one another—"Don't steal from cons," "Don't welsh on a debt," and "Be right."

4. *Be tough and don't lose your dignity.* Although Rule 2 forbids conflict, once it starts an inmate must be prepared to deal with it effectively and thoroughly. Maxims include, "Don't cop out," "Don't weaken," and "Be tough; be a man."

5. *Don't be a sucker.* Inmates are cautioned not to make fools of themselves and support the guards or prison administration over the interest of the inmates—"Be sharp."

Source: Gresham Sykes, *The Society of Captives* (Princeton, N.J.: Princeton University Press, 1958).

conniving against the officials.[15] The right guy does not go around looking for a fight, but he never runs away from one; he acts like a man.

The effects of prisonization may be long-term and destructive. Many inmates become hostile to the legal system, learning to use violence as a means of solving problems and to value criminal peers.[16] For some this change may be permanent; for others it is temporary, and they may revert to their "normal" life after release.

The New Inmate Culture

The importation of outside values into the inmate culture has had a dramatic effect on prison life. Although the "old" inmate subculture may have been harmful because its norms and values insulated the inmate from change efforts, it also helped create order in the institution and prevented violence among the inmates. People who violated the code and victimized others were sanctioned by their peers. An understanding developed between guards and inmate leaders: the guards would let the inmates have things their own way; the inmates would not let things get out of hand and draw the attention of the administration.

The old system may be dying or already dead in most institutions. The change seems to have been precipitated by the black power movement in the 1960s and 1970s. Black inmates were no longer content to play a subservient role and challenged the power of established white inmates. As the black power movement gained prominence, racial tension in prisons created divisions that severely altered the inmate subculture. Older, respected inmates could no longer cross racial lines to mediate disputes. Predatory inmates could victimize others without fear of retaliation. Consequently, more inmates than ever are now assigned to protective custody for their own safety.

In the new culture, African-American and Latino inmates are much more cohesively organized than whites.[17] Their groups sometimes form out of religious or political affiliations, such as the Black Muslims; out of efforts to combat discrimination in prison, such as the Latino group La Nuestra Familia; or from street gangs, such as the Vice Lords or Gangster Disciples in the Illinois prison system and the Crips in California. Where white inmates have successfully organized, it is in the form of a neo-Nazi group called the Aryan Brotherhood. Racially homogeneous gangs are so cohesive and powerful that they are able to supplant the original inmate code with one of their own.

Criminal Justice ⚖ Now ™

Learn more by exploring the "Pseudo–Family" Review and Reinforce activity.

WOMEN IMPRISONED

Before 1960, few women were in prison. Women's prisons were relatively rare and were usually an outgrowth of male institutions. Only four institutions for women were built between 1930 and 1950; in comparison, thirty-four women's prisons were constructed during the 1980s as crime rates soared.

At the turn of the twentieth century, female inmates were viewed as morally depraved people who flouted conventional rules of female behavior. The treatment of white and African-American women differed significantly. In some states, white women were placed in female-only reformatories designed to improve their deportment; black women were placed in male prisons, where they were put on chain gangs and subject to beatings.[18]

As you may recall (chapter 13) the female offender population has increased more rapidly than the male population. There are a number of reasons for this growth. Women have accelerated their crime rate at a faster pace than men. The get-tough policies that produced mandatory and determinate sentencing statutes has also helped reduce the judicial discretion that has traditionally benefited women; women no longer receive the benefits of male chivalry.[19]

Female Institutions

State jurisdictions have been responding to the influx of female offenders into the correctional system by expanding the facilities for housing and treating them.[20] Women's prisons tend to be smaller than those housing male inmates.[21] Although some female institutions are strictly penal, with steel bars, concrete floors, and other security measures, the majority are nonsecure institutions similar to college dormitories and group homes in the community. Women's facilities, especially those in the community, commonly offer a great deal of autonomy to inmates and allow them to make decisions affecting their daily lives.

However, like men's prisons, women's prisons suffer from a lack of adequate training, health, treatment, and educational facilities. Psychological counseling often takes the form of group sessions conducted by laypeople, such as correctional officers. Most trained psychologists and psychiatrists restrict themselves to such activities as conducting intake classifications and court-ordered examinations and prescribing mood-controlling medication. Although many female inmates are parents and had custody of their children before incarceration, little effort is made to help them develop better parenting skills. While most female (and male) inmates have at least one child, less than a quarter actually get an annual visit. Who takes care of these children while their mothers are incarcerated? Most children of incarcerated women are placed with their father, grandparent, other relative, or a family friend. About 10 percent wind up in foster homes or state facilities.

Job-training opportunities are also a problem. Where vocational training exists, it is in areas with limited financial reward, hindering adjustment on release. Female inmates, many of whom were on the economic margin before their incarceration began, find little room for improvement during their prison experience.[22] Surveys also indicate that the prison experience does little to prepare women to reenter the workforce after their sentence has been completed. Gender stereotypes still shape vocational opportunities.[23] Female inmates are still being trained for "women's roles," such as child rearing, and not given the programming to make successful adjustments in the community.[24]

Female Inmates

Like their male counterparts, female inmates are young (most are under age thirty), minority group members, unmarried, undereducated (more than half are high school dropouts), and either unemployed or underemployed.

Incarcerated women also have had a troubled family life. Significant numbers were at-risk children, products of broken homes and the welfare system; over half have received welfare at some time during their adult lives. Many claim to have been physically or sexually abused at some point in their lives. This pattern continued in adult life: many female inmates were victims of domestic violence. It is not surprising that many display psychological problems.[25]

A significant number of female inmates report having substance abuse problems. About three-fourths have used drugs at some time in their lives, and almost half were involved with addictive drugs, such as cocaine, heroin, or PCP. The incarceration of so many women who are low criminal risks yet face a high risk of exposure to HIV (human immunodeficiency virus, which causes AIDS) and other health issues because of their prior history of drug abuse presents a significant problem. One recent study of incarcerated women found that one-third of the sample reported that before their arrest they had traded sex for money or drugs; 24 percent of the women reported trading sex for money or drugs "weekly or more often."[26] Such risky behavior significantly increases the likelihood of their carrying the AIDS virus or other sexually transmitted diseases.

The picture that emerges of the female inmate is troubling. After a lifetime of emotional turmoil, physical and sexual abuse, and drug use, it seems improbable that overcrowded, underfunded correctional institutions can forge a dramatic turnaround in the behavior of at-risk female inmates.

Sexual Exploitation Lack of opportunity is not the only problem faced by female inmates. There are numerous reports of female prisoners being sexually abused and exploited by male correctional workers who either use brute force or psychological coercion to gain sexual control over inmates.[27] Staff-on-inmate sexual misconduct covers a wide range of behaviors, from lewd remarks to voyeurism to assault and rape. The General Accounting Office (GAO) found that the federal government, forty-one states, and the District of Columbia have been forced to pass laws criminalizing some types of staff sexual misconduct in prisons. They found that sexual misconduct persists despite efforts to correct problems and train staff.[28] Because male correctional officers now are commonly assigned to women's prisons, there have also been major scandals involving the sexual exploitation and rape of female inmates. Few if any of these incidents are reported, and perpetrators rarely go to trial. Institutional workers cover for each other, and women who file complaints are offered little protection from vengeful guards.[29]

Adapting to the Female Institution

Daily life in women's prisons differs somewhat from that in male institutions. For one thing, unlike male inmates, women usually do not present an immediate physical danger to staff and fellow inmates. Relatively few engage in violent behavior, and incidents of inmate-initiated sexual aggression, so common in male institutions, are rare in women's prisons.[30] Few female inmates either experience the violent atmosphere common in male institutions or suffer the racial and ethnic conflict and divisiveness.[31] Although female inmates may experience less discomfort than males, that does not mean their experience is a bed of roses. Many still experience fear and are forced to undergo a process of socialization fraught with danger and volatile situations.[32]

The rigid, anti-authority inmate social code found in many male institutions does not exist in female institutions.[33] Confinement for women, however, may produce severe anxiety and anger because of separation from families and loved ones and the inability to function in normal female roles. Unlike men, who direct their anger outward, female prisoners may turn to more self-destructive acts to cope with their problems. Female inmates are

Being separated from their children is particularly difficult for female inmates, so maintaining family ties is an important element of adjustment in women's prisons. Human resource agencies help inmates arrange family visits. Inmates at Fluvanna Correctional Center for Women look into the distance in anticipation of seeing their children arriving during a visit in Troy, Virginia, June 28, 2003. The visit was part of a parenting program for prison mothers and their children sponsored by the Girl Scouts.

© 2005 AP/Wide World Photos

more likely than males to mutilate their own bodies and attempt suicide. For example, one common practice among female inmates is self-mutilation, or "carving." This ranges from simple scratches to carving the name of their boyfriend on their body or even complex statements or sentences ("To mother, with hate").[34]

Another form of adaptation to prison used by women is the make-believe family. This group contains masculine and feminine figures acting as fathers and mothers; some even act as children and take on the role of brother or sister. Formalized marriages and divorces may be conducted. Sometimes one inmate holds multiple roles, so that a "sister" in one family may "marry" and become the "wife" of another inmate. It is estimated that about half of all female inmates are members of make-believe families.[35]

Why do make-believe families exist? Experts suggest that they provide the warm, stable relationships otherwise unobtainable in the prison environment. People both in and out of prison have needs for security, companionship, affection, attention, status, prestige, and acceptance that can be filled only by having primary group relationships. Friends fill many of these needs, but the family better represents the ideal or desire for these things in a stable relationship.

Separate but Unequal

Critics have charged that female correctional institutions do not get the same level of support as male facilities and as a result educational and vocational programs are deficient. Female inmates were not provided with the tools needed to succeed on the outside because the limited vocational training stressed what was considered traditional "women's work": cosmetology, secretarial work, and food services.

To remedy this situation, most state correctional agencies have instituted some sort of vocational training programs for women. Although the traditional vocation of sewing is the most common industrial program, correctional authorities are beginning to teach data processing, and female inmates are involved in such other industries as farming, printing, telemarketing, and furniture repair. Clearly, greater efforts are needed to improve the quality of work experiences for female inmates.

CORRECTIONAL TREATMENT METHODS

Almost every prison facility uses some mode of treatment for inmates. This may come in the form of individual or group therapy programs or educational or vocational training. This section presents a selected number of therapeutic methods that have been used nationally in correctional settings and identifies some of their more salient features.

Individual and Group Treatment

Prison inmates typically suffer from a variety of cognitive and psychosocial deficits, such as poor emotional control, social skills, and interpersonal problem solving; these deficits are often linked to long-term substance abuse. Modern counseling programs help them to control emotions (e.g., understanding why they feel the way they do; dealing with nervousness or anxiety; solving their problems creatively), to communicate with others (e.g., understanding what people tell them; communicating clearly when they write), to deal with legal concerns (e.g., keeping out of legal trouble; avoiding breaking laws), to manage general life issues (e.g., finding a job; dealing with difficult co-workers; being a good parent), and to develop and maintain social relationships (e.g., having good relations with others; making others happy; making others proud).[36]

To achieve these goals, correctional systems use a variety of intensive individual and group techniques, including behavior modification, aversive therapy, milieu therapy, reality therapy, transactional analysis, and responsibility therapy. Under the Bush administration, faith-based rehabilitation efforts have flourished and some have shown to be positive influences on inmate behavior.[37]

Drug Treatment Most prisons have programs designed to help inmates suffering from alcohol and substance abuse issues. One approach is to provide abusers with methadone as a substitute for heroin; some evaluations have shown this method to be effective.[38] Because substance abuse is so prevalent among correctional clients, some correctional facilities have been reformulated into treatment dispensing total institutions referred to as "therapeutic communities." This is the topic of the Policy, Programs, and Issues in Criminal Justice feature on the next page.

Treating the AIDS-Infected Inmate The AIDS-infected prisoner inmate has been the subject of great concern. Two groups of people at high risk of contracting HIV are intravenous drug users who share needles and males who engage in same sex relations, two lifestyles common in prison. Because drug use is common and syringes scarce, many high-risk inmates share drug paraphernalia, increasing the danger of HIV infection.[39]

Although the numbers are constantly changing, the rate of HIV infection among state and federal prisoners has stabilized at around 2 percent and there are about twenty-five thousand HIV-infected inmates.

Correctional administrators have found it difficult to arrive at effective policies to confront AIDS. Although all state and federal jurisdictions do some AIDS testing, only eighteen states and the federal Bureau of Prisons conduct mass screenings of all inmates. Most states test inmates only if there are significant indications that they are HIV-positive. About 40 percent of all state prison inmates have never been tested for AIDS.

Most correctional systems are now training staff about AIDS. Educational programs for inmates are often inadequate because administrators are reluctant to give them information on the proper cleaning of drug paraphernalia and safe sex (since both drug use and sexual relations are forbidden in prison).

Criminal Justice ⚖ Now™
Learn more by exploring the "Getting Tough on Crime" Review and Reinforce activity.

Criminal Justice ⚖ Now™
*Learn more about **Careers in Criminal Justice** by exploring the "On the Job" features **Correctional Treatment Specialist** and **Correctional Counselor**.*

Policy, Programs, and Issues in Criminal Justice

Therapeutic Communities

Because drug abuse is so prevalent among inmates, some institutions have been organized into therapeutic communities (TC) in order to best serve their clientele. The TC approach to substance abuse treatment uses a psychosocial, experiential learning process which relies on positive peer pressure within a highly structured social environment. The community itself, including staff and program participants, becomes the primary method of change. They work together as members of a "family" in order to create a culture where community members confront each other's negative behavior and attitudes and establish an open, trusting and safe environment; TC relies then on mutual self-help. The TC approach encourages personal disclosure rather than the isolation of the general prison culture. Participants view staff as role models and rational authorities rather than as custodians or treatment providers.

Therapeutic communities have several distinctive characteristics:

- They present an alternative concept of inmates that is usually much more positive than prevailing beliefs.
- Their activities embody positive values, help to promote positive social relationships, and start a process of socialization that encourages a more responsible and productive way of life.
- Their staff, some of whom are recovering addicts and former inmates, provide positive role models.
- They provide transition from institutional to community existence, with treatment occurring just prior to release and with continuity of care in the community.

Therapeutic communities are also viewed as a viable alternative to treat the poly-problem inmate who suffers from a variety of social and personal ills such as mental health and substance abuse issues.

The Residential Substance Abuse Treatment (RSAT)

Residential Substance Abuse Treatment (RSAT) is a good example of a therapeutic community program that has been implemented to help substance-abusing inmates in the state of Idaho. It consists of nine to twelve months of rigorous drug treatment provided by a private contractor. Clients are low-risk offenders having a habitual substance abuse problem, a desire to change, a positive attitude, and also have legitimate resources on the outside that will assist them when released.

During their treatment, participants are to better themselves by learning to think before they act in order to change their ways of decision-making. They are required to write down their thoughts and feelings, expressing why they engage in destructive behavior, and how they expect to change their ways with more constructive choices. Participants work on their social, behavioral and vocational skills as well. Clients also take part in a twelve-step model, similar to the programs used by Alcoholics and/or Narcotics Anonymous, group counseling, individual counseling, group meetings, and physical activity.

Critical Thinking

How does the use of a program such as Residential Substance Abuse Treatment jibe with the no-frills movement? Should inmates in a therapeutic community receive treatment and counseling privileges denied to those who have not yet been in trouble with the law?

InfoTrac College Edition Research

To find out more about *therapeutic communities*, use it in a key word search on InfoTrac College Edition. Also, use *correctional treatment* in a similar search.

Sources: Mary Stohr, Craig Hemmens, Diane Baune, Jed Dayley, Mark Gornik, Kirstin Kjaer, and Cindy Noon, "Residential Substance Abuse Treatment for State Prisoners: Breaking the Drug-Crime Cycle Among Parole Violators" (National Institute for Justice: Washington, D.C., 2003); *Therapeutic Communities in Correctional Settings: Appendix B: Revised TCA Standards for TCs in Correctional Settings* (Washington, D.C.: Office of National Drug Control Policy, 1999) www.whitehouse drugpolicy.gov/national_assembly/publications/therap_comm/toc.html, accessed on September 20, 2005; William Burdon, David Farabee, Michael Prendergast, Nena Messina, and Jerome Cartier, "Prison-Based Therapeutic Community Substance Abuse Programs— Implementation and Operational Issues," *Federal Probation 66* (2002): 3–9; Roger Peters, Michelle LeVasseur, and Redonna Chandler, "Correctional Treatment for Co-occurring Disorders: Results of a National Survey," *Behavioral Sciences & the Law 22* (2004): 563–584.

Educational and Vocational Programs

Besides treatment programs stressing personal growth through individual analysis or group process, inmate rehabilitation is also pursued through vocational and educational training. Although these two kinds of training sometimes differ in style and content, they can also overlap when, for example, education involves practical, job-related study.

The first prison treatment programs were in fact educational. A prison school was opened at the Walnut Street Jail in 1784. Elementary courses were offered in New York's prison system in 1801 and in Pennsylvania's in 1844. An actual school system was established in Detroit's House of Corrections in 1870, and the Elmira Reformatory opened a vocational trade school in 1876. Today, most institutions provide some type of educational program. At some prisons, inmates can obtain a high school diploma or a general educational development (GED) certificate through equivalency exams. Other institutions provide an actual classroom education, usually staffed by certified teachers employed full-time at the prison or by part-time teachers who also teach full-time at nearby public schools.

The number of hours devoted to educational programs and the quality and intensity of these efforts vary greatly. Some are full-time programs employing highly qualified and concerned educators, whereas others are part-time programs without any real goals or objectives. Although worthwhile attempts are being made, prison educational programs often suffer from inadequate funding and administration. The picture is not totally bleak, however. In some institutions, programs have been designed to circumvent the difficulties inherent in the prison structure. They encourage volunteers from the community and local schools to tutor willing and motivated inmates. Some prison administrators have arranged flexible schedules for inmate students and actively encourage their participation in these programs. In several states, statewide school districts serving prisons have been created. Forming such districts can make better-qualified staff available and provide the materials and resources necessary for meaningful educational programs.

Every state correctional system also has some job-related services for inmates. Some have elaborate training programs inside the institution, whereas others have instituted prerelease and postrelease employment services. Inmates who hope to obtain parole need to participate in prison industry. Documenting a history of stable employment in prison is essential if parole agents are to convince prospective employers that the ex-offender is a good risk, and postrelease employment is usually required for parole eligibility.[40]

A few of the more important work-related services are discussed in the following sections.

Vocational Training Most institutions provide vocational training programs. In New York, more than forty-two trade and technical courses are provided in organized training shops under qualified civilian instructors. Some of these courses not only benefit the inmate but also provide services for the institution. New York has trained inmates to become dental laboratory technicians; this program provides dentures for inmates and saves the state money. Another New York program trains inmates to become optical technicians and has the added benefit of providing eyeglasses for inmates. Other New York correctional training programs include barber training, computer programming, auto mechanics, auto body work, and radio and television repair. The products of most of these programs save the taxpayers money, and the programs provide the inmates with practical experience. Many other states offer this type of vocational programming.

Despite the promising aspects of such programs, they have also been seriously criticized. Inmates often have trouble finding skill-related, high-paying jobs on their release. Equipment in prisons is often secondhand, obsolete, and hard to come by. Some programs are thinly disguised excuses for prison upkeep and maintenance, and unions and other groups resent the intrusion of prison labor into their markets.

Work Release To supplement programs stressing rehabilitation via in-house job training or education, more than forty-four states have attempted to implement **work release** or **furlough** programs. These allow deserving inmates to leave the institution and hold regular jobs in the community.

Inmates enrolled in work release may live at the institutions at night while working in the community during the day. However, security problems (for example, contraband may be brought in) and the usual remoteness of prisons often make this arrangement difficult. More typical is the extended work release, where prisoners are allowed to remain in the community for significant periods of time. To help inmates adjust, some states operate community-based prerelease centers where inmates live while working. Some inmates may work at their previous jobs, while others seek new employment.

Like other programs, work release has its good and bad points. Inmates are sometimes reluctantly received in the community and find that certain areas of employment are closed to them. Citizens are often concerned about prisoners "stealing" jobs or working for lower than normal wages; consequently, such practices are prohibited by Public Law 89-176, which controls the federal work release program.

On the other hand, inmates gain many benefits from work release, including the ability to maintain work skills, to maintain community ties, and to make an easier transition from prison to the outside world. For those who have learned a skill in the institution, work release offers an excellent opportunity to test out a new occupation. For others, the job may be a training situation in which new skills are acquired. A number of states have reported that few work release inmates abscond while in the community.

Private Prison Enterprise Opposition from organized labor ended the profitability of commercial prison industries, but a number of interesting efforts have been made to vary the type and productivity of prison labor.[41] The federal government helped put private industry into prisons when it approved the Free Venture Program in 1976. Seven states, including Connecticut, South Carolina, and Minnesota, were given grants to implement private industries inside prison walls. This successful program led to the Percy Amendment (1979), federal legislation that allowed prison-made goods to be sold across state lines if the projects complied with strict rules, such as making sure unions were consulted and preventing manufacturers from undercutting the existing wage structure.[42] The new law authorized a number of prison industry enhancement pilot projects. These were certified as meeting the Percy Amendment operating rules and were therefore free to ship goods out of state; by 1987, fifteen projects had been certified.

Today, private prison industries have used a number of models. One approach, the *state-use model*, makes the correctional system a supplier of goods and services that serves state-run institutions. For example, the California Prison Industry Authority (PIA) is an inmate work program that provides work assignments for approximately seven thousand inmates and operates seventy service, manufacturing, and agricultural industries in twenty-three prisons. These industries produce a variety of goods and services, including flags, printing services, signs, binders, eyewear, gloves, office furniture, clothing, and cell equipment. PIA products and services are available to government entities, including federal, state, and local government agencies. Court-ordered restitutions or fines are deducted from the wages earned by

Although some critics want to end **work release,** the program is supported by the ACLU. To reach this site, go to "Web Links" on your Siegel Essentials of Criminal Justice 5e website: http://cj.wadsworth.com/siegel_ess5e.

work release A prison treatment program that allows inmates to be released during the day to work in the community and returned to prison at night.

furlough A correctional policy that allows inmates to leave the institution for vocational or educational training, for employment, or to maintain family ties.

PIA inmates and are transferred to the Crime Victims' Restitution Fund. PIA inmates receive wages between 30 cents and 95 cents per hour, before deductions.[43] In another approach, the free-enterprise model, private companies set up manufacturing units on prison grounds or purchase goods made by inmates in shops owned and operated by the corrections department. In the corporate model, a semi-independent business is created on prison grounds whose profits go to the state government and inmate laborers.[44] Despite widespread publicity, the partnership between private enterprise and the prison community has been limited to a few experimental programs. However, it is likely to grow in the future.

Postrelease Programs A final element of job-related programming involves helping inmates obtain jobs before they are released and keep them once they are on the outside. A number of correctional departments have set up employment services designed to ease the transition between institution and community. Employment program staff assess inmates' backgrounds to determine their abilities, interests, goals, and capabilities. They also help them create job plans essential to receiving early release (parole) and successfully reintegrating into the community. Some programs maintain community correctional placements in sheltered environments that help inmates bridge the gap between institutions and the outside world. Services include job placement, skill development, family counseling, and legal and medical assistance.

© 2005 AP/Wide World Photos

Finding employment can be a key element of a former inmate's adjustment to society. After getting a job offer to work at Dairy Queen, Patricia McCray, right, celebrates with Dorothy Franklin and Bonnie Boyce in Bremerton, Washington. Franklin is the director of the Marilyn Brandenberg Boarding House, a transitional residence for women when they leave prison. McCray and Boyce are residents in the house.

Can Rehabilitation Work?

Despite the variety and number of treatment programs in operation, questions remain about their effectiveness. In their oft-cited research, Robert Martinson and his associates (1975) found that a majority of treatment programs were failures.[45]

Martinson found in a national study that, with few exceptions, rehabilitative efforts seemed to have no appreciable effect on recidivism; his research produced a "nothing works" view of correctional treatment. Martinson's work was followed by efforts showing that some high-risk offenders were more likely to commit crimes after they had been placed in treatment programs than before the onset of rehabilitation efforts.[46] A slew of reviews have claimed that correctional treatment efforts aimed at youthful offenders provide little evidence that rehabilitation can occur within correctional settings. Evidence is scant that treatment efforts—even those that include vocational, educational, and mental health services—can consistently lower recidivism rates.[47]

The so-called failure of correctional treatment has helped promote a conservative view of corrections in which prisons are considered places of incapacitation and punishment, not treatment centers. Current policies stress eliminating the nonserious offender from the correctional system while increasing the probability that serious, violent offenders will be incarcerated and serve longer sentences. This view supports the utility of mandatory and determinate sentences for serious offenders and the simultaneous use of intermediate sanctions, such as house arrest, restitution, and diversion, to limit the nonserious offender's involvement in the system.

Although the concept of correctional rehabilitation is facing serious challenges, many experts still believe strongly in the rehabilitative ideal.[48] Recent analysis of education, vocation, and work programs indicate that they may be able to lower recidivism rates and increase postrelease employment.[49] Inmates who have completed higher levels of education find it easier to gain employment upon release and consequently are less likely to recidivate over long periods.[50] The programs that have produced positive results both in the community and inside correctional institutions contain the following elements:

- Teach interpersonal skills
- Provide individual counseling
- Make use of behavioral modification techniques
- Use cognitive-behavioral therapy
- Stress improving moral reasoning
- Combine in-prison therapeutic communities with follow-up community treatment[51]

Although not all programs are successful for all inmates, many treatment programs are effective and participants, especially younger clients, have a better chance of success on the outside than those who forgo treatment.[52]

Criminal Justice ⚖ Now™

Learn more by exploring the "Prison Vocabulary" Vocabulary Check activity.

GUARDING THE INSTITUTION

Control of a prison is a complex task. On the one hand, a tough, high-security environment may meet the goals of punishment and control but fail to reinforce positive behavior changes. On the other hand, too liberal an administrative stance can lower staff morale and place inmates in charge of the institution.

For many years, prison guards were viewed as ruthless people who enjoyed their positions of power over inmates, fought rehabilitation efforts, were racist, and had a "lock psychosis" developed from years of counting, numbering, and checking on inmates. This view has changed in recent years.

Correctional officers are now viewed as public servants who are seeking the security and financial rewards of a civil service position.[53] Most are in favor of rehabilitation efforts and do not hold any particular animosity toward the inmates. The correctional officer has been characterized as a "people worker" who must be prepared to deal with the problems of inmates on a personal level and also as a member of a complex bureaucracy who must be able to cope with its demands.

Corrections officers play a number of roles in the institution. They supervise cell houses, dining areas, shops, and other facilities as well as perch up on the walls, armed with rifles, to oversee the yard and prevent escapes. Corrections officers also sit on disciplinary boards and escort inmates to hospitals and court appearances.

The greatest problem faced by correctional officers is the duality of their role: maintainers of order and security and advocates of treatment and rehabilitation. Added to this basic dilemma is the changing inmate role. In earlier times, corrections officers could count on inmate leaders to help them maintain order, but now they are faced with a racially charged atmosphere in which violence is a way of life. Today, correctional work in some institutions can be filled with danger, tension, boredom, and little evidence that efforts to help inmates lead to success. Research indicates that next to police officers, the correctional worker's job is the most high-risk job in the United States and abroad.[54] And unlike police officers, correctional officers apparently do not form a close-knit subculture with unique values and a sense of intergroup loyalty. Correctional officers experience alienation and isolation from inmates, the administration, and each other. Interestingly, this sense of alienation seems greatest in younger officers; evidence exists that later in their careers officers enjoy a revival of interest in their work and take great pride in providing human services to inmates.[55] It is not surprising that correctional officers perceive significant levels of stress related to such job factors as lack of safety, inadequate career opportunities, and work overload.[56]

Many state prison authorities have developed training programs to prepare guards for the difficulties of prison work. Guard unions have also commonly been formed to negotiate wages and working conditions with corrections departments.

Female Correctional Officers

The issue of female correctional officers in male institutions comes up repeatedly. Today, an estimated five thousand women are assigned to all-male institutions.[57] The employment of women as guards in close contact with male inmates has spurred many questions of privacy and safety and a number of legal cases. In one important case, *Dothard v. Rawlinson* (1977), the U.S. Supreme Court upheld Alabama's refusal to hire female correctional officers on the grounds that it would put them in significant danger from the male inmates.[58] Despite such setbacks, women now work side by side with male guards in almost every state, performing the same duties. Research indicates that discipline has not suffered because of the inclusion of women in the guard force. Sexual assaults have been rare, and more negative attitudes have been expressed by the female guards' male peers than by inmates. Most commentators believe that the presence of female guards can have an important beneficial effect on the self-image of inmates and improve the guard/inmate working relationship.

Ironically, female correctional officers may find that an assignment to a male institution can boost their career. Recent restrictions on male staff in women's prisons, in the wake of well-publicized sex scandals, have forced administrators to assign women officers to the dormitory areas, the least desirable areas in which to work. Women officers are not similarly restricted in male-only facilities.[59]

Violence is a constant threat in the prison environment, and administrators must be vigilant in order to maintain order. Here, prison guard Tatum Lodish opens a gate in the Berks County Prison near Reading, Pennsylvania. Lodish graduated with a bachelor's degree in criminal justice and the intention of working with troubled teenagers. But for the past eight months, the 23-year-old has been a correctional officer at the prison.

© 2002 AP/Wide World Photos

Criminal Justice ⊕ Now™

*Learn more by viewing the **"U.S. Priest"** "In the News" video clip.*

PRISON VIOLENCE

On August 9, 1973, Stephen Donaldson, a Quaker peace activist, was arrested for trespassing after participating in a pray-in at the White House. Sent to a Washington, D.C., jail for two nights, Donaldson was gang-raped approximately sixty times by numerous inmates. Donaldson later became president of Stop Prisoner Rape, a nonprofit organization that advocates for the protection of inmates from sexual assault and offers support to victims. On July 18, 1996, at the age of forty-nine, Stephen Donaldson died from infections complicated by AIDS, after he contracted HIV through prisoner rapes.[60]

Conflict, violence, and brutality are sad but ever-present facts of institutional life. Violence can involve individual conflict: inmate versus inmate, inmate versus staff, staff versus inmate.

While surveys show that prison administrators deny or downplay its occurrence, sexual assault is a common threat.[61] Research has shown that prison rapes usually involve a victim who is viewed as weak and submissive and a group of aggressive rapists who can dominate the victim through their collective strength; homosexual and bisexual males are at high risk for rapes.[62] Surveys indicate that at least 20 percent of all inmates are raped during the course of their prison stay.[63]

Sexual harassment leads to fights, social isolation, fear, anxiety, and crisis. Nonsexual assaults may stem from an aggressor's desire to shake down the victim for money and personal favors, may be motivated by racial conflict, or may simply be used to establish power within the institution. The problem is so severe that Congress enacted the Prison Rape Reduction Act of 2003, which established three programs in the Department of Justice:

- A program dedicated to collecting national prison rape statistics, data, and conducting research
- A program dedicated to the dissemination of information and procedures for combating prison rape
- A program to assist in funding state programs[64]

© 2003 AP/Wide World Photos

Special units have been created to head off the threat of prison violence. Here, members of a prison tactical team made up of officers from ten different prisons stand watch over inmates at Big Muddy Correctional Center in Ina, Illinois. The team surprised inmates with a drug and weapons sweep that resulted in more than thirty positive drug tests and the recovery of one weapon.

Violence can also involve large groups of inmates, such as the famous Attica riot in 1971, which claimed thirty-nine lives, or the New Mexico State Penitentiary riot of February 1980, in which the death toll was thirty-three. More than three hundred prison riots have occurred since the first one in 1774, 90 percent of them since 1952.[65]

A number of factors can spark such damaging incidents. These include poor staff/inmate communications, destructive environmental conditions, faulty classification, and promised but undelivered reforms. The 1980 New Mexico State Penitentiary riot drew national attention to the problem of prison overcrowding and the conflict which it produced. The prison was designed for 800 but actually held 1,135 prisoners; conditions of overcrowding, squalor, poor food, and lack of medical treatment abounded. The state government had been called on to improve guard training, physical plant quality, and relief from overcrowding but was reluctant to spend the necessary money.

Although revulsion over the violent riots in New Mexico and the earlier riot in New York's Attica prison led to calls for correctional reform, prison violence has continued unabated. About seventy-five to one hundred inmates are killed by their peers each year in U.S. prisons, six or seven staff members are murdered, and some 120 suicides are recorded.

What Causes Violence?

What are the causes of prison violence? There is no single explanation for either collective or individual violence, but theories abound.[66]

Individual Violence

- *History of prior violence.* Before they were incarcerated, many inmates were violence-prone individuals who always used force to get their own way. Some are former gang members who upon entering the institution quickly join inmate gangs.[67] In many instances street gangs maintain prison branches that unite the inmate with their former violence prone peers. Having this connection supports and protects gang members while they are in prison, and it assists in supporting gang members' families and

Criminal Justice ⚖ Now™

Learn more by exploring the ***"Deprivation Model"*** *Review and Reinforce activity and the* ***Prison Society*** *Learning Module.*

associates outside the wall.[68] Gang violence is a significant source of prison conflict.

- *Psychological factors.* Many inmates suffer from personality disorders. Recent research shows that among institutionalized offenders, psychopathy is the strongest predictor of violent recidivism and indifferent response to treatment.[69] In the crowded, dehumanizing world of the prison, it is not surprising that people with extreme psychological distress may resort to violence to dominate others.[70]

- *Prison conditions.* The prison experience itself causes people to become violent. Inhuman conditions, including overcrowding, depersonalization, and the threat of sexual assault are violence-producing conditions. Even in the most humane prisons, life is a constant put-down, and prison conditions are a threat to the inmates' sense of self-worth; violence is an expected consequence of these conditions. Violence levels are not much different in high and low security prisons, indicating that the prison experience itself, and not the level of control, produces violence.[71]

- *Lack of dispute resolution mechanisms.* Many prisons lack effective mechanisms that enable inmate grievances against either prison officials or other inmates to be handled fairly and equitably. Prisoners who complain about other inmates are viewed as "rats" or "snitches" and are marked for death by their enemies. Similarly, complaints or lawsuits filed against the prison administration may result in the inmate being placed in solitary confinement—"the hole."

- *Basic survival.* Inmates resort to violence in order to survive. The lack of physical security and adequate mechanisms for resolving complaints and the code of silence promote individual violence by inmates who might otherwise be controlled.

Collective Violence

- *Inmate-balance theory.* Riots and other forms of collective violence occur when prison officials make an abrupt effort to take control of the prison and limit freedoms. Crackdowns occur when officials perceive that inmate leaders have too much power and take measures to control their illicit privileges, such as gambling or stealing food.[72]

- *Administrative-control theory.* Collective violence is caused by prison mismanagement, lack of strong security, and inadequate control by prison officials. Poor management may inhibit conflict management and set the stage for violence. Repressive administrations give inmates the feeling that nothing will ever change, that they have nothing to lose, and that violence is the only means for change.

- *Overcrowding.* As the prison population continues to climb, unmatched by expanded capacity, prison violence may increase. Overcrowding caused by the rapid increases in the prison population has also been linked to both increases in inmate substance abuse and prison violence.[73]

PRISONERS' RIGHTS

Before the early 1960s, it was accepted that on conviction an individual forfeited all rights not expressly granted by statutory law or correctional policy; inmates were civilly dead. The U.S. Supreme Court held that convicted offenders should expect to be penalized for their misdeeds and that part of their punishment was the loss of freedoms ordinary citizens take for granted.

One reason why inmates lacked rights was that state and federal courts were reluctant to intervene in the administration of prisons unless the circumstances of a case clearly indicated a serious breach of the Eighth Amendment protection against cruel and unusual punishment. This judicial policy is referred to as the **hands-off doctrine.** The courts used three basic justifications for their neglect of prison conditions:

1. Correctional administration was a technical matter best left to experts rather than to courts ill-equipped to make appropriate evaluations.

2. Society as a whole was apathetic to what went on in prisons, and most individuals preferred not to associate with or know about the offenders.

3. Prisoners' complaints involved privileges rather than rights. Prisoners were considered to have fewer constitutional rights than other members of society.[74]

As the 1960s drew to a close, the hands-off doctrine was eroded. Federal district courts began seriously considering prisoners' claims concerning conditions in the various state and federal institutions and used their power to intervene on behalf of the inmates. In some ways, this concern reflected the spirit of the times, which saw the onset of the civil rights movement, and subsequently was paralleled in such areas as student rights, public welfare, mental institutions, juvenile court systems, and military justice.

Beginning in the late 1960s, such activist groups as the NAACP Legal Defense Fund and the American Civil Liberties Union's National Prison Project began to search for appropriate legal vehicles to bring prisoners' complaints before state and federal courts. The most widely used device was the federal Civil Rights Act, 42 U.S.C. 1983:

> Every person who, under color of any statute, ordinance, regulation, custom, or usage of any State or Territory subjects, or causes to be subjected, any citizen of the United States or other person within the jurisdiction thereof to the deprivation of any rights, privileges, or immunities secured by the Constitution and laws shall be liable to the party injured in an action at law, suit in equity, or other proper proceeding for redress.

The legal argument went that, as U.S. citizens, prison inmates could sue state officials if their civil rights were violated—for example, if they were the victims of racial or religious discrimination.

The U.S. Supreme Court first recognized the right of prisoners to sue for civil rights violations in cases involving religious freedom brought by the Black Muslims. This well-organized group had been frustrated by prison administrators who feared its growing power and desired to put limits on its recruitment activities. In the 1964 case of *Cooper v. Pate,* however, the Supreme Court ruled that inmates who were being denied the right to practice their religion were entitled to legal redress under 42 U.S.C. 1983.[75] Although *Cooper* applied to the narrow issue of religious freedom, it opened the door to providing other rights for inmates.

The subsequent prisoners' rights crusade, stretching from 1964 to 1980, paralleled the civil rights and women's movements. Battle lines were drawn between prison officials hoping to maintain their power and resenting interference by the courts, and inmate groups and their sympathizers, who used state and federal courts as a forum for demanding better living conditions and personal rights. Each decision handed down by the courts was viewed as a victory for one side or the other; this battle continues today.

hands-off doctrine The legal practice of allowing prison administrators a free hand to run the institution even if correctional practices violate inmates' constitutional rights; ended with the onset of the prisoners' rights movement in the 1960s.

Substantive Rights

Through a slow process of legal review, the courts have granted inmates a number of **substantive rights** that have significantly influenced the entire correctional system. The most important of these rights are discussed in the following sections.

Access to Courts, Legal Services, and Materials Without the ability to seek judicial review of conditions causing discomfort or violating constitutional rights, the inmate must depend solely on the slow and often insensitive administrative mechanism of relief within the prison system. Therefore, the right of easy access to the courts gives inmates hope that their rights will be protected during incarceration. Courts have held that inmates are entitled to have legal materials available and be provided with assistance in drawing up and filing complaints. Inmates who help others, so-called **jailhouse lawyers,** cannot be interfered with or harassed by prison administrators.

Freedom of the Press and of Expression Correctional administrators traditionally placed severe limitations on prisoners' speech and expression. For example, they read and censored inmate mail and restricted their reading material. With the lifting of the hands-off doctrine, courts have consistently ruled that only when a compelling state interest exists can prisoners' First Amendment rights be modified; correctional authorities must justify the limiting of free speech by showing that granting it would threaten institutional security. In a 2001 case, *Shaw v. Murphy,* the Supreme Court ruled that inmates do not have a right to correspond with other inmates even if it concerns legal advice. If prison administrators believe such correspondence undermines prison security, the First Amendment rights of inmates can be curtailed.[76]

Freedom of Religion Freedom of religion is a fundamental right guaranteed by the First Amendment. In general, the courts have ruled that inmates have the right to assemble and pray in the religion of their choice, but that religious symbols and practices that interfere with institutional security can be restricted. Administrators can draw the line if religious needs become cumbersome or impossible to carry out for reason of cost or security. Granting special privileges can also be denied on the grounds that they will cause other groups to make similar demands. In an important 2005 case, *Cutter v. Williamson,* the Court ruled that the Religious Land Use and Institutionalized Persons Act of 2000, which was intended to protect the rights of prisoners, is not an unconstitutional government promotion of religion.[77] Writing for the majority, Ruth Bader Ginzburg stated, "It confers no privileged status on any particular religious sect, and singles out no bona fide faith for disadvantageous treatment." *Cutter* allows inmates to practice their own religion unless their practices clearly undermine prison security and safety.

Medical Rights In early prisons, inmates' right to medical treatment was restricted through the "exceptional circumstances doctrine." Using this policy, the courts would hear only those cases in which the circumstances totally disregarded human dignity, while denying hearings to less serious cases. The cases that were allowed access to the courts usually represented a situation of total denial of medical care.

To gain their medical rights, prisoners have resorted to class action suits (suits brought on behalf of all individuals affected by similar circumstances, in this case, poor medical attention). In the most significant case, *Newman v.*

substantive rights *Through a slow process of legal review, the courts have granted inmates a number of civil rights, including the rights to receive mail and medical benefits and to practice their religion.*

jailhouse lawyer *An inmate trained in law or otherwise educated who helps other inmates prepare legal briefs and appeals.*

Alabama (1972), the entire Alabama prison system's medical facilities were declared inadequate.[78] The Supreme Court cited the following factors as contributing to inadequate care: insufficient physician and nurse resources, reliance on untrained inmates for paramedical work, intentional failure in treating the sick and injured, and failure to conform to proper medical standards. The *Newman* case forced corrections departments to upgrade prison medical facilities.

It was not until 1976, in *Estelle v. Gamble,* that the Supreme Court clearly mandated an inmate's right to have medical care.[79] Gamble had hurt his back in a Texas prison and filed suit because he contested the type of treatment he had received and questioned the lack of interest that prison guards had shown in his case. The Supreme Court said, "Deliberate indifference to serious medical needs of prisoners constitutes the 'unnecessary and wanton infliction of pain,' proscribed by the Eighth Amendment."[80] Gamble was allowed to collect monetary damages for his injuries.

Cruel and Unusual Punishment   The concept of **cruel and unusual punishment** is founded in the Eighth Amendment of the U.S. Constitution. The term itself has not been specifically defined by the Supreme Court, but the Court has held that treatment constitutes cruel and unusual punishment when it does the following:

- Degrades the dignity of human beings[81]
- Is more severe (disproportional) than the offense for which it has been given[82]
- Shocks the general conscience and is fundamentally unfair[83]
- Is deliberately indifferent to a person's safety and well-being[84]
- Punishes people because of their status, such as race, religion, and mental state[85]
- Is in flagrant disregard of due process of law, such as punishment that is capriciously applied[86]

State and federal courts have placed strict limits on disciplinary methods that may be considered inhumane. Corporal punishment all but ended after the practice was condemned in *Jackson v. Bishop* (1968).[87] Although the solitary confinement of disruptive inmates continues, its prolonged use under barbaric conditions has been held to be in violation of the Eighth Amendment. Courts have found that inmates placed in solitary have the right to adequate personal hygiene, exercise, mattresses, ventilation, and rules specifying how they can earn their release.

In a recent case, *Hope v. Pelzer,* the Supreme Court ruled that correctional officials who knowingly violate the Eighth Amendment rights of inmates can be held liable for damages.[88]

Overall Prison Conditions   Prisoners have long had the right to the minimal conditions necessary for human survival, such as the necessary food, clothing, shelter, and medical care to sustain human life. A number of attempts have been made to articulate reasonable standards of prison care and to make sure they are carried out. Courts have held that, although people are sent to prison for punishment, it does not mean that prison should be a punishing experience.[89] In the 1994 case of *Farmer v. Brennan,* the court ruled that prison officials are legally liable if, knowing that an inmate faces a serious risk of harm, they disregard that risk by failing to take measures to avoid or reduce it. Furthermore, prison officials should be able to infer the risk from the evidence at hand; they need not be warned or told.[90]

cruel and unusual punishment Physical punishment or punishment that is far in excess of that given to people under similar circumstances and is therefore banned by the Eighth Amendment. The death penalty has so far not been considered cruel and unusual if it is administered in a fair and nondiscriminatory fashion.

Although inmates retain the right to reasonable care, if there is a legitimate purpose for the use of governmental restrictions, they may be considered constitutional. For example, it might be possible to restrict reading material, allow strip searches, and prohibit inmates from receiving packages from the outside if the restrictions are legitimate security measures. If overcrowded conditions require it, inmates may be double-bunked in cells designed for a single inmate.[91]

Criminal Justice ⚖ Now™

Learn more by exploring the "Leaving Prison" Animated Artwork.

WWW To reach **the U.S. Parole Commission** website, go to "Web Links" on your Siegel Essentials of Criminal Justice 5e website: http://cj.wadsworth.com/siegel_ess5e.

LEAVING PRISON

At the expiration of their prison term, most inmates return to society and try to resume their lives there. For some inmates, their reintegration into society comes by way of parole—the planned community release and supervision of incarcerated offenders before the expiration of their full prison sentences. In states where determinate sentencing statutes have eliminated discretionary parole, offenders are released after having served their determinate sentence, less time off for good behavior and other credits designed to reduce the term of incarceration. Their release may involve supervision in the community, and rule violations can result in return to prison for the balance of their unexpired sentence.

In a few instances, inmates are released after their sentence has been commuted by a board of pardons or directly by a governor or even the President of the United States. About 15 percent of prison inmates are released after serving their entire maximum sentence without any time excused or forgiven. And despite the efforts of correctional authorities, about seven thousand inmates escape every year from state and federal prisons (the number of escapes is actually declining, due in part to better officer training and more sophisticated security measures).[92]

Regardless of the method of their release, former inmates face the formidable task of having to readjust to society. This means regaining legal rights they may have lost on their conviction, reestablishing community and family ties, and finding employment. After being in prison, these goals are often difficult to achieve.

parole *The early release of a prisoner from imprisonment subject to conditions set by a parole board. Depending on the jurisdiction, inmates must serve a certain portion of their sentences before becoming eligible for parole. The conditions of parole may require the individual to report regularly to a parole officer, to refrain from criminal conduct, to maintain and support his or her family, to avoid contact with other convicted criminals, to abstain from using alcohol and drugs, to remain within the jurisdiction, and so on. Violations of the conditions of parole may result in revocation of parole, in which case the individual will be returned to prison. The concept behind parole is to allow the release of the offender to community supervision, where rehabilitation and readjustment will be facilitated.*

Parole

The decision to **parole** is determined by statutory requirement. In some states parole is granted by a parole board, a duly constituted body of men and women who review inmate cases and determine whether offenders have reached a rehabilitative level sufficient to deal with the outside world. The board also dictates what specific parole rules parolees must obey. In about sixteen other jurisdictions, discretionary parole has been abandoned and the amount of time a person must remain in prison is a predetermined percentage of the sentence, assuming there are no infractions or escape attempts. Referred to as *mandatory parole release*, the inmate is released when the unserved portion of the maximum prison term equals his or her earned good time (less time served in jail awaiting trial). In some states, sentences can be reduced by more than half with a combination of statutory and earned good time. If the conditions of their release are violated, mandatory releasees can have their good time revoked and be returned to the institution to serve the remainder of their unexpired term. The remaining inmates are released for a variety of reasons, including expiration of their term, commutation of their sentence, and court orders to relieve overcrowded prisons.

Sometimes victims and their families can make statements at parole grant hearings in order to sway the parole decision-making process. While many victims demand the offender receive more punishment, that is not always the case. Here, awaiting the decision of the state Parole Board at Denmar Correctional Center in West Virginia, inmate Steven Martin chats with JoAnne Azar, the sister of the man he beat and robbed. With the blessing of Azar, Martin was granted parole after serving fifteen years in prison.

The Parole Board

In those states that have maintained discretionary parole, the authority to release inmates is usually vested in the parole board. State parole boards have four primary functions:

1. To select and place prisoners on parole
2. To aid, supervise, and provide continuing control of parolees in the community
3. To determine when the parole function is completed and to discharge from parole
4. To determine whether parole should be revoked, if violations of conditions occur

Most parole authorities are independent agencies with their own staff and administration, and a few parole boards are part of the state department of corrections. Arguments for keeping the board within a corrections department usually include improved communication and more intimate knowledge about offenders.

The actual (discretionary) parole decision is made at a parole-grant hearing. At this hearing the full board or a selected subcommittee reviews information, may meet with the offender, and then decides whether the parole applicant has a reasonable probability of succeeding outside of prison. Each parole board has its own way of reviewing cases. In some, the full board meets with the applicant; in others, only a few members do that. In a number of jurisdictions, a single board member can conduct a personal investigation and submit the findings to the full board for a decision.

When parole is discretionary, most parole boards will look at the inmate's crime, institutional record, and willingness to accept responsibility before making the release decision. Inmates who maintain their innocence may find that denying responsibility for their crimes places their release date in jeopardy. The requirement that they admit guilt or culpability is especially vexing for those inmates who are actually innocent and who actively refuse to accept their institutional label of "convicted criminal."[93]

The Parolee in the Community

Once released into the community, a parolee is given a standard set of rules and conditions that must be obeyed. As with probation, the offender who violates these rules may have parole revoked and be sent back to the institution to serve the remainder of the sentence. Once in the community, the parolee is supervised by a trained staff of parole officers who help him or her search for employment and monitor the parolee's behavior and activities to ensure that the conditions of parole are met.

Parole is generally viewed as a privilege granted to deserving inmates on the basis of their good behavior while in prison. Parole has two conflicting sides, however. On the one hand, the paroled offender is allowed to serve part of the sentence in the community, an obvious benefit for the deserving offender. On the other hand, since parole is a "privilege and not a right," the parolee is viewed as a dangerous criminal who must be carefully watched and supervised. The conflict between the treatment and enforcement aspects of parole has not been reconciled by the criminal justice system, and the parole process still contains elements of both.

To overcome these roadblocks to success, the parole officer may have to play a much greater role in directing and supervising clients' lives than the probation officer. In some instances, parole programs have become active in creating new postrelease treatment-oriented programs designed to increase the chances of parole success. In other instances, parole agencies have implemented law enforcement–oriented services that work with local police agencies to identify and apprehend parolees who may have been involved in criminal activity.[94]

Intensive Supervision Parole To aid supervision, some jurisdictions have implemented systems that classify offenders on the basis of their supervision needs. Typically, a point or guideline system (sometimes called a *salient factor score*) based on prior record and prison adjustment divides parolees into three groups: (1) those who require intensive surveillance, (2) those who require social service rather than surveillance, and (3) those who require limited supervision.

In some jurisdictions, parolees in need of closer surveillance are placed on **intensive supervision parole (ISP).** These programs use limited caseload sizes, treatment facilities, the matching of parolee and supervisor by personality, and shock parole (which involves immediate short-term incarceration for parole violators to impress them with the seriousness of a violation). ISP clients are required to attend more office and home visits than routine parolees. ISP may also require frequent drug testing, a term in a community correctional center, and electronic monitoring in the home. More than seventeen thousand parolees are under intensive supervision; fourteen hundred of these are monitored electronically by computer.

Although ISP seems like an ideal way of limiting already overcrowded prison populations, there is little evidence that ISP programs are effective; in

intensive supervision parole (ISP) A limited-caseload program for those parolees who need intensive surveillance. Parolees are required to meet more often with parole officers than routine parolees and may also have frequent drug testing, serve a term in a community correctional system, and be electronically monitored.

fact, they may produce a higher violation rate than traditional parole supervision. Limiting caseload size allows parole officers to supervise their clients more closely and spot infractions more easily.[95]

The Effectiveness of Parole

Despite all efforts to treat, correct, and rehabilitate incarcerated offenders, the fact remains that more than half return to prison shortly after their release. Persons released from prison face a multitude of difficulties. They remain largely uneducated, unskilled, and usually without solid family support systems—and to this the burdens of a prison record are added. Not surprisingly, most parolees fail, and rather quickly—rearrests are most common in the first six months after release.[96] Moreover, the cost of their recidivism is acute. One federal survey of 156,000 parole violators who had been sent back to prison concluded that these offenders committed at least 6,800 murders, 5,500 rapes, 8,800 assaults, and 22,500 robberies while under supervision in the community for an average of thirteen months.[97]

To improve parole effectiveness, policy makers might want to see how other countries handle supervision in the community. New Zealand's approach, discussed in the Race, Culture, and Gender in Criminal Justice feature, seems quite effective.

Why Do People Fail on Parole?

Parole failure is still a significant problem, and a growing portion of the correctional population consists of parolees who failed on the outside. Why has the phenomenon of parole failure remained so stubborn and hard to control?

One reason may be the very nature of the prison experience itself. The psychological and economic problems that lead offenders to recidivism are rarely addressed by a stay in prison. Despite rehabilitation efforts, the typical ex-convict is still the same undereducated, unemployed, substance-abusing lower-class male he was when arrested. Being separated from friends and family, not sharing in conventional society, associating with dangerous people, and adapting to a volatile lifestyle probably have done little to improve the offender's personality or behavior.

And when he returns to society, it may be to the same destructive neighborhood and social groups that prompted his original law-violating behavior. It has been estimated 15 to 27 percent of inmates expect to go to homeless shelters upon release from prison.[98] It seems naïve to think that incarceration alone can help someone overcome these lifelong disabilities. By their very nature prisons seek to impose and maintain order and conformity rather than help inmates develop skills such as independence and critical thinking, factors that may be essential once the inmate is forced to cope outside the prison's walls.[99]

It is also possible that parole failure is tied to the releasee's own lifelong personal deficits. Most research efforts indicate that a long history of criminal behavior, an antisocial personality, and childhood experiences with family dysfunction are all correlated with postrelease recidivism.[100] Many releasees have suffered from a lifetime of substance abuse or dependence disorder.[101] A history of physical and sexual abuse has also been linked to recidivism.[102] It is not surprising that recent research (2005) shows that the men who are more likely to return to prison are those who maintain criminal peer associations, carry weapons, abuse alcohol, and harbor aggressive feelings.[103] Another study of youthful ex-offenders trying to make it on the outside found that many experience delayed emotional and cognitive development due to early drug use; most have never learned to use problem-solving or coping skills outside of the correctional setting, and most remain drug-dependent.[104]

Race, Culture, and Gender in Criminal Justice

Monitoring High-Risk Offenders in New Zealand

In New Zealand, the supervision of high-risk offenders (such as sex offenders) after they have served their prison sentence is controlled by the Extended Supervision Order (2004). This order permits local probation services to monitor medium-high and high-risk sexual offenders for up to ten years following their release from prison and/or expiration of their parole. The legislation stipulates that released offenders have to report to a probation officer regularly and, if the need arises, to attend treatment programs and psychological counseling sessions. Offenders may be monitored at home and at their places of employment. They may also be required to wear electronic monitoring devices and obey additional conditions such as prohibiting contact with any children under the age of sixteen or restrictions on places they can attend. Offenders can be charged if they are found in violation of any of these or similar conditions.

In addition, the highest-risk offenders might be placed under home detention–like conditions for the first year after their release. In the most serious cases, electronic monitoring is imposed for the entire period of extended supervision. There is provision for twenty-four-hour monitoring during the first year of extended supervision for the most serious cases.

The extended supervision process includes a thorough psychological assessment, which includes an assessment of the risk to re-offend, a decision to seek an application for extended supervision, submission of the application to the court and, if approved, submission of an application to the parole board to set special conditions.

After release, the probation officer serves as one of the offender's key supports in the community. The officer:

- Ensures that the offender complies with the conditions of the order
- Ensures that the offender attends relapse prevention sessions and other counseling and treatment programs
- Works with family, treatment providers, and support people
- Works with other agencies that might assist the reintegration of the offender, such as welfare benefits, housing, and employment
- Keeps connected to law enforcement
- Assists the offender in dealing with stress by providing a supportive environment to talk, motivate, and provide encouragement
- Assists the offender in identifying solutions and engaging in problem solving

In summary, New Zealand's extended supervision program involves managing the offender in the community under intensive supervision for up to ten years after the completion of the original sentence. It also involves close scrutiny, electronic monitoring, home visits, information-sharing, community-based treatment programs, community safety meetings, and twenty-four-hour monitoring for the higher-risk offender.

Critical Thinking

1. Does ten years of electronic monitoring place too great a burden on any person, no matter what he did, and almost doom him to failure?

2. If a chip were invented which could be implanted in a probationer's body that would allow probation authorities to keep track of his activities, location, and substance abuse intake, would you recommend that it be employed with all probationers? How about those who had committed violent crimes?

InfoTrac College Edition

To learn more about contemporary probation programs, use *probation* and *probation officer* in a key word searches on InfoTrac College Edition.

Source: Donald Evans, "New Zealand's Approach to a High-Risk Offender Supervision Program," *Corrections Today* 67 (2005): 28–30.

Once on the outside, these problems do not easily subside. Some ex-inmates may have to prove that the prison experience has not changed them: taking drugs or being sexually aggressive may show friends that they have not lost their "heart."[105] In contrast, parolees who have had a good employment record in the past and who maintain jobs after their release are the most likely to avoid recidivating.[106]

Ex-inmates may find their home life torn and disrupted when they are finally released. Wives of inmates report that they had to face the shame and stigmatization of having an incarcerated spouse while withstanding a barrage of calls from jealous husbands on the "inside" who tried to monitor their behavior and control their lives. Family visits to the inmate became traumatic and strained relationships because they often involved strip searches and other invasions of privacy.[107] Sensitive to these problems, some states have instituted support groups designed to help inmates' families adjust to their loneliness and despair.[108]

The specter of recidivism is especially frustrating to the American public: it is so difficult to apprehend and successfully prosecute criminal offenders that it seems foolish to grant them early release so they can prey on more victims. This problem is exacerbated when the parolee is a chronic, frequent offender. Research indicates that many of these returning prisoners are less prepared for reintegration and less connected to community-based social structures than in the past.[109] There seems to be a strong association between prior and future offending: the parolees most likely to fail on release are the ones who have failed in the past; chronic offenders are the ones most likely to re-offend. This issue takes on even greater importance when the community-level problems created by returning inmates are considered. This subject is discussed in the Policy, Programs, and Issues in Criminal Justice feature on the next page.

Losing Rights Ex-inmates may also find that going straight is an economic impossibility. Many employers are reluctant to hire people who have served time. Even if a criminal record does not automatically prohibit all chance of employment, why would an employer hire an ex-con when other applicants are available? If they lie about their prison experience and are later found out, ex-offenders will be dismissed for misrepresentation. Research shows that former inmates who gain and keep meaningful employment are more likely to succeed on parole than those who are unemployed or underemployed.[110] One reason that ex-inmates find it so difficult to make it on the outside is the legal restrictions they are forced to endure. These may include bars on certain kinds of employment, limits on obtaining licenses, and restrictions on their freedom of movement. One survey found that a significant number of states still restrict the activities of former felons.[111] Some of the more important findings are listed in Exhibit 14.2.

Exhibit 14.2   Rights lost upon release from prison

- Fourteen states permanently deny felons the right to vote; eighteen states suspend the right until after the correctional sentence has been completed.
- Nineteen states terminate parental rights.
- Twenty-nine states consider a felony conviction to be legal grounds for a divorce.
- Six states deny felons the opportunity for public employment.
- Thirty-one states disallow convicted felons the right to serve on juries.
- Twenty-five states prevent convicted felons from holding public office.
- Federal law prevents ex-convicts from owning guns. In addition, all states except Vermont employ additional legal measures to prevent felons from possessing firearms.
- Forty-six states require that felons register with law enforcement agencies. This requirement is up sharply in recent years; in 1986 only eight states required felons to register.
- Civil death, or the denial of all civil rights, is still practiced in four states.

Source: Kathleen Olivares, Velmer Burton, and Francis Cullen, "The Collateral Consequences of a Felony Conviction: A National Study of State Legal Codes Ten Years Later," *Federal Probation* 60 (1996): 10–17.

Policy, Programs, and Issues in Criminal Justice

The Problems of Reentry

Because of America's two-decade-long imprisonment boom, more than five hundred thousand inmates are now being released back into the community each year. As criminologist Joan Petersilia warns, there are a number of unfortunate consequences to this release back into the community because many of those being released have not received adequate treatment and are unprepared for life in conventional society. The risks they present to the community include increases in child abuse, family violence, the spread of infectious diseases, homelessness, and community disorganization.

The increased reentry risks can be tied to legal changes in how people are released from prison. In the past, offenders were granted early release only if a parole board believed they were rehabilitated and had ties to the community—such as a family or a job. Inmates were encouraged to enter treatment programs to earn parole. Changes in sentencing law have resulted in the growth of mandatory release and limits on discretionary parole. People now serve a fixed sentence and the discretion of parole boards has been blunted. Inmates may be discouraged from seeking involvement in rehabilitation programs (they do not influence the chance of parole), and the lack of incentive means that fewer inmates leaving prison have participated in programs to address work, education, and substance use deficiencies. Nor does the situation improve upon release. Many inmates are not assigned to supervision caseloads once back in the community. About two hundred thousand released inmates go unsupervised each year, three-quarters of whom have been released after completing their maximum sentence and therefore not obligated to be supervised.

Petersilia argues that most leave prison with no savings, no immediate entitlement to unemployment benefits, and few employment prospects. Upon release, some find that they are no longer welcome in subsidized public housing complexes due to the U.S. Department of Housing and Urban Development's "one strike and you're out" policy, where all members of the household are evicted if one member is involved in crime. One year after release, as many as 60 percent of former inmates are not employed in the regular labor market, and there is increasing reluctance among employers to hire ex-offenders. Ex-offenders are commonly barred from working in the fields in which most jobs are being created, such as child care, education, security, nursing, and home heath care. More jobs are also now unionized, and many unions exclude ex-offenders.

Being barred from work opportunities produces chronic unemployment, a status closely related to drug and alcohol abuse. Losing a job can lead to substance abuse, which in turn is related to family violence. Mothers released from prison have difficulty finding services such as housing, employment, and child care, and this causes stress for them and their children. Children of incarcerated and released parents may suffer confusion, sadness, and social stigma, and these feelings often result in difficulties in school, low self-esteem, aggressive behavior, and general emotional dysfunction. If the parents are negative role models, children fail to develop positive attitudes about work and responsibility. Children of

Criminal Justice ⊚⊚ Now™

Learn more by exploring the "Burglary Part 5" Role Play activity.

In general, states have placed greater restrictions on former felons as part of the get-tough movement. However, courts have considered individual requests by convicted felons to have their rights restored. It is common for courts to look at such issues as how recently the criminal offense took place and its relationship to the particular right before deciding whether to restore it.

A number of experts and national commissions have condemned the loss of rights of convicted offenders as a significant cause of recidivism. Consequently, courts have generally moved to eliminate the most restrictive elements of postconviction restrictions.[112]

incarcerated parents are five times more likely to serve time in prison than are children whose parents are not incarcerated.

Prisoners have significantly more physical and mental health problems than the general population. More than three-fourths of the inmates leaving prison in the next year report a history of drug and/or alcohol abuse. Inmates with mental illness (about 16 percent of all inmates) also are increasingly being imprisoned—and then released. Even when public mental health services are available, many mentally ill individuals fail to use them because they fear institutionalization, deny they are mentally ill, or distrust the mental health system. The situation will become more serious as more and more parolees are released back into the disorganized communities whose deteriorated conditions may have motivated their original crimes.

Fear of a prison stay has less of an impact on behavior than ever before. As the prison population grows, the negative impact of incarceration may be lessening. In neighborhoods where "doing time" is more the rule than the exception, it becomes less of a stigma and more of a badge of acceptance. It also becomes a way of life from which some ex-convicts do rebound. Teens may encounter older men who have gone to prison and have returned to begin their lives again. With the proper skills and survival techniques, prison is considered "manageable." Although a prison stay is still unpleasant, it has lost its aura of shame and fear. By becoming commonplace and mundane, the "myth" of the prison experience has been exposed and its deterrent power reduced.

Critical Thinking

1. All too often, government leaders jump on the incarceration bandwagon as a panacea for the nation's crime problem. Is it a "quick fix" whose long-term consequences may be devastating for the nation's cities, or are these problems counterbalanced by the crime-reducing effect of putting large numbers of high-rate offenders behind bars?

2. If you agree that incarceration undermines neighborhoods, can you think of some other, indirect ways that high incarceration rates help increase crime rates?

InfoTrac College Edition Research

Alternatives to prison are now being sought because high incarceration may undermine a community's viability. What do you think?
For some interesting developments, check out these articles on InfoTrac College Edition: Joe Loconte, "Making Criminals Pay: A New York County's Bold Experiment in Biblical Justice," *Policy Review* 87 (January–February 1998), 26, and Katarina Ivanko, "Shifting Gears to Rehabilitation," *Corrections Today* 59 (April 1997), 20.

Sources: Joan Petersilia, *When Prisoners Come Home: Parole and Prisoner Reentry* (New York: Oxford University Press, 2003); "Hard Time Ex-offenders Returning Home After Prison," *Corrections Today* 67 (2005): 66–72; idem, "When Prisoners Return to Communities: Political, Economic, and Social Consequences," *Federal Probation* 65 (2001): 3–9.

SUMMARY

- On entering a prison, offenders must make tremendous adjustments to survive. Usual behavior patterns or lifestyles are radically changed. Opportunities for personal satisfaction are reduced.

- Passing through a number of adjustment stages or cycles, inmates must learn to cope with the new environment.

- Inmates also learn to obey the inmate social code, which dictates proper behavior and attitudes. If inmates break the code, they may be unfavorably labeled.

- Inmates must learn how to cope and deal with sexual and physical predators.

- Women have their own unique inmate culture.

- Psychological problems and sexual exploitation is a problem in women's prisons.
- Inmates are eligible for a large number of treatment devices designed to help them readjust to the community once they are released.
- A number of treatment programs have offered inmates individualized and group psychological counseling. Some make use of the therapeutic community idea.
- There are many educational programs at the high school and even college levels.
- There are vocational training programs. Work furloughs have also been employed.
- Violence is common in prisons. Women often turn their hatred inward and hurt themselves, and male inmates engage in collective and individual violence against others.
- The Attica and New Mexico riots are examples of the most serious collective prison violence.
- In years past, society paid little attention to the incarcerated offender. The majority of inmates confined in jails and prisons were basically deprived of the rights guaranteed them under the Constitution.
- Today, however, the judicial system is actively involved in the administration of correctional institutions. Inmates can now take their grievances to courts and seek due process and equal protection under the law.
- The courts have recognized that persons confined in correctional institutions have rights—which include access to the courts and legal counsel, the exercise of religion, the rights to correspondence and visitation, and the right to adequate medical treatment.
- Most inmates return to society before the completion of their prison sentence. The majority earn early release through time off for good behavior or other sentence-reducing mechanisms.
- Most state jurisdictions maintain an independent parole board whose members decide whether to grant parole. Their decision making is discretionary and is based on many factors, such as the perception of the needs of society, the correctional system, and the client.
- Once paroled, the client is subject to control by parole officers who ensure that the conditions set by the board (the parole rules) are maintained. Parole can be revoked if the offender violates the rules of parole or commits a new crime.
- At one time most inmates were released on discretionary parole, but today changes in sentencing provisions has resulted in a significant increase in mandatory parole releases.
- The problem of prisoner reentry is a national concern.
- Ex-inmates have a tough time adjusting on the outside, and the recidivism rate is disturbingly high. One reason is that many states restrict their rights and take away privileges granted to other citizens.

KEY TERMS

total institution 388
no-frills policy 388
inmate subculture 390
inmate social code 390
prisonization 390
work release 398

furlough 398
hands-off doctrine 405
substantive rights 406
jailhouse lawyer 406
cruel and unusual
   punishment 407

parole 408
intensive supervision parole
   (ISP) 410

REVIEW QUESTIONS

1. Considering the dangers that males face during their prison stay, should nonviolent inmates be placed in separate institutions to protect them from harm?
2. Should women be allowed to work as guards in male prisons? What about male guards in female prisons? Why or why not?
3. Should prison inmates be allowed a free college education while noncriminals are forced to pay

tuition? Why or why not? Do you believe in less eligibility for prisoners?
4. Define parole, including its purposes and objectives. How does it differ from probation?
5. What is the role of the parole board?
6. Should a former prisoner have all the civil rights afforded the average citizen? Explain.
7. Should people be further penalized after they have paid their debt to society? Why or why not?

PART 5

Juvenile Justice

On March 5, 2001, 16-year-old Charles "Andy" Williams went on a six-minute shooting spree at Santana High School in Santee, California, killing Bryan Zuckor, 14, and Randy Gordon, 17, and wounding 11 other students, a teacher, and a campus monitor. Tried as an adult, on August 15, 2002, Williams was convicted and sentenced to 50 years to life in prison. The sentence imposed was the minimum Williams could have received; the 16-year-old will not have a parole hearing until 2051, when he will be 65.

The Williams case is extreme. Typically, youngsters are tried in the juvenile justice system, an independent process that is designed to provide care and treatment to underage youth who are in trouble with the law. Yet, because of the seriousness of his crime, the juvenile justice system was able to transfer him to adult court where he could receive a very long sentence to a high-security prison. Agencies of the juvenile justice system are continually faced with such dilemmas. Because of the importance of their work and the unique contribution they make, the topic of Part 5 is the process of juvenile justice and its agencies. ■

15 THE JUVENILE JUSTICE SYSTEM

CHAPTER 15

The Juvenile Justice System

© 2002 AP/Wide World Photos

KATHRYN SELLERS holds a B.A. in psychology and sociology from the University of Montevallo, an M.S. in psychology from Auburn University at Montgomery, and is completing her M.S. in justice sciences from University of Alabama at Birmingham. After college, she began working as a substance abuse counselor and then became involved in a dual mental health and court officer role when she became a court referral officer. Among her other jobs and interests she is now helping to create programs for juveniles that recognize that they are in the early stages of cognitive and emotional development. Sellers helped develop the Adolescent Intensive Outpatient Program (AIOP) for a tri-county rural area in Alabama. Admitted under court order to the program, teens participate in sessions in which they are asked to tell about themselves—who they are and what is important to

Chapter Outline

Chapter Objectives

1. Be familiar with the early history of juvenile justice
2. Know about the care of children in early America
3. Know who the child savers were and what role they played in the development of juvenile justice
4. Discuss the police processing of juvenile offenders, the use of discretion, and juveniles' legal rights after arrest
5. Understand the issues surrounding the detention process
6. Describe the waiver process
7. Be familiar with the stages in the juvenile trial
8. Discuss the institutions that make up the juvenile correctional process
9. Know something about prevention strategies
10. Be familiar with the debate over retaining the juvenile court

them—in order to get them to focus on positive life experiences. To develop a sense of responsibility, the teen clients help manage the program, work on the budget, the mission, and schedule activities. The approach has been so successful that some clients continued to volunteer after they had met the requirements of the court and graduated from the program.

As a juvenile justice professional, Sellers has enjoyed many diverse opportunities. Currently, she teaches at the college level and is also working with a nonprofit organization and a local juvenile court to assess their use of the state's new information-sharing law, one which requires family court to inform school superintendents if a juvenile is found to have committed a crime that would be considered an A or B felony in adult court.

People like Kathryn Sellers are what make the juvenile justice system unique. Independent of (yet interrelated with) the adult criminal justice system, the juvenile justice system is primarily responsible for dealing with juvenile and youth crime, as well as with incorrigible and truant children and runaways. Conceived at the turn of the twentieth century, the juvenile justice system was viewed as a quasi-social welfare agency that was to act as a surrogate parent in the interests of the child; this is referred to as the **parens patriae** philosophy. Many people who work in the system still hold to the original social welfare principles of the juvenile justice system. In contrast, those who hold a crime control orientation suggest that the juvenile justice system's parens patriae philosophy is outdated. They point to nationally publicized incidents of juvenile violence, such as the shootings at Columbine High School in Colorado, as indicators that serious juvenile offenders should be punished and disciplined rather than treated and rehabilitated. "Why should we give special treatment to violent young juveniles" they ask. "After all, juveniles commit almost 10 percent of all the murders in the United States and about 16 percent of all rapes."[1]

It remains to be seen whether the juvenile justice system will continue on its path toward deterrence, punishment, and control or return to its former role as a treatment-dispensing agency. This chapter reviews the history of juvenile justice and discusses the justice system's processing of youthful offenders.

Criminal Justice ⊛ Now™
*Learn more by exploring the **Parens Patriae** Review and Reinforce activity.*

THE HISTORY OF JUVENILE JUSTICE

The modern practice of legally separating adult and juvenile offenders can be traced back to two developments in English custom and law that occurred centuries ago: the development of Elizabethan-era poor laws and the creation of the English chancery court. Both were designed to allow the state to take control of the lives of needy but not necessarily criminal children.[2]

1. *Poor laws.* As early as 1535 the English passed statutes known as **poor laws,** which in part mandated the appointment of overseers who placed destitute or neglected children with families who then trained them in agricultural, trade, or domestic services; this practice was referred to as *indenture.* The Elizabethan poor laws of 1601 created a system of church wardens and overseers who, with the consent of the justices of the peace, identified vagrant, delinquent, and neglected children and took measures to put them to work. Often this meant placing them in poorhouses or workhouses or, more commonly, apprenticing them until their adulthood. The indenture, or involuntary apprentice, system set the precedent, which continues today, of allowing the government to take control of youths who have committed no illegal acts but who are deemed unable to care for themselves.

2. *Chancery courts.* English chancery courts provided judicial relief to those who had no legal standing or could expect no legal relief because of the corruption and inadequacy of other common law courts. People who felt their rights were being violated could take their cases to the chancery court for review. In this capacity, the chancery court protected the property rights and welfare of more minor children who could not care for themselves—children whose position and property were of direct concern to the monarch. The courts dealt with issues of guardianship and the use and control of property. So if the guardian of an orphaned child wished to sell off his ward's inheritance the chancery court might be asked to review the proceedings and determine if the sale was actually in the child's best interest. Chancery courts operated under the parens patriae philosophy, which held that children were under the protective control of the state

parens patriae *Latin term meaning "father of his country." According to this legal philosophy, the government is the guardian of everyone who has a disability, especially children, and has a legal duty to act in their best interests until the age of majority.*

poor laws *Seventeenth-century laws in England that bound out vagrants and abandoned children as indentured servants to masters.*

and that its rulers were justified in intervening in their lives.[3] In the famous English case *Wellesley v. Wellesley,* a duke's children were taken from him in the name of parens patriae because of his scandalous behavior.[4]

Care of Children in Early America

Poor laws and chancery courts were brought from England to colonial America. Poor laws were passed in Virginia in 1646 and in Connecticut and Massachusetts in 1678 and continued in force until the early nineteenth century. They mandated care for wayward and destitute children. However, those youths who committed serious criminal offenses continued to be tried in the same courts as adults.

To accommodate dependent youths, local jurisdictions developed almshouses, poorhouses, and workhouses. Crowded and unhealthy, these accepted the poor, the insane, the diseased, and vagrant and destitute children. Middle-class civic leaders, who referred to themselves as **child savers,** began to develop organizations and groups to help alleviate the burdens of the poor and immigrants by sponsoring shelter care for youths, educational and social activities, and the development of settlement houses. In retrospect, their main focus seems to have been on extending governmental control over a whole range of youthful activities that previously had been left to private or family control, including idleness, drinking, vagrancy, and delinquency.[5]

The Child-Saving Movement

The child savers were responsible for creating a number of programs for indigent youths, including the New York House of Refuge, which began operations in 1825.[6] Its charter was to protect indigent youths who were at risk to crime by taking them off the streets and reforming them in a family-like environment.[7]

The Granger Collection, New York

Boys on the steps of an abandoned tenement building in New York City, about 1889. The child savers were concerned that, if left alone, children such as these would enter a life of crime. They created the House of Refuge to care for poor and neglected kids. Critics accused them of class and race bias.

The New York House of Refuge, actually a reformatory, opened January 1, 1825, with only six boys and three girls, but within the first decade of its operation 1,678 kids were sent because of vagrancy and petty crimes. Once a resident, a large part of an adolescent's daily schedule was devoted to supervised labor, which was regarded as beneficial to education and discipline. Male inmates worked in shops that produced brushes, cane chairs, brass nails, and shoes. The female inmates sewed uniforms, did laundry, and carried out other domestic work. The reformatory had the authority to bind out inmates through indenture agreements to private employers; most males were farmworkers and most females were domestic laborers.

The Refuge Movement Spreads

When the House of Refuge opened, critics complained that the institution was run like a prison, with strict discipline and absolute separation of the sexes. Such a harsh program drove many children to run away, and the House of

child savers Late nineteenth-century reformers in America who developed programs for troubled youths and influenced legislation creating the juvenile justice system.

Refuge was forced to take a more lenient approach. Despite criticism, the concept enjoyed expanding popularity. In 1826, for example, the Boston City Council founded the House of Reformation for juvenile offenders.[8]

The child savers also influenced state and local governments to create independent correctional institutions to house minors. The first of these reform schools opened in Westboro, Massachusetts, in 1848 and in Rochester, New York, in 1849. Children lived in congregate conditions and spent their days working at institutional jobs, learning a trade where possible, and receiving some basic education. They were racially and sexually segregated, discipline was harsh and often involved whipping and isolation, and the physical care was of poor quality.

In 1853, New York philanthropist Charles Loring Brace helped develop the **Children's Aid Society** as an alternative for dealing with neglected and delinquent youths. Brace proposed rescuing wayward youths from the harsh environment of the city and providing them with temporary shelter and care. He then sought to place them in private homes in rural communities where they could engage in farming and agricultural work outside the influence of the city. Although some placements proved successful, others resulted in the exploitation of children in a strange environment with few avenues of escape.

Criminal Justice ⚖ Now™
*Learn more by going through the **Juvenile Justice System** Vocabulary Check activity.*

■ ESTABLISHMENT OF THE JUVENILE COURT

As the nation expanded, it became evident that private charities and public organizations were not caring adequately for the growing number of troubled youths. The child savers lobbied for an independent, state-supported **juvenile court,** and their efforts prompted the development of the first comprehensive juvenile court in Illinois in 1899. In his recent book *Juvenile Justice in the Making*, historian David Tanenhaus describes how the early child savers fought a long battle against legal and political opponents to get juvenile court legislation passed. He views the juvenile court as the forerunner of both public welfare and grassroots community organizing. He also views the court as the prototype for raising children using expert medical and psychological opinion, which has ranged from Dr. Spock to Dr. Phil.[9] Yet Tanenhaus finds that the early juvenile court represented some of the biases and prejudices of its time: fatherless status offenders were allowed to stay in their homes; motherless ones were sent to institutions.

The Illinois Juvenile Court Act set up an independent court to handle criminal law violations by children under sixteen years of age, as well as to care for neglected, dependent, and wayward youths. The act also created a probation department to monitor youths in the community and to direct juvenile court judges to place serious offenders in secure schools for boys and industrial schools for girls. The ostensible purpose of the act was to separate juveniles from adult offenders and provide a legal framework in which juveniles could get adequate care and custody. By 1925 most states had developed juvenile courts. The enactment of the Illinois Juvenile Court Act of 1899 was a major event in the history of the juvenile justice movement in the United States.

The Development of Juvenile Justice

The juvenile court movement quickly spread across the United States. In its early form it provided youths with quasi-legal, quasi-therapeutic, personalized justice. The main concern was the "best interests of the child," not strict adherence to legal doctrine, constitutional rights, or due process of law. The court was paternalistic, rather than adversarial. Attorneys were not required; hearsay evidence, inadmissible in criminal trials, was commonly employed in the adjudication of juvenile offenders. Children were encouraged to admit their "guilt" in open court in violation of their Fifth Amendment rights.

Children's Aid Society A childsaving organization begun by Charles Loring Brace; it took children from the streets in large cities and placed them with farm families on the prairie.

juvenile court A court that has original jurisdiction over persons defined by statute as juveniles and alleged to be delinquents or status offenders.

Verdicts were based on a "preponderance of the evidence," instead of being "beyond a reasonable doubt." Juvenile courts then functioned as quasi-social service agencies.

Reform Schools Youngsters found delinquent in juvenile court could spend years in a state training school. Though priding themselves as non-punitive, these early reform schools attempted to exercise control based on the concept of reform through hard work and discipline. In the second half of the nineteenth century, the emphasis shifted from massive industrial schools to the cottage system. Juvenile offenders were housed in a series of small cabins, each one holding twenty to forty children, run by "cottage parents," who attempted to create a homelike atmosphere. The first cottage system was established in Massachusetts, the second in Ohio. The system was generally applauded for being a great improvement over the industrial training schools.[10] By the 1950s psychological treatment was introduced in juvenile corrections. Group counseling techniques became standard procedure in most juvenile institutions.

Legal Change In the 1960s and 1970s, the U.S. Supreme Court radically altered the juvenile justice system when it issued a series of decisions that established the right of juveniles to receive due process of law. The Court established that juveniles had the same rights as adults in important areas of trial process, including the right to confront witnesses, notice of charges, and the right to counsel.[11] Exhibit 15.1 illustrates some of the most important legal cases bringing procedural due process to the juvenile justice process.

Exhibit 15.1	**Leading constitutional cases in juvenile justice**

Kent v. United States (1966) determined that a child has the right to an attorney at any hearing to decide whether his or her case should be transferred to juvenile court (waiver hearings).

In re Gault (1967) ruled that a minor has basic due process rights at trial, including: (1) notice of the charges, (2) right to counsel, (3) right to confront and cross-examine witnesses, (4) privilege against self-incrimination, and (5) the right to a transcript of the trial record.

In re Winship (1970) determined that the level of evidence for a finding of "juvenile delinquency" is proof beyond a reasonable doubt.

McKeiver v. Pennsylvania (1971) held that trial by jury in a juvenile court's adjudicative stage is not a constitutional requirement.

Breed v. Jones (1975) rules that a child has the protection of the double-jeopardy clause of the Fifth Amendment and cannot be tried twice for the same crime.

Fare v. Michael C. (1979) held that a child has the protection of the *Miranda* decision: the right to remain silent during a police interrogation and to request that a lawyer be provided to protect his or her interests.

Schall v. Martin (1984) allowed for the placement of children in preventive detention before their adjudication.

New Jersey v. T.L.O. (1985) determined that though the Fourth Amendment protection against unreasonable search and seizure applies to children, school officials can legally search kids who violate school rules (e.g., smoking on campus), though there is no evidence that the student violated the law.

Vernonia School District v. Acton (1995) held that the Fourth Amendment's guarantee against unreasonable searches is not violated by drug testing all students choosing to participate in interscholastic athletics.

Roper v. Simmons (2005) determined that juveniles who commit murder before they turn 18 cannot be sentenced to death.

Sources: *Kent. v. United States*, 383 U.S. 541, 86 S.Ct. 1045, 16 L.Ed.2d 84 (1966); *In re Gault*, 387 U.S. 1, 87 S.Ct. 1248 (1967); *McKeiver v. Pennsylvania*, 403 U.S. 528, 91 S.Ct. 1776 (1971); *Breed v. Jones*, 421 U.S. 519, 95 S.Ct. 1779 (1975); *Fare v. Michael C.*, 442 U.S. 707, 99 S.Ct. 2560 (1979); *Schall v. Martin*, 467 U.S. 253, 104 S.Ct. 2403 (1984); *New Jersey v. T.L.O.*, 469 U.S. 325, 105 S.Ct. 733 (1985); *Vernonia School District v. Acton*, 515 U.S. 646 115 S.Ct. 2386, 132 L.Ed. 2d 564 (1995); *Roper vs. Simmons*, No. 03-633 (2005).

Besides the legal revolution brought about by the Supreme Court, Congress passed the Juvenile Justice and Delinquency Prevention Act of 1974 (JJDP act) and established the federal Office of Juvenile Justice and Delinquency Prevention (OJJDP).[12] This legislation was enacted to identify the needs of youths and to fund programs in the juvenile justice system. Its main goal was to separate wayward, non-dangerous youths from institutions housing delinquents and to remove adolescents from institutions housing adult offenders. In 1996, in a move reflecting the growing national frustration with serious delinquent offenders, the act was amended to make it easier to hold delinquents in adult penal institutions.

Criminal Justice⚖Now™

Learn more by exploring the **Juvenile Justice** *Learning Module.*

juvenile delinquency Participation in illegal behavior by a minor who falls under a statutory age limit.

status offender A juvenile who engages in behavior legally forbidden to minors, such as running away, truancy, or incorrigibility.

▎JUVENILE JUSTICE TODAY

Today, the juvenile justice system has jurisdiction over two distinct categories of offenders: delinquents and status offenders.[13] **Juvenile delinquency** refers to children who fall under a jurisdictional age limit, which varies from state to state, and who commit an act in violation of the penal code. **Status offenders** commit acts forbidden to minors that includes truancy and being a habitually disobedient and ungovernable child (see Figure 15.1). They are commonly characterized in state statutes as persons or children in need of supervision (PINS or CHINS). Most states distinguish such behavior from delinquent conduct to lessen the effect of any stigma on children as a result of their involvement with the juvenile court. In addition, juvenile courts generally have jurisdiction over situations involving conduct directed at (rather than committed by) juveniles, such as parental neglect, deprivation, abandonment, and abuse.

© Sean Clayton/The Image Works

Does scaring youth help keep them out of trouble? Kids who are in the program Shape-Up tour cell house 5, dubbed "The Zoo," at the Colorado Territorial Prison. The two-day program is designed to show delinquent teens what life is like inside prison and how to avoid it. Reviews of such programs have been mixed, and there is some evidence that participants actually commit more crime than nonparticipants!

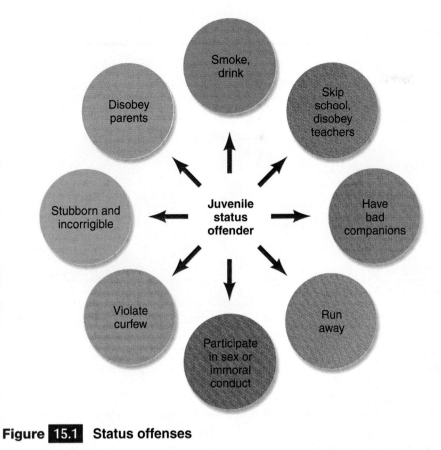

Figure 15.1 **Status offenses**

The states have also set different maximum ages below which children fall under the jurisdiction of the juvenile court. Many states include all children under eighteen years of age, others set the limit at seventeen, and still others at sixteen.

Some states exclude certain classes of offenders or offenses from the juvenile justice system. For example, youths who commit serious violent offenses such as rape or murder may be automatically excluded from the juvenile justice system and treated as adults on the premise that they stand little chance of rehabilitation within the confines of the juvenile system. Juvenile court judges may also transfer, or waive, repeat offenders whom they deem untreatable by the juvenile authorities.

Another trend has been to create family courts, which include a broad range of family and child related issues within their jurisdictions. Family courts are in use or are being considered in more than half of U.S. states. These are designed to provide more individualized client focus treatment than traditional juvenile courts and to bring a holistic approach to helping kids and their families rather than focusing on punishing and/or controlling delinquency.[14] Hawaii's family court jurisdiction is described in Exhibit 15.2.

The juvenile justice system has evolved into a parallel yet independent system of justice with its own terminology and rules of procedure. Exhibit 15.3 describes the basic similarities and differences between the juvenile and adult justice systems. Exhibit 15.4 on page 428 points out how the language used in the juvenile court differs from that used in the adult system.

Today, the juvenile justice system is responsible for processing and treating almost two million cases of youthful misbehavior annually. Each state's system is unique, so it is difficult to give a precise accounting of the justice process. Moreover, depending on local practice and tradition, case processing often varies from community to community within a single state. Keeping this

 www The **Office of Juvenile Justice and Delinquency Prevention** is an excellent resource for information on the juvenile justice system. To reach this site go to "Web Links" on your Siegel Essentials of Criminal Justice 5e website: http://cj.wadsworth.com/siegel_ess5e.

Criminal Justice ⚖ **Now** ™

Learn more by exploring the "Aging Out" Review and Reinforce activity.

Exhibit 15.2   Hawaii's Family Court

Established by statute in 1965, the Family Court's mission is to provide a fair, speedy, economical, and accessible forum for the resolution of matters involving families and children.

Children

The Family Court hears legal matters involving children. These include:

- Delinquency
- Status offenses
- Abuse and neglect
- Termination of parental rights
- Adoption
- Guardianships
- Detention

Domestic Relations

The Family Court also hears domestic relations cases, including:

- Divorce
- Child support
- Paternity
- Uniform child custody jurisdiction cases
- Miscellaneous custody matters

Domestic Violence

Domestic violence cases include:

- Requests for civil restraining orders involving family members
- Persons charged with the offense of abuse of family and household members
- Felony charges limited to offenses against household members

Source: Hawaii State Judiciary, www.courts.state.hi.us/page_server/Courts/Family/153E4A87ED63B9F8EBD8E1142F.html, accessed on Sept. 29, 2005.

in mind, the following sections provide a general description of some of the key processes and decision points in juvenile justice. Figure 15.2 on page 428 illustrates a model of the juvenile justice process.

Criminal Justice ⚖ Now™

Learn more by exploring the "Police Discretion with Regard to Juveniles" Review and Reinforce activity.

POLICE PROCESSING OF THE JUVENILE OFFENDER

According to the Uniform Crime Reports, police officers arrest more than 1.5 million juveniles under age eighteen each year, including almost 500,000 under age fifteen.[15] Most larger police departments have separate, juvenile detectives who handle delinquency cases and focus their attention on the problems of youth. In addition to conducting their own investigations, they typically take control of cases after an arrest is made by a uniformed officer.

Most states do not have specific statutory provisions distinguishing the arrest process for children from that for adults. Some jurisdictions, however, give broad arrest powers to the police in juvenile cases by authorizing the officer to make an arrest whenever it is believed that the child's behavior falls within the jurisdiction of the juvenile court. Consequently, police may arrest youths for behavior considered legal for adults, including running away, curfew violations, and being in possession of alcohol.

Exhibit 15.3	Similarities and differences between juvenile and adult justice systems

Similarities

- Discretion used by police officers, judges, and correctional personnel
- Right to receive *Miranda* warning
- Protection from prejudicial lineups or other identification procedures
- Procedural safeguards when making an admission of guilt
- Advocacy roles of prosecutors and defense attorneys
- Right to counsel at most key stages of the court process
- Availability of pretrial motions
- Plea negotiation/plea bargaining
- Right to a hearing and an appeal
- Standard of proof beyond a reasonable doubt
- Pretrial detention possible
- Detention without bail if considered dangerous
- Probation as a sentencing option
- Community treatment as a sentencing option

Differences

- The primary purpose of juvenile procedures is protection and treatment; with adults, the aim is to punish the guilty.
- Jurisdiction is determined by age in the juvenile system, by the nature of the offense in the adult system.
- Juveniles can be apprehended for acts that would not be criminal if committed by an adult (status offenses).
- Juvenile proceedings are not considered criminal; adult proceedings are.
- Juvenile court proceedings are generally informal and private; adult court proceedings are more formal and are open to the public.
- Courts cannot release to the press identifying information about a juvenile, but must release information about an adult.
- Parents are highly involved in the juvenile process but not in the adult process.
- The standard of arrest is more stringent for adults than for juveniles.
- Juveniles are released into parental custody; adults are generally given bail.
- Juveniles have no constitutional right to a jury trial; adults do. Some states extend this right to juveniles by statute.
- Juveniles can be searched in school without probable cause or a warrant.
- A juvenile's record is generally sealed when the age of majority is reached; an adult's record is permanent.
- A juvenile court cannot sentence juveniles to county jails or state prisons, which are reserved for adults.
- The U.S. Supreme Court has declared that the Eighth Amendment prohibits the death penalty for juveniles under age 18.

Use of Discretion

When a juvenile is found to have engaged in delinquent or incorrigible behavior, police agencies are charged with the decision to release or to detain the child and refer her to juvenile court. Because of the state's interest in the child, the police generally have more discretion in the investigatory and arrest stages of the juvenile process than they do when dealing with adult offenders.

This discretionary decision—to release or to detain—is based not only on the nature of the offense but also on police attitudes and the child's social and personal conditions at the time of the arrest. The following is a partial list of

| Exhibit 15.4 | Comparison of terms used in adult and juvenile justice systems |

	Juvenile Terms	Adult Terms
The person and the act	Delinquent child	Criminal
	Delinquent act	Crime
Preadjudicatory stage	Take into custody	Arrest
	Petition	Indictment
	Agree to a finding	Plead guilty
	Deny the petition	Plead not guilty
	Adjustment	Plea bargain
	Detention facility; child-care shelter	Jail
Adjudicatory stage	Substitution	Reduction of charges
	Adjudicatory or fact-finding hearing	Trial
	Adjudication	
Postadjudicatory stage	Dispositional hearing	Sentencing hearing
	Disposition	Sentence
	Commitment	Incarceration
	Youth development center; treatment center; training school	Prison
	Residential child-care facility	Halfway house
	Aftercare	Parole

factors believed to be significant in police decision making regarding juvenile offenders:

- The type and seriousness of the child's offense
- The ability of the parents to be of assistance in disciplining the child
- The child's past contacts with police
- The degree of cooperation obtained from the child and parents and their demeanor, attitude, and personal characteristics
- Whether the child denies the allegations in the petition and insists on a court hearing[16]

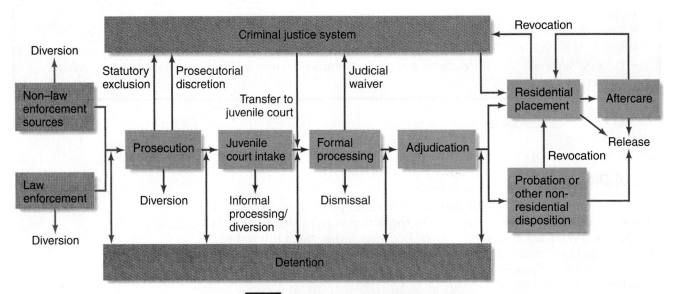

Figure 15.2 Case flow through the juvenile justice system

Source: Office of Juvenile Justice and Delinquency Prevention, www.ojjdp.ncjrs.org, accessed on October 3, 2005.

Legal Rights

Once a juvenile has been taken into custody, the child has the same Fourth Amendment right to be free from unreasonable searches and seizures as an adult does. Children in police custody can be detained prior to trial, interrogated, and placed in lineups. However, because of their youth and inexperience, children are generally afforded more protections than adults. Police must be careful that the juvenile suspect understands his constitutional rights, and if there is some question, must provide access to a parent or guardian to protect the child's legal interests. At one time, police officers could question juveniles in the absence of their parents or an attorney. Any incriminatory statements or confessions could be placed in evidence at trial. That is no longer permissible, and children today have greater protections during police questioning than adults. Police will interrogate a juvenile without an adult present only if they believe that the youth is unquestionably mature and experienced enough to understand her legal rights.[17]

▌THE JUVENILE COURT PROCESS

Criminal Justice⚖Now™
Learn more by exploring the "Mens Rea and Juveniles" Review and Reinforce activity.

After the police have determined that a case warrants further attention, they will bind it over to the prosecutor's office, which then has the responsibility for channeling the case through the juvenile court. The juvenile court plays a major role in controlling juvenile behavior and delivering social services to children in need.

Each year about 2 million youths under 18 are arrested by police, and U.S. juvenile courts process an estimated 1.6 million delinquency cases each year. As Figure 15.3 shows, in 2002, courts with juvenile jurisdiction handled an estimated 1,615,400 delinquency cases). The juvenile court delinquency caseload today is four times as large as it was in 1960.

As Figure 15.4 shows, the number of drug law violation cases increased 159 percent between 1985 and 2002, while public order offense cases increased 113 percent and person offense cases increased 113 percent.[18] In comparison, property offense cases decreased 10 percent during this period. Public order offense cases accounted for nearly half (46 percent) of the growth in the delinquency caseload between 1985 and 2002. Person offense cases made up another 44 percent of the increased number of delinquency cases processed during this time period. So despite a general decline in the crime rate, the juvenile court is now processing more kids than a decade ago for person, drug, and public order offenses.

Among the duties of the juvenile court judge is to decide whether a youngster should remain in pretrial detention or be released to his parents or guardian. Here, Assistant District Attorney Ken Fladager reads the charges to defendant Steven Sedillo, 13, right, and his attorney, Dennis Martinez, during Sedillo's detention hearing in Children's Court in front of Children's Judge John Romero. Ricky Navarette, 16, Fernando Anaya, 13, and Sedillo pleaded innocent on charges in connection with a fire along the Rio Grande.

© 2003 AP/Wide World Photos

The Intake Process

After police processing, the juvenile offender is usually remanded to the local juvenile court's intake division. At this juncture, court intake officers or probation personnel review and initially screen

Figure 15.3
Estimated delinquency cases

Source: National Center for Juvenile Justice, www.ojjdp.ncjrs.org/ ojstatbb/court/qa06204.asp? qaDate=20030811, accessed on June 13, 2005, updated.

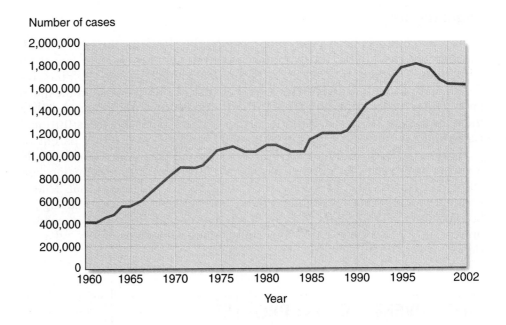

Number of cases

the child and the family to determine if the child needs to be handled formally or whether the case can be settled without the necessity of costly and intrusive official intervention. Their report helps the prosecutor decide whether to handle the case informally or bind it over for trial. The intake stage represents an opportunity to place a child in informal programs both within the court and in the community. The intake process also is critically important because more than half of the referrals to the juvenile courts never go beyond this stage.

The Detention Process

After a juvenile is formally taken into custody, either as a delinquent or as a status offender, the prosecutor usually makes a decision to release the child to the parent or guardian or to detain the child in a secure shelter pending trial.

Figure 15.4
Delinquency cases by offense

Source: National Center for Juvenile Justice, www.ojjdp.ncjrs. org/ojstatbb/court/qa06205.asp? qaDate=20030811, accessed on June 14, 2005, updated.

Criminal Justice ⚖ Now™

Learn more by exploring the "Delinquency Cases by Offense" Animated Artwork.

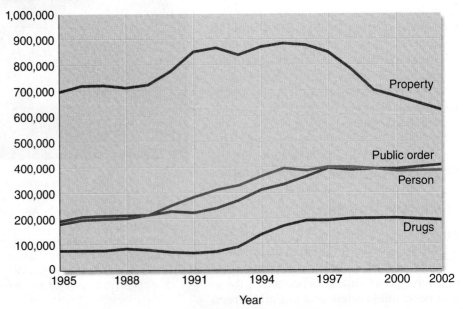

Number of cases

Detention has always been a controversial area of juvenile justice. Far too many children have been routinely placed in detention while awaiting court appearances. Status offenders and delinquents have been held in the same facility, and in many parts of the country, adult county jails were used to detain juvenile offenders. The Juvenile Justice Act of 1974 placed emphasis on reducing the number of children placed in inappropriate detention facilities. Though the act was largely successful, the practice continues.

Despite such measures, hundreds of thousands of youth are placed in pretrial detention each year, most of whom are already living under difficult circumstances. Many have suffered long histories of abuse and mental health problems.[19] The detention decision may reflect a child's personal characteristics and quality of his or her home life rather than dangerousness or flight risk.[20]

As Figure 15.5 shows, the number of delinquency cases involving detention increased 42 percent between 1985 and 2002, from 234,600 to 329,800. The largest relative increase was for drug offense cases (140 percent), followed by person cases (122 percent), and public order cases (72 percent). In contrast, the number of detained property offense cases declined 12 percent during this period. The data also shows a disproportionate number of African-American youth were detained before trial. In 2002, 18 percent of delinquency cases involving white juveniles included detention at some point between referral and disposition; the figure was 25 percent among cases involving black juveniles and 21 percent for cases involving youth of other races. Although black youth were involved in 29 percent of all delinquency cases processed in 2002, they were involved in 36 percent of all detained cases. The disproportionate representation of minority youth in detention is a troubling aspect of juvenile justice.

Legal Issues Most state statutes ordinarily require a hearing on the appropriateness of detention if the initial decision is to keep the child in custody. At this hearing, the child has a right to counsel and may be given other procedural due process safeguards, notably the privilege against self-incrimination and the right to confront and cross-examine witnesses. Most state juvenile court acts provide criteria to support a decision to detain the child. These include (1) the need to protect the child, (2) whether the child presents a serious danger to the public, and (3) the likelihood that the juvenile will return to court for adjudication. Whereas in adult cases the sole criterion for pretrial

Criminal Justice ⚖ Now™
Learn more by viewing the "Swiss Boy Accused of Incest Released" "In the News" video clip.

detention The temporary care of a child alleged to be a delinquent or status offender who requires secure custody, pending court disposition.

Figure 15.5
Detained delinquency cases
Source: Office of Juvenile Justice and Delinquency Prevention, *Statistical Briefing Book,* www.ojjdp.ncjrs.org/ojstatbb/court/ qa06301.asp?qaDate=20030811, accessed on June 14, 2005, updated.

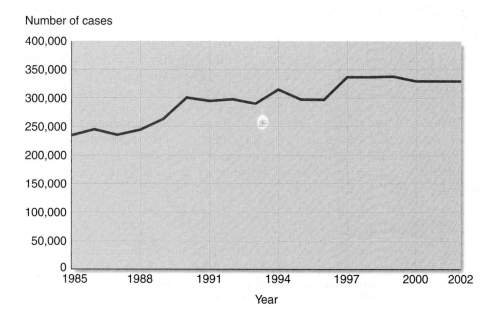

Number of cases

release may be the offender's availability for trial, juveniles may be detained for other reasons, including their own protection. Normally, the finding of the judge that the child should be detained must be supported by factual evidence. In the 1984 case of *Schall v. Martin*, the U.S. Supreme Court upheld the right of the states to detain a child before trial to protect his welfare and the public safety.[21]

Reforming Detention   There has been an ongoing effort to reform detention. The most important reform has been the successful effort to remove status offenders from lockups containing delinquents. After decades of effort, almost all states have passed laws requiring that status offenders be placed in nonsecure shelters, rather than secure detention facilities, thereby reducing their contact with more dangerous delinquent youth.

Another serious problem is the detention of youths in adult jails. The practice is common in rural areas where there are relatively few separate facilities for young offenders.[22] The OJJDP has given millions of dollars in aid to encourage the removal of juveniles from adult lockups. These grants have helped jurisdictions develop intake screening procedures, specific release or detention criteria, and alternative residential and nonresidential programs for juveniles awaiting trial. By 1980, amendments to the act mandating the absolute removal of juveniles from jails had been adopted. Despite such efforts, many states are not complying with the removal provisions and still detain juveniles in adult jails. Adding to their numbers are youths who commit non-serious acts—e.g., runaways—but are apprehended in rural areas where there are no juvenile facilities. There are also states which define the age limit for delinquency as 16 or 17 and therefore treat minors of that age as legal adults. At the time of the last jail census available (June 30, 2004) more than 7,000 persons under age 18 were housed in adult jails. Since jail stays are of short duration, it is likely that hundreds of thousands of minors are held in adult jails each year.

Whatever the actual number jailed today, placing young offenders in adult jails continues to be a significant problem in the juvenile justice system. Juveniles detained in adult jails often live in squalid conditions and are subject to physical and sexual abuse. The practice is widely condemned, but eliminating the confinement of juveniles in adult institutions remains a difficult task.[23]

Bail

If a child is not detained, the question of bail arises. Federal courts have not found it necessary to rule on the issue of a juvenile's constitutional right to bail because liberal statutory release provisions act as appropriate alternatives. Although only a few state statutes allow release on money bail, many others have juvenile code provisions that emphasize the release of the child to the parents as an acceptable substitute. A constitutional right to bail that on its face seems to benefit a child may have unforeseen results. The imposition of money bail might create a serious economic strain on the child's family while conflicting with the protective and social concerns of the juvenile court. Considerations of economic liabilities and other procedural inequities have influenced the majority of courts confronting this question to hold that juveniles do not have a right to bail.

Plea Bargaining

Before trial, juvenile prosecutors may attempt to negotiate a settlement to the case. For example, if the offender admits to the facts of the petition, she may be offered a placement in a special community-based treatment program in lieu of a term in a secure state facility. Or a status offense petition may be substituted for one of delinquency so that the adolescent can avoid being housed in a state training school and instead be placed in a more treatment-oriented facility.

If a bargain can be reached, the child will be asked to admit in open court that he did in fact commit the act of which he stands accused. State juvenile courts tend to minimize the stigma associated with the use of adult criminal standards by using other terminology, such as "agree to a finding" or "accept the petition" rather than "admit guilt." When the child makes an admission, juvenile courts require the following procedural safeguards: (1) the child knows of the right to a trial, (2) the plea or admission is made voluntarily, and (3) the child understands the charges and consequences of the plea.

Waiver of Jurisdiction

Criminal Justice ⚖ Now™
Learn more by exploring the "Waivers to Adult Court" Review and Reinforce activity.

Prior to the development of the first modern juvenile court in Illinois in 1899, juveniles were tried for violations of the law in adult criminal courts. The consequences were devastating; many children were treated as criminal offenders and often sentenced to adult prisons. Although the subsequent passage of state legislation creating juvenile courts eliminated this problem, the juvenile justice system did recognize that certain forms of conduct require that children be tried as adults. Today, most American jurisdictions provide by statute for **waiver,** or transfer, of juvenile offenders to the criminal courts. Waiver is also widely used in juvenile courts in Europe and Great Britain.[24]

In its most basic form, the decision of whether to waive a juvenile to the adult, or criminal, court is made in a **transfer hearing.** The decision to transfer a juvenile to the criminal court is often based on statutory criteria established by the state's juvenile court act, so waiver provisions vary considerably among jurisdictions. Most commonly considered are the child's age and the nature of the offense alleged in the petition. Some jurisdictions require that children be over a certain age (typically, fourteen) before they can be waived. Others mandate that the youth be charged with a felony before being tried as an adult, whereas others permit waiver of jurisdiction to the criminal court regardless of the seriousness of the offense when a child is a chronic offender. In about thirty states, certain offenses, such as murder, have been excluded from juvenile court jurisdiction, creating a mandatory waiver provision for children who have committed those crimes (e.g., murder).

Legal Controls Because of the nature of the waiver decision and its effect on the child in terms of status and disposition, the U.S. Supreme Court has imposed procedural protections for juveniles in the waiver process. In *Kent v. United States* (1966), the Supreme Court held that the waiver proceeding is a critically important stage in the juvenile justice process and that juveniles must be afforded minimum requirements of due process of law at such proceedings, including the right to legal counsel.[25] Then in *Breed v. Jones* (1975), the Court held that the prosecution of juveniles as adults in the California Superior Court violated the double jeopardy clause of the Fifth Amendment if they previously had been tried on the same charge in juvenile court.[26] The Court concluded that jeopardy attaches when the juvenile court begins to hear evidence at the adjudicatory hearing; this requires that the waiver hearing take place prior to any adjudication.

waiver (juvenile) A practice in which the juvenile court waives its jurisdiction over a juvenile and transfers the case to adult criminal court for trial. In some states a waiver hearing is held to determine jurisdiction, while in others juveniles may be automatically waived if they are accused of committing a serious crime such as murder.

transfer hearing The hearing in which a decision is made to waive a juvenile to the criminal court. Waiver decisions are based on such criteria as the child's age, prior offense history, and the nature of the offense.

Youths in Adult Courts Today, all states allow juveniles to be tried as adults in criminal courts in either one of four ways:

1. *Concurrent jurisdiction.* The prosecutor has the discretion of filing charges for certain legislatively designated offenses in either juvenile or criminal court.

2. *Excluded offenses.* State laws exclude from juvenile court jurisdiction certain offenses that are either very minor, such as traffic or fishing violations, or very serious, such as murder.

3. *Judicial waiver.* After a formal hearing at which both prosecutor and defense attorney present evidence, a juvenile court judge may decide to waive jurisdiction and transfer the case to criminal court. This procedure is also known as *binding over* or *certifying* juvenile cases to criminal court.

4. *Reverse waiver.* State laws mandate that certain offenses be tried in adult court. Once the case is heard in the adult court, the trial judge may decide that the offender would be better served by the juvenile court and order a reverse waiver.

Every state has provisions for handling juveniles in adult criminal courts, and the trend is to make the waiver broader.[27] In thirty-one states, once a juvenile is tried in adult court, she is no longer eligible for juvenile justice on any subsequent offense.

The Effect of Waiver The problem of youths processed in adult courts is a serious one. About eight thousand juvenile delinquency cases are now being transferred to the adult courts each year. What is accomplished by treating juveniles like adults? Studies of the impact of the recent waiver statutes have yielded inconclusive results. Some juveniles whose cases are waived to criminal court are actually sentenced more leniently than they would have been in juvenile court. In many states, even when juveniles are tried in criminal court and convicted on the charges, they may still be sentenced to a juvenile or youthful offender institution, rather than to an adult prison. Some studies show that only a small percentage of juveniles tried as adults are incarcerated for periods longer than the terms served by offenders convicted on the same crime in the juvenile court; others have found that waived juveniles actually serve more time behind bars.[28] Some may spend more time in juvenile deten-

Nathaniel Abraham was 11 years old when he fired a shot from a .22 caliber rifle, fatally wounding Ronnie Lee Greene, Jr. The Abraham case received national attention because he was the youngest child in Michigan (and possibly the nation) to be tried for first-degree murder as an adult. Oakland County Judge Eugene Moore sent Abraham to the W. J. Maxey Training Center until the age of 21 and spared him a sentence to an adult prison.

tion awaiting trial. In the end, what began as a get-tough measure has had the opposite effect while costing taxpayers more money.[29]

Transfer decisions are not always carried out fairly or equitably and there is evidence that minorities are waived at a rate that is greater than their representation in the population.[30] About 40 percent of all waived youth are African Americans, even though they represent less than a third (31 percent) of the juvenile court population.[31]

Supporters view the waiver process as a sound method of getting the most serious juvenile offenders off the streets while ensuring that rehabilitation plays a less critical role in the juvenile justice system. Kids are most likely to be transferred to criminal court if they have injured someone with a weapon or if they have a long juvenile court record.[32] No area of juvenile justice has received more attention recently than efforts to redefine the jurisdiction of the juvenile court.[33]

The Trial

There are usually two judicial hearings in the juvenile court process. The first, typically called an **initial appearance,** is similar to the arraignment in the adult system. The child is informed of the charges against him, attorneys are appointed, bail is reviewed, and in many instances cases are settled with an admission of the facts, followed by a community sentence. If the case cannot be settled at this initial stage, it is bound over for trial.

During the adjudicatory or trial process, often called the *fact-finding hearing* in juvenile proceedings, the court hears evidence on the allegations stated in the delinquency petition. In its early development, the juvenile court did not emphasize judicial rule making similar to that of the criminal trial process. Absent were such basic requirements as the standard of proof, rules of evidence, and similar adjudicatory formalities. Proceedings were to be non-adversarial, informal, and noncriminal. Gradually, however, the juvenile trial process became a target of criticism because judges were handing out punishments to children without affording them legal rights. This changed in 1967 when the U.S. Supreme Court's landmark *In re Gault* decision radically altered the juvenile justice system.[34] In *Gault,* the Court ruled that the concept of fundamental fairness is applicable to juvenile delinquency proceedings. The Court granted critical rights to juvenile defendants, most importantly, (1) the notice of the charges, (2) the right to counsel, (3) the right to confront and cross-examine witnesses, (4) the privilege against self-incrimination, and (5) the right to a transcript of the trial record.

The *Gault* decision completely altered the juvenile trial process. Instead of dealing with children in a benign and paternalistic fashion, the courts were forced to process juvenile offenders within the framework of appropriate constitutional procedures. And though *Gault* was technically limited to the adjudicatory stage, it has spurred further legal reform throughout the juvenile system. Today, the right to counsel, the privilege against self-incrimination, the right to treatment in detention and correctional facilities, and other constitutional protections are applied at all stages of the juvenile process, from investigation through adjudication to parole. *Gault* ushered in an era of legal rights for juveniles.

Once an adjudicatory hearing has been completed, the court is normally required to enter a judgment against the child. This may take the form of declaring the child delinquent or a ward of the court or possibly even suspending judgment to avoid the stigma of a juvenile record. Following the entering of a judgment, the court can begin its determination of possible **dispositions** for the child.

initial appearance A juvenile's first appearance before the juvenile court judge in which the charges are reviewed and an effort is made to settle the case without a trial. If the child does not have legal counsel an attorney will be appointed.

disposition For juvenile offenders, the equivalent of sentencing for adult offenders. The theory is that disposition is more rehabilitative than retributive. Possible dispositions may be to dismiss the case; release the youth to the custody of his or her parents; place the offender on probation; or send him or her to an institution or state correctional institution.

Disposition and Treatment

At the dispositional hearing, the juvenile court judge imposes a sentence on the juvenile offender based on her offense, prior record, and family background. Normally, the judge has broad discretionary power to issue a range of dispositions from dismissal to institutional **commitment.** In theory, the dispositional decision is an effort by the court to serve the best interests of the child, the family, and the community. In many respects, this postadjudicative process is the most important stage in the juvenile court system because it represents the last opportunity for the court to influence the child and control his behavior.

To ensure that only relevant and appropriate evidence is considered by the court during trial, most jurisdictions require a separate hearing to formulate an appropriate disposition. The bifurcated hearing process ensures that the adjudicatory hearing is used solely to determine the merits of the allegations, whereas the dispositional hearing determines whether the child is in need of rehabilitation.

In theory, the juvenile court seeks to provide a disposition that represents an individualized **treatment** plan for the child. This decision is normally based on the presentence investigation of the probation department, reports from social agencies, and possibly a psychiatric evaluation. The judge generally has broad discretion in dispositional matters but is limited by the provisions of the state's juvenile court act. The following are typical juvenile court dispositions:

1. Suspended judgment
2. Probation
3. Placement in a community treatment program
4. Commitment to the state agency responsible for juvenile institutional care

In addition, the court may place the child with parents or relatives, make dispositional arrangements with private youth-serving agencies, or order the child committed to a mental institution.

commitment *Decision of judge ordering an adjudicated and sentenced juvenile offender to be placed in a correctional facility.*

treatment *The rehabilitative method used to effect a change of behavior in the juvenile offender, in the form of therapy, or educational or vocational programs.*

Disposition Outcomes In dispositional hearings, juvenile court judges must determine the most appropriate sanction for delinquent youth. Disposition options include commitment to an institution or another residential facility; probation; or a variety of other dispositions, such as referral to an outside agency or treatment program, community service, fines, or restitution. Very often the court imposes some combination of these sanctions. What have been the trends in juvenile disposition? As Table 15.1 shows, the number of adjudicated delinquency cases resulting in residential placement increased by

Table 15.1	Offense profile of cases adjudicated delinquent resulting in out-of-home placement	
Most Serious Offense	**1985**	**2002**
Person	18%	26%
Property	56	37
Drugs	5	10
Public order	22	28
Total	**100%**	**100%**
Cases resulting in out-of-home placement	100,400	144,000

Source: National Center for Juvenile Justice

more than 40 percent between 1985 to 2002 (about 144,000 kids or 10 percent of the total handled in juvenile courts). The number of adjudicated delinquency cases resulting in formal probation more than doubled between 1985 to 2002; about 400,000 kids are put on probation each year.

Juvenile Sentencing Reform

Over the past decade, juvenile justice experts and the general public have become aroused about the serious juvenile crime rate in general and about violent acts committed by children in particular. As a result, some law enforcement officials and conservative legislators have demanded that the juvenile justice system take a more serious stand with dangerous juvenile offenders. In the past two decades, many state legislatures have responded by toughening their juvenile codes. Some jurisdictions have passed mandatory or determinate incarceration sentences for juveniles convicted of serious felonies. The get-tough approach even allows the use of the death penalty for minors transferred to the adult system.[35] Not all jurisdictions, however, have not abandoned rehabilitation as a primary dispositional goal and still hold to the philosophy that placements should be based on the least detrimental alternative. This view requires that judges employ the least intrusive measures possible to safeguard a child's growth and development.[36]

A second reform has been the concerted effort to remove status offenders from the juvenile justice system and restrict their entry into institutional programs. Because of the development of numerous diversion programs, many children who are involved in truancy and incorrigible behavior who ordinarily would have been sent to a closed institution are now being placed in community programs. There are far fewer status offenders in detention or institutions than ever before.

A third reform effort has been to standardize dispositions in juvenile court. As early as 1977, Washington passed one of the first determinate sentencing laws for juvenile offenders, resulting in other states adopting similar statutes.[37] All children found to be delinquent are evaluated on a point system based on their age, prior juvenile record, and type of crime committed. Minor offenders are handled in the community. Those committing more serious offenses are placed on probation. Children who commit the most serious offenses are subject to standardized institutional penalties. As a result, juvenile offenders who commit such crimes as rape or armed robbery are being sentenced to institutionalization for two, three, and four years. This approach is different from the indeterminate sentencing under which children who have committed a serious crime might be released from institutions in less than a year if correctional authorities believe that they have been rehabilitated.

■ THE JUVENILE CORRECTIONAL PROCESS

After disposition in juvenile court, delinquent offenders may be placed in some form of correctional treatment. Although many are placed in the community, more than one hundred thousand are now in secure facilities.

Criminal Justice ⚖ Now™
*Learn more by exploring the **Graduated Sanctions** Review and Reinforce activity.*

Probation

Probation is the most commonly used formal sentence for juvenile offenders, and many states require that a youth fail on probation before being sent to an institution (unless the criminal act is quite serious). Probation involves placing the child under the supervision of the juvenile probation department for the purpose of community treatment. A juvenile may also be required to fol-

The juvenile correctional process relies heavily on community-based treatment programs. Here Project SAW (Service Achievement Work) program coordinator Richard Bethel, with the Mojave County Probation Department, supervises program participants Ryan Dempsey, left, and John Womack, as they install a railing on an exhibit being constructed at the Mojave Museum of History and Arts, May 20, 2004, in Kingman, Arizona. The on-the-job training program, for 16- and 17-year-old juveniles who are on probation and have dropped out of school, puts teens to work in the community.

© 2004 AP/Wide World Photos

low special rules, such as maintain a curfew or attend substance abuse meetings. Alternative sanctions such as community service or monetary restitution may be ordered. Serious offenders can be placed in intensive supervision or under house arrest. Probation can be revoked if the juvenile violates the probation conditions. Similar to the adult system, probation can be revoked if the rules are not followed and the court may impose stricter sanctions.

Juvenile probation is an important component of the juvenile justice system. It is the most widely used method of community treatment in juvenile court. Similar in form and function to adult probation, supervising juveniles in the community combines elements of treatment and control. While some probation officers maintain a social work orientation and want to provide needy kids with an effective treatment plan, others maintain a law enforcement orientation, believing that their clients are offenders who need close monitoring.[38]

Institutionalization

The most severe of the statutory dispositions available to the juvenile court involves commitment of the child to an institution. The committed child may be sent to a state training school or private residential treatment facility. These are usually minimum-security facilities with small populations and an emphasis on treatment and education. Some states, however, maintain facilities with populations over one thousand.

Most state statutes vary when determining the length of the child's commitment. Traditionally, many jurisdictions committed the child up to majority, which usually meant twenty-one years of age. This normally deprived the child of freedom for an extensive period of time—sometimes longer than an adult sentenced for the same offense would be confined. As a result, some states have passed legislation under which children are committed for periods ranging from one to three years.

To better handle violent juvenile offenders, some states have created separate or intermediate juvenile systems. Under such statutes, fourteen- to seventeen-year-olds charged with certain violent felonies are treated as adults, and if convicted, sentenced to new intermediate prisons, separated from both adult and regular juvenile offenders, for terms of two to five years.[39]

Today there are more than 100,000 juveniles being held in either privately run or publicly managed juvenile correctional facilities. About 35 percent are held for person-oriented offenses; about 20 percent for alcohol, drug, and public order offenses; and more than 40 percent for property crimes. Just over 5 percent are confined for a juvenile status offense, such as truancy, running away, or incorrigibility. The efforts made in recent years to keep status offenders out of institutions seem to have paid off.

Population Makeup The typical resident of a juvenile facility is a fifteen- to sixteen-year-old white male incarcerated for an average stay of five months in a public facility or six months in a private facility. Private facilities tend to house younger youths, whereas public institutions provide custodial care for older youths, including a small percentage of youths between eighteen and twenty-one years of age. As already noted, most incarcerated youths are person, property, or drug offenders. A significant and enduring problem is the over-representation of minority youth in juvenile facilities (see Figure 15.6).

Minority youths accused of delinquent acts are less likely than white youths to be diverted from the court system into informal sanctions and are more likely to receive sentences involving incarceration. In some states between 50–75 of juvenile residents are minority group members; in five states and the District of Columbia the proportion is over 75 percent.

While the disproportionate minority representation in juvenile correctional facilities is a very serious matter, it is also reflective of the racial disparity which occurs at every stage of the juvenile justice process. A disproportionate number of minority youth suffer arrest, detention, waivers,

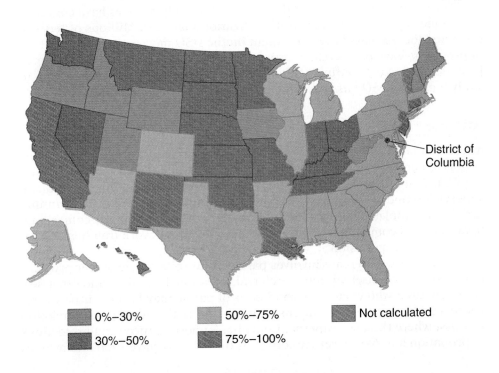

Figure 15.6
Minority proportion of juveniles in residential placement
OJJDP Statistical Briefing Book, www.ojjdp.ncjrs.org/ojstatbb/qa334.html, accessed on October 6, 2005.

District of Columbia

0%–30%   50%–75%   Not calculated

30%–50%   75%–100%

and so on. It is not surprising then that they also face disparity in the probability of incarceration. On the bright side, racial differences have been trending downward, reflecting greater sensitivity to disparity in the justice system and the efforts being made at its correction.

Deinstitutionalization

Some experts in delinquency and juvenile law question the policy of institutionalizing juvenile offenders. Many believe that large institutions are too costly to operate and only produce more sophisticated criminals. This dilemma has produced a number of efforts to remove youths from juvenile facilities and replace large institutions with smaller community-based facilities. The Commonwealth of Massachusetts closed all its state training schools more than twenty years ago (subsequently, however, public pressure caused a few secure facilities to be reopened). Many other states have established small residential facilities operated by juvenile-care agencies to replace larger units.

Despite the daily rhetoric on crime control, public support for community-based programs for juveniles still exists. Although such programs are not panaceas, many experts still recommend more treatment and less incarceration for juvenile offenders. Utah, Maryland, Vermont, and Pennsylvania, for example, have dramatically reduced their reform school populations while setting up a wide range of intensive treatment programs for juveniles. Many large, impersonal, and expensive state institutions with unqualified staff and ineffective treatment programs have been eliminated.

Deinstitutionalizing Status Offenders   There has been an ongoing effort for almost thirty years to deinstitutionalize status offenders (DSO).[40] This means removing noncriminal youths from institutions housing delinquents in order to prevent them from interacting with violent or chronic offenders.

Since its inception, the DSO approach has been hotly debated. Some have argued that early intervention is society's best hope of forestalling future delinquent behavior and reducing victimization. Other experts maintain that legal control over status offenders is a violation of youths' rights. Still others have viewed status-offending behavior as a symptom of some larger trauma or problem that requires attention. These diverse opinions still exist today.

Since Congress passed the JJDP act in 1974, all fifty states have complied with some aspect of the deinstitutionalization mandate. Millions of federal, state, and local dollars have been spent on the DSO movement. Vast numbers of programs have been created around the country to reduce the number of juveniles in secure confinement. What remains to be done, however, is to study the effect DSO has had on juveniles and the justice system.

Aftercare

Aftercare marks the final stage of the formal juvenile justice process. Its purpose is to help youths make the transition from residential or institutional settings back into the community. Effective aftercare programs provide adequate supervision and support services to help juvenile offenders avoid criminal activity. Examples of programs include electronic monitoring, counseling, treatment and community service referrals, education, work training, and intensive parole supervision.

Most juvenile aftercare involves parole. A juvenile parole officer provides the child with counseling, school referral, vocational training, and other services. Children who violate the conditions of parole may have their parole revoked and be returned to the institution. Unlike the adult post-conviction process, where the U.S. Supreme Court has imposed procedural protections in probation and parole revocations, juveniles do not have such due process rights. State courts have also been reluctant to grant juveniles rights in this area and those that have generally refuse to require that the whole array of rights be made available as they are to adult offenders. Since the *Gault* decision, however, many states have adopted administrative regulations requiring juvenile agencies to incorporate due process, such as proper notice of the hearing and the right to counsel in postconviction proceedings.

Preventing Delinquency

Although the juvenile justice system has been concerned with controlling delinquent behavior, there are now important efforts being made to prevent delinquency before it occurs. *Delinquency prevention* refers to intervening in young people's lives prior to their engaging in delinquency in the first place; that is, preventing involvement in delinquency at all. In the past, delinquency prevention was the responsibility of treatment-oriented agencies such as day care providers, YMCA and YWCA, Boys and Girls Clubs of America, and other private and public agencies. Today, there are many community-based treatment programs involving a combination of juvenile justice and treatment agencies. Some focus on the educational experience and attempt to help kids maintain their bond to society by strengthening their attachments to school. The Fast Track program, discussed in more detail in the following Policy, Programs, and Issues in Criminal Justice, is a good example of such a program.

Comprehensive community-based delinquency prevention programs are taking a systematic approach or using a comprehensive planning model to develop preventive interventions. This includes an analysis of the delinquency problem, an identification of available resources in the community, development of priority delinquency problems, and the identification of successful programs in other communities and tailoring them to local conditions and needs.[41] Not all comprehensive community-based prevention programs follow this model, but there is evidence to suggest that this approach will produce the greatest reductions in juvenile delinquency.[42]

A good example of the comprehensive community program is the Children At Risk (CAR) program, funded by the federal government. CAR was

Preventing future delinquency is a key goal of the juvenile justice system. Wyoming Girls' School residents (from left) Christina and Amanda dine with direct care staff member Amber Van Dyke, December 15, 2004, in one of the school's dining rooms. The Wyoming Girls' School is a rehabilitative correctional facility for court-ordered delinquent girls aged 12 to 18.

Policy, Programs, and Issues in Criminal Justice

The Fast Track Project

Fast Track is designed to prevent serious antisocial behavior and related adolescent problems in high-risk children entering first grade. The intervention is guided by a developmental approach that suggests that antisocial behavior is the product of the interaction of multiple social and psychological influences:

1. Residence in low-income, high-crime communities places stressors and influences on children and families that increase their risk levels. In these areas, families characterized by marital conflict and instability make consistent and effective parenting difficult to achieve, particularly with children who are impulsive and of difficult temperament.

2. Children of high-risk families usually enter the education process poorly prepared for its social, emotional, and cognitive demands. Their parents often are unprepared to relate effectively with school staff and a poor home/school bond often aggravates the child's adjustment problems. They may find themselves grouped with other children who are similarly unprepared. This peer group may be negatively influenced by disruptive classroom contexts and punitive teachers.

3. Over time, aggressive and disruptive children are rejected by families and peers, and tend to receive less support from teachers. All of these processes increase the risk of antisocial behaviors, in a process which begins in elementary school and lasts throughout adolescence. During this period, peer influences, academic difficulties, and dysfunctional personal identity development can contribute to serious conduct problems and related risky behaviors.

What Does Fast Track Do?

Fast Track provides intervention based on the assumption that improving child competencies,

parenting effectiveness, school context, and school/home communications will, over time, contribute to preventing antisocial behavior across the period from early childhood through adolescence. To carry out this mission, in four sites across the United States, Fast Track coordinators identified a sample of 445 high-risk children in kindergarten who were identified by their conduct problems at home and at school; a matched control group of 446 youth was also identified. Treatment was provided in a number of phases stretching from first to tenth grade.

Elementary School Phase of the Intervention (Grades 1–5)

- Teacher-led classroom curricula (called PATHS) as a universal intervention directed toward the development of emotional concepts, social understanding, and self-control (including weekly teacher consultation about classroom management); and the following five programs administered to the high-risk intervention subjects:

  - Parent training groups designed to promote the development of positive family/school relationships and to teach parents behavior management skills, particularly in the use of praise, time-out, and self-restraint
  - Home visits for the purpose of fostering parents' problem-solving skills, self-efficacy, and life management
  - Child social skill training groups (called Friendship Groups)
  - Child tutoring in reading
  - Child friendship enhancement in the classroom (called Peer Pairing)

designed to help improve the lives of young people at high risk for delinquency, gang involvement, substance abuse, and other problem behaviors. It was delivered to a large number of young people in poor and high-crime neighborhoods in five cities across the country. It involved a wide range of preventive measures, including case management and family counseling, family skills training, tutoring, mentoring, after-school activities, and community policing. The program was different in each neighborhood. Some of the other

Adolescent Phase of the Intervention Program (Grades 6–10)

- Standard and individualized activities for high-risk youth and families. Group-based interventions were de-emphasized, in order to avoid promoting engagement with deviant peers.
- Curriculum-based parent and youth group meetings were included in the intervention, to support children in their transition into middle school (grades 5–7).
- Individualized services, designed to strengthen protective factors and reduce risk factors in areas of particular need for each youth, which included academic tutoring, mentoring, support for positive peer-group involvement, home visiting and family problem-solving, and liaisons with school and community agencies.

Evaluation of the Fast Track Program

The efficacy of the Fast Track prevention program is tested periodically, by comparing the group of children receiving intervention services to children in the control group, with regard to a wide range of problem-behavior outcomes and their development over time. Significant progress was made toward the goal of improving competencies of the children receiving intervention services and their parents. Compared to the control group, the intervention children improved their social-cognitive and academic skills, and their parents reduced their use of harsh discipline. These group differences also were reflected in behavioral improvements during the elementary school years and beyond. Compared with children in the control group, children in the intervention group displayed significantly less aggressive behavior at home, in the classroom, and on the playground. By the end of third grade, 37 percent of the intervention group had become free of conduct problems, in contrast with 27 percent of the control group. By the end of elementary school, 33 percent of the intervention group had a developmental trajectory of decreasing conduct problems, as compared with 27 percent of the control group. Furthermore, placement in special education by the end of elementary school was about one-fourth lower in the intervention group than in the control group.

Group differences continued through adolescence. Court records indicate that by eighth grade, 38 percent of the intervention group boys had been arrested, in contrast with 42 percent of the control group. Finally, psychiatric interviews after ninth grade indicate that the Fast Track program intervention has reduced serious conduct disorder by over a third, from 27 percent to 17 percent. These effects generalized across gender and ethnic groups, and across the wide range of child and family characteristics measured by Fast Track.

Critical Thinking

1. The success of the Fast Track program has led to its implementation in several school systems across the country, as well as in several schools in Great Britain, Australia, and Canada. Would you want such a program implemented in your local school system?

2. Should the government devote significant resources to helping at-risk kids or might the funds be better off spent on programs that provide advanced training to the academically gifted?

InfoTrac College Edition Research

To read about the effectiveness of the Fast Track program, go to Kristen Lavallee, Karen Bierman, and Robert Nix, "The impact of first-grade 'friendship group' experiences on child social outcomes in the Fast Track program," *Journal of Abnormal Child Psychology 33* (2005): 307–324.

Source: Project overview, Fast Track Data Center, www.fasttrackproject.org/datacenter.htm and www.fasttrackproject.org/fasttrackoverview.htm, accessed on October 4, 2005.

beneficial results for those in the program included less association with delinquent peers, less peer pressure to engage in delinquency, and more positive peer support.[43]

The CAR program is now known as CASASTART, an acronym for the national Center on Addiction and Substance Abuse, Striving Together to Achieve Rewarding Tomorrows. Based at Columbia University in New York, CASASTART is a neighborhood-based, school-centered program aimed at

Policy, Programs, and Issues in Criminal Justice

Should the Juvenile Justice System Be Maintained? Abolished?

Some experts such as David Smith question the efficacy of having a separate juvenile justice system. Looking at international evaluations, he finds that comparative research shows that whether it is passive, treatment-oriented, or lenient, the *juvenile justice system* produces the same level of juvenile delinquency as those that are active, severe, and punitive.

Smith is not alone in his skepticism. In an important work, *Bad Kids: Race and the Transformation of the Juvenile Court,* legal expert Barry Feld makes the rather controversial suggestion that the juvenile court system should be discontinued and replaced by an alternative method of justice. He suggests that the current structure of the juvenile court almost makes it impossible for it to fulfill or achieve the purpose for which it was originally intended.

Feld maintains that the juvenile court system was created in an effort to foster an atmosphere and process that was more lenient than that used against adult criminals. Although this was a worthwhile goal, the court system was doomed to fail even from the beginning, because it was thrown into the role of providing child welfare while at the same time being an instrument of law enforcement, two missions that are often at cross-purposes. During its history, various legal developments have further undermined its purpose—most notably the *In re Gault* ruling, which ultimately led to juveniles receiving similar legal protections as adults and to children being treated like adults in all respects. The juvenile court vision of leniency was further undermined by the fear and consequent racism created by post–World War II migration and economic trends, which led to the development of large enclaves of poor and underemployed African Americans living in northern cities. Then, in the 1980s, the sudden rise in gang membership, gun violence, and homicide committed by juveniles further undermined the juvenile court mission and resulted in legislation creating mandatory sentences for juvenile offenders and mandatory waiver to the adult court. As a result, the focus of the court has been on dealing with the offense rather than treating the offender. In Feld's words, the juvenile court has become a "deficient second-rate criminal court." The welfare and rehabilitative purposes of the juvenile court have been subordinated to its role as law enforcement agent.

Can juvenile courts be reformed? Feld maintains that it is impossible because of their conflicting purposes and shifting priorities. The money spent on serving the court and its large staff would be better spent on child welfare, which would target a larger audience and prevent antisocial acts before they occur. In lieu of juvenile court, youths who violate the law should

both preventing substance abuse and delinquency among high-risk adolescents ages 8 to 13 and reducing drug-related crime in their neighborhoods. The program brings together different organizations including schools, law enforcement, and social service agencies to provide clients with eight different services: tutoring, after-school activities, mentoring, counseling, family services, community policing, juvenile justice intervention, and incentives.

Potentially eligible children are referred to CASASTART by school, social service staff, police, or juvenile court personnel. Staff members (called case managers) then determine whether children meet the criteria of being at high risk of substance abuse and crime. Each case manager works closely on a one-to-one basis with fifteen families. In addition to seeking out participants and coordinating services, CASASTART case managers engage in a full range of activities, including:

- Running after-school or recreation programs
- Arranging for and sometimes transporting family members to appointments

receive full procedural protections in the criminal court system. The special protections given youth in the juvenile court could be provided by altering the criminal law and recognizing age as a factor in the creation of criminal liability. Because youths have had a limited opportunity to develop self-control, their criminal liability should also be curtailed or restricted.

Are these dour assessments of the juvenile court valid and should the court in fact be abolished? No, according to John Johnson Kerbs, who suggests that Feld makes assumptions that may not fit the reality of the American legal system. First, Kerbs finds that it is naïve to assume the criminal courts can provide the same or greater substantive and procedural protections as the juvenile court. Many juvenile court defendants are indigent, especially those coming from the minority community, and it may be impossible for them to obtain adequate legal defense in the adult system. Second, Feld's assumption that criminal courts will take a defendant's age into close consideration may be illusory. In this "get tough" era, it is likely that criminal courts will provide harsher sentences, and the brunt of these draconian sentences will fall squarely on the shoulders of minority youth. Research efforts routinely show that African-American adults are unduly punished in adult courts. Sending juvenile offenders to these venues will most likely further enmesh them in an already unfair system. Finally, Kerbs finds that the treatment benefits of the juvenile courts should not be overlooked or abandoned. There is ample research, he

maintains, that shows that juvenile courts can create lower recidivism rates than criminal courts. Though the juvenile court is far from perfect and should be improved, it would be foolish to abandon a system that is aimed at helping kids find alternatives to crime rather than one that produces higher recidivism rates, lowers their future prospects, and has a less than stellar record of providing due process and equal protection for the nation's most needy citizens.

Critical Thinking

What's your take on this issue? Should the juvenile court be abolished? Since the trend has been to transfer the most serious criminal cases to the adult court, is there still a purpose for an independent juvenile court? Should the juvenile court be reserved for nonserious first offenders?

InfoTrac College Edition Research

Before you make up your mind about the future of juvenile courts, read Joseph V. Penn, "Justice for Youth? A History of the Juvenile and Family Court," *Brown University Child and Adolescent Behavior Letter,* September 2001 v17 i9 p1.

Sources: David Smith, "The Effectiveness of the Juvenile Justice System," *Criminal Justice: International Journal of Policy & Practice 5* (2005): 181–195; Barry C. Feld, *Bad Kids: Race and the Transformation of the Juvenile Court* (New York: Oxford University Press, 1999); John Johnson Kerbs, "(Un)equal Justice: Juvenile Court Abolition and African Americans," *Annals, AAPSS, 564* (1999): 109–125.

- Helping prevent homelessness or utility shutoffs
- Advocating for children and family members in court
- Helping parents resolve problems with schools or social service agencies

The program is now being used in sixty-four sites around the country, including Denver, Colorado, and San Antonio, Texas.[44]

Keep the Juvenile Court?

Over the past century, the juvenile court has struggled to provide treatment for juvenile offenders while guaranteeing them constitutional due process. Over the last century, the juvenile court system has been transformed from a rehabilitative to a quasi-criminal court. Many states are toughening juvenile codes. With limited resources and procedural deficiencies, there is little likelihood of much change in the near future.

The system has been so overwhelmed by violent juvenile crime and family breakdown that some judges and politicians have suggested abolishing the

Criminal Justice⊕Now™

*Learn more about **Careers in Criminal Justice** by exploring the "On the Job" feature "**Gang Information and Apprehension Unit, California Youth Authority.**"*

juvenile system. Even those experts who want to retain an independent juvenile court have called for its restructuring. Crime control advocates want to reduce the court's jurisdiction over juveniles charged with serious crimes and liberalize the prosecutor's ability to try them in adult courts. In contrast, child advocates suggest that the court scale back its judicial role and transfer its functions to community groups and social service agencies.[45] Despite these differing opinions, the juvenile court will likely remain a critical societal institution; there are few viable alternatives. This issue is addressed in the Policy, Programs, and Issues in Criminal Justice feature entitled "Should the Juvenile Court Be Abolished? Maintained?" on pages 444–445.

SUMMARY

- The juvenile justice system is concerned with the care and treatment of delinquent children, and status offenders whose incorrigible behavior makes them beyond the care and protection of their parents.
- Juveniles involved in antisocial behavior come under the jurisdiction of juvenile or family court systems.
- These courts belong to a system of juvenile justice agencies, including law enforcement, child care, and institutional services.
- The juvenile justice system can be traced back to the English poor law system and the chancery court.
- The parens patriae concept meant that that state was responsible for youths who could not care for themselves.
- Needy kids were made into apprentices.
- The English system was brought to America.
- During the nineteenth century, child savers became concerned with the plight of children and created welfare programs such as the Children's Aid Society and the House of Refuge.

- The child savers created the first independent juvenile court in Illinois at the turn of the century.
- Ideally, when a child is brought to the juvenile court, the proceedings are generally non-adversarial and less formal than the adult system.
- In a series of cases, the Supreme Court has granted children procedural safeguards and due process rights.
- The juvenile justice process has many of the same elements of the adult system.
- Kids who are a flight risk or a danger to themselves and others are placed in pretrial detention.
- Juveniles who commit serious crimes can be transferred or waived to the adult system.
- More than 100,000 youths are now in secure custody.
- There have been elaborate and complex efforts to prevent delinquency.
- Some experts believe that the juvenile justice system is antiquated and should be abolished or replaced.

KEY TERMS

parens patriae 420
poor laws 420
child savers 421
Children's Aid Society 422
juvenile court 422
juvenile delinquency 424
status offender 424
detention 431

waiver (juvenile) 433
transfer hearing 433
initial appearance 435
disposition 435
commitment 436
treatment 436

REVIEW QUESTIONS

1. Should status offenders be treated by the juvenile court? Explain. Should they be placed in confinement for such acts as running away or cutting school? Why or why not?

2. Should a juvenile ever be waived to adult court with the possible risk that the child will be incarcerated with adult felons? Why or why not?

3. Do you support the death penalty for children? Explain.

4. Should juveniles be given mandatory incarceration sentences for serious crimes, as adults are? Explain.

5. Is it fair to deny juveniles a jury trial? Why or why not?

6. Do you think the trend toward treating juveniles like adult offenders is desirable? Explain.

Glossary

ABIS (Automated Biometric Identification System) Facial recognition system designed to sift through millions of images to find duplicates prior to issuing an ID or clearing a passport.

actus reus An illegal act. The actus reus can be an affirmative act, such as taking money or shooting someone, or a failure to act, such as failing to take proper precautions while driving a car.

adjudication The determination of guilt or innocence; a judgment concerning criminal charges. The majority of offenders charged plead guilty; of the remainder, some cases are adjudicated by a judge and a jury, some are adjudicated by a judge without a jury, and others are dismissed.

adversarial procedure The procedure used to determine truth in the adjudication of guilt or innocence in which the defense (advocate for the accused) is pitted against the prosecution (advocate for the state), with the judge acting as arbiter of the legal rules. Under the adversary system, the burden is on the state to prove the charges beyond a reasonable doubt. This system of having the two parties publicly debate has proved to be the most effective method of achieving the truth regarding a set of circumstances. (Under the accusatory, or inquisitorial, system, which is used in continental Europe, the charge is evidence of guilt that the accused must disprove; the judge takes an active part in the proceedings.)

al Qaeda A terrorist network strongly opposed to the United States that distributes money and tactical support and training to a wide variety of radical Islamic terrorist groups.

appellate court A court that reconsiders a case that has already been tried in order to determine whether the measures used complied with accepted rules of criminal procedure and were in line with constitutional doctrines.

assigned counsel A lawyer appointed by the court to represent a defendant in a criminal case because the person is too poor to hire counsel.

Auburn system The prison system developed in New York during the nineteenth century that stressed congregate working conditions.

augmented reality (AR) technology Wearable components that supply computer-generated virtual information.

bail The monetary amount for or condition of pretrial release, normally set by a judge at the initial appearance. The purpose of bail is to ensure the return of the accused at subsequent proceedings.

Bail Reform Act of 1984 Federal legislation that provides for both greater emphasis on release on recognizance for nondangerous offenders and preventive detention for those who present a menace to the community.

bench trial The trial of a criminal matter by a judge only. The accused waives any constitutional right to trial by jury.

bill of indictment A written statement charging a defendant with the commission of a crime, drawn up by a prosecuting attorney and considered by a grand jury. If the grand jury finds sufficient evidence to support the indictment, it will issue a "true bill of indictment."

Bill of Rights The first ten amendments to the Constitution.

biosocial theory The school of thought holding that human behavior is a function of the interaction of biochemical, neurological, and genetic factors with environmental stimulus.

blameworthy The culpability or guilt a person maintains for participating in a particular criminal offense.

blue curtain The secretive, insulated police culture that isolates officers from the rest of society.

boot camp A short-term militaristic correctional facility in which inmates undergo intensive physical conditioning and discipline.

broken windows model The term used to describe the role of the police as maintainers of community order and safety.

brutalization effect The belief that capital punishment creates an atmosphere of brutality that enhances, rather than deters, the level of violence in society. The death penalty reinforces the view that violence is an appropriate response to provocation.

Bureau of Alcohol, Tobacco, Firearms, and Explosives (ATF) Federal agency that has jurisdiction over the illegal sales, importation, and criminal misuse of firearms and explosives.

***Carriers* case** A fifteenth-century case that defined the law of theft and reformulated the concept of taking the possession of another.

challenge for cause Removing a juror because he or she is biased or has prior knowledge about a case, or for other reasons that demonstrate the individual's inability to render a fair and impartial judgment in a case.

charge In a criminal case, the judge's instruction to the jurors before deliberation.

child savers Late nineteenth-century reformers in America who developed programs for troubled youths and influenced legislation creating the juvenile justice system.

Children's Aid Society A child-saving organization began by Charles Loring Brace; it took children from the streets in large cities and placed them with farm families on the prairie.

chivalry hypothesis The view that the low female crime and delinquency rates are a reflection of the leniency with which police treat female offenders.

choice theory The school of thought holding that people will engage in delinquent and criminal behavior after weighing the consequences and benefits of their actions. Delinquent behavior is a rational choice made by a motivated offender who perceives the chances of gain outweigh any perceived punishment or loss.

chronic offender A delinquent offender who is arrested five or more times before he or she is eighteen and who stands a good chance of becoming an adult criminal; these offenders are responsible for more than half of all serious crimes.

circumstantial (indirect) evidence Evidence not bearing on the fact in dispute but on various indirect circumstances from which the judge or jury might infer the existence of the fact (for example, if the defendant was seen in the house with wet clothing, that is circumstantial evidence that the person had walked in the rain).

civil law All law that is not criminal, including torts (personal wrongs), contract, property, maritime, and commercial law.

classical theory of crime The view that people choose to commit crime after weighing potential costs and benefits.

collective efficacy Acting cooperatively to solve neighborhood problems. In neighborhoods that maintain collective efficacy, neighbors are active in informal social control activities.

commitment Decision of judge ordering an adjudicated and sentenced juvenile offender to be placed in a correctional facility.

common law Early English law, developed by judges, that incorporated Anglo-Saxon tribal custom, feudal rules and practices, and the everyday rules of behavior of local villages. Common law became the standardized law of the land in England and eventually formed the basis of the criminal law in the United States.

Communications Assistance for Law Enforcement Act (CALEA) A law requiring communication equipment manufacturers to design equipment, facilities, and services that are compatible with electronic surveillance needs.

community service restitution An alternative sanction that requires an offender to work in the community at such tasks as cleaning public parks or working with disabled children in lieu of an incarceration sentence.

community treatment The attempt by correctional agencies to maintain convicted offenders in the community instead of a secure facility; it includes probation, parole, and residential programs.

CompStat A program originated by the New York City police that used carefully collected and analyzed crime data to shape policy and evaluate police effectiveness.

concurrent sentences Prison sentences for two or more criminal acts, served simultaneously and run together.

conflict theory The view that human behavior is shaped by interpersonal conflict and that those who maintain social power will use it to further their own needs.

conflict view of crime (or *critical view of crime*) The belief that the law is controlled by the rich and powerful who shape its content to ensure their continued economic domination of society. The criminal justice system is an instrument of social and economic repression.

confrontation clause The constitutional right of a criminal defendant to see and cross-examine all the witnesses against him or her.

congregate system The Auburn Prison, one of the nation's first correctional facilities, was a congregate system, since most prisoners ate and worked in groups.

consecutive sentences Prison sentences for two or more criminal acts, served one after the other.

consensus view of crime The belief that the majority of citizens in a society share common ideals and work toward a common good and that crimes are acts that are outlawed because they conflict with the rules of the majority and are harmful to society.

constable In medieval England, an appointed official who administered and supervised the legal affairs of a small community.

contingent exclusionary rule A plan that would allow evidence seized in violation of the Fourth Amendment to be used in a court of law.

contract system (attorney) Providing counsel to indigent offenders by having attorneys under contract to the county handle all (or some) such cases.

contract system (convict) The system used early in the twentieth century by which private industry contracted with prison officials for convict labor and set up shops on prison grounds for them to work.

convict-lease system The system whereby the state leased its prisoners to a business for a fixed annual fee and gave up supervision and control.

Court of General Jurisdiction A state or federal court that has jurisdiction over felony offenses and more serious civil cases (i.e., involving more than a dollar amount set by the legislature).

court of last resort A court that handles the final appeal on a matter. The U.S. Supreme Court is the official court of last resort for criminal matters.

courtroom work group The phrase used to denote that all parties in the adversary process work together in a cooperative effort to settle cases with the least amount of effort and conflict.

crime A violation of societal rules of behavior as interpreted and expressed by a criminal legal code created by people holding social and political power. Individuals who violate these rules are subject to sanctions by state authority, social stigma, and loss of status.

crime control perspective A model of criminal justice that emphasizes the control of dangerous offenders and the protection of society. Its advocates call for harsh punishments as a deterrent to crime, such as the death penalty.

criminal justice process The decision-making points from the initial investigation or arrest by police to the eventual release of the offender and his or her reentry into society; the various sequential criminal justice stages through which the offender passes.

criminal procedure The rules and laws that define the operation of the criminal proceedings. Procedural law describes the methods that must be followed in obtaining warrants, investigating offenses, effecting lawful arrests, conducting trials, introducing evidence, sentencing convicted offenders, and reviewing cases by appellate courts.

cross-examination The process in which the defense and the prosecution interrogate witnesses during a trial.

cruel and unusual punishment Physical punishment or punishment that is far in excess of that given to people under similar circumstances and is therefore banned by the Eighth Amendment. The death penalty has so far not been considered cruel and unusual if it is administered in a fair and nondiscriminatory fashion.

cultural transmission The passing of cultural values from one generation to the next.

culture of poverty The crushing lifestyle of slum areas produces a culture of poverty, passed from one generation to the next, marked by apathy, cynicism, feelings of helplessness, and mistrust of social institutions, such as schools, government agencies, and the police.

cybercrime Illegal behavior that targets the security of computer systems and/or the data accessed and processed by computer networks.

cyberterrorism An attack against an enemy nation's technological infrastructure.

cynicism The belief that most people's actions are motivated solely by personal needs and selfishness.

day fees A program requiring probationers to pay in part for the costs of their treatment.

day fine A fine geared to the average daily income of the convicted offender in an effort to bring equity to the sentencing process.

day reporting center (DRC) A nonresidential community-based treatment program.

decriminalization Reducing the penalty for a criminal act but not actually legalizing it.

deinstitutionalization The movement to remove as many offenders as possible from secure confinement and treat them in the community.

demeanor The way in which a person outwardly manifests his or her personality.

Department of Homeland Security (DHS) Federal agency responsible for preventing terrorist attacks within the United States, reducing America's vulnerability to terrorism and minimizing the damage and recovering from attacks that do occur

deposit bail The monetary amount set by a judge at a hearing as a condition of pretrial release, ordering a percentage of the total bond required to be paid by the defendant.

detention The temporary care of a child alleged to be a delinquent or status offender who requires secure custody, pending court disposition.

determinate sentence A fixed term of incarceration, such as three years' imprisonment. Determinate sentences are felt by many to be too restrictive for rehabilitative purposes; the advantage is that offenders know how much time

they have to serve—that is, when they will be released.

deterrent effect Stopping or reducing crime by convincing would-be criminals that they stand a significant risk of being apprehended and punished for their crimes.

developmental theory The view that social interactions developed over the life course shape behavior. Some interactions, such as involvement with deviant peers, encourage law violations, whereas others, such as marriage and military service, may help people desist from crime.

direct examination The questioning of one's own (prosecution or defense) witness during a trial.

directed verdict The right of a judge to direct a jury to acquit a defendant because the state has not proven the elements of the crime or otherwise has not established guilt according to law.

Director of National Intelligence (DNI) Government official charged with coordinating data from the nation's primary intelligence-gathering agencies.

disposition For juvenile offenders, the equivalent of sentencing for adult offenders. The theory is that disposition is more rehabilitative than retributive. Possible dispositions may be to dismiss the case; release the youth to the custody of his or her parents; place the offender on probation; or send him or her to an institution or state correctional institution.

diversion A noncriminal alternative to trial, usually featuring counseling, job training, and educational opportunities.

DNA profiling The identification of criminal suspects by matching DNA samples taken from their person with specimens found at the crime scene.

double marginality The social burden African-American police officers carry by being both minority group members and law enforcement officers

Drug Enforcement Administration (DEA) The federal agency that enforces federal drug control laws.

due process perspective Due process is the basic constitutional principle based on the concept of the privacy of the individual and the complementary concept of limitation on governmental power; a safeguard against arbitrary and unfair state procedures in judicial or administrative proceedings. Embod-

ied in the due process concept are the basic rights of a defendant in criminal proceedings and the requisites for a fair trial. These rights and requirements have been expanded by appellate court decisions and include (1) timely notice of a hearing or trial that informs the accused of the charges against him or her; (2) the opportunity to confront accusers and to present evidence on one's own behalf before an impartial jury or judge; (3) the presumption of innocence under which guilt must be proven by legally obtained evidence and the verdict must be supported by the evidence presented; (4) the right of an accused to be warned of constitutional rights at the earliest stage of the criminal process; (5) protection against self-incrimination; (6) assistance of counsel at every critical stage of the criminal process; and (7) the guarantee that an individual will not be tried more than once for the same offense (double jeopardy).

electronic monitoring (EM) Requiring a convicted offender to wear a monitoring device as part of his or her community sentence. Electronic monitoring is typically part of a house arrest order and enables the probation department to ensure that the offender is complying with court-ordered limitations on his or her freedom.

entrapment A criminal defense that maintains the police originated the criminal idea or initiated the criminal action.

equity The action or practice of awarding each person his or her just due; sanctions based on equity seek to compensate individual victims and the general society for their losses due to crime.

exclusionary rule The principle that prohibits using evidence illegally obtained in a trial. Based on the Fourth Amendment "right of the people to be secure in their persons, houses, papers, and effects, against unreasonable searches and seizures," the rule is not a bar to prosecution because legally obtained evidence may be available that may be used in a trial.

Federal Bureau of Investigation (FBI) The arm of the U.S. Justice Department that investigates violations of federal law, gathers crime statistics, runs a comprehensive crime laboratory, and helps train local law enforcement officers.

felony A more serious offense that carries a penalty of incarceration in a state prison, usually for one year or more. Persons convicted of felony offenses lose such rights as the rights to vote, hold elective office, or maintain certain licenses.

fine   Levying a money payment on offenders to compensate society for their misdeeds.

First Amendment   The U.S. constitutional amendment that guarantees freedom of speech, religion, press, and assembly, and the right of the people to petition the government for a redress of grievances.

foot patrol   Police patrols that take officers out of cars and put them on a walking beat in order to strengthen ties with the community.

forfeiture   The seizure of personal property by the state as a civil or criminal penalty.

furlough   A correctional policy that allows inmates to leave the institution for vocational or educational training, for employment, or to maintain family ties.

general deterrence   A crime control policy that depends on the fear of criminal penalties. General deterrence measures, such as long prison sentences for violent crimes, are aimed at convincing the potential law violator that the pains associated with the crime outweigh the benefits.

Gideon v. Wainwright   The 1963 U.S. Supreme Court case that granted counsel to indigent defendants in felony prosecutions.

globalization   The process of creating transnational markets, politics, and legal systems in order to develop a global economy.

good faith exception   The principle of law holding that evidence may be used in a criminal trial, even though the search warrant used to obtain it is technically faulty, if the police acted in good faith and to the best of their ability when they sought to obtain it from a judge.

grand jury   A type of jury, responsible for investigating alleged crimes, examining evidence, and issuing indictments.

grass eaters   A term to describe police officers who accept payoffs when everyday duties place them in a position to be solicited by the public.

halfway house   A community-based correctional facility that houses inmates before their outright release so that they can become gradually acclimated to conventional society.

hands-off doctrine   The legal practice of allowing prison administrators a free hand to run the institution even if correctional practices violate inmates' constitutional rights; ended with the onset of the prisoners' rights movement in the 1960s.

hearsay evidence   Testimony that is not firsthand but related information told by a second party.

hot spots of crime   Places from which a significant portion of all police calls originate. These hot spots include taverns and housing projects.

house arrest   A form of intermediate sanction that requires that the convicted offender spend a designated amount of time per week in his or her own home—for example, from 5 P.M. Friday until 8 A.M. Monday.

hue and cry   A call for assistance in medieval England. The policy of self-help used in villages demanded that everyone respond if a citizen raised a hue and cry to get their aid.

hulk   A mothballed ship that was used to house prisoners in eighteenth-century England.

hundred   In medieval England, a group of one hundred families that had the responsibility to maintain the order and try minor offenses.

identity theft   Using the Internet to steal someone's identity and/or impersonate them to open a new credit card account or conduct some other financial transaction.

incapacitation   The policy of keeping dangerous criminals in confinement to eliminate the risk of their repeating their offense in society.

indeterminate sentence   A term of incarceration with a stated minimum and maximum length, such as a sentence to prison for a period of from three to ten years. The prisoner would be eligible for parole after the minimum sentence has been served. Based on the belief that sentences should fit the criminal, indeterminate sentences allow individualized sentences and provide for sentencing flexibility. Judges can set a high minimum to override the purpose of the indeterminate sentence.

index (Part I) crimes   The eight crimes that, because of their seriousness and frequency, the FBI reports the incidence of in the annual Uniform Crime Report. Index crimes include murder, rape, assault, robbery, burglary, arson, larceny, and motor vehicle theft.

indigent   Person who is needy and poor or who lacks the means to hire an attorney.

inevitable discovery rule   Evidence seized in violation of the Fifth Amendment's self-incrimination clause may be used in a court of law if a judge rules that it would have been found or discovered even if the incriminating statements had never been made.

in forma pauperis   "In the manner of a pauper." A criminal defendant granted permission to proceed in forma pauperis is entitled to assistance of counsel at state expense.

initial appearance   A juvenile's first appearance before the juvenile court judge in which the charges are reviewed and an effort is made to settle the case without a trial. If the child does not have legal counsel an attorney will be appointed.

inmate social code   An unwritten code of behavior, passed from older inmates to younger ones, which serves as guidelines for appropriate inmate behavior within the correctional institution.

inmate subculture   The loosely defined culture that pervades prisons and has its own norms, rules, and language.

in-presence requirement   The condition that in order to make an arrest in a misdemeanor, the arresting officer must have personally witnessed the crime being committed.

insanity   A legal defense that maintains a defendant was incapable of forming criminal intent because he or she suffers from a defect of reason or mental illness.

intake   The process in which a probation officer settles cases at the initial appearance before the onset of formal criminal proceedings; also, process in which a juvenile referral is received and a decision is made to file a petition in the juvenile court, release the juvenile, or refer the juvenile elsewhere.

intensive probation supervision (IPS)   A type of intermediate sanction involving small probation caseloads and strict monitoring on a daily or weekly basis.

intensive supervision parole (ISP)   A limited-caseload program for those parolees who need intensive surveillance. Parolees are required to meet more often with parole officers than routine parolees and may also have frequent drug testing, serve a term in a community correctional system, and be electronically monitored.

interactionist view of crime Criminal law reflects the values of people who use their social and political power to shape the legal system.

intermediate sanctions The group of punishments falling between probation and prison—"probation plus." Community-based sanctions, including house arrest and intensive supervision, serve as alternatives to incarceration.

internal affairs The branch of the police department that investigates charges of corruption or misconduct made against police officers.

jail A place to detain people awaiting trial, to serve as a lockup for drunks and disorderly individuals, and to confine convicted misdemeanants serving sentences of less than one year.

jailhouse lawyer An inmate trained in law or otherwise educated who helps other inmates prepare legal briefs and appeals.

judicial reprieve The common-law practice that allowed judges to suspend punishment so that convicted offenders could seek a pardon, gather new evidence, or demonstrate that they had reformed their behavior.

jury trial The process of deciding a case by a group of persons selected and sworn in to serve as jurors at a criminal trial, often as a six- or twelve-person jury.

just desert The philosophy of justice asserting that those who violate the rights of others deserve to be punished. The severity of punishment should be commensurate with the seriousness of the crime.

justice of the peace Established in 1326 England, the office was created to help the shire reeve in controlling the county and later took on judicial functions.

justice perspective A view of justice that holds that all people should be treated equally before the law. Equality may be best achieved through the control of individual discretion in the justice process.

juvenile court A court that has original jurisdiction over persons defined by statute as juveniles and alleged to be delinquents or status offenders.

juvenile delinquency Participation in illegal behavior by a minor who falls under a statutory age limit.

Knapp Commission A public body that led an investigation into police corruption in New York and uncovered a widespread network of payoffs and bribes.

landmark decision A decision handed down by the U.S. Supreme Court that becomes the law of the land and serves as a precedent for similar legal issues.

Law Enforcement Assistance Administration (LEAA) Funded by the federal government's Safe Streets Act, this agency provided technical assistance and hundreds of millions of dollars in aid to local and state justice agencies between 1969 and 1982.

legalization The removal of all criminal penalties from a previously outlawed act.

lex talionis (Latin for "law as retaliation") From Hammurabi's ancient legal code, the belief that the purpose of the law is to provide retaliation for an offended party and that the punishment should fit the crime.

life history A research method that uses the experiences of an individual as the unit of analysis, such as using the life experience of an individual gang member to understand the natural history of gang membership.

mala in se A term that refers to acts that society considers inherently evil, such as murder or rape, and that violate the basic principles of Judeo-Christian morality.

mala prohibitum Crimes created by legislative bodies that reflect prevailing moral beliefs and practices.

mandatory sentence A statutory requirement that a certain penalty shall be set and carried out in all cases on conviction for a specified offense or series of offenses.

Manhattan Bail Project The innovative experiment in bail reform that introduced and successfully tested the concept of release on recognizance.

maximum-security prison A correctional institution that houses dangerous felons and maintains strict security measures, high walls, and limited contact with the outside world.

meat eaters A term used to describe police officers who actively solicit bribes and vigorously engage in corrupt practices.

medical model A view of corrections holding that convicted offenders are victims of their environment who need care and treatment to transform them into valuable members of society.

medium-security prison A less secure institution that houses nonviolent offenders and provides more opportunities for contact with the outside world.

mens rea Guilty mind. The mental element of a crime or the intent to commit a criminal act.

minimum-security prison The least secure institution that houses white-collar and nonviolent offenders, maintains few security measures, and has liberal furlough and visitation policies.

misdemeanor A minor crime usually punished by less than one year's imprisonment in a local institution, such as a county jail.

Missouri Plan A way of picking judges through nonpartisan elections as a means of ensuring judicial performance standards.

Mollen Commission An investigatory body formed in New York City in 1993 to scrutinize police misconduct.

monetary restitution A sanction that requires that convicted offenders compensate crime victims by reimbursing them for out-of-pocket losses caused by the crime. Losses can include property damage, lost wages, and medical costs.

moral entrepreneurs People who wage moral crusades to control criminal law so that it reflects their own personal values.

National Commission on Terrorist Attacks Upon the United States An independent, bipartisan commission created in 2002, which prepared an in-depth report of the events leading up to the 9/11 attacks.

National Crime Victimization Survey (NCVS) The ongoing victimization study conducted jointly by the Justice Department and the U.S. Census Bureau that surveys victims about their experiences with law violation.

neighborhood-oriented policing (NOP) Community policing efforts aimed at individual neighborhoods.

no bill The action by a grand jury when it votes not to indict an accused suspect.

no-frills policy A correctional policy that stipulates that prisons are aimed at punishing and not coddling inmates. A "no-frills" orientation usually means a strict regimen of work and discipline, and reduced opportunities for recreation and education.

nolle prosequi The term used when a prosecutor decides to drop a case after a complaint has been formally made. Reasons for a nolle prosequi include evidence insufficiency, reluctance of witnesses to testify, police error, and office policy.

nonindex (Part II) crimes All other crimes except the eight index crimes recorded by the FBI. The FBI records all arrests made by police of Part II crimes.

nonintervention perspective A justice philosophy that emphasizes the least intrusive treatment possible. Among its central policies are decarceration, diversion, and decriminalization. In other words, less is better.

obitiatry Helping people take their own lives.

official crime statistics Compiled by the FBI in its Uniform Crime Reports, these are a tally of serious crimes reported to police agencies each year.

parens patriae Latin term meaning "father of his country." According to this legal philosophy, the government is the guardian of everyone who has a disability, especially children, and has a legal duty to act in their best interests until the age of majority.

parental efficacy The ability of parents to provide support and discipline in a noncoercive manner.

parole The early release of a prisoner from imprisonment subject to conditions set by a parole board. Depending on the jurisdiction, inmates must serve a certain portion of their sentences before becoming eligible for parole. The conditions of parole may require the individual to report regularly to a parole officer, to refrain from criminal conduct, to maintain and support his or her family, to avoid contact with other convicted criminals, to abstain from using alcohol and drugs, to remain within the jurisdiction, and so on. Violations of the conditions of parole may result in revocation of parole, in which case the individual will be returned to prison. The concept behind parole is to allow the release of the offender to community supervision, where rehabilitation and readjustment will be facilitated.

penal harm The view that prison should be a punishing experience and that criminals will be deterred from crime and current inmates will be encouraged to go straight.

penitentiary A state or federal correctional institution for incarceration of felony offenders for terms of one year or more.

penitentiary house A secure correctional facility, based on the Quaker concept that incarcerated criminals should experience penitence.

penumbral crimes Criminal acts defined by a high level of public noncompliance with the stated legal standard, an absence of stigma associated with violation of the stated standard, and a low level of law enforcement or public sanction.

peremptory challenge The dismissal of a potential juror by either the prosecution or the defense for unexplained, discretionary reasons.

phishing Slang for the processes used to acquire personal information used for identity theft and other fraudulent activities.

police brutality Usually involves such actions as the use of abusive language, unnecessary use of force or coercion, threats, prodding with nightsticks, stopping and searching people to harass them, and so on.

police chief The top administrator of the police department, who sets policy and has general control over departmental policies and practices. The chief is typically a political rather than civil service appointee and serves at the pleasure of the mayor.

police-community relations (PCR) Programs developed by police departments to improve relations with the community and develop cooperation with citizens. The forerunner of the community policing model.

poor laws Seventeenth-century laws in England that bound out vagrants and abandoned children as indentured servants to masters.

positive stage During the positive stage of human social development, people embrace rational scientific explanations for observed phenomenon.

preponderance of the evidence The level of proof in civil cases; more than half the evidence supports the allegations of one side.

pre-sentence investigation An investigation performed by a probation officer attached to a trial court after the conviction of a defendant. The report contains information about the defendant's background, education, previous employment, and family; his or her own statement concerning the offense; prior criminal record; interviews with neighbors or acquaintances; and his or her mental and physical condition (that is, information that would not be made public record in the case of guilty plea or that would be inadmissible as evidence at a trial but could be influential and important at the sentencing stage).

presentment The report of a grand jury investigation, which usually includes a recommendation of indictment.

pretrial detention Holding an offender in secure confinement before trial.

pretrial diversion A program that provides nonpunitive, community-based alternatives to more intrusive forms of punishment such as jail or prison.

pretrial procedures Critical pretrial processes and decisions, including bail, arraignment, and plea negotiation

preventive detention The practice of holding dangerous suspects before trial without bail.

prison A state or federal correctional institution for incarceration of felony offenders for terms of one year or more.

prisonization Assimilation into the separate culture in the prison that has its own set of rewards and behaviors. This loosely defined culture that pervades prisons has its own norms, rules, and language. The traditional culture is now being replaced by a violent gang culture.

pro se The defense of self-representation.

proactive policing A police department policy emphasizing stopping crimes before they occur rather than reacting to crimes that have already occurred.

probable cause The evidentiary criterion necessary to sustain an arrest or the issuance of an arrest or search warrant; less than absolute certainty or "beyond a reasonable doubt" but greater than mere suspicion or "hunch." Probable cause consists of a set of facts, information, circumstances, or conditions that would lead a reasonable person to believe that an offense was committed and that the accused committed that offense. An arrest made without probable cause may be susceptible to prosecution as an illegal arrest under "false imprisonment" statutes.

probation A sentence entailing the conditional release of a convicted offender into the community under the supervision of the court (in the form of a probation officer), subject to certain conditions for a specified time. The conditions are usually similar to those of parole. (*Note:* Probation is a sentence, an alternative to incarceration; parole is administrative release from incarceration.) Violation of the conditions of probation may result in revocation of probation.

probation rules Conditions or restrictions mandated by the court which must be obeyed by a probationer.

problem-oriented policing A style of police operations that stresses proactive problem solving, rather than reactive crime fighting.

proof beyond a reasonable doubt The standard of proof needed to convict in a criminal case. The evidence offered in court does not have to amount to absolute certainty, but it should leave no reasonable doubt that the defendant committed the alleged crime.

prosecutor Representative of the state (executive branch) in criminal proceedings; advocate for the state's case—the charge—in the adversary trial, for example, the attorney general of the United States, U.S. attorneys, attorneys general of the states, district attorneys, and police prosecutors. The prosecutor participates in investigations both before and after arrest, prepares legal documents, participates in obtaining arrest or search warrants, decides whether to charge a suspect and, if so, with which offense. The prosecutor argues the state's case at trial, advises the police, participates in plea negotiations, and makes sentencing recommendations.

psychopathic (antisocial, sociopathic) personality Psychopaths are chronically antisocial individuals who are always in trouble, and who do not learn from either experience or punishment. They are loners who engage in frequent callous and hedonistic behaviors, are emotionally immature, and lack responsibility, judgment, and empathy.

public defender An attorney generally employed (at no cost to the accused) by the government to represent poor persons accused of a crime.

public safety doctrine Statements elicited by police violation of the Fifth Amendment's self-incrimination clause may be used in a court of law if a judge rules that the questioning was justified in order to maintain public safety. So, for example, it would be permissible for police to ask a suspected terrorist where he planted a bomb and then use his statement in a criminal trial even though he had never been apprised of his Fifth Amendment (Miranda) rights.

real evidence Any object produced for inspection at the trial (such as a weapon or photograph).

recidivism Repetition of criminal behavior; habitual criminality. Recidivism is measured by (1) criminal acts that resulted in conviction by a court when committed by individuals who are under correctional supervision or who had been released from correctional supervision within the previous three years and (2) technical violations of probation or parole in which a sentencing or paroling authority took action that resulted in an adverse change in the offender's legal status.

recognizance During the Middle Ages, the practice of letting convicted offenders remain free if they agreed to enter a debt relation with the state to pay for their crimes.

rehabilitation perspective A model of criminal justice that views its primary purpose as helping to care for people who cannot manage themselves. Crime is an expression of frustration and anger created by social inequality that can be controlled by giving people the means to improve their lifestyle through conventional endeavors.

release on recognizance (ROR) A nonmonetary condition for the pretrial release of an accused individual; an alternative to monetary bail that is granted after the court determines that the accused has ties in the community, has no prior record of default, and is likely to appear at subsequent proceedings.

residential community corrections (RCC) A nonsecure facility, located in the community, that houses probationers who need a more secure environment. Typically, residents are free during the day to go to work, school, or treatment, and return in the evening for counseling sessions and meals.

restitution A condition of probation in which the offender repays society or the victim of crime for the trouble the offender caused.

restorative justice A view of criminal justice that focuses on crime as an act against the community rather than the state. Justice should involve all parties who are affected by crime—victims, criminals, law enforcement, and the community.

restorative justice perspective A view of criminal justice that advocates peaceful solutions and mediation rather than coercive punishments.

revocation An administrative act performed by a parole authority that removes a person from parole, or a judicial order by a court removing a person from parole or probation, in response to a violation on the part of the parolee or probationer.

risk classification Classifying probationers so that they may receive an appropriate level of treatment and control.

search warrant An order issued by a judge, directing officers to conduct a search of specified premises for specified objects or persons and bring them before the court.

Secret Service Federal law enforcement agency charged with enforcing laws against counterfeiting and protecting the lives of important political figures, including the president and the vice president and their families.

self-defense A legal defense in which defendants claim that their behavior was legally justified by the necessity to protect their own life and property or that of another victim from potential harm.

sentencing circles A type of sentencing in which victims, family members, community members, and the offender participate in an effort to devise fair and reasonable sanctions that are ultimately aimed at reintegrating the offender back into the community.

sheriff The chief law enforcement officer in a county.

shire reeve In medieval England, the senior law enforcement figure in a county; the forerunner of today's sheriff.

shock incarceration A short prison sentence served in boot camp–type facilities.

shock probation A sentence in which offenders serve a short prison term before they begin probation, to impress them with the pains of imprisonment.

six-person jury The criminal trial of a defendant before a jury of six persons as opposed to a traditional jury of twelve persons.

Sixth Amendment The U.S. constitutional amendment containing various criminal trial rights, such as the right to public trial, right to trial by jury, and the right to confrontation of witnesses.

social control The process of external regulation of individual and/or group behavior. Social control can be informal, and applied through sanctions (or rewards) employed by families, neighbors, peers, and so on. There is also formal social control, which is applied by the justice system through the legal process.

social learning The view that behavior patterns are modeled and learned in interactions with others.

social process theory The view that an individual's interactions with key social institutions—family, school, peer group—shape behavior.

social structure theory The view that a person's position in the social structure controls behavior. Those in the lowest socioeconomic tier are more likely to succumb to crime-promoting elements in their environment, whereas those in the highest tier enjoy social and economic advantages that insulate them from crime-producing forces.

specific deterrence A crime control policy suggesting that punishment should be severe enough to convince convicted offenders never to repeat their criminal activity.

split sentence A practice that requires convicted criminals to spend a portion of their sentence behind bars and the remainder in the community.

stalking The willful, malicious, and repeated following and harassing of another person.

stare decisis To stand by decided cases. The legal principle by which the decision or holding in an earlier case becomes the standard by which subsequent similar cases are judged.

state courts of limited jurisdiction/ lower court Generic terms referring to courts that have jurisdiction over misdemeanors and conduct preliminary investigations of felony charges.

status offender A juvenile who has been adjudicated by a judge of a juvenile court as having committed a status offense (running away, truancy, or incorrigibility).

sting operation An undercover police operation in which police pose as criminals to trap law violators.

stop and frisk The situation when police officers who are suspicious of an individual run their hands lightly over the suspect's outer garments, to determine whether the person is carrying a concealed weapon. Also called a patdown or threshold inquiry, a stop and frisk is intended to stop short of any activity that could be considered a violation of Fourth Amendment rights.

Strickland v. Washington The 1984 U.S. Supreme Court decision upholding that defendants have the right to reasonably effective assistance of counsel (that is, competent representation).

strict liability crime Illegal act whose elements do not contain the need for intent or mens rea; usually, acts that endanger the public welfare, such as illegal dumping of toxic wastes.

subculture A substrata of society that maintains a unique set of values and beliefs.

substantive criminal law A body of specific rules that declare what conduct is criminal and prescribe the punishment to be imposed for such conduct.

substantive rights Through a slow process of legal review, the courts have granted inmates a number of civil rights, including the rights to receive mail and medical benefits and to practice their religion.

suicide by cop A form of suicide in which a person acts in an aggressive manner with police officers in order to induce them to shoot to kill.

super-maximum-security prison The newest form of a maximum-security prison that uses high-level security measures to incapacitate the nation's most dangerous criminals. Most inmates are in twenty-three hours per day lockdown.

sureties During the Middle Ages, people who made themselves responsible for the behavior of offenders released in their care.

suspended sentence A prison term that is delayed while the defendant undergoes a period of community treatment. If the treatment is successful, the prison sentence is terminated.

terrorism Premeditated, politically motivated violence perpetrated against noncombatant targets by subnational groups or clandestine agents.

tier system The structure of early prisons having numerous floors or wings that stacked cells one over another.

time-in-rank system For police officers to advance in rank they must spend an appropriate amount of time, usually years, in the preceding rank—that is, to become a captain, an officer must first spend time as a lieutenant.

tithing In medieval England, a group of ten families who collectively dealt with minor disturbances and breaches of the peace.

tort A personal injury or wrong for which an action for damages may be brought.

total institution A regimented, dehumanizing institution such as a prison in which like-situated people are kept in social isolation, cut off from the world at large.

transfer hearing The hearing in which a decision is made to waive a juvenile to the criminal court. Waiver decisions are based on such criteria as the child's age, prior offense history, and the nature of the offense.

treatment The rehabilitative method used to effect a change of behavior in the juvenile offender, in the form of therapy, or educational or vocational programs.

true bill The action by a grand jury when it votes to indict an accused suspect.

truth in sentencing A new sentencing scheme which requires that offenders serve at least 85 percent of their original sentence before being eligible for parole or other forms of early release.

Uniform Crime Report (UCR) The FBI's yearly publication of where, when, and how much serious crime occurred in the prior year.

U. S. Marshals Service Federal agency whose jurisdiction includes protecting federal officials, transporting criminal defendants, and tracking down fugitives.

USA Patriot Act (USAPA) The law designed to grant new powers to domestic law enforcement and international intelligence agencies in an effort to fight terrorism.

venire The group called for jury duty from which jury panels are selected.

verdict A finding of a jury or a judge on questions of fact at a trial.

victim impact statement A postconviction statement by the victim of crime that may be used to guide sentencing decisions.

victimless crime An act that is in violation of society's moral code and therefore has been outlawed—for example, drug abuse, gambling, and prostitution. These acts are linked together because, although they have no external victim, they are considered harmful to the social fabric.

vigilantes A citizen group who tracked down wanted criminals in the Old West.

voir dire The process in which a potential jury panel is questioned by the prosecution and the defense in order to select jurors who are unbiased and objective.

waiver (juvenile) A practice in which the juvenile court waives its jurisdiction over a juvenile and transfers the case to adult criminal court for trial. In some states a waiver hearing is held to determine jurisdiction, while in others juveniles may be automatically waived if they are accused of committing a serious crime such as murder.

Walnut Street Jail In 1790, a separate wing of Philadelphia's Walnut Street Jail was built to house convicted felons. This was the forerunner of the secure correctional system in the United States.

watch system During the Middle Ages in England, men were organized in church parishes to guard at night against disturbances and breaches of the peace under the direction of the local constable.

wergild Under medieval law, the money paid by the offender to compensate the victim and the state for a criminal offense.

widening the net of justice The charge that programs designed to divert offenders from the justice system actually enmesh them further in the process by substituting more intrusive treatment programs for less intrusive punishment-oriented outcomes.

work release A prison treatment program that allows inmates to be released during the day to work in the community and returned to prison at night.

writ of certiorari An order of superior court requesting that the record of an inferior court (or administrative body) be brought forward for review or inspection.

writ of habeas corpus A judicial order requesting that a person detaining another produce the body of the prisoner and give reasons for his or her capture and detention. Habeas corpus is a legal device used to request that a judicial body review the reasons for a person's confinement and the conditions of confinement. Habeas corpus is known as "the great writ."

zero tolerance The practice of seizing all instrumentalities of a crime, including homes, boats, and cars. It is an extreme example of the law of forfeiture.

Notes

Chapter 1

1. This section leans heavily on Ted Robert Gurr, "Historical Trends in Violent Crime: A Critical Review of the Evidence," in *Crime and Justice: An Annual Review of Research*, vol. 3, eds. Michael Tonry and Norval Morris (Chicago: University of Chicago Press, 1981); Richard Maxwell Brown, "Historical Patterns of American Violence," in *Violence in America: Historical and Comparative Perspectives*, eds. Hugh Davis Graham and Ted Robert Gurr (Beverly Hills, Calif.: Sage, 1979), 18–29.
2. Samuel Walker, *Popular Justice* (New York: Oxford University Press, 1980).
3. Ibid.
4. For an insightful analysis of this effort, see Samuel Walker, "Origins of the Contemporary Criminal Justice Paradigm: The American Bar Foundation Survey, 1953–1969," *Justice Quarterly* 9 (1992): 47–76.
5. President's Commission on Law Enforcement and the Administration of Justice, *The Challenge of Crime in a Free Society* (Washington, D.C.: Government Printing Office, 1967).
6. See Public Law No. 90-351, *Title I–Omnibus Crime Control Safe Streets Act of 1968*, 90th Congress, June 19, 1968.
7. For a review, see Kevin Wright, "Twenty-Two Years of Federal Investment in Criminal Justice Research: The National Institute of Justice, 1968–1989," *Journal of Criminal Justice 22* (1994): 27–40.
8. Federal Bureau of Investigation, *Crime in the United States, 2004* (Washington, D.C.: Government Printing Office, 2005), 208.
9. Office of Juvenile Justice and Delinquency Prevention, *Statistical Briefing Book*, http://ojjdp.ncjrs.org/ojstatbb/court/qa06203.asp?qaDate=20030811, accessed on February 10, 2005.
10. For an analysis of this issue, see William Wilbanks, *The Myth of a Racist Criminal Justice System* (Monterey, Calif.: Brooks/Cole, 1987); Stephen Klein, Joan Petersilia, and Susan Turner, "Race and Imprisonment Decisions in California," *Science 247* (1990): 812–816; Alfred Blumstein, "On the Racial Disproportionality of the United States Prison Population," *Journal of Criminal Law and Criminology 73* (1982): 1259–1281; Darnell Hawkins, "Race, Crime Type, and Imprisonment," *Justice Quarterly 3* (1986): 251–269.
11. Herbert L. Packer, *The Limits of the Criminal Sanction* (Stanford, Calif.: Stanford University Press, 1975), 21.
12. Matthew DuRose and Patrick Langan, *Felony Sentences in State Courts, 2002* (Washington, D.C.: Bureau of Justice Statistics, 2004).
13. James Eisenstein and Herbert Jacob, *Felony Justice* (Boston: Little, Brown, 1977); Peter Nardulli, *The Courtroom Elite* (Cambridge, Mass.: Ballinger, 1978); Paul Wice, *Chaos in the Courthouse* (New York: Praeger, 1985); Marcia Lipetz, *Routine Justice: Processing Cases in Women's Court* (New Brunswick, N.J.: Transaction Books, 1983).
14. Samuel Walker, *Sense and Nonsense About Crime* (Belmont, Calif.: Wadsworth, 1985).
15. Malcolm Feeley, *The Process Is the Punishment* (New York: Russell Sage, 1979).
16. John DiLulio, *No Escape: The Future of American Corrections* (New York: Basic Books, 1991).
17. Karen Parker and Patricia McCall, "Structural Conditions and Racial Homicide Patterns: A Look at the Multiple Disadvantages in Urban Areas," *Criminology 37* (1999): 447–448.
18. Francis Cullen, John Paul Wright, and Mitchell Chamlin, "Social Support and Social Reform: A Progressive Crime Control Agenda," *Crime and Delinquency 45* (1999): 188–207.
19. Jane Sprott, "Are Members of the Public Tough on Crime? The Dimensions of Public 'Punitiveness,'" *Journal of Criminal Justice 27* (1999): 467–474.
20. Packer, *The Limits of the Criminal Sanction,* 175.
21. "DNA Testing Has Exonerated 28 Prison Inmates, Study Finds," *Criminal Justice Newsletter,* June 17, 1996, 2.
22. Caitlin Lovinger, "Death Row's Living Alumni," *New York Times,* August 22, 1999, 1.
23. Eric Stewart, Ronald Simons, Rand Conger, and Laura Scaramella, "Beyond the Interactional Relationship Between Delinquency and Parenting Practices: The Contribution of Legal Sanctions," *Journal of Research in Crime and Delinquency 39* (2002): 36–60.
24. Cassia Spohn and David Holleran, "The Effect of Imprisonment on Recidivism Rates of Felony Offenders: A Focus on Drug Offenders," *Criminology 40* (2002): 329–359.
25. *Doe v. Pryor M.D. Ala,* Civ.No. 99-T-730-N, Thompson, J. 8/16/99.
26. This section is based on Paula M. Ditton and Doris James Wilson, *Truth in Sentencing in State Prisons* (Washington, D.C.: Bureau of Justice Statistics, 1999).
27. Herbert Bianchi, *Justice as Sanctuary* (Bloomington: Indiana University Press, 1994); Nils Christie, "Conflicts as Property," *British Journal of Criminology 17* (1977): 1–15; L. Hulsman, "Critical Criminology and the Concept of Crime," *Contemporary Crises 10* (1986): 63–80.
28. Larry Tifft, foreword to *The Mask of Love,* by Dennis Sullivan (Port Washington, N.Y.: Kennikat Press, 1980), 6.
29. Christopher Cooper, "Patrol Police Officer Conflict Resolution Processes," *Journal of Criminal Justice 25* (1997): 87–101.
30. This section leans heavily on Joycelyn M. Pollock, *Ethics in Crime and Justice: Dilemmas and Decisions, 4th Ed.* (Belmont, Calif.: Wadsworth, 2004).
31. International Association of Chiefs of Police, 2005.
32. Allen Beck and Timothy Hughes, *Prison Rape Elimination Act of 2003, Sexual Violence Reported by Correctional Authorities, 2004* (Washington, D.C.: Bureau of Justice Statistics, 2005).

Chapter 2

1. For a general discussion of Marxist thought on criminal law, see Michael Lynch, Raymond Michalowski, and W. Byron Groves, *The New Primer in Radical Criminology: Critical Perspectives on Crime, Power, and Identity,* 3rd ed. (Monsey, N.Y.: Criminal Justice Press, 2000).
2. The National Council on Alcoholism and Drug Dependence, www.ncadd.org (accessed on May 18, 2005).
3. Ibid.
4. The data used in this chapter comes from Federal Bureau of Investigation, *Crime in the United States, 2004* Preliminary Data (Washington, D.C.: Government Printing Office, 2005). Hereinafter cited in notes as FBI, Uniform Crime Report, and referred to in text as Uniform Crime Report, or UCR.

5. Ibid.

6. Duncan Chappell, Gilbert Geis, Stephen Schafer, and Larry Siegel, "Forcible Rape: A Comparative Study of Offenses Known to the Police in Boston and Los Angeles," in *Studies in the Sociology of Sex*, ed. James Henslin (New York: Appleton-Century-Crofts, 1971), 169–193.

7. Dana Peterson, Terrance Taylor, and Finn-Aage Esbensen, "Gang Membership and Violent Victimization," *Justice Quarterly 21* (2004): 793–816.

8. Data from the NCVS used in this chapter comes from Shannan Catalano, *Criminal Victimization 2005* (Washington, D.C.: Bureau of Justice Statistics, 2005). Hereinafter cited as *Criminal Victimization*.

9. Ibid.

10. See, for example, Lloyd Bachman, Patrick O'Malley, and Jerald Bachman, *Monitoring the Future, 2004* (Ann Arbor: University of Michigan, Institute for Social Research, 2005).

11. A pioneering effort in self-report research is A. L. Porterfield, *Youth in Trouble* (Fort Worth, Tex.: Leo Potishman Foundation, 1946); for a review, see Robert Hardt and George Bodine, *Development of Self-Report Instruments in Delinquency Research: A Conference Report* (Syracuse, N.Y.: Syracuse University Youth Development Center, 1965). See also Fred Murphy, Mary Shirley, and Helen Witner, "The Incidence of Hidden Delinquency," *American Journal of Orthopsychology 16* (1946): 686–696.

12. Franklyn Dunford and Delbert Elliott, "Identifying Career Criminals Using Self-Reported Data," *Journal of Research in Crime and Delinquency 21* (1983): 57–86.

13. Leonore Simon, "Validity and Reliability of Violent Juveniles: A Comparison of Juvenile Self-Reports with Adult Self-Reports" (paper presented at the meeting of the American Society of Criminology, Boston, November 1995), 26.

14. Stephen Cernkovich, Peggy Giordano, and Meredith Pugh, "Chronic Offenders: The Missing Cases in Self-Report Delinquency," *Criminology 76* (1985): 705–732.

15. Eric Wish, Thomas Gray, and Eliot Levine, *Recent Drug Use in Female Juvenile Detainees: Estimates from Interviews, Urinalysis, and Hair Analysis* (College Park, Md.: Center for Substance Abuse Research, 1996); Thomas Gray and Eric Wish, *Maryland Youth at Risk: A Study of Drug Use in Juvenile Detainees* (College Park, Md.: Center for Substance Abuse Research, 1993).

16. See, for example, Spencer Rathus and Larry Siegel, "Crime and Personality Revisited: Effects of MMPI Sets on Self-Report Studies," *Criminology 18* (1980): 245–251; John Clark and Larry Tifft, "Polygraph and Interview Validation of Self-Reported Deviant Behavior," *American Sociological Review 31* (1966): 516–523.

17. Charles Katz, Vincent Webb, and Scott Decker, "Using the Arrestee Drug Abuse Monitoring (ADAM) program to further understand the relationship between drug use and gang membership," *Justice Quarterly 22* (2005): 58–88.

18. Mallie Paschall, Miriam Ornstein, and Robert Flewelling, "African-American Male Adolescents' Involvement in the Criminal Justice System: The Criterion Validity of Self-Report Measures in Prospective Study," *Journal of Research in Crime and Delinquency 38* (2001): 174–187.

19. Dean Dabney, Richard Hollinger, and Laura Dugan, "Who Actually Steals? A Study of Covertly Observed Shoplifters," *Justice Quarterly 21* (2004): 693–729.

20. Emily Gaarder and Joanne Belknap, "Tenuous Borders: Girls Transferred to Adult Court," *Criminology 40* (2002): 481–517.

21. Carl Klockars, *The Professional Fence* (New York: Free Press, 1976); Darrell Steffensmeier, *The Fence: In the Shadow of Two Worlds* (Totowa, N.J.: Rowman and Littlefield, 1986).

22. Alfred Blumstein, Jacqueline Cohen, and Richard Rosenfeld, "Trend and Deviation in Crime Rates: A Comparison of UCR and NCVS Data for Burglary and Robbery," *Criminology 29* (1991): 237–248.

23. Clarence Schrag, *Crime and Justice: American Style* (Washington, D.C.: Government Printing Office, 1971), 17.

24. Thomas Bernard, "Juvenile Crime and the Transformation of Juvenile Justice: Is There a Juvenile Crime Wave?" *Justice Quarterly 16* (1999): 336–356.

25. Catalano, *Criminal Victimization*.

26. Kenneth J. Litwin, "A Multilevel Multivariate Analysis of Factors Affecting Homicide Clearances," *Journal of Research in Crime and Delinquency 41*, November 2004: 327–351; Janice Puckett and Richard Lundman, "Factors Affecting Homicide Clearances: Multivariate Analysis of a More Complete Conceptual Framework," *Journal of Research in Crime and Delinquency 40* (2003): 171–193.

27. For example, the following studies have noted the great discrepancy between official statistics and self-report studies: Martin Gold, "Undetected Delinquent Behavior," *Journal of Research in Crime and Delinquency 3* (1966): 27–46; James Short and F. Ivan Nye, "Extent of Undetected Delinquency, Tentative Conclusions," *Journal of Criminal Law, Criminology and Police Science 49* (1958): 296–302; Michael Hindelang, "Causes of Delinquency: A Partial Replication and Extension," *Social Problems 20* (1973): 471–487.

28. Lloyd Johnston, Patrick O'Malley, Jerald Bachman, and J. and J. E. Schulenberg, "Overall teen drug use continues gradual decline; but use of inhalants rises," press release, University of Michigan News and Information Services, Ann Arbor, December 21, 2004.

29. James A. Fox, *Trends in Juvenile Violence: A Report to the United States Attorney General on Current and Future Rates of Juvenile Offending* (Boston: Northeastern University, 1996).

30. Steven Levitt, "The Limited Role of Changing Age Structure in Explaining Aggregate Crime Rates," *Criminology 37* (1999): 581–599.

31. Darrell Steffensmeier and Miles Harer, "Making Sense of Recent U.S. Crime Trend Composition Effects and Other Explanations," *Journal of Research in Crime and Delinquency 36* (1999): 235–274.

32. Daniel Mears, Matthew Ploeger, and Mark Warr, "Explaining the Gender Gap in Delinquency: Peer Influence and Moral Evaluations of Behavior," *Journal of Research in Crime and Delinquency 35* (1998): 251–266.

33. Freda Adler, *Sisters in Crime* (New York: McGraw-Hill, 1975); Rita James Simon, *The Contemporary Woman and Crime* (Washington, D.C.: Government Printing Office, 1975).

34. Finn-Aage Esbensen and Elizabeth Piper Deschenes, "A Multisite Examination of Youth Gang Membership: Does Gender Matter?" *Criminology 36* (1998): 799–828.

35. David Jacobs and Katherine Woods, "Interracial Conflict and Interracial Homicide: Do Political and Economic Rivalries Explain White Killings of Blacks and Black Killings of Whites?" *American Journal of Sociology 105* (1999): 157–190.

36. Robert Agnew, "A General Strain Theory of Community Differences in Crime Rates," *Journal of Research in Crime and Delinquency 36* (1999): 123–155.

37. Bonita Veysey and Steven Messner, "Further Testing of Social Disorganization Theory: An Elaboration of Sampson and Groves's Community Structure and Crime," *Journal of Research in Crime and Delinquency 36* (1999): 156–174.

38. Judith Blau and Peter Blau, "The Cost of Inequality: Metropolitan Structure and Violent Crime," *American Sociological Review 47* (1982): 114–129.

39. Herman Schwendinger and Julia Schwendinger, "The Paradigmatic Crisis in Delinquency Theory," *Crime and Social Justice 18* (1982): 70–78.

40. Michael Gottfredson and Travis Hirschi, "The True Value of Lambda Would Appear to Be Zero: An Essay on Career Criminals, Criminal Careers, Selective Incapacitation, Cohort Studies and Related Topics," *Criminology 24* (1986): 213–234; further support for their position can be found in Lawrence Cohen and Kenneth Land, "Age Structure and Crime," *American Sociological Review 52* (1987): 170–183.

41. Marvin Wolfgang, Robert Figlio, and Thorsten Sellin, *Delinquency in a Birth Cohort* (Chicago: University of Chicago Press, 1972).

42. Marvin Wolfgang, Terence Thornberry, and Robert Figlio, *From Boy to Man, from Delinquency to Crime* (Chicago: University of Chicago Press, 1996).

43. Kimberly Kempf-Leonard, Paul Tracy, and James Howell, "Serious, Violent, and Chronic Juvenile Offenders: The Relationship of Delinquency Career Types to Adult Criminality," *Justice Quarterly 18* (2001): 449–478.

44. Centers for Disease Control, "Homicide Among Young Black Males—United States, 1978–1987," *Morbidity and Mortality Weekly Report 39* (1990): 869–873.

45. Janet Lauritsen and Kenna Davis Quinet, "Repeat Victimizations Among Adolescents and Young Adults," *Journal of Quantitative Criminology 11* (1995): 143–163.

46. Denise Osborn, Dan Ellingworth, Tim Hope, and Alan Trickett, "Are Repeatedly Victimized Households Different?" *Journal of Quantitative Criminology 12* (1996): 223–245.

47. Terry Buss and Rashid Abdu, "Repeat Victims of Violence in an Urban Trauma Center," *Violence and Victims 10* (1995): 183–187.

48. Graham Farrell, "Predicting and Preventing Revictimization," in *Crime and Justice: An Annual Review of Research*, vol. 20, eds. Michael Tonry and David Farrington (Chicago: University of Chicago Press, 1995), 61–126.

49. Cesare Beccaria, *On Crimes and Punishments and Other Writings (Cambridge Texts in the History of Political Thought)*, trans. Richard Bellamy (London: Cambridge University Press, 1995).

50. Lawrence Cohen and Richard Machalek, "A General Theory of Expropriative Crime: An Evolutionary Ecological Approach," *American Journal of Sociology 94* (1988): 465–501.

51. Greg Pogarsky, KiDeuk Kim, and Ray Paternoster, "Perceptual change in the national youth survey: lessons for deterrence theory and offender decision-making," *Justice Quarterly 22* (2005): 1–29.

52. Adrian Raine, "Biosocial Studies of Antisocial and Violent Behavior in Children and Adults: A Review," *Journal of Abnormal Child Psychology 30* (2002): 311–327.

53. Stephen Schoenthaler, *Intelligence, Academic Performance, and Brain Function* (Turlock: California State University Stanislaus, 2000); see also, Stephen Schoenthaler and Ian Bier, "The Effect of Vitamin-Mineral Supplementation on Juvenile Delinquency Among American Schoolchildren: A Randomized Double-Blind Placebo-Controlled Trial," *Journal of Alternative and Complementary Medicine: Research on Paradigm, Practice, and Policy 6* (2000): 7–18.

54. Paul Stretesky and Michael Lynch, "The Relationship Between Lead Exposure and Homicide," *Archives of Pediatric Adolescent Medicine 155* (2001): 579–582.

55. Alan Booth and D. Wayne Osgood, "The Influence of Testosterone on Deviance in Adulthood: Assessing and Explaining the Relationship," *Criminology 31* (1993): 93–118.

56. Nathaniel Pallone and James Hennessy, "Brain Dysfunction and Criminal Violence," *Society 35* (1998).

57. Adrian Raine, Monte Buchsbaum, and Lori LaCasse, "Brain Abnormalities in Murderers Indicated by Positron Emission Tomography," *Biological Psychiatry 42* (1997): 495–508.

58. Leonore Simon, "Does Criminal Offender Treatment Work?" *Applied and Preventive Psychology* (Summer, 1998); Stephen Faraone, et al., "Intellectual Performance and School Failure in Children with Attention Deficit Hyperactivity Disorder and in Their Siblings," *Journal of Abnormal Psychology 102* (1993): 616–623.

59. B. Hutchings and S. A. Mednick, "Criminality in Adoptees and Their Adoptive and Biological Parents: A Pilot Study," in *Biosocial Bases of Criminal Behavior*, eds. S. A. Mednick and Karl O. Christiansen (New York: Gardner Press, 1977).

60. Edwin J. C. G. van den Oord, Frank Verhulst, and Dorret Boomsma, "A Genetic Study of Maternal and Paternal Ratings of Problem Behaviors in Three-Year-Old Twins," *Journal of Abnormal Psychology 105* (1996): 349–357.

61. Michael Lyons, "A Twin Study of Self-Reported Criminal Behavior," and Judy Silberg, Joanne Meyer, Andrew Pickles, Emily Simonoff, Lindon Eaves, John Hewitt, Hermine Maes, and Michael Rutter, "Heterogeneity Among Juvenile Antisocial Behaviors: Findings from the Virginia Twin Study of Adolescent Behavioral Development," both articles in *Genetics of Criminal and Antisocial Behavior*, Ciba Foundation Symposium, eds. Gregory Bock, Jamie Goode, and Michael Rutter (Chichester, England: Wiley, 1995), 61–75 and 128–156, respectively.

62. August Aichorn, *Wayward Youth* (New York: Viking Press, 1965).

63. Paige Crosby Ouimette, "Psychopathology and Sexual Aggression in Nonincarcerated Men," *Violence and Victimization 12* (1997): 389–397.

64. Robert Krueger, Avshalom Caspi, Phil Silva, and Rob McGee, "Personality Traits Are Differentially Linked to Mental Disorders: A Multitrait-Multidiagnosis Study of an Adolescent Birth Cohort," *Journal of Abnormal Psychology 105* (1996): 299–312.

65. Seymour Halleck, *Psychiatry and the Dilemmas of Crime* (Berkeley: University of California Press, 1971).

66. David Eitle and R. Jay Turner, "Exposure to Community Violence and Young Adult Crime: The Effects of Witnessing Violence, Traumatic Victimization, and Other Stressful Life Events," *Journal of Research in Crime and Delinquency 39* (2002): 214–238. See also Albert Bandura, *Aggression: A Social Learning Analysis* (Englewood Cliffs, N.J.: Prentice-Hall, 1973); Albert Bandura, *Social Learning Theory* (Englewood Cliffs, N.J.: Prentice-Hall, 1977).

67. U.S. Department of Health and Human Services, *Television and Behavior* (Washington, D.C.: Government Printing Office, 1982).

68. Richard Kania, "TV Crime and Real Crime: Questioning the Link" (paper presented at the annual meeting of the American Society of Criminology, Chicago, November 1988).

69. David Lykken, "Psychopathy, Sociopathy, and Crime," *Society 34* (1996): 30–38.

70. Steven Smith and Joseph Newman, "Alcohol and Drug Abuse–Dependence Disorders in Psychopathic and Nonpsychopathic Criminal Offenders," *Journal of Abnormal Psychology 99* (1990): 430–439.

71. Ibid.

72. Jack Levin and James Alan Fox, *Mass Murder* (New York: Plenum, 1985).

73. Spencer Rathus and Jeffrey Nevid, *Abnormal Psychology* (Englewood Cliffs, N.J.: Prentice-Hall, 1991), 310–316.

74. Ibid.

75. Samuel Yochelson and Stanton Samenow, *The Criminal Personality* (New York: Jason Aronson, 1977).

76. See, generally, Robert Nisbet, *The Sociology of Émile Durkheim* (New York: Oxford University Press, 1974).

77. Ralph Taylor, *Breaking Away from Broken Windows: Baltimore Neighborhoods and the Nationwide Fight against Crime, Grime, Fear, and Decline* (Boulder, Colo.: Westview Press, 2001).

78. Lincoln Quillian and Devah Pager, "Black Neighbors, Higher Crime? The Role of Racial Stereotypes in Evaluations of Neighborhood Crime," *American Journal of Sociology* 107 (2001): 717–769.

79. Oscar Lewis, "The Culture of Poverty," *Scientific American* 215 (1966): 19–25.

80. William Julius Wilson, *The Truly Disadvantaged* (Chicago: University of Chicago Press, 1987).

81. Jodi Lane and James Meeker, "Social disorganization perceptions, fear of gang crime, and behavioral precautions among Whites, Latinos, and Vietnamese," *Journal of Criminal Justice* 32 (2004): 49–62.

82. C. L. Storr, C.-Y. Chen, and J. C. Anthony, "'Unequal opportunity': Neighbourhood disadvantage and the chance to buy illegal drugs," *Journal of Epidemiology & Community Health* 58 (2004): 231–238.

83. Rebekah Levine Coley, Jodi Eileen Morris, and Daphne Hernandez, "Out-of-School Care and Problem Behavior Trajectories Among Low-Income Adolescents: Individual, Family, and Neighborhood Characteristics as Added Risks," *Child Development* 75 (2004): 948–965.

84. Ibid.

85. Catherine E. Ross, John Mirowsky, and Shana Pribesh, "Powerlessness and the Amplification of Threat: Neighborhood Disadvantage, Disorder, and Mistrust," *American Sociological Review* 66 (2001): 568–580.

86. Michael Reisig and Jeffrey Michael Cancino, "Incivilities in nonmetropolitan communities: The effects of structural constraints, social conditions, and crime," *Journal of Criminal Justice* 32 (2004): 15–29.

87. Steven Messner, Eric Baumer, and Richard Rosenfeld, "Dimensions of Social Capital and Rates of Criminal Homicide," *American Sociological Review* 69 (2004): 882–903.

88. Paul Bellair, "Informal Surveillance and Street Crime: A Complex Relationship," *Criminology* 38 (2000): 137–170.

89. Robert Sampson, Jeffrey Morenoff, and Felton Earls, "Beyond social capital: Spatial dynamics of collective efficacy for children," *American Sociological Review* 64 (1999): 633–660.

90. Ronald Simons, Yi Fu Chen, and Eric Stewart, "Incidents of Discrimination and Risk for Delinquency: A Longitudinal Test of Strain Theory with an African American Sample," *Justice Quarterly* 20 (2003): 827–854.

91. Ibid.

92. Joseph Rankin and L. Edward Wells, "The Effect of Parental Attachments and Direct Controls on Delinquency," *Journal of Research in Crime and Delinquency* 27 (1990): 140–165.

93. John Paul Wright and Francis Cullen, "Parental Efficacy and Delinquent Behavior: Do Control and Support Matter?" *Criminology* 39 (2001): 677–706.

94. Carter Hay, "Parenting, Self-Control, and Delinquency: A Test of Self-Control Theory," *Criminology* 39 (2001): 707–736.

95. Eugene Maguin and Rolf Loeber, "Academic Performance and Delinquency," *Crime and Justice: An Annual Review of Research*, vol. 20, eds. Michael Tonry and David Farrington (Chicago: University of Chicago Press, 1996), 145–264.

96. Ben Brown and William Reed Benedict, "Bullets, Blades, and Being Afraid in Hispanic High Schools: An Exploratory Study of the Presence of Weapons and Fear of Weapon-Associated Victimization Among High School Students in a Border Town," *Crime & Delinquency* 50 (2004): 372–395.

97. David Fergusson, Nicola Swain-Campbell, and L. John Horwood, "Deviant Peer Affiliations, Crime, and Substance Use: A Fixed Effects Regression Analysis," *Journal of Abnormal Child Psychology* 30 (2002): 419–431.

98. Karl Marx and Friedrich Engels, *Capital: A Critique of Political Economy*, trans. E. Aveling (Chicago: Charles Kern, 1906); Karl Marx, *Selected Writings in Sociology and Social Philosophy*, trans. P. B. Bottomore (New York: McGraw-Hill, 1956). For a general discussion of Marxist thought, see Michael Lynch and W. Byron Groves, *A Primer in Radical Criminology* (New York: Harrow and Heston, 1986), 6–26.

99. W. Byron Groves and Robert Sampson, "Critical Theory and Criminology," *Social Problems* 33 (1986): 58–80.

100. Susan Ehrlich Martin and Nancy Jurik, *Doing Justice, Doing Gender* (Thousand Oaks, Calif.: Sage, 1996).

101. For a general review of this issue, see Sally Simpson, "Feminist Theory, Crime, and Justice," *Criminology* 27 (1989): 605–632; James Messerschmidt, *Capitalism, Patriarchy, and Crime* (Totowa, N.J.: Rowman & Littlefield, 1986).

102. See, generally, Sheldon Glueck and Eleanor Glueck, *500 Criminal Careers* (New York: Knopf, 1930); Sheldon Glueck and Eleanor Glueck, *One Thousand Juvenile Delinquents* (Cambridge, Mass.: Harvard University Press, 1934); Sheldon Glueck and Eleanor Glueck, *Predicting Delinquency and Crime* (Cambridge, Mass.: Harvard University Press, 1967), 82–83.

103. Sheldon Glueck and Eleanor Glueck, *Unraveling Juvenile Delinquency* (Cambridge, Mass.: Harvard University Press, 1950).

104. Marvin Krohn, Alan Lizotte, and Cynthia Perez, "The Interrelationship Between Substance Use and Precocious Transitions to Adult Sexuality," *Journal of Health and Social Behavior* 38 (1997): 88.

105. G. R. Patterson, Barbara DeBaryshe, and Elizabeth Ramsey, "A Developmental Perspective on Antisocial Behavior," *American Psychologist* 44 (1989): 329–335.

106. Alex R. Piquero and He Len Chung, "On the Relationships Between Gender, Early Onset, and the Seriousness of Offending," *Journal of Criminal Justice* 29 (2001): 189–206.

107. Rolf Loeber and David Farrington, "Young Children Who Commit Crime: Epidemiology, Developmental Origins, Risk Factors, Early Interventions, and Policy Implications," *Development and Psychopathology* 12 (2000): 737–762.

Chapter 3

1. Some of the historical criminal law concepts discussed here are a synthesis of those contained in Peter Stein, *Roman Law in European History* (London: Cambridge University Press, 1999); Norman Cantor, *Imagining the Law: Common Law and the Foundations of the American Legal System* (New York: Harper Collins, 1999); Jerome Hall, *General Principles of Criminal Law* (Charlottesville, Va.: Michie, 1961).

2. Carriers *Case*, 13 Edward IV 9.pL.5 (1473).

3. See John Weaver, *Warren—The Man, the Court, the Era* (Boston: Little, Brown, 1967); see also "We the People," *Time*, July 6, 1987, 6.

4. *Kansas v. Hendricks*, 117 S.Ct. 2072 (1997); *Chicago v. Morales*, 119 S.Ct. 246 (1999).

5. *City of Chicago v. Morales et al.* 527 US 41 (1999).

6. Daniel Suleiman, "The Capital Punishment Exception: A Case for Constitutionalizing the Substantive Criminal Law," *Columbia Law Review* 104 (2004): 426–458.

7. *Calder v. Bull*, 3 U.S. 386 (1798).

8. Henry Black, *Black's Law Dictionary*, 5th ed. (St. Paul, Minn.: West, 1979), 744, 1150.

9. See, for example, General Laws of Massachusetts, Part II: Real and Personal Property and Domestic Relations. Title III. Domestic Relations, Section 209 (June 30, 2002).

10. Sheldon Krantz, *Law of Corrections and Prisoners' Rights, Cases and Materials*, 3d ed. (St. Paul, Minn.: West, 1986), 702; Barbara Knight and Stephen Early, Jr., *Prisoners' Rights in America* (Chicago: Nelson-Hall, 1986), chapter 1; see also Fred Cohen, "The Law of Prisoners' Rights— An Overview," *Criminal Law Bulletin* 24 (188): 321–349.

11. See *United States v. Balint*, 258 U.S. 250, 42 S.Ct. 301, 66 L.Ed. 604 (1922); see also *Morissette v. United States*, 342 U.S. 246, 72 S.Ct. 240, 96 L.Ed. 288 (1952).

12. New York State Consolidated Laws, Article 270: Other Offenses Relating to Public Safety, Section 270.10: Creating a hazard (2002).

13. *Regina v. Dudley and Stephens*, 14 Q.B.D. 273 (1884).

14. For a history and analysis of these types of defenses, see Eugene Milhizer, "Justification and Excuse: What They Were, What They Are, and What They Ought to Be," *St. John's Law Review 78* (2004): 725–895.

15. William Blackstone, *Commentaries on the Law of England* vol. 1, ed. Thomas Cooley (Chicago: Callaghan, 1899), 4, 26. Blackstone was an English barrister who lectured on the English common law at Oxford University in 1753.

16. Samuel M. Davis, *Rights of Juveniles: The Juvenile Justice System* (New York: Boardman, 1974; updated 1993), chapter 2; Larry Siegel and Joseph Senna, *Juvenile Delinquency: Theory, Practice, and Law* (St. Paul, Minn.: West, 1996).

17. N.A. Criminal Law—Mutual Combat Mitigation—Appellate Court of Illinois Holds That Disproportionate Reaction to Provocation Negates Mutual Combat Mitigation—*People v. Thompson*, 821 N.E. 2d 664 (Ii. App. Ct. 2004), *Harvard Law Review 118* (2005): 2437–2444.

18. 356 U.S. 369, 78 S.Ct. 819, 2 L.Ed.2d 848 (1958); see also *Jacobson v. United States*, 503 U.S. 540, 112 S.Ct. 1535, 118 L.Ed.2d 174 (1992).

19. Matthew Lyon, "No Means No?: Withdrawal of Consent During Intercourse and the Continuing Evolution of the Definition of Rape. By: R." *Journal of Criminal Law & Criminology 95* (2004): 277–314.

20. *Lawrence et al. v. Texas*, No. 02-102, June 26, 2003.

21. Margaret Raymond, "Penumbral Crimes," *American Criminal Law Review 39* (2002): 1395–1440.

22. Marvin Zalman, John Strate, Denis Hunter, and James Sellars, "Michigan Assisted Suicide Three Ring Circus: The Intersection of Law and Politics," *Ohio Northern Law Review 23* (1997): 230–276.

23. 1992 P.A. 270 as amended by 1993 P.A.3, M.C. L. ss. 752.1021 to 752. 1027.

24. National Institute of Justice, *Project to Develop a Model Anti-stalking Statute* (Washington, D.C.: National Institute of Justice, 1994).

25. Sarah Welchans, "Megan's Law: Evaluations of Sexual Offender Registries," *Criminal Justice Policy Review 16* (2005): 123–140.

26. Environmental Protection Agency, Criminal Enforcement Division www.epa.gov/compliance/criminal/index.html, accessed on May 8, 2005.

27. Deborah W. Denno, "Gender, Crime, and the Criminal Law Defenses," *Journal of Criminal Law and Criminology 85* (Summer 1994): 80–180.

28. 384 U.S. 436, 86 S.Ct. 1602, 16 L.Ed.2d 694 (1966).

29. See "Essay," *Time*, February 26, 1973, 95; also, for a tribute to the Bill of Rights and due process, see James MacGregor Burns and Steward Burns, *The Pursuit of Rights in America* (New York: Knopf, 1991).

30. 342 U.S. 165, 72 S.Ct. 205, 95 L.Ed. 183 (1952).

31. Ibid., at 172, 72 S.Ct. at 209.

32. *Sattazahn v. Pennsylvania*, No. 01-7574. Decided January 14, 2003.

Chapter 4

1. United States State Department, "Country Reports on Terrorism April 2005," www.state.gov/documents/organization/45313.pdf, accessed on July 12, 2005.

2. Title 22 of the United States Code section 2656f(d) (1999).

3. Thomas P. M. Barnett, *The Pentagon's New Map: War and Peace in the Twenty-first Century*. (New York: G. P. Putnam's Sons, 2004), 43–46.

4. Edmund Burke, *Reflections on the Revolution in France, 1790* (New York: Penguin Classics; reprint edition 1982).

5. Lindsay Clutterbuck, "The Progenitors of Terrorism: Russian Revolutionaries or Extreme Irish Republicans?" *Terrorism and Political Violence 16* (2004): 154–181.

6. Stephen J. Morgan, *The Mind of a Terrorist Fundamentalist: The Psychology of Terror Cults* (Awe-Struck E-Books, 2001).; Martha Crenshaw, "The Psychology of Terrorism: An Agenda for the 21st Century," *Political Psychology 21* (2000): 405–420.

7. Andrew Silke, "Courage in Dark Places: Reflections on Terrorist Psychology," *Social Research 71* (2004): 177–198.

8. David Weatherston and Jonathan Moran, "Terrorism and Mental Illness: Is There a Relationship?" *International Journal of Offender Therapy & Comparative Criminology 47* (2003): 698–711.

9. Charles Ruby, "Are Terrorists Mentally Deranged?" *Analyses of Social Issues & Public Policy 2* (2002): 15–26.

10. Jerrold Post, "When Hatred Is Bred in the Bone: Psycho-cultural Foundations of Contemporary Terrorism," *Political Psychology 25* (2005): 615–637.

11. This section leans heavily on Anthony Stahelski, "Terrorists Are Made, Not Born: Creating Terrorists Using Social Psychological Conditioning," *Journal of Homeland Security*, March 2004, www.homelandsecurity.org/journal/Articles/displayarticle.asp?article=109, accessed on August 14, 2005.

12. Quintan Wiktorowicz, "A Genealogy of Radical Islam," *Studies in Conflict and Terrorism 28* (2005): 75–98.

13. Ethan Bueno de Mesquita, "The Quality of Terror," *American Journal of Political Science 49* (2005): 515–530.

14. Haruki Murakami, *Underground* (New York: Vintage Books, 2001).

15. Michael Scott Doran, "Somebody Else's Civil War," *Foreign Affairs 81* (January–February 2002): 22–25; Bruce Hoffman, "Change and Continuity in Terrorism," *Studies in Conflict and Terrorism 24* (2001).

16. Ian Lesser, Bruce Hoffman, John Arquilla, David Ronfeldt, and Michele Zanini, *Countering the New Terrorism* (Washington, D.C.: Rand, 1999); Jessica Stern, *The Ultimate Terrorists* (Cambridge, Mass.: Harvard University Press, 1999).

17. Doran, "Somebody Else's Civil War"; Hoffman, "Change and Continuity in Terrorism."

18. Andrew Chen and Thomas Siems, "Effects of terrorism on global capital markets," *European Journal of Political Economy 20* (2004): 349–356.

19. Sanjeev Gupta, Benedict Clements, Rina Bhattacharya, and Shamit Chakravarti, "Fiscal consequences of armed conflict and terrorism in low- and middle-income countries," *European Journal of Political Economy 20* (2004): 403–421.

20. Shaul Mishal and Maoz Rosenthal, "Al Qaeda as a Dune Organization: Toward a Typology of Islamic Terrorist Organizations," *Studies in Conflict and Terrorism 28* (2005): 275–293.

21. Graham Allison, *Nuclear Terrorism: The Ultimate Preventable Catastrophe* (New York: Times Books, 2004).

22. Rand Corporation, "How Prepared Are State and Local Law Enforcement for Terrorism?" www.rand.org/publications/RB/RB9093/, accessed on June 28, 2005.

23. White House press release, November 11, 2002, www.whitehouse.gov/news/releases/2002/11/20021119-4.html, accessed on August 14, 2005. The section on homeland security relies heavily on "The Department of Homeland Security," www.whitehouse.gov/infocus/homeland/index.html, accessed on August 14, 2005.

24. "Homeland Security Secretary Michael Chertoff Announces Six-Point Agenda for Department of Homeland Security," Office of the Press Secretary, July 13, 2005, www.dhs.gov/dhspublic/interapp/press_release/press_release_0703.xml, accessed on July 13, 2005.

25. California Anti-Terrorism Information Center (CATIC), www.ag.ca.gov/antiterrorism/, accessed on August 14, 2005.

26. William K. Rashbaum, "Terror Makes All the World a Beat for New York Police," *New York Times,* July 15, 2002, B1; Al Baker, "Leader Sees New York Police in Vanguard of Terror Fight," *New York Times,* August 6, 2002, A2; Stephen Flynn, "America the Vulnerable," *Foreign Affairs 81* (January–February 2002): 60.

27. Communications Assistance for Law Enforcement Act of 1994, Pub. L. No. 103-414, 108 Stat. 4279.

28. Michael P. Clifford, "Communications Assistance for Law Enforcement Act (CALEA)," *FBI Law Enforcement Bulletin 71* (2002): 11–14.

29. Statement of Michael A. Vatis, Director, National Infrastructure Protection Center, Federal Bureau of Investigation, on Cybercrime before the Senate Judiciary Committee, Criminal Justice Oversight Subcommittee and House Judiciary Committee, Crime Subcommittee, Washington, D.C. February 29, 2000. www.cybercrime.gov/vatis.htm, accessed on July 12, 2005.

30. Ed Frauenheim, "IDC: Cyberterror and other prophecies," CNET News.com, December 12, 2002, accessed on August 14, 2005.

31. Giles Trendle, "An e-jihad against government?" *EGOV Monitor,* September 2002.

32. Computer Security Institute Press Release, "Cyber crime bleeds U.S. corporations, survey shows; financial losses from attacks climb for third year in a row," April 7, 2002.

33. Jeanne Capachin and Dave Potterton, "Online Card Payments, Fraud Solutions Bid to Win," *Meridien Research Report* (Newton, Mass.), January 18, 2001.

34. Ibid.

35. Heather Jacobson and Rebecca Green, "Computer Crimes," *American Criminal Law Review 39* (2002): 272–326.

36. Erik Larson, "Computers Turn Out to Be Valuable Aid in Employee Crime," *Wall Street Journal,* January 14, 1985, 1.

37. Clyde Wilson, "Software Piracy: Uncovering Mutiny on the Cyberseas," *Trial 32* (1996): 24–31.

38. Computer Security Institute (CSI), Ninth Annual Computer Crime and Security Survey www.gocsi.com/forms/fbi/csi_fbi_survey.jhtml

39. Business Software Alliance (BSA) Piracy Study, May 2005, www.bsa.org/globalstudy/upload/2005-Global-Study-English.pdf, accessed on July 11, 2005.

40. Christopher Marquis, "U.S. Says It Broke Pornography Ring Featuring Youths," *New York Times,* August 9, 2001, 6.

41. U.S. Department of Justice Press Release, "Thomas Reedy Sentenced to Life Imprisonment in Child Porn Case," August 6, 2001, www.usdoj.gov/usao/txn/PressRel01/reedy_sent_pr.htm, accessed on August 14, 2005.

42. Saul Hansell, "U.S. Tally in Online-Crime Sweep: 150 Charged," *New York Times,* August 27, 2004, c1.

43. Stephen Baker and Brian Grow, "Gambling Sites, This Is a Holdup," *Business Week,* 3895 (8/9/2004): 60–62.

44. *Metro-Goldwyn-Mayer Studios, Inc. et al. v. Grokster, Ltd. et al.,* No. 04-480. June 27, 2005.

45. Jim Wolf, "Internet Scams Targeted in Sweep: A 10-Day Crackdown Leads to 62 Arrests and 88 Indictments," *Boston Globe,* May 22, 2001, A2.

46. Hansell, "U.S. Tally in Online-Crime Sweep."

47. Barry C. Collin (2004), "The Future of CyberTerrorism: Where the Physical and Virtual Worlds Converge," http://afgen.com/terrorism1.html, accessed on August 14, 2005.

48. Mark Pollitt, "Cyberterrorism—Fact or Fancy?" FBI Laboratory, www.cs.georgetown.edu/~denning/infosec/pollitt.html, accessed on August 17, 2005.

49. Gupta et al., "Fiscal consequences of armed conflict and terrorism."

50. Daniel Benjamin, *America and the World in the Age of Terrorism* (Washington, D.C.: CSIS Press, 2005), 1–216.

51. General Accounting Office, "Critical Infrastructure Protection: Efforts of the Financial Services Sector to Address Cyber Threats Reports to the Technology Committee" (Washington, D.C: January 2003).

52. Yael Shahar, "Information Warfare," Institute for Counter-Terrorism (1997), www.ict.org.il/articles/infowar.htm, accessed on August 17, 2005.

53. Michael Whine, "Cyberspace—A New Medium for Communication, Command, and Control by Extremists," Institute for Counter-Terrorism (1999), www.ict.org.il/articles/articledet.cfm?articleid=76, accessed on August 14, 2005.

54. General Accounting Office, "Critical Infrastructure Protection: Efforts of the Financial Services Sector to Address Cyber Threats."

55. Gabriel Weimann, "Cyberterrorism: The Sum of All Fears?" *Studies in Conflict and Terrorism 28* (2005): 129–150.

56. Heather Jacobson and Rebecca Green, "Computer Crime," *American Criminal Law Review 39* (2002): 273–326; Identity Theft and Assumption Act of 1998 (18 U.S.C. S 1028(a)(7)); Bruce Swartz, Deputy Assistant General, Criminal Division, Justice Department Internet Fraud Testimony Before the House Energy and Commerce Committee, May 23, 2001; Comprehensive Crime Control Act of 1984, PL 98-473, 2101-03, 98 Stat. 1837, 2190 (1984), adding 18 USC 1030 (1984); Counterfeit Active Device and Computer Fraud and Abuse Act Amended by PL 99-474, 100 Stat. 1213 (1986) codified at 18 U.S.C. 1030 (Supp. V 1987); Computer Abuse Amendments Act 18 U.S.C. section 1030 (1994); Copyright Infringement Act 17 U.S.C. section 506(a) 1994; Electronic Communications Privacy Act of 198618 U.S.C. 2510–2520 (1988 and Supp. II 1990).

57. The Computer Fraud and Abuse Act (CFAA) 18 U.S.C. section 1030 (1998).

58. The Digital Millennium Copyright Act, Public Law 105-304 (1998).

59. Title 18, United States Code, section 2319.

60. Title 17, United States Code, section 506.

61. Identity Theft and Assumption Deterrence Act, as amended by Public Law 105-318, 112 Stat. 3007 (October. 30, 1998).

62. ACLU, "*ACLU v. Reno,* Round 2: Broad Coalition Files Challenge to New Federal Net Censorship Law," news release, October 22, 1998.

63. *Ashcroft v. ACLU,* 00-1293, 2002

64. Pub. L. No. 98-473, Title H, Chapter XXI, [sections] 2102(a), 98 Stat. 1837, 2190 (1984).

65. Rand Corporation, Research in Brief, "How Prepared Are State and Local Law Enforcement for Terrorism?" www.rand.org/publications/RB/RB9093/, accessed on July 13, 2005.

Chapter 5

1. James Hawdon and John Ryan, "Police-Resident Interactions and Satisfaction with Police: An Empirical Test of Community Policing Assertions," *Criminal Justice Policy Review 14* (2003): 55–74.

2. Egon Bittner, *The Functions of Police in Modern Society* (Cambridge, Mass.: Oelgeschlager, Gunn & Hain, 1980), 8; see also James Q. Wilson, "The Police in the Ghetto," in *The Police and the Community,* ed. Robert F. Steadman (Baltimore: Johns Hopkins University Press, 1974), 68.

3. George Kelling, *Police and Communities: The Quiet Revolution* (Washington, D.C.: National Institute of Justice, 1988).

4. Sara Stoutland, "The Multiple Dimensions of Trust in Resident/Police Relations in Boston," *Journal of Research in Crime and Delinquency 38* (2001), 226–256.

5. "Law Enforcement Seeks Answers to 'Racial Profiling' Complaints," *Criminal Justice Newsletter 29* (1998): 5.

6. Stephen Rice and Alex Piquero, "Perceptions of Discrimination and Justice in New York City," *Policing: An International Journal of Police Strategies and Management 28* (2005): 98–117.

7. Liqun Cao, James Frank, and Francis Cullen, "Race, Community Context, and Confidence in the Police," *American Journal of Police 15* (1996): 3–15; Thomas Priest and Deborah Brown Carter, "Evaluations of Police Performance in an African American Sample," *Journal of Criminal Justice 27* (1999): 457–465.

8. This section relies heavily on such sources as Malcolm Sparrow, Mark Moore, and David Kennedy, *Beyond 911: A New Era for Policing* (New York: Basic Books, 1990); Daniel Devlin, *Police Procedure, Administration, and Organization* (London: Butterworth, 1966); Robert Fogelson, *Big City Police* (Cambridge, Mass.: Harvard University Press, 1977); Roger Lane, *Policing the City, Boston 1822–1885* (Cambridge, Mass.: Harvard University Press, 1967); J. J. Tobias, *Crime and Industrial Society in the Nineteenth Century* (New York: Schocken Books, 1967); Samuel Walker, *A Critical History of Police Reform: The Emergence of Professionalism* (Lexington, Mass.: Lexington Books, 1977); Samuel Walker, *Popular Justice* (New York: Oxford University Press, 1980); John McMullan, "The New Improved Monied Police: Reform Crime Control and Commodification of Policing in London," *British Journal of Criminology 36* (1996): 85–108.

9. Devlin, *Police Procedure, Administration, and Organization,* 3.

10. McMullan, "The New Improved Monied Police," 92.

11. Elizabeth Joh, "The Paradox of Private Policing," *Journal of Criminal Law & Criminology 95* (2004): 49–132.

12. Wilbur Miller, "The Good, the Bad & the Ugly: Policing America," *History Today 50* (2000): 29–32.

13. Phillip Reichel, "Southern Slave Patrols as a Transitional Type," *American Journal of Police 7* (1988): 51–78.

14. Walker, *Popular Justice,* 61.

15. Christopher Thale, "Assigned to Patrol: Neighborhoods, Police, and Changing Deployment Practices in New York City Before 1930," *Journal of Social History 37* (2004): 1037–1064.

16. Ibid., 8.

17. Dennis Rousey, "Cops and Guns: Police Use of Deadly Force in Nineteenth-Century New Orleans," *American Journal of Legal History 28* (1984): 41–66.

18. Law Enforcement Assistance Administration, *Two Hundred Years of American Criminal Justice* (Washington, D.C.: Government Printing Office, 1976).

19. National Commission on Law Observance and Enforcement, *Report on the Police* (Washington, D.C.: Government Printing Office, 1931), 5–7.

20. Pamela Irving Jackson, *Minority Group Threat, Crime, and Policing* (New York: Praeger, 1989).

21. James Q. Wilson and George Kelling, "Broken Windows," *Atlantic Monthly 249* (1982): 29–38.

22. Frank Tippett, "It Looks Just Like a War Zone," *Time,* May 27, 1985, 16–22; "San Francisco, New York Police Troubled by Series of Scandals," *Criminal Justice Newsletter 16* (1985): 2–4; Karen Polk, "New York Police: Caught in the Middle and Losing Faith," *Boston Globe,* December 28, 1988, 3.

23. Staff of the *Los Angeles Times,* "Understanding the Riots: Los Angeles Before and After the Rodney King Case" (Los Angeles: *Los Angeles Times,* 1992).

24. David H. Bayley, "Policing in America," *Society 36* (December 1998).

25. Ronald Burns, Keith Whitworth, and Carol Thompson, "Assessing Law Enforcement Preparedness to Address Internet Fraud," *Journal of Criminal Justice 32* (2004): 477–493.

26. Kathleen Grubb, "Cold War to Gang War," *Boston Globe,* January 22, 1992, 1.

27. FBI, *Organization,* www.fas.org/irp/agency/doj/fbi/org.htm, accessed on May 25, 2005.

28. Bruce Smith, *Police Systems in the United States* (New York: Harper & Row, 1960).

29. Brian Reaves and Matthew Hickman, *Census of State and Local Law Enforcement Agencies, 2000* (Washington, D.C.: Bureau of Justice Statistics, 2002).

30. Ibid.; Matthew Hickman and Brian Reaves, *Sheriffs' Office 2000* (Washington, D.C.: Bureau of Justice Statistics, 2003).

31. Data in this section come from Reaves and Hickman, *Census of State and Local Law Enforcement Agencies, 2000.*

32. See, for example, Robert Keppel and Joseph Weis, *Improving the Investigation of Violent Crime: The Homicide Investigation and Tracking System* (Washington, D.C.: National Institute of Justice, 1993).

33. Larry Coutorie, "The Future of High-Technology Crime: A Parallel Delphi Study," *Journal of Criminal Justice 23* (1995): 13–27.

34. Bill Goodwin, "Burglars Captured by Police Data Mining Kit," *Computer Weekly,* August 8, 2002, 3.

35. "Forensic Computing Expert Warns Interpol About Computer Crime," *Information Systems Auditor,* August 2002, 2.

36. Lois Pliant, "Information Management," *Police Chief 61* (1994): 31–35.

37. "Spotlight on Computer Imaging," *Police Chief 66* (1999): 6–8.

38. See, generally, Laura Moriarty and David Carter, *Criminal Justice Technology in the Twenty-First Century* (Springfield, Ill.: Charles C Thomas, 1998).

39. Weipeng Zhang, Yan Yuan Tang, and Xinge You, "Fingerprint Enhancement Using Wavelet Transform Combined with Gabor Filter," *International Journal of Pattern Recognition & Artificial Intelligence 18* (2004): 1391–1406.

40. See, generally, Ryan McDonald, "Juries and Crime Labs: Correcting the Weak Links in the DNA Chain," *American Journal of Law and Medicine 24* (1998): 345–363; "DNA Profiling Advancement," *FBI Law Enforcement Bulletin 67* (1998): 24.

41. Ronald Reinstein, *Postconviction DNA Testing: Recommendations for Handling Requests* (Philadelphia: Diane Publishing Co., 1999).

42. "California Attorney General Endorses DNA Fingerprinting," *Criminal Justice Newsletter 1* (1989): 1.

43. *State v. Ford,* 301 S.C. 485, 392 S.E.2d 781 (1990).

44. "Under New Policy, FBI Examiners Testify to Absolute DNA Matches," *Criminal Justice Newsletter 28* (1997): 1–2.

45. "FBI's DNA Profile Clearinghouse Announce First 'Cold Hit,'" *Criminal Justice Newsletter 16* (1999): 5.

46. "South Side Strangler's Execution Cited as DNA Evidence Landmark," *Criminal Justice Newsletter 2* (1994): 3.

47. Ralph Ioimo and Jay Aronson, "Police Field Mobile Computing: Applying the Theory of Task-Technology Fit," *Police Quarterly 7* (2004): 403–428.

48. Brewer Stone, "The High-Tech Beat in St. Pete," *Police Chief 55* (1988): 23–28.

49. "Pen Computing: The Natural 'Next Step' for Field Personnel," *Law and Order 43* (1995): 37.

50. Miller McMillan, "High Tech Enters the Field of View," *Police Chief 62* (1994): 29.

51. Thomas Cowper, "Improving the View of the World Law Enforcement and Augmented Reality Technology," *FBI Law Enforcement Bulletin 74* (2004): 11–14.

52. N.A. "Facial AFIS Launched by Identix," *Biometric Technology Today 11* (2003): 4.

53. Ray Surette, "The Thinking Eye: Pros and Cons of Second-generation CCTV Surveillance Systems," *Policing: An International Journal of Police Strategies and Management 28* (2005): 152–173.

Chapter 6

1. Brian Payne, Bruce Berg, and Ivan Sun, "Policing in Small Town America: Dogs, Drunks, Disorder, and Dysfunction," *Journal of Criminal Justice* 33 (2005): 31–41.
2. Stacey Nofziger and Susan Williams, "Perceptions of Police and Safety in a Small Town" *Police Quarterly 8* (2005): 248–270.
3. Matthew Durose, Erica Schmitt, and Patrick Langan, *Contacts between Police and the Public, Findings from the 2002 National Survey* (Washington, D.C.: Bureau of Justice Statistics, 2005).
4. Brian A. Reaves and Pheny Smith, *Law Enforcement Management and Administrative Statistics, 1993: Data for Individual State and Local Agencies with 100 or More Officers* (Washington, D.C.: Bureau of Justice Statistics, 1995).
5. American Bar Association, *Standards Relating to Urban Police Function* (New York: Institute of Judicial Administration, 1974), standard 2.2.
6. James Hawdon and John Ryan, "Police-Resident Interactions and Satisfaction with Police: An Empirical Test of Community Policing Assertions," *Criminal Justice Policy Review 14* (2003): 55–74.
7. Albert J. Reiss, *The Police and the Public* (New Haven, Conn.: Yale University Press, 1971), 19.
8. James Q. Wilson, *Varieties of Police Behavior: The Management of Law and Order in Eight Communities* (Cambridge, Mass.: Harvard University Press, 1968).
9. George Kelling, Tony Pate, Duane Dieckman, and Charles Brown, *The Kansas City Preventive Patrol Experiment: A Summary Report* (Washington, D.C.: Police Foundation, 1974).
10. Richard Timothy Coupe and Laurence Blake, "The Effects of Patrol Workloads and Response Strength on Arrests at Burglary Emergencies," *Journal of Criminal Justice 33* (2005): 239–255.
11. James Q. Wilson and Barbara Boland, "The Effect of Police on Crime," *Law and Society Review 12* (1978): 367–384.
12. Robert Sampson, "Deterrent Effects of the Police on Crime: A Replication and Theoretical Extension," *Law and Society Review 22* (1988): 163–191.
13. For a thorough review of this issue, see Andrew Karmen, *Why Is New York City's Murder Rate Dropping So Sharply?* (New York: John Jay College, 1996).
14. Robert Davis, Pedro Mateu-Gelabert, and Joel Miller, "Can Effective Policing Also Be Respectful? Two Examples in the South Bronx," *Police Quarterly 8* (2005): 229–247.
15. Lawrence Sherman, James Shaw, and Dennis Rogan, *The Kansas City Gun Experiment* (Washington, D.C.: National Institute of Justice, 1994).
16. Mitchell Chamlin, "Crime and Arrests: An Autoregressive Integrated Moving Average (ARIMA) Approach," *Journal of Quantitative Criminology 4* (1988): 247–255.
17. Stewart D'Alessio and Lisa Stolzenberg, "Crime, Arrests, and Pretrial Jail Incarceration: An Examination of the Deterrence Thesis," *Criminology 36* (1998): 735–761.
18. Perry Shapiro and Harold Votey, "Deterrence and Subjective Probabilities of Arrest: Modeling Individual Decisions to Drink and Drive in Sweden," *Law and Society Review 18* (1984): 111–149.
19. Thomas Marvell and Carlysle Moody, "Specification Problems, Police Levels, and Crime Rates," *Criminology 34* (1996): 609–646; Colin Loftin and David McDowall, "The Police, Crime, and Economic Theory: An Assessment," *American Sociological Review 47* (1982): 393–401.
20. Tomislav V. Kovandzic and John J. Sloan, "Police Levels and Crime Rates Revisited: A County-Level Analysis from Florida (1980–1998)," *Journal of Criminal Justice 30* (2002): 65–76; Steven Levitt, "Using Electoral Cycles in Police Hiring to Estimate the Effect of Police on Crime," *American Economic Review 87* (1997): 270–291.
21. David Jacobs and Katherine Woods, "Interracial Conflict and Interracial Homicide: Do Political and Economic Rivalries Explain White Killings of Blacks or Black Killings of Whites?" *American Journal of Sociology 105* (1999): 157–190.
22. Joan Petersilia, Allan Abrahamse, and James Q. Wilson, "A Summary of Rand's Research on Police Performance, Community Characteristics, and Case Attrition," *Journal of Police Science and Administration 17* (1990): 219–229.
23. Vincent Henry, *The Compstat Paradigm: Management Accountability in Policing, Business and the Public Sector* (New York: Looseleaf Law Publications, 2002).
24. See Belton Cobb, *The First Detectives* (London: Faber & Faber, 1957).
25. For a view of the modern detective, see William Sanders, *Detective Work: A Study of Criminal Investigations* (New York: Free Press, 1977).
26. Mark Pogrebin and Eric Poole, "Vice Isn't Nice: A Look at the Effects of Working Undercover," *Journal of Criminal Justice 21* (1993): 385–396; Gary Marx, *Undercover: Police Surveillance in America* (Berkeley: University of California Press, 1988).
27. Martin Innes, *Investigating Murder: Detective Work and the Police Response to Criminal Homicide* (Clarendon Studies in Criminology) (London, England: Oxford University Press, 2003)
28. John B. Edwards, "Homicide Investigative Strategies," *FBI Law Enforcement Bulletin 74* (2005): 11–21.
29. Robert Langworthy, "Do Stings Control Crime? An Evaluation of a Police Fencing Operation," *Justice Quarterly 6* (1989): 27–45.
30. Mary Dodge, Donna Starr-Gimeno, and Thomas Williams, "Puttin' on the Sting: Women Police Officers' Perspectives on Reverse Prostitution Assignment," *International Journal of Police Science & Management 7* (2005): 71–85.
31. Peter Greenwood and Joan Petersilia, *Summary and Policy Implications*, vol. 1, *The Criminal Investigation Process* (Santa Monica, Calif.: Rand, 1975).
32. Mark Willman and John Snortum, "Detective Work: The Criminal Investigation Process in a Medium-Size Police Department," *Criminal Justice Review 9* (1984): 33–39.
33. Police Executive Research Forum, *Calling the Police: Citizen Reporting of Serious Crime* (Washington, D.C.: Police Executive Research Forum, 1981).
34. John Eck, *Solving Crimes: The Investigation of Burglary and Robbery* (Washington, D.C.: Police Executive Research Forum, 1984).
35. A. Fischer,. "CopLink nabs criminals faster." *Arizona Daily Star,* January 7, 2001; A. Robbins, *PC Magazine 22* (2003); M. Sink, "An electronic cop that plays hunches," *New York Times,* November 2, 2002.
36. Janice Puckett and Richard Lundman, "Factors Affecting Homicide Clearances: Multivariate Analysis of a More Complete Conceptual Framework," *Journal of Research in Crime & Delinquency 40* (2003): 171–194.
37. George Kelling and James Q. Wilson, "Broken Windows: The Police and Neighborhood Safety," *Atlantic Monthly 249* (1982): 29–38.
38. Catherine Coles and George Kelling, *Fixing Broken Windows: Restoring Order and Reducing Crime in Our Communities* (New York: Free Press, 1998).
39. For a general review, see Robert Trojanowicz and Bonnie Bucqueroux, *Community Policing: A Contemporary Perspective* (Cincinnati, Ohio: Anderson, 1990).
40. Police Foundation, *The Newark Foot Patrol Experiment* (Washington, D.C.: Police Foundation, 1981).
41. John Worrall and Jihong Zhao. "The Role of the COPS Office in Community Policing," *Policing: An International Journal of Police Strategies & Management 26* (2003), 64–87.

42. Jihong Zhao, Nicholas Lovrich, and Quint Thurman, "The Status of Community Policing American Cities," *Policing* 22 (1999): 74–92.

43. Albert Cardarelli, Jack McDevitt, and Katrina Baum, "The Rhetoric and Reality of Community Policing in Small and Medium-Sized Cities and Towns," *Policing* 21 (1998): 397–415.

44. Jerome Skolnick and David Bayley, *Community Policing: Issues and Practices Around the World* (Washington, D.C.: National Institute of Justice, 1988).

45. Yili Xu, Mora Fiedler, and Karl Flaming, "Discovering the Impact of Community Policing: The Broken Windows Thesis, Collective Efficacy, and Citizens' Judgment" *Journal of Research in Crime and Delinquency 42 (*2005): 147–186.

46. Quint Thurman, Andrew Giacomazzi, and Phil Bogen, "Research Note: Cops, Kids, and Community Policing: An Assessment of a Community Policing Demonstration Project," *Crime and Delinquency* 39 (1993): 554–564.

47. Walter Baranyk, "Making a Difference in a Public Housing Project," *Police Chief 61* (1994): 31–35.

48. Susan Sadd and Randolph Grinc, *Implementation Challenges in Community Policing* (Washington, D.C.: National Institute of Justice, 1996).

49. Donald Green, Dara Strolovitch, and Janelle Wong, "Defended Neighborhoods: Integration and Racially Motivated Crime," *American Journal of Sociology 104* (1998): 372–403.

50. James Nolan, Norman Conti, and Jack McDevitt, "Situational Policing: Neighbourhood Development and Crime Control," *Policing & Society 14* (2004): 99–118.

51. Herman Goldstein, "Improving Policing: A Problem-Oriented Approach," *Crime and Delinquency 25* (1979): 236–258.

52. Skolnick and Bayley, *Community Policing*, 12.

53. Lawrence Sherman, Patrick Gartin, and Michael Buerger, "Hot Spots of Predatory Crime: Routine Activities and the Criminology of Place," *Criminology 27* (1989): 27–55.

54. Ibid., 45.

55. Dennis Roncek and Pamela Maier, "Bars, Blocks, and Crimes Revisited: Linking the Theory of Routine Activities to the Empiricism of 'Hot Spots,'" *Criminology 29* (1991): 725–753.

56. Sherry Plaster Carter, Stanley Carter, and Andrew Dannenberg, "Zoning Out Crime and Improving Community Health in Sarasota, Florida: 'Crime Prevention Through Environmental Design'" *American Journal of Public Health 93* (2003): 1442–1445.

57. C. Jewett, "Police use bait cars to reduce theft," *Knight Ridder/Tribune Business News*, March 3, 2003; Licensing Road Safety Autoplan Insurance, "Vancouver Police Bait Car Program." North Vancouver, Canada, December 3, 2003.

58. Michael White, James Fyfe, Suzanne Campbell, and John Goldkamp, "The Police Role in Preventing Homicide: Considering the Impact of Problem-Oriented Policing on the Prevalence of Murder" *Journal of Research in Crime & Delinquency 40* (2003): 194–226.

59. Tucson Police Department, Gang Tactical Detail, www.ci.tucson.az.us/police/Organization/Investigative_Services_/Violent_Crimes_Section/Gang_Tactical_Detail/gang_tactical_detail.html, accessed on August 19, 2005.

60. Anthony Braga, David Kennedy, Elin Waring, and Anne Morrison Piehl, "Problem-Oriented Policing, Deterrence, and Youth Violence: An Evaluation of Boston's Operation Ceasefire," *Journal of Research in Crime and Delinquency 38* (2001): 195–225.

61. Bureau of Justice Assistance, *Problem-Oriented Drug Enforcement: A Community-Based Approach for Effective Policing* (Washington, D.C.: National Institute of Justice, 1993).

62. Ibid., 64–65.

63. Jack R. Greene, "The Effects of Community Policing on American Law Enforcement: A Look at the Evidence," paper presented at the International Congress on Criminology, Hamburg, Germany, September 1988, 19.

64. Roger Dunham and Geoffrey Alpert, "Neighborhood Differences in Attitudes Toward Policing: Evidence for a Mixed-Strategy Model of Policing in a Multi-Ethnic Setting," *Journal of Criminal Law and Criminology 79* (1988): 504–522.

65. Mark E. Correia, "The Conceptual Ambiguity of Community in Community Policing: Filtering the Muddy Waters," *Policing: An International Journal of Police Strategies & Management 23* (2000): 218–233.

66. Scott Lewis, Helen Rosenberg, and Robert Sigler, "Acceptance of Community Policing Among Police Officers and Police Administrators," *Policing: An International Journal of Police Strategies & Management 22* (1999): 567–588.

67. Jihong Zhao, Ni He, and Nicholas Lovrich, "Community Policing: Did It Change the Basic Functions of Policing in the 1990s? A National Follow-up Study," *Justice Quarterly 20* (2003): 697–724.

68. Mark Moore and Anthony Braga, "Measuring and Improving Police Performance: The Lessons of CompStat and Its Progeny," *Policing 26* (2003): 439–453.

69. Robin Shepard Engel, *How Police Supervisory Styles Influence Patrol Officer Behavior* (Washington, D.C.: National Institute of Justice, 2003).

70. Amy Halsted, Max Bromley, and John Cochran, "The Effects of Work Orientations on Job Satisfaction Among Sheriffs' Deputies Practicing Community-Oriented Policing," *Policing: An International Journal of Police Strategies & Management 23* (2000): 82–104.

71. Venessa Garcia, "Constructing the 'Other' Within Police Culture: An Analysis of a Deviant Unit Within the Police Organization," *Police Practice and Research 6* (2005): 65–80.

72. Kevin Ford, Daniel Weissbein, and Kevin Plamondon, "Distinguishing Organizational from Strategy Commitment: Linking Officers' Commitment to Community Policing to Job Behaviors and Satisfaction," *Justice Quarterly 20* (2003): 159–186.

73. Michael Palmiotto, Michael Birzer, and N. Prabha Unnithan, "Training in Community Policing: A Suggested Curriculum," *Policing: An International Journal of Police Strategies & Management 23* (2000): 8–21.

74. Lisa Riechers and Roy Roberg, "Community Policing: A Critical Review of Underlying Assumptions," *Journal of Police Science and Administration 17* (1990): 112–113.

75. John Riley, "Community-Policing: Utilizing the Knowledge of Organizational Personnel," *Policing: An International Journal of Police Strategies & Management 22* (1999): 618–633.

76. James Forman, "Community Policing and Youth as Assets," *Journal of Criminal Law & Criminology 95* (2004): 1–48.

77. David Kessler, "Integrating Calls for Service with Community- and Problem-Oriented Policing: A Case Study," *Crime and Delinquency 39* (1993): 485–508.

78. L. Thomas Winfree, Gregory Bartku, and George Seibel, "Support for Community Policing Versus Traditional Policing Among Nonmetropolitan Police Officers: A Survey of Four New Mexico Police Departments," *American Journal of Police 15* (1996): 23–47.

79. Jihong Zhao, Ni He, and Nicholas Lovrich, "Value Change Among Police Officers at a Time of Organizational Reform: A Follow-up Study of Rokeach Values," *Policing 22* (1999): 152–170.

80. Jihong Zhao, Matthew Scheider, and Quint Thurman, "A National Evaluation of the Effect of COPS Grants on Police Productivity (Arrests) 1995–1999," *Police Quarterly 6* (2003) 387–410.

81. Mike Brogden, "'Horses for Courses' and 'Thin Blue Lines': Community Policing in Transitional Society," *Police Quarterly 8* (2005): 64–99.

82. Ling Ren, Liqun Cao, Nicholas Lovrich, and Michael Gaffney, "Linking confidence in the police with the performance of the police: Community policing can make a difference," *Journal of Criminal Justice 33* (January/February 2005): 55–66.

83. William Doerner and Terry Nowell, "The Reliability of the Behavioral-Personnel Assessment Device (BPAD) in Selecting Police Recruits," *Policing 22* (1999): 343–352.

84. See, for example, Richard Larson, *Urban Police Patrol Analysis* (Cambridge, Mass.: MIT Press, 1972).

85. Brian A. Reaves, *State and Local Police Departments, 1990* (Washington, D.C.: Bureau of Justice Statistics, 1992), 6.

86. Philip Ash, Karen Slora, and Cynthia Britton, "Police Agency Officer Selection Practices," *Journal of Police Science and Administration 17* (1990): 258–269.

87. Dennis Rosenbaum, Robert Flewelling, Susan Bailey, Chris Ringwalt, and Deanna Wilkinson, "Cops in the Classroom: A Longitudinal Evaluation of Drug Abuse Resistance Education (DARE)," *Journal of Research in Crime and Delinquency 31* (1994): 3–31.

Chapter 7

1. William Wells, Julie Horney, and Edward Maguire, "Patrol Officer Responses to Citizen Feedback: An Experimental Analysis," *Police Quarterly 8* (2005): 171–205.

2. David Jones, Liz Jones Liz, and Tim Prenzler, "Tertiary Education, Commitment, and Turnover in Police Work," *Police Practice and Research 6* (2005): 49–63.

3. Kathleen Maguire and Ann Pastore, eds., *Sourcebook of Criminal Justice Statistics*, www.albany.edu/sourcebook/pdf/t213.pdf, accessed on May 29, 2005.

4. Maguire and Pastore, eds., *Sourcebook of Criminal Justice Statistics*.

5. Eric Jefferis, Robert Kaminski, Stephen Homes, and Dena Hanley, "The Effect of a Videotaped Arrest on Public Perceptions of Police Use of Force," *Journal of Criminal Justice 25* (1997): 381–95.

6. Richard Lumb and Rondald Breazeale, "Police Officer Attitudes and Community Policing Implementation: Developing Strategies for Durable Organizational Change," *Policing & Society 13* (2003): 91–107.

7. Karen Kruger and Nicholas Valltos, "Dealing with Domestic Violence in Law Enforcement Relationships," *The FBI Law Enforcement Bulletin 71* (2002): 1–7.

8. Robert Loo, "A typology of burnout types among police managers," *Policing: An International Journal of Police Strategies and Management 27* (2004): 156–165.

9. FBI, "Law Enforcement Officers Killed and Assaulted, 2004," press release, May 16, 2005.

10. Jihong Zhao and Nicholas Lovrich, "Determinants of Minority Employment in American Municipal Police Agencies: The Representation of African-American Officers," *Journal of Criminal Justice 26* (1998): 267–278.

11. T. David Murphy and John Worrall, "Residency Requirements and Public Perceptions of the Police in Large Municipalities," *Policing 22* (1999): 327–342.

12. Jack Kuykendall and David Burns, "The African-American Police Officer: An Historical Perspective," *Journal of Contemporary Criminal Justice 1* (1980): 4–13.

13. Ibid.

14. Nicholas Alex, *Black in Blue: A Study of the Negro Policeman* (New York: Appleton-Century-Crofts, 1969).

15. Kim Michelle Lersch, "Predicting Citizen's Race in Allegations of Misconduct Against the Police," *Journal of Criminal Justice 26* (1998): 87–99.

16. Brian A. Reaves and Matthew J. Hickman, *Police Departments in Large Cities, 1990–2000* (Washington, D.C.: Bureau of Justice Statistics, 2002).

17. Nicholas Alex, *New York Cops Talk Back* (New York: Wiley, 1976).

18. David Eitle, Lisa Stolzenberg, and Stewart J. D'Alessio, "Police Organizational Factors, the Racial Composition of the Police, and the Probability of Arrest," *Justice Quarterly 22* (2005): 30–57.

19. Stephen Leinen, *African-American Police, White Society* (New York: New York University Press, 1984).

20. Donald Yates and Vijayan Pillai, "Frustration and Strain Among Fort Worth Police Officers," *Sociology and Social Research 76* (1992): 145–149.

21. Robin Haarr and Merry Morash, "Gender, Race, and Strategies of Coping with Occupational Stress in Policing," *Justice Quarterly 16* (1999): 303–336.

22. Kenneth Novak, Leanne Fiftal Alarid, and Wayne Lucas, "Exploring officers' acceptance of community policing: Implications for policy implementation," *Journal of Criminal Justice 31* (2003): 57–71; Donald Yates and Vijayan Pillai, "Race and Police Commitment to Community Policing," *Journal of Intergroup Relations 19* (1993): 14–23.

23. Bruce Berg, Edmond True, and Marc Gertz, "Police, Riots, and Alienation," *Journal of Police Science and Administration 12* (1984): 186–190.

24. For a review of the history of women in policing, see Dorothy Moses Schulz, "From Policewoman to Police Officer: An Unfinished Revolution," *Police Studies 16* (1993): 90–99; Cathryn House, "The Changing Role of Women in Law Enforcement," *Police Chief 60* (1993): 139–144.

25. Susan Martin, "Female Officers on the Move? A Status Report on Women in Policing," in *Critical Issues in Policing*, eds. Roger Dunham and Geoffery Alpert (Grove Park, Ill.: Waveland Press, 1988), 312–331.

26. *Le Bouef v. Ramsey*, 26 FEP Cases 884 (9/16/80).

27. Michael Birzer and Delores Craig, "Gender Differences in Police Physical Ability Test Performance," *American Journal of Police 15* (1996): 93–106.

28. Reaves and Hickman, *Police Departments in Large Cities, 1990–2000*.

29. James Daum and Cindy Johns, "Police Work from a Woman's Perspective," *Police Chief 61* (1994): 46–49.

30. Mary Brown, "The Plight of Female Police: A Survey of NW Patrolmen," *Police Chief 61* (1994): 50–53.

31. Matthew Hickman, Alex Piquero, and Jack Greene, "Discretion and Gender Disproportionality in Police Disciplinary Systems," *Policing: An International Journal of Police Strategies & Management 23* (2000): 105–116.

32. Robin Haarr and Merry Morash, "Gender, Race, and Strategies of Coping with Occupational Stress in Policing," *Justice Quarterly 16* (1999): 303–336.

33. Merry Morash and Jack Greene, "Evaluating Women on Patrol: A Critique of Contemporary Wisdom," *Evaluation Review 10* (1986): 230–255.

34. Steven Brandl, Meghan Stroshine, and James Frank, "Who Are the Complaint-Prone Officers? An Examination of the Relationship Between Police Officers' Attributes, Arrest Activity, Assignment, and Citizens' Complaints About Excessive Force," *Journal of Criminal Justice 29* (2001): 521–529.

35. Susan Martin, "Outsider within the Station House: The Impact of Race and Gender on Black Women Police," *Social Problems 41* (1994): 383–400 at 387.

36. Ibid., 392.

37. Ibid., 394.

38. Ibid., 397.

39. Ibid.

40. Eric Poole and Mark Pogrebin, "Factors Affecting the Decision to Remain in Policing: A Study of Women

Officers," *Journal of Police Science and Administration 16* (1988): 49–55.

41. Matthew J. Hickman and Brian A. Reaves, "Law Enforcement Management and Administrative Statistics," *Local Police Departments 2000* (Washington, D.C.: Bureau of Justice Statistics, 2003).

42. Brian A. Reaves and Matthew Hickman, *Police Departments in Large Cities, 1990–2000.*

43. Maggy Lee and Maurice Punch, "Policing by Degrees: Police Officers' Experience of University Education" *Policing & Society 14* (2004): 233–249.

44. Bruce Berg, "Who Should Teach Police: A Typology and Assessment of Police Academy Instructors," *American Journal of Police 9* (1990): 79–100.

45. David Carter and Allen Sapp, *The State of Police Education: Critical Findings* (Washington, D.C.: Police Executive Research Forum, 1988), 6.

46. John Krimmel, "The Performance of College-Educated Police: A Study of Self-Rated Police Performance Measures," *American Journal of Police 15* (1996): 85–95.

47. Robert Worden, "A Badge and a Baccalaureate: Policies, Hypotheses, and Further Evidence," *Justice Quarterly 7* (1990): 565–592.

48. See Lawrence Sherman and Warren Bennis, "Higher Education for Police Officers: The Central Issues," *Police Chief 44* (1977): 32.

49. Worden, "A Badge and a Baccalaureate," 587–589.

50. See, for example, Richard Harris, *The Police Academy: An Inside View* (New York: Wiley, 1973); John Van Maanen, "Observations on the Making of a Policeman," in *Order Under Law,* eds. R. Culbertson and M. Tezak (Prospect Heights, Ill.: Waveland Press, 1981), 111–126; Jonathan Rubenstein, *City Police* (New York: Ballantine Books, 1973); John Broderick, *Police in a Time of Change* (Morristown, N.J.: General Learning Press, 1977).

51. Louise Westmarland, "Police Ethics and Integrity: Breaking the Blue Code of Silence," *Policing & Society 15* (2005): 145–165.

52. Malcolm Sparrow, Mark Moore, and David Kennedy, *Beyond 911: A New Era for Policing* (New York: Basic Books, 1992), 51.

53. M. Steven Meagher and Nancy Yentes, "Choosing a Career in Policing: A Comparison of Male and Female Perceptions," *Journal of Police Science and Administration 16* (1986): 320–327.

54. Venessa Garcia, "Constructing the 'Other' within Police Culture: An Analysis of a Deviant Unit within the Police Organization," *Police Practice and Research 6* (2005): 65–80.

55. Michael K. Brown, *Working the Street* (New York: Russell Sage, 1981), 82.

56. Stan Shernock, "An Empirical Examination of the Relationship Between Police Solidarity and Community Orientation," *Journal of Police Science and Administration 18* (1988): 182–198.

57. John Crank, *Understanding Police Culture,* 2nd ed. (Cincinnati, Ohio: Anderson, 2003).

58. Eugene Paoline, "Taking Stock: Toward a Richer Understanding of Police Culture," *Journal of Criminal Justice 31* (2003): 199–214.

59. Crank, *Understanding Police Culture,* 359–363.

60. Egon Bittner, *The Functions of Police in Modern Society* (Cambridge, Mass.: Oelgeschlager, Gunn & Hain, 1980), 63.

61. Richard Lundman, *Police and Policing* (New York: Holt, Rinehart & Winston, 1980); see also Jerome Skolnick, *Justice Without Trial* (New York: Wiley, 1966).

62. Robert Regoli, Robert Culbertson, John Crank, and James Powell, "Career Stage and Cynicism Among Police Chiefs," *Justice Quarterly 7* (1990): 592–614.

63. William Westly, *Violence and the Police: A Sociological Study of Law, Custom, and Morality* (Cambridge, Mass.: MIT Press, 1970).

64. Skolnick, *Justice without Trial,* 42–68.

65. Milton Rokeach, Martin Miller, and John Snyder, "The Value Gap Between Police and Policed," *Journal of Social Issues 27* (1971): 155–171.

66. Wallace Graves, "Police Cynicism: Causes and Cures," *FBI Law Enforcement Bulletin 65* (1996): 16–21.

67. Arthur Niederhoffer, *Behind the Shield: The Police in Urban Society* (Garden City, N.Y.: Doubleday, 1967).

68. Ibid., 216–220.

69. Larry Tifft, "The 'Cop Personality' Reconsidered," *Journal of Police Science and Administration 2* (1974): 268; David Bayley and Harold Mendelsohn, *Minorities and the Police* (New York: Free Press, 1969); Robert Balch, "The Police Personality: Fact or Fiction?" *Journal of Criminal Law, Criminology, and Police Science 63* (1972): 117.

70. Lowell Storms, Nolan Penn, and James Tenzell, "Policemen's Perception of Real and Ideal Policemen," *Journal of Police Science and Administration 17* (1990): 40–43.

71. Carl Klockars, "The Dirty Harry Problem," *Annals 452* (1980): 33–47.

72. Jack Kuykendall and Roy Roberg, "Police Manager's Perceptions of Employee Types: A Conceptual Model," *Journal of Criminal Justice 16* (1988): 131–135.

73. Stephen Matrofski, R. Richard Ritti, and Jeffrey Snipes, "Expectancy Theory and Police Productivity in DUI Enforcement," *Law and Society Review 28* (1994): 113–138.

74. Ellen Hochstedler, "Testing Types: A Review and Test of Police Types," *Journal of Criminal Justice 9* (1981): 451–466.

75. For a thorough review, see Eric Riksheim and Steven Chermak, "Causes of Police Behavior Revisited," *Journal of Criminal Justice 21* (1993): 353–383.

76. Skolnick, *Justice Without Trial.*

77. Carroll Seron, Joseph Pereira, and Jean Kovath, "Judging Police Misconduct: 'Street-Level' versus Professional Policing," *Law & Society Review 38* (2004): 665–710.

78. Helen Eigenberg, Kathryn Scarborough, and Victor Kappeler, "Contributory Factors Affecting Arrest in Domestic and Nondomestic Assaults," *American Journal of Police 15* (1996): 27–51; Leonore Simon, "A Therapeutic Jurisprudence Approach to the Legal Processing of Domestic Violence Cases," *Psychology, Public Policy and Law 1* (1995): 43–79.

79. Peter Sinden and B. Joyce Stephens, "Police Perceptions of Domestic Violence: The Nexus of Victim, Perpetrator, Event, Self, and Law," *Policing 22* (1999): 313–326.

80. Robert Kane, "Patterns of Arrest in Domestic Violence Encounters: Identifying a Police Decision-Making Model," *Journal of Criminal Justice 27* (1999): 65–79.

81. Gregory Howard Williams, *The Law and Politics of Police Discretion* (Westport, Conn.: Greenwood Press, 1984).

82. Dana Jones and Joanne Belknap, "Police Responses to Battering in a Progressive Pro-Arrest Jurisdiction," *Justice Quarterly 16* (1999): 249–273.

83. Douglas Smith and Jody Klein, "Police Control of Interpersonal Disputes," *Social Problems 31* (1984): 468–481.

84. Jones and Belknap, "Police Responses to Battering," 249–273.

85. Robin Shepard Engel, "Patrol Officer Supervision in the Community Policing Era," *Journal of Criminal Justice 30* (2002): 51–64.

86. Westly, *Violence and the Police.*

87. John McCluskey, William Terrill, and Eugene Paoline, "Peer Group Aggressiveness and the Use of Coercion in Police-Suspect Encounters," *Police Practice and Research 6* (2005): 19–37.

88. Peter Liu and Thomas Cook, "Speeding Violation Dispositions in Relation to Police Officers' Perception of the Offenders," *Policing & Society* (March 15, 2005): 83–88.

89. Richard Lundman, "Demeanor or Crime? The Midwest City Police–Citizen Encounters Study," *Criminology 32* (1994): 631–653; Nathan Goldman, *The Differential Selection of Juvenile Offenders for Court Appearance* (New York: National Council on Crime and Delinquency, 1963).

90. Joseph Schafer and Stephen Mastrofski, "Police Leniency in Traffic Enforcement Encounters: Exploratory Findings from Observations and Interviews," *Journal of Criminal Justice 33* (2005): 225–238.

91. David Klinger, "Bringing Crime Back In: Toward a Better Understanding of Police Arrest Decisions," *Journal of Research in Crime and Delinquency 33* (1996): 333–336; "More on Demeanor and Arrest in Dade County," *Criminology 34* (1996): 61–79; "Demeanor or Crime? Why 'Hostile' Citizens Are More Likely to Be Arrested," *Criminology 32* (1994): 475–493.

92. Ambrose Leung, Frances Woolley, Richard Tremblay, and Frank Vitaro, "Who Gets Caught? Statistical Discrimination in Law Enforcement," *Journal of Socio-Economics 34* (2005): 289–309.

93. R. Steven Daniels, Lorin Baumhover, William Formby, and Carolyn Clark-Daniels, "Police Discretion and Elder Mistreatment: A Nested Model of Observation, Reporting, and Satisfaction," *Journal of Criminal Justice 27* (1999): 209–225

94. Karen Kruger and Nicholas Valltos, "Dealing with Domestic Violence in Law Enforcement Relationships," *FBI Law Enforcement Bulletin 71* (2002): 1–7.

95. Richard Lumb and Rondald Breazeale, "Police Officer Attitudes and Community Policing Implementation: Developing Strategies for Durable Organizational Change," *Policing & Society 13* (2003): 91–107.

96. Robert Loo, "A Typology of Burnout Types among Police Managers," *Policing: An International Journal of Police Strategies and Management 27* (2004): 156–165.

97. Yates and Pillai, "Frustration and Strain Among Fort Worth Police Officers."

98. For an impressive review, see Richard Farmer, "Clinical and Managerial Implication of Stress Research on the Police," *Journal of Police Science and Administration 17* (1990): 205–217.

99. Lawrence Travis III and Craig Winston, "Dissension in the Ranks: Officer Resistance to Community Policing and Support for the Organization," *Journal of Crime and Justice 21* (1998): 139–155.

100. Francis Cullen, Terrence Lemming, Bruce Link, and John Wozniak, "The Impact of Social Supports on Police Stress," *Criminology 23* (1985): 503–522.

101. Farmer, "Clinical and Managerial Implications"; Nancy Norvell, Dale Belles, and Holly Hills, "Perceived Stress Levels and Physical Symptoms in Supervisory Law Enforcement Personnel," *Journal of Police Science and Administration 16* (1988): 75–79.

102. Donald Yates and Vijayan Pillai, "Attitudes Toward Community Policing: A Causal Analysis," *Social Science Journal 33* (1996): 193–209.

103. Harvey McMurray, "Attitudes of Assaulted Police Officers and Their Policy Implications," *Journal of Police Science and Administration 17* (1990): 44–48.

104. Robert Ankony and Thomas Kelly, "The Impact of Perceived Alienation of Police Officers' Sense of Mastery and Subsequent Motivation for Proactive Enforcement," *Policing 22* (1999): 120–132.

105. Lawrence Blum, *Force Under Pressure: How Cops Live and Why They Die* (New York: Lantern Books, 2000).

106. Rose Lee Josephson and Martin Reiser, "Officer Suicide in the Los Angeles Police Department: A Twelve-Year Follow-Up," *Journal of Police Science and Administration 17* (1990): 227–230.

107. Yates and Pillai, "Attitudes Toward Community Policing," 205–206.

108. Ibid.

109. Rosanna Church and Naomi Robertson, "How State Police Agencies Are Addressing the Issue of Wellness," *Policing 22* (1999): 304–312.

110. Farmer, "Clinical and Managerial Implications," 215.

111. Peter Hart, Alexander Wearing, and Bruce Headey, "Assessing Police Work Experiences: Development of the Police Daily Hassles and Uplifts Scales," *Journal of Criminal Justice 21* (1993): 553–573.

112. Vivian Lord, Denis Gray, and Samuel Pond, "The Police Stress Inventory: Does It Measure Stress?" *Journal of Criminal Justice 19* (1991): 139–149.

113. Bittner, *The Functions of Police in Modern Society*, 46.

114. "Law-Enforcers on the Rampage," *Economist 375* (April 9, 2005): 31.

115. For a general review, see Tom McEwen, *National Data Collection on Police Use of Force* (Washington, D.C.: National Institute of Justice, 1996).

116. Matthew Durose, Erica Schmitt, and Patrick Langan, *Contacts Between Police and the Public Findings from the 2002 National Survey* (Washington, D.C.: Bureau of Justice Statistics, 2005).

117. Brad Smith, "The Impact of Police Officer Diversity on Police-Caused Homicides," *Policy Studies Journal 31* (2003): 147–162.

118. Brian Thompson and James Daniel Lee, "Who Cares If Police Become Violent? Explaining Approval of Police Use of Force Using a National Sample," *Sociological Inquiry 74* (2004): 381–410.

119. Sandra Lee Browning, Francis Cullen, Liqun Cao, Renee Kopache, and Thomas Stevenson, "Race and Getting Hassled by the Police: A Research Note," *Police Studies 17* (1994): 1–11.

120. Joel Garner, Christopher Maxwell, and Cedrick Heraux, "Characteristics Associated with the Prevalence and Severity of Force Used by the Police," *Justice Quarterly 19* (2002): 705–747.

121. William Terrill, "Police Use of Force: A Transactional Approach," *Justice Quarterly 22* (2005): 107–138.

122. Hannah Cooper, Lisa Moore, Sofia Gruskin, and Nancy Krieger, "Characterizing Perceived Police Violence: Implications for Public Health," *American Journal of Public Health 94* (2004): 1109–1119.

123. Thompson and Lee, "Who Cares If Police Become Violent?"

124. Sean Griffin and Thomas Bernard, "Angry Aggression Among Police Officers," *Police Quarterly 6* (2003): 3–21.

125. Ibid.

126. Kim Michelle Lersch and Tom Mieczkowski, "Who Are the Problem-Prone Officers? An Analysis of Citizen Complaints," *American Journal of Police 15* (1996): 23–42.

127. Samuel Walker, Geoffrey P. Alpert, and Dennis J. Kenney, *Early Warning Systems: Responding to the Problem Police Officer, Research in Brief* (Washington, D.C.: National Institute of Justice, 2001).

128. Michael D. White, "Controlling Police Decisions to Use Deadly Force: Reexamining the Importance of Administrative Policy," *Crime and Delinquency 47* (2001): 131.

129. Kevin Flynn, "New York Police Sting Tries to Weed Out Brutal Officers," *New York Times*, September 24, 1999, 2.

130. Lawrence Sherman and Robert Langworthy, "Measuring Homicide by Police Officers," *Journal of Criminal Law and Criminology 4* (1979): 546–560.

131. Ibid.

132. James Fyfe, "Police Use of Deadly Force: Research and Reform," *Justice Quarterly 5* (1988): 165–205.

133. Richard Parent and Simon Verdun-Jones, "Victim-Precipitated Homicide: Police Use of Deadly Force in British Columbia," *Policing 21* (1998): 432–449.

134. "10 Percent of Police Shootings Found to Be 'Suicide by Cop,'" *Criminal Justice Newsletter 29* (1998): 1.

135. Colin Loftin, David McDowall, Brian Wiersema, and Adam Dobrin, "Underreporting of Justifiable Homicides Committed by Police Officers in the United States, 1976–1998," *American Journal of Public Health 93* (2003): 1117–1121.

136. Sherman and Langworthy, "Measuring Homicide by Police Officers."

137. Brad Smith, "Structural and Organizational Predictors of Homicide by Police," *Policing 27* (2004): 539–557.

138. John MacDonald, Geoffrey Alpert, and Abraham Tennenbaum, "Justifiable Homicide by Police and Criminal Homicide: A Research Note," *Journal of Crime and Justice 22* (1999): 153–164.

139. Jonathan Sorenson, James Marquart, and Deon Brock, "Factors Related to Killings of Felons by Police Officers: A Test of the Community Violence and Conflict Hypotheses," *Justice Quarterly 10* (1993): 417–440; David Jacobs and David Britt, "Inequality and Police Use of Deadly Force: An Empirical Assessment of a Conflict Hypotheses," *Social Problems 26* (1979): 403–412; Smith, "Structural and Organizational Predictors of Homicide by Police."

140. David Jacobs and Jason Carmichael, "Subordination and Violence Against State Control Agents: Testing Political Explanations for Lethal Assaults Against the Police," *Social Forces 80* (2002): 1223–1252.

141. Fyfe, "Police Use of Deadly Force," 181.

142. John MacDonald, Patrick Manz, Geoffrey Alpert, and Roger Dunham, "Police Use of Force: Examining the Relationship between Calls for Service and the Balance of Police Force and Suspect Resistance," *Journal of Criminal Justice 31* (2003): 119–127.

143. Paul Takagi, "A Garrison State in a 'Democratic' Society," *Crime and Social Justice 5* (1974): 34–43.

144. Mark Blumberg, "Race and Police Shootings: An Analysis in Two Cities," in *Contemporary Issues in Law Enforcement*, ed. James Fyfe (Beverly Hills, Calif.: Sage, 1981), 152–166.

145. James Fyfe, "Shots Fired" (Ph.D. diss., State University of New York, Albany, 1978).

146. *Tennessee v. Garner*, 471 U.S. 1, 105 S.Ct. 1694, 85 L.Ed.2d 889 (1985).

147. *Graham v. Connor*, 490 U.S. 386, 109 S.Ct. 1865, 104 L.Ed.2d 443 (1989).

148. Franklin Graves and Gregory Connor, "The FLETC Use-of-Force Model," *Police Chief 59* (1992): 56–58.

149. See James Fyfe, "Administrative Interventions on Police Shooting Discretion: An Empirical Examination," *Journal of Criminal Justice 7* (1979): 313–325.

150. Frank Zarb, "Police Liability for Creating the Need to Use Deadly Force in Self-Defense," *Michigan Law Review 86* (1988): 1982–2009.

151. Warren Cohen, "When Lethal Force Won't Do," *U.S. News & World Report 122* (June 23, 1997): 12.

152. Richard Lumb and Paul Friday, "Impact of Pepper Spray Availability on Police Officer Use-of-Force Decisions," *Policing 20* (1997): 136–149.

153. Tom McEwen, "Policies on Less-than-Lethal Force in Law Enforcement Agencies," *Policing 20* (1997): 39–60.

154. John Cloud, "L.A. Confidential, for Real: Street Cops Accused of Frame-Ups in Widening Scandal," *Time*, September 27, 1999, 44; "L.A.'s Dirty War on Gangs: A Trail of Corruption Leads to Some of the City's Toughest Cops," *Newsweek*, October 11, 1999, 72.

155. Andrew Blankstein, "Jury Awards $6.5 Million in Frame-Up," *Los Angeles Times*, May 26, 2005.

156. Samuel Walker, *Popular Justice*, 2nd ed. (New York: Oxford University Press, 1997): 48–64.

157. Herman Goldstein, *Police Corruption* (Washington, D.C.: Police Foundation, 1975), 3.

158. Knapp Commission, *Report on Police Corruption* (New York: Braziller, 1973), 1–34.

159. Elizabeth Neuffer, "Seven Additional Detectives Linked to Extortion Scheme," *Boston Globe*, October 25, 1988, 60.

160. Kevin Cullen, "U.S. Probe Eyes Bookie Protection," *Boston Globe*, October 25, 1988.

161. Michael Johnston, *Political Corruption and Public Policy in America* (Monterey, Calif.: Brooks/Cole, 1982), 75.

162. William Doherty, "Ex-Sergeant Says He Aided Bid to Sell Exam," *Boston Globe*, February 26, 1987, 61.

163. Alan Feuer and William Rashbaum, "Blood Ties: 2 Officers' Path to Mob Indictments," *The New York Times*, March 12, 2005, A1; Lisa Stein, "Cops Gone Wild" *U.S. News & World Report 138* (March 21, 2005): 14.

164. Ellwyn Stoddard, "Blue Coat Crime," in *Thinking About Police*, ed. Carl Klockars (New York: McGraw-Hill, 1983), 338–349.

165. Lawrence Sherman, *Police Corruption: A Sociological Perspective* (Garden City, N.Y.: Doubleday, 1974).

166. Robert Daley, *Prince of the City* (New York: Houghton Mifflin, 1978).

167. Sherman, *Police Corruption*, 40–41.

168. Samuel Walker, *Police in Society* (New York: McGraw-Hill, 1983), 181.

169. Sherman, *Police Corruption*, 194.

170. Kevin Flynn, "Police Department Routinely Drops Cases of Officer Misconduct, Report Says," *New York Times*, September 15, 1999, 1.

171. Barbara Gelb, *Tarnished Brass: The Decade After Serpico* (New York: Putnam, 1983); Candace McCoy, "Lawsuits Against Police: What Impact Do They Have?" *Criminal Law Bulletin 20* (1984): 49–56.

172. "Philadelphia Police Corruption Brings Major Reform Initiative," *Criminal Justice Newsletter 27* (1996): 4–5.

173. Brown, *Working the Street*, 290.

174. Samuel Walker, *Police Accountability: The Role of Citizen Oversight* (Belmont, Calif.: Wadsworth, 2001); Liqun Cao and Bu Huang, "Determinants of Citizen Complaints Against Police Abuse of Power," *Journal of Criminal Justice 28* (2000): 203–213; Peter Finn, "Getting Along with Citizen Oversight," *FBI Law Enforcement Bulletin 69* (2000): 22–27; Best Practices in Police Accountability website www.policeaccountability.org/issuefacts.htm, accessed on June 1, 2005.

175. *Miranda v. Arizona*, 384 U.S. 436 (1966).

176. *Colorado v. Connelly*, 107 S.Ct. 515 (1986).

177. *Minnick v. Miss.*, 498 U.S. 46; 111 S.Ct. 486; 112 L.Ed.2d. 489 (1990).

178. *Harris v. New York*, 401 U.S. 222 (1971).

179. *Michigan v. Tucker*, 417 U.S. 433 (1974).

180. *Nix v. Williams*, 104 S.Ct. 2501 (1984).

181. *Oregon v. Elstad*, 105 S.Ct. 1285 (1985).

182. *Colorado v. Connelly*, 107 S.Ct. 515 (1986).

183. *Arizona v. Fulminante*, 499 U.S. 279, 111 S.Ct. 1246; 113 L.Ed.2d. 302 (1991).

184. *Moran v. Burbine*, 106 S.Ct. 1135 (1986); *Michigan v. Mosley*, 423 U.S. 96 (1975); *Fare v. Michael C.*, 442 U.S. 23 (1979).

185. *New York v. Quarles*, 104 S.Ct. 2626 (1984).

186. *Colorado v. Spring*, 107 S.Ct. 851 (1987).

187. *Moran v. Burbine*, 106 S.Ct. 1135 (1986).

188. *Davis v. United States*, 114 S.Ct. 2350 (1994).

189. *Oregon v. Elstad*, 105 S.Ct. 1285 (1985).

190. *Missouri v. Seibert* No. 02-1371 (2004).

191. *United States vs. Patane* No. 02-1183 (2004).

192. *Chavez v. Martinez* No. 01-1444. Decided May 27, 2003.

193. Victoria Time and Brian Payne, "Police Chiefs' Perceptions About *Miranda:* An Analysis of Survey Data," *Journal of Criminal Justice 30* (2002): 77–86.
194. Ibid.
195. *Chimel v. California,* 395 U.S. 752 (1969).
196. *Terry v. Ohio,* 392 U.S. 1 (1968).
197. *Illinois v. Wardlow,* 528 U.S. 119 (2000).
198. *Carroll v. United States,* 267 U.S. 132 (1925).
199. *United States v. Ross,* 102 S.Ct. 2147 (1982).
200. *Whren v. United States,* 116 S.Ct. 1769 (1996).
201. Drivers, *Pennsylvania v. Mimms,* 434 U.S. 106 (1977); passengers, *Maryland v. Wilson,* 117 U.S. 882 (1997).
202. Mark Hansen, "Rousting Miss Daisy?" *American Bar Association Journal 83* (1997): 22; *Knowles v. Iowa,* 119 S.Ct. 507 (1998); *Wyoming v. Houghton,* 119 S.Ct. 1297 (1999).
203. *Bumper v. North Carolina,* 391 U.S. 543 (1960).
204. *Ohio v. Robinette,* 117 S. Ct. 417 (1996).
205. Limitations on the plain view doctrine have been defined in *Arizona v. Hicks,* 107 S.Ct. 1149 (1987); the recording of serial numbers from stereo components in a suspect's apartment could not be justified as being in plain view.
206. *Weeks v. United States,* 232 U.S. 383, 34 S.Ct. 341, 58 L.Ed. 652 (1914).
207. *Mapp v. Ohio,* 367 U.S. 643, 81 S.Ct. 1684, 6 L.Ed.2d 1081 (1961).
208. *United States v. Leon,* 468 U.S. 897, 104 S.Ct. 3405, 82 L.Ed.2d 677 (1984).
209. William Greenhalgh, *The Fourth Amendment Handbook: A Chronological Survey of Supreme Court Decisions* (Chicago: American Bar Association Section on Criminal Justice, 1995).
210. Donald Dripps, "The Case for the Contingent Exclusionary Rule," *American Criminal Law Review 38* (2001): 1–47.
211. Jon Gould and Stephen Mastrofski "Suspect Searches: Assessing Police Behavior Under the U.S. Constitution," *Criminology & Public Policy 3* (2004): 315–362.

Chapter 8

1. Matthew Durose and Patrick Langan, *Felony Sentences in State Courts* (Washington, D.C.: Bureau of Justice Statistics, 2004).
2. U.S. Constitution, Art. 3, Secs. 1 and 2.
3. American Bar Association, *Federal Judicial Pay, 2003* (Washington, D.C., 2003) www.uscourts.gov/newsroom/judgespayaction.pdf, accessed on August 24, 2005.
4. Jason Perez-Dormitzer, "Bill Safeguards Restaurants in Obesity-Related Lawsuits," *Providence Business News 18,* March 22, 2004, 5–7.
5. David Klein and Robert Hume, "Fear of Reversal as an Explanation of Lower Court Compliance," *Law and Society Review 37* (2003): 579–607.
6. Roy Schotland, "2002 Judicial Elections," *Spectrum: The Journal of State Government 76* (2003): 18–20.
7. Sari Escovitz with Fred Kurland and Nan Gold, *Judicial Selection and Tenure* (Chicago: American Judicature Society, 1974), 3–16.
8. State Court Statistics, 2001.
9. Judith McFarlane, Ann Malecha, Julia Gist, Kathy Watson, Elizabeth Batten, Iva Hall, and Sheila Smith, "Protection Orders and Intimate Partner Violence: An 18-Month Study of 150 Black, Hispanic, and White Women," *American Journal of Public Health 94* (2004): 613–618.
10. County of Santa Barbara, District Attorney's Office, www.countyofsb.org/da/CriminalDivision/ElderAbuse/elderAbuse.asp, accessed on March 10, 2005.
11. Mason County, Washington, Prosecutors Office, www.co.mason.wa.us/prosecutor/default.shtml, accessed on March 10, 2005.
12. Carol J. DeFrances, *National Survey of Prosecutors, Prosecutors in State Courts, 2001* (Washington, D.C.: Bureau of Justice Statistics, 2002).
13. Jessie Larson, "Unequal Justice: The Supreme Court's Failure to Curtail Selective Prosecution for the Death Penalty," *Journal of Criminal Law & Criminology 93* (2003): 1009–1031.
14. Kenneth C. Davis, *Discretionary Justice* (Baton Rouge: Louisiana State University Press, 1969), 180; see also James B. Stewart, *The Prosecutor* (New York: Simon & Schuster, 1987).
15. Barbara Boland, *The Prosecution of Felony Arrests* (Washington, D.C.: Government Printing Office, 1983).
16. Newman Baker, "The Prosecutor—Initiation of Prosecution," *Journal of Criminal Law, Criminology, and Police Science 23* (1993): 770–771; see also Joan Jacoby, *The American Prosecutor: A Search for Identity* (Lexington, Mass.: Lexington Books, 1980).
17. Jeffrey Spears and Cassia Spohn, "The Effect of Evidence Factors and Victim Characteristics on Prosecutors' Charging Decisions in Sexual Assault Cases," *Justice Quarterly 14* (1997): 501–524.
18. Janell Schmidt and Ellen Hochstedler Steury, "Prosecutorial Discretion in Filing Charges in Domestic Violence Cases," *Criminology 27* (1989): 487–510.
19. Michael Edmund O'Neill, "Understanding Federal Prosecutorial Declinations: An Empirical Analysis of Predictive Factors," *American Criminal Law Review 41* (2004): 1439–1533.
20. Rodney Kingsnorth and Randall Macintosh, "Domestic Violence: Predictors of Victim Support for Official Action," *Justice Quarterly 21* (2004): 301–328.
21. Myrna Dawson and Ronit Dinovitzer, "Victim Cooperation and the Prosecution of Domestic Violence in a Specialized Court," *Justice Quarterly 18* (2001): 593–622.
22. Rodney Kingsworth, John Lopez, Jennifer Wentworth, and Debra Cummings, "Adult Sexual Assault: The Role of Racial/Ethnic Composition in Prosecution and Sentencing," *Journal of Criminal Justice 26* (1998): 359–372; *United States v. Armstrong* 517 U.S. 456 (1996).
23. O'Neill, "Understanding Federal Prosecutorial Declinations."
24. Robert Davis, Barbara Smith, and Bruce Taylor, "Increasing the Proportion of Domestic Violence Arrests that Are Prosecuted: A Natural Experiment in Milwaukee," *Criminology & Public Policy 2* (2003): 263–282.
25. Shaila Dewan, "Prosecutors Say Cuts Force Plea Bargains," *New York Times,* March 10, 2003, B3.
26. Charles D. Breitel, "Controls in Criminal Law Enforcement," *University of Chicago Law Review 27* (1960): 427.
27. Cassia Spohn, Dawn Beichner, and Erika Davis-Frenzel, "Prosecutorial Justifications for Sexual Assault Case Rejection: Guarding the 'Gateway to Justice,'" *Social Problems 48* (2001): 206–235.
28. "Prosecutor Conduct," editorial, *USA Today,* April 1, 1999, 14A.
29. American Bar Association, *Model Rules of Professional Conduct* (Chicago: ABA, 1983), rule 3.8; see also Stanley Fisher, "In Search of the Virtuous Prosecutor: A Conceptual Framework," *American Journal of Criminal Law 15* (1988): 197.
30. Stanley Fisher, "Zealousness and Overzealousness: Making Sense of the Prosecutor's Duty to Seek Justice," *Prosecutor 22* (1989): 9; see also Bruce Green, "The Ethical Prosecutor and the Adversary System," *Criminal Law Bulletin 24* (1988): 126–145.
31. *North Carolina v. Pearce,* 395 U.S. 711, 89 S.Ct. 2072, 23 L.Ed.2d 656 (1969).
32. *Blackledge v. Perry,* 417 U.S. 21, 94 S.Ct. 2098, 40 L.Ed.2d 628 (1974).
33. *Bordenkircher v. Hayes,* 434 U.S. 357, 98 S.Ct. 663, 54 L.Ed.2d 604 (1978).
34. American Bar Association, *Model Code of Professional Responsibility and Judicial Conduct* (Chicago: ABA, 1980), rule 3.8.

35. *Gideon v. Wainwright,* 372 U.S. 335, 83 S.Ct. 792, 9 L.Ed.2d 799 (1963).
36. *Argersinger v. Hamlin,* 407 U.S. 25, 92 S.Ct. 2006, 32 L.Ed.2d 530 (1972).
37. Carol J. DeFrances, *State-Funded Indigent Defense Services, 1999* (Washington, D.C.: Bureau of Justice Statistics, 2001).
38. Ibid.
39. Data compiled by the Bureau of Justice Statistics, www.ojp.usdoj.gov/bjs/id.htm#conviction, accessed on August 24, 2005.
40. *Strickland v. Washington,* 466 U.S. 668, 104 S.Ct. 2052, 80 L.Ed.2d 674 (1984).
41. *Florida v. Nixon,* No. 03-931 (Decided: 12/13/04).
42. The following sections are based on Ron Bowmaster and John Cariotto, "Information Sharing in Nebraska," National Center for State Courts, 2003, www.ctc8.net/showarticle.asp?id=69, accessed on August 24, 2005; Fredric I. Lederer, "The Road to the Virtual Courtroom? Consideration of Today's—and Tomorrow's—High-Technology Courtrooms," *South Carolina Law Review 50* (1999): 799; "Criminal Court Records Go Online," *The Quill 90* (2002), 39; Donald C. Dilworth, "New Court Technology Will Affect How Attorneys Present Trials," *Trial 33* (1997): 100–114.

Chapter 9

1. NA, "Deal Ok'd in Milton Academy Sex Case," *Boston Globe,* June 2, 2005, 3.
2. Gerard Rainville and Brian A. Reaves, *Felony Defendants in Large Urban Counties, 2000* (Washington, D.C.: Bureau of Justice Statistics, 2003).
3. Ibid.
4. Christopher Stephens, "Bail" section of the Criminal Procedure project, *Georgetown Law Journal 90* (2002): 1395–1416.
5. Traci Schlesinger, "Racial and Ethnic Disparity in Pretrial Criminal Processing," *Justice Quarterly 22* (2005): 170–192.
6. This section leans on John Clark and D. Alan Henry, *Pretrial Services Programming at the Start of the 21st Century: A Survey of Pretrial Services Programs* (Washington, D.C.: Bureau of Justice Assistance, 2003).
7. *Stack v. Boyle,* 342 U.S. 1, 72 S.Ct. 1, 96 L.Ed. 3 (1951).
8. Bob Burton, Director of Training and Surety Corporation Liaison, National Institute of Bail Enforcement, personal contact, September 17, 2004.
9. Vera Institute of Justice, *1961–1971: Programs in Criminal Justice* (New York: Vera Institute of Justice, 1972).
10. Chris Eskridge, *Pretrial Release Programming* (New York: Clark Boardman, 1983), 27.
11. Public Law No. 89-465, 18 U.S.C., sec. 3146 (1966).
12. Ellis M. Johnston, "Once a Criminal, Always a Criminal? Unconstitutional Presumptions for Mandatory Detention of Criminal Aliens," *Georgetown Law Journal 89* (2001): 2593–2636.
13. 18 U.S.C., sec. 3142 (1984).
14. See, generally, Fred Cohen, "The New Federal Crime Control Act," *Criminal Law Bulletin 21* (1985): 330–337.
15. *Schall v. Martin,* 467 U.S. 253, 104 S.Ct. 2403, 81 L.Ed.2d 207 (1984).
16. *United States v. Salerno,* 481 U.S. 739, 107 S.Ct. 2095, 95 L.Ed.2d 697 (1987).
17. *Demore v. Kim* (01-1491) 538 U.S. 510 (2003).
18. Doris James, *Profile of Jail Inmates, 2002* (Washington, D.C.: Bureau of Justice Statistics, 2004).
19. Rainville and Reaves, *Felony Defendants in Large Urban Counties, 2000.*
20. Ric Simmons, "Reexamining the Grand Jury: Is There Room for Democracy in the Criminal Justice System?" *Boston University Law Review 82* (2002): 1–76.
21. John Gibeaut, "Indictment of a System," *ABA Journal 87* (2001): 34.
22. Kirke D. Weaver, "A Change of Heart or a Change of Law? Withdrawing a Guilty Plea Under Federal Rule of Criminal Procedure 32(e)," *Journal of Criminal Law and Criminology 92* (2001): 273–306.
23. George Fisher, *Plea Bargaining's Triumph: A History of Plea Bargaining in America* (Palo Alto: Stanford University Press, 2004).
24. George Fisher, "Plea Bargaining's Triumph," *Yale Law Journal 109* (2000): 857–1058.
25. Fred Zacharis, "Justice in Plea Bargaining," *William and Mary Law Review 39* (1998): 1121–1189.
26. Nathaniel J. Pallone, "Without Plea-Bargaining, Megan Kanka Would Be Alive Today,"*Criminology & Public Policy 3* (2003): 83–96.
27. William Stuntz, "Plea Bargaining and Criminal Law's Disappearing Shadow," *Harvard Law Review 117* (2004): 2548–2569.
28. Mike McConville, "Plea Bargaining: Ethics and Politics," *Journal of Law & Society 25* (1998): 526–555.
29. *Hill v. Lockhart,* 474 U.S. 52, 106 S.Ct. 366, 88 L.Ed.2d 203 (1985).
30. *Boykin v. Alabama,* 395 U.S. 238, 89 S.Ct. 1709, 23 L.Ed.2d 274 (1969); *Brady v. United States,* 397 U.S. 742, 90 S.Ct. 1463, 25 L.Ed.2d 747 (1970).
31. *North Carolina v. Alford,* 400 U.S. 25, 91 S.Ct. 160, 27 L.Ed.2d 162 (1970).
32. *Santobello v. New York,* 404 U.S. 257, 92 S.Ct. 495, 30 L.Ed.2d 427 (1971).
33. *Ricketts v. Adamson,* 483 U.S. 1, 107 S.Ct. 2680, 97 L.Ed.2d 1 (1987).
34. *Bordenkircher v. Hayes,* 434 U.S. 357, 98 S.Ct. 663, 54 L.Ed.2d 604 (1978).
35. *United States v. Mezzanatto,* 116 S.Ct. 1480, 134 L.Ed.2d 687 (1995).
36. Stephen P. Lagoy, Joseph J. Senna, and Larry J. Siegel, "An Empirical Study on Information Usage for Prosecutorial Decision Making in Plea Negotiations," *American Criminal Law Review 13* (1976): 435–471.
37. William Stuntz, "The Uneasy Relationship between Criminal Procedure and Criminal Justice," *Yale Law Journal 107* (1997): 10–11.
38. Stephanos Bibas, "Plea Bargaining Outside the Shadow of Trial," *Harvard Law Review 117* (2004): 2464–2543.
39. Keith Bystrom, "Communicating Plea Offers to the Client," in *Ethical Problems Facing the Criminal Defense Lawyer,* ed. Rodney Uphoff (Chicago: American Bar Association Section on Criminal Justice, 1995), 84.
40. American Bar Association, *Standards Relating to Pleas of Guilty,* standard 3.3; National Advisory Commission on Criminal Justice Standards and Goals, *Task Force Report on Courts* (Washington, D.C.: Government Printing Office, 1973), 42.
41. American Bar Association, *Standards Relating to Pleas of Guilty,* 73; see also Alan Alschuler, "The Trial Judge's Role in Plea Bargaining," *Columbia Law Review 76* (1976): 1059.
42. Federal Rules of Criminal Procedure, rule 11.
43. American Bar Association, *Model Uniform Victims of Crime Act* (Chicago: ABA, 1992).
44. George P. Fletcher, *With Justice for Some—Victims' Rights in Criminal Trials* (New York: Addison-Wesley, 1995), 190–193.
45. *Santobello v. New York,* 404 U.S. 257, 92 S.Ct. 495, 30 L.Ed.2d 427 (1971).
46. Barbara Boland and Brian Forst, *The Prevalence of Guilty Pleas* (Washington, D.C.: Bureau of Justice Statistics, 1984), 3; see also Gary Hengstler, "The Troubled Justice System," *American Bar Association Journal 80* (1994): 44.
47. National Institute of Law Enforcement and Criminal Justice, *Plea Bargaining in the United States,* 37–40.

48. For a discussion of this issue, see Michael Tonry, "Plea Bargaining Bans and Rules," in *Sentencing Reform Impacts* (Washington, D.C.: Government Printing Office, 1987).

49. Candace McCoy, *Politics and Plea Bargaining: Victims' Rights in California* (Philadelphia: University of Pennsylvania Press, 1993).

50. Bibas, "Plea Bargaining Outside the Shadow of Trial."

51. Franklyn Dunford, D. Wayne Osgood, and Hart Weichselbaum, *National Evaluation of Diversion Programs* (Washington, D.C.: Government Printing Office, 1982).

52. Sharla Rausch and Charles Logan, "Diversion from Juvenile Court: Panacea or Pandora's Box?" in *Evaluating Juvenile Justice*, ed. James Kleugel (Beverly Hills, Calif.: Sage, 1983), 19–30.

53. John Hepburn, "Recidivism Among Drug Offenders Following Exposure to Treatment," *Criminal Justice Policy Review 16* (2005): 237–259.

Chapter 10

1. *Estelle v. Williams*, 425 U.S. 501, 96 S.Ct. 1691, 48 L.Ed.2d 126 (1976); see also American Bar Association, "Fair Trial and Free Press," in *Standards for Criminal Justice* (Washington, D.C.: ABA, 1993).

2. *Riggins v. Nevada* 504 U.S. 127 (1992).

3. *Sell v. United States* No. 02-5664, June 16, 2003.

4. *Lilly v. Virginia*, 98-5881 (1999).

5. *Pointer v. State of Texas*, 380 U.S. 400, 85 S.Ct. 1065, 13 L.Ed.2d 923 (1965).

6. *Maryland v. Craig*, 497 U.S. 836, 110 S.Ct. 3157, 111 L.Ed.2d 666 (1990).

7. *Duncan v. Louisiana*, 391 U.S. 145, 88 S.Ct. 1444, 20 L.Ed.2d 491 (1968).

8. *Baldwin v. New York*, 399 U.S. 66, 90 S.Ct. 1886, 26 L.Ed.2d 437 (1970).

9. *Blanton v. North Las Vegas*, 489 U.S. 538, 109 S.Ct. 1289, 103 L.Ed.2d 550 (1989).

10. *Lewis v. United States*, 116 S.Ct. 2163 (1996).

11. *Williams v. Florida*, 399 U.S. 78, 90 S.Ct. 1893, 26 L.Ed.2d 446 (1970).

12. Ibid., at 101, 90 S.Ct. at 1906.

13. *Apodica v. Oregon*, 406 U.S. 404, 92 S.Ct. 1628, 32 L.Ed.2d 184 (1972).

14. *Scott v. Illinois*, 440 U.S. 367, 99 S.Ct. 1158, 59 L.Ed.2d 383 (1979).

15. *Shelton v. Alabama*, 122 U.S. 1764 (2002).

16. *Faretta v. California*, 422 U.S. 806, 95 S.Ct. 2525, 45 L.Ed.2d 562 (1975).

17. *Martinez v. Court of Appeal of California*, 120 S.Ct. 684 (2000).

18. See American Bar Association, *Standards Relating to Speedy Trial* (Chicago: ABA, 1995).

19. *Klopfer v. North Carolina*, 386 U.S. 213, 87 S.Ct. 988, 18 L.Ed.2d 1 (1967).

20. Ibid., at 223, 87 S.Ct. at 993.

21. *Doggett v. United States*, 505 U.S. 162, 112 S.Ct. 2686, 120 Rusch.2d 520 (1992).

22. Nicholas A. Pellegrini, "Extension of Criminal Defendant's Right to Public Trial," *St. John's University Law Review 611* (1987): 277–289.

23. *In re Oliver*, 333 U.S. 257, 68 S.Ct. 499, 92 L.Ed. 682 (1948).

24. *Nebraska Press Association v. Stuart*, 427 U.S. 539, 96 S.Ct. 2791, 49 L.Ed.2d 683 (1976).

25. Ibid., at 547, 96 S.Ct. at 2797.

26. Ibid., at 370, 99 S.Ct at 2900.

27. *Press-Enterprise Co. v. Superior Court*, 478 U.S. 1, 106 S.Ct. 2735, 92 L.Ed.2d 1 (1986).

28. *Wilson et al. v. Layne*, Public Law No. 98-83 (1999).

29. *Richmond Newspapers, Inc. v. Virginia*, 448 U.S. 555, 100 S.Ct. 2814, 65 L.Ed.2d 973 (1980).

30. *Globe Newspaper Co. v. Superior Court for County of Norfolk*, 457 U.S. 596, 102 S.Ct. 2613, 73 L.Ed.2d 248 (1982).

31. *Chandler v. Florida*, 449 U.S. 560 (1981); see also American Bar Association, *Criminal Justice Standards, Fair Trial, and Free Press* (Washington, D.C.: ABA, 1992).

32. See *Brinegar v. United States*, 338 U.S. 160, 69 S.Ct. 1302, 93 L.Ed. 1879 (1949); *In re Winship*, 397 U.S. 358, 90 S.Ct. 1068, 25 L.Ed.2d 368 (1970).

33. Ibid., at 174.

34. See *In re Winship*, at 397.

35. Ibid., at 371, 90 S.Ct. at 1076.

36. Brian Kalt, "The Exclusion of Felons from Jury Service," *American University Law Review* 53 (2003): 65–189.

37. George Hayden, Joseph Senna, and Larry Siegel, "Prosecutorial Discretion in Peremptory Challenges: An Empirical Investigation of Information Use in the Massachusetts Jury Selection Process," *New England Law Review 13* (1978): 768.

38. *Batson v. Kentucky*, 476 U.S. 79, 106 S.Ct. 1712, 90 L.Ed.2d 69 (1986); see also Alan Alschuler and Randall Kennedy, "Equal Justice—Would Color-Conscious Jury Selection Help?" *American Bar Association Journal 81* (1995): 36–37.

39. *Powers v. Ohio*, 479 U.S. 400, 111 S.Ct. 1364, 113 L.Ed.2d 411 (1991).

40. *J.E.B. v. Alabama*, 511 U.S. 114 S.Ct. 1419, 128 L.Ed.2d 89 (1994).

41. *Chapman v. California*, 386 U.S. 18, 87 S.Ct. 824, 17 L.Ed.2d 705 (1967).

42. *Douglas v. California*, 372 U.S. 353, 83 S.Ct. 814, 9 L.Ed.2d 811 (1963).

43. *Ross v. Moffitt*, 417 U.S. 600, 94 S.Ct. 2437, 41 L.Ed.2d 341 (1974).

Chapter 11

1. Graeme Newman, *The Punishment Response* (Philadelphia: Lippincott, 1978), 13.

2. Michel Foucault, *Discipline and Punishment* (New York: Vintage Books, 1978).

3. Kathleen Auerhahn, "Selective Incapacitation and the Problem of Prediction," *Criminology 37* (1999): 703–734.

4. Kathleen Daly, "Neither Conflict nor Labeling nor Paternalism Will Suffice: Intersections of Race, Ethnicity, Gender, and Family in Criminal Court Decisions," *Crime and Delinquency 35* (1989): 136–168.

5. Among the most helpful sources for this section were Benedict Alper, *Prisons Inside-Out* (Cambridge, Mass.: Ballinger, 1974); Gustave de Beaumont and Alexis de Tocqueville, *On the Penitentiary System in the United States and Its Applications in France* (Carbondale: Southern Illinois University Press, 1964); Orlando Lewis, *The Development of American Prisons and Prison Customs, 1776–1845* (Montclair, N.J.: Patterson-Smith, 1967); Leonard Orland, ed., *Justice, Punishment, and Treatment* (New York: Free Press, 1973); J. Goebel, *Felony and Misdemeanor* (Philadelphia: University of Pennsylvania Press, 1976); George Rusche and Otto Kircheimer, *Punishment and Social Structure* (New York: Russell & Russell, 1939); Samuel Walker, *Popular Justice* (New York: Oxford University Press, 1980); Newman, *The Punishment Response*; David Rothman, *Conscience and Convenience* (Boston: Little, Brown, 1980); George Ives, *A History of Penal Methods* (Montclair, N.J.: Patterson-Smith, 1970); Robert Hughes, *The Fatal Shore* (New York: Knopf, 1986); Leon Radzinowicz, *A History of English Criminal Law*, vol. 1 (London: Stevens, 1943), 5.

6. *Crime and Punishment in America, 1999*, Report 229 (Washington, D.C.: National Center for Policy Analysis, 1999).

7. Matthew DuRose and Patrick Langan, *Felony Sentences in State Courts, 2002* (Washington, D.C.: Bureau of Justice Statistics, 2004).

8. Silvia Mendes and Michael McDonald, "Putting Severity of Punishment Back in the Deterrence Package," *Policy Studies Journal 29* (2001): 588–610.

9. Steven Levitt, "Understanding Why Crime Fell in the 1990s: Four Factors that Explain the Decline and Six that Do Not," *Journal of Economic Perspective 18* (2004): 163–191; Steven Levitt, "Why Do Increased Arrest Rates Appear to Reduce Crime: Deterrence, Incapacitation, or Measurement Error?" *Economic Inquiry 36* (1998): 353–372.

10. Lawrence Sherman and Richard Berk, "The Specific Deterrent Effects of Arrest for Domestic Assault," *American Sociological Review 49* (1984): 261–272

11. Christopher D. Maxwell, Joel H. Garner, and Jeffrey A. Fagan, *The Effects of Arrest in Intimate Partner Violence: New Evidence from the Spouse Assault Replication Program* (Washington, D.C.: National Institute of Justice, 2001).

12. Robert Davis, Barbara Smith, and Laura Nickles, "The Deterrent Effect of Prosecuting Domestic Violence Misdemeanors," *Crime and Delinquency 44* (1998): 434–442.

13. Patrick Langan and David Levin, *Recidivism of Prisoners Released in 1994* (Washington, D.C.: Bureau of Justice Statistics, 2002).

14. Faith Lutze, "The Influence of Shock Incarceration Program on Inmate Adjustment and Attitudinal Change," *Journal of Criminal Justice 29* (2001): 255–266.

15. Charles Logan, *Criminal Justice Performance Measures for Prisons* (Washington, D.C.: Bureau of Justice Statistics, 1993), 3.

16. Alexis Durham, "The Justice Model in Historical Context: Early Law, the Emergence of Science, and the Rise of Incarceration," *Journal of Criminal Justice 16* (1988): 331–346.

17. Andrew von Hirsh, *Doing Justice: The Choice of Punishments* (New York: Hill and Wang, 1976).

18. Shawn Bushway, "The Impact of an Arrest on the Job Stability of Young White American Men," *Journal of Research in Crime and Delinquency 35* (1998): 454–479.

19. Lawrence W. Sherman, David P. Farrington, Doris Layton MacKenzie, Brandon Walsh, Denise Gottfredson, John Eck, Shawn Bushway, and Peter Reuter, *Evidence-Based Crime Prevention* (London: Routledge and Kegan Paul, 2002); see also Arnulf Kolstad, "Imprisonment as Rehabilitation: Offenders' Assessment of Why It Does Not Work," *Journal of Criminal Justice 24* (1996): 323–335.

20. Francis Cullen, John Paul Wright, Shayna Brown, Melissa Moon, and Brandon Applegate, "Public Support for Early Intervention Programs: Implications for a Progressive Policy Agenda," *Crime and Delinquency 44* (1998): 187–204; Richard McCorkle, "Research Note: Punish and Rehabilitate? Public Attitudes Toward Six Common Crimes," *Crime and Delinquency 39* (1993): 240–252; D. A. Andrews, Ivan Zinger, Robert Hoge, James Bonta, Paul Gendreau, and Francis Cullen, "Does Correctional Treatment Work? A Clinically Relevant and Psychologically Informed Meta-Analysis," *Criminology 28* (1990): 369–404.

21. Paula Ditton and Doris James Wilson, *Truth in Sentencing in State Prisons* (Washington, D.C.: Bureau of Justice Statistics, 1999).

22. Jo Dixon, "The Organizational Context of Criminal Sentencing," *American Journal of Sociology 100* (1995): 1157–1198.

23. Michael Tonry, *Reconsidering Indeterminate and Structured Sentencing Series: Sentencing and Corrections: Issues for the 21st Century* (Washington, D.C.: National Institute of Justice, 1999).

24. *Blakely v. Washington*, 124 S.Ct. 2531 (2004).

25. *United States v. Booker*, No. 04-104 Decided January 12, 2005.

26. Michael Tonry, "The Failure of the U.S. Sentencing Commission's Guidelines," *Crime and Delinquency 39* (1993): 131–149.

27. Sean Nicholson-Crotty, "The Impact of Sentencing Guidelines on State-Level Sanctions: An Analysis Over Time," *Crime & Delinquency 50* (2004): 395–410.

28. Michael Tonry, "Racial Politics, Racial Disparities, and the War on Crime," *Crime and Delinquency 40* (1994): 475–494.

29. Joan Petersilia and Susan Turner, *Guideline-Based Justice: The Implications for Racial Minorities* (Santa Monica, Calif.: Rand, 1985).

30. Henry Scott Wallace, "Mandatory Minimums and the Betrayal of Sentencing Reform: A Legislative Dr. Jekyll and Mr. Hyde," *Federal Probation 57* (1993): 9–16.

31. Paula M. Ditton and Doris James Wilson, *Truth in Sentencing in State Prisons* (Washington, D.C.: Bureau of Justice Statistics, 1999).

32. Matthew Durose and Patrick Langan, *Felony Sentences in State Courts, 2002* (Washington, D.C.: Bureau of Justice Statistics, 2004).

33. Brent Smith and Kelly Damphouse, "Terrorism, Politics, and Punishment: A Test of Structural-Contextual Theory and the Liberation Hypothesis," *Criminology 36* (1998): 67–92.

34. For a general look at the factors that affect sentencing, see Susan Welch, Cassia Spohn, and John Gruhl, "Convicting and Sentencing Differences Among Black, Hispanic, and White Males in Six Localities," *Justice Quarterly 2* (1985): 67–80.

35. Stewart D'Alessio and Lisa Stolzenberg, "Socioeconomic Status and the Sentencing of the Traditional Offender," *Journal of Criminal Justice 21* (1993): 61–77.

36. Cecilia Saulters-Tubbs, "Prosecutorial and Judicial Treatment of Female Offenders," *Federal Probation 57* (1993): 37–41.

37. See, generally, Janet Johnston, Thomas Kennedy, and I. Gayle Shuman, "Gender Differences in the Sentencing of Felony Offenders," *Federal Probation 87* (1987): 49–56; Cassia Spohn and Susan Welch, "The Effect of Prior Record in Sentencing Research: An Examination of the Assumption that Any Measure Is Adequate," *Justice Quarterly 4* (1987): 286–302; David Willison, "The Effects of Counsel on the Severity of Criminal Sentences: A Statistical Assessment," *Justice System Journal 9* (1984): 87–101.

38. Cassia Spohn, Miriam DeLone, and Jeffrey Spears, "Race/Ethnicity, Gender, and Sentence Severity in Dade County, Florida: An Examination of the Decision to Withhold Adjudication," *Journal of Crime and Justice 21* (1998): 111–132.

39. Ellen Hochstedler Steury and Nancy Frank, "Gender Bias and Pretrial Release: More Pieces of the Puzzle," *Journal of Criminal Justice 18* (1990): 417–432.

40. Shimica Gaskins, "Women of Circumstance—The Effects of Mandatory Minimum Sentencing on Women Minimally Involved in Drug Crimes," *American Criminal Law Review 41* (2004): 1533–1563.

41. Dean Champion, "Elderly Felons and Sentencing Severity: Interregional Variations in Leniency and Sentencing Trends," *Criminal Justice Review 12* (1987): 7–15.

42. Darrell Steffensmeier, John Kramer, and Jeffery Ulmer, "Age Differences in Sentencing," *Justice Quarterly 12* (1995): 583–601.

43. Darrell Steffensmeier, Jeffery Ulmer, and John Kramer, "The Interaction of Race, Gender, and Age in Criminal Sentencing: The Punishment Cost of Being Young, Black, and Male," *Criminology 36* (1998): 763–798.

44. *Payne v. Tennessee*, 111 S.Ct. 2597, 115 L.Ed.2d 720 (1991).

45. Robert Davis and Barbara Smith, "The Effects of Victim Impact Statements on Sentencing Decisions: A Test in an Urban Setting," *Justice Quarterly 11* (1994): 453–469;

Edna Erez and Pamela Tontodonato, "The Effect of Victim Participation in Sentencing on Sentence Outcome," *Criminology 28* (1990): 451–474.

46. Rodney Kingsworth, Randall MacIntosh, and Jennifer Wentworth, "Sexual Assault: The Role of Prior Relationship and Victim Characteristics in Case Processing," *Justice Quarterly 16* (1999): 276–302.

47. Tracy Nobiling, Cassia Spohn, and Miriam DeLone, "A Tale of Two Counties: Unemployment and Sentence Severity," *Justice Quarterly 15* (1998): 459–486.

48. Michael Tonry, *Malign Neglect: Race, Crime, and Punishment in America* (New York: Oxford University Press, 1995), 105–109.

49. *Coker v. Georgia*, 433 U.S. 584, 97 S.Ct. 2861, 53 L.Ed.2d 982 (1977).

50. *People v. Stephen LaValle*, Sup.C. #71 (2004).

51. For more on this issue, read Hugo Adam Bedau and Paul Cassell, *Debating the Death Penalty: Should America Have Capital Punishment? The Experts on Both Sides Make Their Best Case* (London: Oxford University Press, 2003).

52. Stephen Markman and Paul Cassell, "Protecting the Innocent: A Response to the Bedeau-Radelet Study," *Stanford Law Review 41* (1988): 121–170.

53. Snell, *Capital Punishment*, 2.

54. Stephen Layson, "United States Time-Series Homicide Regressions with Adaptive Expectations," *Bulletin of the New York Academy of Medicine 62* (1986): 589–619.

55. James Galliher and John Galliher, "A 'Commonsense' Theory of Deterrence and the 'Ideology' of Science: The New York State Death Penalty Debate," *Journal of Criminal Law & Criminology 92* (2002): 307.

56. Steven Stack, "The Effect of Well-Publicized Executions on Homicide in California," *Journal of Crime and Justice 21* (1998): 1–12.

57. David Friedrichs, "Comment—Humanism and the Death Penalty: An Alternative Perspective," *Justice Quarterly 6* (1989): 197–209.

58. Kathleen Maguire and Ann L. Pastore, eds., *Sourcebook of Criminal Justice Statistics, 2002*, www.albany.edu/sourcebook/, accessed on September 1, 2005.

59. For an analysis of the formation of public opinion on the death penalty, see Kimberly Cook, "Public Support for the Death Penalty: A Cultural Analysis" (paper presented at the annual meeting of the American Society of Criminology, San Francisco, November 1991).

60. Alexis Durham, H. Preston Elrod, and Patrick Kinkade, "Public Support to the Death Penalty: Beyond Gallup," *Justice Quarterly 13* (1996): 705–736.

61. See, generally, Hugo Bedau, *Death Is Different: Studies in the Morality, Law, and Politics of Capital Punishment* (Boston: Northeastern University Press, 1987); Keith Otterbein, *The Ultimate Coercive Sanction* (New Haven, Conn.: HRAF Press, 1986).

62. Michael Radelet and Hugo Bedeau, "Miscarriages of Justice in Potentially Capital Cases," *Stanford Law Review 40* (1987): 121–181.

63. House Subcommittee on Civil and Constitutional Rights, *Innocence and the Death Penalty: Assessing the Danger of Mistaken Executions* (Washington, D.C.: Government Printing Office, 1993).

64. David Stewart, "Dealing with Death," *American Bar Association Journal 80* (1994): 53.

65. "The Innocence Protection Act," editorial, *America 187* (September 23, 2002): 2–3.

66. Erik Lillquist, "Absolute Certainty and the Death Penalty," *American Criminal Law Review 42* (2005): 45–92.

67. "A Victim's Progress," *Newsweek*, June 12, 1989, 5.

68. William Doerner, "The Impact of Medical Resources on Criminally Induced Lethality: A Further Examination," *Criminology 26* (1988): 171–177.

69. Elizabeth Purdom and J. Anthony Paredes, "Capital Punishment and Human Sacrifice," in *Facing the Death Penalty: Essays on Cruel and Unusual Punishment*, ed. Michael Radelet (Philadelphia: Temple University Press, 1989), 152–153.

70. Kimberly Cook, "A Passion to Punish: Abortion Opponents Who Favor the Death Penalty," *Justice Quarterly 15* (1998): 329–346.

71. Julian Roberts, "Capital Punishment, Innocence, and Public Opinion," *Criminology & Public Policy 4* (2005): 1–3.

72. Kathleen Maguire and Ann Pastore, *Sourcebook of Criminal Justice Statistics, 1995* (Washington, D.C.: Government Printing Office, 1996), 183.

73. James Unnever and Francis Cullen, "Executing the Innocent and Support for Capital Punishment: Implications for Public Policy," *Criminology & Public Policy 4* (2005): 3–37.

74. Scott Vollum, Dennis Longmire, and Jacqueline Buffington-Vollum, "Confidence in the Death Penalty and Support for Its Use: Exploring the Value-Expressive Dimension of Death Penalty Attitudes," *JQ: Justice Quarterly 21* (2004): 521–546.

75. Gennaro Vito and Thomas Keil, "Elements of Support for Capital Punishment: An Examination of Changing Attitudes," *Journal of Crime and Justice 21* (1998): 17–25.

76. Denise Paquette Boots, Kathleen Heide, and John Cochran, "Death Penalty Support for Special Offender Populations of Legally Convicted Murderers: Juveniles, the Mentally Retarded, and the Mentally Incompetent," *Behavioral Sciences & the Law 22* (2004): 223–238.

77. John Whitehead, Michael Blankenship, and John Paul Wright, "Elite versus Citizen Attitudes on Capital Punishment: Incongruity Between the Public and Policy Makers," *Journal of Criminal Justice 27* (1999): 249–258.

78. William Bowers and Glenn Pierce, "Deterrence or Brutalization: What Is the Effect of Executions?" *Crime and Delinquency 26* (1980): 453–484.

79. Keith Harries and Derral Cheatwood, *The Geography of Executions: The Capital Punishment Quagmire in America* (Lanham, Md.: Rowman and Littlefield, 1997).

80. Lisa Stolzenberg and Stewart D'Alessio, "Capital Punishment, Execution Publicity, and Murder in Houston, Texas," *Journal of Criminal Law & Criminology 94* (2004): 351–380.

81. Jonathan R. Sorensen and Rocky L. Pilgrim, "An Actuarial Risk of Assessment of Violence Posed by Murder Defendants," *Journal of Criminal Law and Criminology 90* (2000): 1251–1271.

82. Rick Ruddell and Martin Urbina, "Minority Threat and Punishment: A Cross-National Analysis," *JQ: Justice Quarterly 21* (2004): 903–931.

83. Marian Williams and Jefferson Holcomb, "Racial Disparity and Death Sentences in Ohio," *Journal of Criminal Justice 29* (2001): 207–218.

84. Jon Sorenson and Donald Wallace, "Prosecutorial Discretion in Seeking Death: An Analysis of Racial Disparity in the Pretrial Stages of Case Processing in a Midwestern County," *JQ: Justice Quarterly 16* (1999): 559–578.

85. Jefferson Holcomb, Marian Williams, and Stephen Demuth, "White Female Victims and Death Penalty Disparity Research," *JQ: Justice Quarterly 21* (2004): 877–902.

86. Lawrence Greenfield and David Hinners, *Capital Punishment, 1984* (Washington, D.C.: Bureau of Justice Statistics, 1985).

87. Gennaro Vito and Thomas Keil, "Capital Sentencing in Kentucky: An Analysis of the Factors Influencing Decision Making in the Post-Gregg Period," *The Journal of Criminal Law & Criminology 79* (1988): 483–508.

88. David Brown, "Man Is Executed in Carolina: Second of a White Who Killed a Black," *Boston Globe*, January 25, 1995, 3.

89. Geoffrey Rapp, "The Economics of Shootouts: Does the Passage of Capital Punishment Laws Protect or Endan-

ger Police Officers?" *Albany Law Review 65* (2002): 1051–1084.

90. Robert Johnson, *Death Work: A Study of the Modern Execution Process* (Pacific Grove, Calif.: Brooks/Cole, 1990).

91. William Bailey, "Disaggregation in Deterrence and Death Penalty Research: The Case of Murder in Chicago," *Journal of Criminal Law and Criminology 74* (1986): 827–859.

92. Gennaro Vito, Pat Koester, and Deborah Wilson, "Return of the Dead: An Update on the Status of Furman-Commuted Death Row Inmates," in *The Death Penalty in America: Current Research*, ed. Robert Bohm (Cincinnati: Anderson, 1991), 89–100; Gennaro Vito, Deborah Wilson, and Edward Latessa, "Comparison of the Dead: Attributes and Outcomes of Furman-Commuted Death Row Inmates in Kentucky and Ohio," in *The Death Penalty in America: Current Research*, ed. Robert Bohm (Cincinnati: Anderson, 1991), 101–112.

93. John Cochran, Mitchell Chamlin, and Mark Seth, "Deterrence or Brutalization? An Impact Assessment of Oklahoma's Return to Capital Punishment," *Criminology 32* (1994): 107–134.

94. William Bailey, "Deterrence, Brutalization, and the Death Penalty: Another Examination of Oklahoma's Return to Capital Punishment," *Justice Quarterly 36* (1998): 711–734.

95. Joseph Schumacher, "An International Look at the Death Penalty," *International Journal of Comparative and Applied Criminal Justice 14* (1990): 307–315.

96. Don Terry, "California Prepares for Faster Execution Pace," *New York Times*, October 17, 1998, A7.

97. See, for example, Ernest Van Den Haag, Punishing Criminals: Concerning a Very Old and Painful Question (New York: Basic Books, 1975), 209–211; Walter Berns, "Defending the Death Penalty," *Crime and Delinquency 26* (1980): 503–511.

98. Thoroddur Bjarnason and Michael Welch, "Father Knows Best: Parishes, Priests, and American Catholic Parishioners' Attitudes Toward Capital Punishment," *Journal for the Scientific Study of Religion 43* (2004): 103–118.

99. Franklin Zimring, *The Contradictions of American Capital Punishment* (London: Oxford University Press, 2003).

100. Vance McLaughlin and Paul Blackman, "Mass Legal Executions in Georgia," *Georgia Historical Quarterly 88* (2004): 66–84.

101. Austin Sarat, "Innocence, Error, and the 'New Abolitionism': A Commentary," *Criminology & Public Policy 4* (2005): 45–53.

102. *Furman v. Georgia*, 408 U.S. 238, 92 S.Ct. 2726, 33 L.Ed.2d 346 (1972).

103. *Gregg v. Georgia*, 428 U.S. 153, 96 S.Ct. 2909, 49 L.Ed.2d 859 (1976).

104. Ibid., at 205–207, 96 S.Ct. at 2940–2941.

105. *Ring v. Arizona*, No. 01-488 (2002).

106. *Coker v. Georgia*, 430 U.S. 349, 97 S.Ct. 1197, 51 L.Ed.2d 393 (1977).

107. *Ford v. Wainwright*, 477 US 399 (1986).

108. *Atkins v. Virginia*, No. 00-8452, 2002.

109. *Roper v. Simmons*, No. 03-0633 (2005).

110. Walter C. Reckless, "Use of the Death Penalty," *Crime and Delinquency 15* (1969): 43; Thorsten Sellin, "Effect of Repeal and Reintroduction of the Death Penalty on Homicide Rates," in *The Death Penalty*, ed. Thorsten Sellin (Philadelphia: American Law Institute, 1959); Robert H. Dann, "The Deterrent Effect of Capital Punishment," *Friends Social Service Series 29* (1935): 1; William Bailey and Ruth Peterson, "Murder and Capital Punishment: A Monthly Time-Series Analysis of Execution Publicity," *American Sociological Review 54* (1989): 722–743; David Phillips, "The Deterrent Effect of Capital Punishment," *American Journal of Sociology 86* (1980): 139–148; Sam McFarland, "Is Capital Punishment a Short-Term Deterrent to Homicide? A Study of the Effects of Four Recent American Executions," *Journal of Criminal Law and Criminology 74* (1984): 1014–1032; Richard Lempert, "The Effect of Executions on Homicides: A New Look in an Old Light," *Crime and Delinquency 29* (1983): 88–115.

111. Jon Sorenson, Robert Wrinkle, Victoria Brewer, and James Marquart, "Capital Punishment and Deterrence: Examining the Effect of Executions on Murder in Texas," *Crime and Delinquency 45* (1999): 481–493.

112. Isaac Ehrlich, "The Deterrent Effect of Capital Punishment: A Question of Life or Death," *American Economic Review 65* (1975): 397.

113. For a review, see William Bailey, "The General Prevention Effect of Capital Punishment for Non-Capital Felonies," in *The Death Penalty in America: Current Research*, ed. Robert Bohm (Cincinnati: Anderson, 1991), 21–38.

Chapter 12

1. For a history of probation, see Edward Sieh, "From Augustus to the Progressives: A Study of Probation's Formative Years," *Federal Probation 57* (1993): 67–72.

2. Ibid.

3. David Rothman, *Conscience and Convenience* (Boston: Little, Brown, 1980), 82–117.

4. See, generally, Todd Clear and Vincent O'Leary, *Controlling the Offender in the Community* (Lexington, Mass.: Lexington Books, 1983).

5. Lauren Glaze and Seri Palla, *Probation and Parole, 2003* (Washington, D.C.: Bureau of Justice Statistics, 2004).

6. Matthew Durose and Patrick Langan, *Felony Sentences in the United States, 2002* (Washington, D.C.: Bureau of Justice Statistics, 2004).

7. Karl Hanson and Suzanne Wallace-Carpretta, "Predictors of Criminal Recidivism Among Male Batterers," *Psychology, Crime & Law 10* (2004): 413–427.

8. *Higdon v. United States*, 627 F.2d 893 (9th Cir., 1980).

9. *United States v. Lee*, No. 01-4485 01/07/03, *United States v. Lee*, PICS N. 03-0023.

10. *United States v. Gallo*, 20 F.3d 7 (1st Cir., 1994).

11. Todd Clear and Edward Latessa, "Probation Officers' Roles in Intensive Supervision: Surveillance versus Treatment," *Justice Quarterly 10* (1993): 441–462.

12. Paul von Zielbauer, "Probation Dept. Is Now Arming Officers Supervising Criminals," *New York Times*, August 7, 2003, 5.

13. Ibid.

14. Hanson and Wallace-Carpretta, "Predictors of Criminal Recidivism Among Male Batterers," (2004): 413–427.

15. David Duffee and Bonnie Carlson, "Competing Value Premises for the Provision of Drug Treatment to Probationers," *Crime and Delinquency 42* (1996): 574–592.

16. Richard Sluder and Rolando Del Carmen, "Are Probation and Parole Officers Liable for Injuries Caused by Probationers and Parolees?" *Federal Probation 54* (1990): 3–12.

17. Patricia Harris, "Client Management Classification and Prediction of Probation Outcome," *Crime and Delinquency 40* (1994): 154–174.

18. Anne Schneider, Laurie Ervin, and Zoann Snyder-Joy, "Further Exploration of the Flight from Discretion: The Role of Risk/Need Instruments in Probation Supervision Decisions," *Journal of Criminal Justice 24* (1996): 109–121.

19. Clear and O'Leary, *Controlling the Offender in the Community*, 11–29, 77–100.

20. *Minnesota v. Murphy*, 465 U.S. 420, 104 S.Ct. 1136, 79 L.Ed.2d 409 (1984).

21. *Griffin v. Wisconsin*, 483 U.S. 868, 107 S.Ct. 3164, 97 L.Ed.2d 709 (1987).

22. *United States v. Knights*, 122 S.Ct. 587 (2001).

23. *Mempa v. Rhay,* 389 U.S. 128, 88 S.Ct. 254, 19 L.Ed.2d 336 (1967).

24. *Morrissey v. Brewer,* 408 U.S. 471, 92 S.Ct. 2593, 33 L.Ed.2d 484 (1972).

25. *Gagnon v. Scarpelli,* 411 U.S. 778, 93 S.Ct. 1756, 36 L.Ed.2d 656 (1973).

26. *United States v. Granderson,* 114 Ct. 1259, 127 L.Ed.2d 611 (1994).

27. Glaze and Palla, *Probation and Parole, 2003.*

28. M. Kevin Gray, Monique Fields, and Sheila Royo Maxwell, "Examining Probation Violations: Who, What, and When," *Crime and Delinquency* 47 (2001): 537–557.

29. Kevin Minor, James Wells, and Crissy Sims, "Recidivism Among Federal Probationers—Predicting Sentence Violations," *Federal Probation* 67 (2003): 31–37.

30. Cassia Spohn and David Holleran, "The Effect of Imprisonment on Recidivism Rates of Felony Offenders: A Focus on Drug Offenders," *Criminology* 40 (2002): 329–359.

31. Joan Petersilia, Susan Turner, James Kahan, and Joyce Peterson, *Granting Felons Probation: Public Risks and Alternatives* (Santa Monica, Calif.: Rand, 1985).

32. Spohn and Holleran, "The Effect of Imprisonment on Recidivism Rates of Felony Offenders."

33. Kathryn Morgan, "Factors Influencing Probation Outcome: A Review of the Literature," *Federal Probation* 57 (1993): 23–29.

34. Michelle Meloy, "The Sex Offender Next Door: An Analysis of Recidivism, Risk Factors, and Deterrence of Sex Offenders on Probation," *Criminal Justice Policy Review* 16 (2005): 211–236.

35. Kathryn Morgan, "Factors Associated with Probation Outcome," *Journal of Criminal Justice* 22 (1994): 341–353.

36. Paula M. Ditton, *Mental Health and Treatment of Inmates and Probationers* (Washington, D.C.: Bureau of Justice Statistics, 1999).

37. "Law in Massachusetts Requires Probationers to Pay 'Day Fees,'" *Criminal Justice Newsletter,* September 15, 1988, 1.

38. Peter Finn and Dale Parent, *Making the Offender Foot the Bill: A Texas Program* (Washington, D.C.: National Institute of Justice, 1992).

39. Nicole Leeper Piquero, "A Recidivism Analysis of Maryland's Community Probation Program," *Journal of Criminal Justice* 31 (2003): 295–308.

40. Todd R. Clear, "Places Not Cases: Rethinking the Probation Focus," *Howard Journal of Criminal Justice* 44 (2005): 172–184.

41. Ariel Hart, "Runaway Bride Enters Plea and Is Sentenced to Probation," *New York Times,* June 3, 2005, A14.

42. Todd Clear and Patricia Hardyman, "The New Intensive Supervision Movement," *Crime and Delinquency* 36 (1990): 42–60.

43. For a thorough review of these programs, see James Byrne, Arthur Lurigio, and Joan Petersilia, eds., *Smart Sentencing: The Emergence of Intermediate Sanctions* (Newbury Park, Calif.: Sage, 1993). Hereinafter cited as *Smart Sentencing.*

44. Norval Morris and Michael Tonry, *Between Prison and Probation: Intermediate Punishments in a Rational Sentencing System* (New York: Oxford University Press, 1990).

45. Michael Tonry and Richard Will, *Intermediate Sanctions* (Washington, D.C.: National Institute of Justice, 1990).

46. Ibid., 8.

47. Stephen Farrall, "Officially Recorded Convictions for Probationers: The Relationship with Self-Report and Supervisory Observations," *Legal and Criminological Psychology* 10 (2005): 121–132.

48. Michael Maxfield and Terry Baumer, "Home Detention with Electronic Monitoring: Comparing Pretrial and Postconviction Programs," *Crime and Delinquency* 36 (1990): 521–556.

49. Sally Hillsman and Judith Greene, "Tailoring Fines to the Financial Means of Offenders," *Judicature* 72 (1988): 38–45.

50. George Cole, "Monetary Sanctions: The Problem of Compliance," in *Smart Sentencing,* 51–64.

51. *Tate v. Short,* 401 U.S. 395, 91 S.Ct. 668, 28 L.Ed.2d 130 (1971).

52. Pennsylvania Department of Corrections, *Day Fines, 2003,* www.cor.state.pa.us/stats/lib/stats/Day_Fines.pdf, accessed on August 1, 2005.

53. Doris Layton MacKenzie, "Evidence-Based Corrections: Identifying What Works," *Crime and Delinquency* 46 (2000): 457–472.

54. John L. Worrall, "Addicted to the Drug War: The Role of Civil Asset Forfeiture as a Budgetary Necessity in Contemporary Law Enforcement," *Journal of Criminal Justice* 29 (2001): 171–187.

55. C. Yorke, *Some Consideration on the Law of Forfeiture for High Treason,* 2d ed. (1746), 26; cited in David Fried, "Rationalizing Criminal Forfeiture," *Journal of Criminal Law and Criminology* 79 (1988): 328–436.

56. Fried, "Rationalizing Criminal Forfeiture," 436.

57. James B. Jacobs, Coleen Friel, and Edward O'Callaghan, "Pension Forfeiture: A Problematic Sanction for Public Corruption," *American Criminal Law Review* 35 (1997): 57–92.

58. Worrall, "Addicted to the Drug War."

59. For a general review, see Burt Galaway and Joe Hudson, *Criminal Justice, Restitution, and Reconciliation* (New York: Criminal Justice Press, 1990); Robert Carter, Jay Cocks, and Daniel Glazer, "Community Service: A Review of the Basic Issues," *Federal Probation* 51 (1987): 4–11.

60. Frederick Allen and Harvey Treger, "Community Service Orders in Federal Probation: Perceptions of Probationers and Host Agencies," *Federal Probation* 54 (1990): 8–14.

61. Gail Caputo, "Community Service in Texas: Results of a Probation Survey," *Corrections Compendium* 30 (2005): 8–12.

62. Sudipto Roy, "Two Types of Juvenile Restitution Programs in Two Midwestern Counties: A Comparative Study," *Federal Probation* 57 (1993): 48–53.

63. Joan Petersilia, *The Influence of Criminal Justice Research* (Santa Monica, Calif.: Rand, 1987).

64. Ibid.

65. Jodi Brown, *Correctional Populations in the United States, 1996* (Washington, D.C.: Bureau of Justice Statistics, 1999), 39.

66. Joan Petersilia and Susan Turner, "Evaluation Intensive Supervision Probation/Parole: Results of a Nationwide Experiment," National Institute of Justice, Research in Brief (Washington, D.C.: National Institute of Justice, 1993).

67. James Byrne and Linda Kelly, "Restructuring Probation as an Intermediate Sanction: An Evaluation of the Massachusetts Intensive Probation Supervision Program," final report to the National Institute of Justice, Research Program on the Punishment and Control of Offenders, Washington, D.C., 1989.

68. James Ryan, "Who Gets Revoked? A Comparison of Intensive Supervision Successes and Failures in Vermont," *Crime and Delinquency* 43 (1997): 104–118.

69. Angela Robertson, Paul Grimes, and Kevin Rogers, "A Short-Run Cost-Benefit Analysis of Community-Based Interventions for Juvenile Offenders," *Crime and Delinquency* 47 (2001): 265–284.

70. S. Christopher Baird and Dennis Wagner, "Measuring Diversion: The Florida Community Control Program," *Crime and Delinquency* 36 (1990): 112–125.

71. Linda Smith and Ronald Akers, "A Comparison of Recidivism of Florida's Community Control and Prison: A

Five-Year Survival Analysis," *Journal of Research in Crime and Delinquency* 30 (1993): 267–292.

72. Robert N. Altman, Robert E. Murray, and Evey B. Wooten, "Home Confinement: A 90s Approach to Community Supervision," *Federal Probation* 61 (1997): 30–32.

73. Joseph Papy and Richard Nimer, "Electronic Monitoring in Florida," *Federal Probation* 55 (1991): 31–33.

74. Peter Ibarra and Edna Erez, "Victim-centric Diversion? The Electronic Monitoring of Domestic Violence Cases," *Behavioral Sciences & the Law* 23 (2005): 259–276.

75. Preston Elrod and Michael Brown, "Predicting Public Support for Electronic House Arrest: Results from a New York County Survey," *American Behavioral Scientist* 39 (1996): 461–474.

76. Brian Payne and Randy Gainey, "The Electronic Monitoring of Offenders Released from Jail or Prison: Safety, Control, and Comparisons to the Incarceration Experience," *Prison Journal* 84 (2004): 413–435.

77. Kevin E. Courtright, Bruce L. Berg, and Robert J. Mutchnick, "The Cost-Effectiveness of Using House Arrest with Electronic Monitoring for Drunk Drivers," *Federal Probation* 61 (1997): 19–22.

78. Brian Payne and Randy Gainey, "The Electronic Monitoring of Offenders Released From Jail or Prison"; Mary Finn and Suzanne Muirhead-Steves, "The Effectiveness of Electronic Monitoring with Male Parolees," *Justice Quarterly* 19 (2002): 293–313.

79. See, generally, Edward Latessa and Lawrence Travis III, "Residential Community Correctional Programs," in *Smart Sentencing*, 65–79.

80. Updated with personal correspondence, Portland House personnel, September 22, 2005.

81. Harvey Siegal, James Fisher, Richard Rapp, Casey Kelliher, Joseph Wagner, William O'Brien, and Phyllis Cole, "Enhancing Substance Abuse Treatment with Case Management," *Journal of Substance Abuse Treatment* 13 (1996): 93–98.

82. Dale Parent, *Day Reporting Centers for Criminal Offenders: A Descriptive Analysis of Existing Programs* (Washington, D.C.: National Institute of Justice, 1990); Jack McDevitt and Robyn Miliano, "Day Reporting Centers: An Innovative Concept in Intermediate Sanctions," in *Smart Sentencing*, 80–105.

83. David Diggs and Stephen Pieper, "Using Day Reporting Centers as an Alternative to Jail," *Federal Probation* 58 (1994): 9–12.

84. For information on the Atlanta program, see www.pap.state.ga.us/metro.htm; see also www.dcor.state.ga.us/COMMISSIONER/PublicRelations/Video_DRC_wmv.htm, accessed on September 26, 2005.

85. David Hartmann, Paul Friday, and Kevin Minor, "Residential Probation: A Seven-Year Follow-Up of Halfway House Discharges," *Journal of Criminal Justice* 22 (1994): 503–515.

86. David Farabee, Yih-Ing Hser Douglas Anglin, and David Huang, "Recidivism Among an Early Cohort of California's Proposition 36 Offenders," *Criminology & Public Policy* 3 (2004): 563–583.

87. Banhram Haghighi and Alma Lopez, "Success/Failure of Group Home Treatment Programs for Juveniles," *Federal Probation* 57 (1993): 53–57.

88. Kathleen Daly and Russ Immarigeon, "The Past, Present, and Future of Restorative Justice: Some Critical Reflections," *Contemporary Justice Review* 1 (1998): 21–45.

89. John Braithwaite, *Crime, Shame, and Reintegration* (Melbourne, Australia: Cambridge University Press, 1989).

90. Gene Stephens, "The Future of Policing: From a War Model to a Peace Model," in *The Past, Present and Future of American Criminal Justice*, eds. Brendan Maguire and Polly Radosh (Dix Hills, N.Y.: General Hall, 1996), 77–93.

91. Kay Pranis, "Peacemaking Circles: Restorative Justice in Practice Allows Victims and Offenders to Begin Repairing the Harm," *Corrections Today* 59 (1997): 74.

92. Carol LaPrairie, "The 'New' Justice: Some Implications for Aboriginal Communities," *Canadian Journal of Criminology* 40 (1998): 61–79.

93. Robert Coates, Mark Umbreit, and Betty Vos, "Restorative Justice Systemic Change: The Washington County Experience," *Federal Probation* 68 (2004): 16–23.

94. David R. Karp and Beau Breslin, "Restorative Justice in School Communities," *Youth & Society* 33 (2001): 249–272.

95. Paul Jesilow and Deborah Parsons, "Community Policing as Peacemaking," *Policing & Society* 10 (2000): 163–183.

96. Gordon Bazemore and Curt Taylor Griffiths, "Conferences, Circles, Boards, and Mediations: The 'New Wave' of Community Justice Decision Making," *Federal Probation* 61 (1997): 25–37.

97. John Braithwaite, "Setting Standards for Restorative Justice," *British Journal of Criminology* 42 (2002): 563–577.

98. Nancy Rodriguez, "Restorative Justice, Communities, and Delinquency: Whom Do We Reintegrate?" *Criminology & Public Policy* 4 (2005): 103–130.

99. David Altschuler, "Community Justice Initiatives: Issues and Challenges in the U.S. Context," *Federal Probation* 65 (2001): 28–33.

100. Lois Presser and Patricia Van Voorhis, "Values and Evaluation: Assessing Processes and Outcomes of Restorative Justice Programs," *Crime and Delinquency* 48 (2002): 162–189.

101. Sharon Levrant, Francis Cullen, Betsy Fulton, and John Wozniak, "Reconsidering Restorative Justice: The Corruption of Benevolence Revisited?" *Crime and Delinquency* 45 (1999): 3–28.

102. Nancy Rodriguez, "Restorative Justice, Communities, and Delinquency."

103. David Karp and Kevin Drakulich, "Minor Crime in a Quaint Setting: Practices, Outcomes, and Limits of Vermont Reparative Probation Boards," *Criminology & Public Policy* 3 (2004): 655–686.

Chapter 13

1. See David Fogel, *We Are the Living Proof*, 2d ed. (Cincinnati: Anderson, 1978); Andrew von Hirsch, *Doing Justice: The Choice of Punishments* (New York: Hill and Wang, 1976); R. G. Singer, *Just Deserts—Sentencing Based on Equality and Desert* (Cambridge, Mass.: Ballinger, 1979). The most widely cited source on the failure of rehabilitation is Robert Martinson; see Douglas Lipton, Robert Martinson, and Judith Wilks, *The Effectiveness of Correctional Treatment: A Survey of Treatment Evaluation Studies* (New York: Praeger, 1975).

2. Thomas Stucky, Karen Heimer, and Joseph Lang, "Partisan Politics, Electoral Competition, and Imprisonment: An Analysis of States Over Time," *Criminology* 43 (2005): 211–247.

3. Francis Cullen, "The Twelve People Who Saved Rehabilitation: How the Science of Criminology Made a Difference," *Criminology* 43 (2005): 1–42.

4. Among the most helpful sources in developing this section were David Duffee, *Corrections: Practice and Policy* (New York: Random House, 1989); Harry Allen and Clifford Simonsen, *Correction in America*, 5th ed. (New York: Macmillan, 1989); Benedict Alper, *Prisons Inside-Out* (Cambridge, Mass.: Ballinger, 1974); Harry Elmer Barnes, *The Story of Punishment*, 2d ed. (Montclair, N.J.: Patterson-Smith, 1972); Gustave de Beaumont and Alexis de Tocqueville, *On the Penitentiary System in the United States and Its Applications in France* (Carbondale: Southern Illinois University Press, 1964); Orlando Lewis, *The Development of American Prisons and Prison Customs, 1776–1845* (Montclair, N.J.: Patterson-Smith,

1967); Leonard Orland, ed., *Justice, Punishment, and Treatment* (New York: Free Press, 1973); J. Goebel, *Felony and Misdemeanor* (Philadelphia: University of Pennsylvania Press, 1976); Georg Rusche and Otto Kircheimer, *Punishment and Social Structure* (New York: Russell & Russell, 1939); Samuel Walker, *Popular Justice* (New York: Oxford University Press, 1980); Graeme Newman, *The Punishment Response* (Philadelphia: Lippincott, 1978); David Rothman, *Conscience and Convenience* (Boston: Little, Brown, 1980).

5. Frederick Pollock and Frederic Maitland, *History of English Law* (London: Cambridge University Press, 1952).

6. Marvin Wolfgang, "Crime and Punishment in Renaissance Florence," *Journal of Criminal Law and Criminology 81* (1990): 567–584.

7. Margaret Wilson, *The Crime of Punishment*, Life and Letters Series, no. 64 (London: Jonathan Cape, 1934), 186.

8. John Howard, *The State of the Prisons in England and Wales*, 4th ed. (1792; reprint ed., Montclair, N.J.: Patterson-Smith, 1973).

9. Alexis Durham III, "Newgate of Connecticut: Origins and Early Days of an Early American Prison," *Justice Quarterly 6* (1989): 89–116.

10. Personal communication, Professor Norman Johnston, February 19, 2002. See his book *Forms of Constraint: A History of Prison Architecture* (Champaign: University of Illinois Press, 2000).

11. David Rothman, *The Discovery of the Asylum* (Boston: Little, Brown, 1970).

12. Orland, *Justice, Punishment, and Treatment*, 143.

13. Ibid., 144.

14. Walker, *Popular Justice*, 70.

15. Ibid., 71.

16. Beverly Smith, "Military Training at New York's Elmira Reformatory, 1880–1920," *Federal Probation 52* (1988): 33–41.

17. Ibid.

18. See Z. R. Brockway, "The Ideal of a True Prison System for a State," in *Transactions of the National Congress on Penitentiary and Reformatory Discipline*, reprint ed. (Washington, D.C.: American Correctional Association, 1970), 38–65.

19. John Roberts, "A Century's Legacy: Five Critical Developments in the Evolution of American Prisons, 1900–2000," *Corrections Today 62* (2000): 102–112.

20. This section leans heavily on Rothman, *Conscience and Convenience*.

21. Ibid., 23.

22. Ibid., 133.

23. 18 U.S.C., sec. 1761.

24. Barbara Auerbach, George Sexton, Franklin Farrow, and Robert Lawson, *Work in American Prisons: The Private Sector Gets Involved* (Washington, D.C.: National Institute of Justice, 1988), 72.

25. Jody Sundt, Francis Cullen, Brandon Applegate, and Michael Turner, "The Tenacity of the Rehabilitative Ideal Revisited: Have Attitudes Toward Offender Treatment Changed?" *Criminal Justice and Behavior 25* (1998): 426–481.

26. See, generally, Jameson Doig, *Criminal Corrections: Ideals and Realities* (Lexington, Mass.: Lexington Books, 1983).

27. Caroline Wolf Harlow, *Prior Abuse Reported by Inmates and Probationers* (Washington, D.C.: Bureau of Justice Statistics, 1999).

28. Paula M. Ditton, *Mental Health and Treatment of Inmates and Probationers* (Washington, D.C.: Bureau of Justice Statistics, 1999).

29. Fred Heinzlemann, W. Robert Burkhart, Bernard Gropper, Cheryl Martorana, Lois Felson Mock, Maureen O'Connor, and Walter Philip Travers, *Jailing Drunk Drivers: Impact on the Criminal Justice System* (Washington, D.C.: National Institute of Justice, 1984).

30. Brandon Applegate, Ray Surette, and Bernard McCarthy, "Detention and Desistance from Crime: Evaluating the Influence of a New Generation of Jail on Recidivism," *Journal of Criminal Justice 27* (1999): 539–548.

31. Ibid.

32. James Stephan, *State Prison Expenditures, 2001* (Washington, D.C.: Bureau of Justice Statistics, 2004).

33. Human Rights Watch, *Prison Conditions in the United States*, www.hrw.org/wr2k2/prisons.html, accessed on September 14, 2005.

34. "Suit Alleges Violations in California's 'Super-Max' Prison," *Criminal Justice Newsletter*, September 1, 1993, 2.

35. James Anderson, Laronistine Dyson, and Jerald Burns, *Boot Camps: An Intermediate Sanction* (Lanham, Md.: University Press of America, 1999), 1–17.

36. Ibid., 328–329.

37. Doris Layton Mackenzie, "Boot Camp Prisons: Components, Evaluations, and Empirical Issues," *Federal Probation 54* (1990): 44–52; see also "Boot Camp Programs Grow in Number and Scope," *NIJ Reports* (November/December 1990): 6–8.

38. Doris Layton Mackenzie and James Shaw, "The Impact of Shock Incarceration on Technical Violations and New Criminal Activities," *Justice Quarterly 10* (1993): 463–487.

39. Mackenzie, Brame, McDowall, and Souryal, "Boot Camp Prisons and Recidivism in Eight States," 352–353.

40. Vanessa St. Gerard, "Federal Prisons to Eliminate Boot Camps," *Corrections Today 67* (2005): 13–16.

41. Correctional Research Associates, *Treating Youthful Offenders in the Community: An Evaluation Conducted by A. J. Reiss* (Washington, D.C.: Correctional Research Associates, 1966).

42. Kevin Krajick, "Not on My Block: Local Opposition Impedes the Search for Alternatives," *Corrections Magazine 6* (1980): 15–27.

43. "Many State Legislatures Focused on Crime in 1995, Study Finds," *Criminal Justice Newsletter*, January 2, 1996, 2.

44. William Bales, Laura Bedard, Susan Quinn, David Ensley, and Glen Holley, "Recidivism of Public and Private State Prison Inmates in Florida," *Criminology & Public Policy 4* (2005): 57–82; Lonn Lanza-Kaduce, Karen Parker, and Charles Thomas, "A Comparative Recidivism Analysis of Releases from Private and Public Prisons," *Crime and Delinquency 45* (1999): 28–47.

45. Charles Thomas, "Recidivism of Public and Private State Prison Inmates in Florida: Issues and Unanswered Questions," *Criminology & Public Policy 4* (2005): 89–99; Travis Pratt and Jeff Maahs, "Are Private Prisons More Cost-Effective Than Public Prisons? A Meta-Analysis of Evaluation Research Studies," *Crime and Delinquency 45* (1999): 358–371.

46. Ira Robbins, *The Legal Dimensions of Private Incarceration* (Chicago: American Bar Association, 1988).

47. Danica Coto, "Medical Care Company Named in Numerous Jail Lawsuits," *The Charlotte Observer*, August 30, 2004.

48. Ahmed A. White, "Rule of Law and the Limits of Sovereignty: The Private Prison in Jurisprudential Perspective," *American Criminal Law Review 38* (2001): 111–147; *Correctional Services Corp. v. Malesko*, 534 U.S. 61, 122 S.Ct. 515 (2001).

49. Lawrence Travis, Edward Latessa, and Gennaro Vito, "Private Enterprise and Institutional Corrections: A Call for Caution," *Federal Probation 49* (1985): 11–17.

50. Patrick Anderson, Charles Davoli, and Laura Moriarty, "Private Corrections: Feast or Fiasco," *Prison Journal 65* (1985): 32–41.

51. Paige Harrison and Allen Beck, *Prisoners in 2003* (Washington, D.C.: Bureau of Justice Statistics, 2004).

52. Caroline Wolf Harlow, *Education and Correctional Populations* (Washington, D.C.: Bureau of Justice Statistics, 2003).

53. Seena Fazel and John Danesh, "Serious Mental Disorder in 23,000 Prisoners: A Systematic Review of Sixty-Two Surveys," *Lancet 359* (2002): 545–561.

54. Todd Clear, *Harm in American Penology: Offenders, Victims, and Their Communities* (Albany: State University of New York Press, 1994).

55. Daniel Nagin, "Criminal Deterrence Research: A Review of the Evidence and a Research Agenda for the Outset of the 21st Century," in *Crime and Justice: An Annual Review*, ed. Michael Tonry (Chicago: University of Chicago Press, 1997).

56. Thomas P. Bonczar and Allen J. Beck, *Lifetime Likelihood of Going to State or Federal Prison* (Washington, D.C.: Bureau of Justice Statistics, 1997).

57. Andrew Lang Golub, Farrukh Hakeem, and Bruce Johnson, *Monitoring the Decline in the Crack Epidemic with Data from the Drug Use Forecasting Program, Final Report* (Washington, D.C.: National Institute of Justice, 1996).

Chapter 14

1. James Stephan and Jennifer Karberg, *Census of State and Federal Correctional Facilities, 2000* (Washington, D.C.: Bureau of Justice Statistics, 2003).

2. Ros Burnett and Shadd Maruna, "So 'Prison Works,' Does It? The Criminal Careers of 130 Men Released from Prison under Home Secretary Michael Howard," *Howard Journal of Criminal Justice 43* (2004): 390–404.

3. Barbara Sims and Eric Johnston, "Examining Public Opinion About Crime and Justice: A Statewide Study," *Criminal Justice Policy Review 15* (2004): 270–294.

4. Richard Berk, Heather Ladd, Heidi Graziano, and Jong-Ho Baek, "A Randomized Experiment Testing Inmate Classification Systems," *Criminology & Public Policy 2* (2003): 215–242.

5. Gresham Sykes, *The Society of Captives* (Princeton, N.J.: Princeton University Press, 1958).

6. David Eichenthal and James Jacobs, "Enforcing the Criminal Law in State Prisons," *Justice Quarterly 8* (1991): 283–303.

7. John Wooldredge, "Inmate Lifestyles and Opportunities for Victimization," *Journal of Research in Crime and Delinquency 35* (1998): 480–502.

8. David Anderson, *Crimes of Justice: Improving the Police, Courts, and Prison* (New York: Times Books, 1988).

9. Christopher Hensley, Mary Koscheski, and Richard Tewksbury, "Examining the Characteristics of Male Sexual Assault Targets in a Southern Maximum-Security Prison," *Journal of Interpersonal Violence 20* (2005): 667–679.

10. Robert Johnson, *Hard Time: Understanding and Reforming the Prison* (Monterey, Calif.: Brooks/Cole, 1987), 115.

11. Wooldredge, "Inmate Lifestyles and Opportunities for Victimization."

12. Leonore Simon, "Prison Behavior and Victim-Offender Relationships Among Violent Offenders," paper presented at the annual meeting of the American Society of Criminology, San Francisco, November 1991.

13. John Irwin, "Adaptation to Being Corrected: Corrections from the Convict's Perspective," in *Handbook of Criminology*, ed. Daniel Glazer (Chicago: Rand McNally, 1974), 971–993.

14. Donald Clemmer, *The Prison Community* (New York: Holt, Rinehart & Winston, 1958).

15. Gresham Sykes and Sheldon Messinger, "The Inmate Social Code," in *The Sociology of Punishment and Corrections*, eds. Norman Johnston, Leonard Savitz, and Marvin Wolfgang (New York: Wiley, 1970), 401–408.

16. Ibid., 439.

17. James B. Jacobs, ed., *New Perspectives on Prisons and Imprisonment* (Ithaca, N.Y.: Cornell University Press, 1983); idem, "Street Gangs Behind Bars," *Social Problems 21* (1974): 395–409; idem, "Race Relations and the Prison Subculture," in *Crime and Justice*, vol. 1, eds. Norval Morris and Michael Tonry (Chicago: University of Chicago Press, 1979), 1–28.

18. Nicole Hahn Rafter, *Partial Justice* (New Brunswick, N.J.: Transaction Books, 1990), 181–182.

19. Meda Chesney-Lind, "Patriarchy, Prisons, and Jails: A Critical Look at Trends in Women's Incarceration," paper presented at the International Feminist Conference on Women, Law and Social Control, Mont Gabriel, Québec, July 1991.

20. Elaine DeCostanzo and Helen Scholes, "Women Behind Bars: Their Numbers Increase," *Corrections Today 50* (1988): 104–106.

21. This section synthesizes the findings of a number of surveys of female inmates, including DeCostanzo and Scholes, "Women Behind Bars"; Ruth Glick and Virginia Neto, *National Study of Women's Correctional Programs* (Washington, D.C.: Government Printing Office, 1977); Ann Goetting and Roy Michael Howsen, "Women in Prison: A Profile," *Prison Journal 63* (1983): 27–46; Meda Chesney-Lind and Noelie Rodrigues, "Women Under Lock and Key: A View from Inside," *Prison Journal 63* (1983): 47–65; Contact, Inc., "Women Offenders," *Corrections Compendium 7* (1982): 6–11.

22. Merry Morash, Robin Harr, and Lila Rucker, "A Comparison of Programming for Women and Men in U.S. Prisons in the 1980s," *Crime and Delinquency 40* (1994): 197–221.

23. Pamela Schram, "Stereotypes About Vocational Programming for Female Inmates," *Prison Journal 78* (1998): 244–271.

24. Morash, Harr, and Rucker, "A Comparison of Programming for Women and Men in U.S. Prisons in the 1980s."

25. Seena Fazel and John Danesh, "Serious Mental Disorder in 23,000 Prisoners: A Systematic Review of 62 Surveys," *Lancet 359* (2002): 545–561.

26. Gary Michael McClelland, Linda Teplin, Karen Abram, and Naomi Jacobs, "HIV and AIDS Risk Behaviors Among Female Jail Detainees: Implications for Public Health Policy," *American Journal of Public Health 92* (2002): 818–826.

27. "Sex Abuse of Female Inmates Is Common, Rights Group Says," *Criminal Justice Newsletter*, December 16, 1996, 2.

28. General Accounting Office, *Women in Prison: Sexual Misconduct by Correctional Staff* (Washington, D.C.: Government Printing Office, 1999).

29. Meda Chesney-Lind, "Vengeful Equity: Sentencing Women to Prison," in *The Female Offender: Girls, Women, and Crime* (Thousand Oaks, Calif.: Sage, 1997).

30. Candace Kruttschnitt and Sharon Krmpotich, "Aggressive Behavior Among Female Inmates: An Exploratory Study," *Justice Quarterly 7* (1990): 370–389.

31. Candace Kruttschnitt, Rosemary Gartner, and Amy Miller, "Doing Her Own Time? Women's Responses to Prison in the Context of the Old and New Penology," *Criminology 38* (2000): 681–718.

32. Mark Pogrebin and Mary Dodge, "Women's Accounts of Their Prison Experiences: A Retrospective View of Their Subjective Realities," *Journal of Criminal Justice 29* (2001): 531–541.

33. Edna Erez, "The Myth of the New Female Offender: Some Evidence from Attitudes Toward Law and Justice," *Journal of Criminal Justice 16* (1988): 499–509.

34. Robert Ross and Hugh McKay, *Self-Mutilation* (Lexington, Mass.: Lexington Books, 1979).

35. Alice Propper, *Prison Homosexuality* (Lexington, Mass.: Lexington Books, 1981).

36. Dianna Newbern, Donald Dansereau, and Urvashi Pitre, "Positive Effects on Life Skills Motivation and Self-

Efficacy: Node-Link Maps in a Modified Therapeutic Community," *American Journal of Drug and Alcohol Abuse 25* (1999): 407–410.

37. Charles McDaniel, Derek Davis, and Sabrina Neff, "Charitable Choice and Prison Ministries: Constitutional and Institutional Challenges to Rehabilitating the American Penal System," *Criminal Justice Policy Review 16* (2005): 164–189.

38. Kate Dolan, James Shearer, Bethany White, Zhou Jialun, John Kaldor, and Alex Wodak, "Four-year follow-up of imprisoned male heroin users and methadone treatment: mortality, re-incarceration and hepatitis C infection," *Addiction 100* (2005): Issue 6, 820–828.

39. Will Small, S. Kain, Nancy Laliberte, Martin Schechter, Michael O'Shaughnessy, and Patricia Spittal, "Incarceration, Addiction and Harm Reduction: Inmates Experience Injecting Drugs in Prison," *Substance Use & Misuse 40* (2005): 831–843.

40. Howard Skolnik and John Slansky, "A First Step in Helping Inmates Get Good Jobs After Release," *Corrections Today 53* (1991): 92.

41. This section leans heavily on Barbara Auerbach, George Sexton, Franklin Farrow, and Robert Lawson, *Work in American Prisons: The Private Sector Gets Involved* (Washington, D.C.: National Institute of Justice, 1988).

42. Public Law 96-157, sec. 827, codified as 18 U.S.C., sec. 1761(c).

43. Courtesy of the Prison Industry Authority, 560 East Natoma Street, Folsom, Calif. 95630-2200.

44. Diane Dwyer and Roger McNally, "Public Policy, Prison Industries, and Business: An Equitable Balance for the 1990s," *Federal Probation 57* (1993): 30–35.

45. Douglas Lipton, Robert Martinson, and Judith Wilks, *The Effectiveness of Correctional Treatment: A Survey of Treatment Evaluation Studies* (New York: Praeger, 1975).

46. Charles Murray and Louis Cox, *Beyond Probation: Juvenile Corrections and the Chronic Delinquent* (Beverly Hills, Calif.: Sage, 1979).

47. Steven Lab and John Whitehead, "An Analysis of Juvenile Correctional Treatment," *Crime and Delinquency 34* (1988): 60–83.

48. Francis Cullen and Karen Gilbert, *Reaffirming Rehabilitation* (Cincinnati: Anderson, 1982).

49. David Wilson, Catherine Gallagher, and Doris MacKenzie, "A Meta-Analysis of Corrections-Based Education, Vocation, and Work Programs for Adult Offenders," *Journal of Research in Crime and Delinquency 37* (2000): 347–368.

50. Mary Ellen Batiuk, Paul Moke, and Pamela Wilcox Roundtree, "Crime and Rehabilitation: Correctional Education as an Agent of Change—A Research Note," *Justice Quarterly 14* (1997): 167–180.

51. David Wilson, Leana Bouffard, and Doris Mackenzie, "A Quantitative Review of Structured, Group-Oriented, Cognitive-Behavioral Programs for Offenders," *Criminal Justice and Behavior 32* (2005): 172–204; Mark Lipsey and David Wilson, "Effective Intervention for Serious Juvenile Offenders: A Synthesis of Research," in *Serious and Violent Juvenile Offenders: Risk Factors and Successful Interventions*, eds. Rolf Loeber and David Farrington (Thousand Oaks, Calif.: Sage, 1998).

52. Paul Gendreau and Claire Goffin, "Principles of Effective Correctional Programming," *Forum on Correctional Research 2* (1996): 38–41.

53. Lucien X. Lombardo, *Guards Imprisoned* (New York: Elsevier, 1981); James Jacobs and Norma Crotty, "The Guard's World," in *New Perspectives on Prisons and Imprisonment*, ed. James Jacobs (Ithaca, N.Y.: Cornell University Press, 1983), 133–141.

54. Claire Mayhew and Duncan Chappell, "An Overview of Occupational Violence," *Australian Nursing Journal 9* (2002): 34–35.

55. John Klofas and Hans Toch, "The Guard Subculture Myth," *Journal of Research in Crime and Delinquency 19* (1982): 238–254.

56. Ruth Triplett and Janet Mullings, "Work-Related Stress and Coping Among Correctional Officers: Implications from the Organizational Literature," *Journal of Criminal Justice 24* (1996): 291–308.

57. Peter Horne, "Female Corrections Officers," *Federal Probation 49* (1985): 46–55.

58. *Dothard v. Rawlinson*, 433 U.S. 321 (1977).

59. Dana Britton, *At Work in the Iron Cage: The Prison as Gendered Organization* (New York: New York University Press, 2003). Chapter 6.

60. Christopher D. Man and John P. Cronan, "Forecasting Sexual Abuse in Prison: The Prison Subculture of Masculinity as a Backdrop for 'Deliberate Indifference,'" *Journal of Criminal Law and Criminology* (2001): 127–166.

61. Christopher Hensley and Richard Tewksbury, "Wardens' Perceptions of Prison Sex," *Prison Journal 85* (2005): 186–197.

62. Christopher Hensley, Mary Koscheski, and Richard Tewksbury, "Examining the Characteristics of Male Sexual Assault Targets in a Southern Maximum-Security Prison," *Journal of Interpersonal Violence 20* (2005): 667–679.

63. Jesse Walker, "Rape Behind Bars," *Reason 35* (2003): 10–12.

64. S. 1435[108]: Prison Rape Elimination Act of 2003; Public Law No: 108-79.

65. David Duffee, *Corrections, Practice and Policy* (New York: Random House, 1989), 305.

66. Randy Martin and Sherwood Zimmerman, "A Typology of the Causes of Prison Riots and an Analytical Extension to the 1986 West Virginia Riot," *Justice Quarterly 7* (1990): 711–737.

67. David Allender and Frank Marcell, "Career Criminals, Security Threat Groups, and Prison Gangs," *FBI Law Enforcement Bulletin 72* (2003): 8–12.

68. Terri Compton and Mike Meacham "Prison gangs: descriptions and selected intervention," *The Forensic Examiner 14* (2005): 26–31.

69. Grant Harris, Tracey Skilling, and Marnie Rice, "The Construct of Psychopathy," in Michael Tonry, ed., *Crime and Justice: An Annual Edition* (Chicago: University of Chicago Press, 2001), 197–265.

70. For a series of papers on the position, see A. Cohen, G. Cole, and R. Baily, eds., *Prison Violence* (Lexington, Mass.: Lexington Books, 1976).

71. Scott Camp and Gerald Gaes, "Criminogenic Effects of the Prison Environment on Inmate Behavior: Some Experimental Evidence," *Crime & Delinquency 51* (2005): 425–442.

72. Bert Useem and Michael Resig, "Collective Action in Prisons: Protests, Disturbances, and Riots," *Criminology 37* (1999): 735–760.

73. Wayne Gillespie, "A Multilevel Model of Drug Abuse Inside Prison," *Prison Journal 85* (2005): 223–246.

74. National Advisory Commission on Criminal Justice Standards and Goals, *Corrections* (Washington, D.C.: Government Printing Office, 1973), 18.

75. *Cooper v. Pate*, 378 U.S. 546 (1964).

76. *Shaw v. Murphy* (99-1613), 2001.

77. *Cutter v. Wilkinson* (03-9877), 2005.

78. *Newman v. Alabama*, 92 S.Ct. 1079, 405 U.S. 319 (1972).

79. *Estelle v. Gamble*, 429 U.S. 97 (1976).

80. Ibid.

81. *Trop v. Dulles*, 356 U.S. 86, 78 S.Ct. 590 (1958); see also *Furman v. Georgia*, 408 U.S. 238, 92 S.Ct. 2726, 33 L.Ed.2d 346 (1972).

82. *Weems v. United States*, 217 U.S. 349, 30 S.Ct. 544, 54 L.Ed. 793 (1910).

83. *Lee v. Tahash*, 352 F.2d 970 (8th Cir., 1965).

84. *Estelle v. Gamble*, 429 U.S. 97 (1976).

85. *Robinson v. California*, 370 U.S. 660 (1962).
86. *Gregg v. Georgia*, 428 U.S. 153 (1976).
87. *Jackson v. Bishop*, 404 F.2d 571 (8th Cir. 1968).
88. *Hope v. Pelzer*, et al., No. 01—309. June 27, 2002.
89. *Bell v. Wolfish*, 99 S.Ct. 1873–1974 (1979); see "*Bell v. Wolfish*: The Rights of Pretrial Detainees," *New England Journal of Prison Law 6* (1979): 134.
90. *Farmer v. Brennan*, 144 S.Ct. 1970 (1994).
91. *Rhodes v. Chapman*, 452 U.S. 337 (1981); for further analysis of *Rhodes*, see Randall Pooler, "Prison Overcrowding and the Eighth Amendment: The Rhodes Not Taken," *New England Journal on Criminal and Civil Confinement 8* (1983): 1–28.
92. *Prison Escape Survey* (Lincoln, Neb.: Corrections Compendium, 1991).
93. Kathryn Campbell and Myriam Denov, "The Burden of Innocence: Coping with a Wrongful Imprisonment," *Canadian Journal of Criminology and Criminal Justice 46* (2004): 139–164.
94. Brian Parry, "Special Service Unit: Dedicated to Investigating and Apprehending Violent Offenders," *Corrections Today 63* (2001): 120.
95. Thomas Hanlon, David N. Nurco, Richard W. Bateman, and Kevin E. O'Grady, "The Response of Drug Abuser Parolees to a Combination of Treatment and Intensive Supervision," *Prison Journal 78* (1998): 31–44; Susan Turner and Joan Petersilia, "Focusing on High-Risk Parolees: An Experiment to Reduce Commitments to the Texas Department of Corrections," *Journal of Research in Crime and Delinquency 29* (1992): 34–61.
96. Patrick A. Langan and David J. Levin, *Recidivism of Prisoners Released in 1994* (Washington, D.C.: Bureau of Justice Statistics, 2002).
97. Robyn L. Cohen, *Probation and Parole Violators in State Prison, 1991: Survey of State Prison Inmates, 1991* (Washington, D.C.: Bureau of Justice Statistics, 1995).
98. James Gondles, "Returning to Society," *Corrections Today 67* (2005): 6–7.
99. Stephen Duguid, *Can Prisons Work? The Prisoner as Object and Subject in Modern Corrections* (Toronto: University of Toronto Press, 2000).
100. James Bonta, Moira Law, and Karl Hanson, "The Prediction of Criminal and Violent Recidivism Among Mentally Disordered Offenders: A Meta-Analysis," *Psychological Bulletin 123* (1998): 123–142.
101. Roger Peters, Paul Greenbaum, John Edens, Chris Carter, and Madeline Ortiz, "Prevalence of DSM-IV Substance Abuse and Dependence Disorders Among Prison Inmates," *American Journal of Drug and Alcohol Abuse 24* (1998): 573–580.
102. Catherine Hamilton, Louise Falshaw, and Kevin D. Browne, "The Link Between Recurrent Maltreatment and Offending Behavior," *International Journal of Offender Therapy & Comparative Criminology 46* (2002): 75–95.
103. Brent Benda, "Gender Differences in Life-Course Theory of Recidivism: A Survival Analysis," *International Journal of Offender Therapy and Comparative Criminology 49* (2005): 325–342.
104. Bonnie Todis, Michael Bullis, Miriam Waintrup, Robert Schultz, and Ryan D'Ambrosio, "Overcoming the Odds: Qualitative Examination of Resilience Among Formerly Incarcerated Adolescents," *Exceptional Children 68* (2001): 119–140.
105. J. E. Ryan, "Who Gets Revoked? A Comparison of Intensive Supervision Successes and Failures in Vermont," *Crime and Delinquency 43* (1997): 104–118.
106. Hanlon, Nurco, Bateman, and O'Grady, "The Response of Drug Abuser Parolees to a Combination of Treatment and Intensive Supervision," 108.
107. Laura Fishman, *Women at the Wall: A Study of Prisoners' Wives Doing Time on the Outside* (New York: State University of New York Press, 1990).
108. Leslee Goodman Hornick, "Volunteer Program Helps Make Inmates' Families Feel Welcome," *Corrections Today 53* (1991): 184–186.
109. Jeremy Travis and Joan Petersilia, "Reentry Reconsidered: A New Look at an Old Question," *Crime and Delinquency 47* (2001): 291–313.
110. Hanlon, Nurco, Bateman, and O'Grady, "The Response of Drug Abuser Parolees to a Combination of Treatment and Intensive Supervision."
111. Kathleen Olivares, Velmer Burton, and Francis Cullen, "The Collateral Consequences of a Felony Conviction: A National Study of State Legal Codes Ten Years Later," *Federal Probation 60* (1996): 10–17.
112. See, for example, *Bush v. Reid*, 516 P.2d 1215 (Alaska, 1973); *Thompson v. Bond*, 421 F.Supp. 878 (W.D. Mo., 1976); *Delorne v. Pierce Freightlines Co.*, 353 F.Supp. 258 (D. Or., 1973); *Beyer v. Werner*, 299 F.Supp. 967 (E.D. N.Y., 1969).

Chapter 15

1. Federal Bureau of Investigation, *Crime in the United States, 2003* (Washington, D.C.: U.S. Government Printing Office, 2004).
2. Material in this section depends heavily on Sanford J. Fox, "Juvenile Justice Reform: A Historical Perspective," *Stanford Law Review 22* (1970): 1187–1205; Lawrence Stone, *The Family, Sex, and Marriage in England: 1500–1800* (New York: Harper & Row, 1977); Philippe Aries, *Century of Childhood: A Social History of Family Life* (New York: Vintage Press, 1962); Douglas R. Rendleman, "Parens Patriae: From Chancery to the Juvenile Court," *South Carolina Law Review 23* (1971): 205–229; Wiley B. Sanders, "Some Early Beginnings of the Children's Court Movement in England," in *National Probation Association Yearbook* (New York: National Council on Crime and Delinquency, 1945); Anthony M. Platt, "The Rise of the Child-Saving Movement: A Study in Social Policy and Correctional Reform," *Annals of the American Academy of Political and Social Science 381* (1979): 21–38; idem, *The Child Savers: The Intervention of Delinquency* (Chicago: University of Chicago Press, 1969); Robert S. Pickett, *House of Refuge: Origins of Juvenile Reform in New York State, 1815–1857* (Syracuse, N.Y.: Syracuse University Press, 1969).
3. Douglas Besharov, *Juvenile Justice Advocacy: Practice in a Unique Court* (New York: Practicing Law Institute, 1974), 2; see also Jay Albanese, *Dealing with Delinquency: The Future of Juvenile Justice* (Chicago: Nelson-Hall, 1993).
4. 4 Eng.Rep. 1078 (1827).
5. Platt, *The Child Savers*, 11–38.
6. See generally, Anne Meis Knupfer, *Reform and Resistance: Gender, Delinquency, and America's First Juvenile Court* (London: Routledge, 2001).
7. This section is based on material from the New York State Archives, *The Greatest Reform School in the World: A Guide to the Records of the New York House of Refuge: A Brief History 1824–1857* (Albany: New York State Archives, 2001); Sanford J. Fox, "Juvenile Justice Reform: A Historical Perspective," *Stanford Law Review 22* (1970): 1187.
8. Pickett, *House of Refuge: Origins of Juvenile Reform in New York State, 1815–1857*.
9. David S. Tanenhaus, *Juvenile Justice in the Making* (New York: Oxford University Press, 2004).
10. LaMar T. Empey, *American Delinquency: Its Meaning and Construction* (Homewood, Ill.: Dorsey Press, 1978), 515.
11. *Kent v. United States*, 383 U.S. 541, 86 S.Ct. 1045, 16 L.Ed.2d 84 (1966); *In re Gault*, 387 U.S. 1, 87 S.Ct. 1428, 18 L.Ed.2d 527 (1967): juveniles have the right to notice,

counsel, confrontation, and cross-examination, and to the privileges against self-incrimination in juvenile court proceedings; *In re Winship*, 397 U.S. 358, 90 S.Ct. 1068, 25 L.Ed.2d 368 (1970): proof beyond a reasonable doubt is necessary for conviction in juvenile proceedings; *Breed v. Jones*, 421 U.S. 519, 95 S.Ct. 1779, 44 L.Ed.2d 346 (1975): jeopardy attaches in a juvenile court adjudicatory hearing, thus barring subsequent prosecution for the same offense as an adult.

12. Public Law 93-415 (1974).

13. For a comprehensive view of juvenile law, see, generally, Joseph J. Senna and Larry J. Siegel, *Juvenile Law: Cases and Comments*, 2d ed. (St. Paul: West, 1992).

14. Erika Gebo, "'Do Family Courts Administer Individualized Justice in Delinquency' Cases?" *Criminal Justice Policy Review 16* (2005): 190–210.

15. Federal Bureau of Investigation, *Crime in the United States, 2003* (Washington, D.C.: Government Printing Office, 2004), 220.

16. Richard J. Lundman, "Routine Police Arrest Practices," *Social Problems 22* (1974): 127–141; Robert E. Worden and Stephanie M. Myers, *Police Encounters with Juvenile Suspects* (Albany: Hindelang Criminal Justice Research Center and School of Criminal Justice, State University of New York, 2001).

17. *Fare v. Michael C.*, 442 U.S. 707 (1979).

18. Juvenile court data in this section was provided by the National Juvenile Court Data Archive National Center for Juvenile Justice, 3700 South Water Street, Suite 200, Pittsburgh, PA 15203. Their website is www.ncjj.org. Special thanks to Anne Stahl, research associate, for her help.

19. Ana Abrantes, Norman Hoffmann, and Ronald Anton, "Prevalence of Co-occurring Disorders Among Juveniles Committed to Detention Centers," *International Journal of Offender Therapy & Comparative Criminology 49* (2005): 179–194.

21. Angela Wolf and Christopher Hartney, "A Portrait of Detained Youth in the State of Hawaii," *Crime & Delinquency 51* (2005): 180–191.

21. *Schall v. Martin*, 467 U.S. 253, 104 S.Ct. 2403, 81 L.Ed.2d 207 (1984).

22. See Juvenile Justice and Delinquency Prevention Act of 1974, 42 U.S.C., sec. 5633.

23. Ira Schwartz, Linda Harris, and Laurie Levi, "The Jailing of Juveniles in Minnesota," *Crime and Delinquency 34* (1988): 131; also Barry Krisberg and Robert DeComo, *Juveniles Taken into Custody—1991* (San Francisco: National Council on Crime and Delinquency, 1993), 25.

24. Catherine Van Dijk, An Nuytiens, and Christian Eliaerts, "The Referral of Juvenile Offenders to the Adult Court in Belgium: Theory and Practice," *Howard Journal of Criminal Justice 44* (2005): 151–166.

25. 383 U.S. 541, 86 S.Ct. 1045, 16 L.Ed.2d 84 (1966).

26. 421 U.S. 519, 528, 95 S.Ct. 1779, 1785, 44 L.Ed.2d 346 (1975).

27. Alan Karpelowitz, *State Legislative Priorities—1995* (Denver: National Conference of State Legislatures, 1995), 10.

28. Dale Parent, *Key Issues in Criminal Justice: Transferring Serious Juvenile Offenders to Adult Courts* (Washington, D.C.: National Institute of Justice, 1997).

29. Barry Feld, "The Juvenile Court Meets the Principle of the Offense: Legislative Changes in Juvenile Waiver Statutes," *Journal of Criminal Law and Criminology 78* (1987): 471–533; see also John Kramer, Henry Sontheimer, and John Lemmon, "Pennsylvania Waiver to Adult Court," paper presented at the annual meeting of the American Society of Criminology, San Francisco, November 1991; authors confirm that juveniles tried in adult courts are generally male, age seventeen or older, and disproportionately minorities.

30. Jeffrey Fagan, Martin Forst, and T. Scott Vivona, "Racial Determinants of the Judicial Transfer Decision: Prosecuting Violent Youth in Criminal Court," *Crime and Delinquency 33* (1987): 359–386; J. Fagan, E. Slaughter, and E. Hartstone, "Blind Justice: The Impact of Race on the Juvenile Justice Process," *Crime and Delinquency 53* (1987): 224–258; J. Fagan and E. P. Deschenes, "Determinants of Judicial Waiver Decisions for Violent Juvenile Offenders," *Journal of Criminal Law and Criminology 81* (1990): 314–347; see also James Howell, "Juvenile Transfers to Criminal Court," *Juvenile and Family Justice Journal 6* (1997): 12–14.

31. Anne L. Stahl, *Delinquency Cases in Juvenile Courts, 1997* (Washington, D.C.: Office of Juvenile Justice and Delinquency Prevention, 2000); Puzzanchera, *Delinquency Cases Waived to Criminal Court, 1988–1998*.

32. Howard N. Snyder, Melissa Sickmund, and Eileen Poe-Yamagata, *Juvenile Transfers to Criminal Court in the 1990s: Lessons Learned from Four Studies* (Washington, D.C.: Office of Juvenile Justice and Delinquency Prevention, 2000).

33. Parent, *Key Issues in Criminal Justice*.

34. 387 U.S. 1, 87 S.Ct. 1428, 18 L.Ed.2d 527 (1967).

35. Victor Streib, *Death Penalty for Juveniles* (Bloomington: Indiana University Press, 1987); also Paul Reidinger, "The Death Row Kids," *American Bar Association Journal 70* (1989): 78; also, "Note: The Death Penalty and the Eighth Amendment: An Analysis of *Stanford v. Kentucky*," *Yale Law Review 35* (1990): 641.

36. See Joseph Goldstein, Anna Freud, and Albert Solnit, *Beyond the Best Interest of the Child* (New York: Free Press, 1973).

37. See Michael Serrill, "Police Write a New Law on Juvenile Crime," *Police Magazine* (September 1979): 47; see also A. Schneider and D. Schram, *Assessment of Juvenile Justice Reform in Washington State*, vols. 1–4 (Washington, D.C.: Department of Justice, Institute of Policy Analysis, 1983); T. Castellano, "Justice Model in the Juvenile Justice System—Washington State's Experience," *Law and Policy 8* (1986): 479.

38. Emily Gaarder, Nancy Rodriguez, and Marjorie Zatz, "Criers, Liars, and Manipulators: Probation Officers' Views of Girls," *JQ: Justice Quarterly 21* (2004): 547–578.

39. "Colorado OKs New Way to Handle Violent Juvenile Offenders," *Criminal Justice Newsletter 9* (1993): 4.

40. National Conference of State Legislatures, *A Legislator's Guide to Comprehensive Juvenile Justice, Juvenile Detention, and Corrections* (Denver: National Conference of State Legislators, 1996).

41. J. David Hawkins, Richard F. Catalano, and associates, *Communities That Care: Action for Drug Abuse Prevention* (San Francisco: Jossey-Bass, 1992).

42. Richard F. Catalano, Michael W. Arthur, J. David Hawkins, Lisa Berglund, and Jeffrey J. Olson, "Comprehensive Community- and School-Based Interventions to Prevent Antisocial Behavior," in *Serious and Violent Juvenile Offenders: Risk Factors and Successful Interventions*, eds. Rolf Loeber and David P. Farrington (Thousand Oaks, Calif.: Sage, 1998).

43. Adele V. Harrell, Shannon E. Cavanagh, and Sanjeev Sridharan, *Evaluation of the Children At Risk Program: Results One Year After the End of the Program* (Washington, D.C.: NIJ Research in Brief, 1999).

44. You can find out more about CASASTART at the following websites: www.casacolumbia.org/absolutenm/templates/PressReleases.asp?articleid=272, http://modelprograms.samhsa.gov/pdfs/FactSheets/CASA.pdf, www.promisingpractices.net/program.asp?programid=107, accessed on September 22, 2005.

45. Fox Butterfield, "Justice Besieged," *New York Times*, July 21, 1997, A16.

Case Index

Note: Italic entries refer to figures, exhibits, and tables.

Subject Index

Note: Italic entries refer to figures, exhibits, and tables.

Photo Credits

This page constitutes an extension of the copyright page. We have made every effort to trace the ownership of all copyrighted material and to secure permission from copyright holders. In the event of any question arising as to the use of any material, we will be pleased to make the necessary corrections in future printings. Thanks are due to the following authors, publishers, and agents for permission to use the material indicated.

Career vignette photos
Permission has been granted by each person whose photo appears at the bottom of the first page of each chapter.

Chapter 1
2: © AP/Wide World Photos; **5:** © Bettmann/Corbis; **10:** © Richard Cohen/Corbis; **17:** © 2005 AP/Wide World Photos; **19:** © 2005 AP/Wide World Photos; **25:** © 2005 AP/Wide World Photos; **27:** © 2005 AP/Wide World Photos

Chapter 2
30: © 2005 AP/Wide World Photos; **34:** © 2005 AP/Wide World Photos; **49:** © AP/Wide World Photos; **52:** © 2002 AP/Wide World Photos; **57:** © 2005 AP/Wide World Photos; **61:** © AP/Wide World Photos

Chapter 3
66: Department of Justice; **69:** © 2005 AP/Wide World Photos; **71:** "Wager of Battel" from *Le Coutume de Normandie,* an illuminated manuscript (1450–1470); **76:** © AP/Wide World Photos; **82:** © 2005 AP/Wide World Photos; **89:** © 2005 AP/Wide World Photos

Chapter 4
92: © Mario Tama/Getty Images; **96:** © Gareth Cattermole/Getty Images; **97:** © AFP/Getty Images; **104:** Robert Nickelsberg/Getty Images; **110:** © J. L. Bulcao/Corbis; **116:** © Reuters/Corbis

Chapter 5
122: © Steve Liss/Time Life Pictures/Getty Images; **125:** © 2002 AP/Wide World Photos; **129:** © Museum of the City of New York/Byron Collection/Getty Images; **132:** © 2000 AP/World Wide Photos; **137:** © 2005 AP/World Wide Photos; **140:** © 2005 AP/World Wide Photos

Chapter 6
148: © 2005 AP/World Wide Photos; **153:** © 2002 AP/World Wide Photos; **155:** © Ed Kashi/Corbis; **159:** © 2002 AP/World Wide Photos; **164:** © 2003 AP/World Wide Photos; **171:** © 2002 AP/World Wide Photos;

Chapter 7
176: © 2005 AP/World Wide Photos; **181:** © Topical Press Agency/Getty Images; **183:** © 2005 AP/World Wide Photos; **195:** © 2003 AP/World Wide Photos; **199:** © 2003 AP/World Wide Photos; **209:** © 2005 AP/World Wide Photos

Chapter 8
218: © 2003 AP/World Wide Photos; **221:** © 2005 AP/World Wide Photos; **231:** © 2005 AP/World Wide Photos; **236:** © Stephen Chenin/Getty Images; **241:** © 2002 AP/World Wide Photos; **244:** © 2003 AP/World Wide Photos

Chapter 9
250: © David McNew/Getty Images; **255:** © 2005 AP/Wide World Photos; **261:** © 2005 AP/Wide World Photos; **262:** © 2003 AP/Wide World Photos; **268:** © 2003 AP/Wide World Photos

Chapter 10
274: © 2005 AP/Wide World Photos; **277:** © 2005 AP/Wide World Photos; **280:** © 2005 AP/Wide World Photos;

286: © 2003 AP/Wide World Photos; **289:** © Nick Ut/Reuters/POOL/Corbis

Chapter 11
292: © Shepard Sherbell/Corbis; **295:** The Granger Collection, New York; **306:** © 2003 AP/Wide World Photos; **307:** © 2005 AP/Wide World Photos; **315:** © 2003 AP/Wide World Photos; **321:** © 2003 AP/Wide World Photos

Chapter 12
326: © 2005 AP/Wide World Photos; **330:** © 2003 AP/Wide World Photos; **333:** © 2003 AP/Wide World Photos; **335:** © 2005 AP/Wide World Photos; **340:** © 2005 AP/Wide World Photos; **343:** © 2005 AP/Wide World Photos; **347:** © 2005 AP/Wide World Photos

Chapter 13
358: © 2005 AP/Wide World Photos; **361:** van Gogh, Vincent: Prisoners' Round (detail), 1890. Pushkin Museum of Arts, Moscow, Scala/Art Resource, New York; **365:** Stock Montage, Inc.; **372:** © 2001 AP/Wide World Photos; **377:** © *Jacksonville Courier*/Zuzana Killiam/The Image Works; **381:** © Robin Nelson/PhotoEdit

Chapter 14
386: © 2005 AP/Wide World Photos; **389:** © 2004 AP/Wide World Photos; **394:** © 2005 AP/Wide World Photos; **399:** © 2005 AP/Wide World Photos; **402:** © 2002 AP/Wide World Photos; **403:** © 2003 AP/Wide World Photos; **409:** © 2005 AP/Wide World Photos

Chapter 15
418: © 2002 AP/Wide World Photos; **421:** The Granger Collection, New York; **424:** © Sean Clayton/The Image Works; **429:** © 2003 AP/Wide World Photos; **434:** © 2003 AP/Wide World Photos; **438:** © 2004 AP/Wide World Photos; **441:** © 2004 AP/Wide World Photos